TERI KWAL GAMBLE & MICHAEL W. GAMBLE

INTERPERSONAL
COMMUNICATION

······ Building Connections Together ······

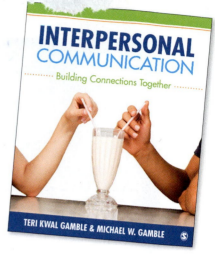

Puts STUDENTS in the Center of Interpersonal Communication

D0073874

"Very engaging. Relatable, Interactive, and Vibrant!"
—Veronica Wicks, Student
Texas Tech University

"Smart and rich content—a nice blend of fields, with an emphasis on what makes Communication unique."
—Kathleen Glenister Roberts
Professor, Duquesne University

INTERPERSONAL
COMMUNICATION
BUILDING
STUDENTS
CONNECTIONS
TOGETHER

INTERPERSONAL COMMUNICATION: *Building Connections Together*
puts students in the center of interpersonal communication by . . .

ACTIVELY engaging students by appealing to their interests in popular culture, media, and technology.

SHOWING students how online connections affect the media generation and the dynamics of the interpersonal experience.

PROVIDING abundant opportunities for students to actively apply and practice what they are learning.

EXPLORING how gender and culture influence interaction.

SHEDDING NEW LIGHT on the everyday interactions and relationships of students.

This text uses an applied approach and an interactive style to engage students. Every chapter considers how media and technology affect the dynamics of relationships and self-expression. The authors also focus on diversity and developing cultural understanding through explorations in every chapter of how gender and culture help shape experiences of interpersonal communication.

INTERPERSONAL COMMUNICATION: *Building Connections Together*
puts students in the center of interpersonal communication through abundant interactive pedagogical features throughout the text, including:

WHAT DO YOU KNOW?

True or False
1. *A conflict-free relationship is not healthy.*
True. Since conflict tests every relationship, lack of conflict is not genuine and is apt to contribute to a relationship's becoming dysfunctional.

Learning Objectives

What Do You Know?

"I liked how it had a true/false section in the beginning of the chapter so you can see what you know before you even read the chapter."

—Margaret Rountree, Student
Old Dominion University

"The 'What Do You Know' sections are excellent because they provide a framework for students to read the chapter. It helps them determine what is most important."

—Todd Lee Goen, Professor
Christopher Newport University

TRY THIS: *The Race Factor*

1. Are the nonverbal reactions of a television character influenced by the race of the other character in a scene? Do the nonverbal reactions displayed by television actors influence racial attitudes in viewers? According to research, the answer to both these questions is yes. The facial expressions and body language of actors are perceived as less favorable when the characters they are interacting with are black. The more negative reactions displayed by the actors adversely affect viewers' attitudes about race. In contrast, when black characters are responded to more favorably than white characters, the attitudes of viewers toward blacks improve. You are the director of television drama. Given these research findings, what instructions would you give your actors?

2. Is your outfit perceived to be a reflection of your race? Again the answer appears to be yes. Research confirms that people make judgments about race based on cues that extend beyond skin color. For example, people are more frequently perceived to be black if they are wearing janitorial attire than if they are wearing other kinds of clothing. The stereotypes we carry with us influence our perceptions of race. Provide an example of a time when you stereotyped a stranger on the basis of her or his apparel.

SOURCES: Valerie Ross, "Color TV," *Scientific American Mind*, July/August 2010, p. 13.

Jonathan B. Freeman, Andrew M. Penner, Aliya Saperstein, Matthias Scheutz, and Nalini Ambady, "Looking the Part: Social Status Cues Shape Race Perception," *PLoS ONE*, 6:9, e25107. doi:10.1371/journal.pone.0025107; also cited in Pamela Paul, "Is Race Reflected by Your Outfit?," *New York Times*, October 16, 2011, p. ST6.

Try This

"My favorite feature is 'Try This.'"
—Wayne Thomas, Student
Old Dominion University

"I really like the 'Try This' because it provides instant ability for students to put into action what they are reading about in the text. Application is often the best way to learn so this is an awesome addition."
—Christa Tess Kalk, Professor
Minneapolis Community & Technical College

"The 'Try This' sections really seemed to spark some good discussion in the class. This allowed students to see their communication as effective or ineffective, appropriate or inappropriate, and allowed them to look inward. It gave them a chance to reflect on how/why they experience difficulties in relationships and how they can better approach conflict."
—Lee Lavery, Professor
Ivy Tech Community College

TRY THIS: *Where Are You on the Grid?*

Think about how you characteristically deal with conflict. Then respond to each of the statements below using the following scale, where 1 indicates that you strongly disagree with the statement and 7 indicates that you strongly agree with it.

Disagree   Agree
1   2   3   4   5   6   7

1. I discuss the problem to reach a mutual understanding.
2. I stick to my argument.
3. I give in to my partner to keep my relationship satisfying.
4. I sometimes sacrifice my own goals so my partner can meet his or hers.
5. I try to find a new solution that will satisfy all our needs.
6. I usually try to win arguments.
7. I do not like to talk about issues of disagreement.
8. I am willing to give up some of my goals in exchange for achieving other goals.
9. I try to get all my concerns and my partner's concerns out in the open.
10. I usually try to forget about issues of disagreement so I don't have to confront my partner.
11. I try to think of a compromise that satisfies both our needs.

...view out in the open.
...sition is right.
...er I usually give in.
...a creative solution we both like.
...for bringing up conflict issues.
...unpleasant issues.
...uments might hurt my partner's feelings.
...nts to make my partner happy.
...eements.
...acceptable to both of us.
...my partner so he or she will see things my way.

25. I believe that you have to "give a little to get a little" during a disagreement.

In order to determine your preferred style of conflict, add your scores for the following items:

3, 4, 16, 20, 21	(accommodating)	
7, 10, 18, 19, 22	(avoiding)	
1, 5, 9, 13, 17	(collaborating)	
2, 6, 12, 14, 24	(competing)	
8, 11, 15, 23, 25	(compromising)	

Higher scores indicate that you possess more of a particular style.

As you consider the Blake and Mouton conflict grid and its five styles, keep your preferred style(s) in mind in an effort to determine if those you habitually use are effective in resolving relational conflict.

SOURCE: This inventory, based on the work of Rahim, Andersen...

INTERPERSONAL COMMUNICATION: *Building Connections Together*

puts students in the center of interpersonal communication through abundant interactive pedagogical features throughout the text, including:

Analyze This

ANALYZE THIS: *Edward de Bono*

Edward de Bono is a physician and leading authority on creative thinking. What does the following excerpt from de Bono's *I Am Right— You Are Wrong* suggest about how the Japanese handle conflict?

Every day the leading executives in the Japanese motor industry meet for lunch in their special club. They discuss problems common to the whole motor industry. But a soon as lunch is over and they step over the threshold of the club, out into the street, they are bitter enemies seeking to kill each other's business by marketing, technical changes, pricing policy, etc. For the Japanese, who do not have the tradition of Western logic, there is no contradiction at all between "friend" and "enemy." They find it easy to conceive of someone as a friend–enemy or enemy–friend.

SOURCE: Edward de Bono, *I Am Right—You Are Wrong*, New York: Viking, 1991, p. 196.

Reflect on This

"...so many opportunities to really engage learning throughout the chapter with reflection questions, application ideas, etc. Excellent!"
—Christa Tess Kalk, Professor
Minneapolis Community & Technical College

REFLECT ON THIS: *The Cell Effect*

Researcher Noelle Chesley wanted to find out if the time people spent on cell-phones enhanced or detracted from their overall feelings of happiness. To answer the question, Chesley surveyed more than 1,200 adults, concluding that a correlation existed: the more time individuals spent on cell-phones the less happy and less satisfied they became with their family relationships. Chesley attributed this, at least in part, to the work lives of people spilling over into their personal lives and causing stress at home.

Consider these questions:

1. Do your experiences confirm Chesley's findings? Does time spent on your cell stress the relationships you share with people important to you, perhaps because you divide your attention, with less attention being paid to the person(s) with you?

2. Do you think Chesley would have found the same results if she had studied the time we spend on tablets or computers? Explain your answer.

3. What recommendations can you offer for alleviating such relationship stressors? For example, would you expect others to abide by rules specifying when to use cell phones or other digital tools?

Source: Noelle Chesley, "Blurring Boundaries? Linking Technology Use, Spillover, Individual Distress, and Family Satisfaction." *Journal of Marriage and Family*, 67, 2005, p. 1237–1238.

and with even more pedagogy like:

- Sections in every chapter which focus on Gender, Culture, Media, and Technology
- **Connect the Case** feature ends chapter with a case study for further application
- SAGE Original Interpersonal Communication Scenario Videos
- **Review This** section at the end of each chapter including a
  - Chapter Summary
  - Chapter Review
  - Check Your Understanding
  - Check Your Skills
  - Key Terms
  - SAGE Student Study Site Details

⑤SAGE puts students and instructors in the center of interpersonal communication with comprehensive online resources

FREE AND OPEN-ACCESS STUDENT SITE

"SAGE's free and open-access site will be the biggest draw for all of those tools since many online accompanying tools usually cost students quite a bit extra. The flashcards and study questions would draw my personal interest the most."

—Lyndsi Earle, Student
Old Dominion University

SAGE provides comprehensive and free online resources at **sagepub.com.gambleic** designed to support and enhance both instructors' and students' experiences.

Students maximize their understanding of introduction to interpersonal communication through the free, **open-access Student Study Site.**

STUDENT RESOURCES INCLUDE:

- SAGE Journal Articles
- SAGE Original Videos
- Web resources
- eFlashcards
- Web quizzes
- Study questions
- Social media guidelines
- Video resources
- Self-assessment quizzes

PASSWORD-PROTECTED INSTRUCTOR TEACHING SITE

Strikes a never-before-seen balance between general education goals AND preparation for Communication majors (links to journal articles in Communication are a major plus)."

—Kathleen Glenister Roberts,
Professor
Duquesne University

SAGE provides comprehensive and free online resources at **sagepub.com.gambleic** designed to support and enhance both instructors' and students' experiences.

Instructors benefit from access to the **password-protected Instructor Teaching Site.**

INSTRUCTOR RESOURCES INCLUDE:

- Test bank

- PowerPoint slides

- Sample syllabi

- Class assignments

- Video resources

- Web resources

- SAGE WATCH THIS scenario videos and video links

- SAGE Journal Articles with articles for every chapter (includes information on how to read and critique a journal article)

- Social media guidelines

INTERPERSONAL COMMUNICATION: *Building Connections Together*

puts students in the center of interpersonal communication by asking them what they think of our text. Here is what they are saying:

WRITING STYLE AND RELATABILITY

"The writing was really easy to comprehend. I really like all the self-assessments. After taking all the self-assessments I could learn a little bit more about myself."

—Juliana Pires, Student
Old Dominion University

"The text is user-friendly, seems to be geared toward an introductory student level, and offers real-life examples that promote understanding/application."

—Lee Lavery, Professor
Ivy Tech Community College

"My favorite chapter was the constructive communication behaviors, and it has helped me by teaching me about the role reversal technique, which I didn't know about before—it will allow me to see the other person's side more clearly."

—Gabriel Lopez, Student
Old Dominion University

ACTIVITIES, ASSESSMENTS, AND FEATURES

"I really liked the GUIDELINES FOR RESOLVING CONFLICT because having the proper knowledge to resolve conflicts can help us to improve our interpersonal skills and communicate better with people, avoiding problems."

—Rosario Villagra, Student
Old Dominion University

"The activities give a better idea of a complex subject. The way the information is written and laid out is simple to understand and involves the reader more. I liked how it had a true/false section in the beginning of the chapter so you can see what you know before you even read the chapter."

—Margaret Rountree, Student
Old Dominion University

"The nonverbal chapter is the best I've seen."

—Todd Lee Goen, Professor
Christopher Newport University

OVERALL TEXTBOOK EXPERIENCE

"...relatable stories and examples, as well as fun learning activities."
—Amanda Osborn, Student
Old Dominion University

"...interesting, easily understood, and I liked the fact that current pop culture examples were mentioned."

—Stacy Evans, Student
Ohlone College

INTERPERSONAL COMMUNICATION: *Building Connections Together* **puts students in the center of interpersonal communication by offering them a lower-priced option**

SAGE VALUE PRICE

"Of course as a college student I think the SAGE value price is great!"
—Melissa Temple, Student
Old Dominion University

"Price is always a concern for students. As educators, we need to make certain our students are getting the best materials possible at a reasonable price."

—Lee Lavery, Professor
Ivy Tech Community College

Costs students $40-$70 LESS than competing Interpersonal Communication texts

INTERPERSONAL
COMMUNICATION

·········· Building Connections Together ··········

TERI KWAL GAMBLE & MICHAEL W. GAMBLE
COLLEGE OF NEW ROCHELLE   NEW YORK INSTITUTE OF TECHNOLOGY

Los Angeles | London | New Delhi
Singapore | Washington DC

Los Angeles | London | New Delhi
Singapore | Washington DC

FOR INFORMATION:

SAGE Publications, Inc.
2455 Teller Road
Thousand Oaks, California 91320
E-mail: order@sagepub.com

SAGE Publications Ltd.
1 Oliver's Yard
55 City Road
London EC1Y 1SP
United Kingdom

SAGE Publications India Pvt. Ltd.
B 1/I 1 Mohan Cooperative Industrial Area
Mathura Road, New Delhi 110 044
India

SAGE Publications Asia-Pacific Pte. Ltd.
3 Church Street
#10 -04 Samsung Hub
Singapore 049483

Acquisitions Editor: Matthew Byrnie
Associate Editor: Nathan Davidson
Editorial Assistant: Stephanie Palermini
Production Editor: Astrid Virding/Eric Garner
Copy Editor: Judy Selhorst
Typesetter: C&M Digitals (P) Ltd.
Proofreader: Wendy Jo Dymond
Indexer: Rick Hurd
Cover Designer: Scott Van Atta
Marketing Manager: Liz Thornton
Permissions Editor: Karen Ehrmann

Printed in Canada

Library of Congress Cataloging-in-Publication Data

Gamble, Teri Kwal.

Interpersonal communication : building connections together / Teri Kwal Gamble, College of New Rochelle, Michael W. Gamble, New York Institute of Technology.

pages cm
Includes bibliographical references and index.

ISBN 978-1-4522-2013-0 (pbk.)

1. Interpersonal communication. 2. Communication—Psychological aspects. I. Gamble, Michael, 1943- II. Title.

HM1166.G36 2013
302—dc23   2012046294

This book is printed on acid-free paper.

13 14 15 16 17 10 9 8 7 6 5 4 3 2 1

Brief Contents

Detailed Contents

CHAPTER 2. THE IMPACT OF SELF-CONCEPT 34

CHAPTER 3. PERCEPTION 60

**CHAPTER 6. NONVERBAL
COMMUNICATION 150**

CHAPTER 7. CONVERSATIONS 188

PART III: DYNAMICS

CHAPTER 8. EMOTIONS 210

CHAPTER 10. POWER AND INFLUENCE 264

CHAPTER 11. CONFLICT 292

PART IV: RELATIONSHIPS IN CONTEXT

CHAPTER 12. RELATIONSHIP DYNAMICS 326

Preface

AN APPLIED APPROACH

Interpersonal Communication: Building Connections Together takes an applied approach to exploring the central role of interpersonal communication in our twenty-first-century lives. Whether with family, friends, or coworkers, in personal or professional contexts, enacted face-to-face and up close and personal or online with technological assistance, *interpersonal communication skills affect the nature and development of all relationships.*

FOCUS ON CULTURE, MEDIA, AND TECHNOLOGY

We had a number of goals in writing this text. First, we wanted to reach students by appealing to their interests in and fascination with popular culture, media, and technology. This volume actively engages students by facilitating their personal observation, processing, and analysis of what occurs as individuals connect interpersonally in the real world and as depicted in popular culture, media, and online. We offer many examples from popular culture and social networking sites to enter students' worlds and meet them where they are.

FOCUS ON ACTIVE LEARNING AND SKILL BUILDING

Second, we wanted to provide numerous opportunities for students to cocreate content and actively apply and practice what they are learning. Exercises in the text encourage students to compose personal observations as they observe and process interpersonal interactions. As a result, *Interpersonal Communication: Building Connections Together* is one text that students will be able to call "their own."

As we noted, this text offers an applied approach. Its strengths are its interactive style and its pedagogy, which affirm the reader as the central player in the life of the textbook. We place our text's emphasis on how we connect with others and on "how we can do it better" so that the book's users will discover how they can employ interpersonal skills to enrich their personal and professional lives.

FUNDAMENTAL PREMISES OF THE TEXT

Premise 1: A text on interpersonal communication should consider how popular culture, media, and technology influence the imagined and actual person-to-person interactions of students. Whether subtly or overtly, the impressions of interpersonal communication that we derive from popular culture and online shape our relationships, influencing our views of self and others, affecting what we expect from relationships, and ultimately influencing how we evaluate the effectiveness of our person-to-person relationships and skills.

Premise 2: A text on interpersonal communication should consider how technology, culture, and gender influence person-to-person interactions. We no longer interact with others solely face-to-face. Thus, a key theme of any new book on interpersonal communication needs to be how online connections affect the "MEdia" generation and the dynamics of the interpersonal experience. We also can no longer expect to communicate solely with people who are mirror images of or just like us. Our world is both too complex and too small, and the people with whom we interact are too diverse, for us even to imagine that we could succeed without understanding how gender and culture influence our person-to-person connections. Thus, by developing two additional text themes, how gender and culture preferences influence interaction, we encourage students to take a step toward improving relationship outcomes. No longer are cultural understanding and sensitivity to difference merely assets; now they are prerequisites of effective and insightful interpersonal communication.

Premise 3: A text on interpersonal communication should consider the effects of the varied contexts of our lives.
Although it is important to consider the content traditionally covered in interpersonal communication courses, it is also important to widen the scope of our consideration to include interactions occurring in the family, in the workplace, and in health care arenas. The ability to interact effectively across our life spans with friends, family members, coworkers and employers, peers, and health professionals is essential for both personal wellness and professional well-being.

ORGANIZATION OF THE TEXT

The book is divided into four main parts: **Foundations**, **Messages**, **Dynamics**, and **Relationships** in Context. We begin with the building blocks of interpersonal communication (Part I: Foundations), then we consider the kinds of information that we share when we connect interpersonally (Part II: Messages), then we look more closely at the variable factors that affect our interpersonal communication (Part III: Dynamics), and finally we explore the full range of relationships that we build together through communication (Part IV: Relationships in Context).

Part I comprises three chapters: Chapter 1, "Interpersonal Communication: A First Look"; Chapter 2, "The Impact of Self-Concept"; and Chapter 3, "Perception." Together, these initial chapters set the stage for our subsequent study of the sharing of messages during interpersonal communication, our consideration of factors influencing how we personally enact interpersonal communication, and, finally, our in-depth exploration of different relational contexts.

Part II includes four chapters: Chapter 4, "Listening"; Chapter 5, "Communicating with Words"; Chapter 6, "Nonverbal Communication"; and Chapter 7, "Conversations." Together these chapters explore the kinds of messages we share during interpersonal communication and whether these messages are listened to and responded to appropriately.

Part III is composed of four chapters: Chapter 8, "Emotions"; Chapter 9, "Trust and Deception"; Chapter 10, "Power and Influence"; and Chapter 11, "Conflict." Each of these chapters looks at a different variable affecting the courses of our relationships.

Part IV concludes the book with three chapters: Chapter 12, "Relationship Dynamics"; Chapter 13, "Intimacy and Distance in Relationships"; and Chapter 14, "Relationships in Our Lives: Family, Work, and Heath-Related Contexts." These chapters explore how the context of a relationship influences its nature and outcomes. Being able to have healthy and meaningful relationships in all spheres of life makes our lives better.

TOOLS FOR LEARNING TOGETHER

We have worked hard to ensure that *Interpersonal Communication: Building Connections Together* fulfills the following four requisites: (1) The text respects and acknowledges student interest in popular culture, media, and technology; (2) the text recognizes the impact that the MEdia age, with its emphasis on self-expression and self-obsession, is having on the interpersonal skills of students and the outcomes of the interpersonal relationships they share; (3) the text expands the communication knowledge base of students, encouraging them to apply interpersonal communication theory and research to their own lives; and (4) the text gives students opportunities to reflect on, practice, and master skills to facilitate their becoming interpersonally competent.

FEATURES

To this end, the text includes pedagogical features that are designed to help students enrich their understanding of fundamental concepts and theories and to help them apply what they have learned to their own interpersonal communication and relationships. The following features reinforce the chapter material and guide students to enhance their interpersonal communication skills:

- Every chapter begins with a list of **Learning Outcomes** that outlines the key objectives of the chapter, followed by an **opening vignette** that introduces the relevance of the chapter content through a contemporary example of interpersonal communication in action.

- At the start of each chapter, students will assess their current understanding of interpersonal communication with a quiz feature titled "**What Do You Know**?" Students can find the answers to the quiz's true/false items printed upside down at the bottom of the box feature, and they will also find these answers revisited in the margins alongside discussion of the relevant topics within the chapter text. This self-quiz prepares students for the content to be covered and for the outcomes they can expect to achieve by chapter's end.

- All chapters offer an array of skills-oriented "**Try This**" boxes, which are introduced regularly to promote active learning and skill building as students make their way through each chapter. The material in these boxes encourages critical inquiry and thought as well as exploration of the role of ethics in interpersonal communication. These boxes feature self-inventories designed to help students assess their learning, skill level, and personal insights into such topics as empathy, reading nonverbal cues, and listening, as well as activities that promote experiential learning and build interpersonal communication skills.

- Every chapter contains one or more "**Reflect on This**" boxes, designed to make the theories discussed in the text come alive. These boxes highlight the research and/or the experiences of professionals whose work has widened the field's understanding of interpersonal communication and, at the same time, guide students in applying the theories' lessons to their own lives.

- Every chapter features "**Analyze This**" boxes, which encourage students to apply critical thinking to examples of interpersonal encounters from literature and popular culture. The material in these boxes is designed to promote discussion and facilitate analysis of interpersonal messages and interpersonal communication in action.

- Near the end of every chapter, "**Connect the Case**" presents a case study that spotlights one or more challenges occurring during interpersonal communication in a face-to-face or mediated environment. Examining these cases involves students in considering chapter content and assessing interpersonal outcomes.

- Special sections in every chapter focus on the topics of **gender**, **culture**, **media**, and **technology**. These sections address how the concepts covered in the chapter intertwine with these underlying themes of the text.

- At the end of every chapter is a **Summary** that connects chapter content to the chapter's **Learning Objectives**. This is followed by a section titled "**Look Back**," which contains two series of questions, "**Check Your Understanding**" and "**Check Your Skills**," that are focused on the concepts and the practical applications the student should have mastered after experiencing the chapter. Page references accompany both sets of questions to guide students back to the relevant sections of the text for further study.

- **Key Terms** are set in boldface throughout the text to highlight important terminology. Students can find the definition for each term on the page where it is introduced in the **Margin Glossary** that runs throughout the text or in the **Glossary** at the end of the book, which collects all of the definitions for a comprehensive review.

ANCILLARIES

Interpersonal Communication: Building Connections Together offers comprehensive ancillary resources for instructors and students, to support teaching and learning in the classroom and beyond.

Instructor Teaching Site: www.sagepub.com/gambleic

A password-protected instructor teaching site provides one integrated source for all instructor materials, including the following key components for each chapter:

- **Test bank**, available in Word format and to PCs and Macs through Diploma software, offers a set of test questions and answers for each chapter. Multiple-choice, true/false, and short-answer/essay questions for every chapter will aid instructors in assessing students' progress and understanding. The software allows for test creation and customization. The test bank is also available in Microsoft Word format.

- **PowerPoint presentations** designed to assist with lecture and review, highlighting essential content, features, and artwork from the book.

- **Sample syllabi**—for semester and quarter classes—provide the instructor with suggested models for creating a course syllabus.

- Carefully selected **Web resources** and **audio and video links** feature relevant content for use in independent and classroom-based exploration of key topics.

- **SAGE Journal Articles:** A "Learning From SAGE Journal Articles" feature provides access to recent, relevant full-text articles from SAGE's leading research journals. Each article supports and expands on the concepts presented in the chapter. This feature also provides discussion questions to focus and guide student interpretation.

Student Study Site: www.sagepub.com/gambleic

An open-access student study site provides a variety of additional resources to build students' understanding of the book content and extend their learning beyond the classroom. Students have access to the following features for each chapter:

- **Self-quizzes** with multiple-choice and true/false questions for every chapter allow students to assess their progress in learning course material independently.

- **eFlashcards** reinforce student understanding and learning of key terms and concepts that are outlined in the book.

- **Study Questions:** Chapter-specific questions help launch discussion by prompting students to engage with the material and by reinforcing important content.

- **Web resources** direct students to relevant online sites for further research on important chapter topics.

- **Video and audio links** feature meaningful content for use in independent or classroom-based exploration of key concepts and skills.

- **SAGE Journal Articles:** A "Learning From SAGE Journal Articles" feature provides access to recent, relevant full-text articles from SAGE's leading research journals. Each article supports and expands on the concepts presented in the chapter. This feature also provides discussion questions to focus and guide student interpretation.

We believe that our instructional package—composed of the text's contents and the pedagogical aids we intersperse both throughout chapters and online—will motivate students to internalize the knowledge and develop the skills they need to make interpersonal connections and develop meaningful and healthy interpersonal relationships, whether their interactions occur face-to-face or online. We hope you agree!

Acknowledgments

How lucky we are to have had the opportunity to work with the very talented professionals at SAGE again! Senior acquisitions editor Matthew Byrnie together with his team, Stephanie Palermini and Nathan Davidson, made writing this book both fulfilling and fun. Matt's creativity and astute understanding of our goals freed us to produce a textbook on interpersonal communication that fulfilled our vision.

We also owe a debt of gratitude to senior project editors Eric Garner and Astrid Virding for so skillfully guiding our efforts, copy editor Judy Selhorst for her careful and insightful reading of the manuscript, assistant editors Megan Koraly and Terri Accomazzo for the many hours of time devoted to working on the ancillaries, senior marketing manager Liz Thornton and market development manager Michelle Rodgerson for using their promotional savvy to bring the book to market, permissions editor Karen Ehrmann for her thoroughness, and designer Scott Van Atta for the text's visual appeal and engaging layout.

We are especially appreciative for our reviewers who so generously and unselfishly shared with us their knowledge and teaching insights; we credit them with helping to produce a book that speaks directly to the needs and interests of students.

Teri & Mike

SAGE is grateful to the following reviewers for providing helpful feedback during various stages of manuscript development:

Andrea R. Acker, Westmoreland County Community College

Luann Okel Adams, Mid-State Technical College

Alicia Andersen, Sierra College

Tim Anderson, Elgin Community College

Laurie Arliss, Ithaca College

Michael Irvin Arrington, University of Kentucky

Leonard Assante, Volunteer State Community College

Lisa Nelson Bamber, Otero Junior College

Polly A. Begley, Fresno City College

Heather Bixler, College of the Sequoias

Ellen Bland, Central Carolina Community College

Derek Bolen, Angelo State University

Diane Boynton, Monterey Peninsula College

Leah Bryant, DePaul University

Jack Byer, Bucks County Community College

Carlotta Campbell, College of Alameda

Chelsea J. Chalk, Ancilla College

Yanrong Chang, University of Texas—Pan American

Yea-Wen Chen, Ohio University

Anita P. Chirco, Keuka College

Margaret K. Chojnacki, Barry University

Karen Clark, Spokane Community College

Colleen Colaner, University of Missouri

William D. Cole, Elizabethtown Community and Technical College

Kathleen Czech, Point Loma Nazarene University

Marianne Dainton, La Salle University

Patricia A. Dobson, Eastern New Mexico University

Aimee DuBois, Normandale Community College

Jill C. Dustin, Old Dominion University

Jen Eden, Northern Illinois University

Leonard M. Edmonds, Arizona State University

Nichole Egbert, Kent State University

Diana Elrod-Sarnecki, Des Moines Area Community College

Bo Feng, University of California, Davis

Diane M. Ferrero-Paluzzi, Iona College

Tracy Frederick, Southwestern College

Sheryl A. Friedley, George Mason University

Daniel D. Fultz, Bluffton University

Joanie Gibbons-Anderson, Riverside City College

Robert J. Glenn, III, Owensboro Community and Technical College

Carlos G. Godoy, Rensselaer Polytechnic Institute

Todd Lee Goen, Christopher Newport University

Alan K. Goodboy, Bloomsburg University

Debra Harper, Lone Star College-Greenspoint Center

Jim Hasenauer, California State University at Northridge

Kristin Haun, Pellissippi State Community College

Leslie A. Henderson, McLennan Community College

Robert Heppler, Broward Community College

Jason Hough, Hartnell Community College

Jessica R. Hurless, Casper College

Rebecca Imes, Carroll University

Kirsten Isgro, State University of New York, Plattsburgh

Robert S. Jersak, Century College

JoAnna Johns, Atlantic Cape Community College

Cynthia B. Johnson, College of the Sequoias

Rod Kenyon, California State University, Chico

Flora Keshishian, St. John's University

J. Clint Kinkead, Dalton State College

Kathryne Kiser, Metropolitan Community College—Longview

Frederick Knight, Eastern New Mexico University Ruidoso Branch Community College

Tony L. Kroll, Tarrant County College

J. Mignon Kucia, Mississippi College

Sandra Lakey, Pennsylvania College of Technology

Karenza Lambert, Ivy Tech Community College

Emily J. Langan, Wheaton College

Kimberly A. Laux, University of Michigan—Flint

Kristen LeBlanc, Texas State University-San Marcos

Jennifer A. Lundberg Anders, West Shore Community College

Kozhi Sidney Makai, Lone Star College—Montgomery

Tracy Marafiote, State University of New York, Fredonia

Barbara J. Mayo, Northeast Lakeview College

Ché V. Meneses, Ohlone College & California State University, East Bay

Michelle Millard, Wayne State University

Nina-Jo Moore, Appalachian State University

Mark T. Morman, Baylor University

Thomas P. Morra, Northern Virginia Community College

Randall Mueller, Gateway Technical College

Kellie L. Mzik, Georgia Military College

Mary E. Nagy, Bloomsburg University

Elizabeth J. Natalle, The University of North Carolina at Greensboro

Christine L. North, Ohio Northern University

Jill O'Brien, DePaul University

Laura Oliver, University of Texas—San Antonio

Chuka Onwumechili, Howard University

Lisa M. Orick-Martinez, Central New Mexico Community College

Steve Ott, Kalamazoo Valley Community College

Kate Pantinas, Ivy Tech Community College

Dennis T. Payne, Texas State University

Douglas C. Pierce, Ridgewater College

Marlene M. Preston, Virginia Tech

Narissra Maria Punyanunt-Carter, Texas Tech University

Terry Quinn, Gateway Technical College

Janice Ralya, Jefferson State Community College

Diane Reuszer, Northeastern Junior College

Nancy Reynolds, Angelina College

Kathleen Roberts, Duquesne University

Sudeshna Roy, Stephen F. Austin State University

Leslie Ramos Salazar, Arizona State University

Kelly Renee Schutz, Ivy Tech Community College

Xiaowei Shi, Middle Tennessee State University

Natalie E. Shubert, Ohio University

Cheryl L. Skiba-Jones, Ivy Tech Community College

Brent C. Sleasman, Gannon University

Garth H. Sleight, Miles Community College

Megan K. Sokolowski, Mid-State Technical College

Jamie Stech, Iowa Western Community College

Tony Strawn, Henderson Community College

Natalie L. Sydorenko, University of Akron

Christa Tess, Minneapolis Community and Technical College

Carl L. Thameling, University of Louisiana at Monroe

Henry J. Venter, National University—Fresno

Dr. Matthew S. Vos, Covenant College

Zuoming Wang, University of North Texas

Lindsey Welsch, Johnson County Community College

Bradley S. Wesner, Nova Southeastern University

Kylene J. Wesner, Broward College

Denise Woolsey, Yavapai College

Alesia Woszidlo, University of Kansas

Ibrahim Yoldash, Indiana University Northwest

Christina Yoshimura, University of Montana

Jason Ziebart, Central Carolina Community College

Phyllis S. Zrzavy, Franklin Pierce University

About the Authors

Teri Kwal Gamble (PhD, New York University; BA, and MA, Lehman College, CUNY) and **Michael W. Gamble** (PhD, New York University; BA and MFA, University of Oklahoma) are professional writers of education and training materials and the coauthors of numerous textbooks and trade books. Their most recent publication is the eleventh edition of their best-selling text *Communication Works* (2012). Among their other books are *Sales Scripts That Sell* (second edition, 2007), *The Gender Communication Connection* (2002), and *Public Speaking in the Age of Diversity* (second edition, 1998). Teri and Michael are also the cofounders of Interact Training Systems, a consulting firm that conducts seminars, workshops, and short courses for business and professional organizations across the United States.

Additionally, Michael served as an officer and taught leadership skills for the U.S. Army Infantry School during the Vietnam War. Together, Teri and Michael also produce training and marketing materials for the real estate industry.

Teri and Michael have two grown children, Matthew, a scientist at Einstein Medical School, and Lindsay, who has completed her MBA and is currently finishing law school. They share their home with twin poodles—Charlie and Lucy.

This is dedicated to the most important people in our lives, our children, Lindsay and her husband Daniel, and Matthew and his love Tong. They define the importance of interpersonal communication.

"I truly believe that life is a contact sport. You never know just who you'll meet and what role they might play in your career or your life."

—Ken Kragen
Communication Consultant

INTERPERSONAL COMMUNICATION:
A First Look

LEARNING OBJECTIVES

After completing this chapter, you should be able to demonstrate mastery of the following learning outcomes:

1. Define interpersonal communication, distinguishing it from other types of communication.

2. Use a communication model to identify the essential elements and transactional nature of the interpersonal communication process.

3. Explain the functions interpersonal communication serves.

4. Describe the characteristics, core principles, and axioms of interpersonal communication

5. Explain how gender and culture affect interpersonal communication.

6. Provide examples of how digital media are reshaping interpersonal contacts.

7. Develop a plan to improve interpersonal communication.

Let's talk about interpersonal communication. How do you decide whether to speak with a person face-to-face or send a text? What if you had to choose between calling and texting? A lot depends on the situation and the other person. Or does it?

According to a report issued by the Pew Internet & American Life Project, we now communicate more often via text. In fact, more than one-third of young adults send on average more than one hundred texts per day, making the text message their focal communication strategy—their "go to" form of interaction.[1] Quite simply, for many of us texting is our dominant daily mode of communicating.[2]

Are you among the two-thirds of people more likely to use your cell phone to text your friend rather than talk to her on the cell? And how do you want your friend to get in touch with you? Do you prefer her to call and talk to you over the phone, or would you rather she text too? Your answer likely depends on how frequently you text and whether you think of texting as easier and more convenient than other communication channels.

We have an abundance of communication choices at our disposal. With so many available options, making the right choice is not always easy, and not necessarily the one most favor. Our goal is to help you explore the benefits your choices present. While recognizing the range of communication technologies open to you, this book will help you improve your skills and develop your abilities to communicate most effectively and appropriately with others—to make sound decisions about how to communicate—whether by text messaging, using social networking sites, calling on a cell phone or landline, instant messaging, e-mailing, or talking face-to-face.

> **How do you decide whether to speak with a person face-to-face or send a text?**

WHAT DO YOU KNOW?

Before continuing your reading of this chapter, which of the following five statements do you believe to be true and which do you believe to be false?

1. Communication is normally intentional.   T   F

2. Interpersonal communication always is between two people.   T   F

3. If you already consider yourself a good communicator, then how you engage others does not need to change.   T   F

4. Interpersonal communication affects your health.   T   F

5. Machines are altering the nature of interpersonal communication.   T   F

Read the chapter to discover if you're right or if you've made any erroneous assumptions.

ANSWERS: 1. F, 2. F, 3. F, 4. T, 5. T

We do it daily. We do it with people we have known all our lives, and we do it with people we have just met. Every day, we engage in interpersonal communication with family, friends, and strangers alike, face-to-face and online, in person and via our phones. Through our personal contacts, we build connections and establish relationships to satisfy our social needs and realize our personal goals. As we relate to others, the messages we send and receive shape us. In fact, there is a direct link between how good we are at communicating and how satisfying or fulfilling we find life.[3] Let's look more closely at the process known as interpersonal communication.

Interpersonal communication is a fact of life.

WHAT IS INTERPERSONAL COMMUNICATION?

Communication is our link to humanity. In its broadest sense, it is a process involving the deliberate or accidental transfer of meaning. One person does or says something, thereby engaging in symbolic behavior, while others observe what was done or said and attribute meaning to it. Whenever you observe or give meaning to behavior, communication is taking place.

WHAT DO YOU KNOW?

True or False

1. *Communication is normally intentional.*

False. Communication is also accidental or unintentional.

Communication:
A process involving both deliberate and accidental transfer of meaning.

Figure 1.1 Texting is Most Common Daily Communication Method for Teens

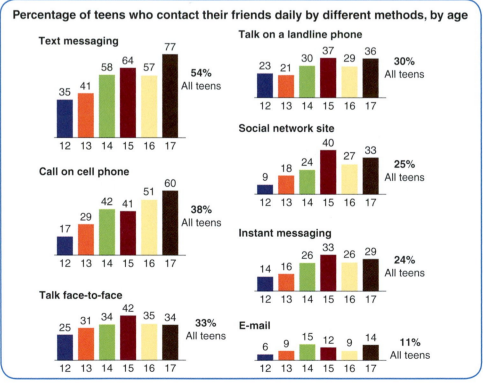

Percentage of teens who contact their friends daily by different methods, by age

Text messaging
35 (12), 41 (13), 58 (14), 64 (15), 57 (16), 77 (17)
54% All teens

Call on cell phone
17 (12), 29 (13), 42 (14), 41 (15), 51 (16), 60 (17)
38% All teens

Talk face-to-face
25 (12), 31 (13), 34 (14), 42 (15), 35 (16), 34 (17)
33% All teens

Talk on a landline phone
23 (12), 21 (13), 30 (14), 37 (15), 29 (16), 36 (17)
30% All teens

Social network site
9 (12), 18 (13), 24 (14), 40 (15), 27 (16), 33 (17)
25% All teens

Instant messaging
14 (12), 16 (13), 26 (14), 33 (15), 26 (16), 29 (17)
24% All teens

E-mail
6 (12), 9 (13), 15 (14), 12 (15), 9 (16), 14 (17)
11% All teens

SOURCE: Based on information from the Pew Internet & American Life Project.

INTERPERSONAL COMMUNICATION IS ABOUT RELATIONSHIPS

There are many kinds of communication. We distinguish one type of communication from others based on the number of persons involved, the formality of the interaction, and the opportunity to give and receive feedback. For example, since **intrapersonal communication** occurs when you think or talk to yourself, it requires only a single communicator—you! In contrast to intrapersonal communication, **interpersonal communication** is the ongoing, ever-changing process that occurs when you interact with another person, forming a **dyad**, which is defined as two people communicating with each other. Both individuals in a dyad share the responsibility for determining the nature of a relationship by creating meaning from the interaction. Thus, anytime we communicate with another person, whether a friend, parent, coworker, or employer, we are communicating interpersonally. It is very common for communicators to use digital media to get their messages across to one another or the public by blogging, texting, tweeting, Instant messaging, e-mailing, or posting in a social networking site such as Facebook (see Figure 1.1).

INTERPERSONAL COMMUNICATION TAKES TWO

First, let's consider the quantitative aspects of our interpersonal interactions. The fact that interpersonal communication takes two people means that it is indivisible. Without the second person, interpersonal communication is impossible. Thus, the parties to interpersonal communication are a duo: a couple, a pair, or perhaps adversaries. From an interpersonal perspective, even groups of three or more individuals are viewed as composites of dyads, effectively serving as the foundations for separate pairings and potential coalitions. Without a dyad, a relationship does not exist, and without a relationship, there is no interpersonal communication.[4] This means that if one person withdraws from the relationship, then that relationship terminates—at least for the time being or until the connection between them is reestablished. The qualitative aspect of interpersonal communication is another story. We measure the quality of an interpersonal relationship along a continuum, with "intimate communication" at one end and "impersonal communication" at the opposite end. The more personally we interact with another person, the more "interpersonal" our relationship becomes. When we engage in interpersonal communication, our goal is to treat one another as genuine persons, not as objects, and to respond to each other as unique individuals with whom we create a distinct relational culture, not as people merely playing roles.[5]

The more personal a relationship becomes, the more interdependent the two people become, sharing thoughts and feelings with each other. Our lives become interconnected, especially when contrasted with how we relate to persons with whom we are uninvolved and to whom we don't reveal much about ourselves. We develop personal relationships because of the intrinsic rewards we derive from them; we find them emotionally, intellectually, and perhaps even spiritually fulfilling. In contrast, we have impersonal relationships usually because of the extrinsic rewards they offer, such as maintaining professional working relationships with others to help us reach our goals. Which kinds of relationships do you have more of, those that are impersonal or those that are personal in nature?

INTERPERSONAL COMMUNICATION IS A LIFELONG PROJECT

The effectiveness of interpersonal relationships depends on the extent to which we practice and exhibit interpersonal skills. While we may be born communicators, we are not born with effective interpersonal skills—those we need to learn. Nor are effective skills static; the same techniques may not work for all people in all situations. The culture of each person, his or her gender, the environment, and the individual's goals will determine how that person approaches and processes interpersonal communication.

Intrapersonal communication: Communication requiring only a single communicator; communication with oneself.

Interpersonal communication: The ongoing, ever-changing process that occurs when one person interacts with another person, forming a dyad; communication occurring within a relationship.

Dyad: Two individuals interacting; a two-person relationship.

Just as every person represents a unique combination of physical, psychological, education, gender, and cultural characteristics that distinguish us from one another, each new relationship teaches us a little bit more about the nature of people and interpersonal communication. Each new relationship increases our comfort at interacting not only with those who share our characteristics but also with those whose attitudes, life experiences, and perspectives differ from ours.

TRY THIS: *Today, Who Is a Stranger?*

When you were a young child, your parents and/or caregivers probably cautioned you not to speak to strangers. However, travel opportunities and social networks such as Facebook make interacting with strangers much more commonplace, even ordinary. Answer the following questions:

1. To what extent, if any, are you more willing to interact with a stranger online than at the mall or when on a trip? Explain.

2. How does the anonymity or privacy of online relationships increase or decrease your level of personal comfort?

3. To what extent, if any, do you think parents or caregivers should restrict the time young children spend interacting online? To what extent, if any, do

you think you should limit the time you spend in social networks?

4. In your opinion, which is more likely to result in a lasting interpersonal relationship—a friendship that begins online, an "old-fashioned" pen-pal type of friendship that depends on U.S. mail delivery, or a relationship that begins with both parties face-to-face? Explain your answer with reasons.

As we grow and learn, we must continually revise and update our personal theories of what works during interpersonal contacts, or our assumptions will compel us to repeat interpersonal scenarios or scripts that are doomed to fail. The effective interpersonal communicator does not take others for granted. Instead of following stereotypes, the effective interpersonal communicator is guided by knowledge and skill.

Our sense of personal identity results from and influences our interpersonal relationships. When we do it well, interpersonal communication helps us work through problems, ultimately enhancing our feelings of self-worth. When we do it poorly, however, rather than enlarging us, it limits our growth and frustrates our achievement of our unique potential.

Whether an interpersonal relationship is productive or not depends on how satisfying the relationship is and how much attention we pay to its health. Having good interpersonal skills can mean the difference between happiness and unhappiness or success and failure in multiple arenas or life contexts—home, job, school, health care settings, and society— as well as across cultures and generations. Enhanced understanding of the factors in play when two people communicate, whether in a personal or a professional relationship, increases an individual's chances of developing **interpersonal competence**—the ability to communicate effectively.[6] We increase communication competence by observing ourselves and others, assessing what we observe, practicing specific behaviors, and then predicting and evaluating the outcomes of our interactions, with the goal of improving our communication skills.

Interpersonal competence:
The ability to use appropriate communication to build and maintain an effective relationship.

As you read the rest of this chapter, consider the following questions about yourself:

1. How effective am I at communicating with people from diverse cultures?

2. Am I equally effective interacting with males and females, and with individuals whose sexual orientations differ from my own?

3. How easy is it for me to develop relationships with people my own age and those of different ages?

4. To what extent am I able to maintain self-control when I interact with others? Under what conditions do I lose control?

5. How, and to what extent, do I use technology in my interpersonal relationships? In what ways is technology changing my interpersonal communication?

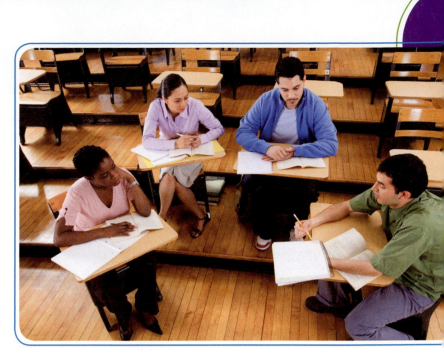

Having good interpersonal skills is key in achieving happiness and success.

Societal problems related to factors such as ethnocentrism, sexism, violence, and health can be lessened, at least to some degree, if we improve our ability to adapt to a changing world and connect interpersonally with others in more effective ways. To this end, we need to explore interpersonal communication, including the field's theories, practice, and contexts. By considering relevant research, putting theory into practice, and applying what we learn to the contexts of our lives, we can develop our interpersonal communication skills. The more we learn, the more extensive our repertoire of acceptable behavioral choices becomes and the more flexible we become, thereby improving our chances to sustain rather than sever needed relationships.

The effectiveness of our personal relationships depends on the communication choices we make. Using communication we present ourselves to others and either work out or compound relationship problems. Because interpersonal relationships can be destructive (yes, they can have a dark or destructive side that causes one or both parties to experience emotional or physical pain), our personal and professional well-being depends on their being effective. Thus, a key goal of this book is to help you build and maintain effective interpersonal connections with a broad array of people.

MODELS OF INTERPERSONAL COMMUNICATION

Whether we are able to exchange messages and negotiate or share meaning during person-to-person encounters depends on how well we handle the essential elements active in the process. For example, depending on the situation, patting someone on the

In the poem *Anonymous*, 21st-century poet Samuel Manashe suggests that when in the company of another person, too often we pretend to be someone we are not, keeping our actual identity secret and hoping to remain unknown or anonymous.

Have you ever asked a question like the one Manashe asks in the poem? Do you suppose anyone has asked such a question about you? How does maintaining anonymity online, for example, affect interaction?

Anonymous

Truth to tell,   *And grow old*
Seldom told   *Self-disguised—*
Under oath,   *Who are you*
We live lies   *I talk to?*

1. How might remaining anonymous be enabling to someone?

2. What could compel you to disguise yourself or wear a mask when interacting with another person on or offline?

3. How would you handle the pain, frustration, and anger caused by feeling the need to suppress your cultural identity or hide your feelings to maintain a relationship?

SOURCE: "Anonymous," from New and Selected Poems of Samuel Menashe copyright © 2005 by Literary Classics of the United States, Inc. All rights reserved. Reprinted by permission.

---

back may be perceived as friendly and supportive or as a form of sexual harassment. There are seven key elements that influence interpretation of this act (see Table 1.1):

1. The *people* involved

2. The *message*(s) that each person sends and/or perceives

3. The *channel*(s) in use

4. The amount of *noise* present

5. The communication *context*

6. The *feedback* sent in response

7. The act's *effect*(s) on the individuals involved

The better we understand these essential elements of interpersonal communication, the more likely we are to improve our interpersonal communication competence and skills. The more we understand how interpersonal communication works, the greater the likelihood it will work for us. So, let us look more closely at each of the elements in play.

PEOPLE

Recall that interpersonal communication between any two people ranges from "impersonal" at one end of an imaginary continuum to "intimate" at the other end.

When you respond impersonally to another person, you communicate with him based on your limited knowledge of the categories in which you place that person—that is, the social groups or the culture to which you believe he belongs—rather than on your personal experience interacting with that individual.

In contrast, when you respond to someone personally, you respond to her as an individual, drawing on your knowledge of her personality to guide your interactions. In other words, your past experience with the individual allows you to differentiate her from the groups to which she belongs. You now take this unique person and her needs into account when you communicate.

As a relationship develops and you get to know someone better, not only can you describe the person's behavior, but you can also more accurately predict how he or she will behave when facing a particular situation or set of circumstances. When you know a person very well, sometimes you can also explain that person's behavior, offering reasons for his or her actions. For instance, when you share an impersonal relationship with someone at work, you can likely describe his behavior—maybe his procrastination in completing an assignment. When you see a supervisor giving him a project to work on, you may be able to predict that he will not complete it on time. Were you to share a more personal relationship with your coworker, however, you might also be able to explain the reasons behind the procrastination—why he is unable to meet a deadline—such as concerns about a child's illness or feelings of inadequacy.

Each party in an interpersonal relationship participates in the functions of sending and receiving messages. Each functions simultaneously as sender and receiver, both parties giving out

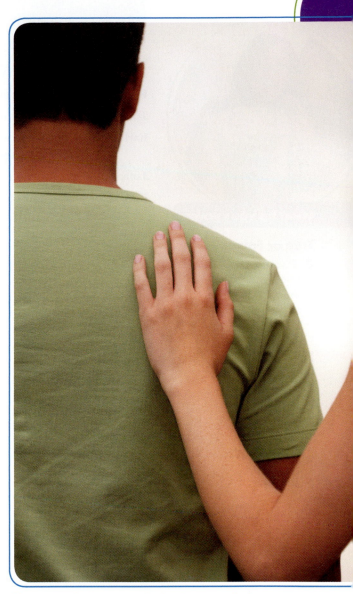

How you pat someone on the back communicates.

TABLE 1.1   The Essential Elements of Interpersonal Communication

People	The senders and receivers of communication messages
Messages	The content of communication
Channels	The media through which messages travel
Noise	Interference with the ability to send or receive messages
Feedback	Information received in exchange for messages
Context	The environmental, situational, or cultural setting in which communication takes place
Effect	The result of a communication episode

and taking in messages. For example, in the following exchange both Jana and Karl give and receive messages:

Jana: I'm so tired. I wish we didn't have to go to the Joneses' party.

Karl: You always feel tired whenever we have plans to go to a party for someone I work with.

Jana: Why do you have to attack me when I say how I feel?

Karl: What's the matter with you? I'm not attacking you. I'm only commenting on what I observe and experience directly.

Jana: Is that all? Give me a break. Don't I have a right to be tired?

Karl: Sure you do. Just tell me one thing. Why do you never feel tired when we're going to a party hosted by your friends?

Interpersonal communication is transactional in nature. It is a process in which transmission and reception occur simultaneously and source and receiver continually influence one another. What we think of each other and what we believe each other to know affect the messages we send.[7] Each party in a dyad simultaneously performs the roles of sender and receiver, also known as a **role duality**. How the individuals perform the roles, or how good they are at sending and receiving, depends on what they bring to the relationship, including their feelings about themselves, their knowledge about communication, and their attitudes, values, and goals. All these elements influence how well a sender encodes his or her thoughts, feelings, emotions, and attitudes by putting them into a form another can relate to, and how the receiver decodes the thoughts, feelings, emotions, and attitudes of the sender by interpreting them into messages.

TRY THIS: *Rating Relationships*

Think about some of the relationships you have had over your lifetime.

1. Identify two of them: the first, an extremely satisfying interpersonal relationship and, the second, an extremely frustrating one.

2. Identify the specific aspects of each relationship that made it satisfying or frustrating for you.

3. After summarizing the characteristics and qualities that differentiate your most satisfying relationship from your most frustrating one, propose steps you might have taken to increase your satisfaction with the relationship you found frustrating.

MESSAGES

We negotiate the meaning we derive from interpersonal communication by sending and receiving verbal and nonverbal **messages**. Whom we speak to, what we choose to speak about, what we do as we interact, the words we use, the sound of our voices, our posture, our facial expressions, our touch, and even our smell constitute the message or the content of our communication. Everything we do as a sender or a receiver has potential message value for the person with whom we are interacting or for someone observing the interaction.

Messages can be conveyed through any one of our five senses: auditory, visual, gustatory, olfactory, or tactile. They can be heard, seen, tasted, smelled, or felt, and they are situational/manipulational, or communicated by the environment. Some messages—such as a caress, a kiss, or the words "I love you"—are more personal than others that could be sent to any

Role duality:
The simultaneous performance of the roles of sender and receiver by the members of a dyad.

Message: The content of communication.

numbers of persons. Some of our messages we send purposefully ("I want to be very clear about this"), while others, such as nervous tics, we emit unconsciously or accidentally ("I didn't know you knew how I felt about this"). Everything we do when interacting with another person has potential message value as long as the other person is observant and gives meaning to our behavior. Whether we frown, jump for joy, move closer, turn away, or go on and on, we are communicating messages that have some effect on someone else.

CHANNELS

Messages travel via a **channel**, a medium that connects sender and receiver, much as a bridge connects two locations. In face-to-face communication, we send and receive messages through the five senses as discussed above. In effect, we may use multiple channels at the same time to communicate a single message. In fact, under most circumstances, interpersonal communication is a multichanneled interaction using visual, auditory, tactile, olfactory, and situational/manipulational means to convey both verbal and nonverbal messages. Consider a first date: to prepare, you make sure you look and smell nice; you choose a quiet setting to ensure you can hear each other; and you generally put your best face forward in both verbal and nonverbal ways in order to say, "I like you and I hope you like me too."

We use each of our five senses to convey messages.

Capable communicators are adept channel switchers. They know how to use sound, sight, touch, taste, smell, and the environment, as well as traditional words and nonverbal signs, to get messages across. However, if you find yourself consistently tuning in on just one channel, you might miss the most salient parts of a message. For instance, if you speak to people only over the phone, you might miss the underlying message when your best friend asks, "Is everything okay? I haven't seen you in a while." While we may prefer to send or receive messages through a particular channel, we should pay attention to and use all of the available channels.

Today, with computer-mediated communication, we have a richness of channels to choose from. In addition to face-to-face contact, we have texting and instant messaging, for example. If one channel is closed or damaged, we can open another to compensate. For instance, rather than assuming that a blind or sight-impaired person will be able to recognize us by our voice, we should also name ourselves. Since the blind person is unable to see the visual cues we use to color in or shade the meaning of a verbal message, we may also need to take special care to ensure that the meanings we want conveyed are contained in the words we choose and the expressiveness of our voice.

Channels are like bridges; they connect us to one another.

NOISE

In communication studies, **noise** includes anything that interferes with or impedes our ability to send or receive a message. Noise distracts communicators by focusing their attention on something extraneous to the communication act. Effective communicators find ways to ensure their messages get through accurately despite any interfering noise.

Noise emanates from both internal and external sources. The words used, the environment, physical discomfort, psychological state, and intellectual ability can all function as noise. As

Channel: A medium or passageway through which a message travels.

Noise: Anything that interferes with or impedes the ability to send or receive a message.

In your opinion does a garage band constitute noise?

the level of noise increases, it becomes more and more unlikely that we will be successful at negotiating or sharing meaning. Among the external sources of noise are the sight, sound, smell, and feel of the environment. A drab room, an overly warm space, a loud siren, an offensive odor, and too many conversations occurring at the same time are all examples of environmental noise.

Among the internal sources of noise are personal thoughts and feelings. Racism, sexism, feelings of inadequacy, hunger, excessive shyness or extroversion, and deficient or excessive knowledge can all interfere with the ability to send and receive messages effectively. Most of us find it easier to cope with external noise than with internal noise because closing a window, for example, is usually a lot easier than opening a mind or changing a personality. Have you created or been influenced by noise in any of your relationships today? Which kind(s) of noise typically cause you the greatest problems? (See Table 1.2.)

FEEDBACK

Feedback is information we receive in response to messages we have sent. It can be both verbal and nonverbal and lets us know how another person is responding to us. Feedback provides clues as to "how we are coming across," whether we were heard through the noise or interference, and how the receiver interpreted our communicative efforts. Feedback reveals whether or not our message was interpreted as we hoped and, if not, which portions of the message need to be resent.

Feedback can be positive or negative. **Positive feedback** enhances behavior in progress. It serves a reinforcing function, causing us to continue our behavior. In contrast, **negative feedback** stops behavior in progress. It serves a corrective function, prompting us to discontinue one or more behaviors because of their apparent ineffectiveness. In this way, negative feedback helps eliminate behavior that others judge inappropriate.

WATCH THIS 1.1
For a video on using communication channels visit the student study site.

Feedback: Information received in exchange for a message sent.

Positive feedback: Responses that enhance behavior in progress.

Negative feedback: Responses that stop behavior in progress.

TABLE 1.2 Types of Noise

Semantic noise	Noise due to the failure to understand the intended meaning of one or more words or the context in which the words are being used (persons speaking different languages, using jargon and "technicalese")
Physiological noise	Noise due to personal illness, discomfort, or a physical problem including speech, visual, auditory, or memory impairment (difficulty articulating, hearing or sight loss, fatigue, disease)
Psychological noise	Noise due to anxiety, confusion, bias, past experience, or emotional arousal that interferes with communication (sender or receiver prejudice, closed-mindedness, rage)
Intellectual noise	Noise due to information overload or underload (over- or underpreparedness)
Environmental noise	Noise due to the sound, smell, sight, and feel of the environment or physical communication space that distracts attention from what is being said or done (cars honking, garbage rotting, people talking at once, cellular or computer interference)

Because we constantly communicate with ourselves (even as we communicate interpersonally), feedback can emanate from both internal and external sources. **Internal feedback** is the feedback you give yourself as you assess your own performance during an interpersonal transaction. **External feedback** is feedback you receive from the other person. Competent communicators are sensitive to both feedback types, since both serve important functions.

Feedback often focuses on a person or a message. We can, for example, comment on a person's appearance or message effectiveness. In addition, we can be totally honest about feedback, offering **low-monitored feedback,** or we can carefully craft a response designed to serve a particular purpose, offering **high-monitored feedback.** Whether our feedback is spontaneous or guarded depends on how much we trust the other person and how much power that person has over our future.

We can also offer immediate or delayed feedback. Immediate feedback instantly reveals its effect on us. For example, after someone tells us a joke, we may laugh really hard. Other times, however, a gap occurs between the receipt of the message and the delivery of feedback. For example, we can nod our head yes or shake our head no every time the other person says something we do or do not agree with. Or we can withhold our reaction until after she or he has finished speaking. When we interview for a job, we are rarely told immediately after the interview whether we will be given the position. Instead, we receive delayed feedback; sometimes days, weeks, or even months pass before we know whether or not the interview was successful.

Feedforward is a variant of feedback. However, instead of being sent after a message is delivered, it is sent prior to a message's delivery as a means of revealing something about the message to follow. Feedforward introduces messages by opening the communication channel and previewing the message. **Phatic communication** (see Chapter 12), that is, a message that opens a communication channel, such as this text's cover or preface, serves as an example of feedforward.

CONTEXT

The environmental and situational or cultural **context** in which the communication occurs (its setting) can also affect its outcome. The environmental context is the physical location of the interaction. The situational or cultural context comprises the life spaces or cultural backgrounds of the parties in the dyad. In many ways, surrounding culture and physical, social, psychological, and temporal settings are integral parts of communication.

The physical setting includes the specific location for the interaction, that is the setting's appearance and condition. A candlelit exchange may have a different feel and outcome from one held in a busy, brightly lit office. The social setting derives from the status relationships and roles assumed by each party. Some relationships seem friendlier and are less formal than others. The psychological setting includes the interaction's emotional dimensions. It influences how individuals feel about and respond to each other. The temporal setting includes not only the time of day the interaction takes place but also the history, if any, that the parties to it share. Any previous communication experience that you and another person have had will influence the way you treat each other in the present. The cultural context is composed of the beliefs, values, and rules of communication that affect your behavior. If you and the other person are from different cultures, the rules you each follow may confuse the other or lead to missing chances for effective and meaningful exchanges. Sometimes the context is so obvious or intrusive that it exerts great control over our interaction by restricting or dominating how we relate to one another; other times it seems so natural that we virtually ignore it.

Internal feedback: A person's response to his or her own performance.

External feedback: Responses received from others.

Low-monitored feedback: Feedback that is sincere and spontaneous; feedback delivered without careful planning.

High-monitored feedback: Feedback offered to serve a specific purpose; feedback that is sent intentionally.

Feedforward: A variant of feedback sent prior to a message's delivery as a means of revealing something about to follow.

Phatic communication: Superficial interaction designed to open the channel between individuals.

Context: The setting in which communication takes place.

How does your current physical setting affect you?

EFFECT

As we interact with each other, we each experience an **effect**—meaning that we are influenced in some way by the interaction. One person may feel the effects more than the other person. One person may react more quickly than the other. The effects may be immediately observable or initially not observable at all.

An effect can be emotional, physical, cognitive, or any combination of the three. As a result of interacting with another we can experience feelings of elation or depression (emotional); we fight and argue or walk away in the effort to avoid a fight or argument (physical); or we can develop new ways of thinking about events, increase our knowledge base, or become confused (cognitive).

There is a lot more to interpersonal communication and its ultimate effects than we may immediately realize. In fact, current relationships may best be considered examples of "unfinished business."[8]

VISUALIZING COMMUNICATION

To be sure, the thinking about interpersonal communication has evolved over the years. The earliest model—a **linear or unidirectional model**—depicted communication as going in one direction only (see Figure 1.2). Questions such as "Did you get my message?," statements such as "I gave you that idea," and acts such as leaving someone a note with instructions give voice to this one-way perspective. While containing many of the elements identified earlier, notice that the linear model omits both feedback and context.

FIGURE 1.2   Linear Model of Interpersonal Communication

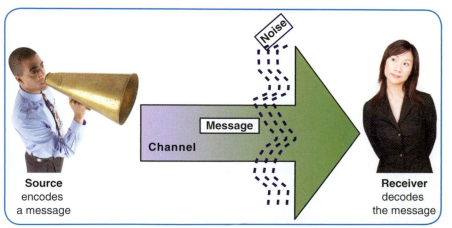

Source
encodes
a message

Noise

Message

Channel

Receiver
decodes
the message

Effect: The result of a communication episode.

Linear or unidirectional model: A representation of communication that depicts it as going in only one direction.

Gradually, a more realistic two-way model—known as an **interaction model**—came to be the model of choice (see Figure 1.3). The interaction model visualizes interpersonal communication not as a one-way event but as a back-and-forth process, much like a game of tennis; it also acknowledges the presence and effects of both feedback and context. However, though more accurate than the one-way model, the interaction model fails to capture the complexity of interpersonal communication, including the reality that interpersonal communication does not involve just a back-and-forth action and reaction as might occur when you send a text and your friend responds.

FIGURE 1.3   Interaction Model of Interpersonal Communication

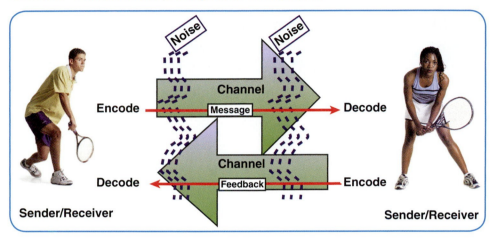

FIGURE 1.4   Transactional Model of Interpersonal Communication

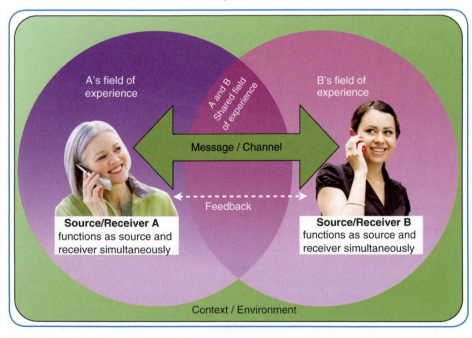

Interaction model:
A representation of communication as a back-and-forth process.

Many communication exchanges involve source and receiver responding to one another simultaneously rather than sequentially. Thus, a more recently developed and even more realistic way to visualize how the elements at work during interpersonal communication dynamically relate to each other is a **transactional model**, as shown in Figure 1.4. The transactional model's strength is that it depicts sending and receiving as simultaneous rather than distinctly separate acts. By doing so, it helps us visualize the vital complexity of interpersonal interaction by showing us that source and receiver send messages to and receive messages from each other at the same time, reflecting the reality of a conversation. (See Table 1.3 for a summary of the various models' strengths and weaknesses.)

TABLE 1.3 Advantages and Limitations of Communication Models

Model	Communication Examples	Advantages	Limitations
Linear	Television and radio E-mail and texts Packaged presentations that do not allow for modifications	Simple and direct	Not useful for most face-to-face encounters
Interaction	Instant messaging Class presentations where content is adjusted based on feedback	Wider applicability	Still discounts receiver's active role in creating meaning
Transactional	Any encounter in which meaning is cocreated	Most realistic depiction of interpersonal communication	Does not apply to texting, tweeting, and posting

HOW DOES INTERPERSONAL COMMUNICATION ENHANCE OUR LIVES?

Communicating interpersonally helps us discover who we are; it fulfills our need for human contact and personal relationships, and it can prompt us to change our attitudes and behavior. In these ways, interpersonal communication serves psychological, social, information, and influence functions.

Transactional model:
A representation of communication that depicts transmission and reception occurring simultaneously, demonstrating that source and receiver continually influence one another.

IT FULFILLS PSYCHOLOGICAL FUNCTIONS

First and foremost, just as we need water, food, and shelter, we need people. When we are isolated or cut off from human contact, our health suffers. In fact, being in at least one good relationship appears to be a prerequisite of physical and psychological well-being.[9] For example, maximum-security prisons used to keep inmates locked alone in their cells for up to twenty-three hours each day. The feelings of isolation the inmates experienced resulted in their becoming restless, angry, violent, and potentially suicidal. When restrictions were loosened, however, and inmates were allowed out of their cells

TRY THIS: *Making Model Sense*

Use the transactional model of interpersonal communication in Figure 1.4 to analyze the following dyadic scenario. Identify how each of the essentials of interpersonal communication included in the model—people, messages, channels, noise, feedback, context, and effect—makes its presence felt during the interaction.

Simona (*approaching a restaurant table*): Hi, Kevin. I thought I recognized the back of your head. How ya doing? Long time no see.

Kevin (*turning, somewhat started*): I recognized your perfume—I used to love it when—(*abrupt break*). It's been a while, hasn't it? When was the last time we got together? Is it a year?

Simona (*smiling*): Longer than that. I haven't heard from or seen you since your divorce from Jan.

Kevin Haven't seen me since the divorce. That makes it almost two years and twenty-four days, then.

Simona Time sure goes fast when you're having fun, doesn't it? Well, you look great. Life's been good to you, huh?

Kevin Yeah. I just got back from six months' troubleshooting in Singapore. I got a promotion, and I'm finally making the kind of money I deserve.

Simona Good for you! Emilio and I still see Jan, you know.

Kevin Do you? How's she doing? I haven't spoken to her in two years, either.

Simona You haven't spoken to your ex since the divorce? Actually, I'm meeting her for lunch today.

Kevin Didn't seem to be anything left to say to her. (*Does a double take*) Did you say you're meeting Jan here? I was just leaving. I've got to get back to the office. I've got a key client coming. It was sure nice running into you.

Simona Sure thing. I'll tell Jan you say hi.

Kevin No. Don't even tell her you saw me. It would just open up her old wounds.

Simona: Why would it do that? She's great, has a great job, and she's seeing one of Emilio's friends. Besides, I'm sure she'd like to know you're doing so well.

Kevin So she picked up the pieces, did she? I didn't think it would happen that fast. She was so broken up, so devastated by my leaving.

Simona Life goes on.

Kevin Guess it does. Well, gotta go. Be good.

Simona (*Under her breath, as he walks away*) What a conceited jerk!

Messages	Simona's message:
	Kevin's message:
Channels	
Noise	
Feedback	Simona's feedback:
	Kevin's feedback:
Context	
Effect	The effect on Kevin:
	The effect on Simona:

for hours each day, able to play sports and mingle and dine with others, their behavior and emotional health improved.[10]

Interpersonal communication also enhances self-other understanding; through our interactions with others, we learn how different individuals affect us. In fact, we depend on interpersonal communication to develop our self-awareness and maintain our sense of self. To quote communication theorist Thomas Hora: "To understand oneself, one needs to be understood by another. To be understood by another, one needs to understand the other."[11]

Because interpersonal communication is a fluid process that depends on constantly changing components, it offers myriad opportunities for self-other discovery. Different contexts help us figure out who likes or dislikes us and why, when and why to trust or distrust someone, what behaviors elicit the strongest reactions, under what conditions we have the power to influence another person, and whether we have the ability to resolve relational conflict.

IT FULFILLS SOCIAL FUNCTIONS

Through interpersonal communication we are able to begin and sustain relationships. Our interpersonal contacts fulfill our social needs to varying degrees. Although we vary greatly in the extent to which we experience these needs, according to psychologist William Schutz our relationships reflect the following in particular:

- Our need for *affection*—to express or receive fondness

- Our need for *inclusion*—to be included or include others as full partners

- Our need for control—to direct or exert influence over the self and others so that we feel we are able to deal with and manage our lives and environment.[12]

Have you ever felt isolated when in a crowd?

When we are in a relationship with someone whose needs complement or balance our own, each of us is able to have our needs met. When our needs are not complementary, however, we are more apt to experience relationship struggles or conflict. Do your experiences confirm this? (We explore the work of William Schutz in more depth in Chapter 12.)

Good interpersonal communication also allows us a glimpse into another person's reality. For example, developing an interpersonal relationship with someone whose culture differs from our own broadens our own point of view. Our interpersonal styles may differ from each other's, but we adapt to the sound, form, and content of their messages and pay attention to how members of different cultures feel about displaying affection, exerting control, defining roles, and meeting goals. While it may be easier to identify with and associate with those who are like us, coming from different cultures does not preclude our learning to share similar meanings.

Interpersonal communication similarly fulfills our need to be *friended* and *to friend* others. (Notice how *friend* has also become a verb.) It helps alleviate feelings of isolation, fulfilling our desire to feel needed, loved, wanted, and capable. Because of this, interpersonal communication may increase our personal satisfaction, helping us feel more positive about ourselves.

IT FULFILLS INFORMATION FUNCTIONS

During interpersonal contacts, as we share information we reduce the amount of uncertainty in our lives. By taking in information we meet the need to acquire knowledge.

Information is not the same thing as communication. Just as more communication is not necessarily better communication, more information is not necessarily better information. Sometimes no information and no communication may be the best course. We can, after all, talk a problem or issue to death. Thus, just as there is a time to talk, there is a time to stop talking and listen.

IT FULFILLS INFLUENCE FUNCTIONS

We use interpersonal communication to influence others—sometimes subtly and sometimes overtly. As we exercise influence, our need to gain compliance is met. Interpersonal communicators are both the users of and targets of persuasion.

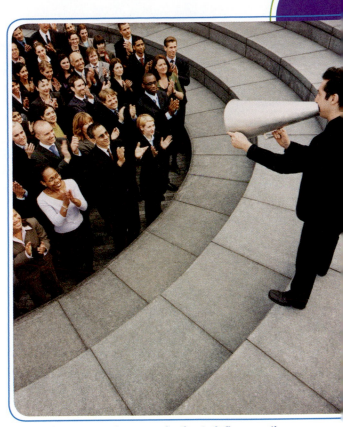

We use interpersonal communication to influence others. Are you aware when others attempt to influence you?

As we observed earlier in this chapter, interpersonal communication is often goal directed. And even though we may not be conscious of it, we often use strategic communication to achieve our goals. We methodically plan how to get what we want. We seek contact with and advice from others whom we believe can help us. This is not to say that human beings are naturally manipulative or deceptive, as neither of these practices supports the interdependent and transactional nature of interpersonal communication.[13] Communication is not something we do to others or have done to us. It is a mutually reinforcing activity we engage in together. How we interact is a two-way affair. We mutually influence each other. We are both affected by what each of us does and says.

How we think about interpersonal communication has evolved from a linear process in which one receiver influences another to an interactional process in which communication by each person precipitates a reaction in the other person to a mutually interactive transaction deriving meaning from the simultaneous sharing of ideas and feelings. From a transaction perspective, no single cause explains how you interpret or make sense of experience. Communication is more complex than that.

Consider three conversations: one you recently had with a significant other, one between you and a friend, and one between you and an acquaintance or coworker you usually don't get together with outside of work. Explain which interpersonal communication functions each interaction fulfilled: psychological, social, information, and/or influence. Be specific in describing and assessing how each interaction illustrates the function(s) you identify.

	Conversation with Significant other	Conversation with a friend	Conversation with a coworker
Psychological			
Social			
Information			
Influence			

UNDERSTANDING INTERPERSONAL CONTACT: CHARACTERISTICS, PATTERNS, AND AXIOMS OF COMMUNICATION

As we see, every interpersonal communication contact shares certain essential elements and serves one or more functions. Every interpersonal communication contact also shares the following:

1. *Key characteristics:* descriptions of the communication that are common across different situations or contexts

2. *Core communication principles:* identifiable behavioral patterns and motivations

3. *Axioms:* the fundamental rules by which communication may be analyzed or explained.

FIVE CHARACTERISTICS OF INTERPERSONAL COMMUNICATION

Let's first explore the noteworthy characteristics of interpersonal communication (see Table 1.4).

TABLE 1.4   Characteristics of Interpersonal Communication

Communication Is . . .	In Other Words . . .
A dynamic process	It is ongoing, continuous, and in a constant state of flux.
Unrepeatable and irreversible	It is unique.
Learned	We find out over time what works for us and what does not work if we remain conscious of the communication.
Characterized by wholeness and nonsummativity	It operates as a complete entity, much like a team functions.

Interpersonal Communication Is a Dynamic Process. By **dynamic process** we mean that interpersonal communication is ongoing or continuous, and in a constant state of flux. All the components continually interact with and affect each other. They are interdependent or interconnected. They depend on and influence one another. What one person says or does influences what the other person says or does. Every interpersonal encounter is a point of arrival from a previous encounter and a point of departure for a future encounter.

Interpersonal Communication Is Unrepeatable. Every interpersonal contact is unique. It has never happened in just that way before, and it will never happen in just that way again. Why? Because every contact changes us in some way and, as a result, can never be exactly repeated or replicated. Try as we might, we can never recapture exactly the same feelings, thoughts, or relationship that existed at a specific point in time. We are no longer exactly the same persons we were before we made contact.

Interpersonal Communication Is Irreversible. In addition to being unrepeatable, interpersonal communication is irreversible. Once we have said or done something to another, we cannot erase its impact. After exhibiting behavior, we cannot simply say, "Forget that!" and substitute a better or more appropriate behavior in its place (though we sometimes would like to try). We cannot rewind or restart communication as we can a TV program recorded on a DVR. We cannot unhear words, unsee sights, or undo acts. They are irretrievable. Presenting a new stimulus does not change the previous stimulus. It merely becomes part of a behavioral sequence.

Once sent, it is virtually impossible to take back an e-mail message.

We Cannot Uncommunicate Online Either. For one thing, a written message provides evidence of the message sent. E-mails are virtually impossible to erase. They remain on servers and workstations, even after we have "deleted" them. So do all entries made on social media sites such as Facebook, Tumblr, Twitter, and LinkedIn. You may try to soften their effects, but you cannot reverse their existence any more than you can try to squeeze toothpaste back into a tube. In fact, the online service Social Intelligence can provide a dossier on every faux pas, every sarcastic comment, every remark containing overt or implied prejudice, and every lewd personal picture you have posted. The Web is forever.[14]

Interpersonal Communication Is Learned. Over time we learn what works for us in an interpersonal relationship and what does not. We can hinder our communication with another person if we remain unconscious of how we affect him or her, and vice versa. Part of the art of interpersonal communication involves recognizing how our words and actions affect others, how their words and actions affect us, and then, based on our observations, making the necessary adjustments.

Interpersonal Communication Is Characterized by Wholeness and Nonsummativity. When we say that the interpersonal relationship is characterized by "wholeness," we are saying that it operates as a complete entity. We consider more than the individuals

Dynamic process: A process that is ongoing, continuous, and in a state of constant flux.

who are in the relationship; we look at the unique ways in which the persons involved influence each other. When we say that interpersonal communication is characterized by "nonsummativity," we are saying that the whole is more than the sum of its parts; interpersonal communication is about more than just its participants per se. We cannot understand a couple by looking at only one-half of the partnership. We cannot understand a family by looking at only one of the children. The nature of the relationship must be examined. The "us" must be explored. The relationship takes on a quality that we cannot understand merely by possessing information about its parts. The system as a whole is simply different from the sum of its parts.[15]

INTERPERSONAL PATTERNS

Interpersonal communication involves understanding patterns of behavior, predicting what others will do and say, and providing reasons for their actions as well as our own.[16] Thus, understanding the patterns of behavior an individual displays, not just a single behavior, provides the basis for understanding the person's interpersonal communication. In other words, a single isolated behavior is not what we need to focus on; rather, we must take into account the entire behavioral sequence.

Interpersonal communication involves not only interpreting but also predicting and accounting for another person's behavior. If we are able to distinguish individuals from a general group, then we recognize their uniqueness and are able to know and understand them. For example, were we to interact with a number of different professors over time yet treat all of them alike, or were we to date a number of different men or women yet not distinguish one date from another, we would not be very effective interpersonal communicators. To the extent that we can predict the behavior of a particular teacher or a specific romantic interest, and account for that behavior, what we term **reasoned sense making**, we can understand that individual more than we might understand other professors, or other dates.

We also reason retrospectively. **Retrospective sense making** means making sense of our own behavior once it has occurred. We interpret our own actions in light of the goals we have or have not attained. We look back on interactions and continually redefine our relationships, which is our way of making sense of them. As our interactions with another person progress, the events of our relationship increase in number, and, as a result, the relationship and how we feel about it changes.

FIVE COMMUNICATION AXIOMS

Identified in a classic study by Paul Watzlawick, Janet Beavin, and Don Jackson, there are five **axioms of communication**, or universally accepted principles, that enable us to understand interpersonal interactions more fully.[17] (See Table 1.5.)

Reasoned sense making: The ability to predict and account for the behavior of a particular person.

Retrospective sense making: The ability to make sense of one's own behavior once it has occurred.

Axioms of communication: A paradigm of universally accepted principles used for understanding communication.

TABLE 1.5   Axioms of Communication

1. You cannot not communicate.
2. Interactions have content and relationship dimensions.
3. Interactions are defined by how they are punctuated.
4. Messages are verbal symbols and nonverbal cues.
5. Exchanges are symmetrical or complementary.

Axiom 1: You Cannot *Not* Communicate. Behavior has no opposite. We cannot voluntarily stop behaving. Even if we consciously decide not to respond, even if we do our utmost not to move a muscle or utter a sound, our stillness and silence are responses. As such, they have message value, influence others, and therefore communicate. No matter how hard we try, we cannot not communicate. Our behavior communicates whenever it is given meaning.

Axiom 2: Every Interaction Has a Content and Relationship Dimension. The content dimension of a message involves the expected response, and the relationship dimension indicates how the message is to be interpreted and reveals what one party to the interaction thinks of the other. For example, a husband says to his spouse, "Get over here right now." The content level, or expected response, is that the spouse will approach immediately. But the message can be delivered in a number of ways: as an order, a plea, a flirtation, or an expression of sexual desire, for example. Each manner of delivery suggests a different kind of relationship. It is through such variations that we offer clues to another person regarding how we see ourselves in relationship to that person.

Axiom 3: Every Interaction is Defined by How It Is Punctuated. Though we often feel as if we can label the beginning and the end of an interaction, pointing to a traceable cause for a specific reaction, in actuality communication has no definitive starting or finishing line. It is difficult to determine exactly what is stimulus and what is response. Consider this example:

> *A woman is usually late getting home from work. When she does get home, she often finds her partner asleep. Both are angry. The woman might observe that she works so much because all her partner does is sleep. The partner might say that all he does is sleep because she's never home.*

Neither of them interprets their own behavior as responses to the behavior of the other. For the woman, her partner's behavior is the stimulus and hers is the response; he causes her behavior. For the partner, it's just the opposite. Whereas he sees the sequence as going from working to sleeping, she sees it as going from sleeping to working; which is it, really?

We all segment experience somewhat differently because we each see it differently. We call the dividing of communication into segments punctuation. The way a communication is punctuated usually benefits the person doing the *punctuating*. Punctuation also reveals how an individual interprets a situation and offers insight into the nature of an interpersonal conflict in particular and the interpersonal relationship in general.

Axiom 4: Messages Consist of Verbal Symbols and Nonverbal Cues. During face-to-face or online interactions, we emit two kinds of messages: discrete, digital verbal symbols or words and continuous, analogic, nonverbal cues. Language is digital because it is composed of discrete words that are coded with meaning, while nonverbal communication is analogic because it is continuous behavior without a beginning or end. According to Watzlawick, Beavin, and Jackson, the content of a message is more apt to be carried via the verbal or digital system, whereas the relationship level of the message is typically carried via the nonverbal or analogic system. Although we can usually control what we say or write, it is much more difficult to control the nonverbal cues we emit. Thus, we may not speak angry words, but our face may betray our rage. As a result, it is easy to lie with words but hard to produce behavior that supports the lie. Nonverbal behavior often gives us away.

Axiom 5: Interactions Are Either Symmetrical or Complementary. Watzlawick, Beavin, and Jackson categorize relationships as either symmetrical or complementary, terms not descriptive of "good" and "bad," but simply two types of relationships into which interactions can be divided. In a symmetrical relationship, the parties mirror each other's behavior. If one person is solicitous, the other is as well. If one person whines, the other does also. In contrast, in a **complementary relationship**, the parties engage in opposite behaviors, with the behavior of one precipitating the behavior of the other. If one person is docile, the other is assertive. If one leads, the other follows. Complementary relationships maximize the differences between the parties, including the different positions each holds in the relationship at a point in time.

Neither symmetrical nor complementary relationships are trouble-free. In a symmetrical relationship the parties run the risk of experiencing "symmetrical escalation." Believing they are "equal," both persons might assert, for example, the right to exert control. Once this starts, each may feel compelled to engage in battle to demonstrate his or her equality. And so a status struggle begins. The main danger facing persons in a symmetrical relationship is a runaway sense of competitiveness.

In contrast, those who share complementary relationships may face a problem called "rigid complementarity"—extreme rigidity. This problem surfaces when one party begins to feel that control is automatically his or hers. For example, an overly protective mother who cannot accept that her child is grown, an employer unable to share leadership, and a teacher who cannot learn from others—all illustrate the rigidness that can develop in people who become locked into self-perpetuating, unchanging, unhealthy patterns of behavior. Switches in power are natural; we need to be prepared for them.

Taken together with the characteristics and principles of communication, the five axioms of communication provide additional knowledge as we seek to enhance our understanding and increase the effectiveness of our interpersonal contacts. Now let's widen our focus.

THE IMPACT OF DIVERSITY AND CULTURE

Because U.S. society is multicultural in makeup and becoming increasingly so, and because cultural values help shape our acceptance of and preference for specific communication styles, it is important that we understand the role cultural prescriptions play in our interpersonal contacts. Here's the challenge: Even though the United States is the most demographically diverse country in the world, how regularly do you take cultural differences into account in your person-to-person interactions?

DIVERSITY AND COMMUNICATION STYLE

Developing **cultural awareness,** the ability to understand the role that cultural prescriptions play in shaping communication, is an asset. Why? Because people we once considered strangers are now our friends and coworkers, and intercultural ignorance too frequently slows our ability to create meaningful interpersonal relationships with people who are culturally different from us.

Whenever cultural variability influences the nature and outcomes of interpersonal communication, culture is having an effect. Learning about other cultures, including their systems of knowledge, belief, values, customs, and artifacts, facilitates

Complementary relationship: A relationship based on difference in which the parties engage in opposite behaviors.

Cultural awareness: The ability to understand the role cultural prescriptions play in shaping communication.

person-to-person interaction. Every culture can be subdivided into cocultures consisting of members of the same general culture who differ in some ethnic or sociological way from the dominant culture. In the United States, African Americans, Hispanic Americans, Japanese Americans, Korean Americans, the physically challenged, homosexuals, and the elderly are examples of cocultural groups. To engage in effective interpersonal communication with members of these and other groups it is important to enhance your knowledge of the norms and rules that characterize their interactions. Remember, the lessons taught to you by your culture are not necessarily the lessons others have been taught by theirs.

Among culture's lessons are how to say hello and goodbye, when to speak and when to remain silent, how to behave when angry, how much eye contact to make when interacting, and how much gesturing and touching is appropriate. If cultural anthropologist Edward T. Hall is right in saying that culture is communication and communication is culture, then culture guides behavior, and we must make the effort to understand someone's culture if we are to understand the person.[18]

Becoming culturally aware increases communication competence.

Determining the answers to the following questions when interacting with someone whose cultural background differs from yours can improve your communication:

1. How do this person's feelings about socialization differ from mine?

2. How does his or her concept of self differ from mine?

3. To what extent do our attitudes, values, and thinking processes differ?

4. To what degree is he or she more or less competitive than me?

5. In what ways does his or her use of nonverbal cues differ from mine?

ORIENTATION AND CULTURAL CONTEXT

While an array of variables distinguish one culture from another, the two we focus on here are (1) individual and collective orientation and (2) high-context and low-context communication.[19]

Individual and Collective Orientation. Cultures that are more individualistic in nature, such as those of the United States, Canada, Great Britain, and Germany, stress individual goals. In contrast, cultures more collectivistic in nature, such as those represented by many Muslim, African, Asian, and Latin American countries, stress group goals.[20] Whereas individualist cultures nurture individual initiative and achievement, collectivist cultures nurture loyalty to a group. In an individualist culture, you are responsible for yourself and maybe your immediate family (the "I" is dominant); in a collectivist culture, you are responsible for the entire group (the "we" is dominant). Likewise, whereas individualist cultures promote competition, collectivist ones stress cooperation.

High-Context and Low-Context Communication. Cultures are also distinguished from each other by their use of high- or low-context communication. High-context cultures are tradition bound; cultural traditions guide members' interactions, causing them to appear to outsiders as overly polite and indirect in relationships. Members of low-context cultures, in contrast, usually exhibit a more direct communication style, one that is verbally explicit. Members of Western cultures tend to use low-context communication, whereas members of Asian and other Eastern cultures typically use high-context communication, preferring to interact indirectly and leaving much unstated.[21] Because they also place a premium on face-saving behavior, members of high-context cultures are much less confrontational as well. Preferring to preserve harmony, they seek to avoid arguing for fear the other person might lose face. For similar reasons, members of high-context cultures are also reluctant to say "no" directly to another person. Thus, members of low-context cultures may have difficulty deciding when and if the "yes" of a member of a high-context culture really means yes.

THE IMPACT OF GENDER

Culture also shapes gender, and gender shapes communication.[22] Socially accepted variations in the definitions and views of masculinity and femininity, gender differences, are taught to us as we grow up. As historian Elizabeth Fox-Genovese writes, "To be an 'I' at all means to be gendered."[23]

GENDER AND COMMUNICATION STYLE

Gender is a social creation that imposes a sense of social order by reflecting the societal characteristics associated with the biological categories of male and female. Subtly or overtly, we are pressured to conform to social norms, encouraged to learn accepted interaction scripts, and usually develop preferences for using different communication styles. Though attitudes have evolved, in U.S. society, for example, women still are generally expected to be more nurturing, sensitive to others' needs, and emotional than men, whereas men are expected to be more independent, assertive, and emotionally restrained than women. Some families even persist in dividing responsibilities along gendered lines, assigning more physically demanding outdoor chores to males while expecting females to clean the home's interior, cook, and care for other family members, including younger siblings and aging parents. Hospitals often wrap baby girls in pink blankets and baby boys in blue blankets. Girls and boys similarly are provided with different kinds of toys—perhaps dolls for girls and action figures for boys. Even schools have been criticized for encouraging students to pursue different curricula depending on their gender. So from the delivery room to the home, to the school, and on to romantic relationships and career paths, we see gender helping to shape lifestyle. However, as we become more conscious of arbitrarily created gendered meanings, we are able to work to reconstruct and broaden our understanding of what is appropriate behavior and what we accept as "normal."

While we all express gender through behavior that we believe is normal for a member of our sex, what we define as normal changes with time. By identifying how arbitrarily created gendered constructions, or conventions, affect interpersonal communication and our relationships, we take a step toward understanding what we hope for when it comes to our interpersonal lives. Do you see your options as unlimited? What tasks do you feel free to

Gender: The socially constructed roles and behaviors that the members of a given society believe to be appropriate for men and women.

perform? What limits, if any, do you believe should be placed on the role gender plays in our social, professional, and family relationships? While all societies promote gender ideologies that specify appropriate behaviors for males and females, what should you do if you believe a gendered construction is privileging, disadvantaging, empowering, or paralyzing you or a partner?

As you proceed through this text, you will have numerous opportunities to answer questions like these. After all, gender is a relational construct that we clarify through person-to-person interaction.

THE IMPACT OF MEDIA AND TECHNOLOGY

According to media guru Marshall McLuhan, the medium is both message and massage.

"The medium is the message." "The medium is the massage." We can trace both of these sayings to the musings of the late media critic and communication theorist Marshall McLuhan. According to McLuhan, the channels of communication affect both the sending and the receiving of messages. The same words convey different messages depending on whether they are sent using face-to-face interaction, print, a cell phone, a video, or a podcast. The medium changes things, altering the message, massaging its contents. For the same reason, ending a relationship in person is different from terminating it via a text. It is now almost five decades since McLuhan predicted that the introduction of new technologies would transform our world into a mobile global village.[24] His prophecy has come true. Technology makes it increasingly possible for us to watch and listen to, introduce ourselves to, and have continuing contact with individuals across the country and around the world without ever leaving our homes. Technology is altering our sense of self, our social norms, our views of reality, our images of success and failure, our happiness, our interpersonal options, and the communication rules we adhere to.

Years ago, Apple's Steve Jobs observed that computers are really personal and should be renamed "inter-personal computers."[25] Today we use them, tablets, or smartphones to log on to Facebook, LinkedIn, or Foursquare so we can connect with others. In the year 2000, the average person spent 2.7 hours a week online. In 2010, that number jumped to 18 hours a week.[26] Now, we live our lives plus sometimes a "second life," enacting a fantasy or alternative life online, perhaps in Farmville, or sharing our interests on Pinterest or other sites. However, when we form a relationship online, we are likely to idealize and create heightened expectations for it, expectations that might not be realized should we actually meet. In fact, online partners feel greater intimacy with and attraction for one another than when they actually meet one another face-to-face.[27] Have any of your online relationships developed into flourishing off-line ones? To what do you attribute their success or failure?

What guidelines do you think people ought to follow when using electronically enhanced communication? For example, have you ever engaged in any of the behaviors identified in the chart below yourself? Would you become annoyed, insulted, or feel at risk if another person engaged in any of the identified behaviors? Use the chart to record your answers.

The behavior	Exhibited the behavior myself	My reaction to another's exhibiting the behavior
Texting while walking in the street		
Texting another person while dining out with a friend		
Answering a cell during a movie		
Talking loudly on your cell on public transportation		
Texting back in response to a missed call		
Talking on a cell with one friend when out with someone who is talking on a cell to another friend		
Not checking into foursquare when solicited		
Tweeting about one friend to another		
Accessing Facebook while watching TV with a significant other		

1. What rules, if any, would you advise we adhere to when using digitally enhanced communication?

2. What makes certain uses of digitally enhanced communication either acceptable or unacceptable in your eyes?

3. How would you react if a rule important to you were violated?

In addition to broadening the network of people we communicate with, for those who experience communication apprehension when face-to-face with another person, technology makes it possible to connect without such fear. We can interact remotely or in person, be anonymous, someone else, or ourselves. If the choice were yours alone, would you opt to increase or decrease the number of your virtual interactions compared to those you experience face-to-face? Why?

As well as spending increased amounts of time online, we are also devoting more time to viewing and talking about reality and other programs. As a result, our mediated experiences are influencing our real-life experiences and relationships. Mediated reality is often sexier or more violent than real-life. Despite this, we sometimes try to apply what we learn from them to our own lives, only to end up disappointed. Our love affairs are rarely as poignant

Which of the two cartoon characters do you believe makes the stronger case and why?

or as passionate as those in the media. Our friends are rarely as attractive, giving, or fun to be with as those we see depicted. Physicians and lawyers are rarely as successful treating or representing us as their fictional counterparts are. Somehow, real life falls short of the lives we encounter either online or via television and film.

A generation ago, parents used to cajole, "Turn off the TV." Their plea has now changed to something like "Turn off the computer and come watch television." Or are your parents as plugged into Facebook and other online sites as you are? Do you or they take the computer to bed as you once did a stuffed animal? The claims we make about Internet addiction are much like the claims people used to make about television being a plug-in drug.

Whether it is the television or a computer, a machine is altering your consciousness and the nature of your interpersonal interactions.[28] And we all need to think about that. In coming chapters we will look at the extent to which it is personalizing or depersonalizing our contacts, fostering or impeding the development of what we call a community. Is it improving or harming your communication with friends and family members? When online, do you gravitate toward cliques of persons who share your interests, or do you seek to widen and diversify your interpersonal community?

ON THE WAY TO GAINING COMMUNICATION COMPETENCE

Even though interpersonal communication is an inevitable part of life, few, if any, of us are as effective or as successful at it as we could be. Therefore, we invite you to treat this class as your interpersonal communication laboratory. Use the information you gain and the skills you practice as guides when you interact with others. There is no such thing as being too good at interpersonal communication. Whatever your capabilities are right now, to help yourself become better at communicating interpersonally, promise yourself you will do the following.

Is the person you present online the same person you present face-to-face?

ADD TO YOUR STOREHOUSE OF KNOWLEDGE ABOUT INTERPERSONAL COMMUNICATION

Your chance of influencing your interpersonal encounters positively depends, at least to some extent, on your knowledge of how interpersonal relationships work. While our relationships vary significantly, with some being plagued by problems and others proceeding smoothly, one of our objectives in this book is to share with you a number of techniques you can use to enhance the quality of your relationships and the satisfaction you derive from them.

RECOGNIZE HOW YOUR RELATIONSHIPS AFFECT YOU

Every one of your relationships affects you in some way. Some influence your sense of others; some alter the quality of your life. Some add to your confidence; others diminish your belief in yourself. While healthy relationships enrich your life, unhealthy ones too often rob you of energy, leaving you demoralized or apathetic. Another goal of this course is to help you understand the complex ways in which interpersonal communication changes you and the complex forces at work during person-to-person contacts. If you understand the challenges you face, identify alternative modes of responding, and learn how to think about your relationships, then you will be better prepared to deal effectively with them.

ANALYZE YOUR OPTIONS

The interpersonal communication choices you make have impacts on you and your partner. Rather than responding automatically, take time to think about your options. What happens in a relationship usually is not beyond your control. In most situations, you have freedom to respond in any number of ways. Every contact you engage in offers opportunities to improve it if you remain flexible and open. Another of our goals is to help you learn to take advantage of this.

INTERACT ETHICALLY, RESPECT DIVERSITY, AND THINK CRITICALLY ABOUT YOUR PERSON-TO-PERSON CONTACTS

Effective interpersonal communicators act ethically in their relationships, demonstrate their respect for diversity, and think critically about the interactions they share. Ethical communicators demonstrate the ability to adhere to standards of right and wrong. They follow appropriate interaction rules, treat other persons as they would like to be treated, and never knowingly harm someone else in an effort to achieve personal goals.

Interpersonal communicators who respect diversity understand culture's role in person-to-person interactions, tolerate difference and dissent, willingly interact with persons from a variety of backgrounds, demonstrate a decreased use of stereotypes to guide behavior, process experience from the viewpoints of others, avoid imposing their cultural values on other persons, and refrain from holding discriminatory attitudes.

Individuals who think critically about their relationships know that communication is complex, and they don't know all there is to know. They are open-minded; reflect on

Researcher Noelle Chesley wanted to find out if the time people spent on cell-phones enhanced or detracted from their overall feelings of happiness. To answer the question, Chesley surveyed more than 1,200 adults, concluding that a correlation existed: the more time individuals spent on cell-phones the less happy and less satisfied they became with their family relationships. Chesley attributed this, at least in part, to the work lives of people spilling over into their personal lives and causing stress at home.

Consider these questions:

1. Do your experiences confirm Chesley's findings? Does time spent on your cell stress the relationships you share with people important to you, perhaps because you divide your attention, with less attention being paid to the person(s) with you?

2. Do you think Chesley would have found the same results if she had studied the time we spend on tablets or computers? Explain your answer.

3. What recommendations can you offer for alleviating such relationship stressors? For example, would you expect others to abide by rules specifying when to use cell phones or other digital tools?

SOURCE: Noelle Chesley, "Blurring Boundaries? Linking Technology Use, Spillover, Individual Distress, and Family Satisfaction." *Journal of Marriage and Family*, 67, 2005, p. 1237–1238.

others' ideas rather than respond impulsively; open themselves to new ideas and new ways of perceiving; challenge themselves to reexamine their beliefs, values, and behaviors; and concern themselves with unstated assumptions in addition to overt discourse. They think things out, analyzing and evaluating outcomes, seeking to understand and remember what worked or didn't, and creating opportunities for their own personal growth together with the personal growth of others.

PRACTICE AND APPLY SKILLS TO IMPROVE INTERPERSONAL PERFORMANCE

This text shares with you skills you can practice to enhance your interpersonal effectiveness. Commit to practicing them. How you present yourself, perceive others, use words and nonverbal cues, listen, progress in a relationship, overcome relational obstacles, demonstrate trust and trustworthiness, and handle your emotions all affect your interaction with friends, family members, coworkers, and health providers. The extent to which you practice and apply the skills we discuss will determine whether you add to your interpersonal behavioral repertoire, demonstrating your interpersonal versatility and resourcefulness.

How omnipresent is technology in your life? Could you live without it? Would you want to?

"After he left my dorm, he texted me, 'I'm sorry, it's over.' That's all he said," Sylvia told her roommate Justine. "How could he end things just like that? Why didn't he talk to me when we were together? I thought everything was fine with us."

Sylvia and Khalil had been together for several months. They had met on campus at the beginning of the semester and had been seeing each other regularly. Sylvia had even invited Khalil to spend Thanksgiving with her at her parent's. They had returned to campus after the holiday and then this happened. "What did I do to cause this?" Sylvia asked Justine. "Do you think he met someone else?"

Sylvia was despondent. Questions raced through her mind. She tried to access Khalil's Facebook page, but he had already defriended her, deleted her pictures, and changed his relationship status to single. She decided to text him back, asking, "What happened? What did I do?" Then she turned off her cell, afraid of what he would text back to her.

Khalil was sitting in his off-campus apartment staring blankly at his iPad. He had just defriended Sylvia and changed his Facebook status. He didn't feel good about it, but he told himself he had no choice. Now she was texting him. He didn't want to read it. "How can I tell her truth?" he wondered. Sure, they had had some great times together—but that was until he went home with her for Thanksgiving dinner. Soon after entering Sylvia's parents' home, Khalil had begun to feel uncomfortable. Her folks were nice enough, but he sensed a certain amount of distance on their part.

By the time they had finished dinner, Khalil was certain that because he was Egyptian, Sylvia's parents had reservations about him. They hadn't done or said anything directly to him; he just had a feeling. Maybe he should have raised his concerns with Sylvia. But he told himself that ending things this way was easier. Was he right? Khalil just didn't know. He turned off his cell.[29]

Demonstrate your understanding by answering these questions:

1. What do you think about the way Sylvia and Khalil handled their situation?

2. What does the behavior of each suggest about his or her communication weaknesses and strengths?

3. Would you have used texting and Facebook in the same way as Sylvia and/or Khalil? Explain your answer.

4. Given the current status of their relationship, what advice would you give each of them?

REVIEW THIS

CHAPTER SUMMARY

1 Define interpersonal communication, distinguishing it from other types of communication. Interpersonal communication occurs between two people who form a dyad. Interpersonal communicators make personal contact, build a connection, and establish a relationship. The process of interpersonal communication is ongoing and ever changing, and occurs whenever we interact with another person, sharing responsibility for creating meaning (what we extract from the interaction) and managing our relationship (determining its nature).

2 Use a communication model to identify the essential elements and transactional nature of the interpersonal communication process. Every interpersonal interaction is transactional in nature, meaning it involves two people who simultaneously function as sender and receiver; it contains messages (the content of communication), channels (the medium or media carrying the message), noise (anything interfering with the reception of a message), feedback (information returned to a message source in response to a message sent), context (the physical, psychological, temporal, and cultural setting for communication), and effect(s) (the emotional, physical, and/or cognitive influence of the communication).

3 Explain the functions that interpersonal communication serves. Interpersonal communication fulfills psychological functions by enhancing self-other understanding; social functions by meeting our needs for affection, inclusion, and control; information functions by promoting the sharing of knowledge and reduction of uncertainty; and influence functions by enabling us to use strategic communication to achieve goals.

4 Describe the characteristics, core principles, and axioms of interpersonal communication. Among interpersonal communication's characteristics are that it is a dynamic process, unrepeatable and irreversible, learned, and noted for its wholeness and nonsummativity. Among the principles underlying interpersonal communication are the importance of using behavioral patterns and both reasoned and retrospective sense making to predict and interpret behavior. The following five axioms add to our understanding of interpersonal relationships: (1) You cannot *not* communicate; (2) every interaction has content and relationship dimensions; (3) every interaction is defined by how it is punctuated; (4) messages consist of verbal symbols and nonverbal cues; and (5) interactions are either symmetrical or complementary.

5 Describe how gender and culture affect interpersonal communication. Gender and cultural prescriptions shape interpersonal communication. Because of their potential to enhance or complicate interpersonal relations, we can demonstrate sensitivity and avoid misunderstandings by increasing our awareness of the culture and gender preferences of others and recognizing the importance of respecting and adjusting to differences.

6 Provide examples of how digital media are reshaping interpersonal contacts. Digital media have broadened our options for communicating interpersonally. They are altering our sense of self, social norms, and views of reality. We send an increasing number of texts, using our cell phones more than ever before. Whether such options are personalizing or depersonalizing interaction is still open to debate.

7 Develop a plan to improve your interpersonal communication. Adding to your storehouse of knowledge about interpersonal communication, critically analyzing how your relationships affect you as well as the behavioral options open to you, committing to interacting ethically, respecting diversity, and thinking critically about person-to-person interactions, together with developing and practicing skills, will make you a more effective interpersonal partner.

✓ CHECK YOUR UNDERSTANDING

1 Can you explain the different kinds of communication you use in a day and how these help meet your needs? (See pages 1–2 and 12–14; and *Try This*, page 18.)

2 Can you give examples of what makes communication interpersonal? (See pages 2–5.)

3 Can you name and define the elements and axioms at work during interpersonal communication by using them to analyze some of your recent communication exchanges? (See pages 20–22.)

4 Can you summarize how communicating online as opposed to face-to-face alters the nature of interpersonal communication? (See pages 25–27; and *Try This*, page 4 and page 26.)

5 Can you write a paragraph describing the steps you will take to enhance your interpersonal skills? (See pages 27–29.)

✓ CHECK YOUR SKILLS

1 Can you identify factors that distinguish your fulfilling and unfulfilling relationships? (See pages 2–4; and *Try This*, page 8.)

2 Can you determine when someone is responding to you personally as opposed to impersonally? (See pages 6–8.)

3 Can you use both feedback and feedforward to improve communication? (See pages 10–11.)

4 Can you use a transactional model of interpersonal communication to analyze an interpersonal communication exchange? (See page 13; and *Try This*, page 15.)

5 Can you provide examples of how one of your relationships fulfills your needs? (See *Try This*, page 18.)

6 Can you illustrate how the axioms of communication make themselves visible in your relationships? (See pages 20–22.)

7 Can you use the questions on page 23 to facilitate communication with a person whose culture differs from your own? (See page 23.)

8 Can you identify the gendered messages communicated to you by your family? (See pages 24–25.)

9 Can you apply your understanding of interpersonal communication when engaging in electronically enhanced communication? (See *Try This*, page 26; and *Reflect on This*, page 29.)

10 Can you use your skills to identify and respond to relationship challenges? (See *The Case of Sylvia and Khalil*, page 30.)

KEY TERMS

Communication   *2*

Intrapersonal communication   *3*

Interpersonal communication   *3*

Dyad   *3*

Interpersonal competence   *4*

Role duality   *8*

Messages   *8*

Channel   *9*

Noise   *9*

Feedback   *10*

Positive feedback   *10*

Negative feedback   *10*

Internal feedback   *11*

External feedback   *11*

Low-monitored feedback   *11*

High-monitored feedback   *11*

Feedforward   *11*

Phatic communication   *11*

Context   *11*

Effect   *12*

Linear or unidirectional model   *12*

Interaction model   *13*

Transactional model   *14*

Dynamic process   *19*

Reasoned sense making   *20*

Retrospective sense making   *20*

Axioms of communication   *20*

Complementary relationship   *22*

Cultural awareness   *22*

Gender   *24*

STUDENT STUDY SITE

Visit the student study site at **www.sagepub.com/gambleic** to access the following materials:

- SAGE Journal Articles
- Videos
- Web Resources
- eFlashcards
- Web Quizzes
- Study Questions

chapter 2

Know thyself.

— Socrates

THE IMPACT OF SELF-CONCEPT

LEARNING OBJECTIVES

After completing this chapter, you should be able to demonstrate mastery of the following learning outcomes:

1. Define self-concept, distinguishing it from the self.

2. Explain reflected appraisal theory, social comparison theory, and confirmation, rejection, and disconfirmation, using them to discuss the role you and others play in shaping the self-concept.

3. Define self-fulfilling prophecy and distinguish between positive and negative Pygmalions.

4. Explain the influence that cultural diversity and gender have on self-concept.

5. Describe how media and technology affect self-concept.

6. Identify how you can change and strengthen your self-concept.

The feature film *The Social Network* presents a fictional characterization of the real Mark Zuckerberg, the entrepreneur who created Facebook. As one writer observed, of significance is the fact that Zuckerberg created *Face*book, and not Footbook or Elbowbook.[1] By starting Facebook, Zuckerberg acted on the belief that it is human for people to want to know what is going on. And we have proven Zuckerberg right. If you are over twelve years of age, you likely are among the more than half of all Americans who use Facebook.

We are not just Facebook's users, however. We are also Facebook's products. We log on to Facebook, post photos that display ourselves as attractively or enticingly as possible, and update our lives for others to share by the minute if we're obsessed, by the hour if we're driven, and by the day if we're typical users.

> What motivates our participation in Facebook? A deep interest in each other, and a desire to be noticed!

What motivates our participation in Facebook? A deep interest in each other and a desire to be noticed. We feel the need to tell about a new shirt, car, promotion, hairstyle, significant other, or status change. Facebook capitalizes on our longing for connection and attention. Zuckerberg understands that we want others to know about us. He understands that showing our face helps us validate our existence—and our concept of self.[2]

WHAT DO YOU KNOW?

Before continuing your reading of this chapter, which of the following five statements do you believe to be true and which do you believe to be false?

1. People with high self-esteem are less likely to be bullies.   T   F

2. Your perceived self is the one others see.   T   F

3. Engaging in face-work improves your looks.   T   F

4. Positive expectations have no impact on performance.   T   F

5. Childhood experiences influence our ideas about gender.   T   F

Read the chapter to discover if you're right or if you've made any erroneous assumptions.

ANSWERS: 1. F; 2. F; 3. F; 4. F; 5. T

How you see yourself affects your relationships with others.

Who are you? What do you think of yourself? Do you consider your relationship with yourself to be a good one? When you evaluate yourself, do you characteristically give yourself a "thumbs-up" or a "thumbs-down"? This chapter offers you the opportunity to develop **self-awareness** by reflecting on and monitoring your own behavior. Use this information to explore the nature of the self; to analyze how culture gender, media, and technology influence its development; and to examine how the intrapersonal level of communication (the individual level, the communicating you do with yourself) affects the choices you make, your behavior, and your relationships.

The poet-philosopher Alan Watts noted, "Trying to define yourself is like trying to bite your own teeth."[3] Exactly how confident are you that you really know yourself? And how willing are you to try to get to know yourself better?

Who you think you are and how you think about yourself in relationship to others influences every one of your interpersonal contacts. What you think of yourself is your baseline, your starting point for communication.

THE SELF-CONCEPT: YOUR ANSWER TO WHO YOU ARE

Where does self-concept come from? While we are not born with a self-concept, over time we certainly develop one. The day a child first says "me," the day she recognizes herself as separate from her surroundings, her life begins to change as she strives to fit into the world as she sees it. In short order, our concept of self—that relatively stable set of perceptions each of us attributes to ourselves—becomes our most important possession.

Beginning in childhood, the **self-concept** is composed of everything we think and feel about ourselves. It is the perceived self—our self-identity—the image we form of ourselves. In fact, self-concept has two key components: self-image and self-esteem (see Table 2.1). **Self-image** is the mental picture you have of yourself—it sums up the kind of person you *think* you are. It is a composite of the roles you claim and the attitudes and beliefs you use to describe who and what you are to others, and your understanding of how others see you. **Self-esteem** is your self-evaluation—your estimation of your self-worth. In many ways it is an indication of how much you like and value yourself, including your feelings, positive and negative, about your abilities, character, and feelings.

With this as background, it becomes apparent that self-concept affects behavior, including what we think possible. As a result, it is important to use every opportunity to think carefully about self-concept.

How you complete the sentences in the "Who Are You?" "Try This" box on page 38, and the categories into which your answers can be grouped, offers clues to your self-concept,

Self-awareness: Personal reflection on and monitoring of one's own behavior.

Self-concept: The relatively stable set of perceptions one attributes to oneself.

Self-esteem: One's appraisal of one's own self-worth.

Self-image: The mental picture one has of oneself.

TABLE 2.1   Looking at Yourself

Self-concept	Everything you think and know about yourself
Self-image	Your mental picture of you
Self-esteem	Your estimation of your self-worth

As you read the following poem by Teri Gamble, consider these questions: What do you think is the significance of the clown's omnipresent rainbow smile? Like the poem's subject, do you ever "play" to people around you? Like the clown, do you ever wonder who you really are?

The rubber man in the spotlight

    Propels himself
    Beyond the reach
    Of reality.
    Midway between today and tomorrow
    He pauses
    Suspended in his reverie by the crowd.

The rubber man in the spotlight

    Warmed by laughter
    Finds a face
    To play to.
    Dancing upon an ever-turning spindle
    He plays to another
    And another, and another.

The rubber man in the spotlight

    Sweeps up the dreams
    That remind him
    Of yesterday.
    Then tumbling out of the ring
    His face frozen in a rainbow smile
    He wonders who he is.

including your self-image and self-esteem. For example, you might conceive of yourself in reference to your gender (male or female), religion or spirituality (Buddhist, Muslim, Jewish, Christian, nonbeliever), race (African American, Hispanic, Asian), nationality (U.S. citizen, Canadian, Chinese), physical attributes (tall, stout), roles (spouse, daughter, sibling, employee), attitudes and emotions (optimistic, dejected, personable), mental abilities (academically challenged, gifted), or talents (musically or artistically proficient). The words you use to express your self-perceptions reveal what you think you are like. In many ways, your answers represent a construct that you have built to make sense of who you are. Remember, however, that the self-concept is not necessarily the same as the self.

HOW ARE THE SELF AND SELF-CONCEPT RELATED?

According to industrial psychologist William Haney, the self and the self-concept differ from each other in a number of ways. First, the self is very fluid and in a state of constant change,

Begin the exploration of your self-concept by answering the following question: Who am I? How many answers can you give? Complete the sentences below with the many different ways you view yourself.

I am _____.   I am _____.

I am _____.   I am _____.

I am _____.   I am _____.

I am _____.   I am _____.

I am _____.   I am _____.

There are many ways to complete the sentences. For example, did you give information about personal traits, such as, "I am spiritual," "I am attractive," or "I am friendly"? Did you describe your social identity, such as "I am a Christian" or "I am Chinese"?

Taken together, your answers describe the elements or specific beliefs that constitute your self-concept. Look back at your answers. What do they reveal regarding how you define yourself? What roles do you see yourself playing? How do you define yourself socially? As you completed the sentences, how did social comparisons influence what you wrote? In what ways, if any, did your past successes and failures as well as other people's judgments play a part in determining your responses?

whereas the self-concept is more highly structured and difficult to change (see Figure 2.1). Second, a portion of the self-concept may not actually be included in the self; this area represents the part of ourselves that we invent. Third, there is much more to the self than is included within the self-concept; this area represents our untapped potential. For example, you may think of yourself as friendly and outgoing, while others see you as snobbish and reserved. You may have the potential to become a leader, but because of your inability to convince others that you would like to work with them, you might not have the opportunity to demonstrate this talent.

To put it another way, the self-concept is a "map" that we create to chart the "territory" that is the self.[4] Our map or mental picture is, at least in part, a result of our interpretations of the messages others send us. As such, it may be accurate or inaccurate, positive or negative. The self-concept is depicted in Figure 2.1 as a rigid, geometric design to indicate that we like to make sense to ourselves. Experiencing uncertainty about the self is not a comfortable state for us, and so we work to develop consistency in the way we perceive ourselves.

HOW ACCURATE IS THE SELF-CONCEPT?

Although change is a constant in life, the thirst for constancy causes us to cling to outdated self-notions even in the face of evidence that renders these notions obsolete. Instead of revising our self-concepts to conform to new information, we do our best to acquire information that confirms what we already believe is true. Our reluctance to let go of set ideas allows outmoded notions about the self to persist. It is understandable that we might resist changing an inaccurate self-concept when the new information available to us is negative, because our self-concept could become

Do you see yourself as you are or as you think you are?

more negative. For example, this could happen when we are no longer considered to be as bright or hardworking as we once were. It is hard to comprehend, however, why we similarly resist changing when the information is positive and would enhance our self-concept, such as when we are no longer perceived to be gawky or unfriendly. By rejecting such information, we deny ourselves a chance for growth and self-renewal. Defending an unrealistic negative or positive self-concept keeps us from making efforts to redefine ourselves. Whether that redefinition would result in a more positive or a more negative picture of who we are does not matter; our cognitive conservatism keeps us from seeing the real need for change and allows us to continue deluding ourselves. Refuting new information that could lead us to change only limits us and obscures our view of how others see us. Conducting a reality check is necessary to validate or invalidate who we think we are. Have you conducted one recently? What did you discover?

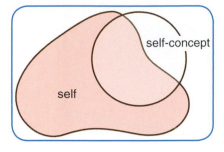

Figure 2.1 The Self and the Self-Concept

self-concept

self

Thus, as we go through life, each of us builds a self-concept that includes feelings of self-worth. The questions each of us must answer include the following: What is my feeling of self-worth? Why? What, if anything, do I want to do about how I feel about myself?

SELF-ESTEEM: ASSESSING SELF-WORTH

When we feel good about our achievements, we also tend to value and feel good about ourselves. Self-esteem, our positive or negative evaluation of our self-concept or sense of personal worth, is important because it can nurture and feed success or make succeeding more difficult. When we achieve or acquire new competencies, our self-esteem grows. In other words, we build self-esteem when we overcome obstacles, acquire specific skills or achievements, or are given increased responsibilities. Feeling good about the self and what we are capable of contributes to our performing well.

Since self-esteem is a measure of the value we place on ourselves, we carry it with us from one interpersonal interaction to another. What is more, we relay our level of self-esteem to others by how we interact with them.

HIGH VERSUS LOW SELF-ESTEEM

People with high self-esteem differ from those with low self-esteem in communication style. They tend to display different eye contact, posture, and expression. Think about your friendly and romantic relationships. How does your opinion of your self-worth affect them?

Individuals with high self-esteem often think better of others, expect others to like them, evaluate their own performance favorably, perform well in front of others, work hard for those who demand it, feel comfortable interacting with superiors, and defend themselves against others' negative appraisals. In contrast, individuals with low self-esteem often disapprove of others, expect others not to like them, evaluate themselves unfavorably, perform poorly in the presence of others, feel threatened by their superiors, and find it hard to defend themselves against those who view them critically, equating criticism with rejection.[5]

When we perceive ourselves as failures, we are more likely to behave in ways that cause us to fail. When we perceive ourselves as successes, we are more apt to act confidently and in ways that bring about success. Every success we have helps build our self-esteem.

SELF-ESTEEM AND PERFORMANCE

When self-esteem is not connected to performance, it can be self-defeating. Feeling good about yourself when you have no reason to—that is, when you have added to neither your

WHAT DO YOU KNOW?

True or False
1. *People with high self-esteem are less likely to be bullies.*
False. High self-esteem may actually increase the tendency to bully.

achievements nor your competencies—can lead to your developing a favorable self-appraisal that will not be matched by others' views of you. Thus, when we talk about the importance of developing self-esteem, we are not talking about merely praising or becoming a cheerleader for you. Rather, we are talking about opening yourself to opportunities that will help you develop your skills and abilities to their fullest potential.

And here's a note of caution—research reveals that individuals with high self-esteem may pose more of a threat to others than persons with low self-esteem.[6] In fact, research indicates that overemphasizing the importance of self-esteem in those who possess an unrealistically inflated self-appraisal can precipitate a culture of bullying characterized by persistent teasing, name-calling, or social exclusion. These findings have led some to argue that there needs to be a balance in the amount of praise given, to prevent inflated perceptions of self-importance in already self-centered individuals.[7] Researchers advise that instead of fostering self-esteem, we should be fostering resilience, because resilience helps people recover from personal disappointments and defeats.[8]

Self-concept, self-worth, and self-esteem are all significant in their influence on how we communicate, but it is important to remember that when they are unrealistically inflated they can pose problems.

HOW OTHERS SHAPE OUR SELF-CONCEPT

Belief in yourself shapes what is possible for you.

While your experiences help shape your self-concept, your self-concept, in turn, helps shape your future experiences. How you see yourself in relation to others both guides and modifies your behavior. Probably, you act differently depending on the people you are with. You may act outgoing when in the presence of one friend but be intimidated by another. You may feel like a star in art class but inferior in chemistry, or vice versa. At any given moment, the nature of your self is affected by the nature of the situation in which you are interacting. And your interactions shape your view of your self. Consequently, your language, attitudes, and appearance are apt to change as you move from one set of conditions to another. In a way, you become different selves as you adapt to perceived changes (see Table 2.2).

WE REFLECT OTHERS' APPRAISALS

Reflected appraisal theory: A theory that states that the self a person presents is in large part based on the way others categorize the individual, the roles they expect him or her to play, and the behaviors or traits they expect him or her to exhibit.

More than a century ago, psychologist William James put it this way: "A man has as many social selves as there are individuals who recognize him and carry an image of him in their mind."[9] In similar fashion, in his **reflected appraisal theory**, psychologist Charles Cooley described the mirrorlike image we derive from our contacts with others and then project into our future experiences. In other words, we build a self-concept that reflects how we think others see us.[10] Thus, as our assessments of situations and people change, we show different sides of ourselves. In fact, we use the views of others to develop our view of ourselves. According to reflected appraisal theory, the self we present is in large part based on the way others categorize us, the roles they expect us to play, and the behaviors or traits they expect us to exhibit. Cooley believed that by reflecting back to us who we are and how we come across, other people function as our mirrors. In fact, he coined the term "looking glass self" to represent the self that comes to us from others. For example, if others see you as a leader, capable, and outgoing, you may reflect their appraisals by viewing yourself in those ways. Of course, the roles we play and how we play them affect both how and with whom we communicate. They all influence the content, objectives, and frequency of our communication contacts.[11]

Feelings about aging may affect notions of self-worth. What messages about the self does our society send people as they age? What messages does it send to the physically challenged as compared to the able-bodied?

Consider these questions:

1. Picture yourself in the future. How do you think your view of yourself would change if you were thirty to forty years older? How do you imagine you would you feel about your appearance? How do you suppose you would feel about your potential to find a good job? How would you feel reporting to someone younger than yourself in your workplace?

2. How would your view of yourself change if instead of being able-bodied you suddenly had to use a wheelchair or vice versa?

3. What steps could you take to foster resilience in yourself when you are faced with forces that challenge your self-conceptions?

TABLE 2.2   Theories Reveal How Others Help Shape Us

Reflected appraisal theory	We build a self-concept that reflects how we think others see us.
Social comparison theory	We assess how we measure up against others.

Of course, not all messages others send us about how they see us carry the same weight. Those sent by our significant others and by individuals whose opinions we respect and trust normally exert more influence on us than do the opinions of strangers and mere acquaintances.

WE COMPARE OURSELVES WITH OTHERS

According to **social comparison theory**, we compare ourselves to others to develop a feel for how our talents, abilities, and qualities measure up to theirs.[12] In other words, in the effort to learn more about ourselves, we use others as measuring sticks, and then we evaluate ourselves in terms of how we think we measure up to them. As we compare ourselves to others, we form judgments of our skills, personal characteristics, and so on. We can, for example, decide whether we are the same as or different from others, whether we are better or worse, stronger or weaker, or more or less creative than those with whom we compare ourselves. Often, as we assess our similarities and differences, we also make decisions regarding the groups we fit into. Generally, we are most comfortable interacting with others we perceive to be like us.[13]

Our self-esteem suffers if we continually feel we fall short when gauging ourselves in relation to others. When this happens, however, it may well be that we have chosen to compare ourselves to an inappropriate reference group. For example, if we compare our looks with those of a supermodel, our musical ability with those of an *American Idol* or Grammy winner, or our athletic prowess with that of an Olympian, we probably are making an unfair comparison and, as a result, will develop an unrealistic assessment of our appearance, talent, or ability. On the other hand, if we compare ourselves with members of a more appropriate reference group, we might be able to inflate rather than deflate our sense of self.

Our accuracy in assessing our self-concept and self-esteem depends on how successful we are at processing experience and receiving feedback. If we pay more attention to our successes than to our failures and more attention to positive reactions than to negative ones, we could end up overinflating our sense of self. On the other hand, if we pay more attention to our failures and give more credence to negative reactions, then our sense of

WHAT DO YOU KNOW?

True or False
2. *Your perceived self is the one others see.*
False. Your perceived self is the image you have of yourself, not the self you aspire to be.

Social comparison theory: A theory affirming that individuals compare themselves to others to develop a feel for how their talents, abilities, and qualities measure up.

True or False

3. *Engaging in face-work improves your looks.*

False. Face-work is what you do to protect your self-image by reducing the negative aspects of yourself that are visible to others.

....

Perceived self: A reflection of one's self-concept; the person one believes oneself to be when one is being honest with oneself.

Ideal self: The self one would like to be.

Impression management: The exercising of control over one's behaviors in an effort to make the desired impression.

Possible self: The self that one might become someday.

Expected self: The self that others assume one will exhibit.

Dramaturgical approach to human interaction: A theory, originated by Erving Goffman, that explains the role that the skillful enacting of impression management plays in person-to-person interaction.

self could deflate. In neither instance would our sense of self conform to reality. Rather than achieving congruence, our sense of self would be inconsistent with both real-life experiences and feedback.

WE HAVE PERCEIVED, IDEAL, AND EXPECTED SELVES

Each of us possesses a perceived self, an ideal or possible self, and an expected self. Sometimes, these views of the self can conflict with one another.

The **perceived self** is a reflection of your self-concept. It is the person you believe yourself to be when you are honest with yourself. Usually, there are some aspects of the perceived self that you wish to keep secret from others. For example, you might hesitate to let others know that you do not think you are good-looking or intelligent, that you are fixated on becoming wealthy, or that you are more concerned for your own welfare than theirs. Your **ideal self** is the self you would like to be. For example, you may want to be likable, and so you try to be a likable person. To accomplish this, you engage in **impression management**; you exercise control over your behavior in an effort to elicit the desired reaction.[14] The **possible self** is the self you might become one day—the one you dream of becoming. You may, for instance, want to be a passionately loved self, an accomplished self, or a rich self. The **expected self** is the one others assume you will exhibit. It is based on behaviors they have seen you display in the past or stereotypes they hold.

Goffman's Dramaturgical Approach. Through his concept known as the **dramaturgical approach to human interaction**, Erving Goffman explains the role that the skillful enacting of impression management plays in person-to-person interaction.[15] If we consider social interaction as a performance and the setting(s) in which interaction occurs as the stage, then the actors (the persons on the stage) play their parts to manage the impressions of others sharing the stage with them, so that they, the actors, may achieve their personal objectives. The more skillful the actors, the more effective they are at convincing others that they are knowledgeable and trustworthy and that they possess a charisma or dynamism that makes them attractive to others.

We can use several dramatic elements to make the best impression in any given scene. First, we can employ *framing*, specifically defining a scene or situation in a way that helps others interpret its meaning in the way we desire. We can also use *scripting*, the identification of each actor's role in the scene. In effect, we convince others on the stage with us to play their roles. Of course, we use *engaging dialogue*—storytelling together with colorful and descriptive language and effective use of nonverbal cues—to guide the responses of the other players. Together, these elements underlie our *performance*.

When performing, we can also choose from among a number of techniques to encourage others to see us as we wish to be seen. For example, we may use *exemplification*, in which we serve as an example or act as a role model for others; *promotion*, in which we elucidate our personal skills and accomplishments and/or a particular vision; *face-work*, in which we take steps to protect our image by reducing the negative aspects of ourselves visible to others; or *ingratiation*, in which we employ techniques of agreement to make others believe us to be more attractive and likable and less threatening, harmful, or pernicious.

Describe a performance, face-to-face or online, that you or another person you know has enacted in an effort to come off as authentic. Were you or the other person successful? Were you or the other person authentic? How do you know?

Imagining a Future Self. According to Kelly McGonigal, author of *The Willpower Instinct*, a disconnection may exist between what we think of ourselves in the present and how we conceive of ourselves in the future—our "future self."[16] Brain scans reveal that the parts of our brain that are active when we think about others are different from the parts of the brain that are active when we think about ourselves. If, however, we feel too little connection to our future self, the same regions that activate when we think of others activate when we think of ourselves in the future. It is as if when we think of our future self we are seeing someone other than ourselves.

Whether you do or do not connect with your future self can affect the decisions you make about your life. When we fail to pay attention to our future self, for example, we may make unethical decisions, such as leaking secrets that could destroy another person, causing ourselves problems both in the present and potentially down the road.[17]

We try to manage the impressions others form of us.

REACTIONS TO YOU: CONFIRMING, REJECTING, AND DISCONFIRMING RESPONSES

As we interact with others, how we feel about ourselves changes. Some people we interact with provide **confirmation** of our opinion of ourselves, communicating with us in ways consistent with our own appraisal of ourselves. How they treat us during our interactions with them reflects the way we think we are. For example, if you believe yourself to be intelligent, confirmers might reflect this by asking you to tutor them.

Others with whom we interact signal **rejection** of our self-appraisals by treating us in ways inconsistent with our sense of self—whether that is good or bad. For example, if you believe yourself to be hardworking but rejecters treat you as if you are lazy, over time their treatment of you might cause you to revise your picture of yourself.

Confirmation: A communication that tells another person that his or her self-image is affirmed.

Rejection: The negation of or disagreement with a self-appraisal.

Disconfirmation: Communication that denies another person's significance.

Self-efficacy: A positive belief in one's own abilities, competence, and potential.

Self-fulfilling prophecy: A prediction or expectation that comes true simply because one acts as if it were true.

Still others give us **disconfirmation** of, or show lack of regard for, our self-appraisals by sending us messages that tell us that as far as they are concerned, we are not even important enough for them to think about; in their eyes, we do not exist—we are irrelevant. Someone who disconfirms you ignores you and goes about her business as if you were not present. By treating other human beings like nonentities, consistent disconfirmers may eventually rob others of their sense of self, without which it becomes virtually impossible for them to relate to the world effectively.[18]

Thus, those around us help shape our self-concepts in both positive and negative ways. Virtually every interpersonal contact we share sends a message regarding our importance, our capabilities, and how others view both our potential and our inadequacies.[19] (See Table 2.3.)

TABLE 2.3   The Self in Relationships

Confirming response	Supports self-appraisal
Rejecting response	Negates self-appraisal
Disconfirming response	Robs the individual of a sense of self

THE SELF-FULFILLING PROPHECY: THE INFLUENCE OF POSITIVE AND NEGATIVE PYGMALIONS

Are you a pessimist or an optimist? Optimists believe they will succeed and persevere; pessimists tend to give up when confronted with challenges. Consequently, pessimists fail more frequently than do optimists, because one's expectations of success often precipitate the expected level of success. Optimists are resilient; they have feelings of **self-efficacy**, possessing a positive belief in their abilities and competence, believing in their own possibilities.[20] Unfortunately, the pessimist's outlook and lack of resilience may lead to failure even as success is within reach. In many ways, both pessimists and optimists live out self-fulfilling prophecies.

A **self-fulfilling prophecy** occurs when we verbalize a prediction or internalize an expectation that comes true simply because we act as if it already were. Thus, our behavior increases the likelihood of an outcome. For example, have you ever been invited to a function you did not want to attend because you expected to be bored? Were you? If you were, to what extent is it possible that your prediction of boredom increased the likelihood of its occurrence?

There are five basic steps in the self-fulfilling prophecy cycle (see Figure 2.2).[21] First, we form expectations of ourselves, others, or events—for example, "Monica won't like me." Second, we communicate the expectation by exhibiting various cues—"so I'll keep my distance from Monica." Third, others respond to the cues we send by adjusting their behavior to match our messages—Monica tells herself, "Ed is stuck up. I don't even want to talk to him." Fourth, the result is that our initial expectation comes true. Because we act as if our belief is true prior to its being confirmed, eventually it *is* confirmed—"It seems that, in fact, Monica does not like me." Fifth, we attain closure as we complete the self-fulfilling prophecy cycle. The way we interpret the actions of others only strengthens our original belief—"Every time I see Monica, I am reminded that she does not like me."

A self-fulfilling prophecy can be either self-imposed or other-imposed. When your own expectations influence your behavior, the prophecy is self-imposed. When the expectations

Pessimists and optimists approach life with divergent outlooks.

Because self-concept is a product of person-to-person interactions, other people can help shape our self-concept by confirming, rejecting, or disconfirming our sense of self.

1. Identify individuals who have confirmed, rejected, or disconfirmed you. Describe the short-and long-term effects of their actions on you.

When someone else . . .	Confirmed your self-concept	Rejected your self-concept	Disconfirmed your self-concept
Short-term effects			
Long-term effects			

2. Identify an instance when you confirmed, rejected, or disconfirmed someone else. Describe what you did or said and the effects of your words and actions on the other person and yourself.

When you . . .	Confirmed someone else's self-concept	Rejected someone else's self-concept	Disconfirmed someone else's self-concept
You said . . .			
The effect was . . .			

3. Identify words and behavior you can use to express your positive regard for someone.

4. Explain how indifference, inattentiveness, and disqualification influence conceptions of the self.

Figure 2.2 The Self-Fulfilling Prophecy Story

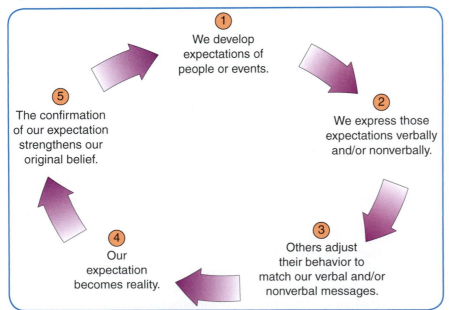

1. We develop expectations of people or events.

2. We express those expectations verbally and/or nonverbally.

3. Others adjust their behavior to match our verbal and/or nonverbal messages.

4. Our expectation becomes reality.

5. The confirmation of our expectation strengthens our original belief.

of others help direct your actions, the prophecy is other-imposed. Either way, we exhibit behavior that we or another person expects.

Among the most widely reported examples of the self-fulfilling prophecy is that used by psychologists Robert Rosenthal and Lenore Jacobson in their classic study *Pygmalion in the Classroom,* named for George Bernard Shaw's play *Pygmalion.* Rosenthal and his associates informed a number of teachers that certain of their students were expected to "bloom"— that is, perform exceptionally well—during the academic years. The teachers were unaware that the student names had actually been selected randomly, and there was no true basis for predicting who would succeed. Despite this, the students who were singled out to bloom did so, improving their IQs and performing at higher levels than would otherwise have been expected.[22] Apparently the teachers functioned as **positive Pygmalions**. Just as playwright Shaw's character Henry Higgins transforms Cockney flower girl Eliza Doolittle into a duchess by showing her his belief that he can help her learn to speak and act like one, the teachers caused the students to live up to the labels placed on them. The teachers' positive expectations positively influenced their treatment of the students. The teachers gave the "about to bloom" students extra positive verbal and nonverbal reinforcement, waited patiently for the students to respond if they hesitated, and did not give them negative feedback when they offered incorrect answers. Thus, the way the teachers behaved influenced the students' perceptions of their own abilities. The "about to blooms" responded to the teachers' prophecies by fulfilling them. Like Eliza Doolittle, the students acted like the persons others perceived them to be.

The Pygmalion effect, as this form of the self-fulfilling prophecy has come to be known, influences performance in a variety of settings, from work-related to educational to social, and it does so in both positive and negative ways. Just as when others hold high expectations for a person, their opinions tend to result in enhanced performance, when **negative Pygmalions** hold low expectations for others, their low expectations typically result in diminished performance. Consequently, managers' expectations can help or hinder worker production, teachers' expectations can boost or deflate student grades, and your own expectations can serve you as an ego maker or breaker. We live up to—and down to— expectations, whether these expectations emanate from others or ourselves. We are what we believe we are. What is important is that we recognize that our self-concept can change. At any point, we can work to strengthen our sense of self-worth.

REVISING YOUR SELF-CONCEPT: REEXAMINING IMPRESSIONS AND CONCEPTIONS

How others treat us and how we treat ourselves influence the person we think we are. Thus, if we wish to change our self-concept, we need to do our part to break with old ways of thinking. We need to update the way we think about ourselves and assess the accuracy of our self-concept. Figuratively speaking, we need to turn on a light inside ourselves so we become more self-aware, recognize the kinds of messages others send us, and be cognizant of messages we typically ignore, discount, or purposefully misinterpret.

While the tendency is to hold on to our existing self-concept—even when it is proved false—this does not mean that we cannot change it. We just have to work to overcome our natural resistance to change. In fact, some of us seek professional help in making meaningful changes. To combat the tendency to cling to an erroneous self-concept, we need to develop the willingness and skills to reevaluate or reinvent ourselves. That way, we will be better able to shed outdated conceptions—one impression at a time.

Positive Pygmalion:
An individual who positively influences one's perceptions of one's own abilities.

Negative Pygmalion:
An individual who negatively influences one's perceptions of one's own abilities.

To start this process, we need to understand how we manage to maintain a self-image that others may regard as unrealistic. For example, we might suppose we are great thinkers while others believe our thinking lacks depth. Perhaps because we are overly concerned with how we come across to others, we put all our energy into presenting ourselves in as favorable a light as possible. When we focus on ourselves, however, we are less likely to notice others' reactions to us, and we may miss feedback cues revealing how they really see us. In addition, sometimes we persist in holding on to an unrealistic self-image because others are reticent to reveal their true responses to us for fear of hurting our feelings. Instead, they tell us what they think we want to hear. Other times, we base our assessment of ourselves on obsolete information—we opt to cling to memories rather than face current realities.

Just as we can view ourselves more favorably than others do, we can also be our own worst critics and view ourselves more harshly than is warranted. For example, we might convince ourselves that we are fat despite others insisting we are a perfect weight. Why do we do this? We might be acting on the basis of outmoded data—information that was true at one time but is no longer true. Or we might receive distorted feedback from an overly critical friend that warps our view of ourselves. Or we might criticize ourselves simply because we believe that is what society expects us to do. We might feel that society prefers we own up to our inadequacies while downplaying our strengths.

When you visualize yourself, do you see a person who can achieve anything or a person with limitations who is likely to fail? Research reveals that conceptions of the self influence self-perspectives of failure.[23] Do you view yourself more positively or negatively than you believe valid? Being too harsh on yourself can keep you from fulfilling your potential. Instead of denigrating yourself, assess your strengths and shortcomings honestly, freeing yourself to reshape your self-image and grow.

DIVERSITY AND CULTURE IN RELATIONSHIPS: HOW IMPORTANT IS THE "I"?

Individuals in most, if not all, cultures have a notion about the self, although the specific notions held vary across cultures, affecting person-to-person interactions in subtle to dramatic ways.[24]

THE SELF IN INDIVIDUALISTIC AND COLLECTIVISTIC CULTURES

In North American and Western European cultures, the word *self* reigns supreme, reflecting the importance individuals place on realizing their personal goals. Members of such **individualistic cultures**, in which individual identity is paramount, value uniqueness and personal identity; they tend to believe in themselves, seek to do their own thing, and shun conformity. In contrast, in the **collectivistic cultures** of Asia, Africa, and Central and South America, where group goals are given a higher priority than individual goals, individuals are more apt to downplay their own goals and emphasize goals set or valued by the group as a whole.[25] Japanese parents, for example, typically refrain from lavishing praise on their children, believing that children who are overpraised are likely to end up being self-centered and not focused enough on the group's needs.

For the members of collectivistic cultures, the self is not the center of the universe. For them, the group—not the individual—is the primary social unit. Where individualistic cultures link success with personal achievement, collectivistic cultures link it to group cohesion and loyalty. This basic difference is underscored by the fact that the "I" in the Chinese written language

Individualistic culture: A culture in which individual identity is paramount.

Collectivistic cultures: Cultures in which group goals are given a higher priority than individual goals.

In his book *Uh-Oh*, philosopher and author Robert Fulghum presents his observations concerning when and how our self-conceptions change:

Ask a kindergarten class, "How many of you can draw?" and all hands shoot up. Yes, of course we can draw—all of us. What can you draw? Anything! How about a dog eating a fire truck in a jungle? Sure! How big you want it?

How many of you can sing? All hands. Of course we sing! What can you sing? Anything! What if you don't know the words? No problem, we make them up. Let's sing! Now? Why not!

How many of you dance? Unanimous again. What kid of music do you like to dance to? Any kind! Let's dance! Now? Sure, why not?

Do you like to act in plays? Yes! Do you play musical instruments? Yes! Do you write poetry? Yes! Can you read and write and count? Yes! We're learning that stuff now.

Their answer is Yes! Over and over again, Yes! The children are confident in spirit, infinite in resources, and eager to learn. Everything is still possible.

Try those same questions on a college audience. A small percentage of the students will raise their hands when asked if they draw or dance or sing or paint or act or play an instrument. Not infrequently, those who do raise their hands will want to qualify their response with their limitations: "I only play piano, I only draw horses, I only dance to rock and roll, I only sing in the shower."

When asked why the limitations, college students answer that they do not have talent, are not majoring in the subject, or have not done any of these things since about third grade, or worse, that they are embarrassed for others to see them sing or dance or act. You can imagine the response to the same questions asked of an older audience. The answer: No, none of the above.

What went wrong between kindergarten and college?

What happened to YES! Of course I can?

Consider these questions:

1. To what extent, if any, do your experiences support Fulghum's observations?

2. What factors do you believe cause us to change our answers to Fulghum's questions as we mature?

3. Based on Fulghum's insights, what advice would you give today's kindergarten and college students?

SOURCE: Robert Fulghum, *Uh-Oh*, New York: Villard Books, 1991, p. 228–229.

Idiocentric orientation: An orientation displayed by people who are primarily individualistic in their ways of thinking and behaving.

Allocentric orientation: A perspective displayed by people who are primarily collectivistic in their thinking and behaving.

looks very much like the word for "selfish."[26] Members of collectivistic cultures gain a sense of identity through their group memberships, not by promoting themselves or stressing how important they are, as members of Western cultures are apt to do.[27] Thus, while some of us have been raised to call attention to ourselves, sing our own praises, and develop ourselves at the group's expense, others of us have been reared to avoid such behavior by nurturing the *interdependent self* instead.[28]

Persons who are primarily individualistic in their thinking and behaving have an **idiocentric orientation**. Those who are primarily collectivistic in the way they think and behave have an **allocentric orientation**.[29] To which group do you belong?

Our unique personal experiences and shared membership in groups influence how we define ourselves. Together with culture, these factors play integral parts in forming our self-concept. Still, care should always be taken against rigidly categorizing people from any given culture, whether individualistic or collectivistic in orientation. Keep in mind that variations occur within countries. For example, in the United States, persons from the South exhibit higher levels of collectivism than do people living the West.[30] In addition, after persons from the Western and Eastern worlds interact with each other, their cultural orientations moderate. In fact, Asian exchange students who have lived in the United States tend to have somewhat more individualized self-concepts than do other Asian students.

Do you think American culture is becoming more individualistic or more communal?

THE SELF IN HIGH- AND LOW-CONTEXT CULTURES

People from different cultures also exhibit different communication style preferences. Individuals belonging to **high-context cultures** tend to be very polite and indirect when interacting with others. In contrast, persons from **low-context cultures** typically exhibit a more direct communication style.[31] When meeting someone for the first time, a person from a low-context culture is likely to ask direct questions in an effort to gather background information and get to know the person; the priority is the discovery and expression of individual uniqueness. Similarly, persons from individualistic cultures feel the need to explain everything and, because of the value they place on assertion, to speak out.

In comparison, persons from high-context cultures hesitate to ask others direct questions, preferring to rely on nonverbal, contextual information. They value silence and reticence, believing that persons of few words are thoughtful, trustworthy, and respectable. As a result, they also are likely to find unsolicited self-disclosures inappropriate. And because they would view such behavior as a sign of disrespect or disloyalty, they are less likely than persons from low-context cultures to criticize one another publicly. When their words hurt another person, they believe they hurt themselves as well.

THE SELF IN HIGH- AND LOW-POWER-DISTANCE CULTURES

Attitudes toward the self also differ along the dimension of **power distance**, or the extent to which individuals are willing to accept power differentials. Persons from high-power-distance cultures, such as Saudi Arabia and India, perceive power as a fact of life. In these cultures, persons in low-power positions are very apt to defer automatically to persons in authority. In contrast, persons from low-power-distance cultures, such as the United States and Sweden, are more likely to emphasize and value their independence even when superiors are present.[32] A general feeling of equality prevails in such cultures (see Table 2.4).

High-context cultures: Cultures in which people tend to be very polite and indirect when interacting with others.

Low-context culture: A culture in which people typically exhibit a direct communication style.

Power distance: The extent to which individuals are willing to accept power differentials.

TRY THIS: *Are You an "I" or Part of a "We"?*

Evaluate how much the statements in categories A and B below reflect how you think and act in regard to yourself and others. Rate each statement as follows: very important, 5; somewhat important, 4; neither important nor unimportant, 3; somewhat unimportant, 2; and not at all important, 1.

Category A:

1. I want to demonstrate my personal worth.

2. I want to be me.   _____

3. I want others to consider me an asset.   _____

4. I want to achieve my personal goals.   _____

Total   _____

Category B:

1. If I hurt you, I hurt myself.

2. I want harmonious relationships.   _____

3. I put the welfare of others before my own welfare.   _____

4. I act in accordance with tradition.   _____

Total   _____

Compare your totals. The higher your Category A total, the greater your idiocentric tendencies. The higher your Category B total, the greater your allocentric tendencies.

TABLE 2.4   Culture and Influences on the Self

Persons with individualistic orientations	Conceive of the individual as the basic social unit Make individual goals a priority Link success and individual achievement
Persons with collectivistic orientations	Conceive of the family/group as the basic social unit Make interdependence/group goals a priority Link success and group achievement
Persons from high-context cultures	Exhibit an indirect communication style Make face-saving a consideration
Persons from low-context cultures	Exhibit a direct communication style Seldom think of face-saving
Persons from high-power-distance cultures	Defer to superiors
Persons from low-power-distance cultures	Value independence

ATTITUDES TOWARD THE SELF ACROSS CULTURES

Even though their cultures may differ, young people throughout the world are likely to share many attitudes regarding the self. Most hope to develop and sustain social relationships, especially with their peers, and most are optimistic regarding their abilities to assume responsibilities for themselves in the future. In the face of the optimism displayed by the majority of young people, between 25 and 30 percent of them also describe themselves as lonely, overwhelmed by life's problems, and frequently sad.[33] Interestingly, Japanese teens are even more likely to attribute these traits to themselves, with 55 percent reporting frequently feeling sad and 39 percent reporting feeling lonely. Japanese young people are also almost twice as likely as young people from other cultures to fear disappointing their parents.[34]

Many years ago, clinical psychologists Darlene Powell Hopson and Derek Hopson, reported that African Americans expressed discontent with the self, finding that as early as the age of three, black children expressed the desire to be white, even expressing a preference to play with white dolls.[35] Do you believe that such self-perceptions are related to African Americans' being victims of racism? Based on your personal experiences, do you believe such feelings still exist today? A more recent study did not find that African Americans had negative attitudes toward the self because of skin tone.[36] Do you believe, however, that negative attitudes toward the self may exist in individuals who are members of marginalized groups, such as the elderly and people who are physically or mentally challenged?

GENDER AND SELF-CONCEPT

If you awoke one day to discover that you had changed into someone of the opposite sex, how would that affect you? In what ways, if any, would this alteration change your plans for the day? The week? The month? The year? What impact would it have on the rest of your life?

As we noted in Chapter 1, *sex* refers to the biological characteristics that define men and women. *Gender,* in contrast, refers to the socially constructed roles and behaviors that the members of a given society believe appropriate for men and women. Thus, gender is a variable that influences how others treat us and how we treat them because of our sex. Our gender becomes integrated into our self-concept, providing us with a **gender identity**, that is, an inner sense of being male or female. The experiences we have during our formative years influence our views of masculinity and femininity, affecting our identities in later years. As we internalize the attributes of maleness and femaleness, what we have come to believe about our gender affects the way we conceive of our self. Transgender activist Chaz Bono has been quoted as saying, "I believe gender is between your ears, not between your legs."

Men and women are likely to see and describe themselves differently. Males generally characterize themselves as possessing initiative, control, and ambition. In contrast, females see themselves as sensitive, concerned for others, and considerate. While appearance plays a major role in the self-image of women, until recently it was not considered integral to the self-image of a man.[39] Young women are still teased about both their looks and their weight more often than are young men, but the macho male, muscular and fit, is making a comeback, placing pressure on men to "bulk up" or be thought of as unmanly.[40]

Unfortunately, in our society, social and cultural expectations cause women to be vulnerable to damage to their self-concepts, in part because of the many conflicting and confused messages they receive.[41] Our society expects those who are feminine to be nurturing,

Gender identity: An inner sense of being male or female.

> **TRY THIS:** *Young and Old*

1. Interview a male relative and a female relative, both of whom are older. Ask them these questions:

   a. Who are you? What roles do you perform? What adjectives describe you?

   b. How has the way you see yourself today changed from how you saw yourself when you were a child, a young adult, and middle-aged?

   c. How do you believe the ways your family and friends see you have changed through the years?

   d. Is there an era of your life you would want to repeat? Why?

2. The following quotations reveal the self-perceptions of two older people. These quotations are not meant to characterize all older people; rather, they are used to illustrate, from their perspective, how aging affects self-perception:

   The young want everything to move fast. They let their impatience show in their eyes. When you are hard of hearing it is worse. People get impatient when you try to join in. They yell in your face. Finally, they just give up on you and act like you are not there because it is too much trouble to try and keep you in the flow of things.[37]

   You ask me if I enjoy remembering things from the past. Well I do. . . . it is as if there are reels of movies in my head, all starting at different eras. I can go back and start one up any time. Different people, dressed differently, living in rooms and houses without electricity. And all starring a different me, of course . . . the past—what I did and accomplished and endured and loved—are all part of who I am.[38]

Compare and contrast the answers your interviewees provided to the questions listed above with the perceptions of these two people.

unassertive, sensitive, caring, deferential, and emotional. As a result of such expectations, society rewards young women for a pleasing appearance, revealing their feelings, being forgiving, and being nice or helpful to others. In contrast, our society expects men to be strong, ambitious, in control of their emotions, and successful; unlike women, men are reinforced for displaying these qualities and achieving results.[42]

Of significance is the finding that our society values male characteristics more highly than female characteristics. Thus, men typically feel better about themselves than do women. The upshot is that many women try harder and harder to attain success by attempting to be it all and do it all. The comedian Carol Leifer perhaps put it best in her act when she said, "I just had a baby an hour ago and I'm back at work already. While I was delivering, I took a course in tax-shelter options."

SEEING THE SELF THROUGH THE MEDIA AND TECHNOLOGY LOOKING GLASS

The products of our modern lives provide the programs, films, music, and applications that help us forge our identities, our sense of self, and who we want to be. From these we learn how to dress, look, interact, and consume. We learn who has power and who does not, who has followers and who does not. The sites and media we frequent also influence our sense of ethnicity and race, gender, and class.

THE IMPACT OF THE MEDIA

Media depictions help us assess what the general public's preferred patterns of behavior and appearance are. They help shape our opinions about how our bodies should look, how males and females should interact, and the meaning of success. The way we interpret their offerings reinforces or negates our own sense of self by influencing our sense of who we are as compared to who we should aspire to be.

Often we are not conscious of the extent to which the media work us over, how much they are "**make-believe media**"—that is, they make us believe.[43] Our concepts of what we should be like or, for that matter, what our relationships should be like, or even more specifically what African Americans, Latino Americans, Asian Americans, and males and females are supposed to be like, are conveyed to us via the media, so much so that some critics complain that the media preempt real life, offering us fabricated views of the world in its place.

Among the media's messages are that violence against women is commonplace; that men are hard, tough, and independent; and that minorities and women are less visible than men. Women, for example, were underrepresented in the one hundred top-grossing films of 2011, which featured fewer female than male protagonists and female characters

Make-believe media: Media offerings that make us believe things that are not necessarily true.

who were younger than the male characters. Women were also less likely than men to be portrayed as leaders and more likely to be identified by their marital status.[44] Other messages are that African American males are either athletes or unlawful, that Asian males are awkward, and that Muslim men are terrorists. Such messages often distort how we see ourselves and influence our perception of what is normal and desirable behavior. In addition, media models adversely affect our evaluations of ourselves as attractive, successful, or smart. And all too often, the thirst the media develop in us for "beautiful thing-hood" turns into painful and enduring feelings of inadequacy when we are unable to acquire the items we covet.[45]

THE IMPACT OF TECHNOLOGY

We derive our sense of self not only from communicating face-to-face but also from communicating online. By using technology we participate in the creation of new worlds and new ways of finding out about ourselves. Interacting in **cyberspace**, we can be ourselves or, at time, someone else—that is, we can exist as personas.

For some of us, the lives we live are more virtual than real. Some of us regularly inhabit virtual worlds, participating in simulations and assuming different personas. We may have a number of e-mail and Twitter addresses and various screen names as we use the Internet to experiment with multiple identities—while concealing our real identities from both friends and strangers with whom we interact online.[46] We might, for example, pose as a member of the opposite sex, conceal our age or ethnicity, hide physical characteristics, or otherwise pretend to be someone we are not. In other words, online we can be genderless, raceless, rankless, and appearanceless.[47]

We also can create parallel identities that facilitate the exploration of murkier aspects of the self, something very different from being an employee part of the day, a student another part of the day, and a family member at home. As psychologist Sherry Turkle notes, "The obese can be slender, the beautiful plain, the 'nerdy' sophisticated" due to the construction of an identity that is not part of their authentic selves. Turkle asserts that instead of developing internally, as a result of our being overly influenced by the opinions of others, the self is being externally manufactured. She contends that when we tweet and communicate via Facebook, we are playing to the crowd—presenting a self that is based on what others respond to positively.[48]

Research shows that we try to present ourselves in as positive a light as possible online—especially, as we noted as the outset of this chapter, when using a social networking site such as Facebook. In effect, we psychologically boost our ego, enhancing our self-esteem.[49] Some researchers believe that Facebook has a dark side, in that it feeds users' narcissistic tendencies by providing opportunities for self-promotion, access to shallow relationships and detached communication, and numerous self-solicitations for support.[50] Other researchers disagree, however, contending that frequency of Facebook use is not associated with narcissism—a trait they assert applies only to those Facebook users who gather unrealistically inflated numbers of friends—but rather with greater openness and lower concern regarding privacy.[51] For avid online game players, spending too much time online can result in depression and anxiety, because failing in game playing becomes as real as failing in real life.[52]

What are you like online? Does communicating online tend to make you more or less social? More or less inhibited? Do you act more or less yourself? Do you assume multiple identities, negotiate identities, or relate as yourself? What have you learned about yourself interacting with others online?

Cyberspace: The virtual space that exists in an online or computer environment.

In Sidney Lumet's award-winning 1976 film *Network*, written by Paddy Chayefsky, the main character, a television news anchorman, speaks these words to his audience:

> Television is not the truth. We lie like hell. . . . We deal in illusions, man. None of it is true. But you people sit there day after day, night after night. . . . We're all you know. You're beginning to think that the tube is reality and your own lives are unreal. You do what the tube tells you to do. You dress like the tube, you eat like the tube, you raise your children like the tube. In God's name, you people are the real thing; we're the illusion!

1. What does the preceding quotation suggest about our relationship with media?

2. Compare and contrast the image you have of each of the following with the image portrayed in the media. Which image do you prefer and why?

   A nurse

   A lawyer

   The police

   A corporate executive

   The wealthy

   Arabs

   Teenagers

   Older people

3. Divide your life into three approximately equal segments. For example, if you are currently twenty-one years old, divide your life into the following segments: ages one to seven, eight to fourteen, and fifteen to twenty-one. From each life segment, select a television program, film/DVD, music video/song, or book that you believe exerted a significant influence on your self-perception and interaction with others. Explain its influence.

4. If you could trade places with any media personality or character, past or present, who would it be and why?

SOURCE: Quote from *Network*, written by Paddy Chayefsky, MGM and United Artists, 1976.

GAINING COMMUNICATION COMPETENCE: WAYS TO STRENGTHEN YOUR SELF-CONCEPT

We all carry a figurative snapshot of the person we think we are wherever we go. Our snapshot is an impressionist collage of merged images: what we think we were like in the past, what we wish we had been like, what we think we are like right now, and what we expect to be like in the future. In many ways, our photo is a composite of how we see ourselves, how we wish we saw ourselves, and how we imagine others see us. Use the following suggestions to improve your mental picture-taking ability and to develop a clearer sense of self.

UPDATE PICTURES

Although changing your mental image of yourself is not easy, it is possible. To do it, remind yourself that a photo captures but a moment in time linked to a particular environment and communication context. Each picture you shoot, however, reveals a

How clear is the picture you have of you?

somewhat different you. Photos are frozen in time. People are not. We change from moment to moment, person to person, year in and year out. Thus, while our memories are important and help us construct our sense of who we are, we need to keep the mental picture we carry with us current. By doing this, we will be better able to discount images that no longer accurately represent us, and thereby avoid focusing on what psychologists refer to as regrets—"the lost lives, lost selves a person could have lived or been if s/he had done a few things differently."[53]

TAKE LOTS AND LOTS OF PICTURES

Watch yourself in action. Review your self-snapshots, periodically taking time to reassess the roles you perform, the statements you use to describe yourself, and the extent to which you approve of your own values and behavior. Are you satisfied as you scroll through them? Do you have realistic goals? It takes courage and open-mindedness to do this.

EXPLORE OTHERS' PICTURES OF YOU

The people we interact with regularly often see the strengths or weakness we tend to either overlook or underplay. While we need not become what others think we are, if we are willing to explore others' perceptions of us, we at least open ourselves to the possibility of change. If we are receptive to how others see us, we may be able to make adjustments and become more effective in other person-to-person contacts.

PICTURE POSSIBILITIES

The self is flexible and changeable. In a constant transitional state, it has the capacity to adapt to changing circumstances and conditions. By asking yourself, "Who am I now?" instead of "Who am I always?" you will be able to take picture after picture of a changing you, someone who opens him- or herself to the possibilities that today and tomorrow offer. As a Xerox executive said in a speech aptly titled "Butterflies, Not Pigeonholes":

GO ▶

WATCH THIS 2.1
For a video on self-concept visit the student study site.

> In a knowledge-driven economy, self-confidence means a willingness to champion new ideas and the resilience to roll with the punches when ideas turn out to be better in the abstract than in reality. Plus, self-confidence provides the persistence to try again from another angle. Self-confidence enables an individual to withstand the criticism of colleagues, to live with the fact that not everyone will like everyone else.
>
> And it gives one the ability to listen to others, to work as part of a team, to be willing to let others share the load . . . and the spotlight, confident that one's contribution to the success of the whole will be recognized.
>
> In short, self-confidence enables people to feel comfortable outside the pigeonholes, to contribute in an ever-changing environment. Without it, the most gifted individual can toil in the shadows, the gifts of provenance never fully realized.[54]

Isn't it better to picture yourself as a butterfly, free, than stuck in a pigeonhole?

"I'll never be able to pass this course," Aisha moaned to herself as she sat at Starbucks staring at her laptop with her text opened beside her. "I've been trying to write this paper all weekend and I'm still on the first page." She sighed deeply, and then rose to get another cup of coffee.

As Aisha sipped her coffee, she began to thumb through the Sunday paper. She stopped to read an article about the Efficacy Institute, a school that provides students with instruction on self-concept. The article noted that studies on "efficacy" suggest that any person can succeed if he or she is motivated and works hard. Efficacy programs help students believe in themselves by repeatedly delivering messages such as "Work hard!" "Think you can!" "Believe in yourself!"

Aisha began to think about her own situation. She had dropped out of college years earlier and had only recently reenrolled. Now she found herself stuck in the same old trap—she didn't think she could do the work. Aisha wondered—should she also enroll at the Efficacy Institute? Aisha remembered how bad she had felt after dropping out of college, and now she was experiencing those same feelings of failure—all because of this paper. Then she had a brainstorm. She typed the following lines on her laptop and posted them on her Facebook wall:

Recipe for Success in College

1. Believe in Your Abilities to Succeed.

2. Work Hard on All Assignments.

3. You can do it!

She stared at the words. Then she started writing. Her head was filled with so many new ideas that her fingers could barely keep up. Could all these ideas have come from the simple lines she had just posted?

Aisha didn't dwell on the question. She was working too hard and writing too fast to ponder that possibility.

What do you think?

1. Do you believe that improving a college student's self-esteem will enable him or her to earn better grades? Why or why not?

2. Are there recipes for success you believe a student should follow to succeed in college? What about in the world of work? In life? If so, describe them, comparing and contrasting your various success recipes.

3. Does *self-talk*—that is, what you tell yourself—influence your chances of succeeding? Explain.

REVIEW THIS

CHAPTER SUMMARY

1 **Define self-concept, distinguishing it from the self.** Self-concept, the baseline for communication, is that relatively stable set of perceptions we attribute to ourselves. Composed of everything we think and feel about the self, it guides our communicative behavior.

2 **Explain reflected appraisal theory, social comparison theory, and confirmation, rejection, and disconfirmation, using them to discuss the role you and others play in shaping the self-concept.** According to reflected appraisal theory, our self-concept reflects how we believe others see us. According to social comparison theory, we compare ourselves to others to develop a feel for how we measure up to them. *Confirmation* supports our self-appraisal, *rejection* negates our self-appraisal, and *disconfirmation* reveals a total disregard for us as a person, suggesting that for the other person, we do not exist, robbing us of a sense of self.

3 **Define self-fulfilling prophecy and distinguish between positive and negative Pygmalions.** A self-fulfilling prophecy is a prediction that increases the likelihood that an anticipated outcome will occur. A positive Pygmalion has positive expectations and fosters positive change in us, while a negative Pygmalion has low or no expectations and fosters diminished performance in us.

4 **Explain the influence that cultural diversity and gender have on self-concept.** Cultural differences influence our self-notions. Whether we are from an individualistic or collectivistic culture, display an idiocentric or an allocentric orientation, or ascribe to masculine or feminine gender prescriptions is derived from the lessons taught us by society and culture.

5 **Describe how media and technology affect self-concept.** Media and technology provide us with information about preferred patterns of behavior and appearance, sometimes causing us to develop unrealistic expectations for ourselves and at times either adversely or positively affecting our feelings of adequacy.

6 **Identify how you can change and strengthen your self-concept.** To strengthen our feelings of self-worth, we need to reassess the nature of our self-concept periodically, visit and revisit others' perceptions of us, and keep ourselves open to the possibility of change.

CHECK YOUR UNDERSTANDING

1 Can you identify the components of self-concept and then use them to describe yourself? (See pages 36–37.)

2 Can you describe how the social comparisons you make with others influence your thoughts about yourself? How does reflected appraisal theory play out in your own life? (See pages 40–42.)

3 Can you name individuals who have served as positive and negative Pygmalions in your life, making you feel better or worse about yourself? Can you explain how you have served as a positive/negative Galatea for yourself? (See pages 44–46.)

4 Can you explain how living in an individualistic or collectivistic culture affects a person's self-concept? What about living in a celebrity-obsessed culture? How about when communicating online? (See pages 47–51.)

5 Can you identify steps you can take to strengthen your self-concept? (See pages 55–56.)

CHECK YOUR SKILLS

1 Can you describe your "perceived identity"? (See pages 36–37 and 42; and **Try This**, page 38.)

2 Can you provide examples of your personal growth and participation in the process of self-renewal? (See page 38.)

3 Can you identify situations that have affected how you see yourself? (See pages 39–40.)

4 Can you name the people and reference groups you use to gauge whether you are a success? (See pages 41–42.)

5 Can you use Goffman's dramaturgical approach to human interaction to make a good impression on others? (See page 42.)

6 Can you point to individuals who have confirmed, rejected, and disconfirmed your sense of self, and describe how you have done the same for others? (See pages 43–44; and **Try This**, page 45.)

7 Can you function as a positive Pygmalion? (See page 46.)

8 Can you determine if you have sufficient self-awareness to reevaluate yourself? (See pages 46–47.)

9 Can you provide examples demonstrating your culture's effects on how you see yourself? (See **Try This,** page 50; and **Try This,** page 52.)

10 Can you use your skills to analyze how self-concept can act to limit or enhance opportunities? (See **The Case of Aisha's Term Paper**, page 57.)

KEY TERMS

Self-awareness 36

Self-concept 36

Self-image 36

Self-esteem 36

Reflected appraisal theory 40

Social comparison theory 41

Perceived self 42

Ideal self 42

Impression management 42

Possible self 42

Expected self 42

Dramaturgical approach to human interaction 42

Confirmation 43

Rejection 43

Disconfirmation 44

Self-efficacy 44

Self-fulfilling prophecy 44

Positive Pygmalion 46

Negative Pygmalion 46

Individualistic cultures 47

Collectivistic cultures 47

Idiocentric orientation 48

Allocentric orientation 48

High-context cultures 48

Low-context cultures 48

Power distance 48

Gender identity 51

Make-believe media 53

Cyberspace 54

STUDENT STUDY SITE

Visit the student study site at **www.sagepub.com/gambleic** to access the following materials:

- SAGE Journal Articles
- Videos
- Web Resources
- eFlashcards
- Web Quizzes
- Study Questions

chapter 3

The future is a foreign country, and we are travelers and explorers.

—Raj Aggarwal,
Frank C. Sullivan Professor
of International Business and
Finance, University of Akron

PERCEPTION

LEARNING OBJECTIVES

After completing this chapter, you should be able to demonstrate mastery of the following learning outcomes:

1. Explain the perception process and its relationship to reality.

2. Define the figure-ground principle, closure, and perceptual constancy.

3. Explain how schemata, perceptual sets and selectivities, and ethnocentrism and stereotypes influence perception.

4. Distinguish among the following perceptual barriers: fact-inference confusions, allness,

indiscrimination, frozen evaluations, snap judgments, and blindering.

5. Discuss how culture, gender, and media and technology influence perceptions of social experience.

6. Identify strategies you can use to enhance your perceptual abilities.

How accurate are the quick perceptions we form of other people? And how good are the decisions we make based on these virtually instant perceptions? Consider speed dating, for example. In speed dating we rely on "thin slicing"—basing our impression of another person solely on an abbreviated behavioral glimpse.[1] During a speed-dating cycle we may interact round-robin style with as many as twelve possible partners, with each individual "date" lasting on average from three to eight minutes. While some believe we should be able to make judgments about how close we want to become with a potential dating partner during such a short time—even as short as 30 seconds—others are not so sure.[2]

Interestingly, researchers report that thin slicing produces accurate judgments.[3] Within 30 seconds, speed-dating participants are able to report either being or not being attracted to someone. The speed daters acknowledge a lack of attraction or negative physical qualities as potential partner turnoffs, with females reporting three times as many negative judgments as do males. The turn-ons they report are physical attractiveness and positive behavior and demeanor, including positive perceptions of a potential date's communication and presentation skills.[4] What is more, participants are likely to report more attraction for those they perceive to share attributes with themselves, whether or not those perceived similarities are accurate.[5] And men report that similarity influences their attraction to a potential partner more than do women.[6]

While we are good at forming rapid, relatively accurate perceptions of others when deciding whom to date, are we as capable of forming quick and accurate perceptions when it comes to making other decisions, including whether a person is racially biased? What do you think?

> In speed dating we rely on "thin slicing" — basing our impression of another person solely on an abbreviated behavioral glimpse.

WHAT DO YOU KNOW?

Before continuing your reading of this chapter, which of the following five statements do you believe to be true and which do you believe to be false?

1. Differences in perception are rare.   T   F

2. We can process unlimited amounts of data each second.   T   F

3. We have a tendency to fill in perceptual gaps.   T   F

4. Dividing people into in- and out-groups improves perceptual accuracy.   T   F

5. "The sun will rise tomorrow" technically is not a statement of fact.   T   F

Read the chapter to discover if you're right or if you've made any erroneous assumptions.

ANSWERS: 1. F; 2. F; 3. T; 4. F; 5. T

To advance the understanding of perception and its role in decision making, Paul Allen, cofounder of the Microsoft Corporation, recently donated $300 million to a project devoted to mapping the brain's circuitry of perception and analyzing the billions of cells and synapses at work in vision, memory, and awareness.[7] Scientists hope that decoding these processes will increase our understanding of how we perceive.

OUR PERCEPTION DEFINES OUR REALITY

Should we believe our eyes? In the effort to answer this question, researchers study the relationships among perception, reality, and performance. When playing well, for example, tennis and baseball players report that the ball looks larger than it does when they are playing poorly. Golfers playing well similarly report that the cup looks bigger than when they are playing poorly. And basketball players say that the hoop appears oversized when their game is on but not so when they are in a scoring slump.[8] Perceive the ball, hole, or hoop to be larger, and you may be on your way to improving your athletic prowess—even if what you perceive is not really there.[9]

However, what if computer artists play with reality by creating an illusion that renders what is actually before your eyes invisible? For example, Cleo Berry, a struggling and overweight actor, accepted $500 from a photographer to pose for some photographs. Unbeknownst to Berry, the photographer sold the photos to the New York City Health Department for use in its antiobesity campaign. To stress that eating fast food and sugary sodas can lead to type 2 diabetes, which can lead to limb amputation, the advertising agency handling the campaign for the health department digitally edited the lower half of Berry's right leg out of the photo. One day, a friend alerted Berry that his image—absent a leg—was all over the Internet and TV. An able-bodied person, Berry was distressed by the use of the manipulated image, in part because the campaign could have used images of an actual amputee instead.[10]

Today it is so easy to reproduce or alter visual images that it has become normal to be skeptical regarding what is real.[11] The yellow line that appears scribbled down the football field on your TV screen is not really there; it is created with a digital pen. The ads you can see behind home plate when you watch baseball on TV are not really there; they are computer-generated effects. Dead celebrities appear in new commercials. And the eyewitness testimony given during trials is wrong about one-third of the time.[12] We do not always agree on what is before our eyes. Our eyes can be deceived.

DO WE SEE THE SAME REALITY?

Our lack of agreement about what we see is particularly apparent when we consider art. For example, take the work of performance artist Marina Abramović, pictured here. Would you call a person sitting still in a room "art"? The fact that answers to this question vary illustrates a key aspect of perception—different people do not always view the same situations in the same ways. For the same reason, people do not agree on the meaning of Edvard Munch's painting *The Scream*. Our perception is a consequence of who we are, where we are, and what we choose to see.

Culture, race, age, gender, geographic location, and life experiences combine to create perceptual gulfs between us

Performance artist Marina Abramović at work. Is this art?

and those whose culture, race, age, gender, geographic location, and life experiences differ from ours. Confronted with issues such as race relationships, gender equity, the economic crisis, and the political divide, many of us see different realities. It is not uncommon for our perceptions of events and people to conflict. In fact, differences in the ways we see, hear, taste, smell, or feel specific stimuli—that is, differences in how we perceive—occur all the time. Is it because we cannot perceive what is really there? Is it because we perceive what we want to perceive? Is it because we never experience the exact same reality as anyone else?[13]

In this chapter we explore such questions as we describe how we perceive our world. By learning more about the perception process, we prepare ourselves to handle the interpersonal problems that perceptual variations and disagreements present. By exploring why different individuals experience the same stimuli differently, we may better understand why they think and act differently as well. Only by getting behind the eye of the "I" can we come to understand why "where we stand depends on where we sit."[14] In other words, social circumstances, experiences, and daily person-to-person interactions affect perception. The experiences we have had as members of particular groups shape how we perceive situations, people, and ourselves by affecting our standpoint. According to **standpoint theory**, persons in positions of power have an overriding interest in preserving their place in the social hierarchy; therefore, they develop views of social life that are likely to be more distorted than those of persons who stand to gain little, if anything, from their positions in the social hierarchy.[15] As a result, it is easier for the powerless to feel inequities than for those who are empowered. In contrast, persons who occupy less powerful or marginalized positions develop keener insights into how society works, if only because they need to develop these understandings to survive.[16]

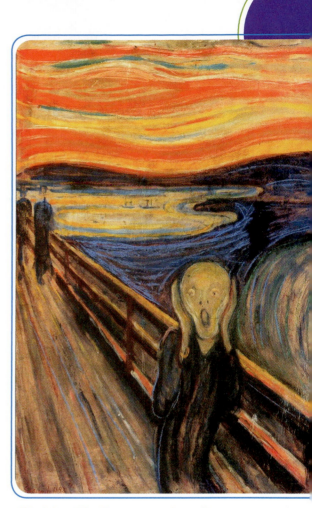

What does *The Scream* mean to you?

By becoming aware of diverse perspectives and interacting with persons whose standpoints differ significantly from our own, we can develop better-balanced perception.[17]

PERCEPTION IN ACTION: THE PROCESS AT WORK

Perception is the process we use to make sense of experience. Through perception, we give meaning to the world, making it our own:

- We actively select or choose to focus on relatively few stimuli.
- We organize or give order to the stimuli.
- We interpret sensory data or explain what we have selected and organized.
- We remember what we have observed.
- We respond.

While waiting to order in a popular restaurant, for example, we may observe two people meeting for lunch, size them up as businesspeople, and decide that they are meeting to close an important deal.

Standpoint theory: A theory that one's place in the power hierarchy influences the accuracy of one's perception of social life.

Perception: The process used to make sense of experience.

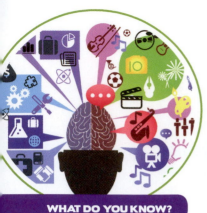

True or False

2. *We can process unlimited amounts of data each second.*
False. The brain can handle only 500 bits of information per second.

We use our perceptual powers to decide what people are like and to give meaning to their behavior. Using the sensory data we take in, we form impressions of others. When engaging in interpersonal perception, we also ask questions about others regarding their relationship to us, draw conclusions about their personalities, and make judgments about their intentions.

According to **uncertainty reduction theory**, we monitor the social environment to learn more about each other.[18] We seek information about each other because if we lack such knowledge, we could fail in our efforts to predict behavior and its consequences. Thus, upon meeting someone, we will choose certain cues to attend to. We might note, for example, that the person is female, older than we are, speaks with a foreign accent, is well groomed, and seems approachable. Our next step would be to organize the information we have gathered so that we are able to store it and/or use it. This is followed by an effort to evaluate and interpret the meaning of our perceptions, which are placed in our memory for retrieval whenever we need or choose to respond.

According to information theorists, although our senses can process approximately 5 million bits of data every second, our brains can handle only about 500 bits per second.[19] Because of our inability to perceive everything, we are compelled to be selective about the stimuli we become aware of.[20] As a result, we focus on certain cues and ignore others. Figure 3.1 illustrates the process of perception in action.

Figure 3.1 The Perception Process

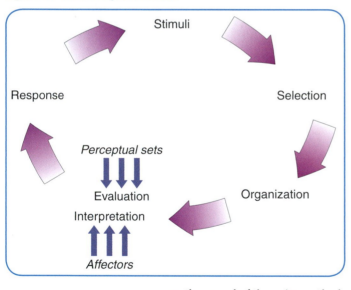

SELECTION

As you read this chapter, stop and look around you. What do you see? What captures your attention? Is it the hum of the refrigerator, the feel of your chair, the color of the walls, or voices coming from another location? Consciously turn your attention to something different. What did you fail to notice initially that now makes an impression on you?

Since we can attend to only a limited number of stimuli from an array of randomly competing stimuli at one time, we choose which persons, situations, or events to perceive. We use all our senses to gather information. Multiple factors influence what we pay attention to and what we ignore, what enters our awareness and what exists unobserved and unnoticed.

When we interact with others, we select the cues on which we focus. Some of us focus on appearance, others on the strength of a handshake, and still others on the sound of the voice or the look in the person's eyes. Whatever we select to focus on, we direct our attention to certain qualities and not others.

Uncertainty reduction theory: A theory that states that individuals learn more about each other by monitoring their social environment.

Usually we focus on a stimulus that is more intense than others or that reflects our motives or interest more than others. For example, we pay attention to a loud noise that disrupts our concentration. Likewise, we overhear a conversation near us in a diner if the two people are speaking about a topic that concerns us. Our interests influence what we perceive, as do our motives. When, for example, we are concerned with our financial situation, we notice more information about how to save money. When considering a new car, we notice the kinds of cars our relatives and friends drive. When we are hungry, we become more aware of food establishments, or we notice the aroma of what someone else is eating. When we are late for an appointment, we might run right past a close friend without even seeing her.

Once our attention is captured, we organize the sensory data to interpret and evaluate them. As we attempt to make sense out of the flood of stimuli competing for our awareness, the personal nature of our selective processes takes over. We do not all experience the same stimuli in the same way. We all have different thresholds of arousal that need to be crossed before a stimulus captures our attention. The cues we select to attend to depend more on the kind of perceiver we are than on what is actually occurring. In addition to our sensory acuity, our loves, hatreds, and desires come into play during the selection process.

According to psychologist Herbert Simon, "A wealth of information creates a poverty of attention."[21] When we direct our attention to some stimuli while choosing to ignore others, we demonstrate **selective perception**. What are the specific cues you tend to focus on when you first meet someone? What do you look for? What do you listen for? Three components of the perceptual process provide answers to these questions:

- **Selective exposure** is our preference for people and messages that confirm our existing beliefs, values, or attitudes, such as paying attention to messages delivered by a candidate we are supporting.

- **Selective attention** is the means by which we focus on certain cues but ignore others, such as not noticing the look of disgust on the face of someone we like.

- **Selective retention** is the practice by which we recall things that reinforce our thinking and forget things we find objectionable, such as recalling positive qualities of persons we like and negative qualities of persons we dislike.[22]

In using any of these, we may bias the perceptual process of selection and end up with distorted views of people or events. For example, think about a relationship you once shared but ended. Once you made the decision to end it, did you begin to notice more about the person that you disliked? This is known as the **horn effect**, which occurs when our perception tends toward the flaws of a person or thing. Compare this phenomenon to what happens when you decide to take a personal relationship to a more serious level. Once you have made this kind of decision, instead of perceiving what is negative about the other person, you are more likely to perceive additional things that you like. The reverse of the horn effect is known as the **halo effect**.

Selective perception helps us create a somewhat limited but more coherent and personally meaningful picture of the world—a picture that conforms to our beliefs, expectations, and convictions.[23]

ORGANIZATION

Just as we use a number of strategies to select what impressions we notice, so we use a number of strategies to facilitate our meaningful organization of these impressions. One strategy is to categorize a stimulus according to the **figure-ground principle**. What we choose to focus on becomes the figure, and the rest of what we experience is the ground. We are able to alternate the figure and ground of what we perceive. In a classroom, for example, if you focus on what a fellow student is doing during your professor's lecture, the student becomes the figure, while the professor recedes into the background. When you focus your attention on the professor, she is the figure, and the rest of the classroom is the ground.

A second organizing strategy we rely on is **closure**. Every time we fill in a missing perceptual piece, we exhibit closure. Look at the stimuli pictured in Figure 3.2. What do you see? Most see a dog and a circle. Because we seek to close gaps, we mentally fill in the incomplete

Selective perception: The aspect of perception comprising selective exposure, selective attention, and selective retention, which enables individuals to see, hear, and believe only what they want to.

Selective exposure: The practice of exposing oneself to people and messages that confirm one's existing beliefs, values, or attitudes.

Selective attention: The means by which one focuses on certain cues while ignoring others.

Selective retention: The recalling of things that reinforce one's thinking and the forgetting of things one finds objectionable.

Horn effect: The perception of negative qualities in a person one dislikes.

Halo effect: The perception of positive qualities in a person one likes.

Figure-ground principle: A strategy that facilitates the organization of stimuli by enabling one to focus on different stimuli alternately.

Closure: The process by which one fills in a missing perceptual piece.

True or False

3. *We have a tendency to fill in perceptual gaps.*

True. We seek to perceive a completed world.

Perceptual constancy: The tendency to maintain the way one sees the world.

Schemata: The mental templates or knowledge structures that individuals carry with them.

Scripts: The general ideas that individuals have about persons and situations and how things should play out.

Affectors: Factors that color responses to stimuli, including, but not limited to, culture, roles, biases, emotional state, past experiences, physical limitations, and capabilities.

figures. We want to perceive a completed world, as it were, so we supply elements that are not really part of the stimuli or messages we process. For example, the assumptions we make about others' motivations help us make sense of our own relationships. We might conclude that a friend invited us to a party only because she needed our help in passing a course. Whether the sense we make is right or wrong, justified or unjustified, it fills in certain gaps. Just as what you choose to notice is up to you, you can choose how to organize what you perceive.

A third organizational strategy we use is **perceptual constancy**—the tendency we have to maintain the same perception of stimuli over time. As a consequence of perceptual constancy, we often see people not as they are but as we have been conditioned to see them. The constancy principle helps explain why we find it difficult to alter a perception once we form it. A large number of our perceptions are learned and then reinforced over time.

Perceptual constancy is facilitated by our use of **schemata**, which are the mental templates or knowledge structures we carry with us, and **scripts**, the general ideas we have about people and situations and how things should play out. We develop schemata and scripts based on both real and vicarious experiences. It is by reverting to schemata that we are able to classify people into manageable categories, according to their appearance, psychological traits, group memberships, and so on. Sometimes schemata, as we will discover later in this chapter, also contribute to stereotyping, which can lead us to see what is not there while too often causing us to ignore what is there.

EVALUATION AND INTERPRETATION

As we evaluate and interpret experience, the meaning we assign to experience is influenced by a number of individual **affectors**—factors that color our responses—including culture, roles, biases, present emotional state, past experiences, and physical limitation or capabilities. If you are looking for a fight, you may perceive an insult. If you are hungry, you may smell food. If you are looking for a date, you are more likely to interpret a statement as a flirtation. Relative to the horn and halo effects, we likely view people with whom we seek a relationship more positively than we view those about whom we have no feelings one way or the other. If, on the other hand, we are in an unhappy relationship, it is likely that we will interpret our partner's behavior more critically than if we were impartial.[24]

Among other variables influencing the interpretation/evaluation process are the degree of involvement we have or expect to have with a person, the knowledge we have relative to the person's intentions, our feelings about ourselves in relation to the other person, and the assumptions we make about human behavior in general and this person's behavior in particular.

MEMORY

Memory is a human construct—a composite of what we read, piece together, experience, and/or want to be true.[25] How we interpret and evaluate a stimulus determines whether or not what we experience enters our memory. What we remember we can retrieve later. The question is, how reliable is what we remember? Can we count on our perceptual abilities to supply us with accurate memories of experience?

Consider this: when Americans were surveyed and asked to recall their memories of what they observed on September 11, 2001, 76 percent of those surveyed in New York and 73 percent of those surveyed nationwide recalled watching television broadcasts of the two planes that struck the twin towers of the World Trade Center.[26] These, however, were false memories. In fact, on that day there was no video of the first plane hitting the tower.

We do not simply reproduce what we store in our memory. Instead of objectively recalling an experience, we attempt to reconstruct a memory at the time of withdrawal. However, as we engage in retrospection or backward reasoning, inaccuracies may creep in. While trying to remember, we infer past occurrences based on who we are and what we now believe and know. We tend to recall information consistent with our schemata and discount or forget information that is not. On the other hand, if information dramatically contradicts any of our schemata, compelling us to think about it, this can lead us to revise the schemata we use.

RESPONSE

Perception is a mixture of external stimulation and an internal state. We actively participate by controlling our responses to stimuli. Effectually, we are both the cause and the controlling force of our perceptions. The result is how we make sense of the world and relate to others.

Attribution theory helps us understand why we respond as we do to persons and events. It also speaks to the fact that we like to be able to explain why others behave as they do. Why, for example, did thirty-two-year-old Anders Behring Breivik murder seventy-seven people in Norway, eight at government buildings in Oslo and sixty-nine at a summer camp? Was it because he was mentally ill? Did he feel alienated from society? Was it his warped view of Christian fundamentalism? Did something go wrong with his upbringing? In an effort to make sense out of what happened, we make educated guesses about what motivated Breivik to commit such crimes. While the circumstances are rarely so dramatic or tragic, we do the same with people we know. We assign meaning to the behavior of others by ascribing motives and causes for their actions. For instance, suppose a couple seated near you in a restaurant get up in the middle of their meal and leave. Why did they leave? Did they have an argument? Did they feel ill? Was the food bad? Was the room too warm? When we attribute behavior to something in the disposition of the people involved, we assume it have an internal cause—that is, we believe it is caused by their characteristics. When we attribute it to something about the situation or environment, we identify an external cause—that is, we believe the behavior to be caused by something outside of them.

Let's say, for example, that your date arrives to pick you up early, and you want to figure out why. Some internal attributions are that he is a stickler for punctuality, that he was eager to see you, and that he did not want you to have to wait for him. Each of these reasons points to an internal characteristic of your date as the cause of the behavior. External attributions are that the traffic was much lighter than it usually is, that he was able to leave work early, and that he did not have to run the errands he thought would be necessary. Each of these point to something in the external environment as causing the behavior.

Figure 3.2 Illustrations of the Closure Principle

The terrorist attack of 9/11 is the most memorable TV event of the past fifty years. But do we remember it as it happened?

Attribution theory: A theory that posits that we assign meaning to behavior by ascribing motives and causes.

In "Childhood," by Frances Cornford, a child's initial perception of old age matures:

> I used to think that grown-up people chose
> To have stiff backs and wrinkles round their nose,
> And veins like small fat snakes on either hand,
> On purpose to be grand.
> Till through the banisters I watched one day
> My grand-aunt Etty's friend who was going away.
> And how her onyx beads had come unstrung.
> I saw her grope to find them as they rolled;
> And then I knew that she was helplessly old,
> As I was helplessly young.

How do you account for the change in the child's perception? Why is it possible to perceive a person, situation, or event one way at a particular point in time and differently at another point in time? What happened that led the child to discover that what she or he saw at one point in time did not tell the entire story?

Identify challenges that stand in the way of your accurately evaluating people, situations, or events. What steps can you take personally to ensure that what you see in a person, situation, or event is not limited to what you are looking for?

SOURCE: Frances Cornford, "Childhood," in *Frances Cornford: Selected Poems,* ed. Jane Dowson. London: Enitharmon Press, 1996. Reprinted by permission.

We use four principles to guide us when we attribute behavior to a particular cause: consensus, consistency, distinctiveness, and controllability. When using the first principle, *consensus,* we consider commonalities of behavior. For instance, we might ask a question such as "Do the friends of my friend also speak with different accents when they are at home as opposed to when they are at work?" If the answer is yes, we are more apt to decide that the exhibited behavior has an external cause.

When focusing on *consistency* to make an attribution, we focus on repeated behavior. For example, if our friend is chronically late for every meal, then there is high behavioral consistency, and we are more apt to attribute the behavior to internal causes.

When focusing on *distinctiveness,* we ask if the person displays similar behavior in different situations. If the answer is yes, we are likely to conclude the behavior has an internal cause.

Finally, when focusing on *controllability,* we are seeking to determine if the person's behavior was or was not under his or her control. For example, if someone is flying in to see you and is delayed because of a mechanical problem with the airplane, the delay was not under her control. She could not have gotten there any faster.

A common error in making attributions is that of assuming that the primary motivation for behavior is in the person, not in the person's situation, a tendency known as the **fundamental attribution error**. When, for example, a friend disappoints us by failing to

Fundamental attribution error: The overemphasis of internal or personal factors.

arrive for a surprise party, we are more apt to conclude that the friend is inconsiderate or does not care than to believe that external factors interfered with his or her ability to attend. We overemphasize internal factors or personality traits, and we de-emphasize or discount the role played by the situation or factors external to the person.[27]

Things change dramatically, however, when we provide reasons for our own behavior. In offering reasons for why we behave as we do, we overemphasize external factors and downplay internal ones. This tendency, known as the **self-serving bias**, functions as a barrier to accurate perception while, at the same time, it helps to raise our own self-esteem during the self-attribution process. We take credit for the positive while denying culpability for the negative. Instead, we attribute the negative to factors beyond our control.

Another perceptual barrier is **overattribution**—the attributing of everything an individual does to a single or a few specific characteristics. For example, we may ascribe a person's alcohol use, preference for certain kinds of friends, and lack of interest in close relationships to the fact that she or he was sexually abused when young.

When it comes to human beings, accounting for behavior can be complex. To understand our own behavior and that of others, we need to do our best to make accurate, reasoned attributions rather than excuse or blame ourselves or other persons based on habitual attribution biases.

FRAMEWORKS OF PERCEPTION

The mental templates and life experiences we bring to any situation strongly affect how we process experience and relate to others. How we organize what we know and the patterns of thought we characteristically display, referred to as schemata, when combined with our preconceived ideas or sets and selectivities along with two other constructs, ethnocentrism and stereotyping, define our perceptions and reveal our perceptual vulnerabilities. What is more, we often enact our perceptions without any conscious awareness.

SCHEMATA

Schemata are the mental templates of characteristics that influence our notions or ideas about other people. Four perceptual schemata, or cognitive frameworks, help us decide what others are like and whether we would like to get to know them better:

1. *Physical constructs* enable us to classify people according to their physical characteristics, including age, weight, and height.

2. *Interaction constructs* point us toward their social behavior cues; for example, are they friendly, arrogant, aloof?

3. *Role constructs* focus on their social position; for example, are they professors, students, administrators?

4. *Psychological constructs* lead us to classify people according to such things as their generosity, insecurity, shyness, and sense of humor.

Which of these schemata are you conscious of using when you first meet someone?

PERCEPTUAL SETS AND SELECTIVITIES

Each of us learns to make sense of the world by organizing the stimuli we perceive uniquely. The lessons that our family, friends, and culture teach us condition us to

Self-serving bias: The overemphasizing of external factors as influences on one's behavior.

Overattribution: The attributing of everything an individual does to a single or a few specific characteristics.

Our tendency to overestimate or attribute another's behavior to dispositional variables while underestimating the impact of existing situational or environmental variables is supported by research. Can you show how this works?

1. Use attribution theory and the fundamental attribution error to provide a rationale that accounts for the following lines from a speech by the Reverend Jesse Jackson:

   Most poor people are not lazy. They catch the early bus. They raise other people's children. They clean the streets. No, no, they're not lazy.

2. Using your understanding of the nature of perception, explain this statement:

   We find causes where we look for them. Then, draw an example from personal experience to illustrate the statement's meaning.

SOURCE: See, for example, Jessica Li Yexin, Katherine A. Johnson, Adam B. Cohen, Melissa J. Williams, Eric D. Knowles, and Chen Zhansheng, "Fundamental(ist) Attribution Error: Protestants Are Dispositionally Focused," *Journal of Personality and Social Psychology*, 102, 2012, p. 281–290; and Didier Truchot, Gwladys Maure, and Sonia Patte, "Do Attributions Change over Time When the Actor's Behavior Is Hedonically Relevant to the Perceiver?," *Journal of Social Psychology*, 143, 2003, p. 202–208.

perceive stimuli in set ways, effectively helping us to construct our social reality. These organizational constructions are known as **perceptual sets and selectivities**; they are established gradually over time and help us decide which stimuli we should attend to. For example, if we are raised in a family that values education, we are likely to perceive learning-related activities more positively than we would if we had been raised in a family that dismisses education as unimportant. Likewise, if we grow up in a home where a particular religious or ethnic group is consistently demeaned, we would be more likely to believe in that group's inferiority.[28] Because past lessons and experiences are part of us at every new encounter, our past influences our interpretations and evaluations of the present.

Education and culture are also variables that influence our perception, helping us make sense of our environment by selecting stimuli significant to us. For example, American culture supports the open expression of opinion, whereas in Japanese culture, talk is not necessarily viewed as good and may be considered a sign of shallowness.[29] Therefore, an American may perceive long silences to be embarrassing and uncomfortable, but a Japanese person accepts periods of silence as perfectly normal. Culture helps to condition us to communicate in distinctive ways. As you will see later in this chapter, it also influences our communication preferences and styles.

Like education and culture, our motivation or internal state also causes us to exhibit our own perceptual selectivities or preferences. For instance, just as thirsty people lost in the desert tend to see water mirages, so hungry people are more apt to see food before their eyes when shown a series of ambiguous pictures than are individuals who are full. Similarly, our financial position can influence our positive or negative perceptions of matters such as the U.S. welfare system and clothing fads.

Perceptual sets and selectivities: Organizational constructions that condition a readiness to perceive, or a tendency to interpret stimuli in ways to which one has been conditioned.

1. To better understand the concept of perceptual sets, quickly read the statements that appear in the following triangles:

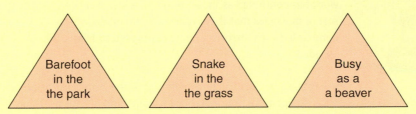

Barefoot in the the park

Snake in the the grass

Busy as a a beaver

2. After you have read them, examine each written statement more carefully. Did you notice the second *the* or *a* in each statement the first time? Because we are conditioned to see words in groups or clusters and not to read individual words, we can actually fail to see what is before our eyes. With the understanding that there is more to perception than meets the eye, what lessons about social perception can you draw from this experience?

3. How do preconceptions or prejudgments (perceptual sets) affect your ability to relate to others? For example, how might your judging a person to be hostile rather than congenial affect your assessment of behavior the person displays that others might see as ambiguous?

ETHNOCENTRISM AND STEREOTYPES

Ethnocentrism is the tendency to perceive what is right or wrong, good or bad, according to the categories and values of our own culture. When we are ethnocentric, we mentally formulate categorizations that make up the perceptions that are familiar and comfortable to our "in-group" and apply categorizations that are unfamiliar and awkward to an "out-group."

While such a process can help us make sense of our world, it also can cause us to narrow our perceptions and use a rigid repertoire of behaviors dependent on the taking of **perceptual shortcuts**, or the use of stereotypes that reduce our communication effectiveness.

Similarly, **stereotypes** are "rigid perceptions which are applied to all members of a group or to an individual over a period of time, regardless of individual variations."[30] Once generalizations become rigid stereotypes, they actually contribute to our losing touch with the real world. Such stereotypes share two key characteristics: (1) they lead us to categorize others on the basis of easily recognized, but not necessarily significant, qualities (for example, noticing a person's ethnicity before anything else, and (2) they lead us to ascribe an array of qualities to most or all members of a group (for example, assuming that all persons of Asian descent are soft-spoken and shy). When our generalizations harden, we are likely to disregard any differences in individuals that set them apart from the stereotyped group.

Stereotyping and **racial profiling** have the potential to plague both interracial and intercultural communication. On the tenth anniversary of the terrorist attacks of 9/11, Geoffrey Canada, educator and president of Harlem Children's Zone, offered an example of what can happen drawn from his observations and reflections on 9/11:

> I don't think many other communities experienced what we experienced in Harlem. We began to have African-American kids beating up Muslim kids,

Ethnocentrism: The tendency to perceive what is right or wrong, good or bad, according to the categories and values of one's own culture.

Perceptual shortcuts: The kinds of perceptions exhibited by lazy perceivers who rely on stereotypes to help them make sense of experience.

Stereotypes: Rigid perceptions that are applied to all members of a group or to an individual over a period of time, regardless of individual variations.

Racial profiling: A form of stereotyping attributed to racism.

True or False

4. *Dividing people into in- and out-groups improves perceptual accuracy.*

False. Dividing people into in- and out-groups leads to stereotyping.

and it shocked all of us. African-American kids thought they were committing some act of patriotism. We began to reach out to the community of those from Northern Africa who live around 125th Street who are mostly Muslim, and create relationships so those folks weren't looking at each other through the prism of stereotypes and wouldn't automatically assume this was a bad person. And that work has continued as these young people have been growing up, [to offset] these sort of messages that they receive via the media, where they're constantly being bombarded with terrorism being connected to Islam. We, as a community, live side by side.[31]

When we stereotype instead of responding to the communication or cues of individuals, we create expectations, assume they are valid, and behave as if they have already occurred. We judge people on the basis of what we believe regarding the group in which we have placed them. We emphasize similarities and overlook differences. Stereotyping leads us to oversimplify, generalize, and grossly exaggerate our observations.

Sometimes we find ourselves in situations requiring that we make decisions based on little information other than appearance. Unfortunately, in addition to making clothing-trait associations, we also are prone to making "feature-trait associations," relying on physical appearance to make judgments regarding both the categories people belong to and the traits they possess. While we may believe we are responding to a specific person, what we are really acting on is a stereotype. For example, for many years certain physical features—dark skin, coarse hair, full lips, and a wide nose—signaled to some people that a person was African American. This was a stereotype that produced a stereotypic judgment. And the more "Afrocentric" an individual's features, the more he or she was ascribed traits stereotypical of African Americans.[32] Colorism researchers report that more prejudice and discrimination are directed against dark-skinned African Americans than against light-skinned African Americans; the latter are more likely to have better jobs and to attain higher levels of education than those with darker skin.[33] Researchers caution that although we may see more African American lawyers and doctors in prime-time television offerings, those characters are lighter skinned than the African Americans who are featured in broadcast/cable news shows as less exemplary characters.

Lazy perceivers rely on stereotyping as their key perceptual process. Because it discourages careful observation and encourages pigeonholing, stereotyping encourages categorization, leading some to observe that stereotyping brings on a malady called "hardening of the categories." When we suffer from such a malady, we insist on having everyone fit into a particular niche, and we fail to recognize that every person is unique in some way and in fact constitutes his or her own category.

Together, schemata, sets and selectivities, and ethnocentrism and stereotypes play major parts in structuring our perceptions. By recognizing their roles and understanding their potential effects, we can prepare ourselves to question whether we are processing experience accurately and are thinking critically and reflectively about the judgments we form.

BARRIERS TO ACCURATE PERCEPTION

In addition to ethnocentrism and stereotypes, a number of other barriers can interfere with our developing accurate perception by causing us to behave unreflectively—that is, to act only on the basis of our personal interests, make erroneous assumptions, and so

forth. Perhaps the best way to eliminate such barriers is to learn to recognize them in our behavior.

Among the factors that can interfere with accurate perception are the following:

1. The failure to recognize the influence of age
2. The failure to distinguish facts from inferences
3. The tendency to think we know it all
4. The penchant for indiscrimination
5. The tendency to freeze our evaluations
6. The tendency to respond to events or persons with snap judgments
7. The wearing of blinders
8. The tendency to judge others more harshly than we judge ourselves

We explore each in turn below.

AGE AND PERSON PERCEPTION

Throughout the life span, we continually change age-group memberships. How old we are at any point in time influences our perceptions of other people.[34] When we are younger, **category-based processing** may affect our attitudes toward an individual we identify as belonging to the category of older adults, for example. In contrast, if we are older and view the target individual as similar to ourselves, rather than rely on stereotypic category-based processing, we may rely on **person-based processing**. Such processing reduces the influence of group attitudes on our perceptual judgments and helps explain why older people, in comparison with people in other age groups, have more complex perceptions of people their age. Because older persons are likely to be more familiar with persons in their age group, they are motivated to use person-based processing when forming impressions of members of their group.[35]

Category-based processing: The processing of information about a person that is influenced by attitudes toward the group into which the person is placed.

Person-based processing: The processing of information about a person based on perceptions of the individual, not on his or her membership in a particular group.

Imagine yourself in the following situation:

You work on campus in one of the chemistry labs from 6:00 P.M. until midnight. It is late in your shift, and you are alone. You are a bit more nervous than usual because there has been an increase in campus crime and students have been warned to travel in pairs. You are relieved when midnight comes and you can close the lab and go home. As you are about to lock the door to the lab, you hear someone yell, "Wait! Don't lock the door!" A person runs down the hall toward you and pleads with you to let him in so that he can complete his work on a class project that is due in the morning. He isn't carrying any student ID; he tells you that he forgot it in his haste to get to the lab. You don't recognize him. Do you trust what he is telling you? Do you let him in?

Would you respond differently if the person were a female? If he or she were elderly? Asian? Latino? Muslim? Dressed shabbily? Wearing designer clothes? Explain your answers.

Young people have the highest level of anxiety about aging.[36] As a result, younger people tend to place older adults into a number of different stereotypes and are likely to perceive them more negatively than they view young and middle-aged adults. Older people, in contrast, have more positive attitudes about their own aging process and perceive other older adults as exhibiting more instrumentality and autonomy. While this may be due to an in-group favoritism effect, the same effect may explain why younger people rate characteristics of people their own age more favorably than do older people.

Gender also affects attitudes toward age. Young women who attribute any negative attitudes toward older people to their own fear of aging tend to stereotype older people less than do other women. In contrast, young men who consider their own fears about aging stereotype older people more than do other men. This may be attributed to the fact that men and women have different mental representations for aging.[37]

FACT-INFERENCE CONFUSIONS

A fact is something we know is true on the basis of observation. Your hair color is brown, for example. An inference is simply a conclusion we draw, whether or not it is supported by facts. If you assume your neighbor is having an affair based solely on the fact that an unfamiliar car comes to her house every few days for an hour or so, you are making an inference.

When we mistake what we infer for something we have observed, we experience **fact-inference confusion**. Inferences have varying degrees of probability of being correct; their validity depends on the facts that underlie them. For instance, "The sun will rise tomorrow" is not technically a statement of fact; it is an inference with a very high probability of being correct. In contrast, if you see a friend talking and laughing with another person and you conclude that the two of them are hooking up, that would be an inference with average to low probability of being correct, because you cannot verify it based on your observations to this point.

Inferences, like assumptions, can have serious consequences for our relationships. They can cause us to jump to erroneous conclusions, create embarrassing moments, and result in our responding inappropriately to others. Thus, we need to take time to evaluate whether we are relying on facts or on inferences when we perceive and interpret another's behavior. The question is not whether we make inferences but whether we are *aware* of the inferences we make. If we are aware that we are inferring and not observing, and we can accurately

WHAT DO YOU KNOW?

True or False
5. *"The sun will rise tomorrow" technically is not a statement of fact.*
True. Because tomorrow's sunrise has not yet been observed, "The sun will rise tomorrow" is an inference.

Fact-inference confusion: The tendency to treat observations and assumptions similarly.

assess the degree of probability that our inferences are correct, we take a giant step forward in improving our perceptions.

ALLNESS

Allness, or thinking that we can know all there is to know about a person, place, or situation, is an attitude that some people carry with them from one relationship to another. Those who "know it all" mistakenly think they can know everything. They exhibit very little tolerance for ambiguity, which causes them to display an unwillingness to withhold judgment.

Thinking we know it all limits our ability to perceive accurately. When we insist that our viewpoint alone is correct, we in effect are saying that any differing perceptions are incorrect. We would be wiser to open ourselves to alternative ways of perceiving. To correct a tendency toward allness, we could add an implied "et cetera" to each of our perceptions— acknowledging that there is more to be known than what we see.

INDISCRIMINATION

When we fail to discriminate *among* individuals, we may end up discriminating *against* an individual. When this occurs, we exhibit **indiscrimination**.[38] In other words, the more we are discriminating and look for differences in all individuals, the less likely it is that we will be prejudiced against the members of any one group or treat people belonging to these groups unfairly.

Accurate perception depends on our being able to identify differences, not just recognize similarities. Too frequently, however, just the opposite happens, increasing our tendency to stereotype. If you remind yourself that no two people are absolutely alike, that every person is unique, your ability to perceive each as an individual will improve.

Using stereotypes as the basis for social exchanges often leads to miscommunication. Too frequently, the way stereotypes play out in behavior leads us to decide that we do not like or

Allness: A perceptual fallacy that allows a person to believe that he or she knows everything about something.

Indiscrimination: A perceptual barrier that causes one to emphasize similarities and neglect differences.

Explain how this poem by John Godfrey Saxe helps illustrate the perceptual fallacy of allness.

It was six men of Indostan
  To learning much inclined

Who went to see the Elephant
  (Though all of them were blind).

That each by observation
  Might satisfy his mind.

The First approached the Elephant,
  And happening to fall

Against his broad and sturdy side,
  At once began to bawl:

"God bless me! But the Elephant
  Is very like a wall."

The Second, feeling of the tusk
  Cried, "Ho! What have we here

So very round and smooth and sharp?
  To me 'tis very clear

This wonder of an Elephant
  Is very like a spear."

The Third approached the animal
  And, happening to take

The squirming trunk within his hands,
  Thus boldly up he spake:

"I see," quoth he, "the Elephant
  Is very like a snake!"

The Fourth reached out an eager hand,
  And fell about the knee;

"What most this wondrous beast is like
Is very plain," quoth he;

"Tis clear enough the Elephant
  Is very like a tree!"

The Fifth, who chanced to touch the ear,
  Said: "E'en the blindest man

Can tell what this resembles most;
  Deny the fact who can

This marvel of an Elephant
  Is very like a fan!"

The Sixth no sooner had begun
  About the beast to grope

Than seizing on the swinging tail
  That fell within his scope:

"I see," quoth he, "the Elephant
  Is very like a rope!"

And so these men of Indostan
  Disputed loud and long,

Each in his own opinion
  Exceeding stiff and strong.

Though each was partly in the right,
  They all were in the wrong![a]

1. What does the poem suggest regarding the dangers of allness?

2. How, in your estimation, does allness affect future evaluations? Explain.

SOURCE: John Godfrey Saxe, "The Blind Men and the Elephant," 1872.

Frozen evaluation: A perceptual fallacy that discourages flexibility and encourages rigidity; an evaluation of a person that ignores changes.

approve of someone before we have even gotten to know her or him. Again, our expectations influence our judgments.

FROZEN EVALUATIONS AND SNAP JUDGMENTS

When we assume that situations and people stay the way they are, always, we make **frozen evaluations**. "Once a poor student," we think, "always a poor student." "Once a thief," we reason, "always a thief." Such statements fail to acknowledge that people can change. If our perception does not permit us to be flexible, but freezes our judgment instead, then we fail in perceiving the constant change that characterizes all of us.

To avoid making such fallacious perceptions, we should date every perception we acknowledge. Doing so will also help prevent us from clinging to our first impressions. Initial perceptions need not be permanent. In fact, maintaining an open mind should be a goal if we are to develop more valid assessments of experience. For example, consider the following initial impression and subsequent reevaluation of perception:

> For years I had seen octopuses as terrible, evil creatures that were intent on grabbing swimmers with their tentacles and dragging them under water to be crushed and drowned.
>
> Now I perceive them as being gentle, inoffensive, intelligent creatures who enjoy playful contacts with swimmers.
>
> Probably I have changed my perceptions of octopuses because of changes in the filters of past experience and mind-set. My early experiences were reading horror stories and seeing horror movies. My mind-set was to believe, as truth, what I read and saw in those media. Also I wanted to believe the horrible stories were true because that enhanced my enjoyment. Later experiences were seeing undersea documentaries by Cousteau and reading books by him. My mind-set now is that I respect what scientists tell me and I expect that they will give me accurate accounts of their research. I saw a movie of one of Cousteau's divers doing a little ballet dance with an octopus he had made friends with. Then I saw the octopus and the diver embrace affectionately as they parted. I also read about a young woman biologist who has made friends with giant octopuses near Seattle. She tickles them and they love it.[39]

Can you think of an experience in your life that led you to form an initial impression that you subsequently changed? For example, you might have believed that a disheveled person seen frequently on a street neighboring your campus was homeless until you discovered that a building at the college was named for him. How challenging is it for you to reevaluate a first impression?

Just as we are apt to make frozen evaluations, we similarly display **snap judgments**, or make instant decisions. In the rush to give meaning to our perceptions, instead of delaying our responses we jump to conclusions, displaying instantaneous and reflexlike—but often incorrect or even dangerous—responses. For example, if we see a friend talking with a police officer, we may rush to judgment and conclude that the officer was giving him a ticket. Accurate perception usually takes time. Better perceivers do not rush to respond; rather, they try to synthesize as many data as possible, explore alternative evaluations of the situation, and thus increase their chances of understanding what is really going on.

Has an instructor ever made a snap judgment about you?

Snap judgment:
An evaluation made without reflection; an undelayed reaction.

BLINDERING

What we tell ourselves about what we perceive can also limit our ability to perceive accurately. In effect, the act of **blindering**—that is, forcing ourselves to see people and situations only in certain ways, as though we are wearing blinders—keeps us from seeing who or what is really before our eyes.

Accurate perception depends on the ability to see what is there without being limited by imaginary restrictions or boundaries. When, for example, scientists stopped searching for the cause of malaria in the air (the word *malaria* comes from the Italian for "bad air") and looked for other causes, they soon traced the origin of the disease to the *Anopheles* mosquito and were then able to find a cure. The following exercise can help you understand the concept of blindering: Draw four straight lines to connect all of the dots below, without lifting your pencil or pen from the page or retracing a line.

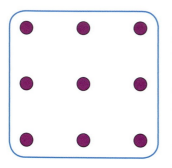

Most people have difficulty completing this exercise because they add a restriction that is not actually there—they assume the figure is a square. (See the solution at the end of this chapter.)

JUDGING OTHERS MORE HARSHLY THAN OURSELVES

Point your finger at a person near you. The gesture feels natural, doesn't it? Now point that same finger at yourself. That doesn't feel quite so natural, does it?

Related to the self-serving bias discussed earlier in this chapter, when perceptual disagreements arise, we tend to assume that the problem in perceiving lies with the other person, rather than with ourselves. We are quite comfortable evaluating our perceptual capabilities more charitably than we judge those of others.

When asked to compare their ability to communicate with that of their peers, parents, professors, significant others, or siblings, most people report communicating at least as well as if not better than others. Thus, whenever communication goes awry, that finger points outward—directly at another person—rather than inward to the self. We shift responsibility for communication problems and perceptual distortions away from ourselves and place it with others with whom we have relationships.

DIVERSITY AND CULTURE: INTERPRETING THROUGH DIFFERENT I'S

We are likely to persist in seeing the world not necessarily as it is but as we have been conditioned to perceive it. Culture and past experience create in us a quest for perceptual constancy—it is easier for us to keep seeing things as we have in the past than it is to revise our perceptions.

The more similar our life experiences, the more similarly we tend to perceive things. The more dissimilar our life experiences, the wider the gap between us with respect to how we see and make sense of things. Not everyone makes sense out of experience in the same way. Cultural habits or selectivities ensure that.

The members of every culture develop particular cultural perspectives or ways of looking at the world. As we have noted, most Americans perceive it to be important to express their uniqueness and independence, whereas in Asian cultures, the group and not the individual is paramount. These contrasting orientations have implications for interpersonal

Blindering: The unconscious adding of restrictions that do not actually exist.

communication. American children are taught to separate from their parents and develop self-reliance, but in cultures that value interdependence over dependence, cooperation, helpfulness, and loyalty are nurtured instead. Thus, persons from these cultures tend to have more close-knit relationships and expect more from others.

We see such differences play themselves out in how we process information as well. The Japanese, for example, develop a wider-angle view of experience than do Americans. They do not see themselves as being at the center of the universe. When students at the University of Michigan and Kyoto University were shown animation of an underwater scene with a "focal fish" and other fish swimming among an array of undersea objects, the Japanese students made more references to the background elements, while the Americans focused on the "focal fish." Americans believe that each person has a separate identity that needs to be reinforced. They value the ethic of competition, the need to be number one. This orientation can cause difficulty for Americans when they need to interact with persons from other cultures who do not share this value and may perceive it as threatening to them.

Culture teaches us a worldview, influencing our assessments of reality. Whether we are judging beauty, evaluating the meaning of success, or reacting to someone's age, culture plays a role. In the United States, for example, we have a culture that values youth and rejects the notion of growing old. Persons in Muslim, Asian, Latin American, Native American, and African cultures do not share this perception. Individuals from different cultures are simply trained to observe the same cues differently; we all interpret what we perceive through a **cultural lens**. Some years ago, researchers used an apparatus resembling binoculars to compare the perceptual preferences of Native Americans and Mexicans. Each subject in the study was shown ten pairs of photographs; one photo in each pair was of an element of Native American culture and one was of Mexican culture. After viewing the paired images through the device, the subjects reported their observations. Results revealed that both the Native American and the Mexican subjects were more likely to report having seen scenes from their own culture.[40]

Race also influences perception. When it comes to views on how much progress we have made since the days of the civil rights movement, a racial divide still exists. For example, when asked who will be hired, whites perceive a level playing field, whereas African Americans believe that discrimination persists. A majority (52 percent) of African Americans, compared with 15 percent of white Americans, believe the United States needs to enact new civil right laws to reduce discrimination.[41] How might such disparate perceptions affect relationships between white people and black people in the United States?

Because we have not all experienced the same life lessons, even within cultures we may not attribute the same meanings to the same sets of conditions or behavioral cues. If we are to relate effectively to one another, we need to take steps to eliminate cultural nearsightedness.

GENDER AND PERCEPTION

Would you see things differently if you were of the opposite sex? Gender, like culture, influences the way we make sense of our experiences. Men and women are conditioned to

Cultural lens: The influence of culture on perception.

Lisbeth Salander, the heroine of the novel and movie *The Girl with the Dragon Tattoo*, has an appearance that challenges conventional images of leading female characters.

perceive different realities, are encouraged to perform in different ways, and prefer to use different communication styles. In addition to influencing how men and women perceive one another, beliefs about gender-appropriate behavior influence how we relate to each other.

From early childhood, both boys and girls are rewarded for using behaviors that conform to their gender; for example, boys are commended for displaying strength and independence, whereas girls are praised for expressing their feelings and being kind to others. We even categorize them differently—men as rational and women as emotional.[42]

As a result of interacting with parents, teachers, peers, and others, we internalize the lessons of appropriate gendered behavior. Such lessons instruct us in how society would like us to behave, framing our perceptions. These constructs, however, can limit how each of us is perceived and may lead to the judging of men and women based on gender expectations rather than on observed cues.

Others' expectations, role model behavior, and stereotyped notions of sex roles reinforce "acceptable" images of male and female behavior. For perceptions of the kinds of behavior appropriate for men and women to change, the messages that institutions, the media, and society feed us need to change.

In addition, we continually monitor ourselves. We sort stimuli, selecting some and rejecting others. The information we store in our internal database helps us build our view of reality and gives our lives a sense of stability. For example, if we develop the perspective that men are persistently more dominant than women, then we use that belief to categorize both genders and predict their actions. However, when our expectations cause us to misperceive others and their intentions, undesirable consequences can result. All too frequently, rigid categorizing creates communication problems and precipitates interpersonal fiascoes.

As thinking men and women, we do not have to accept all the **gender prescriptions** our culture provides. We can reject those that limit our development, and in doing so we can elicit changes in the behavior of others toward us. When we refuse to support a gender-based definition, we in effect participate in redefinition. For example, when one woman encourages another to be more autonomous, she may help that woman to expand her definition of behaviors appropriate for women. As women change their behavior and roles, men may perceive both women and themselves differently and may change as well. In the process, we recast the meanings of masculinity and femininity.

Gender prescriptions: The roles and behaviors that a culture assigns to males and females.

THE MEDIA, TECHNOLOGY, AND PERCEPTION

The media and technology also influence how we perceive social experience. For better or worse, they have the ability to radically change our views of reality. By being mindful of where our perceptions come from—aware of how both media and technology affect our processing of the self, each other, and events—we can better understand and improve our perceptual accuracy.

THE MEDIA AND PERCEPTION

Because the mass media tend to depict us in ways that reinforce cultural views of race, culture, and gender, the more time we spend with the media, the more accepting we tend to become of social stereotypes, and the more likely we are to help perpetuate the unrealistic and limiting perceptions presented to us.

How do stereotypes in media influence our expectations and relationships? First, they help us identify and generalize about what we consider to be appropriate behavior. They offer us categories into which people fit, and they provide us with an array of models in action so that when similar situations arise we think we know how to deal with them. Second, they provide us with perceptual shortcuts; they cause us to forget that we communicate with individuals, not stereotypes, and they contribute to our becoming lazy perceivers—too accepting of the inaccurate or false images presented to us.

What are some of the specific lessons we learn from the media that help shape our perceptions of gender? One lesson, which we glean from the significant underrepresentation of women and older people in leading roles in the media, is that males matter more than women (and younger males matter most) and that women and older people are either not as important or potentially invisible. Even in news programming, stories about men outnumber stories about women.

A second media lesson involves our internalization of stereotypic portrayals of gender. Whereas media offerings present men as active, independent, powerful, and sexually virile, they portray women as the objects of males' sexual desires, incompetent, manipulative, and passive. The media focus on women's looks and their relationships with family members and others. Women are caregivers. Men are typically portrayed taking care of business. They are depicted as providers.

A third lesson concerns the extent to which the media lead us to perceive minority groups inappropriately. Minorities occupy an even smaller media presence than women, for the most part being cast in supporting, not leading, roles and depicted as lazy, unlawful, and dumb, or, in the case of Muslims, as terrorists. Even positive portrayals are based in stereotypes: the media tend to pigeonhole the Asian character as "the smart one" or the African American as "the magical African American friend." African American film director Spike Lee has pointed out the stock character of the "Magical Negro," who serves merely as an enabler to a white character, and comedy sketches featuring such a role have aired on *Saturday Night Live*.

The media also influence our perception by molding our conceptions of the real world and people in ways that are inconsistent with facts. As cultivation theory would predict, for example, heavy television viewers are more likely than those who view little TV to be fearful and to exaggerate the amount of violence in the world.[43] Heavy viewers perceive the world to be meaner and a more dangerous place.[44] Research demonstrates that by distorting our perception of risk, the media induce in us a sense of fear that is out of proportion with any actual danger.[45] In other words, the media are virtually capable of scaring us to death. Such perceptions affect real-life judgments of what is safe, whom we should fear, and whom we are safe with. What steps can you take to counteract the false sense of reality brought to you by media?

Media lessons, which appear to weave their way innocuously into our consciousness, also function to limit our perceptions of ourselves in relation to each other, and, what is worse, they often cause us to misperceive reality. As they perpetuate what is unreal and untrue (even on so-called reality shows), they encourage us to reach for what is impossible. Because we use the media as reference points for what is normal, we are more likely to perceive ourselves, our relationships, and our lives as inferior by comparison. The media present the human body in perfect form and convince us that no one could love us the way we actually are, thus causing us to develop negative images of ourselves. The media's unreal images perpetuate in us unrealistic perceptions of what our lives should be like and cause us to internalize and anticipate unreasonable outcomes from relationships.

TECHNOLOGY AND PERCEPTION

Like media in general, technology is altering self-perception as well as perception of other people and the world. For example, how do we perceive the social connections we have online? Do we see them as pulling us closer into new kinds of communities, or pulling us apart by their ability to separate us from more local, personal interactions? Are we reproducing real social interactions online or creating something altogether different? Is the ease with which we can link with others who share the same interests and goals and confirm our way of thinking creating communities of sameness? Are we sacrificing serendipity for a false sense of companionship?

Violent video games have both positive and negative effects on players. How do they affect you?

Social identity model of de-individuation effects: A theory that states that each individual has different identities that make themselves visible in different situations.

When online, we also make judgments relative to other persons' cultures or gender. According to the **social identity model of de-individuation effects** (known as SIDE), we have different identities that make themselves visible in different situations.[46] When we interact online, the lack of nonverbal cues, especially those related to appearance and sound, cause us to hold on more tightly to what we know about the other person's group affiliations.[47] This could compel us to become more judgmental, to make overattributions (that is, single out one or two characteristics of a person), or to exaggerate the importance of the minimal information we have. We practice closure, often filling in the gaps by using stereotypes. If we assume that people share social categories with us, making them like us, we tend to find them more likable than if we believe they are different.

Technology is changing us in other ways, too. Playing violent games online increases aggressive behavior by causing people to perceive annoying provocations as more hostile.[48] The games also expand the repertoire of aggressive behaviors of users and emotionally desensitize players to aggression and violence.[49] The effects of online gaming are not all negative, however. Playing action games can enhance an individual's ability to pay attention to objects and changes in the environment. Experienced gamers are 30 to 50 percent better than nongamers at perceiving everything happening around them. It appears that gaming not only precipitates better spatial skills but also improves attention skills and facilitates the accurate understanding of a visual landscape.[50]

On the other hand, some observers fear that, because of the vastness of the virtual landscape, interacting online may be limiting our perceptual focus by making it difficult for us to concentrate on any one thing for a sustained period of time. While we watch television, for example, we frequently also use a computing device of some kind to check e-mail, Web surf for information related to what we are watching, or exchange messages with others about what we are viewing.[51] What is more, when we are online, we hurry from one stimulus to another, sneaking peeks at people and sites, paying scant attention to any.[52] The Internet makes multidirectional pulls on our attention, demanding of us a different kind of attention than we are used to giving.[53] In fact, it has been suggested that the distractions caused by social media could cost a company with a thousand workers more than $10 million a year.[54]

The Internet is also affecting how we remember. We pay more attention to and are more likely to remember information if we think we will not be able to find it later. For many, the Internet is becoming a primary system for information storage. We have found a new means of outsourcing memory.[55]

GAINING COMMUNICATION COMPETENCE: ENHANCING YOUR PERCEPTUAL ABILITIES

Your ability to relate to others is affected by how capable a perceiver you are. Understanding the part you play in perception, including how and why you perceive people and events as you do, is essential if you are to experience new and healthy relationships, minimize misunderstandings, and broaden your horizons. What steps can you take to improve your perceptual abilities?

RECOGNIZE THE PART YOU PLAY

Because we are all unique, we each experience a reality that is somewhat different from that experienced by others. Until we acknowledge the part we play in perceiving and making sense of reality, we are apt to experience numerous relational and communication problems. Just because others may not see the world the way we do does not mean their views are wrong. They are merely expressing alternative outlooks. Variations in physiological, psychological, and cultural factors lead us to adopt different perspectives and attribute difference meanings to experience. Perception is not something that happens to us. It is something we do.

You may like a person who seems similar to you and dislike someone who seems different. Your friend's jokes may strike you as funny when you are in a good mood and tasteless when you are preoccupied with a personal problem. By taking stock of yourself, including your emotional state and biases, you accept responsibility for what you bring to the perception process.

BE A PATIENT PERCEIVER

Because we tend to live at an accelerated pace in U.S. society, we may expect things to happen quickly. The emphasis we place on speed can diminish our ability to be patient, contributing to our jumping to conclusions. Patient perceivers, however, do not jump to conclusions, cling to first impressions, or believe they know it all. Instead, they open

TRY THIS: *Facebook in Focus*

Peruse the walls of the Facebook pages of various friends. Then answer these questions:

1. To what extent does each wall contain clues that help others form an initial impression of each person?

2. If you know the person well, how does his or her wall reinforce or contradict your face-to-face perception?

their minds to possibilities, look beyond the obvious, and genuinely attempt to check the accuracy of their interpretations.

Patient perceivers question their perceptual acuity. Ask yourself if there is any chance you could be wrong. By acknowledging that you might have made an error in judgment or misevaluated observed behavior, you motivate yourself to seek further validation. If you take the time and make the effort either to verify your judgment or to prove yourself wrong, you increase your chances of forming more accurate impressions of others and of situations in which you find yourself.

BECOME A PERCEPTION CHECKER

In order to avoid treating interpretations as if they were facts, develop the skill of perception checking. You can do this by relaying a nonevaluative descriptive statement of your observations; that is, observe the behavior of another, describe and interpret what his or her behavior means to you, and put your interpretation into words in the effort to determine if your perception is correct.

For example, imagine you are a participant-observer of the following scene:

> Leila walks into the classroom and flings her books down on the desk. As she takes her seat, you notice that her eyes are narrowed and her face is in a scowl. You are seated directly to her right. You quietly say to her, "Leila, I get the feeling that you're angry about something. Am I right? Can I do anything to help?"

WATCH THIS 3.1
For a video on perception-checking visit the student study site.

Making this initial statement followed by questions that assume nothing is better than asking, "Why are you angry with me?" (Who said she was?) Your goal as a perception checker is to explore Leila's thoughts and feelings, not to prove that your interpretation of what you have observed is right. For example, in response Leila might state, "I'm not angry. I'm upset with myself for not getting the paper done on time." By seeking verification of the impression you received from Leila's nonverbal behavior and giving her the opportunity to share her thoughts and feelings, you reduce your uncertainty about what she is feeling as well as take some of the guesswork out of perception.

Keep in mind that perception checking works best with persons from low-context cultures. Typically, it involves straight talk and direct statements of observation. Persons from high-context cultures might become embarrassed if they are asked so directly about their feelings and the meanings of their actions.

WIDEN YOUR PERCEPTION

Keep the big picture in mind as perceptual clues surface. Avoid jumping to a conclusion based on a single piece of evidence. By cautiously assessing what is happening, you refrain from overattributing meaning to any single behavior or circumstance. While what you may see or hear first (primacy effect) or last (recency effect) may make a great impression on you, you need to search for more evidence so that you do not draw inaccurate conclusions based on the partial picture to which you have access.

SEE THROUGH THE EYES OF ANOTHER

Try to exhibit empathy—that is, experience the world from behind the eyes of another person. This means you need to socially decenter, or take the focus off, yourself and place it on another by considering that person's thoughts and feelings first. Doing this allows you insight into the other person's state of mind and lets you see things from his or her perspective; by stepping into the other person's shoes, you can re-create or vicariously experience what he or she is feeling, and thus develop emotional understanding. When you empathize you also engage in perspective taking—you develop a personal sense of what the person is going through. You imagine what it would be like to be in the person's position. Can you imagine, for example, how your significant other feels when you forget his or her birthday? Can you sense how your supervisor feels when every few weeks you take a day off? While it is easier to feel empathy for those with whom we identify, it is equally important to be able to put yourself into the shoes of a person with whom you may have little in common. Do you find it easy to empathize with others? Some researchers fear that the ability to empathize is on the decline due to the preeminence of social media and its encouragement of self-promotion as opposed to other understanding.[56] Do you believe their fear is justified?

BUILD PERCEPTUAL BRIDGES, NOT WALLS

Although perceptual disagreements can drive us apart, if we exhibit a willingness to experience the world from another person's perspective, we can enhance communication. Rather than argue over whose point of view is right or whose behavior is wrong, it is more productive to understand the factors that create differences in our interpretations and then work to adapt to and bridge those differences.

CONSIDER HOW TECHNOLOGY IS CHANGING HOW WE PERCEIVE

Social transformations are taking place because of the amount of interaction we engage in online. It is important to think about and imagine how virtual interactions are affecting our desire for actual ones and vice versa. For example, consider the following: Could you go an entire day without sending a text message or checking Facebook? Are there times when you should actually speak on your cell phone instead of texting or converse face-to-face instead of posting online? And when posting, do you always consider who will have access to your words and photos and how others might perceive them?

Dax couldn't believe what was happening. Would it never end?

Dax had not been happy when he received the notice to report to the courthouse for jury duty. He was even less happy when he found that he had no valid reason to be excused from the obligation.

The first day he reported, things went just fine. He was called as a member of a panel for a case, but the case was resolved quickly and the jury was dismissed. The second day he was not called during the morning session, so he was able to finish reading a novel. Then it all began.

Dax was called for the jury selection phase of a murder trial. Before he knew it, he was on the jury and the trial had started.

Two days into the trial, Dax began to wonder about the entire process. Could each eyewitness called by both attorneys really have seen the same thing? Twelve different witnesses had been called to testify about what had happened on the street corner where the murder had occurred. All twelve described different versions of the event.

Was this possible? Could so many people not agree on what had happened? Dax wished he could have a chance to question the witnesses himself. Was each of them certain of his or her perception? To what degree did the relationship each did or did not share with the defendant or the victim influence the reports?

Dax was really getting into the trial when the defendant changed his plea to guilty and the jury was dismissed. Though he was released from duty, Dax continued to mull over his confusion about witnesses' perceptions.

Answer these questions:

1. Do you think several people observing one event will perceive it the same way? Why or why not?

2. What is there about the perception process that enables us to observe different realities?

3. How do you explain the differences in the testimony Dax heard at the trial? Do you think any or all of the twelve witnesses who testified lied?

REVIEW THIS

CHAPTER SUMMARY

1 Explain the perception process and its relationship to reality. We do not all perceive reality similarly. Standpoint theory suggests that persons in positions of power have an overriding interest in preserving their place in the social hierarchy. Thus, our view of reality is a consequence of the person we are, where we are, and what we choose to see. Perception is the personally based process we use to make sense of experience. When we perceive, we select, organize, and interpret sensory data in an effort to make sense of and give meaning to our world.

2 Define the figure-ground principle, closure, and perceptual constancy. These are the strategies we use to facilitate perceiving. The figure-ground principle addresses our tendency to focus on a particular person or item while the surrounding context becomes background—that is, we focus on different stimuli alternately. Closure is the process we use to fill in missing perceptual pieces or gaps. Perceptual constancy is our tendency to maintain the way we see the world.

3 Explain how schemata, perceptual sets and selectivities, and ethnocentrism and stereotypes influence perception. Schemata are cognitive frameworks, the mental templates or knowledge structures we carry with us. Perceptual sets and selectivities are organizational constructions that influence our readiness to perceive in predetermined ways; each set or selectivity helps us decide what stimulus to focus on and how to construct our social reality. Ethnocentrism is the tendency to perceive what is right or wrong, good or bad, according to the categories and values of one's own culture. A stereotype is a rigid perception that is applied to members of a group or to an individual over time regardless of individual variations.

4 Distinguish among the following perceptual barriers: fact-inference confusions, allness, indiscrimination, frozen evaluations, snap judgments, and blindering. Each of these makes it difficult for us to perceive people and events accurately. Fact-inference confusions cause us to confuse observations and assumptions. Allness leads us to think we know it all. Indiscrimination causes us to emphasize similarities and neglect differences. When we make frozen evaluations, we ignore change. Snap judgments lead us to jump to conclusions. Blindering causes us to add restrictions where none actually exist.

5 Discuss how culture, gender, and media and technology influence perceptions of social experience. Culture teaches us acceptable ways of looking at our world, as well as acceptable ways of behaving. Gender conditions men and women to perceive different realities, exhibit different behaviors, and use different communication styles. The media also influence our self-perception, as well as our perception of each other, and our social experiences. Because the media tend to reinforce cultural views of gender and ethnicity, they contribute to our becoming more accepting of social stereotypes. Technology is altering the way we perceive social connection, changing our view of what is real, and enhancing our perceptual acuity.

6 Identify strategies you can use to enhance your perceptual abilities. To improve your chances of developing more accurate perceptions, you need to recognize the part you play in perception, develop patience, become a perception checker, see through others' eyes, work to bridge perceptual differences, and carefully consider how technological innovations are affecting your perceptions.

CHECK YOUR UNDERSTANDING

1 Can you provide evidence of your own personal basis of perception? For example, what aspects of your environment are you attending to right now? (See pages 62–63.)

2 Can you offer examples showing how stereotypes have affected your judgments? What do you see as the ethical implications of stereotyping? (See pages 69–72.)

3 Can you describe instances when one or more barriers to perception impeded your response to another person or situation? (See pages 72–78.)

4 Can you offer examples of how attitudes toward masculinity and femininity influence perception? How about media portrayals of race and ethnicity? (See pages 79–83.)

5 Can you describe steps you can take to develop your perceptual ability? In your opinion, is developing accurate perception a moral issue? (See pages 83–85.)

CHECK YOUR SKILLS

1 Can you use standpoint theory to account for your stance toward both wealth inequality and racism? (See page 63.)

2 Can you explain how uncertainty reduction theory helps to explain your behavior on the first day of a class? (See pages 63–64.)

3 Can you provide examples illustrating how selective perception influences your relationships? (See pages 64–65.)

4 Can you use your skills to work through perceptual differences? (See pages 65–67; and *Analyze This*, page 68.)

5 Can you use attribution theory to account for the rationales you offer to explain your own and another's behavior? (See pages 67–69; and *Reflect on This,* page 70.)

6 Can you give examples of how perceptual schemata and sets and selectivities have influenced your

reactions to people and situations? (See pages 69–70; and *Try This*, page 71.)

7 Can you document the impacts of stereotypes on you and on your relationships with others? (See pages 71–72; *Reflect on This*, page 73; and *Try This*, page 74.)

8 Can describe the steps you have taken to prevent perceptual barriers from adversely influencing your responses to people and situations? (See pages 72–78; *Try This*, pages 74 and 75; and *Analyze This*, page 76.)

9 Can you offer examples of the role cultural and gender preferences and media and technology play in your perception of others? (See pages 78–83; *Reflect on This,* page 73; and *Try This*, page 75.)

10 Can you use your skills to identify and respond to specific relationship challenges? (See *The Case of Dax's Trial,* page 86.)

KEY TERMS

STUDENT STUDY SITE

Visit the student study site at **www.sagepub.com/gambleic** to access the following materials:

- SAGE Journal Articles
- Videos
- Web Resources
- eFlashcards
- Web Quizzes
- Study Questions

Solution to Blindering Exercise

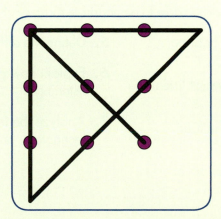

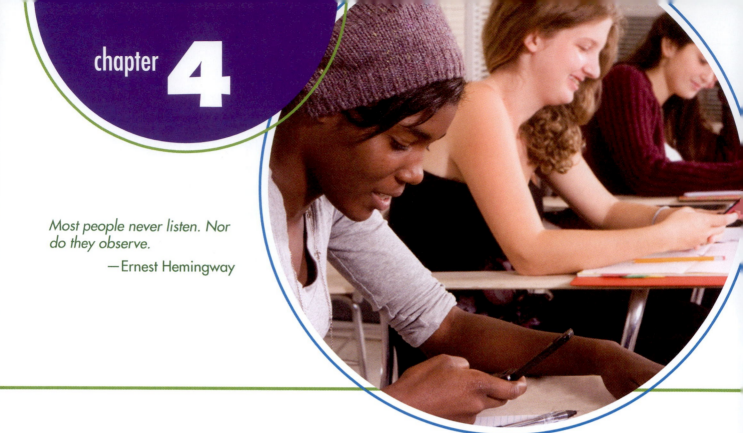

chapter 4

Most people never listen. Nor do they observe.

—Ernest Hemingway

LISTENING

LEARNING OBJECTIVES

After completing this chapter, you should be able to demonstrate mastery of the following learning outcomes:

1. Define and distinguish between hearing and listening.

2. Identify and explain the six stages of listening identified in the HURIER model.

3. Define and distinguish among the four styles and four types of listening.

4. Compare and contrast the behaviors of effective and ineffective listeners.

5. Define the different kinds of feedback.

6. Explain how gender and culture influence listening.

7. Analyze the impacts of media and technology on listening.

Students are known to engage in a number of different activities at the same time—even during class. Be honest. How often do you multitask while trying to listen to and absorb what your instructor or peers are sharing? Perhaps you browse the Web, secretly text a friend, or monitor Facebook—all while listening to a lecture. But is it possible for you to listen effectively while distracted by such competing interests?

Studies have shown that if you multitask during class you may not be listening and absorbing as much as you think.[1] While heavy multitaskers are the people most overconfident about their multitasking abilities, the research reveals that students who multitask during class do not perform as well as those who do not multitask but instead focus on absorbing the lesson.[2] What is more, they often are completely unaware of what they have missed. Multitasking inhibits a person's acquisition of a deep understanding of the information being presented. Concentrating on the task at hand, not multitasking and switching attention between tasks, facilitates effective listening and learning.[3]

> How often do you multitask while trying to listen to and absorb what your instructor or peers are sharing?

WHAT DO YOU KNOW?

Before continuing your reading of this chapter, which of the following five statements do you believe to be true and which do you believe to be false?

1. Most of our waking time is spent listening.   T F

2. If we can hear, we can listen.   T F

3. We hear what we listen for.   T F

4. If after a person tells you about a problem, you say, "It's nothing; don't even waste your time thinking about it," you are helping to legitimate the other person's feelings.   T F

5. A "red-flag word" is patriotic.   T F

Read the chapter to discover if you're right or if you've made any erroneous assumptions.

ANSWERS: 1. T; 2. F; 3. T; 4. F; 5. F

Are you a fan of the video game Angry Birds? If so, you are not alone. A recent version, Angry Birds Space, was downloaded 10 million times in three days. The game and its popularity have at least two lessons to teach us about listening. First, Angry Birds proves that most of us are able to concentrate. In fact, it demonstrates that we will focus intently on something that appeals to us, even if it means skipping a meal just so we can get to the next level of success. Second, the game shows us how feedback can function as a motivator. When we play Angry Birds, the feedback we receive sustains our engagement, virtually compelling us to continue.[4] The question is, how can we use what we learn from Angry Birds to improve our listening?

Most of us spend more of our communication time listening rather than playing Angry Birds or doing anything else—even speaking. You are probably thinking, *"That's not possible! I spend most of my time speaking!"* But that is not what communication research reveals. Studies have found that the average college student spends more than 50 percent of the available communicative time in an average day listening, and the average employee spends more than 60 percent of an average workday listening.[5] Listening clearly consumes more time than any other communication-related behavior. If you add the time you spend listening to various media outlets, research shows that on average young people typically spend ten hours or more consuming media and multitasking with media daily.[6] What is more, the use of digital media complicates things further by helping to distract us. In fact, many of us have grown so accustomed to receiving quick bursts of information, sometimes in the form of tweets, that we expect all messages to be delivered succinctly. Many find it increasingly taxing to listen to more detailed and complex information.[7] That we spend a great deal of each day listening is undeniable—whether we do it well, however, is another issue.[8]

Research reveals that while the average person hears a great deal throughout the day, he or she processes just half of what is said, understands about a quarter of the message, and retains even less of the content. Too frequently, we take listening for granted, and that is not good news for us. It is also not good news for the people we are supposed to be listening to, and it does not bode well for our relationships. When it comes to making relationships work, listening is just as important as other communicative behaviors.

Consider this: How can you afford not to improve your listening ability when we know the following?

1. We are exposed to millions of words every year.

2. We spend a much larger percentage of our waking day listening than we do speaking, writing, or reading.

3. On average, we listen at only 25 percent efficiency; that is, instead of retaining most of what we hear, we lose approximately 75 percent of the conveyed content over a very short time.

4. Listening errors are common. While listening is our most pervasive activity, it is also our least developed communicative skill.

We focus intently when playing Angry Birds.

WHAT DO YOU KNOW?

True or False

1. *Most of our waking time is spent listening.*
True. Listening consumes more of our time than any other communication activity.

5. Listening is not a passive act. Whether we want to gain information, evaluate a message, or merely be entertained, listening requires our active participation.

6. It pays to listen. Listening mistakes carry both personal and monetary costs. In fact, if each U.S. citizen paid just ten dollars for every listening mistake made in a year, the national total would be more than one billion dollars.

7. If we do not give people with whom we interact honest feedback, we forfeit our right to complain about them.

8. Our very existence, as well as the effectiveness of all our person-to-person contacts, depends on our ability to listen and respond appropriately. We rely on our listening skills to develop relationships, make personal and professional decisions, formulate attitudes and opinions, mentally store data for later use, and provide feedback to others.

9. You will spend more time in this class listening than speaking.

This chapter will help you become a better listener.

While we need to develop our abilities to understand and critically evaluate what others tell us, it is equally important for us to develop our abilities to empathize with and provide feedback to those with whom we share relationships. Our relationships will benefit from our learning to recognize those factors that cause us to turn off and stop listening when that is the last thing we should be doing.

DIFFERENCES BETWEEN HEARING AND LISTENING

Effective listeners do not listen only with their ears—they also rely on their minds. To listen well, you need to think effectively. Hearing is the first step in a two-part process.

Hearing is an involuntary, physiological process. Just as we do not need to think to breathe, neither do we need to think to hear. As long as our eardrums are functional, when sound waves hit them, the subsequent vibrations cause the tiny bones of the middle ear—known as the hammer, anvil, and stirrup—to vibrate. Once these vibrations reach our auditory nerves, they are transformed into electrical impulses and automatically processed by our brains, and we hear. What we do with these impulses once we receive them takes us into the complex arena of listening.

In contrast to hearing, **listening** is a voluntary, psychological process. It is "the process of receiving, attending to, and assigning meaning to aural and visual stimuli."[9] As we assign meaning to a spoken message, a number of components come into play, including understanding, remembering, interpreting, and responding. If we do not listen well, we likely will not understand what we hear, and we may pass misinformation on to others. Far too often, instead of listening actively to others, we only *hear* them. Our minds are asleep rather than alert, and we passively receive, rather than actively process, what they are saying. When we listen, however, we not only hear the message but also make sense of it—or at least we try to.

Hearing: An involuntary physiological response in which sound waves are transformed into electrical impulses and processed by the brain.

Listening: A voluntary psychological process consisting of the following stages: sensing, attending, understanding/ interpreting, evaluating, responding, and remembering.

THE DIFFERENCES BETWEEN EFFECTIVE AND INEFFECTIVE LISTENERS

Think of the worst listener you know. What does this person do that suggests to you he or she does not really listen to you? Imagine the person's demeanor when interacting with you.

What is the listener's intention? In this excerpt from *The Seven Habits of Highly Effective People*, Stephen R. Covey describes a specific behavior that hurts a relationship. Identify the behavior and then cite your own examples to illustrate how either you or another person you know has been guilty of acting in the way Covey describes.

"Seek first to understand" involves a very deep shift in paradigm. We typically seek first to be understood. Most people do not listen with the intent to understand; they listen with the intent to replay. They're either speaking or preparing to speak. They're filtering everything through their own paradigms, reading their autobiography into other people's lives.

"Oh, I know exactly how you feel!"

"I went through the very same thing. Let me tell you about my experience."

They're constantly projecting their own home movie onto other people's behavior. They prescribe their own glasses for everyone with whom they interact.

If they have a problem with someone—a son, a daughter, a spouse, an employee—their attitude is, "That person just doesn't understand."

A father once told me, "I can't understand my kid. He just won't listen to me at all."

"Let me restate what you just said," I replied. "You don't understand your son because he won't listen to you?"

"That's what I said," he impatiently replied.

"I thought that to understand another person, you needed to listen to him," I suggested.

"Oh!" he said. There was a long pause. "Oh!" he said again, as the light began to dawn. "Oh yeah! But I do understand him. I know what he's going through. I went through the same thing myself. I guess what I don't understand is why he won't listen to me."

This man didn't have the vaguest idea of what was really going on inside his boy's head. He looked into his own head and thought he saw the world, including his boy.

SOURCE: Stephen R. Covey, *The Seven Habits of Highly Effective People*, New York: Simon & Schuster, 1989, p. 239–240.

What words would you use to describe this person as a listener? Typically, words such as *distracted, inattentive, closed-minded, daydreamer, bored, impatient, nonresponsive,* and *rude* come to mind. Now think of the best listener you know, and select adjectives to describe his or her behavior. Probably among the words you have chosen to describe the best listener are *concerned, open-minded, intelligent, attentive, interested,* and *respectful.* Compare and contrast the words you have selected to describe the best and worst listeners. Which words on the lists you have created would you use to describe your own behavior as a listener? Which words do you imagine others would choose to describe you when you interact with them?

Are you the best listener you could be? We lose when we listen ineffectively, and we stand to gain much when we listen effectively. But what exactly is it that we lose or gain? To find out, first ask and answer the following questions yourself, and then ask them of two other people.

1. What consequences have you suffered when you have displayed a lack of respect for someone you were conversing with?

2. What problems have you encountered after losing your temper with someone else?

3. What challenges have you faced when you have failed to understand what another person was telling you?

4. How has jumping to an incorrect conclusion caused problems for you?

5. What happened when you missed a key conversational segment because you were distracted?

6. How did the person you were conversing with respond upon realizing that you were not really listening?

Being distracted or daydreaming impedes listening.

Listening increases relationship satisfaction. When we fail to listen to each other, our relationships usually experience problems. In contrast, effective listening helps to enhance our relationships by doing the following:

- *Decreasing stress.* Stress levels are reduced as ideas and feelings are communicated clearly and understood as intended.

- *Increasing knowledge.* We learn more about each other when we listen effectively. Each of us learns more about what the other responds to and how the other reacts to our ideas.

- *Building trust.* We all need someone to listen to us. We appreciate those who listen much more than those who fail to give us their complete attention. In fact, careful listening can be a reciprocal act: we pay closer attention to those who do the same for us, and we tend to avoid those who do not.

- *Improving analysis and decision making.* Careful listening can provide you with information and insights that enable you to exercise better judgment. Rather than accepting what is presented at face value, you are more likely to spot faulty reasoning and identify invalid arguments or gross appeals to prejudice when you listen critically. In the process, you protect yourself against others who may act irresponsibly. Careless listeners are more likely to end up accepting the unacceptable.

- *Increasing confidence.* When another person perceives you to be giving him or her your rapt attention and believes that you are open, alert, and actively involved, that person will be more comfortable interacting with you and more likely to share his or her feelings. By listening effectively, you also increase your own confidence and understanding. As you increase your comprehension of another's ideas and feelings, you gain confidence in your ability to respond appropriately.

STAGES OF LISTENING

The **HURIER model** of listening, developed by listening expert Judi Brownell, dean of the School of Hotel Administration at Cornell University, represents a behavioral approach

HURIER model: A model of listening that focuses on the following stages: hearing understanding, remembering, interpreting, evaluating, and responding.

TRY THIS: *How's Your LQ (Listening Quotient)?*

First, fill out the following inventory to gauge your listening effectiveness:

1. Do you ever find yourself labeling either the person you are conversing with or his or her subject as uninteresting? Yes No
2. Do you ever find yourself becoming overstimulated by what someone says to you? Yes No
3. Do you ever jump ahead of the person speaking to you? Yes No
4. Do you ever pretend to pay attention? Yes No
5. Do you ever "turn off" when a message gets complicated? Yes No
6. Do you ever daydream when you are in a conversation with another person? Yes No
7. Do you ever try to process every single word someone says to you? Yes No
8. Do you ever let a person's manner of delivery or mannerisms or gestures interfere with your reception of his or her words? Yes No
9. Do you ever let the environment or personal factors distract you? Yes No
10. Are there some individuals you refuse to listen to? Yes No

Every "yes" response indicates a behavior that can function as an impediment to listening and, as such, merits your attention.

Next, answer questions 1–4 below yourself, then ask two people with whom you interact regularly to fill in the answers to questions 5–8 for you.

1. On a scale of 0 to 100, I give myself a rating of _____ as a listener.

   0   25   50   75   100

2. I would use the following three words to describe myself as a listener:

   _____   _____   _____

3. Others would give me a rating of _____ as a listener.

   0   25   50   75   100

4. Others would use the following three words to describe me as a listener:

   _____   _____   _____

5. One person I asked gave me a rating of _____ as a listener:

   0   25   50   75   100

6. He or she used the following three words to describe me as a listener:

   _____   _____   _____

7. Another person I asked gave me a rating of _____ as a listener:

   0   25   50   75   100

8. He or she used the following three words to describe me as a listener:

   _____   _____   _____

How does your self-rating compare to the ratings others gave to you?

that suggests that listening is a system of interrelated components that includes both mental processes and observable behaviors. The model focuses on six aspects, or stages, of listening: hearing, understanding, remembering, interpreting, evaluating, and responding (see Figure 4.1).[10]

Figure 4.1 Listening Stages

STAGE 1: HEARING

We exist in a world filled with the aural stimuli. Sounds surround us, competing to be noticed, but we choose to pay attention only to the ones that interest us. Eugene Raudsepp of Princeton Creative Research explained the hearing/sensing process by telling the story of a zoologist who is walking with a friend down a busy street filled with the sounds of honking car horns and screeching tires. Turning to his friend, the zoologist says, "Listen to that cricket!" The friend, with astonishment, replies, "You hear a cricket in the middle of all this noise?" The zoologist takes out a coin and flips it in the air. As the coin falls to the sidewalk, a dozen heads turn in response to its "clink." The zoologist responds, "We hear what we listen for."[11]

Attending involves our willingness to focus on and organize particular stimuli. We attend to a sound by concentrating on it, even if just for a moment. Unless the sound holds our attention, we will soon refocus our attention on something else. Consequently, it is not enough to capture another's attention; attention needs to be maintained.[12] This requires developing sensitivity to the interests of those with whom we make contact.

STAGE 2: UNDERSTANDING

During the understanding stage we absorb the meaning of a person's statement or sound. In a sense, we work to decode what is being said using our own reservoir of information, and we refrain from judging the message until we are certain we comprehend it. In an effort to ensure understanding, we might reply to the speaker with questions aimed at clarifying the message's content. Rephrasing or paraphrasing what we have heard also helps us comprehend the message.

STAGE 3: REMEMBERING

During the remembering stage, our brain assigns meaning to the spoken words. Once that is accomplished, we may or may not commit the information to our memory for further use. Here again, we make choices, as we decide what has value and is worth remembering and what we can discard. Of course, if we have intense feelings for the person we are with, or if the message is reinforced, we increase our chances of remembering. Our memory allows us to retain and recall information when we need to. On the other hand, some forgetting is necessary for our mental health.

Two key kinds of memory concern us: short-term memory and long-term memory. We store most of what we hear, if only briefly, in the limited space of our brain's short-term memory bank. Unless we continually use and apply what we store in short-term memory, we will forget it before we can transfer it into our long-term memory bank for use at a much later date. This helps explain why we remember only 50 percent of a message immediately after listening to it and approximately 25 percent after a brief period has elapsed. Our more permanent memory storage facility, long-term memory, plays an important role in listening by connecting new experiences to previous images and information. We remember personal and public events of significance. For example, you likely remember the birthdays of people close to you, as well as where you were when you learned of a loved one's death, or when you survived a natural disaster.

WHAT DO YOU KNOW?

True or False
3. *We hear what we listen for.*
True. We pay attention to what interests us.

Attending: Paying attention; the willingness to organize and focus on particular stimuli.

STAGE 4: INTERPRETING

When we interpret a message, we attempt to make sense of it. In order to interpret effectively, we consider the message from the sender's perspective. Doing this keeps us from imposing our meaning onto another person's ideas. We make the effort to discover how the other person views the situation.

For example, suppose your friend says, "I've had enough!" By listening to his tone of voice and observing his facial expressions you can decide whether your friend is talking about the meal he is eating with you or he is upset by the conversation you are having with him. Each represents a very different interpretation of his words. The meaning you settle on will determine how you respond.

STAGE 5: EVALUATING

When we evaluate a statement, we weigh the worth of and critically analyze what we have listened to, appraising what we were told. We decide if the message has relevance for us or is based on what we know or feel. As with all the stages of listening, we have choices to make. Separating facts from inferences, weighing evidence, and identifying prejudices and faulty arguments are part of the evaluation process. When we fail to evaluate a message effectively, we risk agreeing with ideas or supporting actions that violate our values or have been slanted to earn our support.

For example, when you ask your congressional representative if she supports increasing taxes on those who earn more than one million dollars annually, and she says, "Don't worry about me. I'm okay on that!" she is counting on you to believe she agrees with whatever stance you support. Unless you follow up with additional questions, however, you do not have adequate information to determine where she actually stands on the issue.

STAGE 6: RESPONDING

Responding effectively to the messages we receive through the day affects our overall communication experience. When we respond to someone, we react and provide feedback; we communicate our thoughts and feelings about the received message. We let the person know whether we think the message was communicated successfully or flawed, whether it was "on target" or "missed its mark." In effect, we become the sender's radar. We will address responding in more depth later in this chapter, in our discussion of feedback.

STYLES AND TYPES OF LISTENING

When interacting with others, we are likely to exhibit one of four listening styles: people-oriented, action-oriented, content-oriented, or time-oriented.[13] We are also likely to find ourselves engaged in one of four types of listening: appreciative, comprehensive, critical or deliberative, or empathetic. (See Tables 4.1 and 4.2.) While most of us may prefer to use one style and to listen to a particular kind of content, we probably all use each of the four styles and four types of listening.

STYLES OF LISTENING

Adherents of each of the following listening styles display different attitudes and beliefs about listening. Which one of the following styles is your personal favorite?

People-Oriented Listening. Those who like to focus on the emotions and interests of others prefer the people-oriented style. When you take your time and work to understand what

Researchers assert that listening may well be the most important skill in our communication arsenal because it is necessary for relationship building—in both the personal and professional arenas of life. However, while the research demonstrates listening's value, there are also times when the act of listening itself may pose a danger to the listener and others. Can you think of when this could be the case? Have you ever used your cell phone while driving a vehicle?

According to the research, when the act of listening distracts from the primary responsibility of driving, the listener is endangering her- or himself, passengers, and other drivers or pedestrians. Texting and cell phone use—even when conducted with hands-free devices—cause drivers to lose focus and thus contribute to decreased driving accuracy. The risk faced by drivers who access their cells while driving is four times the risk undistracted drivers face—and similar to to the risk associated with driving while intoxicated. It appears that simply attempting to comprehend a spoken or texted message competes with the driver's need to focus on driving. Thus, driving and listening both require your full attention and should not be placed in competition with each other.

SOURCES: F. E. Gray, "Specific Oral Communication Skills Desired in New Accountancy Graduates," *Business Communication Quarterly,* 73:1, 2010, p. 40–67.

See Marissa A. Harrison, "College Students' Prevalence and Perception of Text Messaging While Driving," *Accident Analysis and Prevention,* 43, 2011, p. 1516–1520; Amy N. Shys, "The Most Primary of Care—Talking about Driving and Distraction," *New England Journal of Medicine,* 362, 2010, p. 2145–2147; and M. S. Just, T. A. Keller, and J. A. Cynkar, "A Decrease in Brain Activation Associated with Driving When Listening to Someone Speak," *Brain Research,* 1205, 2008, p. 70–80.

TABLE 4.1   Styles of Listening

Style	Focus
People-oriented	Emotions and interests
Action-oriented	Clarity, precision, and assumptions
Content-oriented	Facts, details, and ambiguities
Time-oriented	Efficiency and succinctness

others think and feel, you improve your chances of getting to know them well. Thus, the people-oriented style fosters relating to others in more meaningful ways.

Action-Oriented Listening. If you value clarity and preciseness above all else, you are apt to use the action-oriented style often. Action-oriented listeners do not like to feel frustrated by others' indirect messages. They want the persons they speak with to be direct and straightforward.

Content-Oriented Listening. Those who enjoy being intellectually challenged and having to work ideas through practice the content-oriented style. Comfortable listening to messages that are ambiguous and spark debate, content-oriented listeners commonly relate what they are listening to their own views.

Empathetic listening builds strong relationships.

Appreciative listening: Listening engaged in for pleasure.

Comprehensive listening: Listening engaged in to gain knowledge.

Critical or deliberative listening: Listening that involves working to understand, analyze, and assess content.

Empathy: The ability to understand another's thoughts and feelings and to communicate that understanding to the person; the ability to comprehend another's point of view.

Empathetic listening: Listening that involves understanding and internalizing the emotional content of a message.

Time-Oriented Listening. Time-oriented listeners expect the speaker to get to the point. Impatient and efficient, they like others to impart messages that are quick and brief, allowing the listeners to work through them efficiently.

TYPES OF LISTENING

As we have noted, it is doubtful that any of us practice one type of listening exclusively. Still, each of us is likely to prefer one type over others. Which type of listening do you enjoy most?

Appreciative Listening. Sometimes we listen for pleasure—we watch *American Idol,* go to a concert, view a film, or go to a comedy club, actively seeking out an **appreciative listening** activity. Such activities, often experienced with another person, help us unwind or escape.

Comprehensive Listening. When you listen to gain knowledge you engage in **comprehensive listening**. When you ask for directions, listen to a friend's description of her new job, listen to talk radio to get a better idea of current events, or pay close attention to lectures in class, you are listening to derive information. Because your primary purpose is to learn, you listen with an open mind and suspend judgment.

Critical/Deliberative Listening. Have you ever questioned the truth of a message, its usefulness, or the reliability of the person delivering it? Frequently, in addition to working to understand content, we must also analyze it, assess its worth, validity, and soundness, and, ultimately, decide whether to accept or reject it. We perform these functions when we engage in **critical or deliberative listening**.

Empathetic Listening. In Chapter 3, we introduced the topic of empathy. Because **empathy** is also a skill needed for effective listening, we explore it in more depth here.

When another person reaches out to us for support, he needs us to engage in **empathetic listening**. This type of listening is important to master if you seek to build strong interpersonal relationships. For example, when was the last time you called a friend because

TABLE 4.2   Types of Listening

Type	Example	Goal
Appreciative	Listening to music	Be entertained
Comprehensive	Listening to a lecture	Acquire information
Critical/deliberative	Listening to a political debate	Make an evaluation
Empathetic	Listening to a friend talk about a breakup	Therapeutic—to be a sounding board

you needed a sounding board or someone to tell your troubles to? When was the last time you helped someone else work a problem through by offering her or him your ear?

Empathetic listening serves a therapeutic function: it facilitates problem solving, it lends a different, clearer perspective to any given situation, and it helps individuals regain emotional balance. When you listen empathetically, you understand the dilemma another is facing from his or her viewpoint, not yours. You do your best to interpret the situation as if you were the other person.

Those who score high in emotional intelligence are generally better at de-centering themselves while listening. That is, an empathetic person places the focus on another in order to understand that person as he or she desires to be understood. In this way, empathetic listening is a relationship enhancer.[14]

While for some of us empathizing comes naturally, others need to work at it. In general, women are more likely to describe themselves as being empathetic (that is, able to feel what another feels) than are men. Women are more likely than men to report feeling distressed when other persons share their troubles with them. This may explain why all of us, male and female, usually turn to a woman when we need an empathetic listener.[15]

Good listeners are other-oriented. Sometimes, all we need to do is show that we respect and have compassion for the person talking with us. When you listen empathetically, your goal is to understand the other person's thoughts and feelings, so you need to put aside your own thoughts and feelings and listen from that person's point of view. When empathizing you activate three skills: empathetic responsiveness, perspective taking, and sympathetic responsiveness.[16]

When we exhibit **empathetic responsiveness**, we experience an emotional response that corresponds to the emotions the other person is experiencing. For example, when Samira tells Tong that she has to leave school because her family needs her at home, if Tong understands and feels the same regret and sadness that Samira is feeling, she will have done so by using her powers of empathetic responsiveness.

When we employ **perspective taking**, we place ourselves in the shoes of the other person. If Tong imagines herself in Samira's position and understands some of the same emotions, she will have fulfilled the expectations of perspective taking. For example, not only does Samira feel regret and sadness about leaving school, she feels guilty for not wanting to help her family at home. If Tong is able to point this out and perhaps offer a clearer perspective on it, she is practicing this particular type of empathetic skill.

Finally, if Tong feels concern and compassion for Samira because of the situation Samira faces, then Tong also will have succeeded in demonstrating sympathy, or **sympathetic responsiveness**. Sympathetic responsiveness is different from and falls short of empathy because, while the receiver *feels for* the other person, without perspective taking and empathetic responsiveness she does not *feel with* the other person. For example, when you sympathize with and console a friend whose dog has died, even though you have never been in her situation because you are afraid of dogs and you cannot imagine what she is feeling, you are being sympathetically responsive.

What can you do to increase your empathetic abilities? If you are very individualistic, or "I"-oriented, empathizing may not typically be easy for you. You may be so used to being the center of attention that you may find it challenging to look at the world from anyone else's point of view. Yet, if you want to improve your effectiveness at developing meaningful interpersonal relationships, empathizing is a skill you ought to master. Here are six steps you can take to improve your empathy quotient:

Empathetic responsiveness: A listener's experiencing of an emotional response that corresponds with the emotions a speaker is experiencing.

Perspective taking: Adopting the viewpoint of another person.

Sympathetic responsiveness: Feeling for, rather than with, another.

1. Make a concerted effort to become other-oriented, paying careful attention to what others are saying and feeling. If, for example, your partner comes home depressed after a hard day at work, try to imagine how you would feel if you were in his or her situation.

2. Take in the whole scene. Focus not just on words but also on the nonverbal cues that are part of the other person's message. Tune in to how the person walks, sits, looks, and sounds.

3. Work to understand the other person's emotions by questioning the other person and then paraphrasing how you think he or she feels. Your goal is to obtain more details, clarify the nature of the situation, or get at the root cause of what the other person is feeling. When paraphrasing, you might say something like "I guess you are feeling . . . ?" or "So now you are likely feeling . . . ?" By questioning and paraphrasing, you check your perception and ensure that you accurately comprehend how the person feels.

4. While processing the other person's information, repeatedly ask yourself why you believe the other person is experiencing what he or she is, and try to identify what it is that makes you think and feel that this is so. Is it what the person says to you, his or her facial expressions, or something else? By focusing on the person's emotions and the cues you are using to draw your conclusions, you also increase your attentiveness and become better at sensing the other person's emotional state.

5. Again, use the skill of perception checking, discussed above and in the preceding chapter, to facilitate your understanding of what the other person is experiencing. Acknowledge what you think the person has said, and then inquire whether your interpretation is correct.

6. Once you fully understand the other person's feelings, you may still need to provide her or him with emotional comfort and support. Help the other person feel better and/or show that you care about what happens to him or her. When you comfort and support someone, you provide affirmation, acknowledging the person's right to feel as he or she does. You also offer reassurance, consolation, and assistance and, if appropriate, try to cheer the person up or divert his or her attention. And remember that you can comfort someone using both verbal and nonverbal cues.

If you fail at empathizing, usually it is for one of the following reasons:

1. You deny the other person the right to his or her feelings, suggesting that what he or she is feeling is either wrong or inappropriate. You might say something like "You shouldn't be so upset" or "Don't let that get you down." By uttering such a statement, you unwittingly suggest that the person should feel differently—in effect, you "delegitimate" his or her emotions.

2. You minimize the importance of the situation to the other person by saying, "It's no big deal," or "Why are you making a mountain out of a molehill?" Such statements reveal that you really do not understand what the other person is going through.

3. You pass judgment on the other person by saying something such as "Well, you asked for it" or "It's you own fault." Such comments do little more than make the other person defensive.

4. You feel the urge to defend yourself and say something self-centered like "I didn't do it" or "Don't blame me." Defending yourself does nothing to help or support the other person.

5. You place the focus on tomorrow rather than on today. Empathizing occurs in the present, not in the future. While the person who needs your empathy may not remember how bad he or she felt at this moment a decade or a day from now, that is not what he or she wants or needs to hear from you right now.

The closer you feel to the other person, and the more familiar you are with his or her situation, the easier it should be for you to demonstrate empathetic responsiveness. You will likely have to work harder to exhibit genuine empathetic responsiveness toward someone you have known only briefly. By using phrases such as "I'm listening," "I hear you," and "I get it," you can demonstrate your respect, understanding, and acceptance of another person, even someone you do not know very well.[17]

Each type of listening is of value in interpersonal communication. Listening for pleasure relaxes as well as entertains us and helps us develop new insights into our relationships. Listening to derive information sensitizes us to how we can deliver information and clarify understanding. By listening to evaluate information, we learn that just as we evaluate another's behavior, so will that person evaluate ours. And listening to empathize helps us understand what we can do to understand and feel what another person is feeling and, when appropriate, help another person see things through our eyes and appreciate our perspective. When we listen empathetically, the focus is on the other person, not on ourselves.

LISTENING ETHICS

At one time or another, we have all committed an unethical listening act—preferring to pursue our private thoughts, reminisce, or worry about something personal rather than concentrate on what the other person was saying. Unethical listeners believe their own thoughts are more worthy of attention than yours. Thus, in the competition for thinking space, their thoughts win and yours lose. Not listening to another can have serious consequences. For example, imagine what could happen if a physician is more concerned with her own thoughts than with listening to a patient describe his symptoms. And what difficulties might follow if a judge fails to listen attentively to the arguments presented by prosecuting and defense attorneys? Regardless of the role or position of the listener, listening not only fulfills a personal obligation but also confirms a societal bond.

If you are to become a more effective listener, you need to recognize the internal and external factors that lead to deficient listening (see Table 4.3) and then do your part to eliminate them. Ethical listeners do not engage in **nonlistening**—that is, they do not answer any of the following questions with a yes.

DO YOU TUNE OUT?

A listener who does not care about the person with whom he or she is conversing tunes out what the other is saying. When someone tries to start a conversation or share ideas with them or influence them, unethical listeners do not pay attention; they act as if their ears and minds are "out to lunch" or "on vacation." They are preoccupied—too busy thinking

Have you ever gone on "a listening vacation" while another person tried to reach you?

Nonlistening: A kind of deficient listening behavior in which the receiver tunes out.

ANALYZE THIS: *Active and Inactive Listening*

Active listening has a lot in common with perception checking, since it involves feeding back to the speaker your understanding of what the speaker has communicated to you, both in content and in feeling. Active listening holds the key to our engagement with one another in mutually understood messages, both on a cognitive and an emotional level. By providing feedback, we enable the other person to clarify his or her thoughts and emotions.

In listening actively, we pay attention to and respond using both verbal and nonverbal cues. We identify what the speaker has just said and what we think the speaker means. Doing this helps ensure understanding by giving the speaker the chance to clarify misunderstandings or misperceptions on our part. Active listening, however, goes even further than this. When listening actively, we also let the speaker know that we understand his or her feelings and ask questions that provide the speaker with opportunities to talk further.

Consider the following scenario depicting how three of Maya's friends reacted in response to her stating:

> I'm screwed! Dr. Rodriguez wants me to redo this entire paper. I spent so much time researching it, but it's still not good enough for him. He's giving me two days to improve it or I'll get a C. How am I going to get this done? Does he have any idea how busy my life is?

Davilla's response:	Lucky you. At least you got two days. I just got the C.
Dave's response:	Two days isn't so bad. You can do it. All you need to do is focus.
Doreen's response:	Ugh, you worked so hard on that paper! You're totally stressed out, aren't you?

Which of the three friends do you think demonstrated active listening?

Davilla focused on herself. Dave attempted to diminish the problem facing Maya. Only Doreen attempted to promote a meaningful exchange with Maya. Doreen also reflected Maya's feelings, recognizing their legitimacy, while the other two listeners did not.

What exactly did Doreen accomplish with her response? First, she paraphrased Maya's original message, then she showed interest in how Maya was feeling by expressing her understanding of what she must be experiencing. Doreen also accomplished something else: because she made the attempt to cross-check her interpretation, she afforded Maya the chance to let her know if she had gotten it right.

SOURCE: See B. R. Burleson, "Explaining Recipient Responses to Supportive Messages: Development and Tests of a Dual-Process Theory," in S. W. Smith and S. R. Wilson, eds., *New Directions in Interpersonal Communication Research,* Thousand Oaks, CA: Sage, 2010, p. 159–179; and D. Johnson, "Helpful Listening and Responding," in K. M. Galvin and P. Cooper, eds., *Making Connections: Readings in Relational Communication,* Los Angeles: Roxbury, 1996, p. 91–97.

about their own problems or something else. As a result, they fail to focus fully or actively on the messages that others send.

Active listening:
A form of listening that involves the paraphrasing of a speaker's thoughts and feelings.

DO YOU FAKE ATTENTION?

Listeners who do not care about the persons they interact with often engage in pseudolistening—that is, they fake attention. They pretend to listen when nothing could be further from the truth. They look at you, smile or frown appropriately, nod their heads, and even utter sounds such as "hmmm," or "uh-huh." All their external cues tell you they are listening, but they are only pretending to listen. In fact, they let no meaning get through.

TABLE 4.3 Behaviors of Poor Listeners

Behavior	Consequences
Tuning out	Listener's loss of focus and preoccupations make understanding less likely.
Faking attention	Listener's pseudolistening looks and behavior deceive the speaker.
Losing contact opportunities	Listener's misjudging has potential effects on both message relevance and relationship.
Losing control	Listener's emotions and lack of patience lead to ambushes, message distortions, and defensiveness.
Laziness	Listener's lack of effort and refusal to work at listening make comprehension unlikely.
Selfishness	Listener's focus is on the self rather than on the other person.
Being distracted by external factors	Listener's oversensitivity to setting or context interferes with listening.
Wasting time	Listener's failure to use the thought-speech differential to advantage compromises listening effectiveness.
Apprehensiveness	Listener's fear of the new leads to defensiveness.
Burnout	Listener's inability to cope with information overload closes down the mind.

DO YOU IGNORE SPECIFIC INDIVIDUALS?

Before even giving another person a chance, a deficient listener decides that the person looks uninteresting or sounds dull, or that there is no future for a relationship with him or her. Ineffective listeners' tendency to prejudge—uncritically accepting or unfairly rejecting another and his or her ideas—limits their potential for developing meaningful relationships.

DO YOU LOSE EMOTIONAL CONTROL?

Sometimes we let disagreements with another person get in the way of our listening carefully to him or her. Some of us even react so emotionally that we will go out of our way to avoid interacting with someone with whom we disagree or someone who is talking about a subject we do not care about or think might be too hard to comprehend.[18] Sometimes, instead of listening to what the other person says, we distort what we take in until it conforms to what we think he or she should have said. In other words, we manufacture information rather than processing it, shielding ourselves from ideas we would rather not expose ourselves to at all.

Some of the words others speak function as **red-flag words**—words that interfere with our ability to listen because they trigger in us an emotional deafness that causes our listening efficiency to drop to zero as we take an emotional side trip. Among the words and phrases that might contribute to emotional deafness in some of us are *Nazi, you should, you're so slow, entitlement,* and *what's wrong with you?* Are you aware of any specific words or phrases that cause you to erupt emotionally, thereby disrupting your ability to continue interacting meaningfully and calmly with another?

Red-flag word: A word that triggers emotional deafness in the receiver, dropping listening efficiency to zero.

DO YOU AVOID CHALLENGING CONTENT?

Listening is voluntary, and, unfortunately, some of us refuse to volunteer to listen to people whose ideas or manners of expression challenge us. Believing that we will not understand the other person, we do not even give ourselves a chance to exercise our minds.

When was the last time you dismissed another person as uninteresting or unimportant because you told yourself, "I won't understand what she has to say anyway"? Do you turn off possible relationships because you assume that you would have to work too hard to make them succeed? To what extent are you willing to stretch your mind to accommodate the challenge of new ideas instead of merely focusing on those people or ideas that validate your preconceived notions?

ARE YOU EGOCENTRIC?

When was the last time you tuned out and turned off someone you were conversing with because you felt his or her ideas were irrelevant to you? People who are egocentric do this regularly. Seeing themselves as the center of the universe, and seeking only self-satisfaction, they are so wrapped up in themselves that they fail either to realize or to value their interconnectedness with others.

Ironically, egocentric listeners still expect those they converse with to listen to them. While they deny the other person's desire to be listened to, they attempt to monopolize attention by having the other person focus attention on them. Thus, they are self- rather than other-oriented.

DO YOU WASTE POTENTIAL LISTENING TIME?

We think a lot more quickly than we speak. When we converse, we typically speak at a rate of 150 to 200 words per minute. However, we can comprehend upward of 400 to 600 words per minute.[19] The difference between the two is known as the **speech-thought differential**. Ineffective listeners waste this extra time by daydreaming instead of focusing on, summarizing, and asking themselves questions about the substance and meaning of the other person's remarks. They would rather drift off than use the energy it takes to attend closely to what the other person is telling them.

ARE YOU OVERLY APPREHENSIVE?

Apprehensive listeners are fearful of processing or psychologically adjusting themselves to messages that others send to them.[20] For example, have you ever been so fearful of new situations, people, or information that you became overly anxious? Anxiety can cause us to become overly defensive, which, in turn, inhibits effective listening.

ARE YOU SUFFERING SYMPTOMS OF LISTENING BURNOUT?

Sometimes, people who once were effective listeners become ineffective because they are burned out. When exposed to too much information at one time, our minds, unable to cope with information overload, simply close. For example, if you were a psychiatrist or psychologist and had to listen daily to clients' disclosures, you might experience listening burnout and seek to spend your free time not listening so attentively.

Certainly, we cannot listen at full capacity all the time. However, we need to become aware of how often and why we fail to listen and determine what we can do to become better at

Anxiety can inhibit your ability to listen.

Speech-thought differential: The difference between the rate of speech and the rate at which speech can be comprehended.

listening. Because not listening ethically is consequential, being an effective listener has implications for how well we perform our jobs and whether we live up to our relational responsibilities.

HURDLING LISTENING ROADBLOCKS

Listening consumes energy. When you listen actively, your body temperature rises, your palms become moist, and your adrenaline flow increases. Your body actually prepares itself to listen. You are the catalyst in this operation—you set in motion the listening process. Taking to heart the following principles will make your listening efforts more productive:

1. Listening requires your full attention. You can't half listen—the half you miss could be critical.

2. Evaluation follows, it does not precede, reception. Withhold your evaluation until you are certain you have understood the other person's message. Anger and hostility can impede understanding, as can rapture and hero worship. A heightened emotional state impedes your ability to comprehend the other person.

3. The other person's appearance or delivery is not an excuse for not listening. Overlook a speaker's monotone or lack of eye contact. Do not be distracted by a rough or unpolished demeanor. Concentrate on the message. A smooth, polished speaking manner can be equally harmful if you let it blind you to an absence of substance.

4. Likewise, judging another person based on your own existing negative or positive prejudice impedes listening. You either become busy arguing against the other person or are too quickly impressed to accurately process the message being sent.

5. How you listen affects how others feel about you. The better you are at reflecting the feelings of those with whom you interact, and the more adept you are at exhibiting empathetic and supportive behaviors, the more others will want to interact with you.

6. If you seek opportunities to practice skillful listening, you will become a better listener. Listeners are like athletes—daily practice improves their performance.

RESPONDING WITH FEEDBACK

Responding with feedback is an integral part of listening. Thus, developing your abilities to send and receive feedback improves your listening as well.

Think of listening as a collaborative process. Just as none of us functions solely as speaker or receiver, both parties to a conversation have the power to complicate or facilitate listening. Listening is a dialogic, or give-and-take, process in which speakers do not deliver monologues but instead are intimately involved in helping listeners participate in and coordinate what is a joint activity.[21] Stand in the other person's shoes. Tap into his or her interests, needs, and concerns. Contemplate the perceptions he or she has of you. Consider how culture might be influencing you when you are speaking and listening.

DEFINING FEEDBACK

When we listen actively or responsively, we provide the other person with feedback. Recall from Chapter 1 that the term *feedback* implies that we are returning or "feeding back" to another person our reactions to their verbal and nonverbal messages. Whenever you consciously or unconsciously emit a verbal or nonverbal message that another perceives to be a response to something he or she said or did, your message serves as feedback.

During interpersonal communication, you continually provide another person with feedback—and you are not always totally honest when you provide it, either. At times, when you are unhappy in your relationship or bored with a conversation, you may nevertheless put on your "I care for you" face or an "I'm interested" expression and nod adoringly or approvingly. Unfortunately, we can mislead others by providing dishonest feedback.

The feedback you offer another person affects how he or she interprets your relationship. Tiffany Cooper Gueye, CEO of Building Educated Leaders for Life, has noted that the most important thing she can provide to the people she works with is "direct, honest, clear feedback."[22] Many believe the need for such feedback holds in all relationships. Do you?

FEEDBACK OPTIONS

Like communication, feedback is a continuous process. We constantly send feedback, whether or not we intend to. Another person can interpret everything we do or do not do, a raised eyebrow, folded arms, every word we speak or fail to speak, as feedback. Sometimes our feedback is purposeful, because we hope to evoke a specific response. For instance, your partner tells a joke and you laugh heartily because you want him or her to know you enjoyed it and would like him or her to feel comfortable telling you more. On the other hand, sometimes the feedback you send is unintentional and elicits unexpected reactions. Without our consciously realizing it, our words and behavior may provoke responses in another person that we never intended. When facing such an occurrence, we may say something like "That's not what I meant!" or "Don't take it that way!" Other times, a person simply refuses to acknowledge the feedback we sent, choosing instead to ignore it. Have you ever tried to convey your romantic interest to another person without receiving a response? Sometimes another person is not ready, willing, or able to process our honest reaction.

The kind of feedback we offer and the content of the feedback we give another person are dependent on the kind of relationship we share. Our friend, for example, probably expects us to provide feedback on his or her appearance; our boss probably does not. Our partner is likely to give us feedback regarding our relationship strengths; our teachers probably will not. Well-given feedback has positive consequences for our relationships; poorly given feedback does not. Whether your feedback is likely to elicit positive or negative reactions from another person depends on how you answer these three questions:

When given effectively, feedback has positive consequences.

1. Do you offer feedback at the right time?

2. Are you clear and specific about the feedback you give?

3. Is your feedback appropriate, tactful, and conducive to sustaining the relationship?

Feedback May Be Immediate or Delayed. Much of the feedback we send during interpersonal communication is immediate; our reactions occur virtually simultaneously with our reception of a message. Immediate feedback is generally the most effective because our reaction can lose its impact on the other person if we wait too long. Sometimes, however, we may consciously withhold responding. For example, it is wiser to cool down before offering a response to a message that angers you. Feedback sent in anger can damage a relationship.

Interestingly, technology is beginning to influence how quickly feedback occurs in an array of settings, including the workplace. Whereas annual or biannual employee performance reviews have traditionally been the norm, now, because the new generation of workers is used to instant feedback or updates and craves regular feedback, companies such as Facebook have transitioned into offering quarterly, weekly, or even daily feedback sessions. At Facebook, for example, employees are encouraged to ask for and provide feedback regularly, after meetings, presentations, and projects. Asking, "How did it go?" and "What could I do better?" requires only a brief conversation.[23]

Feedback May Be Person- or Message-Focused. We can center feedback on either the person or the message. Feedback such as "You're just about the most compassionate person I know" focuses on the person, while a statement such as "While I understand your position, I believe the reasons you offer are flawed" focuses on the message.

Feedback May Be Low- or High-Monitored. Feedback that is sincere and spontaneous is low-monitored feedback. It occurs constantly through the interpersonal communication process. As we exchange messages, we reveal our responses without consciously monitoring or censoring them. Much of the low-monitored feedback we offer is sent unintentionally and without careful planning or strategizing. In contrast, feedback that we offer to serve a specific purpose is high-monitored feedback. We are more guarded and think about whether our feedback will serve a desired purpose before sending it. For example, if your instructor were to ask you what you think of the course, you would probably monitor your feedback before responding.

Feedback May Be Evaluative or Nonevaluative. When we provide **evaluative feedback**, we announce our opinions or feelings about the matter we are discussing. For example, if a friend asks whether you like his haircut, he is asking for an evaluative response. He might interpret the slight pause before you say, "It looks great," as meaning you don't really like it. When we offer evaluative feedback, we provide positive or negative assessments to another; we let him or her know what we think of his or her ideas, abilities, looks, and so on. By its very nature, evaluative feedback is judgmental; it either confirms or refutes the communication of another.

Positive evaluative feedback keeps people and their communicative behaviors moving in the direction in which they are already heading. For example, if you are flirting with someone who is receptive to your advances, you will tend to continue flirting. Positive evaluative feedback serves a reinforcing function; it causes us to continue acting as we are by enhancing our desire to do so.

Negative evaluative feedback serves a corrective function—it helps reduce undesirable behavior. When we perceive feedback as negative, we are apt to change or modify our behavior accordingly. For example, if you tell an off-color joke and then receive feedback indicating that another person found it offensive, you probably will not tell another. Negative evaluative feedback alerts us to discontinue behavior in progress.

Evaluative feedback: Feedback that reveals one's feelings or reactions to what one heard, providing a positive or a negative assessment.

Unlike evaluative feedback, which tends to be judgmental, **nonevaluative feedback** does not direct the action of another. Instead, we use it when we want to find out more about another person's feelings or when we try to help another person work through his or her feelings. When providing nonevaluative feedback, we refrain from revealing our own personal opinions or judgments. We simply question, describe what we observe, or demonstrate our interest in listening to the person.

Because nonevaluative feedback is nondirective in style, a receiver may perceive it as positive in tone. This is also because we likely reinforce another's behavior when we probe or offer support as he or she works through a problem. In reality, however, nonevaluative feedback goes beyond positive feedback, because it does more than merely reinforce behavior; it also enables others, without our direction, to explore their own thoughts and feelings and arrive at their own solutions. Nonevaluative feedback tends to fall into one of the following categories: probing, understanding, supporting, and "I" messages.

Probing. **Probing** is a nonevaluative technique in which we solicit additional information from another person in an effort to draw him or her out as well as to demonstrate our willingness to listen. For example, suppose a friend who is concerned about a job-related conflict tells you, "I'm really over the edge. My boss keeps pushing and pushing me. I'm going to snap." If you are probing, you might inquire, "What's she doing that is so annoying?" or "What is it about your boss's behavior that particularly concerns you?" or "Why do you think this is happening?" By responding in this way, you give the other person the opportunity to think through the problem while also offering him or her the chance for emotional release. On the other hand, responses such as "Oh, they're all like that," or "Who cares what the boss does?" or "You're stupid for getting upset" could cause your friend to become defensive, preventing him or her from thinking through and discussing the troublesome situation with you.

Understanding. Understanding is an alternative kind of nonevaluative reaction. When we offer understanding, we try to comprehend what the other person is telling us, and we check our interpretations by paraphrasing (restating in our own words) what we have heard. By paraphrasing we show that we care enough about the other person and the problem he or she is facing to be certain we understand the message's meaning. The following examples illustrate the use of paraphrases:

Person 1:   I don't think I'm good enough to get the job.

Person 2:   You mean you think you lack the skills to get promoted?

Person 1:   I am hurt that John trusts Sheila more than he trusts me.

Person 2:   You mean you're jealous of the attention John is paying Sheila?

If we use understanding early in a relationship, we communicate our willingness to listen and the person's important to us. Understanding responses encourage a relationship's development in part by demonstrating our sensitivity to and concern for the other person, and also by allowing the other person more time to describe and detail his or her feelings and perceptions to us.

Supporting. When we respond by supporting, we indicate that we share the other person's perception of a problem as important. For example, suppose your friend comes to you with a problem she believes is extremely serious. Perhaps your friend's concern about the situation has caused her to become agitated, and she says that you couldn't possibly understand her predicament. In offering **supportive feedback** you would do your best to calm her down by

Nonevaluative feedback: Feedback that is nonjudgmental.

Probing: A nonevaluative technique in which one solicits additional information from another.

Supportive feedback: Nonevaluative feedback that indicates that another's problem is viewed as important.

assuring her that that you understand the problem, that her world is not ending, and that you are there to help her work through it.

By offering supportive feedback, we accomplish a number of things: First, we do what we can to reduce the intensity of the other person's feelings. Second, we let him or her know we consider the problem real. Instead of offering comments such as "Why are you worrying about that?" or "It's ridiculous to care about that," we say things like "I can tell you're upset. Let's sit down and discuss it. I'm sure you can find a way to work it out." A friend who is distraught because he or she has just been fired or has just broken up with a lover does not need to be told, "Next time you'll handle things differently," "There's no reason to be so upset," or "I warned you about this." It is much more productive to say instead, "I can tell you're upset. I don't blame you for feeling the way you do." When we provide supportive feedback, we acknowledge the importance of the other person's predicament, but we do not attempt to solve it; we simply listen, show the person we care, and, in so doing, help him or her to discover a solution.

"I" Messages. By delivering nonevaluative feedback in the form of **"I" messages**, we refrain from passing judgment on the other's actions; however, we do reveal our feelings about the situation.

Every time we interact with someone, we have a choice of providing them with evaluative or nonevaluative feedback. Neither form of feedback is always right or wrong. Sometimes, however, our choice can have an adverse effect on our relationship. Do any of these remarks sound familiar? "You're a pain in the neck!" "You're wasting my time!" What do these statements have in common? They contain the word *you.* When we utter such statements, we place blame for something on someone else. When we experience relationship problems, we sometimes resort to name-calling and place blame on others as a means of coping with the situation. Such feedback, however, builds barriers between us, which then become increasingly difficult to remove.

To avoid building these barriers, we can replace "you" messages with "I" messages. Instead of saying, "You're really getting on my nerves"—which could be interpreted by the recipient as "I'm not liked"—explain how you feel. For instance, if you clarify the situation by saying something like "I've just walked in the door and you're asking about our plans for tonight, which stresses me out. I need some time to unwind before talking about tonight," your friend's internal reaction is more apt to be along the lines of "Okay, she's had a really tough day," which is much less likely to evoke a defensive or self-serving reaction to you.

Each of the feedback types we have discussed has its place in our person-to-person contacts. Whether you opt to respond with evaluative or nonevaluative feedback depends on the other person, the situation, and your relationship.

CULTURE'S INFLUENCE ON LISTENING

Listening plays a vital role in the development of our social relationships. Just as culture plays a part in our perception of the self and others, so it plays a part in listening.

Dialogic listening, the process that occurs between people as they respond to one another, is an important focus during interpersonal communication.[24] However, how we engage in dialogic listening differs from culture to culture. For example, in the United States we

When you offer supportive feedback, you acknowledge another person's problem as important.

"I" messages:
Nonevaluative forms of feedback that reveal a speaker's feelings about the situation faced by another person.

Dialogic listening:
Listening that involves give-and-take between persons interacting as they cocreate a relationship.

practice a people-oriented listening style that focuses on the feelings and concerns of the individuals interacting and the social aspects of their interaction. In contrast, those from Eastern cultures tend to practice speculative, metaphoric thinking.[25] Sometimes life's pressures interfere, pushing us away from adopting an open-ended, tentative, and playful attitude toward conversation; instead, we find ourselves pulled in the opposite direction, seeking more certainty, closure, and control. Interestingly, members of Western cultures tend to be less open and tentative in their listening behaviors than do members of Eastern cultures. Reflecting this, the Chinese emphasize the receiving process over the sending process, a demonstration of their concern for interpretation and anticipation.[26]

Cultural attitudes about when it is appropriate to talk and when one should remain silent also play roles. People from Eastern cultures view **silence** as signaling respectability and trust; they believe that words can corrupt an experience and that it is through heart-to-heart communication that people are able to grasp meaning intuitively.[27] They believe people should listen more than talk.[28] Thus, when interacting with persons from Eastern cultures such as China and Japan, persons from Western cultures such as the United States and England need to "listen between the lines"; that is, they would do well to listen to persons from Eastern cultures with more than their ears. When communicating with those from Eastern cultures, Westerners need to understand that what is important may be left unsaid. In other words, the intentions of the speaker may not be spoken directly, but implied. Additionally, because persons from China and Japan have been raised to be comfortable with silence, they simply do not talk as much as Americans do.[29]

Whereas some cultures value succinctness and directness, others value elaboration and exaggeration. For example, members of Arabic cultures commonly use verbal exaggerations and forceful assertions in conversation. Rather than verbally restraining themselves, they release their emotions through language. The ancient Arab proverb "A man's tongue is his sword" suggests that Arabic persons use language as a means of offense, to chastise or punish others, and to boast about their abilities. They may make assertions regarding others' faults and failures, contributing to impressions among persons from non-Arabic cultures that they could be aggressive or threatening.[30] A contrasting Arab proverb, "When you have spoken the word, it reigns over you. When it is unspoken you reign over it," suggests an alternative explanation for how persons of Arabic cultures approach listening. It confirms their hesitation to be negative and their desire to maintain peace. Those who are unaware of this may easily misinterpret the intentions of individuals from Arabic cultures.

As we speak with and listen to members of different cultures, we need to remind ourselves that the meanings we give to words vary based on our experiences and backgrounds. Because culture influences how we use language, it also influences how we listen to and interpret language.

Silence: The absence of vocal communication.

Members of different cultures view feedback differently. In the United States and Europe, for example, individuals prefer direct communication, expecting feedback to be honest and reflective of the feelings of the person giving it. In contrast, members of Asian cultures, such as the Japanese, prefer communicating in a less specific and more indirect way, perhaps because of the value they place on politeness and the maintenance of a positive image. Consequently, members of Asian cultures may expect feedback also to be more indirect, confirming their belief that bluntness could injure the self-esteem of the person to whom feedback is directed. This may happen not just out of concern for others' reactions, however, but because of the understanding that their fate and fortune are bound up with the fate and fortune of others. Of course, at times Americans are also indirect, particularly when discussing sensitive topics or when nervous about another's response. Similarly, in close relationships, interacting with people they know well and trust, members of Asian cultures may choose to be direct.

Asian cultures also instill in members a respect for silence. Silence, rather than talk, communicates. As a result, when interacting with members of Asian cultures, rather than break a silence with talk, persons from other cultures can benefit from learning to use the quiet in a way conducive to feedback once the silence ends.

1. Would you adapt how you offer feedback when interacting with someone from a culture different from yours? Why or why not?

2. In what ways, if any, might using your typical way of offering feedback pose problems for you when you are responding to someone of a different culture? Explain.

3. Pair up with a classmate and discuss a controversial topic of your choice, such as universal health care, capital punishment, or immigration policy. Before you respond to what the other person says, count to four. How does this delay in responding affect your comfort level and the tone of your discussion? Be specific.

SOURCES: See John C. Condon, *With Respect to the Japanese,* Yarmouth, ME: Intercultural Press, 1984, p. 43–44.

See William B. Gudykunst, *Bridging Differences: Effective Intergroup Communication,* 3rd ed., Thousand Oaks, CA: Sage, 1998, p. 173–174.

GENDER'S INFLUENCE ON LISTENING

To what extent, if any, do the listening behaviors of the men and women you know differ? Sociolinguist Deborah Tannen reports that women and men exhibit different listening styles and that they listen for different reasons. To what extent, if any, do your experiences confirm this? According to Tannen, women listen to confirm both the relationship and the person with whom they share a relationship.[31] When a woman processes information, her real goal is to zoom in on an emotional level. This is another reason women excel at empathizing and at identifying another person's communication mood; they are ready, willing, and able to allow others to open themselves up and reveal what is important to them.

In contrast, research reveals that men are more at home with comprehensive listening, hearing a message's facts or informational dimension, and less comfortable handling its emotional content.[32] Men desire to retain power and control; they want to dominate.[33] As a result, they are more likely to listen for solutions so they can give advice rather than empathize. They also are apt to turn off their listening when they come across a problem they cannot solve right away. Unlike women, men generally do not listen to relay support; they want to solve the problem.[34]

Men and women listen for different reasons. Women hear a message's emotional content; men hear the facts.

Empathetic listening, as we learned earlier, is essential for the development and maintenance of a meaningful relationship, so men may need to work to develop and demonstrate empathetic listening skills. They can help others perceive them to have such skills by using more vocal cues when listening, interjecting responsive sounds such as "uh-huh" and "hmmm" into their reactions. Such cues help another person feel listened to.[35] Although early research found that men did not listen to provide emotional support, research completed within the past decade affirms that they do place a value on this kind of listening.[36]

Thus, a number of asymmetries exist in how women and men listen. In interactions between men and women, men tend to spend more time in the speaking role and women in the listening role. If women want to disengage themselves from the role of listener or responder, they probably need to take action, rather than waiting for men to stop speaking. When women exercise their right to enter the conversation, they also relieve men from feeling they have to give a solo conversational performance. Both men and women can expand their behavioral repertoires when it comes to listening.

Not only do men and women listen differently, but also they are listened to differently. For example, when men and women speakers use an equal number of tag questions or qualifiers, listeners still perceive the women to use these speech forms more often.[37] Listeners perceive the speech of men as stronger, more active, and more aggressive than women's speech, which they perceive as more polite, pleasing, and sweet.[38] Even when women and men speak similarly, women's speech is evaluated more negatively—being perceived as aggressive rather than strong, for example. Perhaps if listening were perceived not as a source of power differences between men and women but as a means of relationship building, our ability to process the speech of men and women equitably would improve.

MEDIA AND TECHNOLOGICAL INFLUENCES ON LISTENING

Media and technological innovations are part of our communication landscape. Acknowledging our short attention spans and urge to multitask, they are playing roles in affecting how we listen.

MEDIA INFLUENCES

Critics have long contended that watching too much television shortens the attention spans of viewers. They argue that because we are offered information and entertainment in shorter and shorter segments, partly because programmers fear that if segments were made longer we would lose focus and tune out; our ability to give sustained attention to anything is called into question. Fast-paced editing and rapidly changing images delivering quick bursts of content are the rule.

Consider the advertisements for various brand-name prescription drugs on television, such as a recent one for the antidepressant Cymbalta. The ad features a dad, thin, young, and handsome, twirling his young daughter around their living room, while a newborn baby sleeps nearby. After witnessing the sense of well-being that permeates this scene, viewers suffering from depression are encouraged to ask their doctors to prescribe Cymbalta for them—even though they are also presented with a warning regarding the drug's potentially harmful side effects, as mandated by the U.S. Food and Drug Administration. The ad was successful; an increase in first-quarter sales of 88 percent was attributed to it.[39] The advertiser, it seems, understood the science of attention—that the typical viewer pays attention for only the first 6.5 seconds of a TV ad.[40] The warning about side effects comes later in the ad. Using emotional appeals, the ad quickly captures viewer attention up front—we learn depression hurts, but Cymbalta can help. The detailing of the side effects comes at the point in the ad where we are least likely to pay attention, because we have been led already to imagine the ending. We hear the tone of the voice-over but pay little attention to the words. The warning about potential liver damage is delivered in softened consonants and end sounds, almost a murmur, as the ad's visual imagery changes from tragic to happy—and we know a happy ending is upon us, whereas when the product is introduced and the punch line is delivered at the ad's end, the voice-over diction is slower and the words more carefully enunciated. The makers of this commercial clearly understood how viewers listen and respond to such advertising.

The media have other problematic influences on listening aside from diverting attention. Too frequently on opinion shows, whether on radio or TV, speakers talk over each other, competing for airtime and acting like spoiled children who will not wait their turns to speak. Meaningful discussion has become a rarity on the airwaves and on cable television.

WATCH THIS 4.1
For a video on multitasking and effective listening visit the student study site.

TECHNOLOGY'S INFLUENCES

Given the ubiquity of cell phones, we regularly exercise our ears and mouths—if only because we always can reach someone to listen to us. Still, the question is whether we spend more time listening to be entertained than we do talking to or listening to each other. How frequently, for example, do you respond passively to another person because you are preoccupied with the sounds or messages emanating from one or another communication medium? Some believe that our connections to digital media through smart phones and tablet and laptop computers cause us to focus on the visual rather than the aural—to emphasize the eye over the ear. Do you agree?

With the explosion of texting and around-the-clock Web access, we "listen" more visually, rather than aurally. Texting and e-mailing provide messages devoid of a person's voice or body language. And when we use our cell phones, caller ID lets us decide whose calls we will or will not pick up, while call-waiting lets us keep a person who wants to speak to us waiting for the opportunity to do so. On the other hand, Skype and webcams make it possible for us to see, speak, and listen to people across vast geographic divides for far less than the cost of a traditional landline-based long-distance phone call.

We often multitask when listening. Can your friends tell when your attention is divided?

Additionally, our affinity for technology makes it likely that we will multitask when listening. For example, how often do you find yourself texting, tweeting, or checking e-mail while talking with another person? Unfortunately, because of multitasking, we frequently find ourselves not focusing exclusively on any sole communication channel. Consequently, we often fail to give a person we are with our full attention. In your opinion, should we develop rules specifying when multitasking is and is not socially acceptable? If so, what kinds of rules do you favor? If not, why do you believe such rules unnecessary?

Is it possible for people to face an operating television without really watching it? Likewise, can a person ignore a radio that is turned on? Finally, is it possible for people to speak to each other without listening?

1. How often, would you guess, do individuals with whom you regularly converse "turn off" their listening skills even while they are still in front of you?

2. Do you prefer having an "illusionary listener" to having no listener, much as television and radio stations prefer to have "illusionary viewers or receivers" (persons whose TVs or radios are on but who do not watch or listen) as long as they are counted in their program ratings?

3. Do you consider your Facebook friends to be real or illusionary listeners? Explain.

GAINING COMMUNICATION COMPETENCE: BECOMING A BETTER LISTENER

In this chapter we have explored the role of listening in relationships. You should now recognize that you can never be too good a listener. No matter how effective you believe your listening skills currently are, doing the following can help you become a better listener.

CATCH YOURSELF EXHIBITING A BAD HABIT

Recognition of a fault precedes correction of it. If you monitor your listening behavior, you can catch yourself before you display an undesirable trait. That is the first step toward positive change.

SUBSTITUTE A GOOD HABIT FOR A BAD HABIT

Think about the new listening habits you would like to have. For example, if you are a daydreamer and mentally wander off when someone is speaking to you, encourage yourself to display greater attentiveness and concentration. Visualize yourself listening effectively when conversing. Imagine the positive impact your new behavior will have on your relationships.

LISTEN WITH YOUR WHOLE BODY

Take steps to ensure that your physical mannerisms do not distract or confuse the person you are interacting with. Instead of leaning back with your arms crossed, fidgeting, playing with your hair or jewelry, gazing repeatedly at your watch, or otherwise signaling that you are uninterested in what the other person is saying, make a commitment to convey a more positive listening demeanor. Assume an attentive posture, make good eye contact, and display appropriate facial expressions. In other words, get physically ready to listen. If you look more like an effective listener, you will be apt to behave like one.

CONSISTENTLY USE YOUR EARS, NOT JUST YOUR MOUTH

When you converse with another, shift naturally and frequently from a speaking to a listening mode. Rather than monopolizing the speaking role or spending your time planning what you will say next, make a sincere effort when not speaking to focus on the other person's message when he or she is talking. Rather than completing another's statements because you "know for sure" what he or she is going to say, let the person complete his or her own thoughts. Conversing with another compels us to develop not just a speaking presence but also a listening attitude.

SEE THE OTHER SIDE

One of the greatest detriments to listening is an unwillingness to look at a situation from another's point of view. If you begin a conversation by telling yourself you are willing to see and feel from the other person's perspective, you increase your chances for more meaningful interaction. You may not end up agreeing with what you have heard, but you will be more likely to understand where the thoughts and feelings are coming from.

DON'T LISTEN ASSUMPTIVELY

Every message a person delivers to another person exists in at least four different forms:

1. The message as it exists in the mind of the person speaking to you (his or her thoughts)

2. The message as it is spoken (encoded by the person)

3. The message as the listener interprets it (decoded by you)

4. The message as the listener ultimately remembers it (influenced by personal selectivity or rejection biases)

When passed from person to person, messages become distorted. This happens for a number of reasons. First, it happens because we usually try to simplify the message we hear. Second, because of our apprehensiveness, we may not want to admit that we did not understand what someone told us; instead, we may try to make sense of what we heard by making certain assumptions. This usually results in our adding to, subtracting from, or otherwise altering the message.

PARTICIPATE ACTIVELY

Listening is an active and responsive process, not a passive behavior. Ask questions. Paraphrase what the other person has said, and ask for confirmation of your understanding. In this way you can determine whether you are processing the other person's words and feelings correctly.

Keep in mind that developing effective listening skills is necessary for developing yourself as an effective interpersonal communicator.

CONNECT THE CASE: *The Case of Nonlistening Flora*

"I didn't mean to do it," Flora told Fred, her boss at the factory outlet. "I just misheard you."

Tuesday had begun as a fairly typical day in Flora's busy life. She had attended her morning classes, eaten a late lunch with several friends, and then left campus for a nearby factory outlet store where she was employed as an assistant manager on the evening shift to help pay her way through college.

As she arrived, Flora's boss said, "Be sure and mark the silk designer blouses down to $19.99." It seemed a little low, but who was she to question Fred's instructions? She told Joe, one of the stock workers, to adjust the price immediately.

About an hour later, Adel, a salesclerk, told Flora that the blouses were moving off the shelf. Flora instructed Joe to bring out another case. Indeed, before her shift's end, eager shoppers had purchased the entire contents of five more cases of the silk designer blouses.

As Flora prepared to close the store, she gazed at the now-depleted blouse display and saw the problem: the blouses had been marked down to $9.99 erroneously.

Just then, Fred called Flora to see how things were going. She told him what had happened, and explained, "I told Joe to mark the blouses down to $19.99 like you said, but he mistakenly marked them down to $9.99. He just didn't listen. Should I dock his pay or fire him?"

"Fire him?" came the reply. "I told you to mark the blouses up to $99.99. We've now lost $90 for every blouse we sold tonight! You and Joe are two of the worst listeners ever!"

Flora and her boss reached an agreement. The listening mistake would not be paid for out of Flora's salary all at once; it would be deducted from her paychecks over several weeks.

Flora felt terrible. Lost in thought, she wondered, "How could I have made such a costly mistake?"

Consider these questions:

1. Why do you imagine Flora made the initial listening error?

2. What steps can Flora take to ensure that she listens to others correctly and others listen to her correctly?

3. If you were in Flora's shoes, do you think you would have made the mistake she did, or are you a more proficient listener than she?

REVIEW THIS

CHAPTER SUMMARY

1 **Define and distinguish between hearing and listening.** Hearing is an involuntary physiological process; listening is a voluntary psychological process we use to understand and retain aural messages.

2 **Identify and explain the six stages of listening identified in the HURIER model.** The six stages in the HURIER model are hearing (the physical act of perceiving sound), understanding, (comprehending meaning), remembering (the storing and retrieving of information as needed), interpreting (the assigning of meaning based on the other's perspective), evaluating (assessing the truth and accuracy of a message), and responding (demonstrating to another that you are listening by providing feedback).

3 **Define and distinguish among the four styles and four types of listening.** The four styles of listening are people-oriented (listening to discover commonalities), action-oriented (listening to process errorless, concise messages), content-oriented (listening to be intellectually stimulated), and time-oriented (listening to receive quick and to-the-point communications). The four types of listening are appreciative (listening for enjoyment), comprehensive (listening to gain knowledge), critical (listening to analyze, assess, and decide to accept or reject a message), and empathetic (listening to think and feel as another does by functioning as a sounding board or in a therapeutic role).

4 **Compare and contrast the behaviors of effective and ineffective listeners.** Ineffective listeners tune out, fake attention, lose opportunities for meaningful contact, become overly emotional, look for the easy way out, act in an egocentric manner, are overly sensitive to context, waste time, are overly apprehensive, and/or exhibit symptoms of listening burnout. Effective listeners are active participants in the listening process, asking questions, paraphrasing, and controlling their emotions and biases in the effort to ensure understanding.

5 **Define the different kinds of feedback.** Feedback is a reaction fed back to the source of a message, revealing our response. It can be positive or negative, immediate or delayed, person- or message-focused, low- or high-monitored, and evaluative or nonevaluative. Probing, understanding, supporting, and "I" messages are among the nonevaluative forms of feedback.

6 **Explain how culture and gender influence listening.** Culture affects attitudes toward talk and silence. Gender affects listening style as well as our reasons for listening.

7 **Analyze the impacts of media and technology on listening.** Media and technology are changing how we listen to one another, including whether we multitask or pay full attention to another person when listening.

CHECK YOUR UNDERSTANDING

1 Can you distinguish between hearing and listening when describing your role as a listener? What listening style do you believe you exhibit most frequently? Why do you think this is so? (See pages 93–95 and pages 98–100.)

2 Can you explain how the kind of listening in which someone is engaging influences his or her behavior? What kind of listening do you prefer to engage in? (See pages 101–103.)

3 Can you apply the HURIER model to a personal listening experience? (See pages 95–98.)

4 Can you provide a dialogue (real or hypothetical) that demonstrates one or more listening challenges and the effects of faulty listening? (See pages 103–107.)

5 Can you distinguish between the different kinds of feedback, identifying what makes each valuable? (See pages 107–111.)

CHECK YOUR SKILLS

1 Can you tell when you are hearing but not listening? (See pages 93; and **Analyze This,** page 94.)

2 Can you identify behaviors that make your listening ineffective and take steps to correct your actions? (See pages 93–95 and 103–107; and **Analyze This,** page 104.)

3 Can you prevent yourself from turning listening into a dangerous activity? (See **Reflect on This,** page 99.)

4 Can you use the HURIER model to explain your behavior as a listener? (See pages 95–98; and **Try This,** page 96.)

5 Can you identify the style and type of listening you are using? (See pages 98–103; and **Analyze This,** page 104.)

6 Can you prepare yourself to listen ethically? (See pages 103–107.)

7 Can you use and interpret different kinds of feedback, including "I" messages? (See pages 107–111; and **Try This,** page 112.)

8 Can you offer examples of how culture and gender influence your listening and the listening of a person from a culture other than your own? (See pages 111–114; and **Try This,** page 113.)

9 Can you identify ways in which media and technology serve as listening distractors? (See pages 114–115; and **Try This**, page 116.)

10 Can you use your skills to overcome listening challenges? (See **The Case of Nonlistening Flora,** page 118.)

KEY TERMS

chapter 5

Almost everything we do that concerns other people involves us in conversation.

—Robert E. Nofsinger

COMMUNICATING WITH WORDS

LEARNING OBJECTIVES

After completing this chapter, you should be able to demonstrate mastery of the following learning outcomes:

1. Define language, explaining its uses and distinguishing among semantic, syntactic, and pragmatic codes.

2. Explain the triangle of meaning.

3. Distinguish between denotative and connotative meaning.

4. Discuss the nature of word walls, euphemisms, emotive language, polarizing words, politically correct language, bypassing, and intensional orientation.

5. Explain how language reflects social identity and communication style.

6. Identify how language helps express and reinforce attitudes toward culture, gender, and age.

7. Discuss the interface between language and media and technology.

8. Take steps to use language more effectively.

Have you ever been a bully's target? Bullies don't only attack physically. They also assault verbally. And because bullies are persistent, those who receive such verbal abuse may internalize the bullies' messages—taking them to heart.[1]

The bully picks on a target, using derogatory language to make fun of the person's name, looks, clothes, voice, sexual orientation, or disability. Maybe the bully calls a boy a girl or a fag, or a girl ugly or smelly. The bully spreads rumors to dehumanize the victim. The bully's mean-spirited words, whether delivered face-to-face or in cyberspace, can be as powerful as any weapon, leading some who are bullied to want to die, just to escape their psychological pain.

Tyler Clementi and Dharun Ravi graduated from different New Jersey high schools and, though not acquainted with each other, were assigned to be freshman roommates at Rutgers University. Unfortunately, there was a complete lack of communication between the two. In fact, during the summer before they started college and actually met, Dharun went online to "investigate" Tyler, and he discussed Tyler and the likelihood that he was gay with friends on Facebook and Twitter. Tyler accessed the posts and tweets before arriving on campus and read the rumors Dharun was spreading about him.

A few weeks into their first semester, Dharun tweeted, "Roommate asked for the room till midnight. I went into Molly's room and turned on my webcam. I saw him making

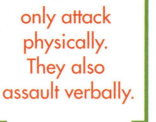

Bullies don't only attack physically. They also assault verbally.

out with a dude. Yay." Dharun and fellow freshman Molly had used a webcam to spy on Tyler and a male friend visiting his dorm, capturing them sharing a kiss. Tyler subsequently read Dharun's words on his Twitter feed. He complained to campus officials and ultimately asked to be moved to another dorm because of Dharun's invasion of his privacy. He also assumed that Dharun had seen his postings on JustUsBoys (a gay website). A few days after he first learned of Dharun's recording of his intimate liaison, like too many others who have been bullied, Tyler Clementi committed suicide, jumping from the George Washington Bridge. Dharun Ravi was tried for invasion of privacy and bias intimidation. On March 16, 2012, a jury found him guilty of committing both crimes.[2]

Despite all their online activity, all their tweets and IMs, in the weeks they had lived together the two roommates had hardly spoken a word *to* each other. Tyler's suicide might have been avoided if he and Dharun had been able to use words to establish what they had in common instead of to target and stigmatize.[3]

A dramatic example of the "dark side" of computer-mediated communication (CMC), this sad story reveals the harm that can be done when we fail to recognize one another's humanity. How much of what was written or said during this episode was rumor—mean, misstated, or misinterpreted? So much of what happens in our lives depends on words and how we use them.

WHAT DO YOU KNOW?

Before continuing your reading of this chapter, which of the following five statements do you believe to be true and which do you believe to be false?

1. Meaning exists in words. T F

2. The personal meaning we have for a word is permanent. T F

3. You can substitute a more polite word for one that is less polite in order to make yourself crystal clear. T F

4. Advertisers realize that words do not easily fool us. T F

5. Spotlighting highlights a person's appearance. T F

Read the chapter to discover if you're right or if you've made any erroneous assumptions.

ANSWERS: 1. F; 2. F; 3. F; 4. F; 5. F

Spoken language is composed of words, and words are what we use to symbolize reality. The words we use reflect and affect our feelings, thoughts, and actions as well as the feelings, thoughts, and actions of others. Our words can comfort, inspire, and make others laugh, and just as easily they can annoy, alienate, and make them cry. We use words to gain interpersonal closeness and to ensure that others keep their distance. Words let us speak of things we have and have not seen or experienced personally, share perceptions of the past, present, and future, and negotiate reality.

Depending on the choices we make, words can clarify or confuse, make meaning apparent or obscure, and cause us literally to miss meaning, humbling us and contributing to our feeling that none of us speaks the same language. Interpersonal effectiveness and word mastery are related. How we use words has an impact on our sense of self and on the nature and development of our relationships. After all, language is the tool we use to form, maintain, and end relationships. Language also makes it feasible for us to cooperate, plan, and share. Without language, we would be far less effective communicators, more isolated, and significantly less social. So, let's talk about language. Let's talk about using words to communicate.

DEFINING LANGUAGE

Language is a code or system of arbitrary symbols that permits a group of people to communicate and share meaning. Without the ability to use words to create verbal messages, we would find interacting with one another far more difficult and certainly more frustrating. If we were unable to use words to express ourselves, how would we talk about our relationships, career goals, or dreams? Yet, as we do with so many other important things, we take words and our ability to use them for granted. Often it is only when we are prevented or restrained from communicating with words that we come to value their utility and importance.

We use language to negotiate meaning, which is at the heart of communication. Because words are symbols, in and of themselves they have no meaning. They are letter combinations or spoken sounds that were arbitrarily selected at some point to stand for the things or referents about which we speak. If enough people agreed, we could create new symbols—new words—to use in place of the ones we currently use. The word *water* is not drinkable. The word *dog* does not bark. The word *love* is not lovable. The word *snow* is not colder than the word *coffee,* any more than the word *coffee* is hotter than the word *pepper.* Meanings for words do not reside in their symbols—their letters or their sounds—but rather in the minds of those who use them. Thus, words are not reality; they merely *represent* reality. In order to understand each other, we must understand the realities represented by our words. Meaning exists in people, not in words. You have your meaning, and other people have their meanings. To the degree that you and others can negotiate your meanings so that they overlap, you will be able to decode each other's messages; you will be able to relate to and understand each other. We will use the model developed by two British literary critics, C. K. Ogden and I. A. Richards, to explain this process further, but first we want to get into and behind the meaning of words.

THE MEANING OF WORDS

How did the words we use to create verbal messages and communicate develop their meanings? To explain how words came to have meaning, we will set the scene by introducing a trio of language codes: the semantic code, the syntactic code, and the pragmatic code (see Table 5.1).

Being unable to use words helps us understand their importance.

WHAT DO YOU KNOW?

True or False

1. *Meaning exists in words.*
False. Meaning exists in people.

Language: A code or system of arbitrary symbols shared by a group and used by its members to communicate with each other.

TABLE 5.1 The Language Code Trio

Semantic Code	Syntactic Code	Pragmatic Code
Denotative and connotative meaning	Conventions and rules (grammar)	Appropriateness based on context
Variability through time and place		

According to the **semantic code**, we agree to use the same symbols to communicate. By agreeing on a set of semantic rules, we make it possible for us to understand each other. The semantic code, which we explore in more depth as we proceed through this chapter, establishes that words have both denotative and connotative meaning, that they vary through time and place, and only represent or symbolize reality. Were we to use symbols in unpredictable ways, perhaps arguing over whether an apple is something to eat or wear on your foot, we would be unable to communicate with each other meaningfully.

The **syntactic code** establishes the conventions that guide our word use. When proper syntax is lacking—that is, when we ignore grammatical rules—we may render our words incomprehensible, even nonsensical. When a person fails to follow widely accepted linguistic or syntactic rules, our impressions of that person may be negatively affected. Until popularized by the music industry, for example, the syntax of the hip-hop community was neither widely accepted nor understood by persons outside the culture, who initially maligned it and blamed it for promoting violence before emulating it. The hip-hop expression "I'm keeping it ghetto," for example, was not widely understood to mean "I'm keeping it real."[4] Understanding and respecting another person's mode of expression, regardless of whether we share the grammatical conventions, is important.

Communicating with words works best when all parties understand and use the same rules. To be pragmatic, we coordinate our efforts and cooperate with each other in order to agree on an appropriate code. When, for example, is it appropriate to tell a joke, and what kind of joke may be told? Are there jokes that you might consider tasteless or denigrating to others? How do you know how a partner will interpret your humor? Answering these questions brings the **pragmatic code** into play. This code requires us to consider the context of an interaction, the interdependent nature of our relationship, and the goal of our exchange to decipher meaning.

When we begin by holding dissimilar perspectives, our interpretations of meaning are also likely to diverge. For example, have you ever observed how the same words can take on different meanings depending on the perspective a person holds? Consider this: You work for a software company that is about to fire fifty employees. Your boss walks by and says, "You look like you've been through the wringer. Why don't you take the rest of the week off?" If you feel secure in your position, you would likely understand that your boss is appreciative of how hard you have been working and is rewarding you with a well-deserved rest. If, on the other hand, you fear being one of the fifty about to be laid off, you might view the boss's comments as the beginning of the end of your employment. If you were in this situation, how would you imagine the boss's words are meant? What pragmatic rules

The context of an interaction provides clues to each person's goal.

Semantic code:
The agreement to use the same symbols to communicate.

Syntactic code:
Conventions that guide word use; the agreement to use the same rules regarding word use.

Pragmatic code:
The agreement to consider the context of an interaction, the interdependent nature of the relationship, and the goal of the exchange in deciphering meaning.

Figure 5.1 The Triangle of Meaning

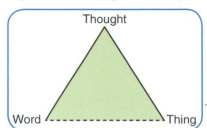

Thought

Word - - - - - - - - Thing

would you use to guide your interpretation of the messages? What is the chance you would jump to the wrong conclusion? In this chapter our focus is on how words influence thoughts, behavior, and action, so the pragmatic code is sure to come into play. Exploring Ogden and Richards's model, the triangle of meaning, will help us understand why misunderstandings occur.

THE TRIANGLE OF MEANING

In their classic work *The Meaning of Meaning,* C. K. Ogden and I. A. Richards use the **triangle of meaning** to illustrate the relationships among words, things, and thoughts (see Figure 5.1).[5] Their model uses a broken line to connect the word and the thing to which the word refers. The broken line underscores that there is an arbitrary relationship between a symbol and its referent; it reminds us that the word is not the thing, and that there is no direct connection between these two points on the triangle. In contrast, by showing that a direct connection exists between words and thoughts and things and thoughts, Ogden and Richards suggest that we attach personal meanings to words and things. Thus, meanings exist in the thoughts or references that we have, not in the symbols we use or their referents. When you say the word *wealth,* for example, it does not necessarily mean the same thing to you that it does to another person. Each of you has different associations that you likely attach to the word based on your stored mental images and personal experiences. Thus, it is quite possible for two of us to use the same word or look at the same referent and give it different meanings. No one else will react to a stimulus— whether a word or a thing—exactly as you do, because no one else has had your exact experiences.

The significance of the triangle is clear: *Meanings exist in thoughts, not in words or things.* For you and another person to understand each other, the sense each of you attributes to the words you are using must overlap. That is, you must both attribute the same meaning to the words being used. When your language is ambiguous or contains what we call **word masks**, misunderstandings may result. When words wear masks, we are apt to misunderstand them. Although in the short run masking meaning may avoid relationship disagreements, in the long run, when the mask is finally taken off the words, the viability and honesty of the relationship may be called into question.

Word walls impede understanding. Have you ever built one?

. . . .

Triangle of meaning: A model that demonstrates the relationships that exist among words, things, and thoughts.

Word mask: Ambiguous language meant to confuse.

Word wall: Language that impedes understanding.

REMOVING SEMANTIC BARRIERS

When we use language to impede understanding, we figuratively build a **word wall**. In Lewis Carroll's *Through the Looking Glass,* Humpty Dumpty explains to Alice how easy it is to build one:

"I don't know what you mean by 'glory,'" Alice said.

Humpty Dumpty smiled contemptuously. "Of course you don't—till I tell you. I meant, 'There's a nice knock-down argument for you!'"

"But 'glory' doesn't mean 'a nice knock-down argument,'" Alice objected.

"When *I* use a word," Humpty Dumpty said in a rather scornful tone, "it means just what I choose it to mean—neither more nor less."

In the real world, we cannot make words mean whatever we want them to. If we do not consider how another person may interpret our words, we are apt to have problems communicating. Although there are a number of semantic barriers that complicate the sharing of meaning, we can overcome them for the most part by identifying the kinds of problems we face when using language, recognizing when they are present, and taking steps to facilitate—not mask—meaning transference.

DIFFERENTIATE DENOTATIVE AND CONNOTATIVE MEANING

Words have both denotative and connotative meanings. A word's **denotative meaning** is its standard dictionary definition. It is the general or objective meaning that members of a particular language community attribute to the word. The more denotations a word has, the greater the possibility for confusion when the word is used. A *run* in baseball is different from a *run* in a stocking, which is different from a 10K *run*. When another person does not understand the denotative meanings of our words, we have a potential semantic barrier.

Connotative meaning, in contrast, is much more subjective, personal, and contextual by nature. Unlike denotative meaning, it is influenced by an individual's personal experience with a word and its referent. Thus, if the person you are speaking with does not share the connotative meaning you have for a word, it becomes even more likely that a semantic barrier will form. A word can have as many connotations as there are people using it; in effect, connotative meanings are limitless. To understand just how limitless, take some time to explore the meanings that commonly used words such as *college, sex, tests,* and *athletes* have for you and your fellow students. (See Try This: Measuring Meaning on page 128.) Because you and your classmates probably do not share the exact same experiences, it is quite likely that you do not share exactly the same connotative meanings for the words. It is important to consider how personal experience influences the connotative meaning carried from person to person, from encounter to encounter.

RECOGNIZE HOW TIME AND PLACE MAY CHANGE MEANING

The meanings that words trigger in people's minds may change with time. Just because we used a word one way at a particular time does not mean that individuals born into a different generation or era will use it in the same way or even be able to understand our message. Our language system is open to expansion and alteration. Words may lose old meanings and evolve new ones, sometimes as often as every year.

Consequently, especially if you are interacting with someone older or younger than yourself, it is important to find out whether the meaning each of you gives to a word matches or misses the other's meaning. The word *gay,* for example, is currently an acceptable term for "homosexual" and has all but shed its past meaning of "happy," "bright," or "merry." Consider how three audiences, one of young adults, one of seniors, and one of elementary school children, might interpret the following words and phrases: *rap, the net, surfing, tool, chill, it's brick*. The point is that definitions do not necessarily stay with words indefinitely, and because time can affect a word's meaning, it is important for us to aware of a word's current meaning.

The meanings of words also may change by geographic region. Thus, a driver whose curiosity causes him or her to slow traffic is called a "rubbernecker" in Texas, a "lookie-Lou" in Los Angeles, and a "gonker" in Detroit.[6] Similarly, a soft drink is known as a "soda" in some parts of the country, a "phosphate" in others, "tonic" elsewhere, and "pop" in other regions. Because of such regional differences, in order to determine meaning you have to consider where you are. Unless you are sensitive to how regional differences affect words, you could find yourself facing a communication gap.

WHAT DO YOU KNOW?

True or False

2. *The personal meaning we have for a word is permanent.*

False. Connotative meaning changes based on personal experience.

WATCH THIS 5.1
For a video on the meaning of words visit the student study site.

Denotative meaning: Dictionary meaning; emotion-free meaning.

Connotative meaning: Subjective meaning; personal meaning.

TRY THIS: *Measuring Meaning*

Below is a seven-point semantic differential scale composed of bipolar terms. The scale, designed to measure how you feel about particular words, is similar to the one developed by psychologists Charles Osgood, George Suci, and Percy Tannenbaum to measure the meaning of words.

1. Score each of the following words using the semantic differential scale below: *college, sex, alcohol,* and *celebrities.* Using the word *college* and the good-bad scale as an example, interpret the seven positions as follows: If your personal meaning for the word *college* gives you an extremely good feeling, place an X as follows:

Good   _X_   ___   ___   ___   ___   ___   ___   Bad

           1   2   3   4   5   6   7

If your meaning of the word *college* gives you an extremely bad feeling, place an X as follows:

Good   ___   ___   ___   ___   ___   ___   _X_   Bad

Proceed in this manner for each word and each polar scale, scoring the four words with four different colored markings on the scale below.

Good	___	___	___	___	___	___	___	Bad
Happy	___	___	___	___	___	___	___	Sad
Strong	___	___	___	___	___	___	___	Weak
Honest	___	___	___	___	___	___	___	Dishonest
Hot	___	___	___	___	___	___	___	Cold
Active	___	___	___	___	___	___	___	Passive
Valuable	___	___	___	___	___	___	___	Worthless
Sweet	___	___	___	___	___	___	___	Bitter
Fast	___	___	___	___	___	___	___	Slow

2. Fill in the numerical score you assigned for each word and each bipolar set of terms in the table below.

Scale	College	Sex	Alcohol	Celebrities
Good/Bad				
Happy/Sad				
Strong/Weak				
Honest/Dishonest				
Hot/Cold				
Active/Passive				
Valuable/Worthless				
Sweet/Bitter				
Fast/Slow				

3. Compare your scores with those of your peers. How do your feelings for each word compare? To what extent, if any, does the sex or age of the respondent appear to affect ratings?

SOURCE: See Charles E. Osgood, George J. Suci, and Percy H. Tannenbaum, *The Measurement of Meaning*, Urbana: University of Illinois Press, 1957.

CONSIDER THE EFFECT OF YOUR WORDS

Words matter. We can choose to use words that are candid and explicit or vague and misleading. Similarly, our words can announce or conceal our true feelings. To influence people's feelings, we may revert to using euphemisms and linguistic ambiguity, emotive language, polarizing language, or language that is politically correct, depending on our message objectives.

EUPHEMISMS AND LINGUISTIC AMBIGUITY

Sometimes we substitute less direct or inoffensive language for language we think may be too blunt or potentially offensive. Such substitutions, called **euphemisms**, mask meaning by "softening the blow" of a message, but because we substitute a pleasant term for a less pleasant one, they also may obscure or fog meaning and alter our receiver's response.[7] As a case in point, few companies *fire* people today—instead, employees are "let go," "laid off," or "given a pink slip." While people in most cultures value politeness, there are cultural variations in how important politeness and honesty are. People from Asian cultures, for example, value politeness in interpersonal relations more than do people in the United States. Eager to spare the feelings of those with whom they are interacting, Asians frequently use euphemisms to soften their words' impact.[8]

While euphemisms help spare feelings, they may also help to obscure or mislead those we speak with by camouflaging the truth. According to American linguist William Lutz, euphemisms wage "linguistic fraud and deception."[9] Politicians also use euphemisms to soften the impacts of government policies. A tax increase becomes "increased revenue," a missile becomes a "peacemaker," a war becomes a "freedom operation," an environmentalist becomes a "conservationist," and global warming becomes "climate change."

The euphemism is not alone in reducing the sting of words; the practice of linguistic ambiguity fulfills a similar function. Purposefully being linguistically ambiguous by saying something that can be taken in at least two ways can help avoid a confrontation. It also can help defuse tense situations, as happened after the United States found itself in a diplomatic crisis with China when a U.S. spy plane collided with a Chinese EP-3E fighter that had been tailing it. The Chinese wanted the United States to issue a *formal* apology, something the U.S. government did not want to do. The solution was found in linguistic ambiguity—via the writing of a nuanced note in which the United States expressed one "sincere regret" over the incident and two "very sorrys," one "sorry" for the loss of the Chinese pilot, and another for making an unauthorized landing—expressions satisfactory to both the United States and China.

RECOGNIZE EMOTIVE LANGUAGE

In contrast to euphemisms, which we use when we want to mask or conceal our real meaning, we use emotive language to editorialize on our feelings. **Emotive language** announces our attitude toward a particular subject of discussion. If, for example, you approve of a friend's cutting back on expenses, you might call her *thrifty*; if you disapprove, you might call her *cheap*. If you like an old piece of furniture you might call it an *antique*. If you don't like it, you might call it *junk*. While the behavior or object being described is the same, the term used to describe it expresses the user's opinion of the behavior. Notice,

Euphemism: Less direct or inoffensive language substituted for blunt language.

Emotive language: Language that announces the user's attitude toward a subject.

In the United States we tend to value directness and "telling it like it is." Still, there are times when, to promote harmony or save face, we consciously revert to speaking indirectly.

1. Provide an example of a time when you chose to use a euphemism rather than speak bluntly. Explain your rationale. What did you accomplish by not speaking directly?

2. Under what circumstances and in what contexts, if any, do you think it would be inappropriate to use linguistic ambiguity? Explain, providing an example. What have you personally accomplished by being strategically ambiguous?

for example, how your reactions change as the words change in the following word trios describing the same things:

War	Defensive response	Massacre
Heavy	Overweight	Obese
Laying off	Firing	Downsizing
Cheat	Evade	Use loopholes
Third World	Undeveloped countries	Backward countries
Aggressor	Axis of evil member	Superpower of concern

In many ways, the word you select to describe a person or an action becomes more a matter of personal feeling than one of objective fact. Now, using the following statements descriptive of a person, demonstrate how you can editorialize on each description by helping others view the subject either more favorably or more unfavorably merely by altering the italicized word:

She's *messy.*

He's *principled.*

I'm *reserved.*

She's *stocky.*

He's *tactful.*

ACKNOWLEDGE THE POWER OF POLARIZING LANGUAGE

Although the vast majority of cases exist between extremes, the English language can lead us to think in extremes. When you view the world and describe it in terms of extremes, you display a tendency to use **polarizing language**; that is, you describe experience in *either-or* terms. How many of these expressions sound familiar to you? "Either you're for us or against us." "Either you're in or you're out." "He's a genius or an idiot." "She's either a patriot or she's a traitor." Either-or thinking conditions us to categorize experience and people according to polar opposites.

Polarizing language: Language that describes experience in either-or terms.

Our language makes it too easy for us to use polarizing thinking and talk. Just see how easy it is to fill in the opposites for each of the following words:

Fat   _____

Happy   _____

Bold   _____

Brave   _____

Tall   _____

Then try filling in two or more words between each pair of opposites. That is more difficult, isn't it? It is harder to find words that express all possibilities, not just the extremes. The world is not black or white, good or bad, beautiful or ugly. It comes in a plethora of shades. Because polarizing leaves out the middle ground, it does not reflect reality; instead, it creates monumental artificial divisions. Overstating the divide between positions causes people to perceive gulfs where none really exist.

BALANCE POLITICALLY CORRECT LANGUAGE

The term *political correctness,* like many other terms, means different things to different people—in fact, it may have different connotations for each of us. For some of us, being politically correct means using words that convey our respect for and sensitivity to the needs and interests of different groups. For others, political correctness means feeling pressured by society to avoid some words for fear of being perceived as offensive to certain groups of people. Still others view political correctness as a form of censorship and a very real danger to free speech. Which of these three views comes closest to your own?

In the film *Borat*, comedian Sacha Baron Cohen plays a fictional journalist from Kazakhstan whose uncensored and unexpected dialogue satirizes political correctness.

In addition to disparaging a person's sex, sexual orientation, age, ethnicity, or race, politically incorrect language also may demean a person's social class or physical or mental abilities. When, for example, one person calls another "white trash" "a retard," or "a spastic," the user's words announce his or her attitude toward the other person while excluding the user from the same group, thereby establishing or enhancing his or her sense of superiority.

Using sexist or non-gender-neutral language is a form of political incorrectness. For example, using the term *congressman* when speaking about any and all members of Congress ignores the reality that women also serve in Congress. Similarly, labeling someone a *fag* or a *dyke* is hurtful and offensive and announces an antipathy toward persons with a particular sexual orientation. In like fashion, using ageist language such as *geezer* indicates little regard or respect for older persons. Using language that is ethnically or racially biased indicates disdain for individuals of particular ethnic or racial heritage and also reveals the stereotypical images the user holds of the members of groups different from their own. Because they demean and disparage others, words like these promote distance rather than interpersonal approachability. For example, sports teams, corporate advertisers, and educational institutions have long used names such as "Redskins," "Braves," and

"Seminoles" as well as logos featuring images of severed heads, tomahawks, Indian chiefs, and Indian princesses to promote their brands and sell products. Native Americans object to the use of such names and symbols as racist, and many institutions have recognized their offensive nature and have stopped using them in recent years.

Language can have repercussions depending on the words and symbols used and who is using them. For example, while one African American may, without blinking an eye, casually refer to another African American as a "nigger" and not have that reference taken pejoratively, it is highly unlikely that a white person's use of the word would be construed in the same way. Members of a group may reclaim and redefine words that were once used to stigmatize or degrade them. One example is the use of the term *queer* by gays and lesbians to positively reference themselves; also, it has become increasingly common for women to refer to themselves as *girls*.

The language we use conveys our feelings and attitudes toward an object of discussion, in large measure reflecting our point of view. In effect, we use language to express and shape attitudes.

BEWARE OF BYPASSING

Bypassing occurs when individuals think they understand each other but actually miss each other's meaning because one or both are using **equivocal language**, words that can have more than one interpretation. Instead of making contact with an agreed-upon meaning, their words simply pass by one another, leaving both parties confused.

Two types of bypassing concern us.[10] The first occurs when people are unaware that they are talking about the same thing or fail to see that they agree with each other because they are using different words or phrasing. For example, a husband and wife argue vehemently over proposed changes in the health care system. One insists that the health care system needs to be "revamped," while the other says that is foolish, since only "small changes" are needed. Neither realizes that what one means by "revamped" is what the other means by "small changes." Too often, we argue because we are unaware that although we appear to disagree, in fact we basically agree. We simply are using different words.

The second and more prevalent type of bypassing occurs when our words suggest we and another person are in agreement when in fact we substantially disagree. While this form of bypassing is often harmless and may even provoke laughter, it can and sometimes does have more serious consequences. Consider that in Britain "knock you up" means "come and see you." What would happen if a young man visiting the United States from England were to tell his American friend that he will "knock her up" before he returns home?

Again, not all bypassing is funny. During World War II, it was thought that the Japanese had decided to ignore the Potsdam Declaration, which called on them to surrender, when the Japanese announced that they would be adhering to a policy of *mokusatsu*. It was only after the atomic bomb was dropped on Hiroshima that interpreters realized that *mokusatsu* could also have been translated as "make no comment at the moment" rather than "reject" or "ignore," as it had been translated initially. The cost of this seeming interpretational error is incalculable.[11]

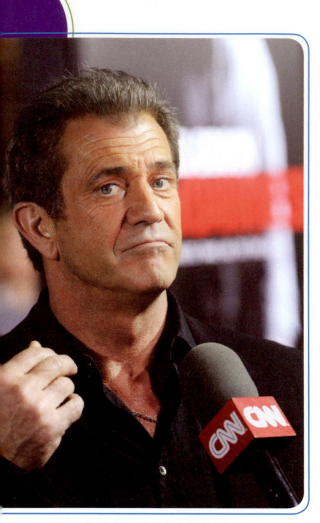

When actor Mel Gibson was alleged to have made controversial remarks characterized as ethnic slurs, civil rights activists called for a boycott of his movies.

Bypassing: A communication problem that occurs when individuals think they understand each other but actually miss each other's meaning.

Equivocal language: Words that may be interpreted in more than one way.

When members of various groups were asked what words they prefer that others use to describe them, the majorities of respondents expressed the following preferences: *older persons* is preferred to *elderly* or *senior citizen, gay* and *lesbian* are preferred for men and women who have affectional orientations toward members of their own sex, *African American* is preferred to *black (African American* places the emphasis on cultural heritage, while *black* focuses on a color), *Hispanic* is preferred to *Latino/a, Inuit* is preferred to *Eskimo, Muslim* is preferred to *Moslem, Asian* is preferred to *Oriental,* and *Native American* is preferred to *Indian.*

The reasons for these preferences vary. For example, the word *Muslim* is preferred to *Moslem* because in Arabic the word *Moslem* actually means "one who is evil and unjust," while the word *Muslim* means "one who submits to God." See if you can discover the rationales for the various groups' preferences for some terms over others.

SOURCES: See M. Schwartz and the Task Force on Bias-Free Language of the Association of American University Presses, *Guidelines for Bias-Free Writing,* Bloomington: Indiana University Press, 1995; J. Lever, "The 1995 *Advocate* Survey of Sexuality and Relationships: The Women," *Advocate,* August 22, 1995, p. 22–30; Michael L. Hecht, Ronald Jackson II, and Sidney A. Ribeau, *African American Communication: Exploring Identity and Culture,* 2nd ed., Mahwah, NJ: Lawrence Erlbaum, 2003.

See Yii-Ann Christine Chen, "Why Do People Say Muslim Now Instead of Moslem?" History News Network, July 8, 2002, http://hnn.us/articles/524.html.

A first step in limiting the damage that bypassing may do to our relationships is to develop an awareness that it can and does occur. If it is possible for another to misunderstand us, he or she probably will. With this in mind, make the effort to become "person-minded" and take the time to make sure that your intended meaning has been understood. The alternative is being "word-minded," which usually results in the protest "I never thought you'd think I meant . . ." or "I was sure you understood me." Recognize the responses your words can precipitate. If you anticipate these responses, then you will be doing your part to prevent mismatched meanings from interfering with effective communication.

Can you create your own cartoon to illustrate the dangers or potential humor caused by bypassing?

DON'T BE MISLED BY LABELS

How label-conscious are you? To what extent do you respond to labels themselves, rather than to what the labels represent?

Linguistic researcher Benjamin Lee Whorf notes that how we define a label or situation dramatically affects our behavior. According to Whorf, words help shape our perceptions of reality, at times even determining the reality we are able to perceive.[12] Thus, because the

1. In your opinion, should an individual pay a price for being politically incorrect and making statements that some judge to have negative moral and social consequences?

2. To what extent, if any, do you believe that the political correctness movement interferes with our rights under the First Amendment, which was expressly designed to protect unpopular speech?

3. How do you believe we can balance the right to say what we want—no matter how provocative or controversial—with watching what we say so that we do not offend others or speaking without regard for how our remarks might play in another context?

4. How do you differentiate and where do you personally draw the line among politically incorrect speech, unpopular speech, and freedom of speech?

WHAT DO YOU KNOW?

True or False

4. *Advertisers realize that words do not easily fool us.*

False. Advertisers count on our being intensionally oriented, or blinded by the labels they use.

Inuit are able to perceive many more different types of snow than have groups that do not live under the same environmental conditions, they have developed many words to label the various types of snow. They have one name for falling snow, *gana,* and another for fluffy fallen snow, *akilukah.* Similarly, avid skiers can label and distinguish among a wide variety of snow types, in contrast to nonskiers, to whom snow is simply snow.

At times, the words we use as labels do not clarify reality but obscure it. When we respond to a label rather than to what the label actually represents, we display what is known as **intensional orientation**. Intensionally oriented individuals are easily fooled by words and labels and as a result fail to inspect what the labels represent. In contrast, when we inspect whatever a label refers to instead of letting the label blind us, we exhibit what is known as **extensional orientation**. Extensionally oriented individuals are "show me," reality-based people who refuse to be conned by words. For example, perfume and cologne manufacturers and advertisers take advantage of our tendencies to be intensionally oriented when they give their products names such as Intimate, Brut, and Obsession. They count on us to buy the products based on our desires—whether to become intimate with another, to be perceived as a manly brute, or to be the object of another's obsession. Other manufacturers and advertisers follow suit with a whole range of consumer products and marketing messages. When we confuse labels with reality, or words with things, we can make major misinterpretations.

LANGUAGE AND RELATIONSHIPS: COMMUNICATION STYLE, WORDS, AND FEELINGS

Intensional orientation: The type of orientation displayed when one responds to a label rather than to what the label actually represents.

Extensional orientation: The type of orientation one displays when not blinded by labels.

Language plays an integral part in expressing social identity.[13] Our preferred speaking style tends to reflect our values and helps emphasize similarities and differences between us. For example, Japanese and Americans display contrasting communication styles. The qualities valued by the Japanese—reserve, formality, and silence—are discouraged by Americans, who generally prefer self-assertion, informality, and talkativeness. For Americans, a key function of speech is to prevent silence.[14] Unlike Americans, who typically use a direct conversational style, the Japanese tend to practice conversational indirectness. From the Japanese perspective, communication failures are the result of receiver deficiencies, not message deficiencies, even when the message contains imprecise and ambiguous words. Because of such culture-based differences, when Japanese and American people interact, there is a potential for tension and bad feeling.[15]

For Americans, social conversation helps establish and maintain friendships. Americans use talk to bring themselves and others together. That is, as communication researcher Steve Duck observes, we talk our relationships into being.[16] Although the use of language serves an information function—it enables us get things done—it also helps us express our feelings about things and each other. In other words, the words we use to describe subjects or persons also displays our attitudes toward them. We can, for example, refer to someone as a *substance abuser,* an *addict,* or a *junkie.* We can call a person *homeless, displaced,* or a *bum.* Our words announce our attitudes. The words *mangy animal, adorable puppy, goofy pup,* and *vicious beast* may all refer to the same dog. Our description of the dog demonstrates our tendency "to snarl" (register disapproval) or "purr" (register approval). In actuality, when we use **snarl words** and **purr words**, we are not describing anything but our preferences. We snarl and purr about people all the time, don't we?

Using social conversation, we talk our relationships into being.

In addition to facilitating the expression of feelings, language can be used to exclude or include others in a conversation. Groups of people who share a profession or a culture different from our own, for example, often make use of "in-group" discussions during which anyone else privy to their conversation may feel quite left out. In contrast, persons who use language that is more inclusive enable everyone present to feel more of a connection to the conversation; they explain terms that may be confusing, translate foreign terms, and use analogies that make it possible for all involved to understand the content more readily.

We can also use language to influence perceptions of power. For example, compare the following statements:

> Um, could I talk to you for a second? I probably shouldn't mention this, and I'm not really sure it's your fault, but I'm kinda upset about the fact that you didn't meet with me at the restaurant like you were supposed to. Can you meet me tomorrow maybe? That is, if you're free?

> I'd like to talk to you. I waited for you at the restaurant and I'm upset that you didn't call when you realized you wouldn't be able to meet me as we planned. While I'm willing to set another date, you need to be more considerate of my time. Just let me know if you can't make the appointment. Okay?

Snarl words: Words that register social disapproval.

Purr words: Words that register social approval.

The speaker in the second example sounds stronger, more in control, and more self-confident than the speaker in the first example, who comes across as weak, powerless, and certainly nonauthoritative.

However, we must be careful not to confuse powerful speech with rude or profane speech. They are quite different. Imagine if the second speaker had stated:

> What's wrong with you? You kept me waiting at the restaurant without so much as a phone call. If you know what's good for you, you'll never do that again!

Effective wordsmiths state their feelings clearly without being rude or using profanities that could be offensive and damaging to a relationship.

We also enact the principles of **communication accommodation theory** during interactions with others.[17] This theory explains that we adjust our language patterns to reflect how we feel about another person. For example, when we feel positively about another person and want to show our interest in and desire to affiliate with him or her, we may adapt our speech style to match theirs. When this is done effectively, the result is **communication convergence**. By matching our vocabulary, speaking rate, and use of pauses to those of the other person, we help build our relationship. For example, if you work in an environment where rough or profane language is the norm, mirroring the swearing patterns of your boss and coworkers may enhance the feelings of connection between you and the group.[18] When two people feel equally positive about each other, they engage in mutual linguistic convergence.

On the other hand, when you admire someone who does not admire you, your attempts at convergence will be unreciprocated—you may speak in a way you believe will succeed in gaining the other person's approval, but he or she may then respond by attempting to stress your differences. Thus, the accommodation principle also works in reverse. When the goal is to stress our differences, we may revert to the strategy of **communication divergence**—that is, purposefully adopting a style of speaking that contrasts with the style of speaking of the person from whom we desire to distance ourselves. How have you used the strategies of communication convergence and divergence in your relationships?

CULTURESPEAK

Words can help us share meaning with others. The more diverse our experiences, however, the more difficult it becomes for us to achieve mutual understanding.

One of the key, but disputed, theories concerning how language reflects culture is the **Sapir-Whorf hypothesis**, developed by the linguist Edward Sapir and his student Benjamin Lee Whorf, which states that language reveals social reality. According to Sapir,

> The real world is to a large extent unconsciously built upon the language habits of the group. No two languages are ever sufficiently similar to be considered as representing the same reality. The worlds in which different societies live are distinct worlds, not merely the same world with different labels attached.[19]

The Sapir-Whorf hypothesis is viewed by some as an expression of **linguistic determinism**, which means that language shapes thinking, and by others as an expression of **linguistic relativity**, which means that languages contain unique embedded elements. According to

---

Communication accommodation theory: A theory that asserts that we adjust our language patterns to reflect how we feel about another person.

Communication convergence: The matching of vocabulary, speaking rate, and use of pauses with another as part of building a relationship.

Communication divergence: The purposeful adoption of a style of speaking that contrasts with the style of speaking of a person from whom one desires to distance oneself.

Sapir-Whorf hypothesis: A theory that proposes that language influences perception by revealing and reflecting one's worldview; language is determined by the perceived reality of a culture.

Linguistic determinism: The view that language shapes thinking.

Linguistic relativity: The view that languages contain unique embedded elements.

Sapir and Whorf, words are not neutral vehicles conveying meaning but rather tools that structure our perception of reality and participate in the construction of our social world. Not everyone speaks or thinks in the same way. Language is not just the content of talk; it is also the content of thought (see Table 5.2).

TABLE 5.2 Sapir-Whorf Hypothesis

Are You a Relativist, a Determinist, or a Nonbeliever?	
Relativist	Language influences thought and feeling.
Determinist	Language conditions us to process experience.
Nonbeliever	Language does not influence thought.

According to linguistic relativists, language influences both human thought and meaning. It mediates between the symbols and the ideas they represent.[20] In fact, Whorf states, "We cut up and organize the spread and flow of events as we do largely because, through our mother tongue, we are parties to an agreement to do so, not because nature itself is segmented in exactly that way for all to see."[21] From this perspective, language defines, rather than reports, experience. It influences how we think and how we perceive the world.

Those who are extreme advocates of the Sapir-Whorf hypothesis believe that we are "at the mercy of the particular language which has become the medium of expression" for our society.[22] Believing that language determines reality, they contend that language conditions users to process experience in a certain way. For example, the Hopi language has no concept of time as an objective entity. This, according to adherents of extreme Whorfianism, affects the Hopi conceptualization of the world. They claim that the way the Hopi rely on preparation, announcing events well in advance, shows a concept of continuous time, in contrast to the segmented time of Western societies. Similarly, famed speech therapist Wendell Johnson observed that very few Indians in one tribe stuttered. Soon after discovering that their language contained no word for stuttering, he concluded that the reason they did not stutter was that the possibility of stuttering never occurred to them.[23]

Those who disagree with the premise of the Sapir-Whorf hypothesis do so by contending that language does not influence thought. In support of this, they cite translatability and the existence of universals. That is, (1) although languages may differ in grammar and syntax, it is still feasible to translate meaning from one language to another, and (2) there are deep grammatical structures that are common to all languages, as observed by another linguist, Noam Chomsky.[24]

Despite having its critics, the Sapir-Whorf hypothesis has influenced the way we conceive of language. Even those who support the hypothesis only weakly and moderately believe that although language may not mandate or determine thought or reality, it does influence us by functioning as a barometer of cultural behavior and offering ways of perceiving and interpreting reality. We may study a culture by examining the words that the members of the culture use. In effect, the languages that groups of people use mirror their experiences. For example, if your talk abounds with words such as *text, tweet,* and *download,* receivers are able to learn something about what is important to you and what your culture is like. However, if the culture of the receivers is one that is not as technologically advanced as yours, they might not understand you.

Language affects thought, and thought affects language use. Viewed from this perspective, language does not imprison its users but rather has the ability to influence the perspective its users adopt, reflecting their worldview and affecting how they interpret experience. In Brazil, for example, a country whose economy depends on coffee, many different words are used for coffee, reflecting the product's importance to Brazilian culture. Similarly, Arabs, who were historically dependent on the camel for transportation, have more words for the animal than do other cultures. According to the Sapir-Whorf hypothesis, the language we use reflects our worldview, our interests and concerns, and what we believe important.

Language also reflects reasoning patterns and expression preferences. For example, people in Western cultures rely on inductive and deductive reasoning to make and understand points; those in the Arab world rely on the expression of personal emotions and the personalization of arguments. Because of these differences, Westerners may have difficulty locating the main idea in an Arab's message, and vice versa.[25] Arab speech is filled with repetitions that highlight an idea's importance. Its stress patterns often confuse Western listeners, causing them to interpret messages as either aggressive or disinterested when they are intended as neither.[26] Likewise, whereas members of Asian cultures are apt to use language sparingly and carefully, preferring to keep their feelings to themselves in an effort to preserve social harmony, members of Spanish and Latin American cultures eagerly engage in conversation and are typically open and willing to share their feelings with others.[27] Thus, our culture influences how we use language.

According to researchers in the field of cultural neuroscience, culture shapes brain activity in addition to language use. They assert that the region of the brain called the medial prefrontal cortex represents the self. For example, when Americans think of the word *me*—their personal identity and traits—the medial prefrontal cortex is activated. For Chinese subjects, however, the same brain region is activated when subjects think of the word for *me* as well as the word for *mother*. Therefore, the research indicates that neural circuitry differs between those raised in cultures that conceive of the self as a part of a larger whole, such as the Chinese, and those raised in cultures that hold the self as autonomous and unique, such as Americans.[28]

We also need to understand how language functions within cocultures. **Cocultures** are groups of people living within a society but outside its **dominant culture** or the mainstream culture. The language within a given coculture will differ in some ways from that of the dominant culture, because it reflects a different reality, including differences in lifestyle, values, and behavior. The special vocabulary that a coculture evolves, its **argot**, enables the members of the coculture to develop both an identity and a sense of community. In American society, for example, members of the African American and LGBT communities use argots to communicate with others within their groups. An argot enables coculture members to use language to maintain a facade of behavior and to cope with any disconnections between their own group and the dominant culture through humor or hostility. In time, some words developed within cocultures begin to be used by the dominant culture. When this happens, members of the cocultures often stop using them. Thus, argots undergo constant change.

Language is a part of identity. In fact, changing how you talk can influence how you think. Thus, sometimes in studying a new language you also open your mind to new ways of looking at the world.[29] The same is true of studying how members of different cultures use language.

Coculture: A group of people who share a culture within a society but outside its dominant culture.

Dominant culture: The culture that has the most power.

Argot: The language used by members of a coculture.

TRY THIS: *The Language-Culture Link*

The advertisements popular in a country provide clues regarding the nature and effectiveness of interpersonal communication there. For example, theorists Richard Brislin and Tomoko Yoshida, authors of *Intercultural Communication Training: An Introduction,* offer the example of a Japanese ad for frozen breaded pork, the tagline of which, they observe, can be translated literally as "A *bento* [box lunch] that can be made with an oven toaster: Strong in the morning, delicious at noon." While this statement may make little or no sense to the uninitiated perceiver, Brislin and Yoshida point out that once you understand the culture, the meaning of the ad becomes clearer:

> To fully understand this advertisement it is necessary for people to know that the Japanese take fairly elaborate lunches to work, school, picnics, and other outings, and that it is important for the lunches to look as though plenty of time had been spent on them. Traditionally, women are expected to make *bentos* for their children, their husbands or, perhaps, for someone they love. If a woman is seen with an elaborate *bento,* many men interpret it as signifying that she will probably make a good wife. Although things are rapidly changing in Japan, and many working women do not have the time to make *bentos,* there is still some romantic significance attached to them. . . . In addition, the phrase "strong in the morning" needs to be understood. The functional equivalent of the phrase in English would be "a morning person," suggesting that even women who are not "morning people" can appear as though they are with the help of this product.

1. Locate an example of an advertisement appearing in a foreign newspaper, foreign magazine, or online site. Even if you do not speak the language used in the ad, describe your understanding of the ad to the best of your ability.

2. Explain how an understanding of the culture of the people to whom the ad is addressed could contribute to an accurate interpretation of the ad's meaning.

SOURCE: Richard Brislin and Tomoko Yoshida, *Intercultural Communication Training: An Introduction*, Thousand Oaks, CA: Sage, 1994, p. 48–49.

GENDERSPEAK

Language is a prime means of communicating cultural views of gender. Once we internalize the transmitted social prescriptions, we then enact them during our relationships. Language can both express and reinforce gender stereotypes and perceptions of power. It is not neutral; rather, it exerts a significant influence on our attitudes toward the self and others.

LANGUAGE CAN DIMINISH AND STEREOTYPE WOMEN AND MEN

Language, for example, can symbolize a devalued perception of women by presenting the experiences of men as the norm and those of women as departures from the perceived standard. Language helps to shape what we see as "normal," "appropriate," or an exception to the rule.[30] Consequently, although male generic language, in theory, was once thought to be inclusive of both women and men, research has revealed that many of us interpreted male generics as including men but excluding women.[31] While they have faded from common usage, male generic terms such as *mankind, businessman,* and *Man of the Year* caused our culture to perceive men as more prominent and numerous than women. To combat such perceptions, many organizations and individuals eventually adopted policies of avoiding the use of male generics and other sexist and non-gender-neutral language.

True or False

5. *Spotlighting highlights a person's appearance.*

False. Spotlighting highlights a person's sex.

Similarly, it used to be common to refer to women as *girls* while refraining from calling men *boys,* leading many to perceive women as childlike. In like fashion, the highlighting of a person's sex, referred to as **spotlighting**, also reinforced the perception that the standard was set by men. Although we rarely hear combinations such as *male physician, male lawyer,* and *male physicist,* terms such as the following remain widely used: *woman doctor, female mathematician.* This practice defines women as exceptions to a norm established by men. Eliminating spotlighting should make it easier to revise gender perceptions.

Language also distinguishes between men and women when our words define them differently. We tend to define men by their independence, activities, status, and accomplishments. We more frequently define women by their appearance and relationships. Defining a person by physical qualities or appearance diminishes that person's achievements. Definitional biases reinforce the idea of women as decorative accessories whose claim to fame is how they look and the idea of men as capable and qualified individuals whose claim to fame is how they perform.

On the other hand, some have asserted that words are also used to emasculate men by promoting a cartoonish idea of them. They point to the new words invented to describe men's fashion as examples: *manties* for male undergarments; *mandals* for sandals designed for men; *manbag, murse,* or *carryall* for a men's version of the purse or pocketbook; and *mewelry* for men's jewelry.[32] How do you feel about these terms?

LANGUAGE PRACTICES REFLECT GOALS AND FEELINGS ABOUT POWER

Key contrasts in the communication practices of females and males demonstrate differences in how they use language. In general, men and women use language to accomplish different goals.[33] Typically, males use it to achieve something or assert themselves, whereas women use it to create and sustain relationships. Men use language to attract and keep an audience, whereas women use it to indicate they are paying attention. Men use language to compete; women use it to collaborate. For women, talk is at the very core of a relationship, not a means to achieve conversational dominance as it is for men.[34]

Because women are more likely than men to exhibit an affiliative, or socially based and mutual, orientation, they are less likely to use words to assert status. Unlike most men, who express ideas firmly and then wait to see if someone challenges them, many women prefer to use language to foster connection, gain support, and display understanding. In contrast to men, women are more likely to interpret challenges to their ideas as personal attacks. Since women are socialized to weigh others' opinions, they also are apt to ask others for their ideas before rendering decisions. Whereas men interpret questions as information requests, women characteristically use questions to keep conversations going. Should a man provide the requested information, the woman typically asks another question, which usually succeeds in frustrating the man. Why is this? When neither understands the other's behavior, the likely result is frustration.[35]

The sensitivity women display to others' reactions probably explains their unobtrusive and smoothing style. In comparison with men, women have a lower threshold for identifying behavior as offensive. This also accounts for why women's speech is often labeled as deferential, as well as why women are prone to offering ritual apologies—saying "I'm sorry" on numerous occasions every day.[36]

Spotlighting: The highlighting of a person's sex for emphasis.

Differences in male and female orientations result in differences in the structure of utterances. Tentative phrases such as "I guess," "I think," and "I wonder if" characterize the speech patterns of women but not those of men. Unlike men, women frequently turn their statements into questions. Thus, a woman might ask, "Don't you believe it would be more effective to put this paragraph in the introduction rather than in the conclusion?" In contrast, a man would deliver a more definitive statement: "It would be more effective to put this paragraph in the introduction rather than in the conclusion."[37]

According to linguist Robin Lakoff, unlike most men, women do not lay claim to their utterances.[38] Additionally, women's tendency to add "tag questions" to their comments contributes to their being perceived as more tentative. While a woman may say, "Mel is right, isn't she?" or It's a great day, isn't it?" men usually make such statements minus the "isn't she" or "isn't it" question tags. Women also reinforce their reputation for tentativeness by prefacing utterances with phrases such as "This probably won't matter, but . . ." and "This probably isn't important, yet. . . ." Some researchers contend that such habits further weaken the impact of the messages women send, while others suggest that the tentativeness noted in women's speech is not a sign of powerlessness but rather reveals their desire to keep conversation open and inclusive.[39]

Linguist Deborah Tannen has coined the term **genderlect** to describe the different languages that men and women use.[40] According to Tannen, the genderlect that women hear and speak is one of connection and intimacy, of seeking to preserve relationships. Men, in contrast, speak and hear a language of status and independence.[41]

Age can account for variations in language use.

AGE AND LANGUAGE

Just as gender and culture help account for language use variations, so does age. Persons who grew up in different generations may experience more difficulty understanding each other than people who grew up in the same generation. Significant age differences may make individuals more prone to misunderstanding one another or to misperceiving what others are telling them.[42]

Research also reveals that young people tend to adjust the language they use when they are interacting with older people. Sometimes, younger persons will feel they have to overaccommodate when interacting with someone significantly older than they are. Reacting on the basis of their stereotype of older persons, younger persons may consciously alter their word choices, making them simpler and more concrete, believing erroneously that older persons have a diminished capacity for conversation. Those who are younger also are likely to think they ought to speak more slowly and in a more nurturing tone when conversing with an older person, which often results in making the older person feel childlike and less capable. Because younger people have the tendency to speak to the elderly as if they are incompetent, the older person may soon *feel* incompetent, which contributes to both individuals, young and old, feeling unfulfilled by their interactions.[43]

Genderlect: Deborah Tannen's term for language differences attributed to gender.

According to **muted group theory**, the group that is dominant in a social hierarchy uses language to shape societal perceptions. As a consequence, those who have less power can find themselves repressed by language. For all practical purposes, their voices are silenced or muted.

Those who control language use also are able to control thought and behavior. Thus, when you change the words used to describe or speak about something you also change the discussion. For example, by calling a law that includes significant limits on individual freedoms the Patriot Act, Congress succeeded in silencing those who questioned the act's contents by implying that nonsupporters were unpatriotic.

1. In what ways, if any, have authorities who have more power than you used language to attempt to mute your voice, and to what extent have you done the same to people whom you perceive to have less power than you?

2. How should we react when someone in power defines a situation as a means of silencing any opposition?

SOURCES: See, for example, Cheris Kramarae, "Classified Information: Race, Class, and (Always) Gender," in Julia T. Wood, ed., *Gendered Relationships,* Mountain View, CA: Mayfield, 1996, p. 20–38; and Cheris Kramarae, *Women and Men Speaking: Frameworks for Analysis,* Rowley, MA: Newbury House, 1981.

See, for example, Ann Burnett, Jody L. Mattern, Liliana L. Herakova, David H. Kahl, Clay Tobola, and Susan E. Bornsen, "Communicating/Muting Date Rape: A Co-cultural Theoretical Analysis of Communication Factors Related to Rape Culture on a College Campus," *Journal of Applied Communication Research,* 37, 2009, p. 465–485; and Cheris Kramarae, "Muted Group Theory and Communication: Asking Dangerous Questions," *Women and Language,* 28:2, 2005, p. 55–61.

Of course, individual accommodations are sometimes necessary. However, even if an older person has a hearing loss, this does not correlate with diminished mental ability. To communicate effectively, we must relate our language to the needs of the individuals with whom we interact rather than basing how we speak on stereotypes. To avoid interacting with an older person in a way he or she could find demeaning, young persons should treat persons of any age group as individuals rather than as members of a social category.

LANGUAGE, MEDIA, AND TECHNOLOGY

As we have seen, how we use language reveals both our attitudes toward and our assessments of the subjects of our discussions and each other. For example, we are more apt to define women by appearance or relationships and men by activities or positions than vice versa. This practice is reflected in countless media examples.

EXPERIENCING MEDIA

Reflecting societal judgments of what is important for each sex, media coverage of female politicians and athletes often contains references to their physical appearance, whereas stories about their male counterparts are more likely to stress their accomplishments rather than their hair, dress, weight, or physical appeal.[44] We also see societal judgments affecting story placement, with stories about women appearing more often in the lifestyle pages rather the front pages of newspapers.[45] And although strides have been made, even

Muted group theory:
A theory that proposes that in a social hierarchy, the dominant group uses language to shape perceptions, effectively silencing or muting those with less power.

when women have careers as physicians or lawyers, they are more apt to be portrayed in stereotypical ways in the media and defined by their marital and familial status. Unfortunately, such practices can tend to increase sexism.

EXPERIENCING TECHNOLOGY

When we interact online, we use words and pictures to encode our on-screen identities: "The way we use these words, the stories (true and false) we tell about ourselves (or about the identities we want others to perceive) is what determines our identities in cyberspace. The aggregation of personae, interacting with each other, determines the nature of the collective culture."[46] We tend to separate ourselves from others online based on our needs and interests, affiliating ourselves with those belonging to communities reflective of our mutual concerns.

As in face-to-face conversation, when you are online the use of language that is inflammatory, insulting, imprecise, or discriminatory can cause problems. What you write, text, or tweet in haste or in anger may reach a wider audience and have more influence than you imagined, causing you potentially serious consequences. For example, when a teacher posted on her Facebook page that she was "a warden for future criminals." The school board of her district scheduled a hearing to consider whether to revoke her tenure.[47] When we are online, we are more apt to share our thoughts without displaying concern for others' feelings. As this chapter's opening examination of the Tyler Clementi and Dharun Ravi tragedy illustrates, we are more likely to comment *about* one another online than to talk *with* one another. Gossip, sexist and homophobic remarks, and trash talk are all too common on the Web—posted for all to read, no longer merely whispered by one person to another. Because young people are addressing issues of race, class, and gender online, they are also likely to reveal their personal struggles, just as they would offline—but not necessarily to their parents.[48]

We send more than a trillion text messages every year.[49] Some believe that the prevalence of texting is causing us to speak in shorter sentences and has the potential to wipe out spoken conversation.[50] Others believe that our use of textspeak is leading us to speak in acronyms, a form of private language.[51] Which of these two positions do you agree with more, if either?

How do your online interactions differ from those you engage in when face-to-face? Some report that they display more enthusiasm during online interactions. Online speech can have a breathless, yet emphatic feel to it—as if users are jumping up and down to capture their receivers' attention.[52]

Some people display more enthusiasm when communicating online than they do in face-to-face interactions. Do you?

Women's use of highly expressive language online projects their desire for connection. While men post about sports games and politics, women use social media more like a public diary, revealing personal bits of their lives, such as relating a funny thing a boyfriend just did and posting questions about their appearance (Does this outfit look okay?).[53]

GAINING COMMUNICATION COMPETENCE: MAKING YOUR WORDS WORK

Taking language for granted can be dangerous. With this in mind, what can you do to master meaning and so improve your relationships? Answering the following questions will help you learn to make your words work.

ARE MY WORDS CLEAR?

Far too often we understand the words we are using, but others do not. If we choose words with the individual we are interacting with in mind, that person will be more apt to respond as we had hoped. Ask yourself the following questions when considering your words' clarity:

- Are the words I am using reflective of the education level of the person with whom I am interacting? For example, you would not give a lecture containing sophisticated computer terminology to a group of first graders.
- Is this person familiar with any technical language (jargon) or argot I might use with members of my particular coculture? For instance, it would be unwise to use medical terminology when explaining an ailment to a patient.

ARE MY WORDS APPROPRIATE?

Our word choice should change as the situation we are in changes and as the individual with whom we are interacting changes. For example, we might use slang when speaking with friends, but we probably would not use it when conversing with our employer or a professor. Whereas obscenities might spew from our mouths when we are letting off steam around a close pal, we probably would censor our remarks when in the presence of a parent, grandparent, or school or corporate officer. Ask yourself the following questions when assessing the appropriateness of your word choice:

- Will my receiver find my words offensive?
- Am I using the right words in the right place at the right time?

AM I USING WORDS THAT ARE CONCRETE?

Our words are concrete when they enable us to describe a feeling, an event, or a circumstance unambiguously—that is, they let us communicate precisely what we mean. When we eliminate vague and confusing words from our conversation and substitute more exact ones, we are able to shape the meaning we transmit to others more effectively. Ask yourself the following questions when evaluating the concreteness of your expression:

- Do my words enable my receiver to formulate a clear picture of my thoughts?
- Do my words communicate my intended feelings?

DO MY WORDS SPEAK TO THE OTHER
PERSON AND REFLECT THE CONTEXT?

Many people use words differently than you do. When this occurs, do not assume they are wrong. Rather, remind yourself that their experiences may have led them to develop different points of view or different ways of thinking about something or someone. When you are sensitive to the person and the context, you increase your chances of "talking the same language."

Keep in mind that the meaning of a word can change from one time period to another and from one culture to another. In the United States, the word *apple* now conjures images of computers, not just of fruit. In the 1970s, when the Ford Motor Company tried to sell its car the Pinto in Brazil, it failed miserably—at least in part because in Brazilian slang the word *pinto* means "tiny male genitals."[54] We all use words, just not necessarily in the same ways.

DO I SHARE "TO ME" MEANING?

Words can confuse or clarify, conceal or reveal meaning. When you take time to share your perception of the "to me" nature of language, you let another person know that you are aware that he or she may not be processing experience the same way you are. That person then also becomes more willing to share his or her "to me" perceptions with you.

You share "to me" meanings by eliminating the accusatory "you" from your vocabulary. By using the word *I* in place of *you,* you effectively describe your own feelings and thoughts instead of berating others for theirs. This simple strategy also allows you to take ownership of your words. For example, instead of telling a friend, "You are selfish. You didn't think about how I would feel when you asked Karen to go shopping with you but not me," you say, "I feel like I didn't matter when you asked Karen to go shopping with you but not me."

If you share your "to me" meanings, this behavior will also actualize the communication strategy of dual perspective talking. Once you acknowledge that everyone has a "to me" meaning and that we all own our feelings and thoughts, you take responsibility for yourself. We do not need to give up our "to me" perspective to respect and understand the perspectives of others. Using "I" or "to me" language decreases the defensiveness of others, opens the door to dialogue, and empowers the self.

DO I RESPECT UNIQUENESS?

No two people, events, or things are exactly alike. Student 1 is not student 2. Political rally 1 is not political rally 2. When we talk in generalities, our words can trip us up and lead us to stereotype. In contrast, identifying differences enables us to demonstrate our respect for uniqueness.

Whenever we make a blanket judgment about others, such as "Lawyers are liars" or "Guidance counselors are teachers who just want out of the classroom," we are thinking in generalities and ignoring differences. Because expecting a behavior can help to precipitate the behavior, we must consciously avoid forming fixed mental pictures of anyone or any group. When we form a fixed mental picture, we fail to notice the unique characteristics that distinguish one person or group from another.

What can you do to ensure you look beyond the category? Indexing generalizations can prevent you from using language to conceal important distinctions between people. When we index generalizations, we acknowledge individual differences within a group. Group member 1 is different from group member 2, who is different from group member 3, and so on. An action as simple as this can help you avoid the problems that stereotyping encourages.

CONNECT THE CASE: *The Case of the Wounding Words*

Like many college students, Aiden gave little thought to how his words affected others. He was shocked to discover that his shouting a few words and then tweeting about it could actually precipitate demonstrations on and off campus. What words had Aiden shouted and tweeted?

One day, when he was disturbed by a group of African American students who in his opinion were socializing much too loudly beneath his window, Aiden had yelled, "Shut up, you water buffalo!" He then posted on Twitter about how annoyed he was. Though it was later learned that Aiden had previously attended a yeshiva where the Hebrew term for "water buffalo" was slang for "foolish person," he was threatened with being prosecuted for racial harassment. Eventually, persecuted by the press, the students who had been outside Aiden's window dropped their charge against him, and the case died down.

However, soon afterward, at a meeting organized to discuss campus sexual harassment policies, one participant, we'll call him or her Lindsay, used a number of hypothetical scenarios to make a point. Featured in the scenarios were two fictional persons referred to as Ethan Stud and Cara Sex Object. While a number of persons present laughed when they heard the names, others were offended and objected vocally, asserting that Lindsay's choice of words was sexist.

Answer the following questions:

1. Are some words so offensively racist or sexist that no one should use them? Explain your stance with reasons.

2. To what extent, and in what ways if any, can the words one person uses to describe another person change our views of both the person using the words and the person the words describe?

3. If you were a friend of Lindsay and Aiden, what advice would you offer each?

4. Are you in favor of political correctness? If so, why, and if not, why not?

NOTE: This case is based on the 1993 racial harassment case of Eden Jacobowitz. See Scott Lanman, "Jacobowitz Settles 'Water Buffalo' Lawsuit," *Daily Pennsylvanian*, September 8, 1997, http://www.thedp.com/index.php/article/1997/09/jacobowitz_settles_water_buffalo_lawsuit.

DO I LOOK FOR GROWTH?

People and situations change. We are constantly in the process of becoming. Your authors are not the same people they were fifteen years ago; our children, Matthew and Lindsay, are not the same people they were last year. And you are not the same person you were just a few short weeks back. Experiences change us. Just as people are not fixed in time, neither are we or our ideas.

Take the opportunity to allow your words to reflect this growth. Demonstrating such flexibility will facilitate more effective interpersonal communication and relationships. Keep in mind that when you make general or static evaluations of others and situations, you deny the reality of change. Static evaluations limit interpersonal effectiveness by preventing you from acknowledging the changes in people and situations.

Check yourself periodically to see if you are holding on to any static evaluations about people or situations that are no longer valid. Dating your observations will remind you that nearly everything—even the meanings of words and our interpretations and reactions to them—changes with time.

REVIEW THIS

CHAPTER SUMMARY

1 Define language, explaining its uses and distinguishing among semantic, syntactic, and pragmatic codes. Language is a system of symbols used by a group of people to communicate. We use language to facilitate social contact, the sharing of perceptions, and the negotiation of meaning. The semantic code consists of our agreed-upon uses of symbols or words. The syntactic code consists of the rules that guide our use of words. The pragmatic code involves the coordination and cooperation necessary to derive meaning.

2 Explain the triangle of meaning. Ogden and Richards's triangle of meaning illustrates the relationships that exist among words, things, and thoughts. The model specifies that there is no direct connection between a symbol and its referent, underscoring the fact that the word is not the thing, and that meaning exists in thoughts, not in words or things.

3 Distinguish between denotative and connotative meaning. A word's denotative meaning is its dictionary definition. A word's connotative meaning is the personal meaning the word has for each individual.

4 Discuss the nature of word walls, euphemisms, emotive language, polarizing words, politically correct language, bypassing, and intensional orientation. When we build a word wall, we use words in a way that impedes understanding and the sharing of meaning. A euphemism masks a communicator's meaning by substituting polite or inoffensive language for blunt, direct language. Emotive language editorializes our feelings. Polarizing language describes the world in extremes. Language that is politically correct is sensitive to the listener's interpretation. Bypassing occurs when we think we understand each other but miss each other's meaning. When we respond to a label rather than to what the label represents, we display intensional as opposed to extensional orientation.

5 Explain how language reflects social identity and communication style. The language we use reflects our values, helping to emphasize the similarities and differences between us, including the nature of our conversations, how we express feelings, and whether our use of words enhances or detracts from our power.

6 Identify how language helps express and reinforce attitudes toward culture, gender, and age. Language exerts a powerful influence on our social identity and perceptions of one another. The language we use to describe one another can cause stereotypes to persist or can foster their eradication.

7 Discuss the interface between language and media and technology. The types of words used to describe people in print, broadcast, and cable media and on the Internet reflect societal judgments of worth and importance.

8 Take steps to use language more effectively. To use language more effectively, we need to ensure that our words are clear, appropriate, and as concrete as possible. We also need to work our way carefully and sensitively through the world of words, be committed to sharing meaning, respect the uniqueness of every individual, and seek opportunities for growth.

CHECK YOUR UNDERSTANDING

1 Can you provide an example that demonstrates how the triangle of meaning works? (See page 126.)

2 Can you provide an example of how time and place influence word choice? Whom do you believe should be held accountable when problems in understanding occur because of time and place differences? (See page 127.)

3 Can you give an example of a time when the use of euphemisms affected one of your relationships? In what ways does masking meaning complicate things? What about the use of polarizing language or displaying an intensional versus extensional orientation? (See pages 129–131.)

4 Can you create a scenario illustrating how gender and/or culture affect your use of language? Can you create another showing how media and/or technology affect your use of language? (See pages 136–141; and pages 142–144.)

5 Can you put into action a plan to improve your command of words? (See pages 144–146.)

CHECK YOUR SKILLS

1 Can you offer examples of how words help you to negotiate meaning? (See pages 124–126; and **Try This**, page 128.)

2 Can you explain how time and place figure into your discussion with another person? (See page 127.)

3 Can you identify when and why you or others use euphemisms, emotive language, polarizing language, and politically correct language? (See pages 129–132; **Try This,** page 130 and page 134; and **Analyze This,** page 135.)

4 Can you take steps to ensure that you and another person do not miss one another's meanings? (See pages 132–133.)

5 Can you determine when intensional orientation interferes with your reactions to persons or products? (See pages 133–134.)

6 Can you share how you use words, including snarl and purr words, to express your social identity? (See pages 135.)

7 Can you tell when you or another is using words to emphasize similarity to or difference from someone? (See pages 136.)

8 Can you account for how your language use reflects and reinforces cultural and gender perspectives and feelings about power? (See pages 136–141; and **Reflect on This,** page 142.)

9 Can you identify how the language featured in media offerings and online may contribute to misrepresentations and misunderstandings? (See pages 142–144.)

10 Can you predict the effects of your words on others? (See **The Case of the Wounding Words,** page 146.)

KEY TERMS

Language *124*

Semantic code *125*

Syntactic code *125*

Pragmatic code *125*

Triangle of meaning *126*

Word mask *126*

Word wall *126*

Denotative meaning *127*

Connotative meaning *127*

Euphemism *129*

Emotive language *129*

Polarizing language *130*

Bypassing *132*

Equivocal language *132*

Intensional orientation *134*

Extensional orientation *134*

Snarl words *135*

Purr words *135*

Communication accommodation theory *136*

Communication convergence *136*

Communication divergence *136*

Sapir-Whorf hypothesis *136*

Linguistic determinism *136*

Linguistic relativity *136*

Coculture *138*

Dominant culture *138*

Argot *138*

Spotlighting *140*

Genderlect *141*

Muted group theory *142*

STUDENT STUDY SITE

Visit the student study site at **www.sagepub.com/gambleic** to access the following materials:

- SAGE Journal Articles
- Videos
- Web Resources
- eFlashcards
- Web Quizzes
- Study Questions

chapter 6

Beware of persons whose bellies do not move when they laugh.

—Chinese Proverb

NONVERBAL COMMUNICATION

LEARNING OBJECTIVES

After completing this chapter, you should be able to demonstrate mastery of the following learning outcomes:

1. Define nonverbal communication, explain its metacommunicative nature, and discuss its functions and characteristics.

2. Define and distinguish among the following kinds of nonverbal messages: kinesics, paralanguage, proxemics, haptics, artifactual communication and appearance, olfactics, color, and chronemics.

3. Compare and contrast the nonverbal communication styles of men and women.

4. Distinguish between contact and noncontact cultures.

5. Describe the impacts of media and technology on nonverbal messages.

6. Identify steps you can take to improve your nonverbal effectiveness.

The motion picture *The Artist* received the Oscar for Best Picture in 2012. This mostly silent black-and-white movie won the hearts of audiences and enthralled the critics, all with hardly any dialogue. Most of the communication that occurs in the movie is nonverbal.

The movie's lead actress, Bérénice Bejo, received an Academy Award nomination for Best Supporting Actress for playing Peppy Miller, a young starlet who in the course of the film becomes a star. In an interview on the experiences she had filming this silent movie, Bejo commented, "I was thinking: '*How am I going to move, how am I going to speak without using my voice?*' By the end of the shooting, I thought: 'That's it, I got it!' I can't explain it; it was physical. We give ourselves so much pressure with words. I like it very much that our intention is not conveyed solely through dialogue but by the body, the walk, the attitude, the precision of each gesture."[1]

The actors did not need to use spoken words to make their characters' messages clear to us. By observing how the actors moved, by paying attention to their facial expressions, by looking at how they sat and adjusted their heads, we understood them—the actors' messages came alive. Relying on such nonverbal cues, we connected with the characters emotionally. We can do this in our daily lives as well.

"How am I going to move, how am I going to speak without using my voice?"

Consider, for example, what these descriptive phrases have in common:

The twinkle in his eye. The edge in her voice. The knowing look of their smiles. The rigidity of his posture. The confidence in her walk. Your hairstyle. Your dress. Where you sit. How closely you stand to another. Your eagerness to arrive.

Each of the phrases highlights a nonverbal cue that offers a clue to the attitudes, feelings, and personality of a person. Despite the presence of such cues, too often we remain unaware of the messages our bodies, our voices, or the space around us sends to others. We simply act and react without considering how actions modify, reinforce, or distort messages.

WHAT DO YOU KNOW?

Before continuing your reading of this chapter, which of the following five statements do you believe to be true and which do you believe to be false?

1. You are a message. T F

2. Words used, not nonverbal cues, are more likely to reveal the telling of a lie. T F

3. Suspicious people are better at spotting deception. T F

4. Your hands reveal more about your feelings than does your face. T F

5. Some women purposefully make their teeth crooked. T F

Read the chapter to discover if you're right or if you've made any erroneous assumptions.

ANSWERS: 1. T, 2. F, 3. T, 4. F, 5. T

This chapter's focus is nonverbal communication. Our concern is transitioning from *what* we say to *how* we say it, for words alone rarely, if ever, lead to our wanting to begin, continue, or end a relationship. By taking time to better appreciate the contributions of nonverbal messages, we take another step forward in expanding our ability to understand person-to-person interaction.

DEFINING NONVERBAL COMMUNICATION

Our interpersonal effectiveness depends on more than words. Nonverbal messages add to or detract from our words. In effect, we become the message, with our nonverbal cues announcing our state of mind, expectations, and sense of self. Our entire beings chatter incessantly, revealing what we really feel and think.

For example, how do you judge another's honesty or trustworthiness? The meaning of these variables is carried predominantly via nonverbal messages, often without our awareness and not under our conscious control. For this reason, nonverbal messages are less likely than words to be intentionally deceptive.[2]

Nonverbal communication is expressed through nonlinguistic means. It is the actions or attributes of humans, including their appearance, use of objects, sound, time, smell, and space, that have socially shared significance and stimulate meaning in others. It includes visual/kinesic cues such as facial expressions, eye movements, gestures, and body orientation; vocal/paralinguistic cues such as volume, pitch, rate, and inflection; proxemic cues such as space and distance; olfactory or smell cues; cues provided via artifactual communication and appearance; cues sent via color; and chronemic or time cues.

Although we may send nonverbal messages deliberately or accidentally, their meaning depends on how they are interpreted. Consequently, they fulfill **metacommunicative functions,** and communicate about communication, clarifying both the nature of our relationship, and/or the meaning of our verbal messages. In fact, researchers conclude that nonverbal cues carry approximately two-thirds of a message's communicative value. Even when used independently of words, as long as an observer derives meaning from them, nonverbal messages speak volumes. Of course, the amount of information conveyed varies according to their clarity, and how receptive and perceptive the receiver is. Based on interpretations of our nonverbal cues, others may decide if they like us, will or will listen to our ideas, or want to sustain or terminate our relationship. The ability to understand and respond to nonverbal messages helps unlock meaning's door.

THE FUNCTIONS AND CHARACTERISTICS OF NONVERBAL COMMUNICATION

As we noted, for us to fully understand the meaning of verbal messages, we also need to understand the meaning of the nonverbal messages that accompany them or occur in their absence. After all, we can change the meaning of our words with the wink of an eye, a certain facial expression, voice tone, bodily movement, use of space, or touch. As our ability to use and interpret nonverbal behavior and contextual cues improves, so will our understanding of interpersonal relationships. Let's see how this works. What do you make of these examples?

Nonverbal communication:
Communication that does not include words; messages expressed by nonlinguistic means; people's actions or attributes, including their use of objects, sounds, time, and space, that have socially shared significance and stimulate meaning in others.

Metacommunicative functions:
Communication about communication.

1. The little boy who hides behind his mother as he says, "*I'm not afraid of the dog.*"

2. The woman who says, "*I love you,*" to her spouse while hugging him and smothering him with kisses.

3. The teacher who asks, "*Any questions?*" and fails to wait for a response before moving on to the next point.

4. The child whose eyes are downcast and shoulders are rounded as she says, "*I'm sorry for breaking the vase.*"

5. The supervisor who, when asked a question by an employee, leans forward with a hand cupped behind one ear.

Each message contains nonverbal cues that help reveal what a person is feeling. As we see, nonverbal cues are integral to communication. As the preceding situations illustrate, they may (1) contradict words, (2) emphasize or underscore words, (3) regulate their flow, (4) complement words, or (5) substitute for or take the place of spoken words (See Table 6.1). Whereas words are best at conveying thoughts or ideas, nonverbal cues are best at conveying information about relational matters such as liking, respect, and social control. To be sure, the meaning of neither verbal nor nonverbal messages should be interpreted without carefully considering the other. Let us review each of the identified functions.

TABLE 6.1 Functions of Nonverbal Communication

Function	Example
Contradicting	Your face is contorted into a grimace. Your eyes are narrowed and eyebrows furrowed. Yet, you are yelling, "I am not upset!" You are sending a mixed/double message.
Emphasizing	You wave your finger accusingly and raise your voice to demonstrate your anger as you say, "It is your fault, not mine." Your behavior provides the italics.
Regulating	After explaining your stance on an issue, you raise and then lower your intonation as you say, "And that's why I feel the way I do." This, together with your silence, signals you are finished speaking and another person may comment. Your behavior influences the flow of verbal interaction.
Complementing	Your head is bowed and your body posture is slouched as your boss tells you how unhappy she is with your job performance. Your nonverbal cues provide clues to the relationship you and your boss share; they also help convey your attitude toward your boss.
Substituting	You run into a friend who asks, "So, how do you like your new job?" You just roll your eyes, using nonverbal cues in place of words.

THE FUNCTIONS OF NONVERBAL COMMUNICATION

1. Nonverbal cues can *contradict* or *negate* verbal messages. When this happens what is said and what is done are at odds. Imagine the man who repeatedly says, "*Hold me,*" but backs away to avoid being held, or the salesperson that just lost a deal, screaming, "*I'm not angry!*" Each of these verbal messages is negated by the source's nonverbal behavior. Each interaction represents a **double-message**—the words say one thing, the nonverbal cues, another.

Double message: The message that is communicated when words say one thing and nonverbal cues another.

We rely on nonverbal cues to emphasize spoken words.

2. Nonverbal cues can *emphasize* or *underscore* a verbal message. For example, when you raise or lower your voice, or slow down your rate of speech so you can deliberately stress a series of words, you are using nonverbal cues to accentuate your words.

3. Nonverbal cues can *regulate* or *control* person-to-person interaction. Using nonverbal cues, we establish the rules of order or "turn-taking" during talk. With eye contact, gestures, and voice we control who should speak next and thus direct the flow of verbal exchanges. The regulatory skills of others influence our judgments of them. For example, if we feel that talking to Eli is like talking to a wall, or that when we talk to Taylor we can't get a word in edgewise, it may be because we do not get the turns or attention that we feel we deserve when we interact with Eli or Taylor.

4. Nonverbal cues can *reinforce* or *complement* a verbal message. With your keys and coat in your hand, you announce, "I have to leave now," as you walk toward your car.

5. Nonverbal cues can *substitute for or take the place of* spoken words. When we don't know what to say to express our sorrow at the death of a friend or a relative, an embrace often suffices. Similarly, when someone asks, *"What do you want to do tonight?"* a shrug of the shoulders frequently is used in place of "I don't know." Often when actions substitute for words, the nonverbal cues function as symbols of the verbal messages because they are widely understood. The up-and-down nod is understood to mean yes, just as forming a T with your hands during a sports event is understood to mean "time-out."

CHARACTERISTICS OF NONVERBAL COMMUNICATION

Nonverbal communication is an essential part of the total communication package. From a nonverbal perspective, you are a lighthouse of information continually sending messages from which others derive meaning.

All Nonverbal Behavior Has Message Value. While we can refrain ourselves from speaking—we literally can shut our mouths—it is impossible for us to stop behaving. Behavior, whether intentional or unintentional, is ongoing.

You cannot stop sending nonverbal messages. As long as someone is aware of your presence and is there to decode your nonverbal communication, it is impossible for you not to communicate. Even if you turn your back on the observer and remove yourself from his or her sight, you are communicating. With this in mind, if someone were to enter the space in which you are now reading, what messages might they derive from your nonverbal demeanor? Are you seated at a desk or reclining on a bed? What does your face suggest regarding your level of interest and degree of understanding?

Nonverbal Communication Is Ambiguous. Although nonverbal cues are continuous and frequently involuntary, others can evaluate them in different ways—that is, what we communicate may be ambiguous and subject to misinterpretation. One nonverbal cue can trigger a variety of meanings. For example, wearing jeans can be symbolic of a relaxed mode of dress or it can be construed as a statement of support for the gay community, as when gay organizations without warning surprise blue jean wearers by posting signs that say "Wear jeans if you advocate gay rights."

We use nonverbal cues to signal our attraction for another person.

Nonverbal cues may not mean what others think they do. There could be any number of reasons why a person looks at a watch, coughs, or rubs his or her eyes. All nonverbal behavior should be interpreted within a specific context.

Nonverbal Communication Is Predominantly Relational. Many find it easier to communicate emotions and feelings nonverbally. We convey liking, attraction, anger, and respect for authority nonverbally. In fact, our primary means of revealing our inner states, that typically are not readily transmitted using words, is through nonverbal communication. For example, we usually look to the face to assess emotional state. We look to the mouth to evaluate contempt. We look to the eyes to evaluate dominance and competence. We base our judgments of confidence and relationship closeness on our reading of gestures and posture, and we listen to the voice to help us evaluate both assertiveness and self-confidence.

Sometimes we are unaware of the nonverbal cues we send; as a result, we inadvertently reveal information we would rather conceal. Without intending it, our nonverbal messages let others know how we feel about ourselves and about them. As our awareness of our nonverbal communication increases, its informational value decreases. In effect, a conscious intention to manage the impression we convey means that we will do our best only to communicate messages that are in our own best interest.

Nonverbal Behavior May Reveal Deception. When a person says one thing but means another, we can use our deception detection skills to determine that the person's behavior

WHAT DO YOU KNOW?

True or False

2. *Words used, not nonverbal cues, are more likely to reveal the telling of a lie.*

False. It is easy to lie with words; it is harder to lie nonverbally.

contradicts his or her words. Under most circumstances, when there is a discrepancy or inconsistency between verbal and nonverbal messages, researchers advise that you believe the nonverbal cues, which are more difficult to fake.[3] Deception clues or leakage can be detected in changes in facial or vocal expression, gestures, or slips of the tongue.[4] In fact, once strong emotions are aroused, these changes may occur automatically, with our words, body, and voice betraying us by thwarting our attempts to conceal them.

Researchers David Buller and Judee Burgoon have conducted an array of studies in which they ask subjects to deceive someone. For example, imagine you face the following situation:

> *You and your BFF have agreed that you would see a new film together during winter break. Prior to the break, however, your significant other surprises you by taking you to see the movie you had agreed to see with your friend. What do you do when you return home for winter break and your friend comes over and says, "We're going to be the last people to see that movie, but I didn't want to see it without you. Can we go tonight?"*

According to Buller and Burgoon's **Interpersonal Deception Theory** you have a number of response choices.[5] If you decide not to tell the truth you could lie to your friend by telling him or her how excited you are to finally be able to go see the movie. In other words, you engage in falsification by creating fiction. Or you could say, "I changed my mind. Let's see something else. I heard that movie got bad reviews." You engage in concealment by keeping from your friend your real reason for not want to go to the film. Or you could practice equivocation by changing the subject and dodging the issue altogether. All three potential responses, however, involve deception. Looking at things from your friend's perspective, do you think you could spot the deception if you were not the person lying but the person being lied to? Buller and Burgoon believe that we make poor lie detectors. Many liars, it seems, strategically monitor and control their deceptive displays giving us only a 60 percent chance of being able to identify when someone is lying to us.[6] In fact, our ability to spot the deception depends on how suspicious we are.

Psychologist Paul Ekman, however, believes that with training it is possible for us to become more skilled at detecting dissemblers. Ekman and his co-researcher, Wallace Friesen, identify forty-three muscular movements that we are capable of making with our face. They also identify more than 3,000 facial expressions that have meaning, compiling them into the **Facial Action Coding System**, or FACS, a virtual taxonomy of facial expressions used to interpret emotions and detect deception. Ekman and Friesen have worked for the CIA, the FBI, and more recently Homeland Security to create experimental scenarios for studying deception that could not only facilitate the counterterrorism work of these organizations but also help their agents correctly identify untruths.[7] Paul Ekman's work was the subject of the pop-culture television program *Lie to Me* that first aired in 2009 and for which he served as a consultant.

WHAT DO YOU KNOW?

True or False

3. *Suspicious people are better at spotting deception.*

True. Because liars often try to conceal displays of deception, being suspicious gives you an edge in identifying such attempts.

Theatrical and media performances demonstrate how possible it is for skilled communicators to control the nonverbal cues they exhibit, thereby persuading audience members to suspend their disbelief and accept the façade. Yet most of us do not spend weeks, days, or hours consciously rehearsing for our daily encounters. Nevertheless, when interacting with another, sometimes we may wish to misrepresent our real feelings or intentions, perhaps by dressing differently, by lying, or by masking an actual facial expression so that we do not insult or embarrass the other person. In general, we are more successful at such deceptions if the other person trusts us. The more a person plans and rehearses a deceptive message, the more confident the person is, and the less guilty the person feels about the deception itself, the less likely it is that others will suspect or uncover the person as a liar. Some people are better deceivers. For example, some occupations such as the law, the diplomatic corps, public relations, politics, and sales require that professionals be able to act differently than they may actually feel. This can pose problems for those of us trying to uncover deception.

If we are watchful, however, we can improve our ability to detect deception attempts. Unskilled liars leak clues.[8] It may be a change in facial expression, a shift in posture, a change in breathing, an unusually long pause, a slip of the tongue, a false smile, an ill-timed gesture, or other leaked nonverbal cue that gives them away (See Table 6.2).

The TV series *Lie to Me* starred Tim Roth as an expert in body language who assists law enforcement in revealing deception. The program was based on the real-life work of psychologist Paul Ekman with the CIA, FBI, and Department of Homeland Security.

TABLE 6.2 Nonverbal Clues to Deception

When telling a lie, you are more apt to do the following:

- Smile falsely, using fewer facial muscles than when exhibiting a genuine smile
- Blink more frequently
- Have dilated pupils
- Rub your hands or arms together, scratch the side of your nose, or cover your mouth
- Shift body posture frequently
- Articulate and pronounce words more carefully
- Speak more slowly and say less than you otherwise would
- Exhibit speech that contains more errors and/or hesitation than is typical for you
- Raise your pitch
- Deliver a mixed message

Your lie is more apt to be discovered if you do the following:

- Intentionally want to conceal your emotions
- Feel intensely about keeping the information hidden
- Feel guilty
- Are unfulfilled by lying
- Are unprepared and unrehearsed

SOURCES: Adapted from R. G. Riggio and H. S. Freeman, "Individual Differences and Cues to Deception," *Journal of Personality and Social Psychology,* 45, 1983, p. 899–915; and Paul Ekman and Mark G. Frank, "Lies That Fail," in Michael Lewis and Carolyn Saarni, eds., *Lying and Deception in Everyday Life*, New York: Guilford Press, 1993, p. 184–200.

Interpersonal deception theory: A theory that explains deception as a process based on falsification, concealment, or equivocation.

Facial Action Coding System: A virtual taxonomy of more than three thousand facial expressions used to interpret emotions and detect deception.

TRY THIS: *It's Not Just What You Say . . .*

We are fascinated with lie detection. Are you able to distinguish a liar from a truth teller? Behavioral slipups can betray those who commit them. For example, if a person is trying to communicate an aura of confidence, but his or her foot shakes uncontrollably, then chances are that others present will determine that the person is anxious or uptight rather than confident or in control.

1. Cite an example of how a friend or coworker's behavior contradicted what she said to you or to another person. Specifically, what behavior(s) exhibited by the person leaked his or her true feelings?

2. Think of the last time you interacted with someone you thought was telling you the truth but whom you now know was lying to you. What was it about this person's behavior that initially caused you to believe that he was being truthful, Now, looking back, how many of the following nonverbal clues to deception do you recall the person exhibiting during your interaction?

   - Pausing
   - Hesitations
   - Rapid speaking rate

   - Self-adaptors, such as touching the face and body
   - Object-adaptors, such as touching to playing with objects
   - Deficient eye contact
   - Averted gazes
   - Excessive blinking
   - Pupil dilation
   - Masked Smiles

3. When have you attempted to use nonverbal messages to conceal your actual intentions or feelings? Were you successful? If you were, what do you attribute your success to? If not, why not?

READING NONVERBAL MESSAGES

To improve your ability to read another person, we explore eight nonverbal message categories including (1) kinesics, (2) paralinguistics, (3) proxemics, (4) haptics, (5) olfactics, (6) artifacts and appearance, (7) color, and (8) chronemics. Though for purposes of examination we will discuss each category separately, the meanings stimulated by behavioral cues falling within these categories do not occur in isolation. Instead, they interact with each other, whether reinforcing or diminishing the impact of the perceived cues (see Table 6.3).

TABLE 6.3   Types of Nonverbal Cues

Messages Are Sent by	
Kinesics	Facial expressions, gestures, eye movement, posture, rate of walk
Paralinguistics	How words are spoken, variations in the voice
Proxemics	How space and distance are used
Haptics	Different types of touching
Clothing and artifacts	Appearance, style
Color	Variations in clothing and environmental colors
Chronemics	Using time to communicate

KINESICS: THE MESSAGES OF MOVEMENT

Kinesics is the study of human body motion. It includes such variables as facial expression, eye movement, gestures, posture, and walking speed. Valuable communicator information is contained in the look on your face, whether you stare or avert your gaze, whether your shoulders are straight or drooped, whether you lips are curved in a smile or signal contempt with a sneer, and whether your gait suggests eagerness or anxiety.

Face and Eye Talk. Picture yourself as part of each of the following scenarios:

> Your spouse has had an operation. You are meeting with the doctor to discuss the prognosis. You search the doctor's face, looking for clues.

> You return home a day late from a business trip. Your spouse meets you at the door. As you approach, your eyes focus on the face of your significant other.

Almost immediately, the face of the doctor or your spouse in each situation could cause you to cry, put you at ease, or frighten you.

The Face. The face is the main channel we use to decipher the feelings of others. Quite simply, faces talk. Chatter oozes out of their every movement. In fact, it is wise to depend on facial cues to facilitate person-to-person interaction.

What do faces reveal? Faces tell us many things, including the following:

1. Whether parties to an interaction find it pleasant or unpleasant

2. How interested an individual is in sustaining or terminating contact

3. The degree of involvement of the parties

4. Whether responses during contact are spontaneous or controlled

5. The extent to which messages are understood and shared

The face is also the prime communicator of emotion. Our ability to read the emotions depicted in facial expressions determines whether we will be able to respond appropriately to others' feelings.

How good are you at reading faces? Do your interpretations of facial expressions have a high or a low degree of accuracy? In general, the ability to read another's face increases with familiarity, an understanding of the communication context, and an awareness of behavioral norms. Not everyone is good at reading facial cues. Deficiency in interpreting facial cues of teachers and classmates, for example, may even be a factor in unpopularity and poor grades. Psychologist Stephen Nowicki notes, "Because they are unaware of the messages they are sending, or misinterpreting how other children are feeling, unpopular children may not even realize that they are initiating many of the negative reactions they receive from their peers."[9]

Since they are the most visible and reliable means we have, we also use facial features to identify others and distinguish one person from another.[10] Just as security analysts use faces to identify potential terrorists, crime victims describe suspects' faces for police artists to draw, parents of missing children describe their children's faces to authorities, and relatives, friends, and acquaintances describe your facial features to others.

WHAT DO YOU KNOW?

True or False

4. Your hands reveal more about your feelings than does your face.

False. The face is the prime revealer of feelings.

Kinesics: The study of human body motion.

Aside from identifying you, your facial appearance influences judgments of your physical attractiveness and approachability.[11] Additionally, your face affects whether others assess you to be dominant or submissive.[12] Thus, we speak of a baby face, a face as cold as ice, a face as strong as a bulldog's, and so on. What words would you use to describe your face, a friend's face, or the face of your significant other?

The Eyes. "Shifty eyes." "Goo-goo eyes." "The evil eye." "Eye to eye." Eye behaviors are a key part of interpersonal communication, as we use our eyes to establish, maintain, and terminate contact. As with all nonverbal cues, the messages you send with your eyes may be interpreted in a variety of ways, but there are three central functions eye movements serve:

1. Eyes reveal the extent of interest and emotional involvement.

2. Eyes influence judgments of persuasiveness and perceptions of dominance or submissiveness.

3. Eyes regulate person-to-person interaction.

Looking others in the eye can help you appear more honest and credible.

The pupils of our eyes are a reliable indicator of emotion. When we take an interest in what another is saying, our blinking rate decreases and our pupils dilate. Of course, the opposite is equally true. When we are uninterested, our pupils contract.[13] Similarly, our pupils dilate when we experience a positive emotion and contract when we experience a negative one. They rarely, if ever, lie, because regulating pupil size is a nonverbal cue beyond our conscious control.

In order for others to find you persuasive, you must refrain from excessive blinking and maintain a steady gaze, that is, neither look down nor look away from the person(s) you are trying to convince; also, you must not exhibit eye flutter. In some cultures, including Arabic, Latin American, and southern European cultures, individuals judge those who look them in the eye as more honest and credible than those who do not. In American culture, when others avoid meeting our eyes or avert their gaze, we are likely to assume that they have something to hide, they lack confidence, or they are unknowledgeable on some matter.[14]

Visual dominance correlates with increased eye contact, whereas frequently averted eyes generate impressions of submissiveness. Like apes, human can "stare down" each other to establish dominance. Look away first, and you may well find that you have become the less powerful player in an interaction. However, again it is important not to draw a wrong conclusion based on a cultural misunderstanding.

Eye contact also indicates whether a communication channel is open. It is much easier to avoid interacting if we have not made eye contact, because once we do, interaction virtually becomes an obligation.[15] When we like one another or want to express our affection, we also increase our eye contact.

FIGURE 6.1 Eye Movements and Cognitive Processing

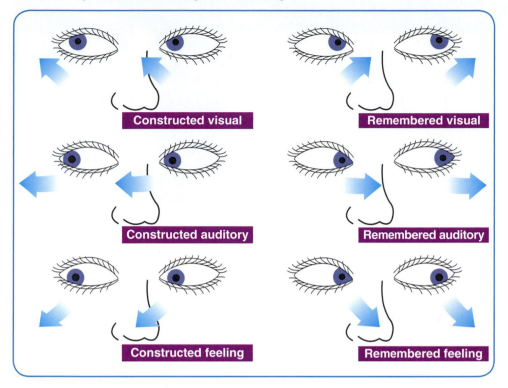

The eyes provide another cue we can use to enhance the establishment of behavior synchrony or behavioral mirroring with another in an effort to establish or advance our relationship. We establish behavioral synchrony by using nonverbal cues that are in sync with the other person's. According to Richard Bandler and John Grinder, a relationship exists between eye movements and thought or cognitive processing—including whether a person is primarily a visual, auditory, kinesthetic, or emotional processor. As a result of their research, Bandler and Grinder were able to identify eye movement patterns and their meanings for right-handed people (the reverse tends to be true for left-handed people) (see Figure 6.1). Since such eye movements reflect a person's preferred sensory modality, you can use them to get on the same wavelength and promote interaction between you—increasing interpersonal intimacy.

While their work is controversial, Bandler and Grindler contend that you can also use eye movements to determine how truthful a person is. If, for example, a person is describing an event experienced firsthand, the person's eyes should move primarily to his or her left (if the person is right-handed), suggesting memory access. If, however, the person looks up and to the right a lot, it may be that he or she is constructing the experience, not recalling it.[16] In addition to providing a window into the soul, revealing a person's emotions to others, the eyes may offer a window into whether or not a person is telling the truth.

Putting on a Face: The Ethics of Face-Work. "Put on a happy face!" instructs a once popular song. Have you ever followed such advice when you did not feel happy inside? Could others tell you were not really happy?

When we use our facial expressions to communicate genuine inner feelings, we exhibit **representational facial expressions**.[17] Conversely, when we consciously control our face to communicate a message meant only for public consumption, for all practical purposes we

Representational facial expressions: Exhibited facial expressions that communicate genuine inner feelings.

In his classic novel *Nineteen Eighty-Four,* author George Orwell alludes to the practice of masking facial expressions in order not to let those in authority know what you are really thinking. The citizens of Orwell's dystopia know that the smallest movement could betray them. Afraid to commit a "facecrime," they make great efforts not to look nervous for fear others will think they have something to hide. They seek to communicate only state-sanctioned feelings; any citizens who fail at this place themselves in danger of being arrested.

Such concerns, of course, have become a part of real life in the twenty-first century. In fact, recently the U.S. Department of Homeland Security had airport security professional trained in how to detect faked facial expressions. However, while we may try to conceal our real feelings, it is not typically because we fear the state's retribution, but instead because we fear that others may not approve of them or may be hurt by them.

1. Can you remember a time when you (or someone near you) were called out for committing a facecrime? What might have led you or the other person to commit the act? What was the outcome?

2. Should the concept of facecrime exist? Explain your position.

SOURCE: *George* Orwell, *Nineteen Eighty-Four* (1949), New York: New American Library, 1983.

---

are giving a performance; hence, our facial expressions are labeled **presentational facial expressions**. It is when we consciously control our facial expressions that we likely are engaging in interpersonal deception.

What techniques do we use to "put on a face"? First, we may qualify our facial expression—that is, we add another expression that modifies the impact of the original expression. Second, we may modulate our facial expression; we simply change it to reflect feelings that are somewhat more or less intense than what we actually feel. Third, we may falsify directly. This requires that we simulate an unfelt emotion, neutralize an emotion by showing none when we actually feel some emotion, or mask a felt emotion by displaying one that we do not really feel.[18] Which of these techniques have you caught yourself using?

When we fake a face, usually we leave an array of clues for astute observers. For example, our "face-work" may lack spontaneity or be out of sync with our words or actions, or we may exhibit involuntary cues, in which an expression appears on our face for only a fraction of a second. What begins as a smile becomes ever so briefly a grimace and then is reengineered back into a smile. We call these fleeting emotional changes, lasting no more than one-eighth to one-fifth of a second, **microfacial** or **micromomentary expressions**. Such expressions reveal our emotional states and typically occur when we attempt to disguise or conceal those states. Thus, a twitch of the mouth or the eyebrow can suggest that the emotion being communicated is not the emotion actually being felt.

Sometimes the simple act of smiling actually evokes a positive mood change in the person smiling. Still, the degree to which people demonstrate susceptibility to deliberately engineered facial expressions varies greatly. On the other hand, the total lack of the physical ability to smile, a condition called *Möbius syndrome,* leaves one with a perpetually grumpy look, making it difficult for individuals afflicted to experience normal interpersonal relationships. Though it may be unintended, the lack of a smile causes others to perceive the unsmiling person as unfriendly or bored.[19]

Presentational facial expressions: Facial expressions that are consciously controlled.

Microfacial/ micromomentary expression: An expression lasting no more than one-eighth to one-fifth of a second that usually occurs when an individual consciously or unconsciously attempts to disguise or conceal an emotion and that reveals an actual emotional state.

Gestures and Posture: The Body in Motion and at Rest. We move and stand in distinctive ways—so distinctive that often others can identify us by our characteristic walk or posture. The movements and alignment of our body communicate. Although some of our body's messages facilitate effective person-to-person interaction, others—whether sent consciously or unconsciously—impede it. What kinds of cues do different bodily movements send?

Cue Categories. Paul Ekman and Wallace Friesen identify five categories of nonverbal behavior that we can use to describe bodily cues: emblems, illustrators, regulators, affect displays, and adaptors.[20] We explore each in turn in the following (see also Table 6.4).

Emblems: Deliberate movements of the body that are consciously sent and easily translated into speech.

Illustrators: Bodily cues designed to enhance receiver comprehension of speech by supporting or reinforcing it.

Regulators: Communication cues intentionally used to influence turn taking and to control the flow of conversation.

TABLE 6.4   Types of Bodily Cues

Cue Category	Description	Examples
Emblems	Deliberate body movements that can translate into speech	Thumbs-up, wave hello
Illustrators	Body cues that support or reinforce speech	Direction pointing
Regulators	Intentional cues to influence turn taking	Head nods, breaking eye contact
Affect displays	Unintentional movements of the body that reflect emotional states of being	Slumping body; relaxed, confident body
Adaptors	Unintentional movements that are frequently interpreted as signs of nervousness	Nose scratches, hair twirling

Emblems are movements of the body that are consciously sent and easily translated into speech, such as a wave that means "come here," a thumbs-up gesture that means "okay," and a wave that means "hello" or "good-bye." We most frequently use emblems when noise or distance makes it less feasible that we will be understood through the use of words alone. Traders on the floor of a stock exchange and sports umpires and coaches on the playing field use emblems regularly; for them, emblems compose a gesture system.[21]

Illustrators are bodily cues designed to enhance receiver comprehension of speech by supporting or reinforcing it. As we do with emblems, we use illustrators consciously and deliberately. For example, when you give someone directions, you use illustrators to facilitate your task. When you want to stress the shortness of a member of a basketball team compared to the average height of team members, you use your hands to emphasize the difference.

Regulators are cues we use intentionally to influence turn taking— who speaks, when, and for how long. For example, gazing at someone talking to you and nodding your head usually encourages the person to continue speaking, while leaning forward in your seat, tensing your posture, and breaking eye contact traditionally

The person in this picture is using an illustrator to clarify the directions he is giving.

signals that you would like a turn. If we ignore or remain unaware of another's use of regulators, the other person may accuse us of rudeness or insensitivity. Your use or misuse of regulators reveals much about your social skills.[22]

Affect displays are movements of the body that reflect emotional states of being. While our face, as we have noted, is the prime indicator of the emotion we are experiencing, it is our body that reveals the emotion's intensity. Typically, we are less aware of our affect displays because often we do not intend to send many of them. People who "read" our bodies on the basis of its demeanor can judge how we genuinely feel.[23] For example, you might describe another person's body as slumping and defeated, still and motionless, relaxed and confident, or proud and victorious. Those of us who characteristically show a lack of affect or feeling make it especially difficult for others to relate to us meaningfully.

As we do with affect displays, we unintentionally use **adaptors** that involuntarily reveal information about our psychological state at the same time they meet our own physical or emotional needs. Adaptors include movements such as nose scratches, hand over lips, chin stroking, and hair twirling. Individuals interacting with us or observing us interpret these as signs of nervousness, tension, or lack of self-assurance.

Decoding the Body's Messages. Others form impressions of us and may judge us to be more or less likable, assertive, or powerful based on observations of our physical behavior. Watching a person's body can help us answer questions such as the following:

Do individuals like or dislike one another? When we like each other, we tend to exhibit open postures and more direct body orientation, and we stand more closely together than when we do not. Our bodies are also relatively relaxed, and our gestures are uninhibited and natural. Such cues tend to stimulate interaction. In contrast, if we do not like each other, our bodies emit very different cues. Instead of facing each other directly, we exhibit incongruent and indirect body orientations. We are also likely to avoid sustained eye contact and display a high degree of bodily tension and rigidity. It is harder to like someone who is closed off or all wrapped up in him- or herself.

Is a person being assertive or nonassertive? An assertive person's nonverbal behavior is more relaxed and expansive than the nonverbal behavior of someone who is nonassertive.

Affect displays:
Unintentional movements of the body that reflect the intensity of an emotional state of being.

Adaptors:
Unintentional movements of the body that reveal information about psychological state or inner needs, such as nervousness.

Typically, a nonassertive person adopts a rigid posture, exhibits an array of nervous gestures, avoids sustained eye contact, and hunches his or her shoulders in a protective or closed stance. In contrast, the assertive counterpart exhibits comfortable eye contact and employs illustrators in place of confidence-deflating adaptors that announce vulnerability.

Is an individual powerful or powerless? If you have an erect but relaxed posture, gesture dynamically, feel free to stare at others, and interject your own thoughts even if it means interrupting another person, you are likely to be perceived as powerful. On the other hand, visible bodily tension, a downward gaze, and closed posture will contribute to perceptions of you as powerless.

Thus, whether or not we want to approach or avoid another person, and whether we assess him or her to be confident or anxious, powerful or powerless, is often influenced by the bodily cues we receive. Our bodies talk constantly about how we feel about ourselves and how we feel about others. Even when we try to "stonewall" someone in an effort to cut off our communication, our body continues talking.

GO ▶

WATCH THIS 6.1
For a video on effective nonverbal cues visit the student study site.

PARALINGUISTICS: THE MESSAGES OF THE VOICE

The messages that you send with your voice are known as **paralanguage**. Often it is not what you say but how you say it that determines an interaction's outcome. We rely on vocal cues to help us determine the real meaning of spoken words. Such cues are especially important when we are deciding whether someone is being sarcastic. The words "Yeah, right" convey different meanings depending on whether they are spoken sincerely or sarcastically, and our interpretation of these words influences how we respond to the person who said them.

The tone of your voice can help you communicate what you mean to convey, or it can reveal thoughts you mean to conceal. It can reinforce or negate the words you speak. The sound of your voice communicates, revealing to others your emotional state, attitudes, personality, status, and interaction maintenance, or turn-taking, needs. How you speak influences how others interpret your intentions, as well as how credible, intelligent, or attractive they judge you to be.[24] With this in mind, respond to the following questions:

The sound of your voice affects how others respond to your words.

- Does my voice enhance or detract from the impression I make?

- Does my voice support or contradict my intended meaning?

- If I were interacting with me, would I want to listen to the sound of my voice?

Paralanguage:
Messages sent using only vocal cues.

Among the elements of paralanguage are pitch, volume, rate, articulation, pronunciation, hesitations, and silence. Each plays a part in the impressions others form of you.

Pitch. Pitch is the highness or lowness of the voice; it is similar to pitch on a musical scale. We associate higher pitches with female voices and lower pitches with male voices. We also develop vocal stereotypes. We associate low-pitched voices with strength, sexiness, and maturity, and high-pitched voices with helplessness, tension, and nervousness. Although we each have a modal or habitual pitch—one that we use most frequently when we speak—we also vary our pitch to reflect our mood and interest in conversing. For example, we often lower our pitch when sad and raise it when excited. In contrast, if we are bored, we may speak in a monotone that reflects our lack of interest. A lively animated pitch encourages interaction, whereas a monotone discourages it.

It is the voice's pitch that others use to determine whether you are making a statement or asking a question or whether you are expressing concern or conviction. Your pitch expresses your emotional state; for instance, it can communicate anger or annoyance, patience or tolerance.

Volume. The power of your voice, its loudness or volume, also affects perceptions of intended meaning. While some whisper their way through encounters, others blast through them. An individual who is typically loud may alienate others; such a person is often viewed as overbearing or aggressive. In contrast, if you are soft-spoken, others may interpret your behavior as timidity. Thus, your volume can over- or underwhelm, thereby causing others to turn you off in an effort to turn you down or to lose interest in your words simply because they cannot Comfortably hear them.

Effective Interpersonal Communicators Regulate Volume in an Effort to Promote Meaningful Interaction. Your volume should reflect the nature of your message, the size and acoustics of the space you are in, your proximity to the other person, and any competing noise or conversations. Typically, we increase volume to stress particular words and ideas and to reflect the intensity of our emotions. Similarly, a sudden decrease in volume can add suspense or sustain another's attention. Volume that is varied is most effective.

Rate. Speaking rate is the third vocal cue affecting the communication of meaning. Most of us speak at an average rate of 150 words per minute. When we speed up our speech, exceeding 275 to 300 words per minute, it is difficult for others to comprehend what we are saying, and our message thus becomes virtually unintelligible. In contrast, if we speak too slowly, others may perceive us as tentative or lacking in confidence or intelligence. An overly deliberate speaking pace contributes to boredom, lack of attentiveness, and unresponsiveness in others. Rate also affects others' judgment of our intensity and mood. As your rate increases, so do assessments of your level of emotional intensity.[25] When talking about more serious subjects, we often slow down; on the other hand, our speaking rate usually accelerates as we shift to talking about lighter topics. In many ways, rate reflects the pulse of your words. It quickens to relay agitation, excitement, and happiness, and it falls to convey seriousness, serenity, or sadness.

Articulation and Pronunciation. The sound attributes of articulation and pronunciation affect message intelligibility as well as perceptions of credibility. **Articulation** is the way you pronounce individual sounds. Ideally, even during person-to-person contact, the sounds of your speech are sharp and distinct. When you fail to utter a final sound (a final *t* or *d*, for example), fail to produce the sounds of words properly, or voice a sound in an unclear, imprecise way (*come wimme* versus *come with me, dem* versus *them, idear* versus *idea*), perceptions of your credibility drop.

Articulation: How individual words are pronounced.

While the focus of articulation is on the production of speech sounds, the focus of **pronunciation** is on whether you say the words themselves correctly. When you mispronounce a word, you may suffer a loss of credibility, and those listening to you may find it more difficult to make sense of what you are saying.

Hesitations and Silence. Hesitations and silence are the final paralinguistic variables we will consider here. Knowing when to pause is a critical skill. When nervous or tense, we may exhibit a tendency to fill all pauses, often by inserting meaningless sounds or phrases such as *uh, you know,* or *okay* in the effort to fill voids. These **nonfluencies**, or hesitation phenomena, disrupt the natural flow of speech and adversely affect how others perceive your competence and confidence.

In addition to slowing the rate of speech and emphasizing key ideas, brief periods of silence or pauses give us a chance to gather our thoughts. This is not to suggest that a pause's message is always positive. Sustained pauses—significantly extended periods of silence—allow us to give another the "silent treatment," a means by which we ignore a person, saying to him or her without using words, "As far as I am concerned, you do not exist." We also tend to become silent during moments of extreme anxiety or annoyance.

PROXEMICS: SPACE AND DISTANCE TALKS

Our use of space and distance also reveals how we feel about ourselves and what we think of others. As with kinesics and paralinguistics, space and distance communicate.

Generally, we use physical proximity and distance to signal either desire to communicate or disinterest in communicating. The closer we stand, the greater the chances are that we like

Pronunciation: The conventional treatment of the sounds of a word.

Nonfluencies: Hesitation phenomena; nonlinguistic verbalizations.

one another. Proximity or lack of it also indicates how dominant or submissive we are in a relationship. The more dominant we feel, the more likely we are to move closer to another; in contrast, the more submissive we feel, the less likely we are to decrease our interaction distance. Perceptions of friendliness or unfriendliness and extroversion or introversion, as well as our privacy and social contact needs, are also reflected in our spatial relationships. As we study how we use space and distance to communicate, keep in mind that a gap may exist between the messages we intend to send using space and distance and the messages that others actually receive and interpret.

The father of proxemics research, Edward T. Hall, coined the term **proxemics** to indicate that "proximity" influences human interaction. The word itself refers to how we use the personal space around us as we interact with others as well as how we structure the space around us in our homes, offices, and communities (territory).[26]

Spatial Relationships: Near or Far. Hall identified four distances that distinguish the kinds of interactions we have and the relationships we share during them (it should be noted that Hall's research involved only white Americans):

Intimate distance	Contact to 18 inches
Personal distance	18 inches to 4 feet
Social-consultative distance	4 to 12 feet
Public distance	12 feet to the limit of sight

Intimate distance ranges from skin contact to 18 inches from another person. At this distance physical touching is normal. While we usually share such closeness with those we trust and with whom we share an emotional bond, this is also the distance used for physical combat and sexual harassment. For example, have you ever had someone physically "in your face" to the point that you wished he or she would just "back off"? At times, in crowded spaces such as elevators, buses, or theater lobbies, we have to put up with intimate distance between ourselves and strangers—people we would not ordinarily stand so near.

Personal distance, which ranges from 18 inches to 4 feet, is less proximate or personal than intimate distance. While we can still hold or shake the hand of another at this distance, we are most likely merely to converse informally. We use this distance at social events such as receptions or when talking between classes or during coffee breaks. If we unilaterally close the gap between personal and intimate distance, we may make the person we are interacting with feel uncomfortable. On the other hand, if we widen the distance between us, we may make him or her feel rejected.

Proxemics: The study of how space and distance are used to communicate.

Intimate distance: From skin contact to 18 inches from another person; the distance usually used by people who trust each other or who share an emotional bond or closeness.

Personal distance: distance: From 18 inches to 4 feet from a person; the distance at which we are most apt to converse informally.

The amount of distance we maintain between us reveals the nature of our relationship.

Social distance extends from 4 feet to 12 feet. At this distance we are less apt to talk about personal matters, more able to keep another at arm's length, and thus more likely to conduct business or discuss issues that are neither private nor of a personal nature. Many of our discussions during meals, conferences, or meetings are held within social distance range. Often we use objects such as desks or tables to maintain appropriate distance in these settings. Usually, the more distance we keep between us, the more formal our interaction becomes.

Public distance (12 feet and beyond) is the distance we use to remove ourselves physically from interaction, to communicate with strangers, or to address large groups. Public distance is much less likely than smaller distances to involve interpersonal communication.

People from different cultures maintain the same four categories, but not necessarily the same distances. For example, Latin Americans use the smallest conversational space, European Americans use more space than Latin Americans do, and African Americans use even more impersonal space than European Americans do.[27] In addition, as common sense tells us, cultural and family backgrounds also influence our use of space and personal body boundaries. Unlike the United States, where land tends to be plentiful and family size averages three or four, in countries where land is scarcer and families are larger, people live in tighter spaces, spaces that by our standards might be small or confining.

What happens when we violate distance norms? **Expectancy violation theory** researchers tell us that the outcomes of such violations can be positive. For example, if we perceive the approaching person closing the distance between us as attractive or a high-reward source, our evaluation of him or her may become more favorable, especially if the distance violation is accompanied by other behaviors, such as compliments.[28] More frequently, however, we may feel uncomfortable or violated when another person invades our personal space.

Understanding proxemics affords us opportunities to improve our relationships. By becoming aware of how space communicates, we attune ourselves to the nature of acceptable and unacceptable proxemic behavior. Although some studies reveal that "spatial invasions" may, under some conditions, achieve positive outcomes, we ought not be too quick to dismiss the fact that spatial violations have also led to lawsuits and violence.

Places and Their Spaces: Decoding the Environment. Three kinds of environmental space concern us: fixed-feature space, semi-fixed-feature space, and informal space (see Table 6.5).[29] Each affects communication in different ways.

Fixed-feature space involves the permanent characteristics of an environment—including walls, doors, built-in cabinets, windows, in-ground pools, roads, and paths—that functionalize it and determine how we will use it. For example, window placement often determines the front of a classroom, swimming pools provide opportunities for increased interaction, and aisles in shopping malls and stores route customers in an effort to promote sales.

Social distance: From 4 feet to 12 feet from another person; the interpersonal distance we usually use to conduct business or discuss nonpersonal issues.

Public distance: A distance of 12 feet and beyond; the distance we use to remove ourselves physically from interaction, to communicate with strangers, or to address large groups.

Expectancy violation theory: A theory that addresses our reactions to nonverbal behavior and notes that violations of nonverbal communication norms can be positive or negative.

Fixed-feature space: Space as defined by the permanent characteristics of an environment.

TABLE 6.5 It's about Space

Type of Space	Represented by	Example
Fixed-feature space	Permanent characteristics of the environment	Walls, Doors
Semi-fixed-feature space	Movable objects	Plants, Furniture
Informal or non-fixed-feature space	Our space	Personal bubble

Semi-fixed-feature space uses movable objects such as furniture, plants, temporary walls, and paintings to identify boundaries and either promote or inhibit interaction. For instance, desks can reduce contact, while chairs facing each other can increase it. Compare the amount of interaction occurring in a physician's waiting room, where chairs line a wall, with the amount of interaction occurring in restaurants, where chairs are positioned to encourage conversation. Some rooms say, "Use me," and actually bring people together, while others say, "Look at me," and keep people out.

When is it acceptable for another person to invade your territory?

Informal space or **non-fixed-feature space** is the space we carry around with us. It is invisible, highly mobile, and enlarged or contracted at will as we try to keep individuals at a distance or bring them closer. The amount of personal space we claim, the size of our personal bubble, changes as we move from interaction to interaction, relationship to relationship.

Territoriality: Yours and Mine.

Territoriality is another proxemics variable related to our use of informal space. Each of us lays claim to, or identifies as our own, spatial areas that we seek to protect or defend from intrusion. We devise various means to accomplish this, some more formal than others: nameplates, fences, stone walls, assigned chairs, or signs that say things such as "My Room." While it may not be logical to claim certain spaces, it is typical. Think of how often you have stopped someone from taking a specific seat, saying, "That's my chair," or "Don't sit there—that's Dad's seat."

Semi-fixed-feature space: Space in which movable objects are used to identify boundaries and promote or inhibit interaction.

Informal space or non-fixed-feature space: The invisible space each person carries around.

Territoriality: The claiming or identifying of space as one's own.

Haptics: The study of how touch communicates.

Problems may develop when another invades territory we have identified as ours. Sometimes we fight over spaces, or we get upset when someone uses space we think is ours without our permission. To restore our comfort and prevent another from continuing to occupy our space, we may chastise a person who, without our authorization, put his or her things on our desk or in our room.

In professional settings, territory claimed tends to reflect status. CEOs and company presidents typically are accorded more favorable and larger office spaces than are managers. The former also are able to employ more markers, such as outer offices with assistants, to keep others out. While higher-status individuals can enter the spaces of lower-status people unannounced, the opposite is rarely true.

HAPTICS: TOUCH

In the discussion on proxemics, we noted that intimate space extends from the point of touch to 18 inches. **Haptics**, or touch, is usually involved in our closest relationships. While always part of sexual communication, touch also plays a role in helping us develop closer relationships and is a key ingredient in the establishment and maintenance of many of our personal relationships.

Touching signals the desire for closeness. As children we likely were introduced to various touching no-no's. For example, we might have been instructed to keep our hands to ourselves around people—and not to touch when around breakable items. However, touch remains an important tool in interpersonal communication, and the messages it communicates, as we shall see, are varied.

The amount of touching we do or find acceptable is, at least in part, culturally conditioned. As with proxemics, a set of norms governs our use of touch. When others violate these norms, we may experience discomfort. Although some cultures promote only limited touching, others promote more frequent touch. Members belonging to a given culture generally conform to its established norms. In the United States, for instance, it is more acceptable for women to touch each other than it is for men to touch each other.[30] Touch also correlates positively with openness, comfort with relationships, and the ability to express feelings.[31]

Touch is an element of our closest relationships.

We use touch for different purposes: to communicate attitude or affect, to encourage affiliation, and to exert control or power.[32] To demonstrate our concern for others, we often touch them. In some ways, beginning early in our lives, touch serves a therapeutic function. Infants wither emotionally and physically when not touched, and they thrive when picked up and held. Our entrance into and our exit from this world typically involve touch. Unfortunately, although touch is our most effective means of demonstrating affect or support, and it is important for the maintenance of both physiological and psychological health, as we get older we are often touched less.

Touch also helps us exert status or power in relationships. People of higher status usually initiate touch. Thus, it is more likely you will see the CEO pat a worker on the shoulder than vice versa.[33] The person who initiates touch is also the one who usually controls or directs the interaction. The person touching typically is perceived to have more power and to be more assertive than the person he or she is touching. Thus, the touching act itself implies power. Sometimes, however, rather than communicating liking or concern, touch signals dislike, dominance, aggression, or abuse; shoves, pokes, and slaps fall into this category.

The amount of consensual touching two people do indicates how much they like each other. Touch is part of relationship development and is used as a guide to gauge the amount of intimacy desired. We touch those we like and try not to be touched by those we dislike.

Touch also marks greetings and leave-takings. Even a handshake can be social and polite or friendly and warm.

ARTIFACTUAL COMMUNICATION AND APPEARANCE

What clothing or jewelry do you like to wear? What do your appearance, hairstyle, and mode of dress and personal adornments suggest to others about you? Do others find your bodily appearance and attire pleasing and appropriate?[34] And how does what you wear affect you?

Artifactual communication and appearance influence our reactions. In the early stages of a relationship, what we wear and how we look affect first impressions and may even lead to our being accepted or rejected. In addition, the clothing and jewelry we wear can cause others to form judgments regarding our success, character, power, and competence. Typically, we respond more positively to those we perceive to be well dressed than to those whose attire we find questionable or unacceptable. In the past, Americans were more apt to respond to requests from well-dressed individuals, including those in uniform, than they were to listen to or emulate individuals whose dress suggested lower status or a lack of authority,[35] but things may be changing. During the past few presidential campaigns, candidates have dressed more casually in the effort to come off as accessible and as "empathetic, regular Joes."[36]

Unfortunately, many believe we live in a looks-based culture. They may be right. It appears that tall men, slender people, and attractive women are awarded a premium for their height, thinness, and beauty. For example, when it comes to height, taller people seem to win elections and jobs. Men actually make almost $800 a year more for every extra inch of height. When it comes to weight, individuals who are obese or overweight are treated more unkindly, with heavier people earning less than slim people or people of average weight. In like fashion, persons others judge to be unattractive receive lower salaries than do persons judged attractive. Attractiveness also appears to be a factor for people facing prison, with less attractive people receiving longer sentences than their more attractive peers.[37]

Recent research has also discovered that what we wear affects our cognitive processes, reflecting the findings of a new scientific field called "embodied cognition." According to a study conducted by Hajo Adam and Adam D. Galinsky, because of this, if you wear a white coat you believe belongs to a physician, your ability to pay attention improves significantly. If, however, you think the same white coat belongs to a painter, no such improvement occurs. Quite simply, the clothing we have on not only influences how others see us but, by transforming our psychological state, also affects how we think about ourselves.[38]

What we wear and how we look helps others form impressions of us. What do the artifacts you wear suggest to others about you?

Are you, for example, familiar with the television hit *Mad Men*? Acknowledging the show's popularity, a recent news headline proclaimed "Now You Can Look Like the Drapers." The story reported on a major national retailer's decision to introduce a *Mad Men* line, with clothing and accessories based on the show offered for sale to the public. The hit status of *Mad Men* made the clothing of the 1960s the style to wear in the second decade of the twenty-first century![39] If you wanted to look like Betty Draper, you might have bought A-line dresses, while Don Draper made the thin tie and fitted jacket into a statement. Some fans even created avatars of themselves dressed as their favorite *Mad Men* characters, and others adopted the actual hairstyles worn by the characters they most admired. Some used all their nonverbal wiles to capture the essence of the series, even purposefully mimicking the speech cadences and gestures of characters.

The craze for retro fashion tells a story. Back in *Mad Men* days, clothing echoed gender roles and helped prepare us for the transition from domestic roles for women to roles that were more progressive, as many women of the day forsook meekness, cherishing their new independence.[40] The show's costumers are conscious and deliberative in their use of fashion as nonverbal message.

OLFACTICS: SMELL

Who smells good to you? How good do you smell to others? Through the years, the desire to use and appeal to the sense of smell or **olfactics** has spawned numerous industries offering products such as perfumes and colognes, mouthwashes and deodorants, household disinfectants, scented candles, and aromatherapy oils. Unlike the members of some cultures, Americans are into masking their natural bodily odors, preferring to use smell as an attractor by substituting pleasant for unpleasant smells in the effort to trigger emotional reactions, sexual arousal, romance, or friendship. For example, women prefer men who smell similar to them.[41] Gay men respond to smell much as women do, and in ways that are distinct from those of heterosexual men.[42]

Smell and the recall of good and bad memories go hand in hand. When something bad happens, for example, our sense of smell sharpens, as if going on high alert to warn us of impeding danger.[43] Of course, we also have good memories related to the presence of pleasing smells, such as freshly baked cookies and flowers blooming.

COLOR: ASSOCIATIONS AND CONNECTIONS

Color talks both to and about us. The colors we surround ourselves with and the colors we wear affect us both physically and emotionally. For example, research has found that when a person is exposed to pure red for extended periods, the nervous system is excited, and blood pressure, respiration rate, and heart rate rise. In contrast, when the person is similarly exposed to dark blue, a calming effect occurs, and blood pressure, respiration, and heart rate fall.[44] Color may help compel us to move more quickly or slowly, help us relax, or cause us to become agitated. People who regularly wear red tend to be more active, outgoing, and impatient than those who avoid the color.

Fast-food chains, product marketers, department stores, and law enforcement agencies use our predictable reactions to various colors as behavioral conditioners. For example, because the color green encourages oral interaction, it is common practice for investigators to question suspects in green rooms, or in rooms where the lighting is green. Of course, green also prompts

Slick sixties fashions are an important part of the popularity of the television drama *Mad Men*. The costumes evoke the spirit of the era and communicate the characters' personalities.

Smell can attract or repel. How do you use smell in your efforts to attract others?

Olfactics: The study of the sense of smell.

Color affects us both physically and emotionally. How does the color red affect you?

ecological associations. Table 6.6 indicates how marketers use color to target consumers.[45] In which group would you place yourself?

Colors do not evoke the same meanings in all cultures. For example, whereas in the United States and European countries brides routinely wear white, in Asian countries white is the color of mourning and so not considered suitable for weddings. In India, if a bride wears white, at least a touch of another color is usually added. In Ghana blue signifies joy; in Iran it has negative connotations. In the United States yellow suggests caution or cowardice; in China it represents wealth. Korean Buddhists reserve the color red for writing a person's name upon his or her death. What meanings do different colors have for you?

In their efforts to influence our reactions to color, some paint companies give their colors new names. For example, Sherwin-Williams has a color called Synergy (a shade of green), and Ace Paint has Hey There (a yellowish color)—words that give new meaning to color.[46] The names of the colors suggest how they are likely to influence communication.

CHRONEMICS: THE COMMUNICATIVE VALUE OF TIME

Chronemics is the study of how we use time to communicate. Some of us are preoccupied with time, while others regularly waste it. Some of us are typically early, while others are chronically late. Some of us approach life with a sense of urgency, while others prefer a more leisurely pace. Some of us are early birds, functioning best in the morning, while others, night owls, perform best at night.

TABLE 6.6 Color Matters

First, look only at the color palette in the first column. Rank the colors shown, from the color you prefer most (your favorite) to the color you prefer least.

Once you have completed your ranking, consider the accompanying color preference descriptions. To what extent, if any, do you think they accurately describe you?

Color	Meaning/Personality	Communicates
Gray	Neutrality	Noninvolvement, concealment, or lack of commitment
Blue	Calmness	Contentment, being at peace
Green	Growth	Persistence, high self-esteem, constancy
Red	Energy	Intensity, conquest, fullness of living
Yellow	Happiness	Lack of inhibition, a desire for change
Violet	Enchantment	Longing for wish fulfillment, a desire to charm others
Brown	Security	Need for physical ease and contentment, for release from discomfort
Black	Nothingness	Surrender, renunciation

SOURCE: Based on Max Luscher, *The Luscher Color Test*, translated and edited by Ian Scott, New York: Random House, 1969.

Chronemics: The study of how humans use time to communicate.

FIGURE 6.2 How Often Are You Late for Work?

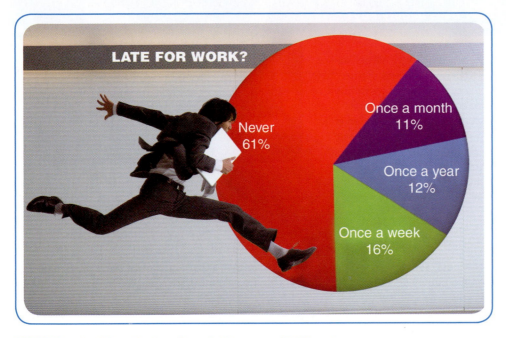

SOURCE: Based on information from CareerBuilder survey of 7,780 workers.

Misunderstandings, miscalculations, and disagreements involving time can create communication and relationship problems. What does it mean to be "on time"? How is the concept of punctuality construed? To be "on time" for a job interview may be interpreted differently from what it means to be "on time" for a cocktail party. The latter usually allows more flexibility.

We also structure time in an effort to ensure we accomplish needed tasks. How long we are willing to wait to meet with someone or for something to occur is also a reflection of our status and the value we place on what we are waiting for. Status affords us greater power to control both our own time and others' time. The more status a person has, the longer others with less status will wait to see him or her.[47]

Our culture influences how we use and think about time. In some cultures people live for today, but in others they are waiting for tomorrow. Thus, even the meaning of the phrase "a long time" is influenced by how a culture's members conceive of time.

CULTURE AND NONVERBAL BEHAVIOR

Our culture modifies our use of nonverbal cues. For example, individuals who belong to **contact cultures,** such as Saudi Arabia, France, and Italy, relish the intimacy of contact; when interacting, they tend to display their warmth, closeness, and availability to one another, tend to be comfortable standing close to each other, seek maximum sensory experience, and touch each other frequently. In contrast, members of **noncontact cultures** or lower-contact cultures, such as Scandinavia, Germany, England, Japan, and the United

Contact cultures: Cultures that encourage nonverbal displays of warmth, closeness, and availability.

Noncontact cultures: Cultures that discourage the use of nonverbal displays of warmth, closeness, and availability.

Research reveals a connection between perceived attractiveness, mating, and income. In Daniel S. Hamermesh's book *Beauty Pays: Why Attractive People Are More Successful,* the accomplished economist explains why he believes attractive people make more money than unattractive people—some $230,000 more over the course of their lives. According to Hamermesh, this is true even in professions where beauty should not be an issue, such as education and sports. Additionally, Hamermesh reports that men suffer more monetarily for being labeled unattractive than do women, with women earning some 3 percent less and men earing a whopping 22 percent less than more attractive cohorts.

Consider these questions:

1. If we know the cost of unattractiveness, should those judged below average on the beauty scale be protected in the same way we protect people from racism and sexism?

2. Have you ever penalized another or been penalized in some way yourself for your looks? Explain.

SOURCES: For example, see Mads Meier Jaeger, "A Thing of Beauty Is a Joy Forever"? Returns to Physical Attractiveness over the Life Course," *Social Forces*, 89, 2011, p. 983–1003; and P. Prokop and Peter Fedor, "Physical Attractiveness Influences Reproductive Success of Modern Men," *Journal of Ethology*, 29, 2011, p. 453–458.

Daniel S. Hamermesh, *Beauty Pays: Why Attractive People Are More Successful,* Princeton, NJ: Princeton University Press, 2011.

States, place more value on privacy and are more likely to discourage the behaviors exhibited by higher-contact culture members.[48]

Individuals who grow up in different cultures may display emotion or express intimacy in different ways. For example, members of Mediterranean cultures tend to display uninhibited, exaggerated highly emotional reactions, expressing grief or happiness with open facial displays, magnified gestures, and vocal cues supportive of their feelings. In contrast, neither the Chinese nor the Japanese readily reveal their feelings in public, preferring to display less emotion, maintain more self-control, and keep their feelings to themselves; for these reasons, they often remain expressionless.[49]

Even when members of different cultures use the same nonverbal cues, they may not mean the same thing. In the United States, for instance, a nod symbolizes agreement or consent, while in Japan it means only that a message was received.

Misunderstandings become more likely when we fail to understand that persons around the world and from different cocultures use nonverbal cues that adhere to cultural rules that are different from ours. For example, individuals from Latino cultures tend to avoid making direct eye contact with another person as a sign of respect or attentiveness, a cue that persons from the main U.S. culture may misinterpret as a sign of inattentiveness or disrespect.[50] Like those from Latino cultures, individuals from Asian cultures also lower their eyes as a means of signaling respect. While African Americans are apt to use more continuous eye contact than European

Americans when speaking, they tend to use less when listening.[51] They also prefer authority figures to avert their gaze.[52] When it comes to public displays of fervent emotion, however, African Americans tend to be comfortable with such behavior, while some members from the mainstream culture may regard such displays as inappropriate because they violate their expectation for self-control and restraint.[53] Culture influences other kinds of nonverbal cues as well. For example, while a timepiece may be a great gift to give someone in the United States, in China clocks are associated with death and funerals, so making a gift of a clock may be interpreted as a sinister act.[54] And while Americans are prone to spending money to straighten less-than-perfect teeth to improve their smiles, in Japan a new fashion has women paying to have their teeth purposefully made crooked—a look called *yaeba,* favored by men and suggesting the woman is not perfect. This practice is thought to make the women more girl-like and approachable, sexualizing them in the process. Just as women in the United States use Botox to change their appearance and make themselves more acceptable to men, Japanese women use *yaeba* to maintain a youthful appearance.[55]

For us to interact effectively with individuals from different cultures, we need to make the effort to identify and understand how culture shapes nonverbal communication. Acknowledging that one communication style is not intrinsically better than any other can help foster more successful multicultural exchanges.

GENDER AND NONVERBAL BEHAVIOR

Just as we learn language from others, we pick up the proper use of nonverbal cues from them as well. In fact, our nonverbal interaction style likely contributes to our gendered identity, because the preferred styles of men and women tend to reflect a number of gendered patterns. Researcher Judith Hall suggests that "'male' and 'female' are roles, each with its set of prescribed behaviors."[56] As a result, men and women commonly use nonverbal communication in ways that reflect societal expectations. For example, men are expected to exhibit assertive behaviors that demonstrate their power and authority; women, in contrast, are expected to exhibit more reactive and responsive behavior. Thus, it should not surprise us that men talk more and interrupt women more frequently than vice versa.[57]

Men are also more apt to be dominant during interactions. The measurement of visual dominance involves comparing the percentage of time spent looking while speaking with the percentage of time spent looking while listening. When compared with women, men display higher levels of looking while speaking and lower levels of looking when listening. Thus, the **visual dominance ratio** of men usually is higher than that of women, again reflecting the ability of nonverbal cues to reinforce perceptions of social power.[58]

Men and women also differ in how they use space and touch. Men tend to use space and touch to assert their dominance over women. As a result, men are much more likely to touch women than women are to touch men. Women thus are more apt to be the recipients of touching actions than they are to be the initiators. Men usually also claim more personal space than do women, and when they walk with women, they are more likely to take a position in front of the women than behind them. Thus, usually, males are the "touchers" and not the "touchees" and are the leaders rather than the followers. In general, when it comes to same-sex touch, it is considered more appropriate for women to touch other women than for men to touch other men. Men, it appears, have more of a concern with being perceived as homosexual than women do.[59]

Visual dominance ratio: A figure derived by comparing the percentage of looking while speaking with the percentage of looking while listening.

1. Are the nonverbal reactions of a television character influenced by the race of the other character in a scene? Do the nonverbal reactions displayed by television actors influence racial attitudes in viewers? According to research, the answer to both these questions is yes. The facial expressions and body language of actors are perceived as less favorable when the characters they are interacting with are black. The more negative reactions displayed by the actors adversely affect viewers' attitudes about race. In contrast, when black characters are responded to more favorably than white characters, the attitudes of viewers toward blacks improve. You are the director of television drama. Given these research findings, what instructions would you give your actors?

2. Is your outfit perceived to be a reflection of your race? Again the answer appears to be yes. Research confirms that people make judgments about race based on cues that extend beyond skin color. For example, people are more frequently perceived to be black if they are wearing janitorial attire than if they are wearing other kinds of clothing. The stereotypes we carry with us influence our perceptions of race. Provide an example of a time when you stereotyped a stranger on the basis of her or his apparel.

SOURCES: Valerie Ross, "Color TV," *Scientific American Mind,* July/August 2010, p. 13.

Jonathan B. Freeman, Andrew M. Penner, Aliya Saperstein, Matthias Scheutz, and Nalini Ambady, "Looking the Part: Social Status Cues Shape Race Perception," *PLoS ONE,* 6:9, e25107. doi:10.1371/journal.pone.0025107; also cited in Pamela Paul, "Is Race Reflected by Your Outfit?," *New York Times,* October 16, 2011, p. ST6.

One of the nonverbal behaviors that women display more than men is smiling. Accustomed to using a smile as an interactional tool, women even smile when under stress.[60] In contrast, men, who are customarily taught to display less emotion than women, are likely to suppress their facial expressions, thereby conveying their sense of reserve and self-control. Gender differences in behaviors such as smiling do not necessarily cross over to cocultures. Unlike their Caucasian counterparts, African American women do not tend to smile more than African American men. Feminine socialization functions differently in the African American community. Women also commonly display their feelings more overtly than do men. In general, women are more expressive and exhibit higher levels of involvement during person-to-person interaction. Women also use nonverbal signals to draw others into conversation to a greater extent, perhaps smiling at them or opening their hands in the direction of others to solicit comments. While women characteristically demonstrate an interest in affiliation, men generally are more interested in establishing the strength of their ideas than in sharing the floor.[61] On the other hand, women tend to be better interpreters of nonverbal messages.

When it comes to use of artifacts, use of color, and clothing, men and women are likely to reflect the stereotyped characteristics attributed to the sexes. For instance, women use artifacts such as jewelry, cosmetics, and hair adornments that help reinforce the image of a woman as a decorative object. Similarly, men's clothing tends to be less colorful and more functional than women's clothing. Men's clothing is more likely than women's to promote utility, activity, and ease of movement, and it does not call the same kind of attention to the body as does women's clothing. Consequently, women are perceived as more sexual.[62]

Despite these habitual proclivities, in recent years some men have taken to wearing heels and some women have taken to wearing classic male oxfords. In fact, in France, the wearing of high-heeled shoes, by men as well as women, used to be perceived as a sign of nobility.

Today, they help men bring a look to dance floor clubs. While it appears to be acceptable for women to wear shoe styles that were previously reserved for men, how long do you think it will be before contemporary society finds it acceptable for men to wear stilettos?[63] Interestingly, men are also wearing "wristwear" (not called bracelets) and carrying "holdalls" (not referred to as purses and less and less as "murses").[64]

Remember, according to standpoint theory (discussed in Chapter 3), it was women's subordinate societal status that compelled them to become better message decoders so that they could accurately predict the behavior of the more dominant or powerful men.[65] On the other hand, as Carol Gilligan notes, since women are more concerned than men with relationship maintenance, it follows that they are likely to develop an enhanced sensitivity to nonverbal cues that facilitate and sustain relationship development.[66]

How would you describe what this man is wearing over his shoulder? Would you change the terminology were a woman wearing it?

NONVERBAL CUES AND FLIRTING: EXPRESSING INTEREST OR DISINTEREST

Flirting is a means of self-promotion as well as a vehicle to express your interest in another. As we now realize, making an impression on someone starts not when you begin to speak, but rather with your appearance, posture, manner of moving, and gestures.

How do males and females signal interest in potential partners? Males signal their interest by preening and stretching (actions that makes them seem larger). They also are likely to stiffen their stance and flex their muscles. Men may also talk in a low voice and are likely to stand or sit with their hands on their belt or belt buckle. Females, in contrast, display nonverbal actions designed to make them appear smaller. They may play with or flick their hair, tilt their heads, exposing their necks, and even display their inner wrists. They also are apt to glance, gaze, primp, preen, pout, lip lick, smile, giggle, laugh, and nod in agreement. Both men and women flash or raise their eyebrows slightly to indicate their interest, make eye contact (even from across the room) or exhibit sideway glances, and play with accessories such as earrings, necklaces, or neckties. They also tend to lean in closer, exhibit open body language, gaze at the other's lips or jaw, laugh, and lightly touch the other's arm or knee.[67]

TRY THIS: Top Billing

Fascination with name brands and celebrity culture has transformed the clothing industry. Many people wear clothing like a billboard—using what they have on to promote their personal status, express affection for a celebrity, or endorse an issue or cause. For example, we wear clothing or carry artifacts emblazoned with the logos of popular designers, effectively providing free advertising for those labels. We wear copies of outfits worn by celebrities. We wear T-shirts promoting our attitudes toward an array of subjects, from opposition to animal cruelty to support for a political candidate.

1. In your opinion, are men and women more apt to use clothing in this manner?

2. Why do you think this is so?

To slow down or de-escalate a flirtation, the woman may turn her body away, cross her arms across her chest, or avoid meeting the other's eyes. Both men and women use departing, excuses involving friends, answering or pretending to answer a cell phone, ignoring, and facial expressions of disinterest to deter or end a flirtation. When terminating a flirtation, men tend to be less polite than women. Of course, the consequences of unwanted flirtation can be serious, especially if it is interpreted as sexual harassment or becomes obsessively intrusive.[68]

Gender influences men's and women's use of nonverbal cues as they define their expectations for each other, express their feelings about and toward one another, and convey their interest in pursuing or not pursuing an interpersonal relationship. By sensitizing yourself to the differences associated with gender, you can reduce misunderstandings and increase your personal communication effectiveness.

MEDIA, TECHNOLOGY, AND NONVERBAL MESSAGES

All too often, the media and technology help to legitimate stereotypical nonverbal displays. Their contents depict a plethora of open sexual appeals, portrayals of women obsessed with men, and male-female interactions in which the men are physically dominant and the women are subordinate. They also include numerous repetitions of the message that "thin is in."

For example, in her video series *Killing Us Softly,* Jean Kilbourne explores how media representations help convey gender norms for dominance and subordination. Kilbourne argues that advertising, the primary storyteller in our culture, takes agency away from women. According to Kilbourne, by exploiting the social anxieties women have and espousing the American value that transformation is possible, advertisers encourage women to be excessively thin. Kilbourne also warns that the images advertisers use undermine how women see themselves while at the same time participating in the normalization of violence directed at them by men. In support of her position, Kilbourne offers examples of how advertisements sexualize women, turn women into body parts, contain numerous instances of silenced women, depict women competing against one another, trivialize the power women have, appear to condone violence against women, and feature few older women. Kilbourne further observes that advertising's objectification and sexualization of men is also on the rise.[69]

After repeated exposure to such media messages, men and women come to believe and ultimately emulate what they see and hear. Thus, females are primed to devote considerable energy to improving their appearance, preserving their youthfulness, and nurturing others, while males learn to display tougher, me, men are typically portrayed as superior to women, who are usually shown in various stages of undress. In the media, nonverbal behaviors portray women as vulnerable and men in control.[70]

The repetition of such myths can cause us to feel dissatisfied and inadequate. If we rely on the media for messages about what is and is not desirable in our relationships and interactions, we may find it difficult to be ourselves.

Flirting is a means of self-promotion as well as a means of expressing our interest in another.

Even mediated vocal cues suggest that it is the male and not the female who is the authority. In up to 90 percent of all advertisements, male voices are used in voice-overs—even when the product being sold is aimed at women. Interestingly, however, when the medium changes and we segue to the computer, we find that computer voices are mostly female, as exemplified by the voice-activated feature called Siri—the iPhone virtual assistant. The reason: research reveals that people find women's voices more pleasing. This is also the rationale for the use of female voices in most navigation systems—except those sold in Germany, where German men refuse to take directions from a woman.[71]

The continued growth of the use of computer-generated virtual reality simulations is cause for some concern. While facilitating our feeling as if we are really interacting in different, but make-believe, environments and even giving us the opportunity to change our gender, such simulations are also being used to enforce violent gender scenarios resulting in women being threatened and killed. Even when erotic rather than violent, computer games all too often reinforce the notion that men have physical control over women.

In the effort to help eliminate some of the ambiguity of online communication, individuals use **emoticons**—relational icons—to increase the expressiveness of their written messages by revealing the user's physical or emotional state. Additionally, they employ a kind of shorthand, using abbreviations such as ROFL (rolling on the floor laughing) or LOL (laughing out loud), to describe their reactions to a partner. Still, despite advances in virtual reality programs, it is impossible to reach out and actually touch someone on the computer screen.[72] The use of emoticons is not without criticism. As one person wrote, "If anybody on Facebook sends me a message with a little smiley-frowny face or a little sunshine with glasses on them, I will de-friend them. I also de-friend for OMG and LOL. They get no second chance. I find it lazy. Are your words not enough?"[73]

When we are interacting online, sometimes words are not enough.

What is more, soon we will no longer merely look like we are talking to ourselves when wearing tiny wireless earpieces connected to our smartphones; we may soon also be able to don "Google glasses"—thick-framed eyeglasses that will project information and entertainment onto the lenses—which may well cause us to exhibit bizarre body language as we seek to avoid the virtual things projected before us.[74] Can you imagine how an onlooker will interpret the flailing of your arms? While Google glasses may be the next big thing, right now facial recognition software lets us use only visual cues to tag someone on Facebook.

Emoticons: Text-based representations of facial expressions and moods.

TRY THIS: *Can You Read the Cues?*

Back in 1959, anthropologist Edward T. Hall coined the expression "the silent language" to describe nonverbal communication. Halls writings on nonverbal communication attracted significant attention, both scholarly and popular. Hall argued that when we fail to decode the manners, gestures, and subtle protocols that accompany words, we leave ourselves vulnerable to miscommunications of one kind or another.

Today we spend significant communicative time interacting online in social networks. It is estimated that high school students alone devote in excess of nine hours a week to social networking. Add texting, blogging, and tweeting on top of that. In our increasingly text-dependent world, more and more communication involves the exchange of written words alone. The prevalence of texting and other forms of messaging leaves a dearth of opportunities to learn to read posture, facial expressions, intonation, and eye movements—all the expressive behaviors of nonverbal communication that are so essential for mutual understanding.

1. In your opinion, are we in danger of losing the "silent fluency" that comes from experiencing face-to-face communication, a needed key in reading another's behavior? Explain your answer.

2. How do you suggest we ensure that such skills are acquired?

3. To what extent do you believe that using FaceTime and Skype, enablers of face-to-face interaction over cell phones and computers, solve some of these issues? How does reading someone's face when you are virtually face-to-face with him or her compare with reading faces when you are really face-to-face?

SOURCE: *Mark* Bauerlein, "Why Gen-Y Johnny Can't Read Nonverbal Cues," *Wall Street Journal,* September 28, 2009, p. W11.

GAINING COMMUNICATION COMPETENCE IN NONVERBAL COMMUNICATION

In Chapter 1, we noted that human beings cannot *not* communicate, because all behavior has message value. In fact, nonverbal behavior affects credibility ratings. Thus, it is important to learn to use nonverbal messages to enhance your personal credibility, likability, and attractiveness, and, at times, to establish dominance. By using nonverbal cues appropriately, you can create a more favorable impression and aid in the development of your relationships. If we are to enhance our abilities to develop effective interpersonal relationships, we need to be fully aware of the nonverbal messages we send and receive.

PAY ATTENTION TO NONVERBAL MESSAGES

By tuning in to nonverbal messages, we can enhance our awareness of how others respond to us. Nonverbal communication is a "relationship language." It expresses how we feel about one another. Even though it may be a challenge to interpret how people really feel, if only because they may not want us to know, the key to understanding people is to observe them in action and listen to the sound of their voices as they interact with you. For example, when in your company, do other people lean toward you or pull away? Face you directly or indicate a desire to avoid interpersonal involvement by facing away from you? Do their facial expressions suggest they are happy you are around, interested in pursuing a relationship, fearful to approach you, or angry with you? Is their posture relaxed, indicating they feel comfortable, or uptight, indicating that they feel you or the situation pose a threat? What do their voices reveal? Do they speak in a friendly manner? Are they trying to use their voices to hide what they are really feeling? Similarly, what does their use of touch, space, and distance suggest about your relationship? What about their use of clothing, color, and time? As you observe others, you pick up and interpret nonverbal cues that reveal their attitudes and feelings.

WHEN UNCERTAIN ABOUT A NONVERBAL CUE'S MEANING, ASK!

What a particular nonverbal cue signifies in one culture may not transfer to another culture. For example, psychologist Aaron Wolfgang reports,

> I remember when I was doing some filming in a marketplace in Palermo, a group of men motioned to my crew with their arms extended, palms down and fingers moving back and forth. We thought it meant, "Go away." As we prepared to leave, one of the men came forward, smiled, and taking our arms invited us for some wine. We found out later that the gesture meant, "Come here."[75]

To avoid misinterpretation, it is important to pay attention to differences in cultural background.

Even if you and those with whom you interact come from the same culture, it is important to remember that nonverbal cues can have multiple meanings. Because of the ambiguity of nonverbal cues, it is a good idea to check your perception, perhaps by paraphrasing, to determine if your interpretation is correct. By asking for verbal clarification of your observations, you increase the chances for mutual understanding.

REALIZE INCONSISTENT MESSAGES HAVE COMMUNICATIVE VALUE

When words and facial expressions, gestures, postures, or vocal cues contradict each other, rely more on the nonverbal information you are receiving than on the words. Even though the words may be precisely what we want or expect to hear, we must also heed unintended mixed or inconsistent messages to help us decide, for example, whether the other person is incompetent, nervous, or a liar.

MATCH THE DEGREE OF CLOSENESS YOU SEEK WITH THE NONVERBAL BEHAVIOR YOU DISPLAY

Nonverbal behavior should be compatible with the kind of relationship sought. Touch, for example, typically varies according to duration, location, and strength, depending on our relationship with another person. Similarly, intimacy and distance also correlate with relationship type. Thus, your proximity to the other person and the amount of touching you use should be compatible with the kind of relationship you seek. The more intimate your relationship is, the closer you will want to be to each other. The less intimate you are with another person, the greater the distance you are likely to keep between you. Should you find yourself in close proximity with someone with whom you are not emotionally close, you can use nonverbal cues to compensate for your discomfort. For example, you may decrease eye contact, helping to psychologically increase the distance between you.

Similarly, if you are separated from someone with whom you feel emotionally close, you can find ways to use nonverbal cues to close the distance gap, perhaps increasing eye contact, waving, or smiling. Among the other nonverbal cues you can use that reveal the closeness of a relationship are cues related to chronemics or time. You reveal your closeness to and comfort with another person by spending more time together.

MONITOR YOUR NONVERBAL BEHAVIOR

Monitoring your own nonverbal behavior is a critical component of interpersonal goal attainment. By engaging in self-reflection, you will be better able to judge if you are using nonverbal cues to project the message you hope to send. For example, how well do you use facial expressions and body movements to foster relationships you want to pursue and terminate relationships you want to end? Are you effective at using the environment to invite or better control opportunities for person-to-person interaction? What does your proximity to the other person and your use of touch suggest about the nature of your relationship? When you want to change the tenor of a relationship from one that is close to one that is more restrained, or vice versa, what nonverbal cues do you characteristically put into play? How do they affect your partner?

ACKNOWLEDGE THAT ABILITIES TO ENCODE AND DECODE NONVERBAL MESSAGES VARY

Some of us are better at regulating, expressing, and interpreting nonverbal behavior than are others. There appears to be a positive correlation between our ability to enact nonverbal messages and our ability to receive and decipher them—skills that also are linked with a Extroverts also have an advantage when it comes to picking up nonverbal cues because they are comfortable in making contact, participating in social encounters, and observing others.

Even more important, the more we hone our nonverbal abilities, the more likely it is that others will perceive us as socially adjusted and that we will be able to exert social influence and have satisfying relationships.[77]

Sam entered the conference room. He couldn't put his finger on what was up, but things just didn't feel right to him as he observed the people already present in the room. At the head of the impressive mahogany table sat his company president. Senior vice presidents sat to the president's right and left, and several managers—including Sam's immediate supervisor—lined the table's sides.

There was one seat open. As Sam approached, he couldn't help but feel uneasy. Sure, the people at the table were drinking coffee, smiling, checking their smartphones, consulting their tablets, texting, and chatting among themselves. As Sam took his seat, not one person looked up or said a word to him.

Sam asked himself why he was feeling uncomfortable. Was it because the president had not yet acknowledged Sam's presence? Was it because no one had greeted him except maybe his immediate supervisor, who Sam thought had acknowledged him with a perfunctory hello by nodding her head? Whatever it was, Sam felt like an outsider.

Then the president looked up—and made eye contact directly with Sam. Everyone else stopped whatever he or she was doing and looked Sam's way too. The president called the meeting to order, explaining that there was but a single agenda item—Sam.

Sam's heart sank. How could he have missed it? Had there been other cues besides the lack of eye contact that he had overlooked? Was this going to be the end of his career? Here they were, he told himself, about to fire him, and he had had no clue that any problem existed before now.

At that moment, the president reached under the table and brought out a bottle of champagne. Sam, he announced, was being promoted and would now be senior vice president in charge of his entire division. Slowly, a smile appeared on Sam's face, and Sam rose to shake hands with all assembled, including his soon-to-be former supervisor.

Answer these questions:

1. Have there been times when you have felt just as uncomfortable as Sam did on entering a room but could not identify what caused you to feel that way?

2. What steps can we take to ensure that we pick up and do not misread nonverbal cues?

REVIEW THIS

1 **Define nonverbal communication, explain its metacommunicative nature, and discuss its functions and characteristics.** Nonverbal communication consists of the actions or attributes of human beings, together with the use of objects, sounds, time, and space that have socially shared significance and stimulate meaning in others. Because nonverbal communication helps clarify the nature and meaning of verbal messages, it also fulfills metacommunicative functions. Nonverbal cues can add to, negate, accent, regulate, or replace verbal messages. As such, they are an integral part of the total communication package. Nonverbal behavior also has message value, is ambiguous, is predominantly relational in nature, and provides clues to deception.

2 **Define and distinguish among the following kinds of nonverbal messages: kinesics, paralanguage, proxemics, haptics, artifactual communication and appearance, olfactics, color, and chronemics.** Kinesics is the study of body motion, including expressions, gestures, eye movement, posture, and rate of walk. Paralinguistics includes a consideration of vocal cues, such as how words are spoken and the impact of vocal variations. Proxemics is the use of space and distance. Haptics includes an exploration of different kinds of touch. Artifactual communication and appearance involve the significance of clothing, personal adornments, beauty, height, and weight for our feelings and others' reactions to us. Olfactics is the study of the sense of smell. Color has effects on us both psychologically and physically. Chronemics explores the communicative value of time.

3 **Compare and contrast the nonverbal communication styles of men and women.** Most men and women use nonverbal communication in ways that reflect societal expectations for persons of their respective genders. Thus, men exhibit assertive behaviors and women are more responsive and reactive.

4 **Distinguish between contact and noncontact cultures.** Contact cultures value the intimacy of contact by promoting interaction and displays of warmth, closeness, and availability. Noncontact cultures value privacy and the maintenance of distance.

5 **Describe the impacts of media and technology on nonverbal messages.** Media and technology frequently participate in the legitimation of stereotypes. When interacting online, some individuals use emoticons to try to replace the nonverbal cues that would be present in face-to-face interaction.

6 **Identify steps you can take to improve your nonverbal effectiveness.** By paying attention to nonverbal cues, paying attention to cultural differences, being alert for inconsistent messages, matching nonverbal behavior and relationships so they are compatible, monitoring our nonverbal behavior, and recognizing that we vary in our abilities to encode and decode nonverbal messages, we improve the likelihood of communicating effectively.

CHECK YOUR UNDERSTANDING

1 Can you offer an example of metacommunication in action? How, for example, might you use it to better understand the nature of a relationship? (See pages 152–154.)

2 Can you create a scenario illustrating the role nonverbal cues play in creating a false impression? Why do you think people believe that it is easier to lie with words than with nonverbal cues? (See pages 155–158.)

3 Can you explain the kinds of messages conveyed by personal appearance? What about those that voice and use of space and distance communicate? (See pages 172–174.)

4 Can you offer two examples of nonverbal messages in action, one demonstrating how gender or culture influences the use and interpretation of nonverbal cues, and the other demonstrating the role that media and technology play in nonverbal messaging? (See pages 175–182.)

5 What can you do to enhance your ability to send and receive nonverbal messages? (See pages 182–184.)

CHECK YOUR SKILLS

1 Can you use nonverbal cues to identify when someone is attempting to deceive you? (See pages 155–157; and *Try This*, page 158.)

2 Can the ability to read faces accurately improve your relationships? (See pages 159–162; *Analyze This,* page 162; and *Try This*, page 182.)

3 Can you use your eyes to increase your visual dominance and establish behavior synchrony? (See pages 161–162.)

4 Can correctly interpreting another's body messages help you make judgments regarding that person's liking, assertiveness, and power? (See pages 163–165; and *Try This*, page 164.)

5 Can you use paralinguistic cues to help identify the meaning inherent in spoken words? (See pages 165–167, and *Reflect on This*, page 167.)

6 Can you use space and distance to clarify intentions? (See pages 167–170.)

7 Can you recognize the attractiveness effect? (See pages 172–173; and *Reflect on This*, page 176.)

8 Can you use nonverbal messages to help bridge culture and gender differences? (See pages 175–179; and *Try This*, page 178.)

9 Can you assess when media and technology are helping to legitimate the use of stereotypical nonverbal displays? (See pages 181–183.)

10 Can you account for the misreading of nonverbal cues? (See pages 182–184; and *The Case of Surprised Sam*, page 185.)

KEY TERMS

Nonverbal communication   *152*

Metacommunicative functions   *152*

Double message   *153*

Interpersonal deception theory   *157*

Facial Action Coding System   *157*

Kinesics   *159*

Representational facial expressions   *161*

Presentational facial expressions   *162*

Microfacial/micromomentary expressions   *162*

Emblems   *163*

Illustrators   *163*

Regulators   *163*

Affect displays   *164*

Adaptors   *164*

Paralanguage   *165*

Articulation   *166*

Pronunciation   *167*

Nonfluencies   *167*

Proxemics   *168*

Intimate distance   *168*

Personal distance   *168*

Social distance   *169*

Public distance   *169*

Expectancy violation theory   *169*

Fixed-feature space   *169*

Semi-fixed-feature space   *170*

Informal space or non-fixed-feature space   *170*

Territoriality   *170*

Haptics   *170*

Olfactics   *173*

Chronemics   *174*

Contact culture   *175*

Noncontact culture   *175*

Visual dominance   *177*

Emoticons   *181*

STUDENT STUDY SITE

Visit the student study site at **www.sagepub.com/gambleic** to access the following materials:

- SAGE Journal Articles
- Videos
- Web Resources
- eFlashcards
- Web Quizzes
- Study Questions

"I truly believe that life is a contact sport. You never know just who you'll meet and what role they might play in your career or your life."

—Robert Morley (1908–1992), actor

CONVERSATIONS

LEARNING OBJECTIVES

After completing this chapter, you should be able to demonstrate mastery of the following learning outcomes:

1. Define small talk, conversation, and conversational turn taking and enumerate the skills shared by good conversationalists.

2. Identify the five parts of a conversation.

3. Describe how cultural and gender differences influence feelings and perceptions of the nature and value of conversation.

4. Discuss how media and technology are helping to reinforce or change both the substance and the nature of conversation.

5. Identify specific steps you can take to improve your conversational skills.

Fans of popular television shows love to connect with one another to engage in conversation and analysis both during and after the airing of every episode. They relish conversing about and deconstructing their favorite programs together—often using Facebook posts, tweets, and the opportunities provided by call-in after-shows such as *Talking Dead,* a follow-up program devoted to discussion of *The Walking Dead.* Apps such as IntoNow and Miso similarly encourage social discussion via online chatter. Years ago, prior to widespread use of the Internet and particularly the advent of social media, popular programs were the topics of workplace "watercooler conversations" on the mornings after new episodes aired, but now viewers can converse with many others about their favorite shows even while watching the shows. Each new online chat venue functions as a substitute for those conversations that in the past would have been held around the proverbial office watercooler.[1]

Posting comments about television programs on Twitter, Facebook, and other social platforms grew 146 percent from April 2011 to April 2012.[2] And the tweeting does not happen just during the commercials. It happens whenever there is an OMG (Oh my God) moment in a show. The shows most discussed online are those that air live—*American Idol, Dancing with the Stars,* and *The Voice,* as well as sports and award shows. Scripted series, however, also generate their fair share of online conversation. Fans thrive on sharing reactions—viewing has been turned into a social experience.

While many of us talk online about television shows or other subjects simply because we enjoy doing so—treating such discussion as an add-on to the chatting we do face-to-face—others, because of social anxiety, prefer connecting online to interacting face-to-face all the time.[3]

> Have you ever found yourself tongue-tied at a party, afraid you would say something stupid?

Consider this: Have you ever found yourself tongue-tied at a party, afraid you would say something stupid? According to a recent *Wall Street Journal* article, this is a pretty common occurrence. Many of us find conversing or speaking up in the presence of others hard to do, especially if we think our social status is in question.[4] When we compare ourselves to others and judge ourselves to fall short, we may be struck silent and clam up.

WHAT DO YOU KNOW?

Before continuing your reading of this chapter, which of the following five statements do you believe to be true and which do you believe to be false?

1. Rules guide conversation.　　　　　　　T　F

2. A skilled conversationalist can control a conversation's direction.　　T　F

3. Conversations are essentially the same everywhere in the world.　　T　F

4. Once you have said something wrong in a conversation, you can never repair the damage.　　T　F

5. Texting is taking the place of face-to-face conversations.　　T　F

Read the chapter to discover if you're right or if you've made any erroneous assumptions.

ANSWERS: 1. T, 2. T, 3. F, 4. F, 5. T

While making **small talk** or engaging in spontaneous conversation with another person may come naturally to some of us, for others it poses problems. Yet it is by talking to others that we lay the foundation for most of our interpersonal relationships. Because most people enjoy being in the company of a good communicator, one of the most important skills you can master is that of carrying on an effective conversation. A good conversationalist is adept at approaching others, starting a conversation, listening, changing a topic to one of interest or importance to him or her, and gracefully ending the interaction.

THE IMPORTANCE OF CONVERSATIONAL CONTACT

Personal relationships depend on conversation. When deprived of opportunities to converse face-to-face, we devise other means.

Conversation facilitates the establishing of interpersonal relationships. As such, it plays a critical role in our lives. For example, some years ago, in an effort to reduce the likelihood that prison inmates would share information about how to commit different crimes, prison reformers reduced the amount of conversation inmates were able to have with each other. The result was very interesting: "The prisoners spent much of their time tapping out coded messages on walls and pipes, devising means of passing information to one another, and working out other clever ways of communicating."[5] Even when the inmates were denied opportunities to be face-to-face, they found other ways to converse. So have we—when not face-to-face, we connect to converse, primarily by texting.

Retired Navy captain Gerald Coffee, one of hundreds of American pilots shot down over North Vietnam and held as a prisoner of war in a facility known as the "Hanoi Hilton" during the Vietnam War, offers a moving example that illustrates the lengths human beings will go to in order to compensate for face-to-face **conversation deprivation**. In his book *Beyond Survival*, Coffee describes an ingenious method he and his fellow prisoners used to communication with one another within the prison walls. The prisoner who previously had occupied the small cell that was now Coffee's had scratched a five-by-five grid into the wall. The grid, as illustrated below, displayed a system for using taps to represent the letters of the alphabet; users could indicate letters by tapping, giving the locations down and then across.

	1	2	3	4	5
1	A	B	C	D	E
2	F	G	H	I	J
3	K	L	M	N	O
4	P	Q	R	S	T
5	U	V	W	Y	Z

After learning this system, prisoners were able to maintain contact with one another by covertly tapping coded messages.[6] "Hi," for example, would be tapped as follows:

XX XXX   XX XXXX

(2-3)   (2-4)

H   I

Assess how you feel about striking up a conversation with another person. Using a scale of 1 to 5, where 1 represents an extremely negative response and 5 represents an extremely positive response, answer each question below as honestly as possible.

1. How much do you enjoy yourself in situations that compel you to mingle and strike up conversations with people you don't know well or at all?

2. How much do you enjoy engaging in small talk?

3. Do you look forward to spending a lot of time talking with others?

4. How comfortable are you around people who don't talk a lot?

5. How at ease are you sharing personal information with others when face-to-face?

What do your answers suggest regarding whether or not you are conversationally apprehensive?

Because of the grid, the prisoners were able to compensate for a lack of aural communication and thereby maintain their sense of connection to others. Try using the "Hanoi Hilton" grid to tap out some words. How important would such a system be for you were it the only means you had to carry on a conversation?

While connection and conversation are mainstays of human interaction, if unchecked, the extremely extroverted may equate any conversational opening with a rush to speak and a desire to put oneself out there, rather than thinking reflectively before speaking, a quality introverts, who may find nonstop socializing stressful, are more apt to display.[7] Thus, being comfortable in the spotlight is not the sole requisite for being an effective conversationalist; another important element is a desire to share real-life experiences.[8]

WHAT DO YOU KNOW?

True or False
1. *Rules guide conversation.*
True. The rules of conversation reflect accepted social practices.

WHAT IS CONVERSATION?

Conversation is defined as a relatively informal social interaction in which the parties involved exchange the roles of sender and hearer, or receiver, collaboratively and spontaneously.[9] During conversations there is no set time limit for each party to speak or listen; the participants determine the time frame themselves. However, describing conversational exchanges as spontaneous does not mean that conversations are random or without rules. In fact, **conversational rules** reveal the behaviors we prefer and would like to prohibit in various social situations.[10] For instance, if someone says, "Hello," how do you respond? Typically, with a "Hi," or a "Hello, how are you?" Rules guide much of person-to-person behavior. Reflect for a moment on the rules you use to guide you in answering the following questions: Do American fathers kiss their sons on the lips? When you are angry with your employer, how do you speak to him or her? We tend to rely on learned social and conversational rules to guide us as we interact.

As we explore conversation, we can also apply what we have learned about verbal and nonverbal messages directly to our daily interactions and our efforts at relationship

Conversation: A relatively informal social interaction in which the roles of speaker and listener are exchanged in a nonautomatic fashion under the collaborative management of all parties.

Conversational rules: Behaviors that are established, preferred, or prohibited during social exchanges.

TRY THIS: *The Elevator*

What rules do most people follow regarding conversing with others in elevators?

1. While in an elevator (in an office building or apartment complex), break a rule you usually follow and observe how the other person reacts. For example, does he or

she respond in kind, refrain from responding, or exhibit some other noteworthy behavior?

2. Why do you imagine such elevator rules exist?

WHAT DO YOU KNOW?

True or False
2. *A skilled conversationalist can control a conversation's direction.*
True. Skilled conversationalists effectively regulate interaction by managing turn taking and topic shifts.

Conversational structure: The typical format for conversation, comprising the greeting, topic priming, the heart of the conversation, preliminary processing, and the closing.

building. After all, as relationship expert and researcher Steve Duck notes, "If you were to sit and list the things that you do with friends, one of the top items on the list would surely have to be 'talking.'"[11] By exploring the dynamics of conversational exchange, we can enhance our ability to engage in everyday talk wherever our conversations occur—whether on the playing field, at work, at home, during a date, or at a social gathering. While many of our conversations are primarily spontaneous, casual interactions with others that involve no preplanned agenda, others are more pragmatic and involve a specific goal on the part of at least one of the conversational parties. Which kinds of conversations do you engage in more?

CONVERSATION: GAMES AND PLAYERS

Some theorists suggest that conversation is a kind of game and that we can therefore apply the same rules we use when playing a game or a favorite sport to our conversational interactions.[12] Adopting this approach, Robert Nofsinger, a communication researcher who studies conversation, notes, "The idea is to apply what we know about ordinary, everyday games (chess, checkers, tic-tac-toe, card games, competitive sports, and so on) to the conduct of conversation."[13] When we use this analogy, we find people making moves, taking turns, and aiming to achieve some goal. We also find them using specific tactics, employing strategies, and devising game plans.

According to Nofsinger, talk produces the moves of conversation. When we talk, however, we do not simply *say* something, we also *do* something. Our talk, for example, may direct others, invite others to approach us, signal our acceptance or rejection of another, or insult another. How we act and respond or subsequently conduct our conversations depends on our understanding or interpretation of conversational events.

While the rules of board games and sports games are codified and written down so that they may be enforced easily—and violators can be corrected or penalized for breaking the rules—rules of everyday conversation do not usually appear in print. There are topics we may consider taboo when we interact with some people but that we consider acceptable when we converse with others. We simply are able to change the rules to guide our conversations from day to day and from minute to minute.

CONVERSATIONAL STRUCTURE

Most conversations adhere to a general five-stage **conversational structure**: the greeting, topic priming, the heart of the conversation, preliminary processing, and the closing (see Table 7.1). We address each stage in turn in the following.

TRY THIS: *Conversational Analysis*

Watch and record a brief segment of a film or TV show focusing on interpersonal relationships in which two characters converse. For example, you might use an excerpt from *Modern Family, How I Met Your Mother, Jersey Shore, The Simpsons*, or a soap opera. Then analyze the recorded conversation as follows:

1. Describe the nature, purpose, and results of the conversation.

2. Describe how the communicators regulate their interaction, including who appears to be in control of interaction ebb and flow. Be sure to note how turn taking is managed, who asks questions, who interrupts, and who shifts topics.

3. Discuss the degree to which the characters conversing appear to be involved in the conversation. Identify the cues you have relied on to distinguish involved from uninvolved characters.

4. For both parties to the conversation, evaluate their conversational adaptability (flexibility), responsiveness (the extent to which they appear to know what to say, understand their role, and feel part of the interaction), perceptiveness (the extent to which they demonstrate an awareness of how the other perceives them and responds to them), and attentiveness (the extent to which they listen carefully to the other party or are preoccupied with personal thoughts).

5. Evaluate whether any party to the conversation displays conversational narcissism—that is, exhibits cues suggesting that a participant is overly self-concerned—and how the presence or absence of this quality affects the outcome of the interaction.

6. Identify which conversational participant exhibits more empathy—that is, which is best able to show his or her conversational partner that emotions are shared and the situation is understood.

7. Evaluate whether the goals of the conversation are achieved and at what, if any, cost.

TABLE 7.1 The Stages of a Conversation

Stage	Functions
Greeting	Ask a question. or Tell something about yourself. or Deliver a compliment. or Make a cute/flippant statement. or Say something innocuous. or Issue a direct invitation.
Topic priming	Provide feedforward by previewing the nature of and reason for the conversation. and Ask one or more open-ended questions.
Heart of the conversation	Introduce and then discuss the conversation's focus or goal by exchanging comments.
Preliminary processing	Reflect back on the conversation in an effort to evaluate conversational progress.
Closing	Let the other person know the conversation is ending. Express appreciation. Summarize topics discussed.

Greetings are conversational openers.

The Greeting. Phatic communication is a message that opens up the communication channel, thereby enabling two people to begin interacting. By creating an opening for conversation, the greeting serves that function. The interpersonal greeting is our routine way of beginning or initiating conversation with someone, and we usually are able to adjust it based on our perception of a relationship with a specific person, our mood, and how we imagine the other person will respond. We cannot, however, script our opening lines in advance. There are no lines guaranteed to establish a relationship. "Didn't I meet you in Istanbul?" and "Do you have an aspirin?" and "Bet I can make you laugh" have all been tried, and they have worked in some instances but not others. Even our favorite line to use at a business function—"You look like someone I should know. My name is . . ."—doesn't come complete with a guarantee.

Conversational analyst Thomas E. Murray has identified three different categories of conversational openers:

1. Questions ("How are you?")

2. Advertisements ("My name is . . .")

3. Compliments ("I like your suit")[14]

Researcher Chris Kleinke also identifies three types of openers:

1. Cute/flippant ("Is that really your hair?")

2. Innocuous ("What do you think of the band?")

3. Direct ("Since we're both eating alone, would you like to join me?")[15]

Note that each of these approaches relies on a question. While men and women both use indirect opening lines, women particularly tend to dislike the use of cute and flippant openers by men.

Whatever type of greeting we employ, we use it to let others know that we are accessible and would like to converse. Normally the person we greet will return our greeting in a similar way. When this does not happen—when the other person responds coolly or with caution to our greeting or conversational overture—we can usually tell that something is wrong, that the other person does not want to establish contact, that he or she is shy or fears establishing contact, and that we will have to work harder and be more creative if we hope for a more sustained conversation.

Topic Priming. We prime a conversation by keeping the communication channels between us open and by previewing for the other person what the topic or focus of our conversation will be. For example, we might say, "I need your input. What do you think of X?" or "I need to share some bad news with you," or "This isn't easy for me to say, and you may not like to hear it, but . . ." Priming prepares the person we are conversing with for what is to follow.

If we are unable to find a topic to discuss with another person, our conversation ends after the greeting. In general, we usually end up talking about one of three kinds of topics: ourselves, the other person, or a particular situation. Sometimes we test a particular topic, not by merely making a statement but by asking a question: "I liked what you said today at lunch. What do you think businesses should be doing to avoid having to downsize their operations?" or "I've been looking for a place to buy a new tablet. I noticed you have one. Do you have any suggestions?" or "I see you're reading a book by Stieg Larsson. What do you think of his trilogy?" By asking **open-ended questions**, which allow the respondent free rein in answering, rather than **closed-ended questions**, which force the respondent to choose a specific response, we are better able to involve and interest another person in conversing with us.

Gregory Stock, author of *The Book of Questions,* notes that far too frequently we exchange small talk without becoming involved in deeper conversation. To combat this dilemma, he suggests that we ask questions that are more "dangerous," that perhaps we have never been willing to ask before, and that might provoke more interesting reactions in others. The following are examples of such questions, as suggested by Stock:

- For a person you loved deeply, would you be willing to move to a distant country, knowing there would be little chance of seeing your friends or family again?

- Would you accept $1,000,000 to leave the country and never set foot in it again?

- What would constitute a "perfect" evening for you?[16]

We err in conversation when we cut short the priming stage or extend it beyond what is considered appropriate. If we get stuck in the priming stage, our conversational partner may wonder if we really have anything to discuss—that is, if we have a purpose or focus or are totally disorganized. On the other hand, if we omit this stage and head straight for our goal, the other person may judge us to be rude, insensitive, or interpersonally deficient.

The Heart of the Conversation. At the heart of our conversation, we find its focus or goal. Perhaps we want to share new information with another person. Or perhaps we want to persuade him or her to act or think in a specific way. Maybe we want to offer the person our help—perhaps even just a friendly ear. Whatever our specific goal, in this part of our conversation we get to the heart of the matter—why we opened the conversation in the first place, and why we did our best to prepare the other person for what was to come next.

How good we are at getting to and explaining the heart of our conversation is directly related to **conversational maintenance** skills, which will be discussed a little later in this chapter. The substance of the conversation involves conversational partners exchanging speaker and listener roles.

Preliminary Processing. The preliminary processing stage is the flip side of topic priming. Here, instead of preparing the other person for what is to come, we process what has just

At the heart of every conversation is its focus or goal.

Open-ended question: A question that allows the respondent free rein in answering.

Closed-ended question: A question that forces the respondent to choose a specific response.

Conversational maintenance: Preservation of the smooth and natural flow of conversation.

occurred between us. We consider the effects that our conversation has had on each of us and, based on our assessment of the other person's response, we may decide to adjust or alter our message and strengthen or modify our content. During this stage we may also assess how much we have learned about the other in an effort to determine the extent to which we have been able to reduce our uncertainty about him or her.

As we review our conversation's progress, we may realize that while we feel that we have accomplished our conversational purpose, our partner may not agree. Thus, we may need to take a step back instead of forward and complete our discussion.

The Closing. The closing is the reverse of the greeting. We now take our leave, say goodbye, signal that we are no longer accessible, and separate ourselves from the other person, sometimes briefly and sometimes forever. How we take our leave often lets the other person know whether we intend to meet with him or her again. "It was good to catch up about you and Joe, but I've got to go now, or I'll be late for my appointment" or "I really enjoyed hearing about your trip. When can I see you again?" or "I'm sorry to hear you haven't been feeling well. I'll call you tomorrow to see how you're doing"—each kind of closing sends a message that is very different from a mere good-bye.

Renowned communication scholar Mark Knapp and his colleagues note that a good closing to a successful conversation serves three functions:

1. It lets the other party know that the conversation is nearing an end and thus signals the impending inaccessibility of one party.

2. It is supportive in tone and contains expressions of appreciation for the conversation and the desire to renew contact.

3. It summarizes the main topics discussed.[17]

Closings based on these three rules leave both parties feeling good about the possibilities for continued contact.

Sometimes we merge conversational stages—the processing and closing stages may be combined, for example—or we may mutually agree to skip a stage because the time we have together is short. Thus, our five-stage model of conversation is just that—a model—a representation of how a conversation forms, builds, and concludes. Not all conversations contain all five steps. However, if you listen and observe carefully, you should be able to identify at least some, if not all, of these stages during many of your conversations. You will probably realize that the conversations you find most fulfilling and least frustrating are those that develop sequentially according to the five-stage model.

CONVERSATIONAL MANAGEMENT

Conversational turn taking:
The simultaneous exchanging of the speaker and listener roles during a conversation.

When a conversation flows smoothly and naturally, the roles of speaker and listener are performed simultaneously by both parties, with each party engaging in **conversational turn taking**—the alternating of speaking and listening during conversation as each takes a speaking turn, cooperating and engaging in dialogue to fulfill the conversation's purpose.

How does one get a turn to speak during a conversation? Is this something that we can can determine ahead of time? Do perceptions of wealth or status play a role? What behaviors promote conversational dialogue?

TURN TAKING: MAINTAINING AND YIELDING THE FLOOR

We regulate our conversations by using and responding to turn-maintaining and turn-yielding signals. **Turn-maintaining signals** include both paralinguistic and kinesic cues. For example, we may vocalize pauses (*ummm, uhhh*) to indicate we have not yet completed a thought, inhale a breath to suggest we have more to say, exhibit a gesture that suggests we are not yet finished, or avoid making direct eye contact with the other party until we are fully ready to surrender our speaking turn.

Turn-yielding signals let our conversational partner know that we are prepared to let him or her speak. For example, we may make direct eye contact, ask a question requiring a response, nod in the other person's direction, drop our pitch, or remain silent. When someone interrupts or overlaps what we consider to be our turn, we may become upset or agitated, fight to maintain our turn allocation, or reluctantly yield it prematurely.

Turn-taking control does not rest in the hands of one person. An individual who is listening may also exert regulatory control over conversational turn taking by emitting **turn-requesting signals** or **turn-denying signals** that let the person speaking know whether the listener would like to switch roles. To signal interest in having a speaking turn, the listener might use a vocalized filler such as *umm* or *ah,* merely open his or her mouth as if to interject a thought, lean forward and look directly at the speaker, or gesture for attention with his or her hand. Similarly, the listener may signal a reluctance to take over the speaking role by avoiding eye contact with the speaker, shaking his or head to indicate that he or she has nothing to add, engaging in some activity that is incompatible with a speaking role (such as taking copious notes), closing his or her eyes, coughing, or exhibiting a gesture that encourages the speaker not to yield the floor but to continue speaking instead. The use or absence of **backchannel signals**, or verbalizations we use to tell another person that we are listening, also contributes to the continuing or ending of talk.

THE COOPERATION PRINCIPLE

For both parties to be satisfied with a conversation, they need to cooperate. According to the cooperation principle, conversations are most satisfying when the comments of the conversational partners are consistent with the conversation's purpose. Based on this premise, researchers offer the following conversational maxims: quality, quantity, relevancy, and manner.[18]

According to the **quality maxim**, persons engaged in conversation should not offer a comment if they know it to be false. The parties to a conversation should offer only information they know is truthful. Information that is deceptive, deliberately misleading, or distorted has no place in conversation. Offering an opinion when you have no knowledge of the topic or are only speculating is inappropriate. Violating this maxim leads to distrust.

The **quantity maxim** tells us to provide as much information as is needed to communicate the meaning of our message and continue the conversation. This means neither party talks too much or too little. Each should avoid single-word responses but say what is needed to deliver the message while allowing the other person to continue the conversation. Persons who fail to provide others with the information they need violate this maxim. Monopolizing the conversation and failing to give another his or her chance to speak undermines cooperation.

The **relevancy maxim** asks that we not go off on tangents or purposefully digress and switch subjects when the other party still wants to actively discuss our initial topic. Interjecting irrelevant comments illustrates uncooperativeness. Effective conversationalists work instead to sustain conversational coherence by relating their comments to previous remarks

Turn-maintaining signals: Paralinguistic and kinesic cues that suggest that a speaker is not yet ready to give up the speaking role.

Turn-yielding signals: Paralinguistic and kinesic cues that indicate the readiness of a speaker to exchange the role of speaker for the role of listener.

Turn-requesting signals: Paralinguistic and kinesic cues that let a speaker know that a listener would like to switch roles.

Turn-denying signals: Paralinguistic and kinesic cues that signal a reluctance to switch speaking and/or listening roles.

Backchannel signals: Verbalizations one uses to tell another person that one is listening.

Quality maxim: The premise that persons engaged in conversation do not offer comments known to be false.

Quantity maxim: The premise that persons conversing provide as much information as is needed to communicate a message's meaning and continue the conversation.

Relevancy maxim: The premise that persons engaged in conversation do not purposefully go off on tangents or digress.

WHAT DO YOU KNOW?

True or False

3. *Conversations are essentially the same everywhere in the world.*
False. Culture influences conversation.

Manner maxim:
The premise that when conversing one should use diction that is appropriate to the receiver and the interaction's context.

Monologue: A communication process lacking in interactivity, during which one person speaks while another person listens.

Dialogue: An interactive process involving speaking and listening.

and by rarely interrupting to switch subjects.[19] They prefer to ask relevant questions that others enjoy answering.

According to the **manner maxim**, diction should be appropriate to the receiver and the interaction's context; that means using terms the other party understands and providing background information to avoid confusion. Conversation is informal, but that does not mean it should be disorganized. Adherence to this maxim requires organizing thoughts to facilitate sharing meaning.

These four maxims apply to conversations occurring between persons living in the United States. Person from other cultures may adhere to other maxims, such as the *maxim of face-saving,* which would require the parties to a conversation to avoid arguing with, contradicting, embarrassing, or correcting one another. In addition, the *maxim of politeness* might require that persons avoid self-praise or taking credit for an accomplishment, focusing the spotlight on the other instead.[20] While it is particularly common for persons from Asian cultures as well as the British to adhere to the foregoing two maxims, people from all cultures value face-saving and politeness.[21] Being impolite or committing a face-threatening act (an FTA) would likely jeopardize any relationship.

THE DIALOGUE PRINCIPLE

When conversing with another person, we often display a preference for **monologue,** in which we speak while the other person listens, or **dialogue,** in which we both speak and listen. Unlike dialogue, monologue involves little, if any, conversational ebb and flow, lacks interactivity, and expresses minimal concern for the thoughts and feelings of the other person. Instead, the monologist is self-centered, spends a lot of time talking about him- or herself (this is especially apparent on social media sites such as Facebook and Twitter), and exhibits an obsession with achieving personal conversational goals and objectives. Approximately 40 percent of our everyday talk is devoted to letting others know our thoughts and feelings.[22] Why do we find it so enjoyable to talk about ourselves? Harvard University neuroscientists have suggested that self-disclosure becomes its own reward,

ANALYZE THIS: *Relationship Turns*

Read the following excerpt from Lorraine Hansberry's play *A Raisin in the Sun*, paying special attention to the nature of turn taking and the state of conversational cooperation exhibited:

Mama: *(Still quietly)* Walter, what is the matter with you?

Walter: Matter with? Ain't nothing the matter with *me*!

Mama: Yes there is. Something eating you up like a crazy man. Something more than me not giving you this money. The past few years I been watching it happen you. You get all nervous acting and kind of wild in the eyes—*(Walter jumps up impatiently at her words)* I said sit there now, I'm talking to you!

Walter: Mama—I don't need no nagging at me today.

Mama: Seem like you getting to a place where you always tied up in some kind of knot about something. But if anybody ask you 'bout it you just yell at 'em and bust out the house and go out and drink somewheres. Walter Lee, people can't live with that. Ruth's a good, patient girl in her way—but you getting to be too much. Boy, don't make the mistake of driving that girl away from you.

Walter: Why—what she do for me?

Mama: She loves you.

Walter: Mama—I'm going out. I want to go off somewhere and be by myself for a while.

Mama: I'm sorry 'bout your liquor store, son. It just wasn't the thing for us to do. That's what I want to tell you about—

Walter: I got to go out, Mama—

(He rises.)

Mama: It's dangerous, son.

Walter: What's dangerous?

MAMA: When a man goes outside his home to look for peace.

As you reflect on what you have read, consider this question: What do the turn taking and yielding behaviors of Mama and Walter tell us about their relationship? Do they adhere to the cooperation principle?

triggering the same sensations in the brain as food and money.[23] What is more, we would rather talk about ourselves even when we are promised an incentive of food or money for speculating about other people.[24] What we love is for other people to listen to us.

Effective communication, however, is dialogic and requires that communicators exhibit concern for each other and their relationship. The conversational parties display respect for each other, invite each other to participate actively in the conversation, display an accepting manner, request clarification of the other person's perspective, and show empathy by adopting an other-oriented perspective that helps the other person feel understood.

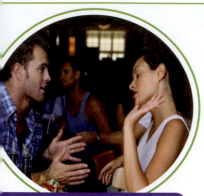

REPAIRING CONVERSATIONAL DAMAGE

Every now and then we commit or are on the receiving end of a **conversational blunder**—a faux pas—during which something we find objectionable is said. When this occurs, a prime means of repairing the damage done by the blunder is to offer an excuse or a disclaimer designed to lessen the potential negative consequences of the remark. For instance, after insulting a friend or being overly critical of a peer, we might offer an excuse such as "I'm really sorry. It's been a long day, and my exhaustion got the better of me" or "I don't know why I said that. Can you forgive me? I'm just stressed because of what's happening at work."

To avoid committing such blunders we need to remind ourselves that, as we converse, it is important to engage in dual perspective talking. This requires that, while we not abandon our own feelings, we make a concerted effort to take the other person's feelings into account as we interact. Conversations help define relationships.

Insensitivity is not the only cause of conversational blunders. Sometimes **prejudiced talk** also damages conversations. Prejudiced talk includes the making of racist, sexist, or ageist comments in public.[25] Because it emphasizes differences rather than similarities, such talk functions to separate, distance, and enhance feelings of power for the user of the questionable language rather than unite, bring individuals from diverse groups closer together, or equalize the perceived power bases from which they operate. Because most of us try to present ourselves as unprejudiced when we interact with others, we are apt to preface prejudiced talk with a disclaimer in which we claim not to be prejudiced. As noted earlier, however, once we speak them aloud, we cannot easily take back our words. The damage is done, and the persons in the relationship will feel its effects.

CULTURAL DIFFERENCES AND CONVERSATION

Culture and conversation are related. Our culture influences our beliefs about the nature and value of conversation. For example, conversation is more important to European Americans than it is to native-born Chinese or Chinese Americans. For that reason, European Americans are much more likely to initiate and engage in conversations with others than are Chinese Americans. Whereas European Americans view talk as a tool to gain social control, the Chinese view the absence of talk, or silence, as a control strategy.[26] From their collectivist perspective, talk is not necessary for relationship development, whereas from the individualist perspective held by European Americans, it is.

The difference between high-context cultures such as those of Asia and Africa and low-context cultures such as those of the United States and most Western European countries is also reflected in the word choices of members. During their conversations, members of low-context cultures are more likely to utter words such as *absolutely, positively,* and *most definitely,* while members of high-context cultures are more likely to use fewer categorical words while employing more provisional language, such as *maybe, possibly,* and *probably.*[27] These practices are reflective of contrasting worldviews—the Western worldview being linear and the non-Western worldview being relational and therefore focused on avoiding the use of more extreme wordings.[28] Do your experiences confirm this observation?

The Japanese share the collectivist perception; in general, they tend to trust those who are silent more than those who talk a lot. The Japanese value social discretion; they believe that talking can be dangerous to a relationship because it may precipitate social disapproval that may unnecessarily contribute to the embarrassment of others.[29] Consequently, rather than risk interpersonal consequences or express disagreement or anger with another, the Japanese prefer to remain silent.

In contrast, people from Arab cultures tend to engage others in conversation much more directly and to use an abundance of overassertions or exaggerations when conversing.[30] Often, for example, a simple no is construed by other Arabs to mean yes, and thus, Arabs must rely on verbal exaggeration to make or drive home a point.[31]

Puerto Rico, a collectivist, high-context culture, shares a number of characteristics with Asian cultures. Like Asians, Puerto Ricans typically do their best to reduce the risk of any conversational confrontation, preferring to be more imprecise and indirect when it comes to clarifying a message's meaning rather than explicit and direct. What is *not* said in a conversation with someone from Puerto Rico may be more significant than what is said.[32]

Feelings about turn taking also vary among cultures. Because they value succinctness rather than verboseness, for example, people from Asian cultures tend to take short turns when conversing and try to distribute turns evenly.[33] In contrast, North Americans tend to take longer turns, which they distribute unevenly, with the participant who initiated a topic characteristically attempting to monopolize conversation. To the extent that we understand such differences, we increase our chances of facilitating effective conversations with people from diverse cultures.

GO ▶

WATCH THIS 7.1
For a video on effective conversation skills visit the student study site.

GENDER DIFFERENCES AND CONVERSATION

Men and women view and define conversation differently. A number of the differences are attributable to the value men place on instrumental behavior and their preference for engaging in organized activities or interacting in groups and the value women place on talk and their preference for engaging in one-on-one, person-to-person communication.[34] Underscoring this basic difference, linguist Deborah Tannen notes that for men, conversations "are negotiations in which people try to achieve and maintain the upper hand if they can, and protect themselves from others' attempts to put them down and push them around," whereas for women, conversations "are negotiations for closeness in which people try to seek and give confirmation and support, and to reach consensus. They [women] try to protect themselves from others' attempt to push them away."[35] As a result, women and men often misunderstand each other's intentions. Women wonder why men are not interested in discussing a situation's details, and men wonder why women want to waste their time talking about trivial matters.

Conversation is a collaborative effort.

Conversation is a collaborative effort. Everything that happens during conversation is the doing of the participants, including interrupting. For interruption to succeed, one speaker begins speaking before being yielded the floor, and another speaker must stop speaking as a result. Men and women differ in the amount of interrupting they do during their conversations with each other. Interrupting provides the interrupter with an opportunity to violate the turn-taking system, exercise his or her conversational power, and assume greater conversational control.

Who do you think interrupts more—men or women? Typically, the interrupter is male.

In this excerpt from her book *Gender and Discourse,* researcher and sociolinguist Deborah Tannen focuses on a gender-based conversational perception:

> A joke has it that a woman sues her husband for divorce. When the judge asks her why she wants a divorce, she explains that her husband has not spoken to her in two years. The judge then asks the husband, "Why haven't you spoken to your wife in two years?" He replies, "I didn't want to interrupt her."

> This joke reflects the commonly held stereotype that women talk too much and interrupt men. On the other hand, one of the most widely cited findings to emerge from research on gender and language is that men interrupt women far more than women interrupt men. This finding is deeply satisfying insofar as it refutes the misogynistic stereotype and seems to account for the difficulty getting their voices heard that many women report having in interactions with men. At the same time, it reflects and bolsters common assumptions about the world: the belief that an interruption is a hostile act, with the interrupter an aggressor and the interrupted an innocent victim. Furthermore, it is founded on the premise that interruption is a means of social control, an exercise of power and dominance.

Consider this: To what extent do your experiences support or contradict the observations of Tannen and others? Explain your answers using specific examples.

SOURCES: See V. Chand, "Linguistic Anthropology," *Current Anthropology,* 46, 2005, p. 261–362.

Deborah Tannen, *Gender and Discourse,* New York: Oxford University Press, 1994, p. 54–55.

However, in other situations, interruptions can be construed not as power plays but as a sign of conversational or social comfort, where one party feels free to interrupt the other and the interrupted party does not feel infringed on and does not resent the interruption.[36] When this occurs, there is a conversation duet or supportive cooperative overlapping, which actually greases a conversation's wheels, encouraging and reinforcing the speaker, rather than an attempt at conversational domination, which can and often does bring conversation to a halt.[37]

MEDIA AND TECHNOLOGY TALK

Media and technology have changed how we converse in person as well as via computers and smartphones. As we observed in the introduction to this chapter, technology increases opportunities for communication. The question is, however, whether we are sacrificing meaningful conversation for mere connection—a concern expressed by author, psychologist, and MIT professor Sherry Turkle. Turkle observes that we have become too comfortable being "alone together."[38] Technology frees us to be with each other and somewhere else simultaneously. We want to pay attention to what interests us, but not

ANALYZE THIS: *Don't Finish My Thoughts*

Read the following selection from Henrik Ibsen's classic play *A Doll's House*, in which Torvald Helmer and his wife, Nora, whom he has always treated as though she were a child, are engaged in a conversation:

Nora: *(Looking at her watch.)* It's not so late yet. Sit down, Torvald; you and I have much to say to each other. *(She sits at one side of the table.)*

Helmer: Nora—what does this mean? Your cold, set face—

Nora: Sit down. It will take some time. I have much to talk over with you. *(Helmer sits at the other side of the table.)*

Helmer: You alarm me, Nora. I don't understand you.

Nora: No, that is just it. You don't understand me; and I have never understood you—till to-night. No, don't interrupt. Only listen to what I say.—We must come to a final settlement, Torvald.

Helmer: How do you mean?

Nora: *(After a short silence.)* Does not one thing strike you as we sit here?

Helmer: What should strike me?

Nora: We have been married eight years. Does it not strike you that this is the first time we two, you and I, man and wife, have talked together seriously?

Helmer: Seriously! What do you call seriously?

Nora: During eight whole years, and more—ever since the day we first met—we have never exchanged one serious word about serious things.

Helmer: Was I always to trouble you with the cares you could not help me to bear?

Nora: I am not talking of cares. I say that we have never yet set ourselves seriously to get to the bottom of anything.

Helmer: Why, my dearest Nora, what have you to do with serious things?

Nora: There we have it! You have never understood me—

1. What can you tell about Nora and Torvald's relationship from this brief conversation?

2. Have you ever initiated a conversation similar to this one that signaled a turning point in a close relationship?

3. If so, did the person you were addressing attempt to interrupt you? Did you attempt to interrupt him or her? How did each of you respond?

SOURCE: Henrik Ibsen, *A Doll's House* (1879), translated by William Archer, in *Six Plays by Henrik Ibsen*, New York: Barnes & Noble Classics, 2003, p. 311–312.

necessarily the person we are with. Even as we connect, Turkle notes, we hide. She quotes the words of a wistful sixteen-year-old: "Someday, someday, but certainly not now, I'd like to learn how to have a conversation."[39] Far too many of us are not comfortable conversing face-to-face. We wear headsets connected to smartphones and computers, keeping even people who are near us at a distance. According to Turkle, no matter how valuable Twitter and Facebook are, connecting with others through them does not substitute for

TRY THIS: *Squawk Talk*

Think about the ways your conversation or your expectations for conversation have been influenced by broadcast programs and films. To what extent, if any, do you think we use such offerings to learn how to talk to each other and what to talk about?

1. Cite an example of conversation initiation, topic focusing, and termination used in a television sitcom or drama, film, or talk show that you have copied or used in conversation with another person. Compare and contrast the results you achieved with the media results.

2. Listen to or view a talk show. Count the number of times the show's host or guests attack, embarrass,

and/or insult each other; raise their voices; interrupt each other; or otherwise display anger, frustration, or impatience with one another.

3. In your opinion, does poor conversational behavior make "good" radio or television? If yes, why? If no, how do you account for the popularity of shows featuring such behavior?

conversation—the means of communicating that calls on us to see things from another's perspective.[40] Unfortunately, even when conversing face-to-face, we sometimes fail to achieve that goal.

MEDIA TALK

The nature of conversation on radio and television talk shows has coarsened over the years. Even during presidential debates, the candidates talk over one another. Instead of mirroring the "constructive buzz of the public square," too frequently participants demonstrate their incivility. On programs such as *The O'Reilly Factor, Imus in the Morning,* and *The Rush Limbaugh Show,* hosts and guests commonly use insults, speech that degrades, and pronouncements that encourage defensiveness or hostile reactions. Hosts and guests repeatedly verbally attack and chronically interrupt one another, exhibit little patience for alternative points of view, belittle each other, and raise their voices so that they literally yell at and talk over each other. While at the same time offering few examples of genuine, well-mannered, and well-informed conversation, the media provide a multitude of negative models of conversation for listeners and viewers to emulate when interacting with each other.[41]

TECHNOLOGY TALK

Advances in technology are contributing to many of us finding it difficult to imagine person-to-person contact apart from electronic connections. Cyberspace is constantly in our hands or worn over our ears. Legions of people walk down the street or sit in cafés communicating with others who are not physically present in the same space. We have the ability to converse with virtually anyone, no matter where he or she is located, at any time. And when we do so, we are more apt to be blunt, sometimes even cruel, than we are in face-to-face encounters.

For some of us, talking face-to-face or on cell phones is passé; we prefer texting—even when the person we want to text shares an environment we are in. Some of us think nothing of interrupting a face-to-face conversation to respond to someone who is not present, but who is calling, texting, or tweeting us. For some reason, the person reaching out via technology tends to be given priority to interrupt our "real-world" conversations. Some observers have asserted that face-to-face conversation may be in

WHAT DO YOU KNOW?

True or False

5. *Texting is taking the place of face-to-face conversations.*
True. Many prefer texting to conversing orally.

jeopardy, that we may be jettisoning verbal communication. In fact, surveys conducted by the Pew Research Center have found that text messaging on a smart phone is teenagers' favored means of communicating, with half of teens sending sixty or more text messages daily (up from fifty in 2009) and one-third sending more than one hundred.[42]

Describe how you feel when someone with whom you're conversing multitasks while interacting with you.

Prior to **computer-mediated communication**, or CMC, we were typically aware of whom we were conversing with. When we tweet or post online, however, we may be doing so without full knowledge of everyone who will read and react to our words because the person(s) we intend our posts for can send them on to others without our permission or knowledge.

In addition, technology makes it commonplace for us to multitask. We often find ourselves participating in multiple conversations simultaneously. While we sometimes do the same when engaged in face-to-face discussions, in those instances usually those with whom we are interacting are aware of our side conversations. This is not necessarily true when we go online; when online we can conduct an array of conversations with a number of persons, each of whom might believe we are interacting solely with him or her while we text others, talk on our cell, or tweet yet someone else. While our attention is divided, somehow we manage to keep numerous conversational threads going. It is as if we keep our finger on the shoulders of a number of people, tapping away, to keep them in our conversational sphere. Unlike person-to-person conversation, however, Twitter gives you a microphone, a means of listening in on millions of conversations daily.[43]

How is all this media multitasking affecting us? It may be hurting some of us—especially teenagers—socially and emotionally. In fact, face-to-face time correlates with higher levels of social confidence.[44] It may well be that watching others' faces lets us better interpret their emotions, which makes us feel more comfortable socially and more emotionally engaged. Looking at people, not just devices and not just via Skype, is key.[45]

Unlike our contributions to face-to-face conversations, blog entries can be reread and revised before we post them.

Blogging provides another means we use to compose our thoughts and share our ideas with others. Years back, people recorded their secret wishes, regrets, social problems, and the like in personal diaries. Today, we use blogs (a term derived from *Web logs*) to write about our problems, vent, relieve stress, and permit others to respond. For the most part, reader responses to personal revelations tend to be supportive, helping the blogger put things in perspective.[46] As with all forms of conversation, however, while we can use a blog to comment on our hopes, likes and dislikes, opinions, and other views, we can also use it to spread rumors and gossip.[47] Bloggers tend to write on a regular basis, but unlike face-to-face conversations, which are for the most part spontaneous, blog entries can be reread and revised before they are posted for others to read and respond to.

Computer-mediated communication: Communication that uses computers as a means of linking individuals.

Whereas face-to-face conversations have clear beginnings and endings, a conversation begun in cyberspace may terminate without our full awareness. In other words, our conversational partner can disengage without notifying us. How do you feel when, in the midst of an online chat, you discover that you literally are talking to yourself? Would you prefer that your partner clue you in to his or her departure, perhaps by typing "gotta go"? What if a partner you had been talking to face-to-face simply walked away without so much as a word? Are the two situations comparable? While the latter is unexpected, sadly, more and more people are accepting abrupt technological disconnections as normal. Do you?

GAINING COMMUNICATION COMPETENCE: IMPROVING YOUR CONVERSATION SKILLS

Developing the skills noted in the following can facilitate your ability to participate in and manage conversations more effectively.

DEVELOP METACONVERSATIONAL ABILITIES

Just as metacommunication is communication about communication, **metaconversation** is conversation about conversation. Be willing to talk with your conversational partner about *how* you talk to one another. Share your insights about intentions, messages sent, perceived contradictions or inconsistencies, and impressions of each others' thoughts and feelings. It is important to commit to developing a greater understanding of the factors involved in effective conversation.

DEVELOP AWARENESS OF HOW CULTURE AND GENDER DIFFERENCES AFFECT CONVERSATION

In practicing your skills, be aware of how culture and gender differences may influence your conversational style and reaction to each other. What works in China may not work in the United States or in Muslim countries. To facilitate interaction with people whose cultural background or gender differs from your own, you need to open yourself to and respect the differences that exist, maintain a flexible rather than rigid outlook, and engage in conversation to increase your understanding of one another. This means that you need to be unconditionally accepting of differences; you should not make others feel that they have to conform to your preferences for you to interact with them.

STRIVE TO IMPROVE CONVERSATION INITIATION, MANAGEMENT, AND TERMINATION ABILITIES

Every communicator shares responsibility for beginning, managing, and terminating conversations. This means we are each responsible for performing speaking and listening functions, and we are each responsible for ensuring that we take advantage of conversational opportunities.

To that end, you need to monitor your own behavior in addition to monitoring the behavior of the person you are conversing with. Demonstrate your concern for others in addition to your concern for yourself. Practice active listening, be sensitive to expressions that signal turn-taking preferences, find ways to communicate your personal involvement and your interest—or your lack of personal involvement and disinterest—in appropriate ways, and terminate or attain conversational closure in a manner that is confirming and nonoffensive, leaving the door open for possible future encounters.

Metaconversation:
Conversation about conversation.

CONNECT THE CASE: *The Case of the Company Party*

It would be one of those company parties—the kind where you don't really know anyone, so you stand around and feel awkward and totally unconnected. Even though he wasn't the chitchatty type, Alberto knew he was expected to attend. He told himself that it meant he would have to spend time interacting with people he really didn't want to spend any extra time with. He had no interest in them, just as they probably had no interest in him.

Alberto thought about trying to get out of going to the party. He considered using the old "car trouble" excuse, but he dismissed that idea quickly because it was trite and seemed too obvious. He had gone so far as to mention to a coworker that he wasn't feeling well, but he knew that his not showing up at the party would only create more problems for him. So a little while after testing out the "sickness" excuse, he had said he felt better.

Alberto saw no way out. He had to go. He hated the thought of going so much that he went so far as to briefly consider quitting his job to avoid having to be put in these uncomfortable situations time and again. But giving up his job really wasn't feasible.

From the moment Alberto arrived at the party, he felt out of place, just as he thought he would. Not one person approached him, and he didn't approach anyone either. He longed to find a quiet little corner, sit down, and do his best to look introspective. He considered interacting with the catering staff so that he wouldn't stand out as unapproachable. He took out his cell and pretended to text.

Suddenly, seemingly out of nowhere, a person Alberto had never spoken to before stood before him. Alberto was dumbstruck. He could think of nothing to say. He opened his mouth, hoping some interesting words would come out, but his nerves got the better of him. Alberto was a wreck. As he excused himself, uttering something about having just received an emergency text, and hurried to leave the room, an even sicker feeling consumed him. Looking at the framed picture on the wall of the hallway, Alberto realized that the person he had just turned his back on was the company's president and chairman of the board.

Consider these questions:

1. If you were Alberto's friend, what advice would you give him about how to survive and thrive at a company party or similar function?

2. Have you ever been in a situation similar to the one Alberto found himself in? How did you handle it? How would you handle it now?

REVIEW THIS

CHAPTER SUMMARY

1 Define small talk, conversation, and conversational turn taking and enumerate the skills shared by good conversationalists. Small talk is spontaneous conversation; it facilitates our making contact with others. Conversation is a "relatively informal social interaction in which the roles of speaker and hearer are exchanged in a nonautomatic fashion under the collaborative management of all parties."[48] Conversational turn-taking facilitates the maintenance and flow of a conversation. Affecting turn taking are turn-maintaining and turn-yielding signals, turn-requesting and turn-denying signals, and backchannel signals.

2 Identify the five parts of a conversation. Most conversations proceed in the following five stages: greeting, topic priming, heart of the conversation, preliminary processing, and closing. Each stage serves different functions and occupies an important place in the conversation's life.

3 Describe how cultural and gender differences influence feelings and perceptions of the nature and value of conversation. Both cultural and gender differences influence our attitudes about the nature and value of conversation. For example, while the members of some cultures view talk as a means of gaining social control, others use silence for this purpose. Whereas for men conversations are negotiations for achievement, for women they are negotiations for closeness.

4 Discuss how the media and technology are helping to reinforce or change both the substance and the nature of conversation. Media talk shows are providing models of incivility, leading to the coarsening of conversations. New technologies are widening the kinds of conversations we are having, freeing us to conduct multiple conversations simultaneously, some of which are face-to-face and some of which take place in cyberspace.

5 Identify specific steps you can take to improve your conversational skills. By working to increase your understanding of conversations and taking the time to develop your conversational skills, you can enrich your potential for developing meaningful relationships.

CHECK YOUR UNDERSTANDING

1 Can you offer an example that displays the role small talk plays in relationship building? (See page 190.)

2 Can you create a scenario illustrating the difference between an effective and an ineffective conversationalist? (See pages 190–191.)

3 Can you deconstruct a recorded conversation by identifying its parts? (See pages 192–196.)

4 Can you describe specific ways in which gender, culture, media, and technology affect your conversational exchanges? (See pages 200–206.)

5 Can you devise a plan to enhance your conversational skills? (See page 206.)

CHECK YOUR SKILLS

1 Can you engage in conversation comfortably with a new acquaintance? (See pages 191–192 and page 195; *Try This,* page 191; and *Try This,* page 192.)

2 Can you apply the rules of everyday conversation when interacting with others? (See pages 190–193 and 196–200; and *Try This,* page 193.)

3 Can you identify the phases of a conversation? (See pages 193.)

4 Can you use an appropriate conversational opener to signal your accessibility? (See page194.)

5 Can you use both open- and closed-ended questions, depending on your conversational goals? (See pages 194–195.)

6 Can you close a conversation skillfully? (See page 196.)

7 Can you use and respond competently to turn-taking signals? (See page 197; and *Try This,* page 198.)

8 Can you adjust the nature of your conversation to reflect the culture- and gender-influenced preferences of another person? (See pages 200–201; *Reflect on This,* page 202; and *Analyze This,* page 203.)

9 Can you distinguish between appropriate and inappropriate conversation in media offerings and online social interactions? (See pages 202–206; and *Try This,* page 204.)

10 Can you diagnose and overcome conversational challenges? (See *The Case of the Company Party,* page 207.)

KEY TERMS

Small talk   *190*

Conversation deprivation   *190*

Conversation   *191*

Conversational rules   *191*

Conversational structure   *192*

Open-ended question   *195*

Closed-ended question   *195*

Conversational maintenance   *195*

Conversational turn taking   *196*

Turn-maintaining signals   *197*

Turn-yielding signals   *197*

Turn-requesting signals   *197*

Turn-denying signals   *197*

Backchannel signals   *197*

Quality maxim   *197*

Quantity maxim   *197*

Relevancy maxim   *197*

Manner maxim   *198*

Monologue   *198*

Dialogue   *198*

Conversational blunder   *200*

Prejudiced talk   *200*

Computer-mediated communication   *205*

Metaconversation   *206*

STUDENT STUDY SITE

Visit the student study site at **www.sagepub.com/gambleic** to access the following materials:

- SAGE Journal Articles
- Videos
- Web Resources
- eFlashcards
- Web Quizzes
- Study Questions

chapter 8

Emotions are contagious.

—Karl Jung

Anyone can be angry—that is easy. But to be angry with the right person to the right degree, at the right time, for the right purpose, and in the right way—that is not easy.

—Aristotle

EMOTIONS

LEARNING OBJECTIVES

After completing this chapter, you should be able to demonstrate mastery of the following learning outcomes:

1. Describe the benefits of emotional intelligence and the consequences of emotional ineptitude.

2. Explain the role that emotions play in emotion contagion.

3. Compare and contrast emotion states and emotion traits.

4. Identify how emotions can contribute to relationship facilitation or relationship debilitation.

5. Describe how culture and gender affect the expression of emotion.

6. Discuss how the media and technology serve as both models and channels for the emotions we exhibit.

7. Identify steps you can take to share emotions more effectively.

Surprise—your friend dyed her hair an interesting shade of purple! Sadness—your grandfather's cancer is incurable. Anger—your BFF has been secretly going out with your significant other. Fear—you hear a gunshot right outside your home. Emotions are powerful forces that help to mark the high and low points of our lives. Falling in love, having a baby, grieving, experiencing an act of violence personally or vicariously—all these arouse our emotions. Our emotional responses reveal what we care about and what we think is of consequence.

Because our emotions may move us in ways we do not anticipate, sometimes they also get the better of us.[1] They may, for example, affect our judgments and our ability to make rational decisions.[2] This can happen, for example, if we overidentify with another person's pain or joy, or

> **Emotions are powerful forces that help to mark the high and low points of our lives.**

become paralyzed by fear.[3] When we are overwhelmed with emotion, we can find it challenging to control our reactions. And when handled poorly, emotions can have frightening effects, sometimes leading us to the dark side of emotional experience, where visceral fear and anger take over and rationality disappears. Daniel Goleman notes numerous examples of this happening in his often-cited book *Emotional Intelligence*.[4] When a student goes on a violent rampage after being insulted by another student, a motorist experiences road rage after being cut off by another motorist, or a Neighborhood Watch member responds to a perceived threat by "standing his ground" and shooting a weaponless teenager, we are witness to the effects of out-of-control, badly managed emotions.

WHAT DO YOU KNOW?

Before continuing your reading of this chapter, which of the following five statements do you believe to be true and which do you believe to be false?

1. Feeling depressed affects your breathing.　　　　　　T　F

2. Anger is the briefest of all emotions.　　　　　　　　T　F

3. We feel closer to those people we laugh with.　　　　T　F

4. The use of Botox contributes to emotional expressiveness.　　T　F

5. On Twitter, good news travels faster than bad news.　　　　T　F

Read the chapter to discover if you're right or if you've made any erroneous assumptions.

ANSWERS: 1. T; 2. F; 3. T; 4. F; 5. F

How we feel about a situation influences our emotional response.

Emotional intelligence helps us maintain emotional balance. It also helps us keep our relationships healthy. When in possession of emotional intelligence we motivate ourselves to persist in the face of frustration, to control impulses and delay gratification, and to regulate our moods so we keep distress from swamping our ability to think, to empathize, and to hope.[5] In contrast, **emotional ineptitude**, or the inability to control an emotional response, is the root cause of many relationship problems. Once we have an emotional outburst, we may regret it, but the relational damage is done.

In this chapter, we explore steps can we take to prevent relational damage, including how we can recognize our feelings and better understand our emotions so that when we respond, we don't end up hurting ourselves. By shaping our emotional habits, we take steps to prevent either out-of-control or festering emotions from destroying our relationships—overtly or insidiously.

WHAT ARE EMOTIONS?

Emotions are the feelings we experience in reaction to our surroundings and others. Emotions are our stimuli for responding to the differences we perceive between the self and the environment.[6] For example, if we sense a personal gain from a relationship, we are apt to feel confident. On the other hand, if we feel threatened by the relationship, we are apt to feel anxious. Thus, it is how we feel about the interpersonal situation that influences our emotions, feelings, and emotional response to the situation.

Our emotions are accompanied by physiological changes within our bodies and physical changes in our appearance. Some emotions, such as anger, increase respiration and heart rate and may cause us to become tense and flushed and to raise our voices or strike out at those around us. Other emotions have the opposite effects. For example, depression slows respiration and may cause us to visibly pale, sit sullenly, or cry uncontrollably.

By becoming more aware of our emotional responses to people and events and others' responses to us, we become more aware of what it is about the relationships we share that is important to us. For example, we may enjoy being with some people because they make us laugh. Laughter is believed to correlate with feelings of well-being, primarily because of the release of endorphins—brain chemicals known for their feel-good effect.[7]

As noted in our discussion of perception in Chapter 3, not everyone responds to the same stimulus in the same way or with the same intensity. Each of us experiences unique physical and psychological sensations as our emotions affect us in complicated ways. By focusing on both response differences and similarities, we can learn about our unique emotional style and how we can best cope with our feelings.[8] As one theorist observes, "The joyful person is more apt to see the world through 'rose colored glasses,' the distressed or sad individual is more apt to construe the remarks of others as critical, and the fearful person is inclined to have *tunnel vision,* that is, to see only the frightening object."[9] Thus, our emotions help color our relationships.

Emotional intelligence: The ability to motivate oneself or to persist in the face of frustration; to control impulse and delay gratification; to regulate one's mood and keep distress from swamping the abilities to think, empathize, and hope.

Emotional ineptitude: The inability to handle and control one's emotional responses.

Emotions: The feelings one experiences in reaction to one's surroundings.

Developmental psychologist Howard Gardner believes that at the very core of intrapersonal and interpersonal intelligence are the ability to gain "access to one's own feelings and the ability to discriminate among them and draw upon them to guide behavior," together with the "capacities to discern and respond appropriately to the moods, temperaments, motivations, and desires of other people."[10] By developing a broader awareness of and sensitivity to feelings through "mindfulness mediation," we also can cultivate greater **resilience**, an ability to cope with and recover quickly from disappointments.[11]

WHY EMOTIONAL INTELLIGENCE IS IMPORTANT

Emotional intelligence is a form of **social intelligence**—the ability to understand and relate to people.[12] According to Gardner both intrapersonal and interpersonal intelligence are integral components of social intelligence.

With intrapersonal intelligence, we are able to recognize our own emotions and manage them by finding ways to handle such feelings as fear, anxiety, anger, and sadness. What is more, we learn to display emotional self-control, which frees us to channel our emotions in the service of a goal. By knowing ourselves, we are more likely to recognize similar emotions in others, a skill that strengthens interpersonal intelligence.

Monitoring our own emotions is critical for developing self-understanding. When emotionally intelligent, we monitor our own and others' emotions, discriminating among the emotions we experience and using what we discern to guide our thinking and actions.[13] For example, does arguing with a friend ruin the rest of your day? If a dinner engagement is canceled, do you feel depressed for hours? How quickly do you recover from disappointments? Once we get in touch with our true feelings, we can learn to control them; failing to develop such awareness leaves us at their mercy. Learning to manage our emotions enables us to develop the resilience necessary for us to bounce back from setbacks and upsets. With greater resilience, we are better able to shake off feelings that debilitate and/or de-energize us.

The ability to employ the appropriate emotions in pursuit of a goal is also a useful skill. By displaying emotional self-control and a willingness to delay gratification, we facilitate goal realization.

As you learned in the discussion of listening in Chapter 4, empathy, the ability to tune in to what others are feeling and to feel with them, is an important interaction skill. Those who are **emotionally tone-deaf** usually do not have as many fulfilling relationships as do the emotionally attuned. In fact, to become interpersonally effective, we need to develop our ability to manage emotions in others as well as in ourselves.[14]

THE LOOK AND FEEL OF EMOTIONS

Years ago, there was a hit song titled "The Look of Love." Have you ever stopped to consider what love actually looks like? When we are in love, our facial expressions and body language often reveal our emotions to others. (See Chapter 6 on nonverbal communication.) In fact, while different cultures may have rules that guide emotional displays, the physical expressions associated with particular emotions appear to be virtually universal. For that reason, even without understanding another's language, we are often able to identify the emotion the person is expressing—we can tell whether he or she is angry, feels threatened, or feels at ease and is having a good time.

According to nonverbal communication expert Paul Ekman, particular facial patterns support the expression of each emotion.[15] Let us see how this works for a number of selected emotions.

Resilience: The ability to cope with and recover quickly from disappointments.

Social intelligence: The ability to understand and relate to people.

Emotionally tone-deaf: Unable to listen empathetically.

True or False
2. *Anger is the briefest of all emotions.*
False. Surprise is the briefest of all emotions.

Surprise! Surprise is the briefest of all emotions, flitting quickly across our faces. We express surprise by lifting our eyebrows, creating horizontal wrinkles across the forehead, slightly raising our upper eyelids, and usually opening the mouth in an oval shape. The lifting of the eyebrows also allows us to take in a larger visual area and enables more light to strike the retina. Surprise may transform into happiness if the stimulus that caused it leads to something favorable; it also may transform into anger or fright if the event that created it in the first place leads to a perceived threat or outrage.

Anger. Anger is an emotion that has garnered a lot of attention because of the damage it can do if poorly handled. We feel anger when someone interferes with our ability to pursue or attain a goal, restraining us, physically or psychologically, by holding us back or by causing us to feel that we are incapable or unworthy. Actions of others that reveal disregard for our feelings or disdain for us may also produce in us feelings of anger and hostility. When we experience anger or hostility, we usually lower our eyebrows and draw them together to create a scowl or a frown. Often we stare at the object or person that elicited these feelings and tightly compress our lips or draw them back in a squarelike shape to reveal our clenched teeth. Our face may redden, and the veins in our neck and head may become more visible to others. As anger surges through us, blood flows to our hands, making it easier for us to grasp a weapon or, should we desire to do so, strike out; our heart rate increases, and adrenalin prepares us for possible action.[16]

Because contemporary American society discourages overt expressions of anger, we might conclude that expressing anger is dangerous and unhealthy. If communicated properly, however, it is neither. In fact, while it may be unhealthy to express a lot of anger often, it is better to express some anger than to avoid expressing anger at all. Research has found that the moderate expression of anger, compared with little or no expression, cuts the risk of heart attack and stroke in half.[17] Persons who do not express their anger at all have been found to be more likely to exhibit passive-aggressive behavior or a negative and hostile personality. It is important that we learn constructive ways to express angry feelings, using assertiveness rather than aggressiveness. Also of value is learning how to redirect angry feelings and calm down.

Lashing out unthinkingly takes a toll on a relationship.

When we express our feelings aggressively to a person about a situation that angers us, we lash out unthinkingly, escalating both our and the other person's anger and aggression. If we are hotheaded and have a low tolerance for frustration, we may respond inappropriately. On the other hand, when we respond to persons or situations that anger us by keeping our feelings hidden, suppressing them, and turning them inward, we often find ourselves feeling chronically grumpy and irritable as a result.

Repressed or prolonged anger is also unhealthy. A more effective response to anger is to figure out what triggered it so that we can express our angry feelings assertively by clarifying for the person(s) involved what our needs are and how they can be met without harming anyone else. This requires that we be able to calm down before responding so that we can control not just our outward behavior but also our internal responses. By relaxing, perhaps by doing some deep breathing or visualizing appropriate imagery, we can calm down angry feelings. Expressing angry feelings in assertive ways—ways that are respectful of our own needs and feelings as well as those of others—rather than in aggressive or suppressive ways is the healthiest means of dealing with anger.

A number of techniques, including cognitive restructuring, problem solving, and humor, have been shown to be useful in the management of anger. *Cognitive restructuring* involves changing the way we think. If, for example, we commonly react by swearing when we become angry because we exaggerate the situation, telling ourselves that this is the worse thing that could happen, we need to change that dramatic response by toning it down and reminding ourselves that this is not the end of the world. While we may feel frustrated, getting angry is not going to help. Instead, we need to adopt a more balanced perspective, identify the problem, and focus on facing and handling it. This involves mapping out a plan and monitoring progress toward it. Humor can also defuse anger that is in danger of escalating out of control. This is not to suggest that we laugh away the problem by making light of the situation or becoming overly sarcastic. Rather, humor is useful for helping us to avoid taking ourselves or the situation too seriously.[18]

Happiness. Like anger, happiness has received particular attention in recent years as researchers have explored happiness's impacts and have tried to gauge the happiness of people living in different countries.[19] In contrast to anger, happiness is the feeling that pulls our lips back and curves them gently upward in a smile. Our cheeks rise and the corners of our lips create wrinkles (some call them dimples) that run from the nose and eyes and out beyond our lips and cheeks. The key biological change during a happy state is increased activity in the brain center that inhibits negative feelings and increases our sense of energy. Social laughter, a nonverbal expression of happiness, not only contributes to interpersonal bonding and feelings of closeness but is also a source of health and well-being.[20] Just the physical act of laughing triggers an increase in endorphins, brain chemicals that, as noted earlier, contribute to our feeling good. In fact, in the devastating aftermath of the terrorist attacks of September 11, 2001, many Americans made simple happiness a top priority, their "new bottom line."[21] In recent years, researchers in an array of fields have sought to unravel the secrets of happiness.[22]

Thus, how much you smile and laugh is an indication of how happy you feel. In general, people who share a healthy romantic relationship are happier than those who do not. Additionally, happy people are likely to be more creative and productive. They also tend to have strong bonds with friends and family members. Interestingly, the frequency of positive experiences in life is more important than their intensity. Having many positive experiences enhances feelings of happiness. In fact, happiness researcher Daniel Gilbert asserts that happiness is the sum of hundreds of small things.[23] Nurturing social connections is one of them.

Can you predict what will make you happy and how long the feeling of happiness will last? Sadly, most of us are not terribly accurate at predicting either what will make us happy or how long our happiness will persist. In fact, few experiences—whether good or bad—affect us for longer than a few months. Yet, resilience and the ability to produce "synthetic happiness," or the happiness we create even when we do not get what we want, make it possible for us to make the best of every experience.[24] It seems that we are able to look for and find things that can make our lives happier.

Sadness. When we experience the opposite of happiness, sadness, we often exhibit a loss of facial muscle tone. We arch the inner corners of our eyebrows upward and draw them

WHAT DO YOU KNOW?

True or False
3. *We feel closer to those people we laugh with.*

True. People who laugh together are more likely to bond.

together. We may also raise our lower eyelids and draw down the corners of the mouth, and our lips may tremble. Accompanying sadness are a drop in energy and a slowing of the body's metabolism. What precipitated your last bout of sadness?

Fear. When we experience fear, we raise our eyebrows slightly as we draw them together. We open our eyes wider than usual, and our lower eyelids tense. We stretch our lips back tightly, and the center of the forehead wrinkles. Our body tells us that something is wrong. When did you last experience fear?

Disgust. Think of what your face looks like when you take a bite of a lemon. While this is not exactly the face of disgust, it comes close. Unquestionably, feelings of disgust do more than upset your stomach. Finding something disgusting alters your behavior, affecting virtually all aspects of your interpersonal relations, from romance to how close you get to others to whom you choose to sit near.[25]

Emotions: Primary, Mixed, and Contagious. Sometimes putting on the facial expression associated with an emotion can actually precipitate the feelings that the expression represents. In other words, facial expressions are not merely the visible signs of emotions: in some instances, they may in fact be the *cause* of emotions.[26] As the mind can influence the body, the body can also influence the mind.

Psychiatrist Robert Plutchik asserts that there are eight primary emotions: surprise, anger, fear, sadness, disgust, acceptance,

Figure 8.1 Wheel of Emotions

Primary emotions are inside the wheel.
Mixed emotions are outside the wheel.

SOURCE: Based on Robert Plutchik, "Emotions: A General Psychoevolutionary Theory," in Klaus R. Scherer and Paul Ekman, eds., *Approaches to Emotion*, Hillsdale, NJ: Lawrence Erlbaum, 1984, p. 197–218.

anticipation, and joy. According to Plutchik, these eight emotions can combine, like paint on a canvas, to form the following mixed emotions: remorse, a mixture of disgust and sadness; love, a combination of joy and acceptance; awe, a blend of fear and surprise; submission, a mixture of acceptance and fear; disappointment, a combination of sadness and surprise; contempt, a combination of anger and disgust; optimism, a blend of anticipation and joy; and aggressiveness, a mixture of anger and anticipation (see Figure 8.1).[27] Does your experience support or contradict the hierarchy of primary and secondary emotions that Plutchik describes? With a greater understanding of the amalgams of emotions we experience—mixtures involving emotions that sometimes conflict with one another—we can describe our feelings more accurately, develop a keener awareness of how they affect us, and process and respond to them appropriately.

It is also possible for us to catch a mood much as we catch a cold. We call this **emotion contagion**. People expose us to their moods in much the same way they pass their germs on. The better able we are to tune in to the moods of others—the more empathetic we are—the better our chances of catching the mood of the person with whom we are communicating. Highly empathetic people tend to develop emotional support and unconsciously mirror or imitate the moods and emotions of others.[28] People who are weak at both sending and receiving moods tend to have more relationship problems than do those who are more emotionally expressive and receptive.

Relationships don't experience emotions; we do.

EMOTIONS AFFECT EVALUATIONS

Although relationships affect our emotions, a relationship itself does not experience emotions—*we do*. When we feel good or experience what we perceive to be a positive emotion when interacting with another person, we tend to attribute that feeling to the other person and to the kind of relationship we share.[29] But when we feel a particular emotion, such as depression or rage, persistently, we are exhibiting an emotion trait. An **emotion trait** exists when we experience a specific emotion during person-to-person interactions regardless of whom we are interacting with.[30]

We are constantly experiencing some emotion. During any interpersonal encounter, we have various thoughts or feelings about the person with whom we are interacting and the situation itself. These thoughts elicit an **emotion state**, an emotional process of limited duration lasting from second to hours and varying in level of feeling from mild to intense.[31] This contrasts with the emotion trait, which persists for a long time. Examples of emotion states are the temporary sadness and happiness that come from hearing certain kinds of news.

Women report being in negative moods or emotion states about twice as often as do men and, as conflicting as it may seem, also report being in positive moods about twice as often as do men.[32] One reason cited for the disparity between women's and men's reports is that women's moods simply tend to be more intense than men's.[33] In addition, we generally seek to interact with those who share our mood. As a result, our moods tend to perpetuate themselves. Further, our moods influence our perceptions of the future. After viewing a comedy, for example, we are likely to evaluate our relationships and careers more positively that we do after viewing a tragedy. Thus, a good or bad mood can create in us an optimistic or pessimistic frame of mind and, in turn, influence how positively or negatively we view others and our future.

Emotion contagion: The passing of a mood from person to person, influenced by individuals' ability to respond to emotion in kind or to exhibit a parallel response.

Emotion trait: An emotion that persists during person-to-person interactions regardless of whom one is interacting with.

Emotion state: An emotion of limited endurance.

TRY THIS: *Emotional Checkup*

1. Which of the emotions on the following list do you recall experiencing during the past month? List them on a separate sheet of paper. (If necessary, add other emotions not listed here.)

Accepted	Angry	Anticipatory
Anxious	Apathetic	Apprehensive
Ashamed	Bewildered	Bored
Calm	Concerned	Confident
Confused	Contemptuous	Curious
Depressed	Desperate	Disappointed
Disgusted	Eager	Ecstatic
Embarrassed	Envious	Excited
Fearful	Guilty	Happy
Hostile	Hurt	Impatient
Insecure	Jealous	Joyful
Loving	Optimistic	Outraged
Paranoid	Pessimistic	Proud
Rejected	Relieved	Remorseful
Sad	Shy	Supported
Surprised	Stressful	Sympathetic
Tense	Useful	Useless
Vengeful	Vicious	Violent
Worried		

2. Go back through your list and place a checkmark next to each of the emotions you experience most frequently.

3. Think about the specific people you tend to be with when you experience your most frequent emotions. Write their names next to the appropriate emotions.

4. Review the emotions and the names you have written. What relationship variables can you point to as being the cause or precipitating factor for each emotion?

5. Finally, complete these sentences:
   I am anxious when I interact with _____.
   I am confident when I interact with _____.
   I am frustrated when I interact with _____.
   I am embarrassed when I interact with _____.
   I am happy when I interact with _____.
   I am stressed when I interact with _____.

Answering such questions can help us to identify which of our relationships are associated with our feeling particular emotions. The terms we use to label our feelings are based on our interpretations of the situations we experience.

RELATIONSHIPS AND EMOTIONS

Emotions can facilitate or impede the development of healthy relationships. **Coping** involves the management of our emotions. We use two key coping strategies. First, we may try to remove the problem. This is often difficult—if not impossible—to accomplish when it involves another human being. For example, when we are angry with someone, it is not always practical or desirable for us simply to remove the person from our surroundings. The second, more feasible and usually more effective, means of coping involves changing the way we interpret a situation and our emotional response to it. In the following subsections, we look at ways of coping with emotions.

ARE YOUR EMOTIONS FACILITATIVE OR DEBILITATIVE?

When we perceive that our interactions support our well-being, we usually experience positive or **facilitative emotions**, and we act in ways that permit our emotions to help our relational goals. When we perceive that others impede our well-being, we usually experience negative or **debilitative emotions**, and the actions accompanying these feelings typically get in the way of our developing a healthy relationship or realizing our relational goals.[34]

Although we all experience an array of emotions in our relationships, those most closely associated with relationship facilitation or goal attainment are compassion, happiness, hope, love, pride, and relief. Those most closely associated with debilitation, or that lead to our failing to attain our relational goals, are extreme anxiety, disgust, envy, terror, guilt, jealousy, paranoia, rage, sadness, and shame.

Both facilitative and debilitative emotions run the gamut of different types of feelings, but they differ from each other in two key ways—intensity and duration. We tend to feel debilitative emotions more intensely and for longer periods than facilitative emotions. Because of this, debilitative emotions interfere with our ability to engage in productive interactions. For example, although some anger can serve as a motivational force and even propel us to act, anger that is out of control—rage—typically reduces our ability to act rationally and, therefore, usually impedes our ability to make things better. Thus, how we experience and express our emotions can be facilitating or debilitating and can significantly affect our relationships with others.

WHAT DO YOU TELL YOURSELF?

How you interpret events often holds the key to handling your emotions. Consider the following two situations:

> Imagine you are walking by a friend's house. Suddenly your friend opens the door, throws a rock at you, and starts shouting obscenities at you. How do you respond?

> Imagine that instead of walking by a friend's house, you are walking by a mental institution in which your friend is a patient. When your friend hurls the same rock and shouts the same obscenities at you, will your reaction be the same?[35]

You would probably think about and react to these two situations differently. Whereas in the first situation you might feel angry and upset, most likely in the second you would feel saddened and distraught. Your interpretations cause you to experience different feelings.

What you tell yourself about the nature of your experiences determines whether you feel outrage or sympathy, compassion or disdain for others. We interpret the actions of others based on our feelings and the reasons we use to explain their behavior. Recall from

Coping: The managing of emotions.

Facilitative emotion: An emotion that promotes effective functioning.

Debilitative emotion: An emotion that impedes a person's ability to function effectively.

Chapter 3's discussion of perception that attribution theory describes how we infer and explain the causes of social behavior—that is, our belief regarding whether a specific behavior is due to a person's personality or to the situation the person finds him- or herself in affects our evaluation of that person. In other words, what we determine to be the reasons for someone else's behavior—rightly or wrongly—directly influences our perception of and feelings toward that person.[36]

WHAT DO YOU TELL ANOTHER PERSON?

How do you tell others what you are feeling? How do you explain your anger without becoming angry? How do you explain your disappointment without withdrawing into a shell? By making the effort to describe your feelings, rather than enact them, you increase your chances of keeping lines of communication open and improving your relationship.

When we describe our feelings, we are also communicating how we would like the other person to treat us as well as the effect that person's behavior is having on us. By sharing

What do these lines from a William Blake poem reveal about the power of our emotions?

I was angry with my friend:

I told my wrath, my wrath did end.

I was angry with my foe.

I told it not, my wrath did grow.

1. Do you agree with Blake? Is the expression of anger always beneficial?

2. In your own experiences with anger, have you found that verbally expressing it helps you purge yourself of anger, or does it cause you to feel even angrier? Explain.

SOURCE: William Blake, "A Poison Tree." 1794.

such information, we give that individual the opportunity to decide whether her or his behavior toward us is appropriate or is having the intended effect. For example, if you politely tell Lindsay that you get exasperated when she doesn't stop talking long enough to listen to you, maybe next time you interact she will seek a response from you instead of merely delivering a monologue. If you tell Ken that you are delighted to go with him to his friend's party, he is more likely to ask you again than if you say you will go but aren't really happy about it. When we share feelings, we make the other person more aware of how his or her actions affect us. But remember, **describing feelings** and **displaying feelings** are not the same thing. When we describe our feelings, we are not judging the other person. In contrast, an overt display of feelings—such as shouting, "That was the most stupid thing you've ever done!"—conveys an evaluation.

Emotions help structure our view of the world. When we are angry, we see the world as offensive; when we are fearful, we see it as threatening; when we are in love, we see it as beautiful. Those who do not share our perceptions of certain behavior will not experience the same emotions we do, but they are probably still capable of understanding our perceptions.

Though we find it easier to share positive emotions than negative ones, and we are reluctant to send messages that could hurt or embarrass another, it is important that we let someone know when we are angry with or disappointed in him or her. Because emotion is one of the most consequential outcomes of interaction, it is necessary that we let others know what causes us to feel as we do.[37] When our relationship partners understand how we feel, they are in a better position to make appropriate interpersonal choices regarding how best to interact with us.

WHAT IS YOUR EMOTIONAL ATTACHMENT STYLE?

Some of us easily express our emotions, whereas others prefer to be more reserved. Researcher Amir Levine, for example, differentiates among three styles of attachment: avoidant, anxious, and giving.[38] Persons with an avoidant attachment style tend to feel overwhelmed if bombarded with too much emotion. Too much physical and emotional closeness is likely to irritate them, making it difficult for them to be emotionally supportive.

WATCH THIS 8.1
For a video on coping skills visit the student study site.

Describing feelings:
Revealing how another's behavior affects one without expressing any judgment of that behavior.

Displaying feelings:
Overtly enacting one's feelings.

Avoidant people also are apt to devalue their relationship partners by joking about their habits or weight. In contrast, persons who display an anxious attachment style typically are uncomfortable communicating feelings, yet are constantly looking for cues of rejection in their partners. They want their partners to notice when they are upset or acting out and take corrective action without their having to give voice to their feelings. Emotional givers tend to be secure in showing affection; they enjoy being on both the sending and receiving ends of displays of love and are comfortable showing intimacy.[39]

What style of emotional expresser do you think you are? Identifying your style and recognizing the style another person displays can help prepare you to handle emotional challenges with more understanding as well as support you in the effort to cope with disappointments.

CULTURE AND THE EXPRESSION OF EMOTION

Climate may affect cultural variations in emotional expressiveness. It appears that persons from warmer places tend to be more emotionally expressive than persons living in cooler climates.[40] Despite this, as we have discussed, there are basic emotions that we all experience regardless of where we live. Not matter what our cultural background, at one time or another we all feel anger, disgust, fear, happiness, and sadness. As members of a multicultural society and citizens of a shrinking world, we must understand how our own cultural filters influence how we assess the behavior and the propriety of emotions displayed by persons from cultural groups other than our own. What generates our feelings and how expressive we are at displaying or revealing them are affected, in part, by the rules and norms of our culture.

For instance, the Japanese generally refrain from expressing negative emotions in public.[41] This is because members of collectivistic cultures, such as Japan, China, and India, place great value on preserving harmony and consequently discourage the expression of any negative feelings that could create disharmony among the group's members. In contrast, members of highly individualistic cultures, such as the United States and Canada, are comfortable "telling it like it is"—revealing their feelings to others.[42] In such cultures, always withholding feelings or keeping them secret so that others are unable to tell when you are hurt, happy, or sad is, for the most part, regarded as both inappropriate and an ineffective way to manage feelings. Similarly, traditional Mexican culture encourages the open display and discussion of emotion; in fact, Mexican Americans who maintain their allegiance to traditional Mexican culture are even more likely than other Americans to express negative emotions openly.[43]

When individuals from collectivistic and individualistic cultures interact with one another, the former might easily perceive the latter as too frank or direct. Similarly, those from individualistic cultures may perceive members of collectivistic cultures as not completely forthcoming, in part due to the importance collectivistic cultures place on helping all parties in an interaction save face.[44] **Face-saving**, or the preservation of dignity, is so important that should persons from individualistic cultures violate this norm when interacting with members of collectivistic cultures, the relationship they share can suffer.

When we are sensitive to another's cultural beliefs regarding emotional expression, we equip ourselves with the skills we require to modify how we express our own emotions.

Sharing positive emotions is easier than is sharing negative ones.

Face-saving: The preservation of a person's dignity; may involve giving indirect answers to avoid hurting or embarrassing another person.

Consider this example of a negotiation between two businesspeople, one Japanese and one American. After you read it, identify what you believe the problem was.

> Phil Downing . . . was involved in setting up a branch of his company that was merging with an existing Japanese counterpart. He seemed to get along very well with the executive colleagues assigned to work with him, one of whom had recently been elected chairman of the board when his grandfather retired. Over several weeks of discussion, Phil and the chairman of the Japanese branch had generally laid out some working policies and agreed on strategies that would bring new directions needed for development. Several days later . . . the young chairman's grandfather happened to drop in and he began to comment on how the company had been formed and had been built up by the traditional practices, talking about some of the policies the young executives had recently discarded. Phil expected the new chairman to explain some of the innovative and developmental policies they had both agreed upon. However, the young man said nothing; instead, he just nodded and agreed with his grandfather. Phil was bewildered and frustrated . . . and he started to protest. The atmosphere in the room became immediately tense. . . . A week later the Japanese company withdrew from the negotiations.

Phil failed to understand that the fact that the Japanese company's chairman had saved face for his grandfather by agreeing with him did not negate the agreements the chairman had earlier negotiated with Phil. Phil's overt protest and disagreement with the grandfather caused the grandfather to lose face, and the young chairman was now unwilling to do business with him. What would you have done in Phil's place?

SOURCE: Richard W. Brislin, Kenneth Cushner, Craig Cherrie, and Mahealani Yong, *Intercultural Interactions: A Practical Guide,* Beverly Hills, CA: Sage, 1986, p. 155–156.

GENDER AND THE EXPRESSION OF EMOTION

There are numerous differences between women and men in the handling of feelings. Because some men are taught to be more emotionally reserved than women, many males tend to be less expressive. As a result, some researchers say that men's friendships lack the emotional depth that characterizes women's friendships.[45] However, others counter that men lack neither feelings nor emotional depth; rather, they prefer to express their feelings and develop closeness with others through *doing* rather than through talking, through activities rather than through self-disclosure.[46]

Men and women vary in both expressiveness and sensitivity to others' emotions. Women are more likely than men to reveal a wide range of feelings, precipitating the stereotypes of women as overly expressive and of men as inexpressive. For example, women are known to cry more than men. Most would expect them to feel better after a good cry, but this is not necessarily the case. In one study, the mood of women on a crying day was found to be worse than on one during which they did not cry. Surprisingly, the negative mood characteristic of crying days persisted for the two subsequent days as well. The researchers found, in addition, that the less dark the woman's mood, the more likely crying was to help. What also helped was crying in the presence of another person. Crying in front of a group, as compared to a single individual, however, made things worse.[47]

In contrast to women, men try not to reveal feeling frightened, sad, lonely, or embarrassed. On the other hand, men tend to unabashedly reveal their strengths. As a

Men and women are likely to express feelings and closeness differently.

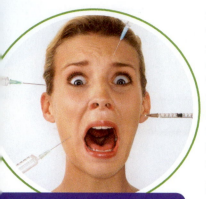

result, observers are less accurate in discerning men's emotions than they are in discerning women's.[48] Women are also better than men at noticing the clues that others provide regarding their emotions.[49] Thus, women tend to outperform men at decoding the emotions of others.[50] However, when it comes to the ability read others' feelings, men and women who use Botox to reduce facial lines may be at an equal disadvantage; research suggests that Botox dulls the user's ability to understand others' emotions. We read emotions partly by mirroring facial expressions, and because the drug paralyzes users' facial muscles, they cannot make a number of the facial movements normally active in facial expression mimicking. Thus, Botox not only impedes a user's ability to express emotions but may also impede the ability to empathize with another.[51]

Most women tend to prefer intimate talk, whereas most men prefer instrumental demonstrations of commitment.[52] By recognizing and understanding this stylistic difference, members of both sexes can take a giant step forward in being able to relate effectively to each other. This difference may also explain why, when under stress, both men and women report wanting to be with a woman friend, and why both men and women are in general more comfortable revealing feelings to women than to men.[53] These differences are played out in online communication as well, with women more likely than men to use emoticons as emotional clarifiers.[54]

MEDIA AND TECHNOLOGY: CHANNELING FEELINGS

The media and technology provide both the models and the channels we use daily to form attitudes about the most effective ways to handle and display our feelings. What we view in the media and the technologies we prefer affect both our willingness to communicate our emotions and the means we employ to express them.

MEDIA MODELS

Similar to what you learned in the chapter on perception, **media models**, the images that we see on television, in advertising, and in movies, have the potential to affect our emotions. Heavy television viewers (those who watch more than four hours a day) have different attitudes and hold different beliefs than do light viewers (those who watch fewer than two hours daily). For example, heavy viewers hold an exaggerated view of the prevalence of violence in society and believe that older people are fewer in number and less healthy today than in years past. In general, heavy television viewers perceive the world to be a meaner and more sinister place than do light viewers, believing that, if given the chance, people will take advantage of you because they are looking out only for themselves. The opinions that heavy viewers hold reflect the fictional world that television brings to them, not the world in which they actually live.[55] The fearfulness they experience, however, is all too real.

What we see in the media influences what we believe and how we evaluate experience, affecting how we feel and express our feelings. For example, heavy television viewers are less likely to presume innocence on the part of those accused of crimes and tend to take more of a hard line when serving on juries than do light viewers. This helps them handle the anger they feel about the perceived prevalence of societal violence. They also develop more fear

Media models: The images depicted in the mass media.

TRY THIS: *Sharing Feelings*

Think of a specific male and a specific female friend, sibling, or parent. Using a scale of 1 to 10, where 1 represents little if any comfort and 10 represents complete comfort, indicate how comfortable you are sharing the following feelings with each:

	Male	Female
A problem you have with him or her		
A problem you have with someone else		
Anger directed toward him or her		
Anger directed toward someone else		
A recent disappointment directed at him or her		
A recent disappointment directed at someone else		
Fears about him or her		
Fears about someone else		
What he or she does that makes you feel insecure		
What someone else does that makes you feel insecure		
What he or she does that causes you stress		
What someone else does that causes you stress		
What he or she does that makes you happy		
What someone else does that makes you happy		

1. With which of the two persons you have chosen are you most comfortable sharing your emotions? To what extent, if any, does gender appear to be a factor?

2. Which emotions are easiest for you to share with a female? With a male? Which are the hardest to share with a female? With a male? How do you account for the differences or similarities?

3. What general conclusions can you draw regarding individuals sharing emotions with person(s) of the same or opposite gender?

---

of crime than do light viewers and, due to repeated exposure to slasher-type programming, have less sympathy or empathy for rape victims. For heavy viewers, television serves as a vital source of information for constructing their image of the world.[56]

Media models also have the potential to influence our behavior. We simply are more likely to do what we have seen. After viewing a dramatized suicide, we may come to feel that suicide may be a reasonable way to deal with the problems life presents; after watching a televised fight, we may conclude that physical violence is an acceptable way to deal with disappointment.

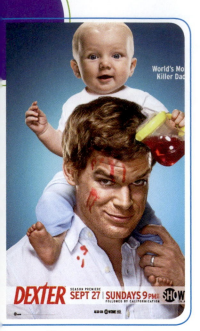

The amount of television we watch influences our emotions and our perceptions of the world.

Telepresence: The sense of physically being in a different place or time through virtual reality.

Emoji icons: Whimsical pictures used to supplement emoticons.

TECHNOLOGICAL CHANNELS

We are in control of both channels of mass and personalized communication. We now can call up television programs and movies on demand and view them whenever we want to on our tablets or smartphones. What is more, we are now able to create our own interactive media experiences.

We are no longer merely watchers; we are active participants. We may experience media versions of real worlds, or we can enter a virtual world. For a long time, we have vicariously experienced other worlds by watching television programs and movies and playing computer games, but virtual reality does something these media do not: it endows us with **telepresence**—it takes our body with us into another world, giving us the sense of physically being in a different place or time, allowing us to participate more fully in sensory experiences that elicit feelings and emotions we otherwise might never have experienced. Just as NASA and the military use virtual reality environments to train crews and members of the armed services for space travel and war, we can use virtual reality environments to train for future communication encounters unlike any we have had to date. How would you describe your use of virtual reality? Do you use it to escape from reality into a world of fantasy? Do you use it to help you more fullyprocess the human experience? Do you find participating in virtual reality experiences emotionally bankrupting, emotionally enriching, or emotionally neutral?

Social networking sites such as Twitter have given researchers new media to investigate. For example, they have found that social networks composed of company workers and family members facilitate the sharing of emotion, and that Twitter messages containing negative emotions are retweeted more frequently than other messages, leading them to conclude that bad news travels faster than good news.[57] Researchers who explored the Twitter messages posted by more than two million people in eighty-four countries discovered that the emotional tones of these messages exhibited similar patterns, not only through the day but also through the week and alternating seasons. After analyzing the posts and their accompanying emoticons, the researchers concluded that our moods reflect a shared underlying biological rhythm that transcends culture. We tend to be happiest on weekends, and we usually awaken in a good mood that deteriorates as the day progresses and then drifts upward again after dinner.[58] Still, some researchers caution that tweets may reveal what the tweeter thinks the follower wants to hear rather than the tweeter's actual feelings.[59] Do your experiences confirm these findings?

Of course, emoticons, an array of text-based representations of facial expressions and moods, are available to help us express our emotions in cyberspace when we aren't using a webcam or Skype and are unable to see or hear the nonverbal cues of the person we are interacting with (see Figure 8.2). For clarity's sake, we sometimes also include statements describing our feelings. In addition to emoticons, some also use whimsical pictures known as **emoji icons**, or emojis. Cousins of emoticons, these colorful pictorial creations are a bit more elaborate in their communication of emotion, and so let users convey more feeling in their messages. Long popular in Asia, emojis may suffer in translation. For example, in Japan, the emoji of a smiling coil of human waste expresses dissatisfaction. This may not resonate with people in the United States. Other emojis may be more easily understood by Americans, such as one titled "Titanic" that depicts both a ship's anchor and a broken heart.[60]

TRY THIS: *Modeling*

First, identify a media offering that you believe convinced you that a certain way of behaving was legitimate or appropriate. For example, have any television programs or films affected your way of dressing or manner of speaking?

1. Explain how what you viewed influenced how you felt and expressed your feelings, and as a result affected your response to a real-life situation.
2. To what degree, if at all, did the emotional rewards obtained by the mediated characters also accrue to you?
3. If given the opportunity, would you act the same or differently today? Explain.

Second, answer the following questions regarding the media models provided by extremely angry talk-show hosts, guests, and music artists:

4. In your opinion, what effect, if any, do such models have on you and other members of the viewing and listening public? Do you think they help educate us? Do you think they harm us?
5. What do you believe we stand to gain and/or lose from listening to hosts and other celebrities who make their living demonstrating an inability to handle their emotions, becoming aggressive, lashing out, and giving in to verbal impulses that trample on others' rights?

Also related to the expression of emotion through technological channels is **flaming**, or the losing of emotional self-control while sending a message online, which can lead to **flame wars**, or the exchange of out-of-control online messages. Sometimes we express our anger online by CAPITALIZING ALL OUR WORDS. Other times, our loss of control is signaled by our use of obscene or inappropriate language. And yet other times, we are just plain nasty and resort to derogatory words and vile insults.

Figure 8.2 Emoticons

:-1)	smiley with a mustache
:D	big smile
;-	wink
:*	kiss
:**:	returning kiss
:-J	tongue in cheek or joking
()	hug
:-(	sad
:'(	crying

Finally, how we use technology and what we use it for reveals our feelings about it as a conduit for interpersonal communication. When your smartphone or computer goes down, for example, are you relieved by the fact you are no longer connected, or do you panic because you may be unreachable and not able to reach anyone else for the time being? Does forgetting your phone completely stress you out? Technology can arouse us, involve us, affect our relationships with others, or leave us cold. For example, one researcher examined the brain activity of subjects viewing both religious images and consumer images involving brands such as Apple. The brain activity was strikingly alike for both stimuli. Another experiment demonstrated a "synesthesia" (cross-sensory effect), with subjects having activation in both the audio and visual cortices of their brains when they were exposed separately to audio and video of a ringing and vibrating iPhone. What is more, subjects' brains responded to their phones' sounds just as they did to the presence of a loved one. For some, technology appears to be a love affair.[61]

Flaming: The losing of emotional self-control while sending a message online.

Flame war: An exchange of out-of-control online messages.

GAINING COMMUNICATION COMPETENCE: COMMUNICATING EMOTION

A number of factors facilitate our accurately communicating our feelings. Among these are the ability to think productively about feelings, the ability to use precise language in talking about them, the willingness to accept ownership and responsibility for our feelings, the willingness to reveal the breadth or range of our feelings, and the ability to gauge the right time and place to discuss them.

RECOGNIZE THAT THOUGHTS CAUSE FEELINGS

The rational-emotional approach to emotion management posits that in order to turn off debilitative feelings and replace them with feelings that are facilitative, we first need to learn how to change unproductive thinking.[62] According to rational emotive behavior therapy founder and cognitive behavior psychologist Albert Ellis, the negative *beliefs* we hold about events and people, and not the actual events or people, cause us mental anguish and lead to mental and even physical discomfort. How we react emotionally to a person or event—that is, how we interpret the event or the behavior of a person—elicits different feelings in us and different consequences in our behavior. The key to understanding our feelings is to review our self-talk—our continuous internal monologue about what is occurring, the thought process that takes place before an emotion is expressed—and analyze whether the thoughts we have debilitate or facilitate our interactions and relationships.[63]

Do you panic when your smartphone fails or your computer crashes?

By taking responsibility for our own emotions and actions and by monitoring our emotional reactions to specific persons or situations, we can get in touch with our feelings. Once we realize how we feel, we can look for factors that trigger debilitative reactions in us. We need to record our self-talk; specifically, we need to identify the irrational beliefs we hold, explain why they are a product of irrational thinking, and choose as an alternative a more rational and realistic way of thinking for the next time we are faced with the same person or situation. Why should we allow our feelings to debilitate us when we can use them as facilitators instead? According to Albert Ellis, we create our own moods and emotional states with the words we use during self-talk.[64] We can reframe events by using different words to describe what has occurred. A person who persistently places a pessimistic frame around events will debilitate him- or herself, whereas a person who places an optimistic frame around events helps to facilitate instead. Persons who are optimists when young have been found to be in better health in middle age than those who had been pessimists.[65]

CHOOSE THE RIGHT WORDS

Many of us have a hard time letting others know exactly what we are feeling: we say we feel "good," "okay," or "bad." By relying on words that are not as specific as they could be or that do not adequately describe our emotions, we make it more difficult for others to understand us. If we can figure out what triggers a particular emotion, often, we can be more specific when we talk about it. We can also try to find words to describe what we feel happening to us: for example, we might say, "I feel like a robot, robbed of my personal identity"; "I feel like a trained seal"; or "I feel like an eagle." In addition, we can describe what we would like to do in response to our feelings: "I feel like sticking my head in the sand" or

"I feel like coming right over and kissing you." It is important that we work hard to describe our feelings and their intensity.

SHOW THAT YOU ACCEPT RESPONSIBILITY FOR YOUR FEELINGS

It is important to acknowledge that you own your feelings. To do this you need to identify yourself as the feelings' source. This means that you need to start your comments with "I," not "you." Instead of saying, for example, "You're always embarrassing me," you need to say, "I get embarrassed when . . ." Remember, no one can make you feel an emotion that you refuse to feel.

SHARE FEELINGS FULLY

Often what we feel is an amalgam of emotions rather than one single emotion. For example, we may feel anger, confusion, embarrassment, and sadness at the same time. To call such feelings simply anger would be misleading and not candid. To refuse to discuss what we are feeling at all could be even worse. Once the feelings have surfaced they will continue to exist, and they will not go away even when we try to ignore them. You ought to be able to share all feelings fully in the interest of openness.

DECIDE WHEN, WHERE, AND TO WHOM TO REVEAL FEELINGS

When you are angry is not the best time to let others know just how angry you are. Often it is wiser to wait a bit, collect your thoughts, and consider the best way to express your feelings to whoever you believe triggered your anger.

Deciphering our emotions and deciding how to deal with them can be a lengthy process. Be sure before you start a discussion of your feelings that you will have the time needed for a fair consideration of them.

DESCRIBE THE RESPONSE YOU SEEK

It is helpful if the person you are speaking to understands how you want him or her to respond to your expression of feelings. For example, you might end your statement by noting, "I need you to help me unwind after a busy day." By revealing how we feel, how we see things, and how we would like things to change, we take steps toward achieving a greater state of relational health and set the stage for continued relational growth.

CONNECT THE CASE: *The Case of Late Jean*

John was furious. Jean had promised she would be home for dinner on time for once. But once again, she was more than an hour late.

John had rushed home from work just so that they would be able to spend some time together, but here he was spending it alone. Obviously, he told himself, Jean does not consider our relationship as important as I do. Clearly, he reasoned, she always puts her work before me.

John felt disappointed. His emotions mixed together: annoyance fused with resentment, exasperation turned into outrage. His once adoring and caring spouse for some reason preferred work to being in his company. She was becoming more like a boarder, he told himself, not acting like a wife. Feeling dejected and almost desperate, he picked up his cell to text her.

Just as he was about to press "send" the front door opened. It was Jean—and she was carrying a bottle of his favorite dinner wine. "Sorry honey," she said. "I meant to be here an hour ago, but one thing led to another, and before I knew it, time got away from me."

After considering this case from the perspective of both John and Jean, answer the following questions:

1. If you were John, what would be the next words out of your mouth? Why?

2. Does Jean's bringing home John's favorite wine solve the problem? Does it to some extent help to alleviate the problem? Or is the wine an attempt to camouflage or conceal the problem? What do you think?

REVIEW THIS

CHAPTER SUMMARY

1 Describe the benefits of emotional intelligence and the consequences of emotional ineptitude. By learning to understand and handle our emotions—that is, by making a commitment to become emotionally intelligent—we increase our potential for sharing meaningful, effective relationships. On the other hand, when we display emotional ineptitude, or an inability to discuss or cope with our emotions, we contribute to continued relationship difficulties.

2 Explain the role that emotions play in emotion contagion. We use our faces and bodies to reveal emotion, and these displays may be mirrored by others. Some people are better than others at both communicating and reading emotions.

3 Compare and contrast emotion states and emotion traits. We are always experiencing some emotion. An emotion state is an emotional process of limited duration that varies in both duration and intensity. An emotion trait is an emotion state that persists beyond a period that is considered appropriate.

4 Identify how emotions can contribute to relationship facilitation or relationship debilitation. Emotions are reactions that influence our appraisals of interpersonal situations. The emotions we feel are accompanied by physiological changes in our bodies and physical changes in our appearance. By becoming more aware of our emotional responses and the emotional responses of others, we become more aware of what is important to each of us in our relationships as well as the extent to which our emotions help color our relationships.

5 Describe how culture and gender affect the expression of emotion. Among the emotions that members of all cultures experience are anger, disgust, fear, happiness, and sadness. However, both individual emotional expressiveness and contributing factors may vary across cultures. Men and women vary in both emotional expressiveness and sensitivity to the emotions of others.

6 Discuss how the media and technology serve as both models and channels for the emotions we exhibit. Media models affect our internalization and display of emotion. Technological channels allow us to personalize and control our interactive experiences as well as monitor our emotional responses.

7 Identify steps you can take to share emotions more effectively. The following factors facilitate the accurate communication of feelings: recognizing that our thoughts cause feelings, choosing the right words to describe our feelings, showing that we accept responsibility for our feelings, being able to share feelings fully, knowing when and where to reveal feelings, and describing the response we seek.

CHECK YOUR UNDERSTANDING

1 Can you offer examples to illustrate the difference between an emotionally intelligent and an emotionally inept response? (See pages 212–213.)

2 Can you describe what it feels like to be happy, sad, or angry and use your description to explain the processes of cognitive restructuring and emotion contagion? (See pages 213–217.)

3 Can you compare and contrast an emotion trait with an emotion state and assess the extent to which each has influenced your interaction in a relationship? (See page 217.)

4 Can you create a scenario illustrating how gender and culture affect the handling of emotion and another depicting the roles that media and technology play in affecting the internalization and display of emotion? (See pages 222–227.)

5 Can you compile a list of recommended strategies for improving the sharing of emotions? (See pages 227–229.)

CHECK YOUR SKILLS

1 Can you communicate your emotional intelligence? (See pages 212–213.)

2 Can you use your face and body to reveal your emotions accurately? (See pages 213–216; *Reflect on This,* page 216; and *Try This,* page 218.)

3 Can you manage your emotions when presented with a challenge? (See pages 219–220; *Try This,* page 220; and *Analyze This,* page 221.)

4 Can you describe your feelings so others understand them? (See pages 220–221.)

5 Can you explain how your attachment style affects your interactions? (See pages 221–222.)

6 Can you adjust your emotional expressiveness to reflect another person's cultural and gender preferences? (See pages 222–224; *Try This,* page 223; and *Try This,* page 225.)

7 Can you assess the effects that the media and technology have on your emotions? (See pages 224–227; and *Try This,* page 227.)

8 Can you use self-talk to understand your feelings? (See page 228.)

9 Can you make clear how you expect others to respond to your expressions of emotion? (See pages 228–229.)

10 Can you appropriately interpret and handle the emotional challenges a relational partner presents? (See *The Case of Late Jean,* page 230.)

KEY TERMS

STUDENT STUDY SITE

Visit the student study site at **www.sagepub.com/gambleic** to access the following materials:

- SAGE Journal Articles
- Videos
- Web Resources
- eFlashcards
- Web Quizzes
- Study Questions

chapter 9

A friend in need is a friend indeed.

—William Hazlitt

TRUST AND DECEPTION

LEARNING OBJECTIVES

After completing this chapter, you should be able to demonstrate mastery of the following learning outcomes:

1. Define trust and explain the bases for it.

2. Explain cost-benefit theory, including its relationship to trust.

3. Identify factors contributing to the development of supportive and defensive interpersonal climates.

4. Describe how lying affects interpersonal relationships.

5. Discuss how gender and culture influence the development of trust.

6. Describe how media portrayals and technology can foster or impede the development of relationships based on trust.

7. Identify and use behaviors that promote the development of trusting relationships.

While we expect our significant other to tell us the truth, 92 percent of us admit to lying to our romantic partner.[1] In fact, our romantic partner is the person to whom we are mostly likely to tell our biggest lies. It is all too common for one or both partners in a romantic relationship to attempt to deceive the other, each believing that it is possible to succeed at keeping the partner from discovering the deceit. However, often this turns out not to be the case.

An example is the case of then Congressman Anthony Weiner, who in 2011, speaking to the press, was compelled to confess that he had not been honest with himself or his wife about the fact that he had tweeted revealing photos of himself to various women.[2] Why had Representative Weiner sought to deceive not only his partner but the public as well? Likely motivating factors were his concern for his marital relationship, his need to try to maintain a positive image in the eyes of his constituents, and his desire to avoid punishment.[3] Weiner's deceit, however, resulted in problems in his marriage, destroyed his image,

> In fact, our romantic partner is the person to whom we are mostly likely to tell our biggest lies.

and led to unavoidable punishment. Once the deception was uncovered, Weiner had to come clean. His deception proved to be costly. Disgraced, Weiner put his political career on hold, resigning from Congress. He stated that he was going to devote himself to trying to repair his marital relationship, hopefully finding a way to restore his then pregnant wife's trust in him and committing to reviving their emotional connection.

A similar scenario, though fictional, was portrayed in the television series *The Good Wife*. In this instance, the "good wife's" politician husband had an affair that he attempted to keep secret from her, only to have her discover his indiscretion. The wife's discovery resulted in lower levels of relational satisfaction, decreased commitment, and retaliation on her part; she had an affair of her own with a law partner in the firm for which she worked.

Deception breeds mistrust and more deception, factors harmful to the building of strong relationships.

WHAT DO YOU KNOW?

Before continuing your reading of this chapter, which of the following five statements do you believe to be true and which do you believe to be false?

1. When you trust your partner, your relationship is safe.   T   F

2. Trust violations hurt the body.   T   F

3. Being unforgiving can cause you to become depressed.   T   F

4. Most students lie to their parents.   T   F

5. Liars use more indirect language than do truth tellers.   T   F

Read the chapter to discover if you're right or if you've made any erroneous assumptions.

ANSWERS: 1. F, 2. T, 3. T, 4. T, 5. T

How can you tell when to trust or not trust another person? What behaviors lead you to place your trust in some of the people you know, but not in the others? Interpersonal deception is not limited to romantic relationships. A deception may occur in any of our personal relationships. For example, when surveyed, even trusted physicians admitted to lying to their patients about the state of the patients' health and prospects for recovery; some also came clean about their failure to disclose a conflict of interest when prescribing a drug.[4] If lying is so common, who is to be trusted?

WHAT IS TRUST?

We all think we know the meaning of **trust**—displaying the willingness to rely or depend on another person. Sometimes our trust is merited, and we are rewarded for it; other times, however, we misplace our trust, resulting in our feeling disappointment or becoming disillusioned with a relationship partner.

We place our trust in others for a variety of reasons. We may rely on others because we expect them to perform basic services for us, such as make breakfast or drive us to work. Sometimes we expect them to give us direction, such as helping us pick out what to wear for an interview or helping us choose our classes.

A deception can occur in any relationship, even one shared with a trusted medical practitioner.

Still other times we expect others to meet our emotional needs—commiserate with us when we are sad or celebrate with us when we are happy. The degree to which another fulfills our expectations determines whether we will depend on or trust that particular person again. As the maxim says, *Fool me once, shame on you. Fool me twice, shame on me.*

Although we all freely use the word *trust,* not everyone can express clearly what the word means to them personally. Try expressing what it means to you. Then consider the following excerpt from Antoine de Saint-Exupéry's *The Little Prince,* in which the fox tries to explain to the little prince what trust means to him by telling the prince, who is seeking friends, that he will permit the prince to "tame" him, much as we tame and then enjoy the friendship of a pet:

"What does that mean—'to tame'?"

"It is an act too often neglected," said the fox. "It means to establish ties."

"'To establish ties'?"

"Just that," said the fox. "To me, you are still nothing more than a little boy who is just like a hundred thousand other little boys. And I have no need of you. And you, on your part, have no need of me. To you, I am nothing more than a fox like a hundred thousand other foxes. But if you tame me [if we establish ties], then we shall need each other. To me, you will be unique in all the world. To you, I shall be unique in all the world.[5]

Trust: The belief that one can rely on another; made up of two components: trusting behavior and trustworthy behavior.

Essential for relationship satisfaction, trust grows over time. Once you trust another person, your willingness to make yourself vulnerable by engaging in personal disclosures increases, primarily because you have confidence in the person's dependability and believe you can reliably predict how the person will respond.

THE BASES OF TRUST

How does establishing personal ties serve as a basis for building trust? The amount of trust we place in another is, in large measure, based on our perception of that person's character. In other words, when we judge someone to be of good character, we are likely to have faith in that person's (1) integrity, (2) motives, (3) consistency of behavior, and (4) discretion.

When we trust someone because of his or her integrity, we think the individual possesses a basic honesty that permeates our relationship. When we trust another's motives, we trust that person's intentions—that is, we do not believe that he or she would exhibit malevolent behavior toward us. When we trust someone on the basis of the consistency of his or her behavior, we feel that we know that person well enough to predict his or her actions. Finally, when we trust another on the basis of his or her ability to be discreet, we conclude that the person will not intentionally violate our confidence or disclose information about us to anyone who could harm us.

When you place your trust in another, you display your willingness to rely on that person.

To foster the development of a mutually trusting relationship, we need to create an interpersonal climate that reduces the chances of rejection or betrayal, which each of us fears. This is not always easy, but the establishment of trust is essential for every relationship's maintenance and well-being.

THE COMPONENTS OF TRUST

Trust is an amalgam of two basic components: confidence in another person's behavior (or what we call **trusting behavior**) and behavior exhibited by the other person that confirms our confidence (also known as **trustworthy behavior**). Only when both components are present can trust be said to exist. In fact, these behaviors are reciprocal: trusting precipitates trustworthiness, and vice versa. The faith you place in another person therefore will either grow or weaken over time.

Trusting Behavior. Trusting behavior involves three elements. First, we expect another person to behave in a way that can have either harmful or beneficial results. For example, your friend can choose either to embarrass you in front of others or to do her best to make you look good. Second, we are aware that whether the outcome is positive or negative depends on the other person's actions. Whether you end up being embarrassed or looking good is in your friend's control. Third, we think the other person will behave in ways that produce beneficial results. You are confident that your friend is more more apt to try to make you look good. In other words, you think that your friend's behavior has "positive" predictability.

Trustworthy Behavior. Trustworthy behavior similarly requires that three conditions be satisfied. First, we become aware of the motivational preferences of another person. You realize that your coworker wants to impress his boss, for example. Second, we recognize

Trusting behavior: Behavior that accords with the belief that another will not take advantage of one's vulnerabilities.

Trustworthy behavior: Behavior that does not take advantage of another's vulnerabilities.

1. Take a moment to identify three people whom you trusted or depended on recently and three people who recently trusted or depended on you.

2. Consider the relationship you shared with each of the three persons you trusted and enter the information in the chart below. For each person identified, indicate whether your trust in the person was justified and explain why or why not.

Name	Behavior You Expected the Person to Exhibit	Extent to Which Your Expectations Were Fulfilled

3. Consider the relationship you shared with each of the three persons who placed their trust in you and enter the information in the chart below. For each person, explain why you think he or she should or should not have trusted you.

Name	Behavior Expected of You	Extent to Which You Believe You Fulfilled the Expectation

Examine both of your charts. What does your analysis of each reveal about your trust choices?

---

that the other person has confidence in us and is relying on us to help him or her accomplish this. You understand that your coworker is counting on you to help him look good to the boss. Third, we respond by exhibiting the expected behavior. You make it a point to tell the boss how much you enjoy working with your coworker.

FAILED TRUST

If any ingredient for trusting or trustworthy behavior is missing, trust, in the real sense of the word, cannot exist. While trust takes time to develop, it is, unfortunately, relatively easy to destroy. When individuals depend on each other, each party in the relationship is taking a risk; the element of risk means that either party to the relationship can be personally harmed or diminished as a result of the other's behavior. When you place your faith in another, you recognize that it is possible for this person to use your strong belief in him or her against you. If this occurs, it usually shatters your trust.

Unfortunately, we cannot trust everyone we know.[6] Inappropriately relying on another can sometimes cause us as many problems as mistrusting a person who merits our trust. Thus, you would be wise to avoid depending on another person who repeatedly behaves in a way that brings you pain or causes you to feel rejected or betrayed. When you say, "I don't trust Ralph," for example, you probably mean that when you trusted him in the past, he disappointed you. In effect, you no longer feel you can predict what Ralph will do in a

WHAT DO YOU KNOW?

True or False

1. *When you trust your partner, your relationship is safe.*

False. Trust is easy to destroy.

given situation. In contrast, it makes sense for you to continue relying on a person whose behavior you believe you can predict with relatively consistent accuracy.

Because trust is a gamble, it always carries some risk. According to psychologist Abraham Maslow, people who believe in themselves and others tend to make "growth" choices. Maslow describes such individuals as self-actualizers who are close to fulfilling their unique potential as human beings.[7] The trusting behavior of self-actualizers permits them to experience the world fully and vividly, for they have the ability to be open and honest with others and themselves. Because trust can lead us to reveal important information about ourselves, it can also help us improve our self-awareness and understanding. Thus, trust, openness, and self-actualization go hand in hand.

As you have probably learned from experience, there are numerous reasons to sustain or end a relationship. Once we feel we can no longer trust another person, our relationship is in jeopardy. The absence of trust, an ingredient essential to the sharing of intimate information, causes reciprocation of disclosures to cease, thereby precipitating relationship failure. Trust is like interpersonal glue. When it is present, parties psychologically stick together. The relationship is perceived to have value. When it is missing, however, the potential costs of the relationship are perceived to outweigh its potential benefits.

FORGIVENESS: REBUILDING A RELATIONSHIP AFTER TRUST IS BETRAYED

What happens when you are hurt as the result of an interpersonal transgression committed against you by someone close to you? Are you likely to respond by holding a grudge and being resentful or by forgiving the other person? The choice is yours.

Researchers have described forgiveness as the sense of peace and understanding that we experience when we stop blaming another person for a perceived wrong and instead interpret the transgression less personally, pardoning the other person.[8] Forgiveness is not equivalent to condoning unkindness; rather, it is a manifestation of the personal control we have over our lives, just as deciding whether or not to take offense in the first place is a choice.[9]

In order to repair and rebuild a relationship that has been jeopardized by our betrayal by a person whom we trusted, we need to find a way to forgive the person who has hurt us so that we are able to let go of negative feelings.[10] According to research findings, the act of forgiveness involves a multistage problem-solving process similar to the one associated with grief. In the forgiveness process, initially the person feels anger and hurt but then finds a way to excuse the specific offense, putting forth more personal and situational understanding of the offender and of him- or herself.[11] The forgiveness process may be broken down into four stages:

1. Experiencing self-justified anger

2. Recognizing that anger does not feel good and desiring to repair the damage to the relationship

3. Realizing that forgiveness has beneficial effects and choosing to let go of anger fairly quickly

4. Making the proactive choice to rarely if ever get angry

One of Edward Albee's plays, *Who's Afraid of Virginia Woolf?*, contains numerous examples of the negative outcomes of misplaced trust. During the course of an evening spent at the home of George and Martha, guests Nick and Honey and their hosts engage in some rather heavy "social" drinking. While the wives are elsewhere, George discloses some personal information about his youth to Nick. Nick reciprocates by telling George that he was forced to marry Honey because she had a hysterical pregnancy. As the evening progresses, George perceives that Nick has humiliated him; he therefore decides to "get the guest." In the presence of Honey and Martha, George reveals the story Nick had confided in him. Honey, quickly sickened, rushes from the room. The scene ends with Nick vowing to get revenge for George's behavior.

1. Cite an incident in which you witnessed or participated in an interaction in which someone who was trusted acted in an untrustworthy manner. What did you and others learn as a result?

2. Describe a relationship you share that is based on trust. Identify the trusting and trustworthy behaviors exhibited by you and your relationship partner and the factors in your relationship that permitted a climate of trust to develop.

3. Describe a second relationship that you mistakenly believed to be based on trust. Identify the trusting and trustworthy behaviors that were missing, and describe the negative consequences that resulted from the situation. Account for factors in your relationship that prevented or inhibited the development of a climate of trust.

We do not all follow these four stages in the same way. There are some people in our lives for whom we have such love that we will always be at Stage 4. And there are others who have hurt us so badly that we might spend years at Stage 1. The choice, however, is ours.[12]

Willingness to forgive also may be influenced by gender. For example, when Stanford University psychologists solicited volunteers to participate in a study on forgiveness, they found it easy to attract female participants but had difficulty attracting men. In the effort to determine why men were hesitant to participate, one of the researchers, Dr. Carl Thoresen, randomly asked a group of men about it. The consensus among the men was that the word *forgiveness* is too soft and acquiescing, suggesting that the forgiving person is being a doormat. The men advised the researchers to use the harsher, more masculine-sounding word *grudge* in place of the word *forgiveness* in their solicitations. Once the researchers started distributing flyers reading "Got a grudge?" male participants surfaced.[13]

Persons unable to forgive a violation of trust put themselves in danger of experiencing not just emotional difficulties and interpersonal problems but also impaired cardiovascular, neurological, and immune systems. When another's actions hurt us, we experience the hurt not just in our minds but also in our bodies. The more readily we experience anger or hurt, the more our bodies secrete "stress chemicals" that over time exact their price, taking a toll on our health.[14] Persons who are unwilling to forgive experience more depression and are likely to have less fulfilling relationships than those who are more forgiving. Holding on to resentment may have adverse impacts on a person's health. In the words of Nelson Mandela, "Resentment is like drinking poison and waiting for it to kill your enemy." In contrast, giving up grudges improves both emotional and physical well-being. By accepting not only others' flaws but also our own, we increase our chances of deriving satisfaction from our relationships. Learning to forgive yourself is as important as learning to forgive others.

COST-BENEFIT THEORY: THE PRICE WE ARE WILLING TO PAY FOR A RELATIONSHIP

Our relationships thrive or falter as a consequence of the energy we are willing to expend on them; they succeed or fail based on what we are willing to do with and for one another. For example, we may expect a high level of trust, commitment, respect, and even love to characterize a relationship when we have worked to hold up our side of it. When expectations such as these are met, we find the relationship satisfying; however, when they go unfulfilled, we find the relationship lacking.

According to **cost-benefit theory,** also known as social exchange theory, we work to sustain those relationships that give us the greatest total benefit.[15] We can represent this concept by constructing a relational balance sheet on which we keep track of the rewards we receive from our relationships and the costs we must pay to obtain the rewards. We can represent the relational equation as follows:

$$\text{Perceived Relationship Rewards} - \text{Perceived Relationship Costs} = \text{Perceived Relationship Benefits.}$$

The perceived relationship rewards are the positive outcomes we hope to acquire from our relationships, such as increased self-esteem, an enhanced sense of security, and better coping skills. The perceived relationship costs are the price we pay, or the personal energy that we must expend, if we hope to reap any of the rewards. Typical costs include the time we need to invest to make a relationship work, psychological and physical stress, and damage to our self-image. The perceived relationship benefits are the difference between rewards and costs: either a net gain or a loss, if the costs turn out to be more than the rewards.

We can see how this equation works by considering some sample relationships. Let's say you want to develop a closer relationship with a person you have been dating for a few weeks; to acquire a benefit of intimacy in that relationship, you have to be willing to trust that person enough to self-disclose or reveal personal information to him or her. On the other hand, what if you are seeking social acceptance? In that case, you might have to adopt certain beliefs, attitudes, and values. Similarly, to acquire friends, you need to be a good friend. In each case, to obtain a benefit, you have to pay a price; that is, you need to expend energy to ensure that you receive a desired result.

Cost-benefit theory tells us that we will work to continue a relationship only as long as the benefits we perceive ourselves to be receiving outweigh our emotional expenditures. As we compare and contrast the profits and costs of one relationship, we also establish a **comparison level for alternatives** with which to weigh the profits and costs of that relationship against those we might derive from another. If we believe we can easily find another person to give us whatever a current partner is not providing, we are likely to extricate ourselves from an unsatisfactory relationship and enter a new and potentially more rewarding one; in contrast, if we believe such a person *cannot* easily be found, we are more likely to stay in the relationship even though it carries with it great costs and the potential for significant loss.[16]

DEFINING THE RELATIONAL SITUATION

Trusting and trustworthy behaviors will thrive or wither depending on a relationship's situation or climate. Whether we perceive a relationship as cooperative or competitive, supportive or defensive, makes a difference.

Cost-benefit theory: A theory that states that we work to sustain relationships that give us the greatest total benefit and that a relationship will be sustained only as long as perceived benefits outweigh emotional expenditures; also known as social exchange theory.

Comparison level for alternatives: A comparison of profits and costs derived from one relationship with those that might be derived from another relationship.

TRY THIS: *Relationship Balance Sheet*

Review two relationships, one that you recently ended and one that you are in currently. Conduct a cost-benefit analysis for each, identifying both the rewards you receive(d) and the costs you accrue(d). Estimate the net benefit for each.

	Relationship You Ended	**Relationship You Are in Currently**
Rewards you receive(d)	_____	_____
	_____	_____
	_____	_____
Costs you accrue(d)	_____	_____
	_____	_____
	_____	_____
Net benefit	_____	_____
	_____	_____
	_____	_____

On the basis of your analysis, what do you think led you to end the first relationship? What is your forecast for the future of the present relationship?

Whether a relationship is perceived as cooperative or competitive, supportive or defensive, affects its nature.

COOPERATIVE AND COMPETITIVE RELATIONSHIPS

How we define a relational situation affects whether we develop trust. If we view our relationship as primarily *competitive,* then we each are more apt to try to protect ourselves when communicating with one another, and the rule of "everyone for him- or herself" may play itself out. If, on the other hand, we view our relationship as primarily *cooperative,* we eliminate the dog-eat-dog nature of the situation, and sharing, interdependent efforts, and trust become more likely. Defining an interpersonal relationship as competitive precipitates defensive and threatening behavior on the part of the communicators, whereas defining it as cooperative precipitates supportive, nonthreatening behaviors and the exchange of messages that are more honest. In cooperative interpersonal relationships, communication channels are open rather than closed.

The goals we bring to each relationship affect how trusting we are. If we perceive our goals to be congruent, then it is easier to create a cooperative atmosphere. But if we perceive our goals to be contradictory, then we are more apt to display competitive mind-sets.

In order for cooperation to take place, certain requirements need to be met. It is important for us to agree that we each have an equal right to satisfy our needs. Additionally, we have to ensure that conditions allow each of us to get what we want at least some of the time. For this to occur, we need to discourage the use of power plays that rely on techniques such as threatening, yelling, and demanding. What is more, neither of us should attempt to manipulate the other by holding back information or dissembling. When two persons are interacting cooperatively, one party does not aim to "win" or to "beat" or "outsmart" the other. Unlike **competitive relationships, cooperative relationships** do not depend on one person gaining an edge over the other and do not promote defensiveness or lying.

SUPPORTIVE AND DEFENSIVE RELATIONSHIPS

One of the first problems we face when entering into a new relationship is that of developing the ability and willingness to trust.[17] For trust to develop we need to feel valued. Valuing is communicated to us by messages a person sends that make us feel recognized, let us know that our ideas and feelings are important, and project interest in what we think and how we feel. When valuing is not communicated, usually we take steps to protect ourselves from being hurt. The result may be a **defensive climate** because a party to the relationship perceives or anticipates a threat. Such a threat need not be physical; more typically, it takes the form of a comment or behavior by one person that the other person perceives as a direct attack on the image that he or she is trying to project.

When we are insecure about a relationship, we are likely to experience a negative feeling and respond by exhibiting a defensive reaction. For example, you might respond to a threat to your image by counterattacking and becoming verbally aggressive toward the other person: "Who made you king?" or "What gives you the right to say what I should and should not do?" In effect, with such a response, you take the focus off yourself and shift the blame to the other person.

We might also defend ourselves from attack by distorting what the other person says in such a way that we are able to preserve our sense of self. We rationalize the attack by creating an explanation that is untrue but self-protective. Or we try to compensate for

Competitive relationship: A relationship characterized by the presence of defensive and threatening behavior; a relationship in which one party aims to win, or to beat or outsmart the other party.

Cooperative relationship: A relationship based on supportiveness, sharing, interdependent efforts, and trust.

Defensive climate: The climate that results when a party to a relationship perceives or anticipates a threat.

the criticism by pointing out one or more strengths we have that we contend are more important than the weakness pointed out to us. Instead of deflecting an attack, we could choose simply to avoid one by avoiding people we believe pose a threat to our image. None of these attempts at image preservation are particularly healthy responses.

To minimize or eliminate the arousal of defensiveness in our relationships, we need to understand what causes us to become defensive in the first place and substitute supportive behaviors. In a classic article, Jack R. Gibb identifies six such defense-causing behaviors and isolates six contrasting behaviors that, when exhibited, help create a **supportive climate** that will reduce the threat level individuals experience; these behaviors are listed in Table 9.1 and are discussed in the following sections.[18]

Evaluation versus Description. A relationship may run into trouble if one party makes **evaluative statements**. If, as a result of our manner of speaking, tone, or words, we seem to be judging the other person, he or she is likely to be wary of our intentions. For example, once we label another's actions using overly critical descriptors such as *stupid, ridiculous,* or *absurd,* the development or continuance of a positive communication climate is impeded. The following are examples of evaluative statements that are judgmental in tone and phrased in ways that can easily provoke defensiveness:

"I don't think you know what you're talking about."

"This car is filthy!"

"You call that a joke?"

In contrast to evaluative statements, **descriptive statements** recount a person's particular observable actions without labeling them good or bad, right or wrong. When we use descriptive language, we do not admonish another to change his or her behavior but

TABLE 9.1   Categories of Behavior Characteristic of Defensive and Supportive Climates

Defensive Climate	Supportive Climate
1. Evaluation Judgmental statements impede communication	1. Description Neutral statements promote communication
2. Control orientation Promotes resistance	2. Problem orientation Promotes cooperation
3. Strategy Presence of a hidden agenda	3. Spontaneity Deception-free
4. Neutrality Communicates indifference	4. Empathy Communicates concern
5. Superiority Encourages jealousy or resentment	5. Equality Encourages trust
6. Certainty Encourages perceptions of inflexibility	6. Provisionalism Encourages perceptions of flexibility

Supportive climate:
A climate in which the level of threat that individuals experience is reduced.

Evaluative statements:
Judgmental pronouncements.

Descriptive statements:
Statements that recount observable behavior without judgment.

simply report or question what we saw, heard, or felt. The following statements are descriptive and focused on the speaker's thoughts and feelings:

> "I would like to understand how you came to that conclusion."

> "I get upset when the car looks like this because I'm the one who cleans it up."

> "When you tell jokes that embarrass me I turn all red."

Describing what concerns you instead of going on the attack is usually more productive than is being judgmental.

Control versus Problem Orientation. Communication perceived as an effort to exert control also provokes defensiveness rather than trust. In other words, if your intent is to control another person—to get someone to do something or to change his or her beliefs—you are apt to encounter resistance. How much resistance you meet depends, in part, on the openness with which you approach the other person and the degree to which your behavior causes the other to question or doubt your motives. If we conclude that someone is trying to control us, we tend also to conclude that the other believes we are ignorant and unable to make decisions. A problem orientation, on the other hand, promotes just the opposite response. When we communicate that we have not already formulated a solution and are not going to attempt to force an opinion on the other person, that person feels freer to cooperate to solve the problem.

How two people argue affects their relationship.

A control orientation is communicated with more than just words; the person exerting control also uses voice tone, gestures, and/or facial expressions to send a clear message that he or she has more power, has secured more rights, or is more intelligent than the other person—a message the other person is likely to find disconfirming and objectionable. In contrast, a problem-solving demeanor, accompanied by problem-solving words, is much less likely to trigger defensiveness. For example, consider the difference between asking another person to decide where to dine, what movie to see, how to spend shared vacation funds, or what candidate to vote for and issuing a declaration such as "Well, I like Barbados more than Aruba, and since my bonus is paying for the vacation, I'll decide where to go." In such an instance, the problem-oriented individual would say, "It appears that we both have different vacation destinations in mind. Let's see if we can identify a locale where we can enjoy ourselves together." This kind of approach keeps the relationship intact rather than provoking disharmony.

WATCH THIS 9.1
For a video on control vs. problem orientation visit the student study site.

Strategy versus Spontaneity. Our defensiveness is likely to increase if we feel another person is trying to put something past us. No one enjoys being conned or made the victim of a hidden agenda. We become suspicious of strategies we discover have been concealed or are underhanded. We do not like it when someone makes a decision for us and then tries to make us feel that we made the decision. Once we feel manipulated, we tend to become defensive and self-protective. In contrast, honest, spontaneous behavior, free of deception, helps reduce defensiveness. Under such conditions we exhibit less doubt regarding the other's motivations, and trust is more likely to develop.

With this in mind, consider a situation in which a person says, "Would you help me out if I told you it was really important?" and also fails to reveal what "helping out" means. We

In Tennessee Williams's renowned play *A Streetcar Named Desire*, we meet a character named Blanche DuBois. Blanche, we realize, depends on an array of defensive behaviors to maintain a false image and protect her sense of self. Blanche puts it this way: "I don't want realism. I want magic. I try to give that to people. I misrepresent things to them. I don't tell the truth. I tell what ought to be truth." Blanche can't stand the truth anymore than she can "stand a naked light bulb." Blanche's inner feelings and outward acts tend to create equally defensive postures in her brother-in-law, Stanley Kowalski. Their resulting circular response pattern becomes increasingly destructive when Stanley confronts her with the harsh truth about her various "boyfriends":

Stanley: This millionaire from Dallas is not going to interfere with your privacy any?

Blanche: It won't be the sort of thing you have in mind. This man is a gentleman and he respects me. *(Improvising feverishly)* What he wants is my companionship. Having great wealth sometimes makes people lonely! A cultivated woman, a woman of intelligence and breeding, can enrich a man's life—immeasurably! I have those things to offer, and this doesn't take them away. Physical beauty is passing. A transitory possession. But beauty of the mind and richness of the spirit and tenderness of the heart—and I have all of those things—aren't taken away, but grow! Increase with the years! How strange that I should be called a destitute woman! When I have all of these treasures locked in my heart. *(A choked sob comes from her)* I think of myself as a very, very rich woman! But I have been foolish—casting my pearls before swine!

Stanley: Swine, huh?

Blanche: Yes, swine! Swine! And I'm thinking not only of you but of your friend, Mr. Mitchell. He came to see me tonight. He dared to come here in his work clothes! And to repeat slander to me, vicious stories that he had gotten from you! I gave him his walking papers . . .

Stanley: You did, huh?

Blanche: But then he came back. He returned with a box of roses to beg my forgiveness! He implored my forgiveness. But some things are not forgivable. Deliberate cruelty is not forgivable. It is the one unforgivable thing in my opinion and it is the one thing of which I have never, never been guilty. And so I told him, I said to him, "Thank you," but it was foolish of me to think that we could ever adapt ourselves to each other. Our ways of life are too different. Our attitudes and our backgrounds are incompatible. We have to be realistic about such things. So farewell, my friend! And let there be no hard feelings . . .

Stanley: Was this before or after the telegram came from the Texas oil millionaire?

Blanche: What telegram? No! No, after! As a matter of fact, the wire came just as—

Stanley: As a matter of fact there wasn't no wire at all!

Blanche: Oh, oh!

Stanley: There isn't no millionaire! And Mitch didn't come back with roses 'cause I know where he is—

Blanche: Oh!

Stanley: There isn't a goddamn thing but imagination!

Blanche: Oh!

Stanley: And lies and conceit and tricks!

Blanche: Oh!

Stanley: And look at yourself! Take a look at yourself in that worn-out Mardi Gras outfit, rented for fifty cents from some rag-picker! And with the crazy crown on! What queen do you think you are!

Blanche: Oh—God . . .

Stanley: I've been on to you from the start! Not once did you pull any wool over this boy's eyes! You come in here and sprinkle the place with powder and spray perfume and cover the light-bulb with a paper lantern, and lo and behold the place has turned into Egypt and you are the Queen of the Nile! Sitting on your throne and swilling down my liquor! I say—Ha!—Ha! Do you hear me? Ha-ha-ha! *(He walks into the bedroom.)*

Consider these questions:

1. What defensive behaviors do Blanche and Stanley display in this excerpt from the play?

2. Why do you imagine they feel the need to act the way they do?

3. What causes us to become defensive rather than supportive of one another?

might feel that something is being kept from us, and we might begin to feel that we are being set up. We might develop a similar feeling if someone begins a request for help with words like these: "Remember when you needed me to help you move?" Instead of trying to manipulate others with premeditated comments, it is better to be open and honest. For example, saying "I could really use your help to prepare for this exam" is a natural, straightforward, and nonmanipulative way of asking for another's assistance.

Neutrality versus Empathy. Another behavior that can increase defensiveness is neutrality. For the most part, we like and need to feel that others see us as worthwhile, value our presence, like us, and are willing to take the time to establish a meaningful relationship with us. If instead of communicating warmth and concern the person with whom we are interacting communicates neutrality or indifference, we may interpret this as worse than rejection, concluding that the individual has no interest in us or that he or she perceives us as a nonperson. Comments such as "In that class, I'm only a number" and "The boss doesn't even know me by name" indicate that someone is bothered by a perceived indifference. In contrast, empathy erases feelings of indifference by implying care and regard for others. When you accept another's feelings, you send a message of concern and respect; "I can see that you're hurting and I understand why" and "It sound like you're feeling undervalued by your boss" are empathetic statements.

Superiority versus Equality. The development of either defensiveness or trust in interpersonal relationships is also influenced by behaviors showing superiority or equality. Defensiveness is aroused in us if the person with whom we are communicating expresses feelings of superiority about social position, power, wealth, intellectual aptitude, appearance, or other such characteristics. Upon receiving such a message, we are apt to react by competing with the sender, becoming jealous, or ignoring the message altogether. On the other hand, by communicating a message of equality, another person can forestall defensive reactions in us and encourage our trust.

Persons with whom we are communicating are likely to become defensive in response to any message we send suggesting that we are in a one-up position and that they are not as good as

When feelings of indifference replace warmth, relationships suffer.

we are. Sometimes how we deliver a message conveys our feelings of superiority and lets others conclude that we literally are "looking down our nose at them." When someone says something to us such as "I know more than you do on this subject" or "You should shop where I shop," the words convey an attitude of superiority and are apt to elicit a response protecting our self-esteem. If similar information had been communicated to us in a way that did not make us feel inadequate, we would probably be less likely to get our guard up. The more secure we feel, the easier we find it to treat others as equals.

Certainty versus Provisionalism. When someone expresses absolute or total certainty about a disputed issue, we may become defensive. We are suspicious of individuals who think they have all the answers, view themselves as our "guides" through life rather than our fellow travelers, and belittle or reject ideas we offer. In contrast, an attitude of provisionalism, or open-mindedness, by not requiring that someone win an argument, defend ideas to the bitter end, or be right all the time, is more likely to encourage trust to develop.

When we communicate an attitude of provisionalism, we make it possible for others to perceive us as flexible and open. We neither feel nor convey the need "to be right." Saying something such as "Only a nerd would think this assignment is fun" or "You're not going to get me to change my mind, because I know my decision is right" closes the door to continued discussion because the speaker appears to be unwilling to consider other positions. Alternatively, prefacing remarks with something such as "The way I look at the assignment . . ." or "The way I came to my decision is . . ." encourages further discussion.

Various nonverbal cues support the development of either a defensive or a supportive interpersonal climate; these are summarized in Table 9.2 on page 250. As you review the cues, consider the extent to which a defensive or supportive climate characterizes each of your relevant social or job-related relationships.

DECEPTION AND RELATIONSHIP ETHICS

An old Moroccan proverb says "Why are you lying to me who is your friend?" What does the word *lie* mean to you? To whom have you recently lied? Who has recently lied to you? What kinds of situations do you feel justify lying on your part? What circumstances do you believe justify someone else's lying to you? How do you react when you catch someone in a **lie**? How do you react when caught in a lie? How does lying or being lied to affect a relationship? How common is it?

To examine your practices when it comes to lying, complete the five sentences that follow:

Lie: The deliberate distortion or concealment of information; the intentional deception of another person to convince him or her of something one knows to be untrue.

1. A lie is _____.

2. I would lie to _____.

3. I would lie if _____.

4. In the past week I lied _____ times.

5. In the past week I was caught lying _____ times.

TRY THIS: *Cornered*

First, think of several interpersonal encounters you have shared during which you believe the other person succeeded in challenging the image you were trying to project. For example, how would you respond if a professor or employer criticized you for performing poorly? Or how would you feel if a friend told you that you were never there when needed but always put yourself first? If the criticism was justified, you would more than likely feel defensive. Create a list of people who have put you on the defensive. Identify aspects of yourself that these individuals caused you to defend and the means you used to protect yourself from their perceived attacks. Use the chart below to record your observations.

Individuals Who Have Made Me Feel Defensive	What About Me the Person Found Fault With	What I Did to Protect Myself

Next, think of several interpersonal encounters during which you sent one or more messages to someone that led him or her to feel a threat to his or her image. How did each person respond to your criticism? What consequences did your behavior have for your future relationship with each? Use the chart below to record your observations.

Individuals Whose Image I Threatened	What I Did to Precipitate the Threat	How the Person Responded	Relationship Consequences

Finally, consider the defensiveness-producing situations from the perspective of each party. What advice would you give the person whose image was threatened regarding how to handle feelings of defensiveness? What would you say to the person doing the threatening regarding how to reduce the level of threat projected?

It is difficult to determine how pervasive lying is in U.S. culture because the nature of lying is to deceive others without their noticing. Still, when surveyed, more than eight in ten students confessed to having lied to a parent about something important, despite the fact that 92 percent of the students in the same survey said they believe their parents want them to behave ethically.[19]

WHY DO WE LIE?

Deliberately lying by distorting the truth is committing an overt lie; concealing sensitive information is committing a covert lie—a practice all too common in person-to-person interaction.[20] Whenever we hope to convey a false impression or convince another to believe something about us, someone else, or something else that we ourselves do not believe, we are lying. Whether we want to admit it or not, our goal is to intentionally deceive the other person into accepting what we know to be untrue; our verbal and nonverbal communicative intent is to mislead the other person, either by providing false information or by purposefully failing to provide the relevant information he or she needs to make a

TABLE 9.2   Nonverbal Symbols That Can Contribute to the Development of a Supportive or Defensive Climate

Behavior Producing Defensiveness	Behavior Producing Supportiveness
1. Evaluation Maintaining extended eye contact Pointing at the other person Placing your hands on your hips Shaking your head Shaking your index finger	1. Description Maintaining comfortable eye contact Leaning forward
2. Control Sitting in the focal (central) position Placing your hands on your hips Shaking your head Maintaining extended eye contact Invading the personal space of the other person	2. Problem orientation Maintaining comfortable personal distance Crossing your legs in the direction of the other person Leaning forward Maintaining comfortable eye contact
3. Strategy Maintaining extended eye contact Shaking your head Using forced gestures	3. Spontaneity Leaning forward Crossing your legs in the direction of the other person Maintaining comfortable eye contact Using animated natural gestures
4. Neutrality Crossing your legs away from the other person Using a monotone voice Staring elsewhere Leaning back Maintaining a large body distance (4½–5 feet)	4. Empathy Maintaining close personal distance (20–36 inches) Maintaining comfortable eye contact Crossing your legs in the direction of the other person Nodding your head Leaning toward the other person
5. Superiority Maintaining extended eye contact Placing your hands on your hips Situating yourself at a higher elevation Invading the other person's personal space	5. Equality Maintaining comfortable eye contact Leaning forward Situating yourself at the same elevation Maintaining a comfortable distance
6. Certainty Maintaining extended eye contact Crossing your arms Placing your hands on your hips Using a dogmatic voice	6. Provisionalism Maintaining comfortable eye contact Nodding your head Tilting your head to one side

True or False

4. *Most students lie to their parents.*

True. Eight out of ten students surveyed reported having lied to a parent.

decision or come to an understanding.[21] When we lie, we try to manipulate someone into making choices he or she would not otherwise make. By manipulating the truth, partners manipulate each other.

It is rare for us to tell only a single lie. Once we tell a lie, we are compelled to work hard to cover our tracks. As your experience probably reveals, to sustain a lie, we frequently have to tell another, and another, and another. Thus, whenever we lie, we usually are left with a significant amount of mending. We spend a lot of time and energy concentrating on those we told what lies to and why. Some think that lying, for any reason, is morally and ethically wrong. Others hold that the motive for lying matters: Is harm intended? Still others believe it is a lie's outcome that merits consideration. What do you believe?

At times we fail to realize that under some circumstances a truth that hurts someone can be as harmful as a lie. Now and again, we succeed in taking away false beliefs from those who need them to survive. Wittingly or unwittingly, when we do this we can do as much damage as callous liars. For example, if someone believes she is attractive to others, but you find her unappealing and a bore, would you say so? Some people need their illusions; they need their magical thinking.[22] If you analyze your life, it may become clear that some of your relationships rely on the silent agreement made between parties that certain illusions will be sustained and certain memories will be suppressed. This, too, is a form of trust.

In the TV series *Nurse Jackie*, ER nurse Jackie (Edie Falco) long concealed both her affair with hospital pharmacist Eddie (Paul Schulze) and her addiction to prescription drugs.

WHITE LIES: MOTIVATION MATTERS

What does the phrase *white lie* mean to you? A white lie is a minor falsehood that is not meant to harm or injure anyone. Individuals use white lies to provide moral support or cheer, or to maintain the "humanness" of the social relationship

A relationship based on deception is likely to fail.

itself. An example is telling your roommate you like her haircut even if you don't because you know she does, or telling your little brother you didn't go by the toy store on your way home because you know he would be upset if he knew you had. Would you mind if someone told you such a white lie?

LYING TO OURSELVES: DEFENSIVE STRATEGIES

We do not lie only to others; we also lie to ourselves, employing a number of defensive strategies to protect ourselves from having to face the truth. For example, according to his biographer, Steve Jobs believed, up until the very end, that he would beat his cancer.[23] It seems we need illusions to feel good about ourselves and to maintain a sense of continuity in our lives.[24] Persons who lie to themselves commonly employ three defense mechanisms: displacement, repression, and rationalization.

Displacement. When we release our anger or frustration by communicating our feelings to people or objects we perceive to be more accessible and less dangerous than whoever or whatever precipitated the feelings in the first place, we practice **displacement**. For example, you yell at a younger brother or sister when you really want to yell at your boss.

Repression. We use the self-protective strategy of **repression** when situations are too painful or unpleasant to face. We "forget" the stimulus that has disturbed us by denying its existence. For example, if someone was subjected to verbal abuse as a child, he or she might "solve" any problems that such abuse might engender by pretending it never happened. Although the facade erected would say "nothing is wrong," in reality, feelings of anger and aggression would be building, and in time, resentment might surface and affect the individual's present-day relationships.

Rationalization. When we use **rationalization**, we give ourselves a logical or reasonable explanation for our unrealistic pictures, thoughts, or feelings. For instance, workers who receive poor assessments from their managers might tell themselves "everyone gets poor assessments." Persons who interview for a position but are not hired might convince themselves that they didn't really want the job.

Thus, beneath deception and lying are strong feelings and the desire to protect our emotional well-being. Our lies may be self-serving, or they may be motivated by our desire to demonstrate caring and support for others.[25]

RELATIONAL COUNTERFEITERS

What motivates us to create a **counterfeit relationship**—one based on deception that will invariably lead to interpersonal failure? What causes us to lie? While there are many reasons for lying, two appear most prevalent: to gain a reward or to avoid a punishment. Specifically, lying is motivated by our desire to protect our self-esteem, continue to meet our basic needs, initiate or preserve desired affiliations, and attain personal satisfaction.[26] Achieving these goals is rewarding; having them taken away can be punishing. While we most frequently lie to protect ourselves, many of our lies are designed to protect someone with whom we have a relationship, and a smaller number benefit a third party (see Table 9.3). Thus, lies help us negotiate situations that have exposed us or another person to levels of vulnerability exceeding our comfort zone.

Displacement: A defense mechanism through which one releases anger or frustration by communicating feelings to people or objects perceived to be more accessible and less dangerous than the person who precipitated the feelings.

Repression: The forgetting or denial of disturbing stimuli.

Rationalization: The provision of a logical or reasonable explanation for an unrealistic thought or feeling.

Counterfeit relationship: A relationship based on a lie.

TABLE 9.3 Who Lies?

Where do you fit into the following statistical data on lying?
More than 10 million taxpayers "lie on their tax forms," according to the IRS.
Approximately 80% of all job seekers' résumés are misleading.
It is estimated that 70% of all doctors lie on their bills to health insurance providers.
100% of dating couples surveyed reported lying to each other in about one-third of their conversations.
20%–30% of middle managers surveyed admitted to writing fraudulent internal reports.
95% of participating college students surveyed were willing to tell at least one lie to a potential employer to win a job, and 41% had already done so.
We are lied to about 200 times each day.
Most people lie to others once or twice a day and deceive about 30 people per week.
The average rate of lying is 7 times per hour if you count all the times people lie to themselves.
We lie in 30% to 38% of all our interactions.
College students lie in 50% of conversations with their mothers.

SOURCE: Data in this table are derived from information contained in the 2000 U.S. Census and on the websites of the U.S. Census Bureau (http://www.census.gov) and the U.S. Bureau of Labor Statistics (http://www.bls.gov).

THE EFFECTS OF LYING

How does lying affect a relationship? If discovered, lying can destroy the very basis of a relationship. Imagine a relationship, no matter how effective in other respects, in which you could never trust the authenticity of the other person's messages—never believe his or her words or gestures. Imagine feeling that you have been taken advantage of, treated as a pushover, or duped. Such a relationship would be difficult to sustain simply because you would probably suspect the other person's motives, resent how he or she treated you, and feel disappointed in both of you—your partner for lying and you for believing the lies—and, as a result, you would be much more likely to question the veracity of any and all information he or she passed on to you in the future. Because you feel wronged, you reinterpret and reevaluate your past, present, and future with this person in light of the lies, and you are wary of every fully trusting this person again.

Although "bending the truth" to keep peace in a relationship may be a common practice, doing so can also reveal that the relationship is in trouble and not likely to last. By sucking trust out of a relationship, lies destroy it; after you discover a partner's lies, it is much less likely that you will take the risk of displaying the vulnerability required for trust to grow between you and this person in the future. Once this occurs, a climate of distrust characterizes the relationship. In fact, an inability to trust one's partner is the reason most commonly given for a relationship's deterioration and dissolution, and it is the partner who discovers that he or she has been lied to who typically ends things.

A little more than three decades ago, disagreeing with prevailing notions of the importance of facing the truth, psychologist Richard S. Lazarus asserted that illusion and deception have important roles to play in mental health.

Lazarus observed that many people believe facing the truth, however painful, is necessary to live successfully, that to have "authentic" relationships, we have to be absolutely honest with one another and ourselves. Dissenting, Lazarus noted that many poets, playwrights, and novelists base their work, as he did, on the opposite notion—that we need our illusions. Lazarus embraced the view that illusion and self-deception have positive value, if only because they are part of the fabric of our lives. He pointed out that we hold countless unexamined and idiosyncratic beliefs about ourselves that we pass down unchallenged to succeeding generations even though they have no basis in reality. According to Lazarus, we pilot our lives in part by illusions and by self-deceptions that give life meaning and substance.

What do you think of Lazarus's position? What illusions do you believe are key in the life of someone close to you?

SOURCE: Richard S. Lazarus, "Positive Denial: The Case for Not Facing Reality," *Psychology Today*, November 1979, p. 47.

THE EFFECTS OF GOSSIP

How do you feel about gossip? Have you ever begun a conversation with a friend with words such as these: "Have you heard the latest?" If you have, then more than likely you have spread gossip. Whether you are a man or a woman, telling a friend a juicy story or sharing a rumor lets the other person know that you trust him or her enough to share your confidence. While many believe that gossip is negative, much of it is benign small talk, peppered with statements such as "Did you know Kaleisha got a really great grade on her presentation?" and "Can you believe that Paula and Sean are engaged? I never thought they'd get back together after she left him for Raul." This kind of gossip is basically harmless because no secrets are being revealed. What is being talked about is public information. Although many believe erroneously that women gossip more than men, the opposite is actually true: men gossip at least as much as women, especially on their cell phones. Men, however, give gossip another label, calling it "shop talk."[27]

While many people today consider gossip wrong, until the 1800s, gossip was seen as denoting friendship. Now, more than two centuries later, a number of psychologists once again contend it is a natural activity and critical to human survival. Chances are we all gossip. In fact, if you review your conversations during the past twenty-four hours, you may discover that a large number of them consisted of gossip. Gossip can be a powerful socializing force.[28]

In their book *Gossip: The Latest Scoop,* Jack Levin and Arnold Arluke note that gossip functions like social grooming, setting the boundaries of social behavior and letting us know when we have crossed a line. As such, it may hold one key to our understanding the social environment, help us develop

After lies about Olive (Emma Stone) spread around campus in the movie *Easy A*, she fights back against the gossip by sewing a red letter A to all of her clothing, like Hester Prynne in *The Scarlet Letter*.

and maintain relationships, cement social ties, and bond with other members of our social group.[29] In *Grooming, Gossip, and the Evolution of Language,* Robin Dunbar provides support for these notions, contending that verbal communication evolved from a need to indulge in gossip, ultimately reducing stress and enhancing feelings of social cohesion.[30] Dunbar asserts that we humans gossip because, unlike other primates, we do not groom each other; instead, we use speech to maintain contact. For Dunbar *gossip* is a synonym for *social communication.* Humans learned to talk so we could talk about each other.

This is not to suggest that gossip does not have a darker side. Gossip's potential to be harmful can be seen in cyberbullying—the sustained use of digital technology to post mean-spirited online messages designed to threaten, embarrass, harass, or torment—which challenges the resilience of its targets. Postings filled with rage and hate messages abound on Internet sites. Some have precipitated suicides; these deaths attributed to online aggression are sometimes called **cyberbullicides**.[31] Cyberbullies, who often remain anonymous, post false rumors, start offensive websites, post information designed to encourage others to laugh at their targets, and otherwise harass their targets relentlessly.

Thus, while gossip can have a prosocial side, it also can be unethical, malicious, and vicious. It is particularly egregious when the information being shared is inaccurate and directed at those not present to defend themselves. Sometimes the gossiper is particularly subtle and deceptive, pretending to be sympathetic to the subject of the gossip while actually trying to do harm. When used in this way, gossip can do untold damage. Sometimes gossip functions like a boomerang—the characteristics the gossiper attributes to a target end up rebounding back to the gossiper.

CULTURE AND TRUST

Our expectations and predictions regarding how members of various cultural groups will communicate with us may facilitate or impede the development of trust when we actually interact with members of these groups. Some of us are less apt to trust someone we perceive to be different from us than to trust someone we think similar. For example, consider that people from Western cultures such as the United States expect friends to maintain approximately an arm's-length distance when conversing. When people enter our private space, we feel uncomfortable and violated and are unlikely to enter a trusting relationship with them. In contrast, many members of Arab cultures expect friends to stand so close they can smell each other's breath. In fact, some people in Arab cultures believe that not to allow a friend to smell one's breath is insulting and may lead to decreased trust and intimacy.[32]

Remember that ethnocentrism—the perception that one's culture is superior to all others—also limits development of trusting relationships among persons identifying with different cultural groups. When ethnocentric, members of one group conclude that members of others groups have inferior values and that they should maintain a social distance from them. As a result, rather than trying to understand members of other groups, which would facilitate the growth of trust, they evaluate the behavior and manner of communication of the outsiders negatively. Ethnocentric feelings make it difficult to dispel preconceptions, impede the personalization of communication, make satisfying conversations of self-disclosure difficult, limit acceptance of "outsiders," and hinder development of trusting relationships among persons of difference.[33]

The more ethnocentric someone is, the more anxious he or she is about interacting with members of other cultures; when we are fearful, we are less likely to expect such interactions to have positive outcomes and less willing to trust. For relationships between

Cyberbullicide:
Suicide committed in response to online aggression.

persons from diverse cultures to thrive, the individuals involved at least "need to act *as if* a sense of trust were justified, and set their doubts aside."[34] Until we feel we can trust one another, it is unlikely our relationship will become close.

People from different cultures also differ in emotional expressiveness. In the United States, for example, people operate from the premise that expressing feelings is positive and, as a result, are particularly emotionally expressive, but members of other cultures may be much less likely to be emotionally expressive and much more likely to mask their emotions and behave in ways that belie their actual feelings. It becomes difficult to trust others if we attribute their lack of expressiveness to a desire to deceive and believe that they want to lead us astray.

GENDER AND TRUST

In your opinion, is the Web like a "backyard fence, a place for virtual neighbors to build trust and intimacy"?[35] When you feel the need to talk to someone you trust, do you go online to see which of your friends is available to chat? Your answers to these questions may differ depending on whether you are male or female.

On the other hand, all of us, whether male or female, want close friends whom we can trust. Women generally like to share feelings and men typically enjoy sharing activities,[36] but both kinds of interaction can engender trust—they might simply be considered alternate paths to its development. Unless there is reason to doubt trust in a relationship, men assume trust and rarely discuss it, whereas women are likely to talk about a relationship's dynamics more overtly.

For men and women to trust each other, they need to recognize each other's concerns and interpret each other's behavior appropriately. When we support each other, making ourselves emotionally reliable and mutually attentive, we enhance trust. Women are more likely than men to sense when a partner is in trouble and provide an empathetic response. Men, upon sensing something is wrong, tend to respond by attempting to change the subject. While from a female perspective such a response may be interpreted as a lack of caring or understanding, when viewed from a male perspective it is construed as appropriate.[37]

Because of our mismatched perceptions of communication, the kinds of lies we tell also may be influenced by gender. Whereas men tend to tell self-centered lies, the lies of women tend to focus on others' feelings. Women generally put a positive spin on events or falsely derogate themselves to make another feel more confident; men are apt to pretend to be more put off than they actually are to manipulate others into acting the way they want.[38]

Just as women talk to preserve relationships, sometimes they also pretend not to detect a lie so they do not have to put a relationship in jeopardy. Because of this practice, some believe that women are more self-deceptive than men. Men, in contrast, tend to be more apt to confront deception, or at the very least to let on that they are aware another person is trying to deceive them.[39]

MEDIA, TECHNOLOGY, AND LESSONS ON TRUST

The messages of the media and technology influence whom we are willing to trust. Because we consume them daily, media and technology leave their imprint on our relationships, often without our being aware they have done so.

We foster trust by being emotionally reliable and mutually attentive.

THE MEDIA AND TRUST

Of the many influences on how we view different groups in society, the media are among the most powerful. Integrated into our daily lives, media messages are repeated to us incessantly. They communicate images of the sexes, older persons, businesspeople, medical professionals, ethnic groups, and so forth, and a significant percentage of the messages encoded in the media help sustain stereotypical or unrealistic perceptions regarding who is trustworthy.[40]

For too long the media were prone to categorizing women as either good or bad. "Good" women typically were portrayed as deferential and focused on home and family, while "bad" women were depicted as hard, cold, aggressive, ambitious, embittered, and not to be trusted.[41] In addition, media portrayals of women may be undermining the ability of women to trust each other.[42] For example, in advertising, films, and television, women and girls often are presented as being in competition with each other—often for men. Such depictions may cause women to become suspicious of one another, contributing to their inability to trust each other and leading others to stereotype women as "catty."

Similarly, the media have all too frequently handled minority groups by either stereotyping or neglecting them.[43] For instance, until recently, the portrayal of Native Americans in the U.S. media was consistently inaccurate, depicting them as bloodthirsty, marauding savages who were not to be trusted.[44] Likewise, the media still often portray minorities and people from less developed countries in extremes: African Americans as incapable, shiftless, or inferior; Hispanics as illegal aliens; and Italians as mobsters. The media also portray overweight people as lazy, older people as childlike and helpless, and the disabled as problems. By unfairly labeling or stigmatizing individuals, media portrayals may negate the human value of honesty, perpetuate misinformation, lead to human degradation, and adversely influence person-to-person understanding.

There is danger in sharing our deepest secrets and vulnerabilities online.

TECHNOLOGY AND TRUST

With the ever-increasing popularity of social networking, more and more of us are spending more and more time online. We communicate with our fingertips, sharing our deepest secrets—virtually at warp speed. Technology helps speed up romance by compelling people to communicate verbally at the same time that it helps de-emphasize distracting visual signals such as frowns, smirks, and rolling eyes, which can inhibit in-person contact.

Social networking sites and other online venues find people revealing secrets and sharing vulnerabilities much sooner than they would in more traditionally formed relationships. The traditional love letter has all but disappeared. Online communication, however, may lack the security or inherent privacy that the sealed letter once promised. In fact, we might compare our social network pages more to postcards: we shouldn't be surprised when a post or e-mail we write is read by persons other than the one for whom it was intended. People who imagined they were disclosing personal information to one intended recipient have been devastated to find that others to whom they had no intention of revealing such information were privy to it. Consequently, while technological innovations have made us more accessible to each other, they also have made us more accessible to everyone.

On the other hand, for some, the Web encourages the sharing of personal information that they might have found too difficult to communicate were they actually required to do so face-to-face. Somehow, using technology to communicate helps reduce our inhibitions and frees us to reveal information we would otherwise hesitate to share.

This leads us to pose three questions that each of us should ask ourselves before we entrust others with our more intimate disclosures on social networking sites:

1. If we would not discuss something on the richest channel available to us—face-to-face communication—should we be revealing the information at all?

2. How much of the real meaning of our disclosures is being lost in the electronic translation of personal information?

3. To what extent should we trust social networking sites to ensure our privacy at the same time they reduce our inhibitions and link us more closely to each other?

Whereas we may have been taught to assume that members of the community in which we live are trustworthy, online communities are a different story. We know many of the people we interact with online only by their screen names, making it more difficult for us to establish genuine trusting relationships. As one writer queried, "Is technology making us intimate strangers?"[45] When we otherwise interact with persons who surrender their fictional identities so that we can verify who they really are, the establishment of trust becomes easier.

Still, since so much interaction has moved online, it would be a benefit if we were able to spot online deception. According to information technology and deception specialist Jeffrey

Figure 9.1 Countries with the Highest Percentages of Adults Who Use Social Networking Sites

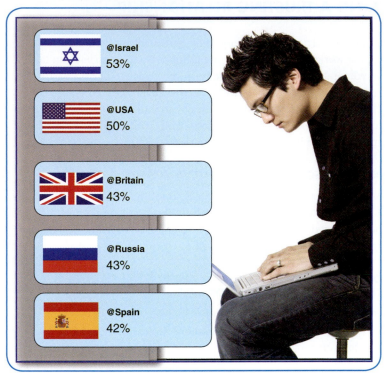

@Israel
53%

@USA
50%

@Britain
43%

@Russia
43%

@Spain
42%

SOURCE: Based on information from Pew Research Center.

Hancock, "Most people believe that given the opportunity, everything else equal, people will lie more online than they would face-to-face."[46] Lies told online are motivated by the same human needs as are any other lies, but their quantity may be greater. Research on deception in online dating reveals that approximately 80 percent of people embellish their profiles with "small" fibs, such as a man representing himself as six feet tall when he is really three inches shorter or a woman claiming that she weighs a bit less than she really does. In such cases, those who tell the fibs find that the potential cost of being caught is outweighed by the self-presentation benefit of having others find them more appealing because they are thought to be taller or slimmer than they really are. Lying in an online dating profile is a means to create interpersonal attraction. The requirement to post photos of themselves online, however, does make people less likely to lie.[47]

How can you spot a lie when searching online for a potential date? Online prospects who are being less than honest are less likely to refer to themselves as "I"; use indirect adjectives, such as "not boring" rather than "exciting"; and keep their descriptions brief. Using these criteria, researchers were able to identify liars about 65 percent of the time.[48]

Another online trend practiced by young couples is the sharing of passwords to e-mail and social networking accounts, which facilitates opportunities to read each other's private e-mails and texts and may be seen as a means of proving their trust in one another. A danger of this practice is the potential for each person to reveal the secrets of the other should the relationship turn dark or end. While the former partners may change their passwords, a lot of damage can be done before the password change is accomplished.[49]

GAINING COMMUNICATION COMPETENCE: NURTURING A TRUSTING RELATIONSHIP

As our examination of trust reveals, being trustworthy means working to build a real relationship, not working to get to know the other person just so you can take advantage of his or her vulnerabilities. When you use your knowledge to harm a partner, you destroy your partner's trust in you. Fear, distrust, and other defensive feelings are common blocks to the functioning and self-actualizing abilities of an individual, as well as barriers to the development and maintenance of a good relationship. Thus, the key to building trust in a relationship is to behave in a trustworthy manner.

BE WILLING TO DISCLOSE YOURSELF TO ANOTHER PERSON

Like self-disclosure, trust is a reciprocal process. Trusting behavior on your part can often lead to trusting behavior in another. Thus, self-disclosing to another can help the other come to know you, understand you, and realize that he or she must also take a risk if a relationship based on mutual trust is to develop.

LET THE OTHER PERSON KNOW YOU ACCEPT AND SUPPORT HIM OR HER

When you reduce threats to the ego of another individual, you increase the level of trust between you and create a **supportive environment**. If the other person feels accepted by you and feels that you perceive him or her as a significant human being who is worthy of your time and attention, then he or she will be less likely to experience anxiety about being placed in a vulnerable position. Such feelings of acceptance will also deter others from attempting to defend themselves by lying or concealing the truth. They simply will have no reason to do so. Thus, support and acceptance encourage trust and honesty.

DEVELOP A COOPERATIVE/SUPPORTIVE RATHER THAN A COMPETITIVE/DEFENSIVE ORIENTATION

Working to "win" in a relationship can destroy it. The definition of a relationship affects how easily trust may be built or, indeed, whether it will be built at all. If your primary aim is to increase your personal gain, even though that means sacrificing the well-being of a partner, the degree of trust your partner is willing to put in you will diminish rapidly. You will be perceived as a manipulator. In contrast, healthy relationships depend on the problem-solving abilities of the individuals involved. Skillful problem solving presupposes a nonmanipulative orientation. If individuals choose to compete with each other instead of cooperating, trust simply will not develop.

TRUST ANOTHER WHEN WARRANTED

Taking inappropriate risks can cause as many problems as never being willing to take a risk. In other words, always trusting people who do not merit your trust is as dysfunctional as never trusting anyone. Persons who consistently trust exploitative people find themselves taken advantage of and will not build relationships based on trust. Instead, you must be willing question the other person's motives and behavior openly. The other person may learn to respect you for feeling strong enough or capable enough to call a halt to the duplicity. Remember, trust is sustained only if both parties to a relationship behave in trustworthy ways.

WHAT DO YOU KNOW?

True or False

5. *Liars use more indirect language than do truth tellers.*

True. The speech of liars contains less specificity than does the speech of people who are not lying.

Supportive environment: An environment that builds trust and maintains each person's sense of worth.

Fifty houses! Angela was devastated. She had shown the Williams family fifty houses over the summer—and now this!

At the end of the spring term, Angela had completed a real estate sales course. A summer job selling houses had seemed like a great idea. She liked people, the hours were flexible, and the potential for earning high commissions as a sales agent with a company in her hometown was great. Of course, the downside was that there would be no pay if she failed to make a sale, but Angela figured that was too remote a possibility for her to take seriously.

Selling was not an easy job. There were houses to preview, owners to call, and buyers to show houses to seven days a week. After working days and evenings for six weeks with no success, Angela finally found "live" buyers—Rita and Tom Williams—who desperately wanted to buy a $600,000 home in an upscale neighborhood. All was not lost. The fee she would earn from selling them a house would pay most of her school expenses for the next year.

Angela worked tirelessly, taking Rita to houses in the morning and showing Tom the same houses in the evening. She got to know their three-year-old son, Evan, better than she knew her own nieces and nephews. Evan was a nice kid; it wasn't his fault that he often got carsick and threw up in her backseat . . .

Rita and Tom had finally narrowed it down to two homes. Angela was sure she could close the deal before September, when she would return to college. Showing them fifty houses had been exhausting, but now that she could see the bright light at the end of the real estate tunnel, she decided it had been fun.

Then Rita called. She and Tom had also been looking at houses with another real estate agent. In fact, they had already made an offer on a house that had been accepted several days ago; they would be closing on it soon. They had continued to look at houses with Angela just to convince themselves that the one they had made the offer on was the best they could find. Now they were convinced that they had made the right choice. Unfortunately, nothing Angela showed them had compared to the one they had decided to bid on. Rita thanked Angela for all her help.

Angela dropped the phone. How could Rita and Tom do this to her? Because of the time she had spent with them, Angela had worked the entire summer without earning a cent.

"Whom can I trust?" she cried to her sales manager. Just then, the door opened and a couple walked in. They wanted to look at homes. The sales manager introduced them to Angela.

Consider these questions:

1. Should Angela trust the new couple and show them houses?

2. What could Angela do, if anything, to ensure that the trust she might place in these new buyers would not be misplaced?

CHAPTER SUMMARY

1 Define trust and explain the bases for it.
Trust is the belief that you can depend on another person to act in your best interest. It consists of two basic components: trusting behavior and trustworthy behavior. Whether trust exists influences the nature of a relationship. The amount of faith we have in one another is based in large measure on our perceptions of each other's character. Among character-based sources of trust are trust in the other's integrity, consistency of behavior, and discretion.

2 Explain cost-benefit theory, including its relationship to trust. According to cost-benefit theory, we work to sustain relationships that enable us to maximize the profit side of our relational balance sheets. As long as the benefits we receive from our relationships outweigh our emotional expenditures, we will work to sustain them.

3 Identify factors contributing to the development of supportive and defensive interpersonal climates. Whether a relationship is defined as cooperative or competitive plays a part in determining whether the individuals involved develop trust. An interpersonal relationship that is competitive precipitates defensive and threatening behavior in interactions, whereas a cooperative relationship tends to precipitate more supportive and honest communication.

4 Describe how lying affects interpersonal relationships. Deception, or the effort to manipulate truth, affects the nature and outcomes of a relationship. Although some people differentiate between white lies and bigger lies, all lies help us negotiate situations that expose us to levels of vulnerability exceeding our comfort zones.

5 Discuss how gender and culture influence the development of trust. Culture and gender play roles in determining whom we trust. The presence of ethnocentrism and gender preferences influence perceptions of who can be trusted.

6 Describe how media portrayals and technology can foster or impede the development of relationships based on trust. Stereotyped portrayals in media affect our views of different groups in society, fostering unrealistic perceptions of who is and is not trustworthy. Technology and social networks facilitate the sharing and disclosure of personal information, leading us to trust persons who may not deserve to be trusted.

7 Identify and use behaviors that promote the development of trusting relationships. For trust to develop you need to be willing to disclose yourself to another person, let the other person know you accept and support him or her, develop a cooperative orientation, and believe that trusting behavior will be reciprocated and is, therefore, appropriate.

✔ CHECK YOUR UNDERSTANDING

1 Can you provide examples that highlight the nature of both trusting and supportive relationships? (See pages 236–239 and 243–248.)

2 Can you create a scenario illustrating how lying and/or a willingness or unwillingness to forgive may affect a relationship? (See pages 239–240.)

3 Can you develop a story to explain the value of cost-benefit theory? (See page 241.)

4 Can you create a list of ways in which your culture, your gender, or your preference for particular media offerings and social networks could influence your feelings about trust? (See pages 255–259.)

5 Can you identify behaviors you can adopt to foster more trusting relationships? (See page 260.)

CHECK YOUR SKILLS

1 Can you use a set of criteria to help you judge when someone is or is not trustworthy? (See pages 236–239; and **Try This,** page 238.)

2 Can you take appropriate action when a person you trusted proves to be untrustworthy, including but not limited to forgiving the trust violation? (See pages 239–240; and **Analyze This,** page 240.)

3 Can you use cost-benefit theory to evaluate a personal relationship? (See page 241; and **Try This,** page 242.)

4 Can you appropriately define a relationship as cooperative or competitive? (See pages 242–243; and **Try This,** page 243.)

5 Can you correctly evaluate when you or others are being defensive and introduce behaviors conducive to the creation of a supportive climate? (See pages 243–248; **Analyze This,** pages 246–247; and **Try This,** page 249.)

6 Can you use behaviors that build trust in order to limit the potential damage that lying can do to a relationship? (See pages 248–253; and **Reflect on This,** page 254.)

7 Can you recognize when gossip turns dangerous? (See pages 254–255.)

8 Can you identify how cultural and gender preferences influence willingness to trust? (See pages 255–257; and **Try This,** page 256.)

9 Can you point out how media offerings and online sites undermine or encourage trust in others? (See pages 257–259.)

10 Can you use your skills to handle relational issues based on trust? (See **The Case of the Trusting Agent,** page 261.)

KEY TERMS

Trust 236

Trusting behavior 237

Trustworthy behavior 237

Cost-benefit theory 241

Comparison level for alternatives 241

Competitive relationship 243

Cooperative relationship 243

Defensive climate 243

Supportive climate 244

Evaluative statements 244

Descriptive statements 244

Lie 248

Displacement 252

Repression 252

Rationalization 252

Counterfeit relationship 252

Cyberbullicide 255

Supportive environment 260

STUDENT STUDY SITE

Visit the student study site at **www.sagepub.com/gambleic** to access the following materials:

- SAGE Journal Articles
- Videos
- Web Resources

- eFlashcards
- Web Quizzes
- Study Questions

Our ultimate freedom is the right and power to decide how anybody or anything outside ourselves will affect us.

—Stephen R. Covey

POWER AND INFLUENCE

LEARNING OBJECTIVES

After completing this chapter, you should be able to demonstrate mastery of the following learning outcomes:

1. Define power.

2. Compare and contrast the following types of power: reward, coercive, expert, legitimate, referent, and persuasive.

3. Define and distinguish among attitudes, beliefs, and values.

4. Discuss the persuasive forces that help elicit compliance.

5. Explain balance theory and cognitive dissonance and their roles in interpersonal persuasion.

6. Discuss how gender differences influence the exercise of power.

7. Explain the ways in which media and technology influence both the perception and the exercise of power.

Can you imagine someone having the power to make you do something you absolutely do not want to do? For example, do you think you would obey an authority figure who asked you to inflict pain on a stranger, or on a friend for that matter?

Power has a dark side. A half century ago, the psychologist Stanley Milgram conducted a series of studies on obedience. Over and over again, Milgram demonstrated that a large number of his well-intentioned subjects delivered what they thought were increasingly painful electric shocks to another person in what the subjects believed was an experiment about learning. Unbeknownst to the subjects, however, the "learner" was actually an actor who was only pretending to receive the painful shocks.[1]

> **We all have some power that we use in our daily interactions.**

Some fifty years later, Milgram's experiments were replicated. Again, more than half the participants agreed to proceed past the point of what they thought was real pain.[2] These studies showed that human beings have the capacity to act destructively without being coerced. They merely comply with the instructions of those in authority. They cede their personal power to those they believe are in control.

Milgram's subjects had a choice, though, and so do we. We all have some power that we use in our daily interactions. By better understanding the relationship between power and influence, we can more capably respond to perceived power imbalances in our interpersonal relationships.

WHAT DO YOU KNOW?

Before continuing your reading of this chapter, which of the following five statements do you believe to be true and which do you believe to be false?

1. Giving perks reflects a need to influence behavior.　　T　F

2. Asking someone to do something for you that he or she can easily do works about half the time.　　T　F

3. We feel obligated to return a favor.　T　F

4. If someone pays you $100 to speak in support of a person or an issue that you do not support, you are more likely to come to support the person or issue than if the person pays you only $10 for your efforts.　　T　F

5. If you always do as you are told, you likely are a member of a culture with a low-power-distance preference.　　T　F

Read the chapter to discover if you're right or if you've made any erroneous assumptions.

ANSWERS: 1. T; 2. F; 3. T; 4. F; 5. F

Spider-Man's heroic deeds are motivated by a phrase attributed to his Uncle Ben: "With great power comes great responsibility."

Power, the potential to influence, plays a role in every relationship—though ideally not in ways that are abusive or exploitative.[3] Whether you are interacting with a close friend and exerting an equal amount of power, with an employer who exerts more power than you, or with a spouse who acquiesces to your every request, power is present. Power affects our respect for others, our fear of others, our feelings of confidence or dependence, and even our decisions about whose company we seek. It determines which individuals we are able to control, which are able to control us, and whether we are comfortable being in or out of control. Although the amount of power we are able to exert depends on our relationship with the other person, we can all gain from understanding the nature of personal power.

THE CONTROL FACTOR: EXPLORING THE BALANCE OF POWER IN RELATIONSHIPS

Sometimes we feel in control or powerful in a relationship, while other times we feel out of control or powerless. When we cede control or feel powerless, our feelings of vulnerability increase. In contrast, when we make a power grab and succeed, we feel more influential. We test the balance of power routinely in our relationships. The amount of power we have is less important than how we use it: Do we use power for our self-benefit or to benefit both parties in the relationship?

FEELING POWERFUL VERSUS POWERLESS

If you find yourself feeling powerless a lot of the time, chances are that you are unhappy and unsatisfied with your relationships. When we lose the ability to control what happens to us, we also lose the ability to direct our future, and others end up directing our lives. When this happens, others influence our decisions, and they also may make choices for us—choices that may or may not be in our best interest.

Are You Socially Anxious? Your emotions influence how powerful or powerless you feel. For example, if you feel nervous or overly emotional in social situations, you may suffer from social anxiety, which probably makes it more difficult for you to project a powerful image. Those who are socially anxious find it difficult to enjoy themselves in public. They are likely to feel that others are evaluating them, finding fault with them, or judging them. Because the anxiety felt by the socially anxious is so painful, some who experience this problem decide to stay away from social situations and avoid others altogether, which makes it unlikely that they will influence anyone.

The socially anxious are especially fearful of authority figures, such as bosses and supervisors at work or anyone they perceive to be better or more important than they are. Upon meeting authority figures, people with social anxiety may experience a lump in the

Power: The potential to influence others.

throat and their facial muscles may freeze up. Because their focus is on *not failing* and *not giving themselves away,* they are unlikely even to remember what was said in conversation.[4]

Are You on a Power Trip? At the extreme, some emotions can send you on a *power trip*—you feel so capable and secure that you imagine you can manipulate others to do whatever you want with little effort. The term *Machiavellian* refers to people who use a variety of ploys to make choices for and control others. If you score high in **Machiavellianism**, you have the drive to control others. If you score low in Machiavellianism, you are likely less controlling and more susceptible to the interpersonal persuasion of others.[5]

WHERE DOES POWER COME FROM?

Power is relational. The person who has power derives it from the social relationship itself. Another person assents, overtly or covertly, to the use of power. The greater our power, the greater our ability to make things happen and to prevent those things we do not want to happen from happening. When we have power, we simply are better able to control what happens to us when in the company of others. Your judgment of the amount of power you have or another has is based on the resources you or the other control and determines the extent to which either one of you feels dependent in the relationship.

POWER CATEGORIES

When we have power, we possess a resource others value.[6] Researchers have identified six categories of power that we use to control and influence others: reward, coercive, expert, legitimate, referent, and persuasive (see Table 10.1).[7] The extent to which we use each of these resources or currencies of power in our relationships reveals our influence preferences.

TABLE 10.1 Types of Power

Type	Definition	Example
Reward power	One party in the relationship controls something valued by the other party.	Instructors hold reward power over their students in the form of grades.
Coercive power	One party in the relationship can deliver negative consequences in response to the actions of another.	Individuals who threaten to boycott a business unless certain actions are taken hold coercive power over the business owners.
Expert power	One party in the relationship possesses special knowledge or skill that another individual believes he or she needs.	Physicians hold expert power in the eyes of patients in the form of specific diagnoses or treatments.
Legitimate power	Because of his or her position, one party in the relationship is able to control the other party.	Employers hold legitimate power over their employees.
Referent power	Because of the respect and admiration accorded him or her, one party in the relationship is able to convince others.	An older sibling may have referent power over a younger brother or sister.
Persuasive power	One party in the relationship is able to persuade another to believe or act as he or she wants.	Through the use of logic, well-conceived and developed arguments, and emotional appeals, lawyers hold persuasive power over jurors.

Machiavellianism: The drive to control others.

TRY THIS: *What's Your Power Orientation?*

The amount of Machiavellianism you possess influences whether you are more or less likely to try to control others. Persons scoring high on the following test for Machiavellianism are apt to be more strategic and manipulative in their interpersonal efforts than are persons who score low. The latter are more likely to exhibit a problem-solving orientation when faced with an interpersonal power moment.

For each statement below, select a numerical response from the following scale and write it down next to the statement.

Disagree a lot	Disagree a little		Agree a little	Agree a lot
1	2	3	4	5

1. The best way to handle people is to tell them what they want to hear. ____

2. When you ask someone to do something for you, it is best to give the real reason for wanting it rather than giving reasons that might carry more weight. ____

3. *Anyone who completely trusts anyone else is asking for trouble.* ____

4. It is hard to get ahead without cutting corners here and there. ____

5. It is safest to assume that everyone has a vicious streak, which will come out when given a chance. ____

6. One should take action only when it is morally right. ____

7. Most people are basically good and kind. ____

8. There is no excuse for lying to someone else. ____

9. Most people more easily forget the death of their father than the loss of property. ____

10. Generally speaking, people won't work hard unless they're forced to do so. ____

To determine your score, follow these steps.

Reverse the scores on items 2, 6, 7, and 8 as follows:

If you responded with	Change it to
5	1
4	2
3	3
2	4
1	5

Add together your answers for all questions, being certain to use the reverse numbers for questions 2, 6, 7, and 8.

If your total score is between 35 and 50, you are likely a high Machiavellian; if you score between 10 and 15, you are probably a low Machiavellian. The majority of people's responses fall between these extremes.

Do you believe that your results on this test accurately describe you? Do your results support or contradict research findings that men generally are more Machiavellian than women, older adults tend to have lower scores than younger adults, and those with higher scores tend to be in professions that require one to exert control over others? To what extent, if any, do you see your score reflected in how you interact with others and your decisions regarding whether or not to exert power over the choices others make?

SOURCE: From R. Christie and F. L. Geis, Studies in Machiavellianism. Academic Press 1970. © Elsevier Science & Technology Books.

Reward Power. The person in a relationship who controls something valued by the other person in the relationship is said to hold **reward power**. The person with reward power knows what the other person wants, is able to retain or provide it, lets the other know this ability exists, and reveals what the other needs to do for the reward to be released. Rewards may be tangible (job, money, "perk") or intangible (friendship, security, love). The extent to which one person values the rewards determines the amount of power the other is able to exercise. If you have the ability either to deliver positive consequences or to remove negative ones, you will be more likely to get another person to comply with your requests. When you control physical or emotional resources, you have power. Every relationship implies some degree of reward power. The more fulfilling we find a relationship, the more we perceive it to have such power.

Coercive Power. Unlike reward power, **coercive power** is typically associated with force. Individuals with coercive power can deliver negative consequences or remove positive ones in response to another's actions. When using coercive power, people need to be prepared both to escalate the threats they make and to have others resent or dislike them for threatening them in the first place. To exercise coercive power, you need to identify the specific consequences another fears most, have the ability to mete out those consequences at will, let the other person know you have that ability, and convince him or her that unless he or she behaves as you want, you will act accordingly.

By exercising psychological coercive power, someone can compel us to maintain a relationship we might otherwise choose to end. Because we fear the punishment the other person can inflict—whether that fear is of being ignored, demeaned, or something else— the threats made can be a powerful interpersonal motivator.

Expert Power. A person who has **expert power** is presumed to possess a special knowledge or skill others believe they need. Expert power holders have the ability to influence us because of their training, background, or accomplishments. Such power is further enhanced when we believe the expert source to be unbiased, with nothing to gain personally from influencing us. For example, a physician may persuade us to follow specific instructions concerning our health once we are convinced that her credentials allow her to dispense such medical advice, we believe in the correctness of her prescription, and we trust that she will not profit unduly if we follow her advice. If, on the other hand, we find that a presumed expert will profit personally as a result of gaining our compliance, that person's perceived expertise will decline in our eyes. If, for instance, a salesperson recommends you purchase a product for which he will earn a higher fee, you might doubt his actual expertise.

Legitimate Power. When a person's position enables him or her to control another, that person has **legitimate power**. Most of us believe that some people have a right to exert power over us merely because of the roles they perform, who they are, or the positions they hold. For example, students perceive their teachers to have legitimate power, law-abiding citizens perceive the police to have legitimate power, and employees perceive their employers to have legitimate power. Often used to reduce conflict, legitimate power convinces those with less power to adhere to the requests of the more powerful.

Referent Power. When someone has **referent power**, we do as he or she requests because we identify with, respect, or like him or her, and we want the person to like us. The relationship is a simple one. As our desire to be like someone increases, so does that individual's referent power in our eyes. The more attractive we find someone and the more we respect and admire him or her, the greater our tendency to mirror that person's behavior and do as he or she wants rather than contradict his or her actions and fail to conform with his or her wishes. Thus, a person who serves as our referent can get us to do many things we might not otherwise ordinarily do.

Reward power: Power based in the fact that one party in a relationship controls something valued by the other party.

Coercive power: The ability to deliver negative consequences in response to the action of another; power derived from force or the threat of force.

Expert power: Power derived from having special knowledge or skills that another thinks he or she needs.

Legitimate power: The type of power in which one party in a relationship controls the other.

Referent power: Power that is based in other persons' respect for or identification with the power holder.

Being able to develop logical arguments can increase your power.

Persuasive Power. Sometimes a person has power because of his or her ability to persuade by conveying information in well-thought-out arguments. The individual's power is based on the logic or reasonableness of his or her arguments or the demonstrated superiority of his or her knowledge. **Persuasive power** enables one person to persuade another through the presentation of well-reasoned arguments. Those who possess persuasive power need not be experts; they only need to know how to use speech powerfully and reason intelligently.

Although we can use any of these types of power in a relationship, some are more effective and less damaging than others to the sense of self of the less powerful member. By analyzing the types of power that characterize your meaningful relationships, you gain insight into how balanced or unbalanced, personally costly or beneficial, and effective or ineffective the use of power and personal influence is in your life.[8]

EXERCISING PERSUASION

How often do you succeed in exercising power and persuading others to see things your way? How often do you give in to another whom you perceive to have more power and agree to do things his or her way? Successful persuaders understand the attitudes, beliefs, and values others hold dear and use these to accomplish their persuasive goals. Once we identify how we can best influence others, our interpersonal effectiveness may improve markedly.

When seeking to influence another, usually we try to modify that person's thinking, feelings, or behavior so it becomes more compatible with ours. Seeking to exert personal influence is normal, but some of us become so preoccupied with the effort that our central aim in our relationships becomes to create similarity of thought, feeling, and behavior.

To this end, let us explore the roles that attitudes, beliefs, and values play in this process, and how attitudes, beliefs, and values are internalized, maintained, or changed through interaction.

THE ROLE OF ATTITUDES

Although we cannot see, hear, or touch an attitude, we can see, hear, and touch the behavior that results from holding that attitude. We use verbal and nonverbal cues to communicate attitudes. Facial expressions, postures, and gestures are attitude revealers. Each time we socialize, attend class, or go to a meeting, our attitudes are on display. They affect who we are and how we relate.

What Is an Attitude? Most psychologists define an **attitude** as a mental set or readiness to respond that causes us to react in a particular way to a given stimulus. Each of our attitudes represents a predisposition to react positively or negatively toward certain people, ideas, things, or situations. In other words, our attitudes represent our evaluations. They help us sort our perceptions into categories ranging from extremely favorable to extremely unfavorable.

In large measure, our attitudes determine our communication preferences and behavior. They lead us to behave in certain ways and increase the likelihood that specific kinds of reactions will occur.

Persuasive power:
The ability of one party in a relationship to persuade the other party to act in a desired way.

Attitude: A mental set or readiness that causes one to respond in a particular way to a given stimulus.

1. In your relationships, the more powerful person is the one in control of the situation. Think of five current relationships.

   A. For each, identify the relationship's nature—that is, is it based primarily on friendship, family ties, work, or health needs?

   B. Compare and contrast the amount of power you perceive you and the other person to wield. In each instance, who is the more powerful person and why?

   C. Indicate your perceptions of the amount of power each of you has on the continuum below by marking the points for each of the five relationships. In which of your relationships is power balanced? In which is it imbalanced? How do you account for the differences?

   You have more power.   Power is balanced   The other person has more power.

2. Each of the six categories of power comes into play as we relate to one another in different arenas of our lives, including work.

   A. With reference to the work arena, describe how employers and employees use each power category to solve work-related problems.

   B. Which category do you find yourself using most frequently/effectively to motivate others to think or behave in ways you would like? Explain.

   C. Which type of power do you find works best on you? Why?

Where Do Our Attitudes Come From? We act according to pictures we carry in our heads—pictures that do not necessarily correspond with reality. To understand why we hold the attitudes we do, we can try to "dig out" the roots of our pictures. As we do this, we will identify the forces that help us create and sustain them.

The roots of our attitudes extend in many directions. Among the forces feeding them and contributing to their growth are family, religion, education, economic and social class, and culture:

- *Family:* Few of us escape the strong influences our family members exert. Our parents communicate their attitudes, and eventually we acquire and hold at least a number of them. Research confirms: "It is the family that bends the tender twig in the direction it is likely to grow."[9]

- *Religion:* Religion affects both believers and nonbelievers. In fact, its impact has become even more widespread in recent decades, with churches striving to influence attitudes on such social issues as abortion, the roles of men and women, violence in media, and economic disparities.

- *Education:* We attend school for more years now than ever before. Many of us start before we are five years old and attend until we are well into our twenties or older. In addition, adults are returning to school in record numbers, either to complete or to advance their education. What we are taught, who teaches us, articles and books we are assigned to read, the films and other media products we are shown, the websites we use—all help shape our attitudes.

- *Economic and social class:* Our economic and social backgrounds also shape our attitudes. Our economic status helps determine the social arena we frequent. The company we keep and the amount of money we have influence our thoughts about the world and its problems.

- *Culture:* We learn our culture. It is transmitted to us, and the messages it considers important are constantly reinforced. Culture is "our theory of 'the game' being played in our society."[10] Once we share a culture, we also share similar meanings.

- Our culture, passed on to us by our family, friends, and the groups we belong to, helps coordinate our behavior and the norms and rules we live by.

Few of us escape the strong influences of family members.

Beliefs: The building blocks of attitudes; one's assessment of what is true or false, probable or improbable.

THE ROLE OF BELIEFS

Although the term *attitude* is sometimes used interchangeably with the term *belief,* the two are distinguishable. While we internalize many attitudes, we form an even greater number of beliefs.

What Are Beliefs? Beliefs are to attitudes as bricks are to buildings. In other words, **beliefs** are the building blocks of attitudes; they provide the basis or foundation for our attitudes.

Whereas attitudes are measured on a favorable-unfavorable or good-bad continuum, beliefs are measured on a true-false or probable-improbable continuum. Thus, if we say that we think something is true, we really are saying that we believe it. Beliefs help us describe how we view our environment and reality.

Why do we believe or fail to believe what others say to us? Why do we believe or fail to believe our physician? Our friends? Our coworkers? The media? We believe information for a variety of reasons. Sometimes we believe it because we read it somewhere or saw it on the news, and we have "blind faith" in what we read or see in the media, never recognizing that authors and reporters may be wrong or biased. Other times, we believe information because an authority "says it is so," because our best friend says it is so, because "everyone else believes it," or simply because "that's the way it really is." Our beliefs are not necessarily logical. Rather, in large part, we hold them as a result of what we want or need to believe, what we are able to believe, or what others teach us to believe. For reasons such as these, we do not always require proof to believe. Instead, we allow our beliefs to influence our interpretations; we use them to manipulate or distort what we see and hear. We act in ways that are consistent with what we think is true. As a result, at least to some degree, what we believe restricts what we perceive.

Our belief system is made up of everything with which we agree.[11] It includes all the information and biases we have accumulated since birth. Formed along with our belief system is our disbelief system. It is composed of all the things with which we disagree. Together, the two systems influence our processing of information.

TRY THIS: *Assessing Attitudes and Surveying Beliefs*

1. Use each of the paired scales that follow to indicate your evaluations of the people and issues listed. For example, if you hold an extremely favorable attitude toward the concept or person being evaluated, then you would indicate that by circling the words "extremely favorable" on the first scale as well as by choosing a 90 or a 100 on the positive scale and a 0 or a 10 on the negative scale.

Physicians

Scale 1	Extremely favorable		Fairly favorable		Neutral		Fairly unfavorable		Extremely unfavorable	
Scale 2										
Positive 0	10	20	30	40	50	60	70	80	90	100
Negative 0	10	20	30	40	50	60	70	80	90	100

Marriage

Scale 1	Extremely favorable		Fairly favorable		Neutral		Fairly unfavorable		Extremely unfavorable	
Scale 2										
Positive 0	10	20	30	40	50	60	70	80	90	100
Negative 0	10	20	30	40	50	60	70	80	90	100

Your best friend

Scale 1	Extremely favorable		Fairly favorable		Neutral		Fairly unfavorable		Extremely unfavorable	
Scale 2										
Positive 0	10	20	30	40	50	60	70	80	90	100
Negative 0	10	20	30	40	50	60	70	80	90	100

Your boss

Scale 1	Extremely favorable		Fairly favorable		Neutral		Fairly unfavorable		Extremely unfavorable	
Scale 2										
Positive 0	10	20	30	40	50	60	70	80	90	100
Negative 0	10	20	30	40	50	60	70	80	90	100

Your parents

Scale 1	Extremely favorable		Fairly favorable		Neutral		Fairly unfavorable		Extremely unfavorable	
Scale 2										
Positive 0	10	20	30	40	50	60	70	80	90	100
Negative 0	10	20	30	40	50	60	70	80	90	100

Premarital sex

Scale 1	Extremely favorable			Fairly favorable			Neutral			Fairly unfavorable			Extremely unfavorable		
Scale 2															
Positive	0	10	20	30	40	50	60	70	80	90	100				
Negative	0	10	20	30	40	50	60	70	80	90	100				

Long-distance relationships

Scale 1	Extremely favorable			Fairly favorable			Neutral			Fairly unfavorable			Extremely unfavorable		
Scale 2															
Positive	0	10	20	30	40	50	60	70	80	90	100				
Negative	0	10	20	30	40	50	60	70	80	90	100				

Divorce

Scale 1	Extremely favorable			Fairly favorable			Neutral			Fairly unfavorable			Extremely unfavorable		
Scale 2															
Positive	0	10	20	30	40	50	60	70	80	90	100				
Negative	0	10	20	30	40	50	60	70	80	90	100				

Telecommuting

Scale 1	Extremely favorable			Fairly favorable			Neutral			Fairly unfavorable			Extremely unfavorable		
Scale 2															
Positive	0	10	20	30	40	50	60	70	80	90	100				
Negative	0	10	20	30	40	50	60	70	80	90	100				

A. Which type of scale was most useful to you in clarifying the nature of your attitudes? Why?

B. To what extent did your attitudes show absolute conviction (0 on one measure, 100 on the other)?

C. To what extent were your attitudes mixed or ambivalent?

2. Develop a list of five things you believe and five things you disbelieve about someone important to you. Identify your reasons for each belief. Describe how each belief influences your behavior toward the person, affecting what you do or say. Explain how your behavior might change if you did not believe what you say you believe and believed what you say you do not believe.

DEFINING AND CHARACTERIZING VALUES

Like attitudes and beliefs, our values influence our communication. Let us examine how values affect our relationships (see Figure 10.1). We define **values** as ideas about what is important in our lives. Our values represent our feelings about the worth of something.

In the classic book *Types of Men,* German philosopher and psychologist Eduard Spranger argues that we each have one predominant value system drawn from the following six major value types:[12]

- *Theoretical:* Values the pursuit and discovery of truth, the intellectual life
- *Economic:* Values that which is useful, practical
- *Aesthetic:* Values form, harmony, and beauty
- *Social:* Values love, sympathy, warmth, and sensitivity in relationships
- *Political:* Values competition, influence, and personal power
- *Religious:* Values unity, wholeness, and a sense of purpose above human beings

Our values provide us with a relatively persistent framework for deciding what we think is right or wrong, which goals to aspire to, whose company to seek, whom to listen to, and how to live. They provide us with criteria for evaluating the people in our lives, including their ideas and actions. They indicate what we find desirable and to what extent, and, consequently, they influence what we are willing to strive for.

GAINING COMPLIANCE IN INTERPERSONAL RELATIONSHIPS

Because we are always forming new relationships and encountering new experiences, we may find it necessary or perhaps expedient to change or adjust our attitudes. Sometimes, for example, we interact with another whose actions conflict with our beliefs. When this occurs we may try to take steps to reduce or eliminate the conflict. We work hard to gain compliance so that we are able to maintain internal consistency or balance among our actions, feelings, and beliefs.

STRATEGIES FOR COMPLIANCE GAINING

We use a variety of persuasive strategies to gain compliance from others. For example, we may attempt to influence another toward a particular action, attitude, or belief by making a direct request such as "Will you drive me to the library so that I can get a book I need on genetics?" This is the most straightforward way to gain compliance. Studies demonstrate that simply asking someone for something with which he or she can easily comply succeeds 90 percent of the time. For example, in one study, when a person asked those waiting in a line if she could cut ahead of them because she was in a rush, most acquiesced. More than 60 percent also let the person in when the reason offered was weak: "I have to make some copies."[13]

Adding supportive evidence can strengthen a request: "I really would like to be able to put the latest research into my report, and to do that I need the new genetics book the library is holding for me." Or we might offer a trade, such as "If you drive me to the library,

FIGURE 10.1 Interpersonal Influencers

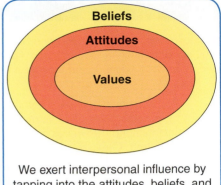

We exert interpersonal influence by tapping into the attitudes, beliefs, and values of others.

Values: One's ideas about what is important in life.

ANALYZE THIS: *The Diary of a Young Girl*

The following is a page from *Anne Frank: The Diary of a Young Girl.* How would you compare it to your journal, your Facebook page, or a page from a blog you write? To what extent do our innermost thoughts and feelings help reveal our values?

Saturday, 15 July, 1944

"For in its innermost depths youth is lonelier than old age." I read this saying in some book and I've always remembered it, and found it to be true. Is it true then that grownups have a more difficult time here than we do? No. I know it isn't. Older people have formed their opinions about everything, and don't waver before they act. It's twice as hard for us young ones to hold our ground, and maintain our opinions, in a time when all ideals are being shattered and destroyed, when people are showing their worst side, and do not know whether to believe in truth and right and God.

Anyone who claims that the older ones have a more difficult time here certainly doesn't realize to what extent our problems weigh down on us, problems for which we are probably much too young, but which thrust themselves upon us continually, until, after a long time, we think we've found a solution, but the solution doesn't seem able to resist the facts which reduce it to nothing again. That's the difficulty in these times: ideals, dreams, and cherished hopes rise within us, only to meet the horrible truth and be shattered.

It's really a wonder that I haven't dropped all my ideals, because they seem so absurd and impossible to carry out. Yet I keep them, because in spite of everything I still believe that people are really good at heart. I simply can't build up my hopes on a foundation consisting of confusion, misery, and death. I see the world gradually being turned into a wilderness. I hear the ever approaching thunder, which will destroy us too. I can feel the sufferings of millions and yet, If I look up into the heavens, I think that it will all come right, that this cruelty too will end, and that peace and tranquility will return again.

In the meantime, I must uphold my ideals, for perhaps the time will come when I shall be able to carry them out.

Yours, Anne

WHAT DO YOU KNOW?

True or False

3. *We feel obligated to return a favor.*
True. The norm of reciprocity predicts the return of favors.

I'll cook you a great dinner." The norm of reciprocity—the fact that we feel obligated to return another's favor, even if the person is someone we are not crazy about—often elicits compliance.[14]

On the other hand, instead of trying to strike a deal, we might try to coerce the other person into complying by threatening him or her with a punishment for inaction: "I can't believe you're hesitating. I'm only asking you to drive me to the library, not around the world. If you don't take me, I won't go with you to that dinner that's so important to you."

Similarly, we might describe another benefit—that is, we might offer one or more reasons that help the other person perceive what he or she stands to gain from helping us: "If I get that book, I'm much more likely to get a good grade, which will lead to my qualifying for a research assistantship, which means I won't have to get a second job, and I'll have more time to spend with you."

At times, however, we might find it more desirable to use an indirect approach during which we make emotion-laden statements designed to help us maintain face: "You know I really want to get a good grade on my research assignment, but I won't be able to do it without that book. I just wish I could get to the library." Or we might aim to instill empathy for our plight by appealing to the other's love and concern for our welfare: "Come on," we

TRY THIS: *Graphing Your Values*

The box below describes six different types of people.

1. Read all the descriptions and then rank them from 1 to 6, with 6 representing the description that most closely resembles you and 1 representing the description that least resembles you.

A.	You value the pursuit and discovery of truth—the intellectual life.
B.	You value that which is useful and practical.
C.	You value form, harmony, and beauty.
D.	You value love, sympathy, warmth, and sensitivity in relationships with people.
E.	You value competition, influence, and personal power.
F.	You value unity, wholeness, and a sense of purpose above human beings.

2. Next, plot the numbers you just entered in the preceding box in the appropriate places on the graph below. For example, if you gave sentence A a 4, put an X in the box at 4A. Once you connect your Xs you will have your personal value profile—a visual representation of six dimensions of your personal system of values. Note the graph's high and low points. These reveal which of the six types of values are most and least central in your life. Provide examples that help demonstrate the graph's accuracy or inaccuracy by revealing the extent to which your responses have been influenced by those values most important to you.

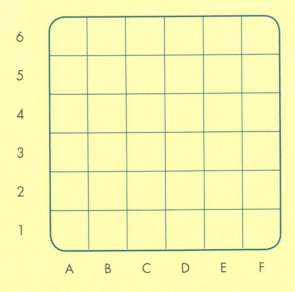

3. Use the following charts to compare and contrast the rankings of males and females in your class. Enter the numbers of males and females who made each choice in the appropriate columns.

Males

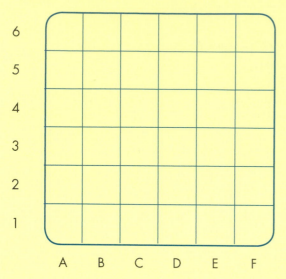

Females

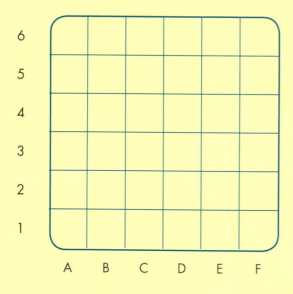

4. To what extent, if any, did you find a difference in rankings by sex? To what do you attribute this difference or lack of difference?

5. In what ways can you apply the information you have learned about yourself and others from this exercise? Identifying whether an individual's value system is theoretically, economically, aesthetically, socially, politically, or spiritually based can facilitate interpersonal persuasion; when you understand a person's value system, you have valuable information about his or her susceptibility to personal influence attempts.

might say, "We always help each other out because my doing well is important to you and your doing well is equally important to me."[15] Successfully persuading others increases our sense of personal power and helps to facilitate our psychological balance (see Table 10.2).

TABLE 10.2 Compliance-Gaining Strategies

Which of the interpersonal persuasion strategies do you consider ethical? Which are you comfortable using? Which have you found work the best?	
Strategy	**Example**
Make a direct request.	Will you drive me to the airport and pick me up when I return?
Strengthen a request with supporting evidence.	Will you drive me to the airport so that we can complete our discussion of what needs to be done while I'm away? And will you pick me up when I return so that you can fill me in on how things went while I was gone?
Strike a deal/offer a trade.	If you drive me to the airport and pick me up when I return, I'll treat you to a great dinner at that restaurant you wanted to go to.
Exert coercion.	I can't believe that you haven't offered to drive me to the airport and pick me up. If you don't help out, I'll complete the report while I'm away and I won't put your name on it.
Identify compliance benefits.	If you drive me to the airport and pick me up when I return, I'll be more likely to have time to get your ideas on the project you'd like to be involved in, which means I'll be able to recommend you to the president.
Use emotion-laden statements.	I really want to be able to recommend to the president that you be a part of the special team that's being formed, but I won't be able to unless I'm able to learn more about how you think. I just wish you'd take me to the airport and pick me up when I return so I'll be able to do a good job with that recommendation.
Instill empathy with an appeal directed at your welfare.	Come on. Take me to the airport and pick me up. I know that you care about how I do on this trip. If I'm rested, my chances of succeeding are greater. I know that's important to you.

STRATEGIES FOR BALANCING ATTITUDES

Balance is a state of psychological health or comfort in which our actions, feelings, and beliefs are related in a way we like them to be. When we are in a balanced state, we are content and satisfied. When our actions, feelings, and beliefs are not related to one another as we want them to be, instead of experiencing satisfaction we experience discomfort and tension. If given a choice between feeling relatively secure and free from anxiety or feeling distraught and tense, we prefer the former.

We can illustrate our need for consistency by referring to a model of attitude change called **balance theory**, developed by Fritz Heider.[16] In Heider's model, *P* refers to one person, *O* stands for another person, and *X* represents the subject under discussion or consideration:

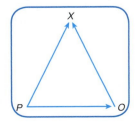

Balance theory: A mode of attitude change that demonstrates the desire to live in a state of equilibrium.

Do you feel balanced?

Imagine yourself as person *P*. We can symbolize your relationship with *O* and *X* with plus and minus signs. A plus sign signifies a positive feeling or attitude; a minus signifies a negative feeling or attitude. According to Heider, we expect people we like to like what we like and people we don't like to dislike what we like. In other words, Heider asserts that we feel comfortable when people we feel positively toward hold the same attitudes we do and when people we feel negatively toward hold different ones. Thus, whenever the model contains three pluses or one plus and two minuses, the interpersonal relationship is balanced. For example, you like dining out (+), you like David (+), and David likes dining out (+). Your relationship is balanced. On the other hand, your relationship is also balanced if you don't like dining out (–), you like David (+), and David doesn't like dining out (–).

When our relationships are balanced, we exist in a state of equilibrium; people we share relationships with think the same way we do. When our relationships are unbalanced, however, we exist in a state of disequilibrium. Things don't fit together as would want them to or as we expect. Thus, we try to make adjustments to restore balance.

At times, each of us purposefully avoids interacting with another person because we fear we will dislike or disagree with him or her. This is one way we try to maintain a state of consistency or balance. At other times, however, we are unable to avoid interacting with someone who threatens our balance. This is especially true if we really like another person and our relationship with him or her is important to us. When a relationship we value is endangered by inconsistencies that cause us discomfort, we can attempt to restore balance in a number of ways. First, we can change our attitude toward the problem. We can reassess our stand and decide that our original judgment was in error. Second, we can try to change the other person by giving him or her information that supports our point of view. Third, we can withdraw from considering this issue with the other person. We simply decide that whether we agree on the issue is not of vital importance to our relationship. Fourth, we can misinterpret the other's position, convincing ourselves that the person does not really mean what he or she is saying—that is, we convince ourselves that the person really agrees with us. When this happens, the person who is the liar and

When knowledge and behavior conflict, dissonance exists.

the person lied to are one and the same. Finally, we can choose to view the imbalance as an asset, telling ourselves that it demonstrates the maturity of our relationship. We then can disagree without feeling excessive discomfort.

The theory of **cognitive dissonance** offers another approach to explain how we compensate when we find ourselves doing things that fail to fit with what we know or have opinions that fail to fit with other opinions we hold.[17] According to Leon Festinger, the theory's formulator, dissonance is an aversive drive that propels us toward consistency. In other words, once we have acted, we feel compelled to bring our beliefs into harmony with our actions. For example, imagine that you are a heavy smoker who knows about all the medical reports on the dangers of smoking. Your knowledge conflicts with your behavior. According to Festinger, something has to give: either you will give up smoking or you will alter your belief that smoking will harm you, whichever action is easiest. Or imagine that you spent significant time and effort pursuing a goal that failed to deliver the results you anticipated. What do you do? The time and effort have been spent. Most probably, you convince yourself that the outcome wasn't that bad after all. Remember the fable of the fox who tried to reach the grapes but couldn't? He convinced himself that had he reached them, the grapes would have been too sour to eat!

Festinger identifies three mental means we use to ensure that our actions and attitudes support each other. The first, selective exposure, reduces dissonance by ensuring we avoid information and people likely to contradict our beliefs (as briefly discussed in Chapter 3). This explains why a political rally is likely to attract mostly members of the party holding the rally. The second, the **need for reassurance**, ensures that we will seek out information and social support confirming that we made the right decision. This explains why, after being persuaded to make a significant purchase such as a car, you might pore over copies of *Consumer Reports,* seek a friend's feedback, or notice that others have bought cars like yours too. The third, **minimal justification for action**, suggests that small rather than large incentives are more effective at creating dissonance and inducing attitude change. Of the three mental processes, the third runs counter to what we might expect. What it reveals, however, is that when the incentive to alter behavior is small, we really do have to change our attitude to bring it in line with our behavior. Doing so also allows us to appear reasonable to ourselves. Our attitudes, it seems, follow our behavior when we have invested substantial effort. Thus, if you know someone who exhibits a behavior or holds an opinion that you find objectionable, the way to reduce the dissonance you feel is not to promise your friend significant rewards for changing or dire consequences if he or she fails to change. Instead, you are more likely to succeed if you offer your friend just enough encouragement to alter his or her current behavior or way of thinking.

ROUTES TO INTERPERSONAL INFLUENCE

Which influence route do you travel—a peripheral or shorthand route, or a central, more thoughtful route? Before you answer, realize that we are exposed to so many persuasive messages during interpersonal encounters that we virtually are certain to take the lazy approach unless the subject is one in which we are personally involved.

Those of us who are relatively easily influenced are likely to respond to what psychologist Robert Cialdini calls **trigger cues**—cues that stimulate "click, whirr" programmed responses to persuasive appeals.[18] These cues take six forms: reciprocation ("You owe me one"), consistency ("This has always worked before"), social proof ("The whole administration is in favor of this approach"), liking ("Love me, support my ideas"), authority ("Because I want you to"), and scarcity ("Hurry, before it's no longer possible

Cognitive dissonance: An aversive drive propelling one toward consistency.

Need for reassurance: The need to seek out information to confirm a decision.

Minimal justification for action: The principle that small rather than large incentives are more effective at creating dissonance and inducing attitude change.

Trigger cues: Cues that stimulate "click, whirr" programmed responses to persuasive appeals.

TRY THIS: *Tensions and Tactics*

1. According to theorist Fritz Heider, when two people interact in relation to an event or object of mutual concern, the intrapersonal and interpersonal situations they find themselves in are either balanced or not. An unbalanced situation precipitates tension, motivating a change in attitude in an effort to restore balance. Persuasion, according to balance theory, operates subsequent to an unbalanced situation and a "felt tension." The triangles below represent balanced and unbalanced states. First, for each situation, recall a personal experience in which you as person *P* and another person identified as *X* existed in either a balanced or imbalanced situation due to your matching or mismatching attitudes relevant to some object (*O*) of mutual concern. Then, for each unbalanced situation, specify the steps you and/or the other took in an effort to restore balance, describing how the "felt tension" contributed to interpersonal persuasive efforts on either your part or your partner's.

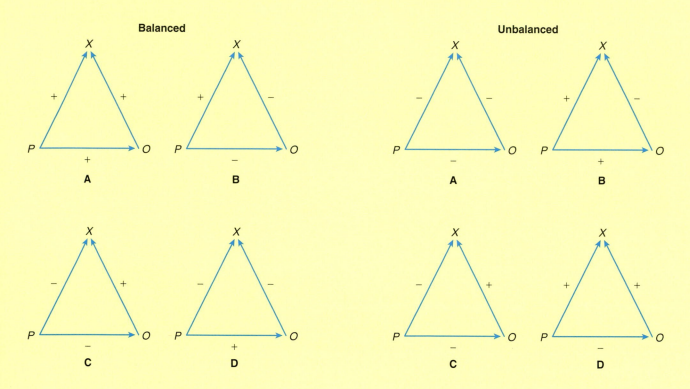

2. Think through the people you have encountered during the past week. Which of these people did you deliberately seek out? Which had you tried to avoid? What about your online relationships? Did you engage in "interpersonal censorship," that is, were there people whom you attempted to avoid coming into contact with electronically (not engaging them on Facebook or Twitter or via text)? How did this work out for you?

for you to do so"). Trigger cues lead us to take a cognitive shortcut, or a peripheral route, one that requires little or scrutiny, effort, or thought.

According to psychologists Richard Petty and John Cacioppo, "A more thoughtful alternative cognitive process, the central route, involves message elaboration, the careful thinking about issue-relevant arguments contained in a persuasive communication."[19] Once we travel this route, a number of other factors, among them our motivation and ability to concentrate and resist distractions, determine our success.

DIVERSITY, VALUES, AND RELATIONAL POWER

According to theorist Geert Hofstede, culture influences and modifies four value dimensions: individualism-collectivism, uncertainty avoidance, masculinity and femininity, and power distance. One of the key variables determining human action is whether one's primary orientation is individual or collective in nature. In individualistically oriented countries such as the United States, Great Britain, and Australia, the individual is of central importance; independence is stressed, with personal goals taking priority over allegiance to a group; personal achievement is rewarded; and uniqueness is an asset. In collectivistically oriented countries such as Taiwan, Colombia, and Pakistan, the individual is dependent on the in-group, the views and needs of the in-group are valued over the views and needs of the individual, a "we" consciousness prevails, and the individual sacrifices personal rights and places trust in group decisions.[20] A number of cocultures in the United States, including Mexican American and African American cultures, are collectivistically oriented.[21]

The second key variable for Hofstede is uncertainty avoidance, or the extent which persons within a culture perceive uncertainty or ambiguous situations as threatening. This orientation, predominant in countries such as Japan, Portugal, and Greece, leads people to develop written rules and regulations and hold rituals and ceremonies that add structure to life. In contrast, countries such as the United States, Denmark, and Ireland, with their low tolerance for structure, have a low need for uncertainty avoidance. These countries instead value initiative and risk more highly.

By "masculinity and femininity," Hofstede refers to the extent to which a country values masculine (male-oriented) or feminine (female-oriented) traits. Among the countries that value such masculine traits as ambition, achievement, and the acquisition of money are Ireland, Japan, and Mexico. In countries such as these, men are taught to be assertive, ambitious, and domineering. In contrast, femininity-valuing cultures such as Sweden and the Netherlands stress caring, nurturing, and sexual equality.[22]

Different cultures endow the parties to a relationship with different levels of social power or status. In some cultures, for example, wealth gives individuals more power, whereas in others age, education, occupation, and even family background are more important than wealth as sources of power. Whereas some cultures minimize social or class inequalities, others emphasize them, sometimes even asserting that each person has a protected place in the culture's social order, that hierarchical relationships are appropriate, and that individuals with high social status have the right to use their power as they see fit. Such variations are a measure of power distance, the extent to which the culture's members believe that institutional and organizational power should not be shared equally and that all decisions by power holders must be accepted.[23] A **power-distance index** (PDI) indicates where a culture rests on the power-distance scale. At one end of the scale are cultures such as Israel and Denmark, which believe in minimizing social or class imbalances, challenging authority figures, and using power only for legitimate purposes. On the other end of the scale are Saudi Arabia and Syria, which prefer the maintenance of large power distances (see Table 10.3).

GO ▶

WATCH THIS 10.1
For a video on interpersonal influence visit the student study site.

Power-distance index: A measurement of where a culture rests on the power-distance scale.

TABLE 10.3 Power Distance and Behavior

Behaviors Characteristic of Low-Power-Distance Cultures	Behaviors Characteristic of High-Power-Distance Cultures
Minimizing class and social differences	Treating power as a fact of life
Challenging authority figures	Accepting inequalities in society
Using power for legitimate purposes only	Bypassing subordinates in decision making

Individuals who grow up in high-power-distance cultures learn not to question authority. They expect to be told what to do and tend to conform readily to established norms. They learn to do as they are told without questioning why—at least not outwardly. In such cultures power is a fact of life; thus, the use of coercive or referent power is common.

In contrast, persons who grow up in low-power-distance cultures value their independence and are less apt to conform to others' expectations. Because they believe power should be used only when appropriate, they prefer expert or legitimate power. The members of these cultures need to understand why they should follow others' directions.

In some cultures individuals are encouraged to take power when they feel it is rightfully theirs rather than allowing others to have power over them. In other cultures such verbal assertions of the right to power on the part of individuals are repressed. Members of cultures that have nonverbal rather than verbal traditions do not tell others that they seek power; rather, these individuals believe that they can intuit where power lies. Thus, for such people, power does not need to be claimed. If they have power, others will know. Unlike North American cultures, where power can be enhanced through communication, in Eastern cultures, members believe such communication is unnecessary and out of place.[24] Whatever the cultural background, however, when females are questioned about power relationships, they describe men as being more concerned both with power and with content than with relational issues.[25]

Our interpersonal relationships benefit when we understand how views of power differ across cultures. Developing a clearer vision of the kinds of power people in different cultures value and the extent to which the members of a culture will or will not engage in conflict with persons in power enhances our ability to interpret another's responses to power; this is especially important when the individual is from a culture different from our own.

GENDER AND THE BALANCE OF POWER

Society's tendency to view women as less powerful than men influences our everyday relationships. In fact, some women and men maintain the traditional belief that men should be more powerful, earning more money and achieving more status than women.[26] When these expectations go unmet, relationships may suffer. Current economic realities place increased pressure on men as it becomes harder for them to be the sole or prime wage earners in their families.

Although women now contribute significantly to family income, they still perceive themselves to have primary responsibility for seeing that domestic responsibilities are met.

Inequitable workloads can lead to relationship resentment, dissatisfaction, and dissolution. In contrast, more equitable distribution of out-of-home and in-home work leads to more relationship satisfaction and stability.[27]

Women are expected to be work specialists, home specialists, health specialists, and life-cycle specialists, persons adept at coping with crises during any life stage. Women are supposed to monitor relationships and make sure things get done when scheduled, yet accede to or comply with the preferences or beliefs of their partners whenever their opinions differ. Thus, while women may be gaining increased access to resources, some hesitate to use those resources independently.[28]

Generally, men engage in more efforts to exert control and dominate in relationships than do women. However, it could be that women conceive of power differently. Powerful women should not be thought of as men wearing dresses. Instead of practicing male patterns of behavior, many women seek alternative means of gaining, maintaining, and exerting power. Thus, in contrast to most men, when questioned about their perception of power in relation to their positions in society, most American women do not epitomize attributes such as control and domination—so prominent in the traditional power displays of men—but instead practice power based on a model of personal authority, empowerment, or reciprocal empowerment.[29]

Sexual harassment, defined as "unwelcome sexual behavior that takes place in person or electronically," represents an abuse of power affecting men and women.[30] Being subjected to inappropriate sexual comments or jokes, inappropriate touching, sexual intimidation, receiving unwelcome sexualized photos through texts or e-mail, and having sexual rumors or pictures spread are included among examples of sexual harassment. In a national survey of middle and high school students conducted during the 2010–2011 school year, girls reported being harassed more than boys—56 percent compared with 40 percent, with boys more frequently identified as the harassers. Of the students surveyed, 48 percent said they had been harassed during the academic year, some both on- and offline; 44 percent reported being harassed in person, while 30 percent reported online incidents of harassment.[31]

Sexual harassment also affects men and women at work, with male-female, male-male, and female-female harassment reported. Although more formal processes exist for reporting sexual harassment today than in the past, and many employers have instituted antiharassment policies and workshops, each year thousands of incidents of sexual harassment are still reported to local, state, and federal agencies. That so much sexualized aggression—attributable to inequitable power and assumed workplace prerogatives—still occurs is evidence of continued gender discrimination in the workplace.[32]

Sexual harassment is an abuse of power that occurs too frequently in the workplace.

. . . .

Sexual harassment: Unwelcome sexual behavior that takes place in person or electronically.

Researchers report that working women with children have larger workloads than the respective dads, logging five more hours of in-home work each week and approximately ten hours fewer than stay-at-home moms. Years back, researchers reported that in families where both partners worked full-time, the women averaged more than twenty-six hours a week in household labor, while the men averaged ten. When housework and employment hours were combined, women averaged sixty-nine hours a week, while men averaged fifty-two hours. Thus, while not yet equal, the workloads of men and women appear to be on a trend toward equalizing. In fact, a recent study conducted for the Families and Work Institute confirmed that men now experience even more work-family conflicts than women. Despite these improvements, however, some women remain dissatisfied, pointing out that whatever leisure time they have is often interrupted, while men appear better at protecting their leisure time from interruption contamination.

With this information as background, consider how power is distributed in your family today and answer the following questions. Then ask a peer in your major field the same questions and compare and contrast the responses you receive with your own.

1. How many hours per week does each family member work?

2. How many hours per week does each family member spend performing household chores?

3. Which members of the household are given the power to decide who engages in what activities, how money is spent, how leisure time is spent, and so forth?

4. When claiming leisure time, which family member's leisure time is subject to more interruptions?

5. To what extent, if any, do you perceive in the family a relationship between the exercise of power and gender?

SOURCES: See the December 2009 issue of *Social Forces* and results of the 2010 American Time Use Survey from the U.S. Bureau of Labor Statistics, http://www.bls.gov/news.release/archives/atus_06222011.pdf.

See Daphne Spain, *Gendered Spaces.* Chapel Hill: University of North Carolina Press, 1992.

Ruth Davis Konigsberg, "Chore Wars," *Time,* July 21, 2011, p. 45–49.

Kerstin Aumann, Ellen Galinsky, and Kenneth Matos, *The New Male Mystique,* Families and Work Institute, Corporate Leadership Circle Conference Call, September 8, 2011, http://www.familiesandwork.org/site/support/110908_clc_ppoint.pdf.

Konigsberg, "Chore Wars," p. 45.

MEDIA, TECHNOLOGY, AND POWER SHIFTS

How complicit are the media and technology in shaping perceptions of relational power? The media present us with numerous models of people on the giving and receiving ends of power. Technology facilitates the spreading of influence. Both affect how we respond to and use power in personal encounters.

MEDIA POWER

Because women are consistently underrepresented in the media,[33] we may be left with the impression that men hold the power, are typically in charge, occupy more high-status positions, and set the cultural standards. Men, not women, are held up to us by the media as authorities. Even in news broadcasting, more men than women hold the position of anchor, reinforcing the impression that men belong in positions of authority. This perception is reinforced by commercials, where male voice-overs predominate, supporting the impression that women depend on men for direction.[34] In contrast, when women are portrayed in power positions, they are often depicted as lonely or embittered. Thus, we too frequently are led to believe that men are entitled to exert power over others, while women are not.[35]

The power that is left to women appears to be sexual power. Women are generally encouraged to hone their powerlessness, while men are encouraged to develop their aggressiveness and strength. Exceptions may be found in recent years, however. For example, in the popular film *The Hunger Games,* which is based on the extremely successful young adult novel of the same title by Suzanne Collins, the audience is presented with a heroic female lead whose power stems not from her sexualization or beauty but rather from her skill and athletic prowess—she is portrayed as capable, cunning, and compassionate.[36] Such a lead character has proved very popular, especially among teens.

The power of Katniss Everdeen (Jennifer Lawrence), the heroic female lead of the film *The Hunger Games*, comes not from her sexualization or beauty but rather from her skill and expertise.

In depictions of power and powerlessness in the media, minorities fare even worse than women. Minority men sometimes still are cast in stereotypical roles, presented as lazy and unable to handle authority, and minority women are still depicted as misusing power in their efforts to dominate others or as sex objects. In addition, the media too often present distorted depictions of older people that reinforce notions that they are sickly and less powerful members of society.

TECHNOLOGICAL POWER

The Internet is often looked to as a power equalizer. It can be color- and gender-blind. As a result, women, minorities, and older persons are apt to find themselves with wider audiences and receiving more respect when online than when off. In fact, the Internet is empowering, giving users a sense of interpersonal power as it enables them to share ideas and concerns and otherwise feel more in control and less isolated and lonely. By reducing the time that people spend with other media, are computers decreasing the amount of power the traditional media exert? By taking time from face-to-face interaction, is technology helping to insulate you from more intimate settings? What do you think?

Technology has the potential to create magic as well as magnify danger. When it comes to computer and video games, for example, often players must take part in virtual violence to prevail. Unfortunately, too often, this reinforces cultural views of men as aggressors, females as sexual objects, and violence as a turn-on.[37]

Perhaps one of the most serious dangers of technology's ability to create an imbalance of power is the penchant of some users to engage in cyberbullying. Again, **bullying** is defined as repeated verbal or physical attacks or emotional harassment committed by one or more persons to intimidate or cause harm to one or more victims. Promoting their own power at others' expense, bullies equate power with force. Among some of the reasons people report being bullied are their looks, sexual orientation, race/ethnicity, religious beliefs, and lack of money.[38] Bullying is by no means new, but the advent of the Internet has extended the bully's reach. Online, intimidating messages such as "I hate you. No one can stand you. Why don't

Bullying: Repeated verbal or physical attacks or emotional harassment committed by one or more persons to intimidate or cause harm to one or more victims.

Cyberbullying extends the bully's reach, magnifying the harm to a victim.

you kill yourself like everyone hopes?" are instantly accessible to millions and thereby magnify the bully's potential to harm his or her victim(s). Cyberbullying is a prime example of the misuse of power. A number of teenagers, including Phoebe Prince and Tyler Clementi (both of whom you may have read about in the news), have committed suicide, or what we have previously called cyberbullicide, allegedly because they were subjected to relentless malicious taunting and other actions by cyberbullies.[39] Neither necessarily face-to-face with their victims nor accountable for their actions as a result of their anonymity, cyberbullies experience extreme online disinhibition effects, leading to their feeling even freer to disparage, slander, or threaten others with violence and fill their victims' world with fear. Online bullies doctor photographs, post embarrassing videos, and use texts, webcams, and cell phone cameras to put technology to malicious use. Unlike a video game, bullying can be deadly. What actions do you think should be taken to address the dangers of cyberbullying and empower the victims of cyberbullies?

GAINING COMMUNICATION COMPETENCE: CONTROLLING RELATIONSHIPS

You can increase your interpersonal communication competence by adhering to the following guidelines concerning power.

USE POWER WISELY

You have the option to use different kinds of power in your relationships. How you choose to use your power says a lot about the nature of each one. What kinds of power bind others to you, willingly and unwillingly? What kinds of power enable you to make the most of relational opportunities? What kinds limit or debilitate you? Having a range of effective power and influence strategies can make it easier for you to satisfy your relational needs.

UNDERSTAND HOW BELIEFS, VALUES, AND ATTITUDES AFFECT INTERACTIONS

Your interactions with others are facilitated when you understand your own attitudes, beliefs, and values as well as theirs. For example, how do you respond when your significant beliefs are challenged? While some beliefs are more meaningful to you than to others, the more central a belief is, the harder each of you works to defend it, the less willing you are to change it, and the more resistant you become to compliance-gaining efforts.

CAPITALIZE ON THE NEED FOR BALANCE

Recognize the extent to which your drive for consistency influences the nature and tone of your interpersonal relationships. When we want to convince another to think and feel as we do, we can create or point out an imbalance in his or her life, and then demonstrate how thinking or feeling as we do will help restore a sense of internal consistency.

CONNECT THE CASE: *The Case of the Power Moment*

Tilda was given the task of assessing the productivity and performance of employees in various divisions of the company where she works. Included among those she would have to report on was her live-in boyfriend, Larry, who is a division head. Tilda's boss told her to deliver copies of a preliminary report to all division heads once the report was complete, prior to its being disseminated to him and to a wider company audience.

After reading Tilda's preliminary report, which was somewhat critical of a number of people in his division, Larry hit the roof. If his people were targets of criticism, the clear implication was that he was not doing his job. When Larry told Tilda his reaction and concerns, she became defensive and insisted that the information in her report was accurate. Larry cautioned Tilda that if she didn't alter her report, he would end their relationship. It was that important to him.

Larry didn't want his anger to become evident to others at work, so he interacted with Tilda at work with the same level of professionalism he had always exhibited. Their private communication was another matter, however. All week, when they were at home together, Larry pressured Tilda to revise the report, pointing out time and again the errors he believed she was making and reminding her of the consequences she would face if she failed to comply.

Tilda was in emotional turmoil. What should she do?

Consider the following questions:

1. If you were Tilda, how would you respond to Larry's ultimatum?

2. What steps might Tilda and Larry take to resolve their impasse?

REVIEW THIS

CHAPTER SUMMARY

1 Define power. Power is the ability to influence and control others. It is dependent on the resources one is able to control.

2 Compare and contrast the following types of power: reward, coercive, expert, legitimate, referent, and persuasive. When a person has reward power, he or she controls something another person values. With coercive power, one person can deliver negative consequences to another. A person with expert power possesses special knowledge or skill that another thinks he or she needs. With legitimate power, one party's position lets him or her control another. A person has referent power when another respects and admires him or her. A person with persuasive power is skilled at using logic, well-conceived arguments, and emotional appeals to persuade others to believe or behave as he or she desires.

3 Define and distinguish among attitudes, beliefs, and values. An attitude is a mental set or readiness to respond in a predetermined way to a particular stimulus. Beliefs are the building blocks of attitudes. They are one's assessment of what is true or false, probable or improbable. Values represent our ideas of what is important in life.

4 Discuss the persuasive forces that help elicit compliance. Attitudes, beliefs, and values affect the nature and tone of relationships. Communicated through behavior, they influence whose company we seek, with whom we are most comfortable, and what we need to do to maintain a state of internal consistency or balance. We employ an array of compliance-gaining strategies in our efforts to influence others.

5 Explain balance theory and cognitive dissonance and their roles in interpersonal persuasion. Balance theory is a model of attitude change that demonstrates our desire to live in a state of equilibrium. Cognitive dissonance is an aversive drive that propels us toward consistency. Interpersonal persuasion occurs first by creating imbalance and then finding a solution that restores balance.

6 Discuss how gender differences influence the exercise of power. Gender expectations reinforce the belief that men should be powerful. In general men engage in more efforts to exert control, while women practice reciprocal empowerment. Abuses of power, including sexual harassment, affect men and women in school and in the workplace.

7 Explain the ways in which media and technology influence both the perception and the exercise of power. The media present men more often than women in positions of power. The Internet affords power to those with access. For some, technology is interpersonally empowering, and it also decreases the amount of power other media exert. For others, technology exacerbates the creation of imbalances of power, contributing to cyberbullying.

CHECK YOUR UNDERSTANDING

1 Can you provide examples of appropriate and inappropriate uses of different kinds of power? What kind(s) of power do you think you wield? (See pages 266–270.)

2 Can you explain how the attitudes, beliefs, and values of two people could influence the course of their relationship? (See pages 270–275.)

3 Can you explain the relationship between power and compliance? (See pages 275–279.)

4 Can you offer scenarios to illustrate the roles that balance theory and cognitive dissonance play in interpersonal persuasion? (See pages 279–281.)

5 Can you identify ways in which culture, gender, the media, and technology influence perceptions of power in the United States? In what ways are the messages sent positive? In what ways are they negative? (See pages 283–288.)

CHECK YOUR SKILLS

1 Can you assess both your level of social anxiety and your level of Machiavellianism and measure how each influences your views toward power? (See pages 266–267; and *Try This,* page 268.)

2 Can you correctly choose which of the six categories of power to exercise when presented with the opportunity? (See pages 267–270; and *Try This,* page 271.)

3 Can you use your understanding of another's attitudes, beliefs, and values to accomplish a persuasive goal? (See pages 270–275; *Try This,* page 273; and *Analyze This,* page 276.)

4 Can you vary the strategies you use to gain compliance depending on the nature of the situation? (See pages 275–279.)

5 Can you use both balance theory and cognitive dissonance theory to better understand why you feel comfortable or uncomfortable in a relationship? (See pages 279–281; and *Try This,* page 282.)

6 Can you identify when someone uses a trigger cue on you? (See pages 281–283.)

7 Can you use your understanding of the culture and gender practices of others to better manage your approach and response to power? (See pages 283–285; *Try This,* page 285; and *Reflect on This,* page 286.)

8 Can you recognize and respond appropriately when you or another person is being sexually harassed? (See page 285.)

9 Can you point to media offerings and practices as well as websites that reinforce or subvert the effective and appropriate use of power? (See pages 286–288.)

10 Can you manage a disagreement over the exercise of power in a relationship? (See *The Case of the Power Moment,* page 289.)

KEY TERMS

Power *266*

Machiavellianism *267*

Reward power *269*

Coercive power *269*

Expert power *269*

Legitimate power *269*

Referent power *269*

Persuasive power *270*

Attitude *270*

Beliefs *271*

Values *275*

Balance theory *279*

Cognitive dissonance *281*

Need for reassurance *281*

Minimal justification for action *281*

Trigger cues *281*

Power-distance index *283*

Sexual harassment *285*

Bullying *287*

STUDENT STUDY SITE

Visit the student study site at **www.sagepub.com/gambleic** to access the following materials:

- SAGE Journal Articles
- Videos
- Web Resources

- eFlashcards
- Web Quizzes
- Study Questions

Not everything that is faced can be changed, but nothing can be changed until it is faced.

—James Baldwin

CONFLICT

LEARNING OBJECTIVES

After completing this chapter, you should be able to demonstrate mastery of the following learning outcomes:

1. Define conflict and discuss its nature, explaining the difference between functional and dysfunctional conflict.

2. Identify conflict sources.

3. Identify conflict resolution and management strategies.

4. Compare and contrast the following conflict expression styles: assertive, nonassertive, and aggressive.

5. Explain culture's influence on conflict.

6. Discuss differences and similarities in how men and women approach and handle conflict.

7. Discuss how media portrayals and technology affect perceptions of conflict.

8. Identify how to resolve conflict effectively.

Which aspiring actor will win the role of a lifetime—the opportunity to play the fabled star Marilyn Monroe in a new theatrical production about her life? That's the question explored in *Smash*—a television drama series that tracks the battles that ensue during preparations and rehearsals for a new Broadway musical about the legendary star. In each episode, the writers and composers, the rival leading ladies competing to play the coveted role, their assorted significant others, and the director find themselves embroiled in any number of conflicts.

For example, the women vying for the role of Marilyn are as different from each other as they can be, but they often find themselves forced to be together in very uncomfortable, conflict-inducing situations. The temperamental director, often confrontational and aggressive, is the source of many of the disagreements between the cast members and those of importance to them. By putting his cast members in humiliating and painful situations just to see how they react, he exposes his callousness and their weaknesses.

> Fictional conflicts and those occurring in "reality" television shows . . . often are contrived to make the show more interesting by developing a compelling storyline.

Fictional conflicts and those occurring in "reality" television shows such as *The Amazing Race*, *The Apprentice*, and *Survivor* often are contrived to make the shows more interesting by developing compelling story lines. Frequently, one or more of the characters are shown losing control, unable to find a way to resolve the conflicts they face.

Nonetheless, despite all the contrivances of televised drama, we can learn much about the handling of conflict by watching the different characters in action and thinking through how we would respond to particular conflicts were we in the characters' situations.[1]

WHAT DO YOU KNOW?

Before continuing your reading of this chapter, which of the following five statements do you believe to be true, and which do you believe to be false?

1. A conflict-free relationship is not healthy. T F

2. Some interpersonal conflicts take on a life of their own, with participants unable to control them. T F

3. Some interpersonal arguments are less destructive than others, but all of them have negative consequences. T F

4. Most people have a stylized way of dealing with conflict that is unique to their own context and culture. T F

5. Movies and video games have a powerful influence on how we learn to deal with conflict. T F

Read the chapter to discover if you're right or if you've made any erroneous assumptions.

ANSWERS: 1. T, 2. F, 3. F, 4. T, 5. T

While conflict has a dark side that can surface in a number of ways—as bullying, interpersonal violence, or outright war—the reality is that conflict need not become dysfunctional. An inevitable part of life, conflict touches us all sooner or later. Every one of our relationships of any significance has conflict—whether we want it to or not. In fact, a conflict-free relationship is a paradox. When a relationship is conflict-free, it probably is not genuine.[2]

Conflict develops for a variety of reasons. It's how you handle it that matters.

THE MEANING OF CONFLICT

Conflict can be a positive or a negative experience. Given that conflict is an everyday occurrence, it makes sense that we should learn how to handle conflict constructively, so its presence improves our relationships. In this chapter we explore the nature of interpersonal conflict, how it arises, how it affects you, and what you can do to manage it more effectively.

CONFLICT DEFINED

Interpersonal conflict is a struggle between interdependent parties that occurs whenever one individual's thoughts or actions are perceived to limit or interfere with those of another individual.[3] For example, when you and a friend want to play the same position on a team, or apply for the same job, or ask the same person to be your date to a wedding, your attempt to maximize your personal satisfaction or meet your needs may interfere with your friend's ability to do the same. Because both parties to the conflict are aware of a disagreement and recognize the incompatibility of their goals, each does his or her best to prevail. It does not matter if their goals are not in fact incompatible; what matters is that one or both of them perceive the goals to be mutually exclusive and believe that there is not enough of something to satisfy both of them.[4]

CONFLICT IS BASED ON INTERACTION

Conflict develops for a variety of reasons and assumes a variety of forms. Whatever its origin, however, one thing is certain: interpersonal conflict is based on interaction. Conflict is created and maintained through behavior, and it tests every relationship. How do you react upon discovering you are in conflict? Do you tend to become aggressive and strike out at the other person, compete with him or her, suppress your feelings, negotiate the situation, or deal with it directly? Do you escalate the conflict, seek to avoid it, demonstrate your inflexibility, or use constructive patterns that allow you to manage it effectively?

FEELINGS ABOUT CONFLICT

Were it not for conflict, we would have no meaningful relationships. Although we may not look at conflict as a positive, when we come to realize that it is a means to grow and develop in our interpersonal relationships, we are on the way to finding satisfying solutions to our problems rather than letting the problems escalate and destroy our relationships.

Where have your feelings about conflict come from? Dictionaries tell us that conflict is disagreement . . . war, battle, collision . . . suggesting that conflict is a negative force that leads to undesirable consequences. Some of us may also believe that conflict is one of the prime causes of divorce, disorder, or relational violence, and that disagreeing, arguing, or fighting with another either will dissolve whatever relationship exists or prevent one from forming. Others may have been taught that nice people don't fight or make waves. And still others may fear that if they don't smile and act cheerful, they won't be liked. The more awful we think conflict is, the worse it gets. It is not conflict that creates problems, however, but the way we approach and deal with it.[5] In and of itself, conflict is neither a positive nor a negative force. How we perceive it and handle it—whether the conflict is functional or becomes dysfunctional—determines, at least in part, the health of our interpersonal relationships and our satisfaction with them.[6]

Functional Conflict. Conflict can have real benefits. When we handle conflict so that it helps us develop insights into our relationships and develop more effective means of relating to one another, the conflict is functional. **Functional conflicts** build in us a clearer understanding of each other's needs, attitudes, or beliefs; they serve to strengthen and cement relationships.

According to conflict experts, when handled well, conflict performs a number of valuable functions:

1. Conflict helps us learn better ways of handling future conflicts and thereby reduces or eliminates the probability of more serious conflicts.

2. Conflict fosters innovation by helping us acquire new ways of looking at things, new ways of thinking and behaving.

3. Conflict develops in us a renewed sense of cohesiveness and togetherness by increasing our understanding of one another as well as our perceptions of closeness and trust.

4. Conflict provides invaluable opportunities for us to assess the viability of our relationships.

5. Conflict, once resolved, helps to strengthen relationships.[7]

When approaching conflict with a functional orientation, you are willing to listen to opposing viewpoints, open to changing troublesome behaviors, and accepting of differences in others. Functional conflicts are constructive; they do not damage relationships.

Dysfunctional Conflict. As we noted in the opening to this chapter, when handled poorly, a conflict may escalate and become dysfunctional, precipitating a destructive outcome. While not necessarily resulting in the death of one of the parties, **dysfunctional conflict** can create serious problems for a relationship, often resulting in personal pain, emotional strain or schisms, and lasting resentment. Individuals engaged in dysfunctional conflict characteristically rely on threats, deception, force, and violence to achieve their goals, which typically include the desire to defeat or hurt the other person. The parties to a dysfunctional conflict tend to demonstrate rigid inflexibility. They attempt to meet their own needs and serve their own interests by undercutting the other person and making him

When a conflict turns dysfunctional, it can lead to lasting resentment.

Functional conflict: A conflict that develops a clearer understanding of needs, attitudes, or beliefs.

Dysfunctional conflict: Conflict that creates one or more serious relationship problems.

TRY THIS: *Thinking through Conflict*

Review several situations in which you and another were in conflict, and examine the feelings you had at those times. Then use the following scales to measure those feelings. For example, for the first item, "good" versus "bad," if you feel that the conflict was completely good, circle 1. If you feel that the conflict was completely bad, circle 5. If you feel neutral about the conflict, circle 3.

Conflict

Good	1	2	3	4	5	Bad
Rewarding	1	2	3	4	5	Threatening
Normal	1	2	3	4	5	Abnormal
Constructive	1	2	3	4	5	Destructive
Necessary	1	2	3	4	5	Unnecessary
Challenging	1	2	3	4	5	Overwhelming
Desirable	1	2	3	4	5	Undesirable
Inevitable	1	2	3	4	5	Avoidable
Healthy	1	2	3	4	5	Unhealthy
Clean	1	2	3	4	5	Dirty

Compute your score by adding up the numbers you have circled.

Total Score _____

If your score is:

10–14	You think conflict is definitely a positive experience.
15–20	You think conflict can be helpful.
21–30	You don't like to think about conflict; you have very ambivalent feelings toward it.
31–40	You think conflict is something to avoid.
41–50	You think conflict is definitely a negative experience.

How do you imagine the scores of males and females compare? If possible, collect the scores of all the students in your class and compute the averages for males and females. How does your score compare to the average score for your sex? What conclusions, if any, can you draw from this?

---

or her look bad. As a result, dysfunctional conflict tends to grow worse, become destructive, and badly damage or destroy relationships.[8]

Crazymaking behavior, a conflict-producing technique that can figuratively "drive a partner crazy," is often at the root of dysfunctional conflict. For example, visualize the outcome of the following conversation between a husband and wife after the husband has been waiting at taxi stand for his wife, who arrives late:

He: Why were you late?

She: I tried my best.

Crazymaking behavior: Behavior believed to be at the root of dysfunctional conflict.

He: Yeah? You and who else? Your mother is never on time either.

She: That's got nothing to do with it.

He: The hell it doesn't. You're just as sloppy as she is.

She: You don't say! Who picks your dirty underwear off the floor every morning?

He: I happen to go to work. What do you do all day?

She: I'm trying to get along on the money you don't make, that's what I do all day.

He: Why should I knock myself out for a lazy ingrate like you?

This exchange illustrates the technique of "gunnysacking," signifying that the user saves all of his or her complaints, as though stuffing them in a gunnysack, and then makes a mess of things by emptying the sack during a heated moment, allowing an abundance of complaints to cascade out. When we visit our "psychiatric museums" and drag irrelevant past issues—such as the mother-in-law mentioned in the preceding dialogue—into a conflict, we end up venting pent-up aggressions and exchanging insults. Thus, after being served remarks about her mother by her husband, the wife retaliates with complaints about her husband's lack of substantial income.

People who are crazymakers typically display passive-aggressive behavior, catching a person off guard, confusing him or her, and arousing anger. Instead of addressing a relational complaint constructively, crazymakers resort to insidious approaches. Among examples of other kinds of crazymaking behavior are "guiltmaking," "beltlining," avoiding, and withholding. Guiltmaking occurs when one party makes the other party responsible for causing pain: "It's okay; don't worry about me," whines the guiltmaker. Beltlining involves the voicing of comments that "hit below the belt," such as bringing up a person's unattractive physical attributes or perceived lack of intelligence. Avoiding occurs when a party to a conflict refuses to face an issue, leaving the other person frustrated because no one will face the problem. Finally, withholding involves the keeping back of affection, humor, a material possession, or some other desirable thing or behavior because of the conflict. Any one of these inappropriate responses to conflict can contribute to the buildup of relationship resentments.[9] (See the following subsection on conflict-generating behaviors for additional discussion of the kinds of behaviors that fuel conflict.)

In lieu of enacting crazymaking behavior, when a conflict arises, follow these five guidelines:

1. Be specific when you introduce a complaint.

2. Ask for change that will make the situation better.

3. Be tolerant of your partner.

4. Attack the issue, not the other person.

5. Think about what you have to say before you say it.[10]

Thus, conflicts can have either constructive or destructive outcomes depending on the interactive communication strategies the parties employ in the effort to resolve their differences. The first step toward handling conflict more effectively is to be open to its possible positive value.

CONFLICT'S SOURCES

Anyone can start a conflict. Conflict can also occur in any setting. Forces within us that oppose each other can build to create a conflict, or we may find ourselves experiencing tension as outside forces combine to create conflict. An **intrapersonal conflict** originates within a single person. For example, a person who is going to school full-time while raising children may feel conflicted about whether to spend time studying or watching his or her child's Little League game. Interpersonal conflict originates between two or more interdependent people. For example, conflict occurs between people in all types of interpersonal relationships: parents and children, siblings, coworkers, friends, and lovers.

Interpersonal conflict can result from real or imagined differences.

INTERACTIONS AMONG INDIVIDUALS

Interpersonal conflict involves a communication situation in which the people involved are interdependent—that is, the actions or beliefs of one person are likely to have some impact on the other person.[11] Conflict is apt to occur in the following situations:

1. When we perceive *individual difference* in beliefs, opinions, perceptions, values, needs, assumptions, interests, or goals. For example, you believe that taking personal risks and relocating to accept a new job is necessary for you to grow and develop in your career, whereas your partner believes that stability and roots are more important. The difference in the way you and your partner think is apt to produce conflict.

2. When we observe a *scarcity of certain resources* or rewards such as time, money, power, popularity, space, or position. For example, you may feel that the sharing of a bank account with your partner is keeping you from realizing your personal goals. If you had your own bank account, you tell yourself, you would be better able to fulfill your personal needs. Thus, the shared bank account becomes a source of relational conflict.

3. When we *engage in a rivalry* or compete with someone else. For example, if you and a friend are applying for the same job, conflict may arise between you.

4. When we *disagree over how to define a relationship*. For instance, you and a partner may define your roles in your relationship differently. While you want to stay just friends, he or she wants more. Your disagreement over the nature of your relationship can trigger conflict between you.

5. When we *misinterpret another's intent*. When you misunderstand the intentions of another person, you may assume certain things that can lead to conflict. For instance, if a friend does not call because she is planning to surprise you, but you erroneously think that she is simply avoiding talking to you or seeing you, your beliefs may result in conflict.

Intrapersonal conflict: Conflict that originates within a single person.

A conflict can result from real differences or from a misunderstanding, anger, or expecting too much or too little from another person.

CONFLICT-GENERATING BEHAVIORS

When another person acts to block your goals, those actions may generate conflict. Among the behaviors that are apt to precipitate relational conflict are preemptive striking, forcing, and blaming.

Preemptive Striking. As one partner walks through the door, without warning, the other partner attacks him or her verbally or physically. Because the just-entering partner is unprepared to handle the conflict, the conflict is likely either to escalate or to be postponed by the entering person's immediate departure.

Forcing. When one partner forces his or her position on the other, conflict is apt to develop. We do not like to feel compelled to do something, nor do we enjoy feeling that we cannot extricate ourselves from a situation. When this occurs, a relationship may suffer serious damage.

Blaming. When one partner blames the other for some wrong suffered, conflict between the two is likely inevitable. Blame does nothing to resolve a relationship problem, but it does expose the raw feelings that one party is experiencing. Blame relies on the delivery of messages that attack rather than messages that attempt to resolve disagreements.

Placing blame is an ineffective means of resolving a relationship problem.

CLASSIFYING CONFLICTS

Classifying a conflict can help us better understand the cause of the conflict. Once we understand a conflict's cause, we can address it more effectively. We can classify an interpersonal conflict in several different ways: by the nature of the goal of the parties, by the conflict's level of intensity, and by the general character of the conflict. We explore each in turn below.

The Nature of the Goal. We can categorize conflict based on whether the parties involved seek a **shareable goal** or a **nonshareable goal**. A goal is shareable if each participant to the conflict possesses some of it; it is nonshareable if it must be fully claimed and possessed by only one of them. Two people competing for the highest score on a test are competing for a shareable goal; two people competing for the same job are competing for a nonshareable goal.

The Intensity Level of the Conflict. The level of intensity we bring to a conflict depends on how strongly we feel about winning. Those engaged in a **low-intensity conflict** usually do not seek to undermine one another; instead, they devise a strategy to help control their communications that permits the discovery of a solution beneficial to each. A disagreement about where to eat dinner may constitute a low-intensity conflict. In a **medium-intensity conflict**, although each person wants to win, winning itself is seen as sufficient. Those involved do not seek to hurt each other in the process. Competing with a friend to be captain of a sports team may create a medium-intensity conflict. In contrast, in a **high-intensity conflict** one party to the conflict aims to harm or at least seriously debilitate the other. Winning is no longer enough; victory must be total. Two people engaged in a highly contested divorce may find themselves in a high-intensity conflict.

Shareable goal: A goal that both parties to a conflict can possess.

Nonshareable goal: A goal that can be fully claimed and possessed by a single individual only.

Low-intensity conflict: Conflict in which the parties involved devise strategies to create a solution beneficial to both.

Medium-intensity conflict: Conflict in which each of the persons involved wants to win.

High-intensity conflict: Extreme conflict in which one party aims to destroy or debilitate the other.

Complete the Inventory of Verbal Aggressiveness using the following scale:

1 = almost never true
2 = rarely true
3 = occasionally true
4 = often true
5 = almost always true

_____ **1.** I try not to attack someone's intelligence when I attack his or her ideas.

_____ **2.** In order to counter a person's stubbornness, I use insults.

_____ **3.** I try to preserve another's self-concept as I try to influence him or her.

_____ **4.** When someone has no reason that I can see for refusing to complete a task that I think is important, I tell him or her how unreasonable s/he is.

_____ **5.** When others do things I perceive as stupid, I'm gentle in telling them what I think.

_____ **6.** I attack the characters of others when I think they deserve it.

_____ **7.** When I don't like how someone is behaving, I insult him or her to wake him or her up.

_____ **8.** Even when I think another's ideas are stupid, I'll try to make him or her feel good about him- or herself.

_____ **9.** When people are fixed in their ways of thinking or acting, I lose my temper and say things to them I shouldn't say.

_____ **10.** I take criticism well and do not retaliate by criticizing another.

_____ **11.** I enjoy telling others off after they insult me.

_____ **12.** When I do not like someone, I try not to show it.

_____ **13.** To stimulate their intelligence I enjoy belittling people who do what I consider to be stupid things.

_____ **14.** I try not to harm another person's self-concept even when I attack his or her ideas.

_____ **15.** I go out of my way not to offend those I try to influence.

_____ **16.** When others are cruel or mean, I attack their characters in an effort to correct their behavior.

_____ **17.** I won't engage in an argument that involves personal attacks.

_____ **18.** Yelling and screaming work to involve others I am trying to influence when all else fails.

_____ **19.** When I am unsuccessful refuting another's position, I'll make him or her feel defensive to try to weaken his or her resolve.

_____ **20.** When an argument becomes a personal attack, I try to change the subject.

Follow these steps to compute your verbal aggressiveness score:

1. Add the scores on items 2, 4, 6, 7, 9, 11, 13, 16, 18, 19.

2. Add the scores on items 1, 3, 5, 8, 10, 12, 14, 15, 17, 20.

3. Subtract the step 2 score from 60.

4. Add the score from step 1 to the score you computed from step 3.

If you scored between 59 and 100, you are highly verbally aggressive.

If you scored between 39 and 58, you are somewhat verbally aggressive.

If you scored between 20 and 38, you are rarely verbally aggressive.

Does your score surprise you? Do you think it would surprise those you interact with frequently? Ask them. Do their responses confirm or contradict your beliefs? If you scored high in verbal aggressiveness, what might you change about the way you share your ideas with others to avoid becoming verbally combative?

SOURCE: Inventory of Verbal Aggressiveness adapted from Dominic A. Infante and Charles J. Wigley III, "Verbal Aggressiveness: An Interpersonal Model and Measure," *Communication Monographs*, Volume 53, March 1986, p. 64. Reprinted by permission of Taylor & Francis Ltd., http://www.tandf.co.uk/journals/titles/03637751.html, and Professor Dominic A. Infante.

The Character of the Conflict. In addition to the intensity level, it is important to consider the character of the conflict—the basic disagreement at the root of the problem. When we categorize a conflict by its character, we identify it as a pseudoconflict, a content conflict, a value conflict, or an ego conflict.

A **pseudoconflict**, while not really a conflict, gives the appearance of one. It occurs when one person mistakenly believes that both parties to the conflict cannot simultaneously achieve their goals. Typically, pseudoconflicts revolve around erroneous either/or judgments (either you or I win) or around simple misunderstandings in which one or both parties fail to perceive that they actually agree. The parties to a pseudoconflict resolve it when they realize there actually is conflict. For example, suppose Allie and Buffy are going to spend an evening watching DVDs. Allie wants to watch one DVD, and Buffy wants to watch another. If one of them is willing to delay watching the one she wants until a bit later, they can watch both. In this way, both parties' goals can be met.

Pseudoconflicts can also exist due to misunderstandings resulting from lack of clarity. For example, a person who is chronically late can be handled with little difficulty, as the following cell phone exchange illustrates:

Maya: I'm running late. I won't be there for a while.

Elijah: What do you mean by "a while"? What time do you think you'll get here? I have a number of things to do today and not enough time to do them.

Maya: It should be about twenty minutes.

Elijah: Oh, that's pretty soon, but it does give me time to run an errand before you arrive. See you in twenty minutes.

How strongly we feel about winning affects the intensity of our conflict.

A **content conflict** occurs when two parties disagree over matters of fact: the definition of a term, the solution to a problem, or accuracy of information. Once they accept that facts can be verified, inferences tested, definitions checked, and solutions evaluated against established criteria, they are then able to settle their conflict rationally. If you and a partner disagree about how much money is in your joint savings account, a trip to the bank can resolve your disagreement.

A **value conflict** occurs when the parties hold disparate views on an issue important to each—entitlements, for example. A person who values individual independence and self-assertion (standing up for one's rights while respecting the rights of others) is apt to have different opinions of entitlements than someone who believes that we are all ultimately accountable for the well-being of others. If both can agree that it is all right to disagree, they will be able to discuss the issue, share insights, understand each other's positions, and learn from each other, even though they might continue to disagree.

Of all the conflict categories, an **ego conflict** has the greatest potential to ruin a relationship. Persons involved in an ego conflict seek to win at all costs because they think that losing will damage their self-worth or prestige or others' perception of their competence. Because they believe that their credibility is on the line, it is no longer the issue itself that is important. Rational decision making suffers as both strive to win to protect their egos. For example, when each of two friends believes that he or she is the best person to run for class president, and neither will back down, they will likely engage in an ego conflict.

Pseudoconflict: A situation that, while not an actual conflict, gives the appearance of one.

Content conflict: A conflict that revolves around a matter of fact.

Value conflict: Conflict that revolves around the importance of an issue.

Ego conflict: A conflict that revolves around an individual's self-worth.

Conflict-generating behaviors affect each of us differently and elicit different kinds of responses as we seek to cope with or alleviate them.

CONFLICT MANAGEMENT STYLES

A number of different paradigms have been defined to help us understand and represent the strategies we use as we try to resolve conflicts. Among the most widely used is Blake and Mouton's **conflict resolution grid**. Theorists Robert Blake and Jane Srygley Mouton originated the concept of preferred conflict resolution style.[12] By identifying five distinct types of conflict behavior and placing them on a grid, they were able to represent graphically the different ways people resolve conflicts. The grid depicts the extent to which individuals employ *assertive strategies* to satisfy their own concerns or *cooperative strategies* to satisfy the concerns of another as a means of resolving a conflict. You can use Blake and Mouton's approach to help you select the behavioral strategy most appropriate for resolving a specific conflict.

The grid, as shown in see Figure 11.1, has two scales. The vertical scale, assertiveness, measures the extent to which a person acts to attain personal goals, and the horizontal scale, cooperativeness, represents the extent to which that person exhibits behavior intended to satisfy a concern for others. The interface between the two scales represents how strongly an individual feels about each component—that is, how the person's concern is apportioned or how he or she behaves. On the basis of this measure, Blake and Mouton identified five **conflict styles**: avoiding, competitive, compromising, accommodative, and collaborative. We discuss each in turn in the following.

Avoiding. A person with an **avoiding style** (1, 1 on the grid) is unassertive and uncooperative. The person's approach to conflict is to withdraw, or "lose and walk away." He or she may actually physically flee or leave the scene of the conflict. The avoider aims to maintain the appearance of indifference. Avoiders view conflict as a useless, potentially

Figure 11.1 Blake and Mouton's Conflict Resolution Grid

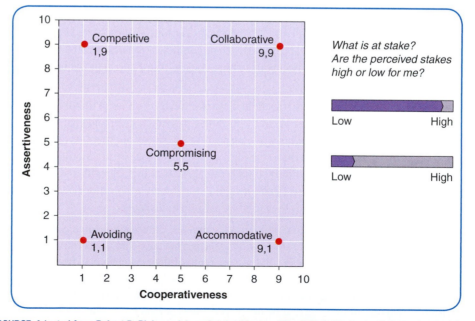

SOURCE: Adapted from Robert R. Blake and Jane Srygley Mouton, "The Fifth Achievement," *Journal of Applied Behavioral Science*, Vol. 6, No. 4, 1970, p. 418. Copyright © 1970 by NTL Institute for Applied Behavioral Science.

Conflict resolution grid: A model that measures an individual's preferred style of handling conflict.

Conflict styles: Individuals' characteristic approaches to conflict with respect to measures of assertiveness and cooperativeness.

Avoiding style: A style of resolving conflict that is unassertive and uncooperative.

punishing endeavor. Rather than face it and have to handle the frustrations that may accompany it, they physically and mentally separate themselves from the situation. By withdrawing and refusing to deal with the conflict, they relieve themselves of the psychological relational burdens it imposes. Avoiders also give up their personal goals and sometimes their relationships.

Competitive. A person with a **competitive style** (1, 9) is high in assertiveness and low in cooperation. Competitors strive to force their position on others; they aim to attain personal goals while ignoring others' concerns. Competitors possess a "win-lose" mind-set, exhibiting an overwhelming need to win or to defeat those they are in conflict with. They fight to defend their positions, often confronting others, attacking their self-concepts, and compelling them to concur by physical force or psychological domination. Competitors do this despite the costs incurred, the harm caused, or the fact that others may find them destructive in their handling of conflict. Bullies, for example, exhibit such behaviors.

When in a conflict, how assertive and cooperative are you?"

Competitive style adherents seek to maximize the importance of their needs by minimizing the needs of others.[13] In their fight to achieve dominance, competitors threaten, accuse, name-call, confront, deny responsibility for wrongdoing, and generally do everything they can to prove how right they are. Primarily because of their lack of motivation to treat their partners appropriately, those who use the competitive style exhibit low levels of effective communication.[14]

Compromising. Someone who has a **compromising style** (5, 5) is in the middle range in both assertiveness and cooperativeness. Compromisers aim to find the middle ground by working to permit each party to a conflict to gain something. While that may happen, each also gives up something to reach the agreement. Also known as "sharing" or "horse-trading," this style leaves users only partially satisfied, and because of this it is sometimes referred to as the "lose-lose" approach. Part of a goal or a relationship is sacrificed to reach agreement—for the common good.

Compromisers typically appeal to fairness and negotiate trade-offs to find a reasonable quick solution to the conflict they face. As such, compromising is only moderately effective, requires both parties to sacrifice, and precludes the search for more creative solutions.

Accommodative. Persons with an **accommodative style** (9, 1) are unassertive and cooperative. Accommodators typically "give in and lose." Because they are likely to overvalue the maintenance of relationships and undervalue the attainment of their own goals, accommodators' main concern is to do what they must to smooth things over and ensure that others accept them, like them, and maintain a relationship with them. Because they believe conflict should be avoided in favor of harmony, accommodators are appeasers; in an effort to preserve the relationship, they smooth over disagreements and conceal ill feelings. Their actions can precipitate an uneasy, tense relational state characterized by a weak, self-sacrificing approach and nervous laughter.

Indirect and passive in how they approach conflict, accommodators tend to trivialize it by glossing over differences and downplaying disagreements. The style is perceived as generally ineffective, if only because its users usually feel powerless and fail to meet their personal goals, adding to the strains their relationships are under.

Competitive style: A style of resolving conflict that is high in assertiveness and low in cooperation.

Compromising style: A style of resolving conflict that is in the middle range in both assertiveness and cooperativeness.

Accommodative style: A style of resolving conflict that is unassertive and cooperative.

Collaborative. A person with a **collaborative style** (9, 9) is high in both assertiveness and cooperativeness. Collaborators exhibit a "win-win" orientation; they are problem solvers, actively seeking to satisfy their own goals as well as those of others. Users of this style seek to integrate the needs of both parties to the conflict so that each attains full satisfaction with the solution. Collaborators see conflict as a means of improving relationships. Problem solvers, they recognize that conflict is normal and can be helpful, believing that every person involved in a conflict holds an opinion that deserves to be aired and considered. Collaborators openly discuss differences without resorting to personal attacks. They seek to discover a solution that achieves both their goals and those of the other(s). Collaborators tend to be highly competent communicators who keep lines of communication open, thereby preserving and promoting opportunities for sharing and continued interaction.

Each of the five conflict styles has its place and can be useful given different relationships, circumstances, and contexts. You might, for example, use one strategy or another at different times and with different partners. How you manage conflicts is affected by the importance of your personal goals versus the importance of your relationships. For example, avoidance may be the best approach when a conflict is minor, or when the risk you face by confronting it is too great. Likewise, accommodation may be an appropriate choice when the conflict's outcome is more important to the other person than to you. Forcing may be an appropriate strategy when you do not need the continued goodwill and cooperation of the other person. By becoming more mindful of such possibilities, we can vary our responses according to what will work best in particular situations. While the most constructive strategy finds the parties to a conflict collaborating, taking part in a search for a solution that will make both of them happy, the strategy they actually use will depend on their personal assessment of the specific conflict. In other words, by understanding Blake and Mouton's conflict resolution behaviors, we become better equipped to select the approaches or behavioral strategies most appropriate for resolving various kinds of conflicts.

Collaborative style:
A style of resolving conflict that is high in both assertiveness and cooperativeness.

TRY THIS: *Where Are You on the Grid?*

Think about how you characteristically deal with conflict. Then respond to each of the statements below using the following scale, where 1 indicates that you strongly disagree with the statement and 7 indicates that you strongly agree with it.

Disagree   Agree

1	2	3	4	5	6	7

1. I discuss the problem to reach a mutual understanding. _____

2. I stick to my argument. _____

3. I give in to my partner to keep my relationship satisfying. _____

4. I sometimes sacrifice my own goals so my partner can meet his or hers. _____

5. I try to find a new solution that will satisfy all our needs. _____

6. I usually try to win arguments. _____

7. I do not like to talk about issues of disagreement. _____

8. I am willing to give up some of my goals in exchange for achieving other goals. _____

9. I try to get all my concerns and my partner's concerns out in the open. _____

10. I usually try to forget about issues of disagreement so I don't have to confront my partner. _____

11. I try to think of a compromise that satisfies both our needs. _____

12. I argue until my ideas are accepted. _____

13. It is important to get both our points of view out in the open. _____

14. I try to convince my partner that my position is right. _____

15. I try to meet my partner halfway. _____

16. If the issue is very important to my partner I usually give in. _____

17. I attempt to work with my partner to find a creative solution we both like. _____

18. I usually let my partner take responsibility for bringing up conflict issues. _____

19. I would rather not get into a discussion of unpleasant issues. _____

20. I avoid bringing up certain issues if my arguments might hurt my partner's feelings. _____

21. I might agree with some of my partner's points to make my partner happy. _____

22. I avoid talking with my partner about disagreements. _____

23. I try to find a "middle ground" position that is acceptable to both of us. _____

24. I try to influence my partner so he or she will see things my way. _____

25. I believe that you have to "give a little to get a little" during a disagreement. _____

In order to determine your preferred style of conflict, add your scores for the following items:

3, 4, 16, 20, 21	(accommodating)	_____
7, 10, 18, 19, 22	(avoiding)	_____
1, 5, 9, 13, 17	(collaborating)	_____
2, 6, 12, 14, 24	(competing)	_____
8, 11, 15, 23, 25	(compromising)	_____

Higher scores indicate that you possess more of a particular style.

As you consider the Blake and Mouton conflict grid and its five styles, keep your preferred style(s) in mind in an effort to determine if those you habitually use are effective in resolving relational conflict.

SOURCE: This inventory, based on the work of Blake and Mouton, appears in "Put Yourself to the Test," in Laura K. Guerrero, Peter A. Andersen, and Walid A. Afifi, *Close Encounters: Communication in Relationships*, Thousand Oaks, CA: Sage, 2011, p. 336–338.

COMMUNICATION BEHAVIOR IN THE FACE OF CONFLICT

As we seek to resolve conflict, we need to avoid using the kinds of behavior that destroy relationships. By eliminating destructive communication behaviors from our repertoire and substituting constructive communication behaviors in their place, we will be better able to manage interpersonal conflict.

DESTRUCTIVE COMMUNICATION BEHAVIORS

When a conflict first develops, one of the variables affecting its outcome is whether participants intend to cooperate or compete with each other. If both bring a competitive

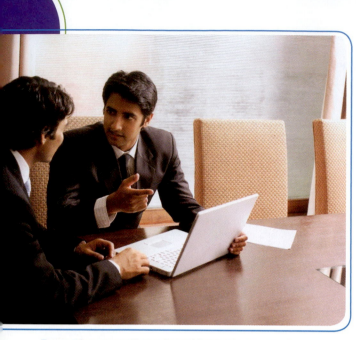

Expressing yourself openly and honestly can create a "win-win" opportunity.

Role reversal:
Imagining or acting by one party in a relationship or an exchange that he or she is the other party.

orientation to the conflict, each will likely be ego involved, perceiving his or her self-concept at stake and viewing winning the conflict as an affirmation of personal worth. When parties to a conflict are deceitful rather than open, when they fail to respect each other or view each other as equals, when they do not try to understand the conflict from the other's point of view, when they neglect to ask questions, or when they ignore or fail to clarify the assumptions under which they are operating, they also are likely rely on strategies that suppress rather than encourage the free exchange of ideas. As a result, they will impede, not facilitate, the identification of a mutually satisfactory solution.

Parties to a conflict who lack openness usually are unconcerned with the other's feelings, believing that it is unnecessary that each party to the conflict benefit from a positive outcome. Instead, they place blame on the other in an effort to absolve themselves of any responsibility for creating the conflict in the first place. In addition, they are apt to use power techniques that further inhibit freedom of expression while trying to inflict psychological pain on the other person or damage his or her self-image.

For better or worse, competing with, even striving to defeat, another person we are in conflict with is common in U.S. society. Common phrases support this orientation: people speak of "outsmarting" another, of getting "one up," of doing whatever is necessary to win at the sport of social "gamesmanship."

CONSTRUCTIVE COMMUNICATION BEHAVIORS

When parties to a conflict define it as mutually noncompetitive—a "win-win" opportunity— they express themselves openly and honestly, view each other as equals, and respect and work to understand each other's positions. In order for both parties to win, they must use effective listening techniques (see Chapter 4) and perception validation techniques (see Chapter 3) to ensure understanding of the other's perspective. They must encourage a free exchange of ideas, engage in open discussion of alternatives, and integrate their needs in their effort to identify a mutually satisfactory solution.

As a result of using constructive conflict resolution behaviors, each party avoids behaving in a way that could escalate the situation by causing the other to become defensive or combative. Instead, each seeks to view the conflict through the other's eyes. Employing **role reversal** is one way to learn conflict resolution strategies. Through this technique, in which each person imagines him- or herself as the other, the parties come to understand each other, discover creative ways to integrate their interests and concerns, and work toward a common goal. Once statements such as "You're wrong," "You're stupid," "I hate you," and "That's ridiculous" are replaced with statements such as "What you believe is not what I believe," individuals are on their way to developing a cooperative conflict resolution orientation based on effective communication.

To be sure, we all compete with others at one time or another. In school, we compete for grades. At work we compete for promotions. In social settings we compete for attention, friendship, and even love. The question is, how do we behave and what kind of expressive style do we exhibit when facing a conflict?

DESC SCRIPTS

A strategy that can help manage and resolve conflict is the **DESC script**, a means of expressing our feelings and understanding the feelings of another person.[15] DESC is an acronym for *describe, express, specify,* and *consequences.* In every DESC script, the parties to the conflict are the characters, the conflict is the plot, the time and place of the interaction is the setting, and the words exchanged, along with nonverbal cues, are the message.

Describe. You initiate a DESC script by *describing* to the other party why a situation troubles you, doing so as specifically and objectively as possible. While describing the situation, you also give yourself the opportunity to examine and define your personal needs and goals. Once you identify what you perceive as negative about the situation, you are in a better position to resolve it. It is important that your words describing the situation be simple, concrete, specific, and unbiased. For example, instead of yelling, "You're always embarrassing me!" try saying, "I don't like to be embarrassed in front of my friends." Instead of assuming you understand someone's motives and saying, "You're infatuated with Danielle; when she's around you wish I'd disappear," observe, "The last two times we've been with Danielle, you've ignored me."

How successful are you at expressing your feelings?

Express. The second step in the DESC approach is to *express* how you feel about the situation. Here it is important to use personal statements that make it clear you are expressing what *you* feel and what *you* think. The key to making a personal statement is to use the pronouns *I, me,* or *my;* for example, use phrases such as "I feel," "I believe," "My feelings are," "It appears to me." You can name a feeling: "I feel disappointed" or "I feel angry." You can use comparisons: "I feel invisible." Or you can indicate the type of action your feelings prompt you to display: "I feel like running away." By disclosing your feelings, you help the other become aware of your position without alienating him or her.

Specify. Once you have described the problem and expressed your feelings, the next step is to discuss changing. You *specify* how you would like to see the situation resolved. In effect, you request that the other person stop behaving one way and start behaving another. For instance, "When you know you will be late, please call to warn me."

Consequences. All behavioral changes have *consequences* in the form of punishments or rewards. In the last phase of DESC, you spell out the consequences of the status quo, the change, or both. When possible, you should emphasize positive rather than negative outcomes. For example, it is probably more effective to say, "If you stop belittling me in front of Nick and Alisha, I'll feel better and we'll have more fun," than it would be to say, "If you continue to make fun of me, I'll have to start making fun of you."

DESC script: A strategy for expressing one's own feelings and understanding the feelings of others; DESC is an acronym for describe, express, specify, and consequences.

The following example illustrates how one person, Emma, used a DESC script in an attempt to resolve the relationship difficulties she was having with her friend Destiny and reconcile with her:

WATCH THIS 11.1
For a video on using DESC scripts visit the student study site.

Describe: Destiny, we hardly see or speak to each other any more. It's been weeks since we've talked or gone out for a drink.

Express: I feel bad about how our schedules are making it difficult for us to get together, especially since I value your friendship, and I want us to stay in touch.

Specify: Can we get together for a latte and see how we can make more time for each other?

Consequences: If we can find a way to schedule friendship breaks like others schedule coffee breaks, I think we'd feel better and not find ourselves so stressed.

Similarly, an employee, Cole, had the following conversation with his employer, Alexa, in an effort to refuse what he perceived as her unreasonable demand.

Describe: We have been swamped with work every day, yet almost every evening right before I'm ready to leave you have asked me to complete a number of extra special assignments as well. I'm becoming exhausted.

Express: I feel overworked, overstressed, and overwhelmed.

Specify: I typically complete the morning's assignments about a half hour before I break for lunch. If you let me know then what additional work you need me to do, and which assignment has the highest priority, I'll take care of it then.

Consequences: I can handle my regular responsibilities and the extra work without becoming stressed or overwhelmed if you'll give me enough notice. I think that would make us both feel relieved.[16]

As we see, by using DESC scripts Emma and Cole managed their conflicts in a healthy and mature way. They expressed their feelings clearly and directly, making it possible for the persons they addressed to respond in kind.

YOUR EXPRESSIVE STYLE: NONASSERTIVE, AGGRESSIVE, OR ASSERTIVE

You have choices when facing conflict-producing situations: you can choose to respond nonassertively, aggressively, or assertively (see Figure 11.2). The choice you make ultimately determines the conflict's resolution. Let's explore the characteristics of each approach. For example, you can respond to each of the following situations by letting another person take advantage of you (you respond nonassertively), attacking the other person (you respond aggressively), or by standing up for your rights (you respond assertively). Which kind of response would you use?

- Your friend is taking a class in public speaking. She asks to borrow the speech you gave when you were enrolled in a similar course.

- You are in line waiting to buy concert tickets and another person pushes in front of you.

- You are not given the promotion you believe you are due.

- You are chosen to represent your school at a national conference that you have neither the time nor the desire to attend.

Figure 11.2 Expressive Style Scale

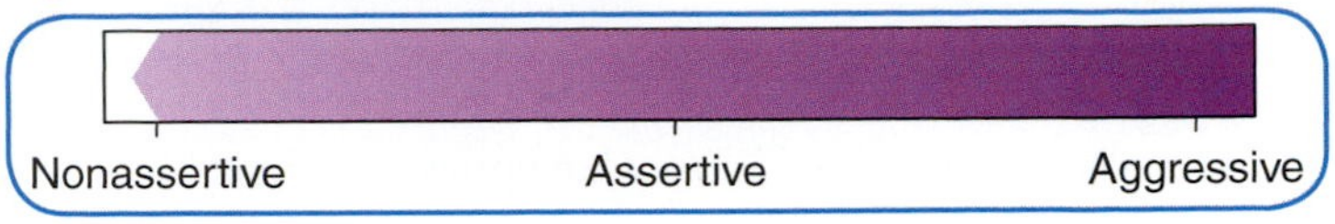

Nonassertive   Assertive   Aggressive

TRY THIS: *A Self-Assessment*

Respond to the statements below to assess the extent to which you characteristically respond assertively to interpersonal conflict. Use the following scale to evaluate the degree to which each statement typifies your behavior.

For each statement, assign a score of 5 to 1, according to the following criteria:

5   You almost always display the behavior.

4   You display the behavior about 75 percent of the time.

3   You have a 50-50 chance of displaying the behavior.

2   You sometimes, but not frequently, behave this way.

1   You almost never display the behavior.

You and a friend disagree over who works harder to make your friendship work. You

_____   try not to make your friend feel guilty.

_____   calmly let your friend know what upsets you about his or her behavior.

_____   avoid blaming your friend for any relationship problems.

_____   look directly at your friend when talking to him or her.

_____   make no assumptions about how your friend feels.

_____   question your friend in an effort to avoid misunderstanding him or her.

_____   avoid using sarcasm as a communication strategy.

_____   refrain from becoming anxious about discussing the problem.

_____   use appropriately forceful voice tone, body language, facial expressions, and gestures to support your feelings.

_____   avoid cursing and using obscenities to make your point.

_____   present your thought in an organized manner.

_____   consider the impact of your actions.

_____   **Total**

You and your boss disagree over the kind of job you're doing. You

_____ try not to make your boss feel guilty.

_____ calmly let your boss know what upsets you about his or her behavior.

_____ avoid blaming your boss for any relationship problems.

_____ look directly at your boss when talking to him or her.

_____ make no assumptions about how your boss feels.

_____ question your boss in an effort to avoid misunderstanding him or her.

_____ avoid using sarcasm as a communication strategy.

_____ refrain from becoming anxious about discussing the problem.

_____ use appropriately forceful voice tone, body language, facial expressions, and gestures to support your feelings.

_____ avoid cursing and using obscenities to make your point.

_____ present your thought in an organized manner.

_____ consider the impact of your actions.

_____ **Total**

You and a professor disagree about a grade. You

_____ try not to make your professor feel guilty.

_____ calmly let your professor know what upsets you about his or her behavior.

_____ avoid blaming your professor for any relationship problems.

_____ look directly at your professor when talking to him or her.

_____ make no assumptions about how your professor feels.

_____ question your professor in an effort to avoid misunderstanding him or her.

_____ avoid using sarcasm as a communication strategy.

_____ refrain from becoming anxious about discussing the problem.

_____ use appropriately forceful voice tone, body language, facial expressions, and gestures to support your feelings.

_____ avoid cursing and using obscenities to make your point.

_____ present your thought in an organized manner.

_____ consider the impact of your actions.

_____ **Total**

To determine your total score, add the values in each of the sections above.

If you consistently score near 60 for each situation, you are likely comfortable handling conflict. If you consistently score near 12, you likely are not. Reexamine each set of responses. With which person were you most effective? Most ineffective? Why? Circle the items to which you responded with a 1, 2, or 3. These are the behaviors you may want to work on.

NONASSERTIVENESS

When we are fearful or hesitate to express our feelings and thoughts, we exhibit a **nonassertive expression style** in which we do not try to satisfy our own concerns. By adopting such an avoidance-based strategy, we allow others to intimidate us and usually ensure that our own feelings will remain bottled up inside us and that our needs will go unmet. Out of fear, we fail to let another know of our displeasure, and we do not take whatever steps are needed to improve an unsatisfying relationship. We offer excuse after excuse, never quite finding the right time or the right words to express how we really feel, and we avoid confronting the individual or situation that is causing us discomfort. Using a nonassertive style can contribute to your paying too much for a meal, performing a favor when you cannot really spare the time, or staying in a relationship you find demeaning. Why would you not assert yourself?

Why We Do Not Assert Ourselves. A number of factors account for nonassertiveness. Sometimes it is inertia—we are merely lazy; it is, after all, easier to do nothing. Assertion takes energy. At other times, it is not laziness, but merely that we do not care enough about the conflict to assert ourselves. What is at stake is either not important enough or not salient enough to move us to take constructive action. At still other times, it is *fear* that compels us to adopt a nonassertive style. We may, for example, fear rejection, making another person angry, or making someone unhappy with us. Shyness is also a factor. People who are shy devote a lot of time to worrying about what others think of them, less time letting others know what they think, and more time as victims.

Nonassertive Language. Suppose someone who is shy (Person A) wants another person (B) to help plan a friend's party. Their conversation might proceed like this:

A: Um, hey, this really isn't important, but you know Angela's birthday is coming up and I was wondering if you would be willing to take a few minutes and help me plan a party for her.

B: *(Head buried in a book)* Can't do it now. I'm busy.

A: Oh, sure. Sorry.

How would you describe the behavior pictured? Can you tell a story about it?

Various nonverbal and verbal behaviors are associated with shyness and nonassertiveness. Nonassertive nonverbal cues include downcast eyes or evasive eye contact, excessive head nodding, body gestures such as hand wringing, slouched posture, and a low, whining, hesitant, or giggly voice. Nonassertive verbal behaviors include fillers like "uh," "um," and "you know"; negators such as "This really isn't important, but," and "You'll probably think I'm stupid"; qualifiers such as "just" and "I guess"; an overuse of apologetic words; and a disconnected speech pattern. Generally, nonassertive behaviors reduce the impact of what is said. That is one reason individuals fearing rejection resort to them—their aim is to appease others.

AGGRESSIVENESS

In contrast to people who are nonassertive, people who exhibit an **aggressive expression style** express their needs, wants, and ideas openly, even if doing so hurts another person. In the effort to stand up for themselves, those who are aggressive often ignore or violate

Nonassertive expression style: An style of communication characterized by hesitation in expressing one's feelings and thoughts.

Aggressive expression style: A style of communication involving the open expression of one's needs, wants, and ideas even at the expense of another person.

Sue Sylvester (Jane Lynch, left) is known for her aggressive communication style and her penchant for tracksuits on the series *Glee*. Here, Sue meets her match in rival teacher Brenda Castle (Molly Shannon, right).

the rights of others with whom they conflict. As a result, aggressive people get more of their needs met than do nonassertive people—but at someone else's expense. The aggressor's aim is to dominate and win; merely breaking even is not enough.

Why We Act Aggressively. People act aggressively for a number of reasons. First, we may lash out simply because we feel vulnerable; we make an effort to protect ourselves from the perceived threat of powerlessness. Second, unresolved, emotionally volatile experiences can trigger an aggressive reaction, causing an overreaction when we face conflict. Third, we may believe that the only way to get our ideas and feelings across is through aggression. For some reason, we may convince ourselves that others will not listen to or react to our words if we are mild-mannered. And finally, we may not understand how to channel or handle aggressive impulses. Our aggressive style may be related to repeated past instances of nonassertive behavior. The hurt, disappointment, bewilderment, and sense of personal violation that accompany nonassertion may have reached a boiling point. No longer able to contain our feelings, we abruptly vent them. As a result, aggression may do damage to or even destroy a relationship.

Aggressive Language. The message sent by the aggressive person is selfish: "This is how I feel about . . . You're dumb for feeling differently." "This is what I want; what you want doesn't count and is of no consequence to me." Now suppose a person exhibiting an aggressive style (Person A) were to attempt to convince a friend (Person B) to help plan a party for a friend. Their conversation might go like this:

A: I'm fed up with you. I'm sick of listening to you tell me you don't have time to plan this party. You'd better make time for me now!

B: *(Head buried in a book)* Can't do it now. I'm busy.

A: You're wrong. You can do it now. You're just selfish. You don't have time for anyone but yourself.

B: Not so.

A: That's a lie. Who always does everything? I do. All you ever do is read or watch videos. You're just a lazy bum! I'm sick and tired of talking to you.

B: Oh, just cool down.

Compared to the nonassertive person, who starts hesitantly, the aggressive person begins by attacking and uses nonverbal and verbal cues in support. Nonverbal cues include "stare-down" messages; a raised, harsh, strident voice; a cold, sarcastic, or demeaning tone; excessive finger pointing and fist pounding; and a willingness to invade another's personal space. The aggressive person's message also spells p-u-t-d-o-w-n. Aggressors often interrupt or answer before another finishes speaking and use threats such as "You'd better," "If you don't stop," or "I'm warning you." They are also prone to making evaluative judgments and spouting accusative statements such as "That's bad," "You're wrong," and "Your approach is inferior," and degrading comments such as "You can't be serious," "You're joking," and "Shut up." In some exchanges the conversation escalates out of control because the aggressor's target feels the need to retaliate. When his happens, they reach a stalemate, and no one wins.

ASSERTIVENESS

While the nonassertive person wants to avoid conflict, even at the cost of sacrificing needs and wants, and the aggressive person wants to dominate, even if this domination causes another harm, the person exhibiting an **assertive expression style** wants to communicate honestly, clearly, and directly, and to stand up for what he or she believes without harming anyone—including him- or herself.

By asserting yourself, you meet more of your interpersonal needs, make more of your own decisions, and think and say what you believe without apologizing, dominating, infringing on another's rights, or violating another's dignity. You also protect yourself from becoming a "victim." Behaving in this way promotes a healthy interpersonal climate for the handling of conflict.

Acting assertively tends to be rewarding. When we accomplish our goals and act in our own best interest without harming or depreciating someone else, we feel good. The same holds true when we elicit a positive response from another and can openly express our feelings and thoughts.

Learning Assertive Behavior. Learning assertive skills can help you refrain from sending nonassertive or aggressive messages when doing so would be inappropriate. By attending to feelings and using specific verbal and nonverbal skills, you can resolve interpersonal conflict. Nonassertive persons create a power imbalance by giving everyone more rights than they give themselves, and aggressive persons create an imbalance by giving themselves more rights than others. Assertive individuals try to balance social power and thereby equalize the nature of their relationships.

Assertive Language. As with nonassertion and aggression, particular nonverbal and verbal cues characterize assertion. An important one is good eye contact. When we avoid eye contact we send the message that we are nervous, anxious, uncomfortable, or even incompetent. When we stare at another, our gaze suggests we hold the person in contempt. However, when we look at another with interest and focus on him or her during a conversation, we communicate our concern. Likewise, a strong, well-modulated steady voice signals we are in control and sincere. We saw in Chapter 8 that using "I" language helps others accept responsibility for their feelings. In similar fashion, the verbal characteristics of assertive individuals include an ability and willingness to send "I" messages and "we" messages. Those who are assertive let us know what they think and feel ("I want," "I don't like"). They are willing to cooperate for a relationship's betterment ("Let's," "We can"). When we communicate assertively we also use empathetic statements of interest such as "What do you think?" or "How do you see this?" Absent from the assertive person's conversations are wishy-washy statements such as "I guess," fillers such as "um," and self-demeanors such as "I know this sounds dumb, but . . ." In addition, when we display an assertive style, we don't offer blame

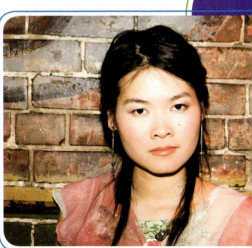

When you assert yourself, you make more of your own decisions.

Assertive expression style: A style of communication that is honest, clear, and direct.

statements or send "you" messages. Instead, we express ourselves in personally fulfilling and interpersonally effective ways.

The assertive approach is exhibited in the following exchange, during which an assertive person (Person A) attempts to convince another (Person B) to help him plan a party for a friend.

A: It's March and that means it's time to begin planning Tim's party.

B: *(Head buried in a book)* Can't do it now. I'm busy.

A: I think the party will have a better chance of succeeding if we give ourselves plenty of time to get organized.

B: It's going to be impossible for me to give it much thought.

A: I've already jotted down some preliminary ideas. I hope you'll look at them when you finish the chapter you're reading.

B: Do I have to do it today?

A: Is there another day that would be better for you?

B: Oh, I don't know.

A: Well, let's talk about it when you complete your reading. Are we agreed?

B: All right.

A: Good! It shouldn't take more than 30 minutes, and I'll really feel better when we've at least gone over these ideas.

The ability to communicate assertively usually puts you at an advantage when you are involved in a conflict. Your perception of your role in a relationship affects your choice of conflict resolution strategy. Each of the following examples offers responses representing nonassertive, assertive, and aggressive approaches. Which would you offer for each situation? Answer honestly.

> You and Sheila work for the same company. Sheila asks you to pick her up and drop her off at the train every day. You feel this will cause you unnecessary delays. You respond:

> **1.** "Um, well, I guess it's possible . . . Oh, all right." (nonassertive)
> **2.** "You're kidding! You really have nerve! Why should I do that for you?" (aggressive)
> **3.** "I understand you get tired of having to walk to the station every day, but still, I'd rather not commit myself to picking you up and driving you there every day. I'd be glad to help you once or twice a week." (assertive)

> Your physician makes a sexist remark while examining you. You respond:

> **1.** "Who the hell do you think you are?" (aggressive)
> **2.** (With a laugh) "Oh, now really, doctor!" (nonassertive)
> **3.** "I think that remark is sexist. I can't believe you meant it." (assertive)

> You are attending a business meeting concerning possible changes at your company. One of the people in attendance speaks up to urge the committee not

to change the existing system, and she gives inaccurate data in an attempt to convince committee members of her position. You disagree. You respond:

1. (Shouting) "You're a liar! You've distorted everything on purpose!" (aggressive)

2. (Speaking quietly only to the person seated next to you) "What she said isn't really accurate." (nonassertive)

3. "I see why you're worried about changing the total system, but I believe we can preserve its integrity and still develop innovative approaches." (assertive)

For each situation, was your chosen response assertive, nonassertive, or aggressive?

As these examples illustrate, we can be assertive, nonassertive, or aggressive in various ways. When we interact with someone, we can communicate our nonassertiveness by demeaning ourselves, by keeping silent, or by hesitating when we state a position. We can communicate our aggressiveness by being openly hostile, sarcastic, or rude. And we can communicate our assertiveness by standing up for our rights, opening expressing our beliefs, and stating our positions openly and directly. Although there is no one way you need to act in every interpersonal conflict, each choice you make regarding how to act influences the eventual outcome of the conflict.

CULTURE AND CONFLICT RESOLUTION

Because culture is the lens through which we view the world, cultural background appears to influence our response to conflict. For example, people from individualist cultures such as the United States prefer to deal directly with conflict, whereas those from collectivist cultures such as Japan are more comfortable dealing indirectly with it.[17] People from individualist cultures use controlling and overt confrontational strategies, whereas people from collectivist cultures prefer to use smoothing or avoidance strategies in the effort to help those they are in conflict with save face.[18]

In the United States, an emphasis is placed on the individual's rights, mainly on whether a person's needs are given their proper due. In contrast, most Latin American and Asian countries emphasize the concerns of the group rather than the rights and needs of individuals.[19] In one study, university students from different cultures were asked if they would permit aggressive behavior in their children to help protect what they perceived rightfully to be theirs. The highest percentage of affirmative responses came from U.S. parents (61 percent).[20]

We also distinguish cultures by whether they use high- or low-context communication. Cultures using high-context communication are tradition-bound and emphasize politeness and indirectness in relationships. In contrast, members of low-context communication cultures exhibit a more direct communication style. Thus, people from low-context cultures such as the United States are likely to communicate openly and directly, whereas members of high-context cultures such as Japan and Korea prefer to avoid confrontation and to preserve a sense of harmony in an effort to help others maintain their self-esteem.[21]

Because of the inevitability of conflict in relationships, people from different cultures need to recognize and acknowledge their differences. By becoming less ethnocentric and more culturally aware and competent, we can learn to handle conflict with people from different

Edward de Bono is a physician and leading authority on creative thinking. What does the following excerpt from de Bono's *I Am Right—You Are Wrong* suggest about how the Japanese handle conflict?

Every day the leading executives in the Japanese motor industry meet for lunch in their special club. They discuss problems common to the whole motor industry. But a soon as lunch is over and they step over the threshold of the club, out into the street, they are bitter enemies seeking to kill each other's business by marketing, technical changes, pricing policy, etc. For the Japanese, who do not have the tradition of Western logic, there is no contradiction at all between "friend" and "enemy." They find it easy to conceive of someone as a friend–enemy or enemy–friend.

SOURCE: Edward de Bono, *I Am Right—You Are Wrong*, New York: Viking, 1991, p. 196.

cultures as effectively as we handle conflict with persons from our own culture. The next time you are involved in a conflict with someone from a different culture, ask yourself:

1. Which of my behaviors is my partner having difficulty understanding or accepting?

2. Which of his or her behaviors am I having difficulty with?

3. To what extent is this person more or less cooperative or competitive than me?

4. To what degree is this person more or less open, direct, and assertive or more or less reticent, indirect, and nonassertive than me?

By making an effort to understand how the experiences of people from other cultures lead them to develop perspectives on conflict that differ from yours, you can appreciate and embrace the flexibility necessary to resolve conflict.[22]

When it comes to age as a cultural variable, developing the ability to empathize can bridge the generation gap that fuels many intergenerational conflicts. Older people complain that members of younger generations stereotype them as "old geezers," making them feel worthless and discarded. Members of the "sandwich generation" complain about the burden they have to shoulder in both caring for their own children and "parenting" their aged parents, who have numerous "aches and pains" and—from their adult children's perspective—rarely seem to be content. If members of the older and younger generations could empathize with one another—that is, identify with and understand each other's feelings and motives—and could share their thoughts, a fuller, more meaningful understanding might develop between them.[23]

GENDER AND CONFLICT RESOLUTION

Can women and men work together effectively to resolve conflict? Do they share the same priorities when it comes to alleviating conflict? Adult men and women tend to respond dissimilarly to conflict. Women, it appears, specialize in communication that builds support, while men tend to focus on task-related issues.[24] However, both kinds of behavior can actually complement each other and work in unison to resolve conflict.

Neither men nor women may be aware of their contributions to or strategies for conflict resolution. As they grow up, boys are taught to use communication to solve problems and to assert their points of view. They see talk as a means of establishing superiority and winning others' respect. For women, conversation provides the means to work out conflicts and relationship problems. Whereas men use talk to negotiate for power and influence, women use it to build connections and include others. Men put priority on outcomes, and women put it on the relationship itself. As a result, while men may be better at staying focused on the goal gained from resolving a conflict, women are likely better prepared to interpret the feelings, moods, and needs of those they are in conflict with. They are better at asking questions and avoiding the putdowns that make conflict resolution unnecessarily difficult.[25]

Men and women differ in how committed they are to conflict resolution. Men are sometimes more quick than women to withdraw from conflict. Women may want to talk it out, but men may simply want to be done with it—something they often achieve by leaving.[26] At times, men and women both are likely to overreact to or withdraw from conflict because of a physiological response that causes them to lose control and experience rage. *Flooding* occurs when the man or woman becomes surprised, overwhelmed, or disorganized by the partner's expression of negative emotion.[27] During flooding, a person's heart rate increases and blood pressure rises, and he or she finds it hard to process incoming information. Fight or flight is the usual response. While stress or physical exertion may trigger emotional flooding, humor and affect may help allay its impact. Women also tend to do more compromising and accommodating than men, who are likely to use somewhat more forceful and direct means to get their way. Men and women need to be aware that they tend to bring different orientations to conflict that influence their responses.

An unconventional "hookup" relationship model and the struggle against falling in love with one another fuels conflict between Adam (Ashton Kutcher) and Emma (Natalie Portman) in the romantic comedy film *No Strings Attached.*

MEDIA, TECHNOLOGY, AND CONFLICT RESOLUTION: MODELS OR MADNESS

How we arrive at a solution when involved in an interpersonal conflict is revealing. For example, we can try one approach after another and then weigh the consequences of potential options, or we can rely on the power of example and then enact what we have observed, effectively learning vicariously. Media and technology facilitate the vicarious approach, providing abundant models of people embroiled in conflict. They also supply the means to communicate about and spread conflict, at times contributing to conflicts going viral. As such, both media and technology play parts in helping and hindering conflict resolution.

MEDIA PORTRAYALS: MODEL THE WAY

According to **social learning theory**, we learn at least some of what we know by observing others and then modeling the behavior of those we have observed. Thus, through observation and modeling of mediated characters we acquire a wide range of behaviors and solutions to potential problems that we otherwise might not have had the resources,

Social learning theory: A theory that asserts that we learn at least some of what we know by observing others and then modeling the behaviors that we have observed.

inclination, or time to figure out. In this way, media offerings (including video games) can lead us to practice certain behaviors while also inhibiting our use of others.

Both broadcast and cable television offerings, news and entertainment, involve depictions of different kinds of conflicts. News stories, for example, may describe the nature and outcomes of gang violence, union-management disputes, political rivalries, or a war's battles. Entertainment shows abound with conflicts resulting from family disputes, love entanglements, and disagreements over job-related issues such as promotions and/or money. Some of these conflicts have positive outcomes, and others have negative ones. All, however, affect our attitudes toward the means used to resolve them. We learn what works and what doesn't.

Media offerings influence attitudes toward conflict in another way as well. A program may improve on "real life" by tying up into neat packages situations that in reality would leave us feeling confused or would require more effort to resolve. To suit entertainment needs, for example, most television programs fit time slots of 30, 60, or 120 minutes—not exactly reflecting the reality of how long it takes to resolve conflict. Few, if any, conflicts go unresolved within those time blocks. Rarely are we left hanging or in despair. Instead, we are presented with fabricated versions of conflict resolution. To be sure, most of us realize that drama and real life are different. Some people, however, may not be able to adequately separate fantasy from reality.

TECHNOLOGY: REAL AND UNREAL

Call of Duty and Battlefield are popular video game franchises that have morphed into cultural institutions. These games realistically simulate high-tech military combat—vividly re-creating the experiences of fighting in a war. How does taking war and turning it into a computer game affect us, especially when the line between warrior and civilian is often unclear and the visuals are frighteningly close to YouTube footage of the wars in Iraq and Afghanistan?[28] While some believe these games trivialize military conflict and have little cultural impact, others believe they are akin to movies, such as *The Hurt Locker* and *Black Hawk Down,* that comment on war. Real war, however, is not "fun" or "entertaining," and those who play these games find them both fun and entertaining.

In your opinion, what does playing computer games teach us about conflict? Whether or not we take these games seriously, to what extent might they be influencing the approaches we use to handle conflict in our personal and professional lives? Could they influence us to use destructive approaches to conflict resolution when less aggressive, more accommodating approaches might be wiser? Could such games be encouraging us to display more aggressive behavior in our personal relationships? What about games that reward players for killing those who are innocent, members of law enforcement, or prostitutes or for displaying skill using a range of weapons, or in which players assume the role of a criminal or a hunted and hated character rather than the protagonist?

Research has found that immediately after playing violent games, the possibility that the player will interpret a mild or ambiguous provocation in a hostile fashion increases, as do the player's general arousal level and dominant behavioral proclivities. In effect, through playing such games players learn aggressive life scripts and come to de-emphasize negative reactions to conflict and violence.[29]

During online interactions, the heated discussion of real-world political, social, religious, or economic issues may result in flaming (communication that is hostile and insulting, as discussed in Chapter 8). From a conflict perspective, flaming is an outgrowth of one person's perception that the other is being patently unfair. It typically provokes angry responses that sometimes result in flame wars between the parties, ultimately drawing in many more participants who perpetuate the online harassment. Some attribute flaming to de-individuation and a general lack of awareness of the feelings of others, asserting that in U.S. culture we spend so much time online that we have individualized our leisure time, reducing our dependence on others and precipitating what has been called the "bowling alone" syndrome—the doing of more things on our own.[30] What do you think? And to what extent, if any, does social networking ameliorate this?

On the other hand, newer technologies are not without their benefits for conflict resolution. In fact, at times their availability can help users defuse rather than heat up a conflict. For example, individuals who are very angry at one another may find that texting and instant messaging actually foster their communication. These means allow people with a conflict to interact while avoiding the shouting match that would likely take place if they were in the same room rather than online. By slowing things down a bit and freeing them to think things through before responding, communicating in cyberspace may help to lower the tension level and reduce the number of potentially hurtful and thoughtless retorts they might otherwise make to one another.

Some contend that the opposite is true, insisting that an **online disinhibition effect** makes the escalation of conflict more likely. They assert that people are more willing to say what they really think, more willing to speak out or misbehave, online than they are in person.[31] According to this argument, striking out at another person online feels less like a confrontation than would telling that person the same thing over the phone or face-to-face. Being too frank can in turn provoke the target of that frankness to retaliate with vitriolic remarks, and so on.

To what extent, if any, do your experiences support either of these perspectives?

Online disinhibition effect: The willingness to say what one really thinks or to misbehave when online.

First, view a film (e.g., *The Ides of March, Bully, Real Steel, The Avengers*) or television program (e.g., *Game of Thrones*) or play a computer game (e.g., Mortal Kombat) that focuses on the handling of interpersonal conflict.

1. Describe the nature of the conflict presented in the film or game.

2. Discuss how the characters attempt to handle the conflict, identifying both their negative and positive behaviors.

3. Describe the outcome of the conflict and the extent to which its resolution strengthened or weakened the relationship of the characters.

4. Explain your views regarding the ethics and viability of the means used to resolve conflict in film and games.

Next, select a current issue of a major newspaper, an online news site, or a broadcast/cable news show.

1. Identify articles/stories focused on conflict of different kinds. For example, stories may be devoted to gang fights, domestic violence, management-labor disputes, class warfare, or war.

2. Keep a tally of which conflict-focused articles/stories have positive slants and which have negative slants, which have positive resolutions and which have negative resolutions.

3. Discuss what your findings suggest regarding the coverage of conflict.

4. How might the nature of news coverage influence reader/viewer attitudes toward the effect and value of conflict?

GAINING COMMUNICATION COMPETENCE: GUIDELINES FOR RESOLVING CONFLICT

By applying principles of effective communication, we can resolve interpersonal conflict more productively. Using effective communication techniques can help us reduce the likelihood that our behavior will escalate a conflict. Learning to handle conflict successfully is an obtainable goal leading to increased self-confidence, improved relationships, and a greater ability to handle stressful situations. The following guidelines summarize how we can use interpersonal skills to resolve conflict.

RECOGNIZE THAT CONFLICT CAN BE RESOLVED RATIONALLY

Sometimes when we step back from a situation, we find the perspective needed to realize that we can resolve a conflict. A conflict might be settled rationally if we do not withdraw when we should confront, smooth when we should merely compromise, or force when it would be more appropriate for us to smooth. At times, deciding who needs a goal most and letting that person have it is the rational choice. Similarly, withdrawing or postponing a discussion of the conflict until you are in control of your emotions can be the most rational decision, just as smoothing or apologizing when you feel that to engage in conflict would be wrong may well be the most rational way to end the conflict. Of course, meeting in the middle and facing the conflict head-on are also valid. Recognizing when to use which behavior and sensing when a behavioral choice will be productive or not are first steps in learning to handle conflict more effectively. Being able to switch approaches according to what will work best is a key to conflict resolution.

AGREE ABOUT HOW TO DEFINE THE CONFLICT

Once we acknowledge that we can handle a conflict rationally, we are ready to identify the reason for the conflict by asking questions such as, What is the nature of our conflict? Which of us feels more strongly about the issue? What can we do about it? Communication during this stage will be more effective if, when sharing feelings and reactions, we send "I" messages ("I don't like having to do all the work") rather than "you" messages and avoid sending blame messages ("You will destroy us"). This stage has no place for labeling, accusing, or insulting. Instead, both sides need to be specific regarding the reasons for the conflict and in explaining what is needed to find a beneficial solution—a solution in which neither will lose and both will win. In other words, if we find a way to define the conflict as a mutual problem rather than as a win-lose battle, it will be easier to resolve. Defining a conflict is like baking a cake: without the right ingredients, the recipe won't work.

EXCHANGE PERCEPTIONS: DESCRIBE, EXPRESS, SPECIFY, AND NOTE BEHAVIORAL CONSEQUENCES

To the extent each party proposes a solution that underscores the intention to cooperate, defensiveness and egocentrism levels are reduced. Such a solution requires that each person understand the other's perspective and be able to keep it as well as his or her own in mind as the sides resolve the differences between them. To settle a conflict, each party must understand—but not necessarily agree with—the motivation behind the other's actions. Only by taking the perspective of another can we invent an array of possible solutions (propose options for mutual gain) based on a clear understanding of each side and the emotional force underlying each position.

To avoid gunnysacking, deal with the conflict expeditiously. Bear in mind the biblical warning: "Let not the sun go down upon your anger" (Ephesians 4:28). Failing to take such measures only prolongs or intensifies the core conflict.

ASSESS ALTERNATIVE SOLUTIONS AND CHOOSE THE ONE THAT SEEMS BEST

After conceiving possible solutions, we must assess which solution each of the parties considers best. Consider which alternative is best: Will one solution lead to a one-sided "win" at the other's expense, will everyone "lose," or will everyone "win"? Make a note of which solutions are totally unacceptable and those that are mutually acceptable. The conflict is resolved when the parties select a solution that satisfies each of them and to which they agree to abide. Usually, this is the solution with the most advantages and fewest disadvantages for each side—the one that appears to be the most fair when measured against agreed-on criteria.

IMPLEMENT AND EVALUATE THE SELECTED SOLUTION

During this stage we test the chosen solution. We identify who is doing what, when, where, and under what conditions. We seek to know whether the adopted solution has alleviated the conflict's causes and whether the outcome has been as rewarding as anticipated. If it has not, then it is time to restart the conflict resolution process. Agreements that do not improve the ability of the parties to relate typically fail because they usually are inconsistent with, rather than supportive of, each person's needs and goals.

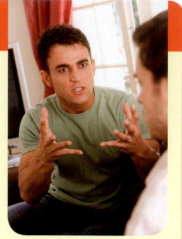

Jim and Jack share an apartment. After reading their story, decide whether their pairing was a match or a mismatch.

Jim likes to rise early and enrolls for 8:00 a.m. classes. Jack likes to sleep in; he carries a heavy late-afternoon and evening course load. Jim likes a quiet place to study. Jack loves to read with his expensive speakers blasting music. Jim is a neat freak. Jack leaves his things wherever he happens to drop them.

As roommates, Jim and Jack shared a relationship that could be described as tenuous at best, until . . .

It was about 2:00 a.m. Jim had been asleep for about three hours. Jack arrived home and immediately turned on his music—it was blaring so loud that it virtually knocked Jim out of bed. Jim yelled at Jack to turn the speakers off and put his headset on. Jack yelled back at Jim to get a life. Jim was so angry that he hurled a book across the room; it hit the ceiling and set off the fire alarm. As the engines arrived, Jack and Jim began to wonder if they might consider alternatives to screaming and throwing things at each other.

Now, consider these questions:

1. In your opinion, will Jack and Jim survive a year together?

2. What will need to happen for them to develop a more positive and cooperative relationship?

3. How would you advise these roommates to resolve their conflict?

REVIEW THIS

CHAPTER SUMMARY

1 Define conflict and discuss its nature, explaining the difference between functional and dysfunctional conflict. Conflict is inevitable in any relationship. Anyone can start a conflict, and a conflict can occur in any setting. It can involve a single person (intrapersonal conflict) or two or more people (interpersonal conflict). Conflict occurs whenever the thoughts or actions of one person are perceived by another to limit or interfere with his or her own thoughts or actions. Once aware of their disagreement and the incompatibility of their goals, both parties to the conflict try to prevail. Conflicts that are functional are constructive; they help us better understand one another as well as strengthen our relationships. Conflicts that are dysfunctional damage or even destroy relationships.

2 Identify conflict sources. Conflicts arise from perceived individual differences, scarcity of resources, rivalries, relationship disagreements, and misinterpretations. Every conflict can be described according to the nature of the goal of the parties (shareable or nonshareable), the conflict's level of intensity (low, medium, or high), and the general character of the conflict (pseudoconflict, content conflict, value conflict, or ego conflict).

3 Identify conflict resolution and management strategies. Among the most popular means to depict preferred conflict resolution styles is Blake and Mouton's conflict resolution grid. The five styles identified in the grid are avoiding, accommodative, competitive, compromising, and collaborative. A DESC script is a strategy to help manage and resolve conflict. DESC is an acronym for *describe, express, specify,* and *consequences.*

4 Compare and contrast the following conflict expression styles: assertive, nonassertive, and aggressive. A person who approaches conflict nonassertively attempts to avoid it, even if this means giving up his or her own needs and wants. A person who approaches conflict aggressively aims to dominate in a relationship, even if this means hurting the other party. A person who approaches conflict assertively communicates honestly, clearly, and directly about the conflict, standing up for what he or she believes without harming the other party or him- or herself.

5 Explain culture's influence on conflict. Persons from individualist, low-context communication cultures prefer to deal directly with conflict, whereas persons from collectivist, high-context communication cultures are more comfortable dealing with conflict indirectly.

6 Discuss differences and similarities in how men and women approach and handle conflict. Males tend to pursue their own self-interests without orienting themselves to a partner's perspective; females tend to attempt to meet others' needs. Men focus on problem-solving and task-related issues, while women try to build support as they work out relationship problems.

7 Discuss how media portrayals and technology affect perceptions of conflict. We acquire attitudes, emotional responses, and styles of conduct by modeling what we observe on television, in films, and in games. Communicating online may also lower the tension level associated with face-to-face conflict. At the same time, television and film may delude us into thinking that conflicts can be resolved quickly.

8 Identify how to resolve conflict effectively. To resolve conflict, we must recognize that conflict can be resolved rationally, agree on a definition of the conflict, exchange perceptions, communicate tentative solutions illustrating cooperative intentions, choose the best solution, implement it, and evaluate it.

✔ CHECK YOUR UNDERSTANDING

1 Can you deconstruct a specific conflict situation by identifying the parties to the conflict, the sources of the conflict, the goal(s) sought, the nature of the conflict, and its resolution? (See pages 270–275.)

2 Can you differentiate between functional and dysfunctional conflict? Which kind do you experience most frequently in your close relationships? (See pages 294–298.)

3 Can you create scenarios illustrating the differences among nonassertive, assertive, and aggressive approaches to a conflict-laden situation? (See pages 279–283.)

4 Can you provide examples of how gender, culture, and media and technology influence both attitudes toward and behaviors exhibited during conflict? (See pages 315–320.)

5 Can you assess your own conflict management skills? (See pages 320–321.)

✔ CHECK YOUR SKILLS

1 Can you approach conflict in a way that yields positive results? (See pages 294–298; and *Try This*, page 296.)

2 Can you avoid displaying crazymaking behavior? (See pages 296–298.)

3 Can you use clues to predict when a conflict is likely to occur? (See page 299.)

4 Can you identify factors contributing to relational conflict? (See pages 298–301; and *Try This*, page 300.)

5 Can you choose an appropriate conflict management style to resolve a conflict? (See pages 302–305; and *Try This*, pages 304–305.)

6 Can you differentiate between constructive and destructive communication behaviors? (See pages 306–307.)

7 Can you respond assertively when facing a conflict-producing situation? (See pages 313–315; and *Try This*, pages 309–310.)

8 Can you take cultural background and gender into account when in conflict with another? (See pages 315–317; and *Analyze This*, page 316.)

9 Can you account for how media and technology affect responses to conflict? (See pages 317–319; *Reflect on This*, page 318; and *Try This*, page 320.)

10 Can you use your skills to identify and respond to conflict when it challenges a relationship? (See *The Case of the Jousting Roommates*, page 322.)

KEY TERMS

Interpersonal conflict   *294*

Functional conflict   *295*

Dysfunctional conflict   *295*

Crazymaking behavior   *296*

Intrapersonal conflict   *298*

Shareable goal   *299*

Nonshareable goal   *299*

Low-intensity conflict   *299*

Medium-intensity
conflict   *299*

High-intensity conflict   *299*

Pseudoconflict   *301*

Content conflict   *301*

Value conflict   *301*

Ego conflict   *301*

Conflict resolution grid   *302*

Conflict styles   *302*

Avoiding style   *302*

Competitive style   *303*

Compromising style   *303*

Accommodative style   *303*

Collaborative style   *304*

Role reversal   *306*

DESC script   *307*

Nonassertive expression
style   *311*

Aggressive expression
style   *311*

Assertive expression
style   *313*

Social learning
theory   *317*

Online disinhibition
effect   *319*

STUDENT STUDY SITE

Visit the student study site at **www.sagepub.com/gambleic** to access the following materials:

- SAGE Journal Articles
- Videos
- Web Resources
- eFlashcards
- Web Quizzes
- Study Questions

To suggest that one simply starts a friendship, courtship, romantic partnership or marriage and "off it goes" is simple-minded. It is like believing that one can drive down the street merely by turning the ignition key, sitting back, and letting the car take care of itself.

—Steve Duck

RELATIONSHIP DYNAMICS

LEARNING OBJECTIVES

After completing this chapter, you should be able to demonstrate mastery of the following learning outcomes:

1. Discuss the functions relationships serve, identifying the characteristics that distinguish one relationship from another.

2. Use Rawlins's friendship model and Sternberg's triangle of love to explain the relationship spectrum, distinguishing among acquaintanceships, friendships, and romantic relationships.

3. Use Knapp and Vangelisti's relationship model to describe the stages a romantic relationship may pass through.

4. Describe the factors that influence interpersonal attraction.

5. Identify how culture, gender, the media, and technology influence relationship development.

6. Identify specific techniques that can facilitate our mastery of relationship dynamics.

Relationships fascinate us! The success of the *Real Housewives* franchise on the Bravo cable television network—including *The Real Housewives of New York*, *The Real Housewives of New Jersey*, *The Real Housewives of Beverly Hills*, *The Real Housewives of Atlanta*, and *The Real Housewives of Orange County*, just to name some of the *Real Housewives* genre offerings—attests to this; these shows are among the most highly rated programs on television. We avidly watch as the women featured on these shows and their spouses or significant others, assorted friends, and family members develop their relationships, experiencing relationship highs and lows. We observe as the characters figure out the ground rules for each relationship and make decisions whether to take a particular relationship to another level, to work through the relationship's challenges, or to terminate it.

In the second season of *The Real Housewives of Beverly Hills*, for example, one cast member, Taylor Armstrong, had to confront the unexpected death of her estranged husband, Russell. Prior to his apparent suicide, the marital troubles Russell and Taylor experienced provided much of the drama in the series' first season, as did the impending divorce of Camille Grammer from her now former husband, actor Kelsey Grammer.

Relationship dramas—both the ups and the downs—are at the heart of all the offerings in the *Real Housewives* franchise. Each program presents a case study focused on evolving relationship dynamics. We are privy to weddings, breakups, and squabbles among family members and friends. Some featured relationships fall apart quickly, others experience significant alternations, and a number are shown as just beginning. While some of the story lines are likely manufactured, they still afford us the chance to compare the dynamics of the relationships featured in them with our own—past and present. And as we revise our feelings toward the people in our lives with whom we share real relationships, how we feel about the characters on these shows also changes over time. And sometimes, as Andy Cohen, Bravo's senior vice president in charge of original programming and development notes, our greatest satisfaction comes when we think, "I would never do that!"[1]

> Each program presents a case study focused on evolving relationship dynamics. We are privy to weddings, breakups, and family and friend squabbles.

WHAT DO YOU KNOW?

Before continuing your reading of this chapter, which of the following five statements do you believe to be true and which do you believe to be false?

1. Happy people tend to live longer than unhappy people. T F

2. As time passes, passionate love increases. T F

3. "What's up?" is a question that opens a communication channel between two people. T F

4. By talking about *my* friends instead of *our* friends, partners are able to bond more easily. T F

5. Less talk about fewer topics increases a relationship's strength. T F

Read the chapter to discover if you're right or if you've made any erroneous assumptions.

ANSWERS: 1. T; 2. F; 3. T; 4. F; 5. F

Our happiness depends on our satisfaction with our relationships.

Relationships are the fabric of our lives. In fact, how happy we are depends on how satisfied we are with our relationships.[2] Whether we are friends or family, linked romantically or through our careers, relationships matter. As a foundation for a better understanding of the impacts of relationships, let us begin by clarifying what constitutes a relationship.

WHY DO WE NEED RELATIONSHIPS?

The term *relationship* refers to a wide array of social connections that to varying degrees meet your interpersonal needs. When we speak of interpersonal relationships we are concerned with the relationships we share with our parents, significant other, siblings, friends, employer or employees, physician, and instructors, among others. The kind of interpersonal communication you use when relating with another person reflects the nature, importance, and effectiveness of that particular relationship in your life.

The expectations we have for a relationship depend on its nature as well as on the specific needs we want it to fulfill. For example, we likely have different relational expectations for a doctor, a coworker, a friend, a lover, and a family member. As a result, we probably use different rules to guide our behavior in relating to each of them, and we measure each relationship's effectiveness according to somewhat different criteria that we establish based on our goals for the particular relationship.

Your goals for a relationship reflect the kind of interaction you expect to share. When interacting with a physician, for example, your goals are more than likely different from those you have when interacting with a friend. Your expectations for a work relationship are probably different from those for a romantic relationship. Despite this, however, you might see certain commonalities in the way you approach others and communicate during your interactions.

Relationships help meet personal needs and goals. Perhaps we are lonely and seek an outlet from our isolation. Maybe we feel a need to release pent-up tensions, discuss our interests, or share concerns and feelings. Perhaps we want to change another's beliefs or attitudes. Or maybe we aspire to learn more about ourselves. Whatever our personal reasons for reaching out to another human being, the desire to interact with and develop meaningful relationships lives in us all, helping to define our humanness. We need interpersonal contact to survive. Table 12.1 summarizes the key functions relationships serve.

RELATIONSHIPS PRESERVE HAPPINESS AND HEALTH

There is a correlation between happiness and relationship effectiveness. There is also a correlation between happiness and how long we live, with those who report feeling happy living up to 35 percent longer.[3] Unhappiness, which can be caused by problems such as depression, marital conflict, family violence, and job dissatisfaction, sometimes results from a lack of relational attention and poorly handled relationship problems.[4] Family, friends, and associates, however, can function as social support and help us get through the stresses and challenges of life events.

Relationships: Social connections, of many different kinds, that, to varying degrees, meet our interpersonal needs.

TABLE 12.1   Relationships Function to Help Us Meet Our Personal Goals

Relationships . . .
Preserve our happiness and health.
Prevent our isolation.
Meet our needs for inclusion, control, and affection.
Offer a point of reference we use in checking whether our behavior and emotional responses are culturally acceptable.
Function as a communication pipeline.
Maintain our sense of worth.

WHAT DO YOU KNOW?

True or False

1. *Happy people tend to live longer than unhappy people.*
True. Happy people live up to 35 percent longer than those who report being unhappy.

Not only do relationships help preserve our mental well-being, but they also affect us physically.[5] People involved in problematic relationships experience more medical problems than do those with better-functioning relationships.[6] The incidence of heart attacks and traffic accident injuries is higher among people whose relationships are failing than it is among those whose relationships are thriving.[7] Mortality rates, in fact, are higher for those whose social support systems are lacking, who do not feel part of a group or a family, or do not feel that they "fit in" somewhere.[8] Persons with terminal illnesses tend to die sooner if they have only a small group of friends rather than a large array of family members and friends on whom they can rely for support. Widowed men who do not remarry have higher mortality rates than those who do. The resilience of women also declines after a spouse's death. The immune systems of widows are weaker than those of their married counterparts. Lonely people die sooner and younger. This is more of a problem for men than for women because men usually have fewer close friendships.[9]

RELATIONSHIPS PREVENT ISOLATION

All of us need person-to-person contact. When cut off from others, we suffer. Even our dreams reflect our desire to end loneliness and feelings of isolation or estrangement. For example, hermits are prone to hallucinating that other people are present and speaking to them, the bereaved are apt to imagine their dead loved ones are there with them, and those who are incarcerated dream about meeting their family members, friends, and other people on the outside.[10] When our social surroundings fail to reflect our wishes, we try to manufacture situations that do reflect them, even if only subconsciously. Humans have the need to belong.[11]

RELATIONSHIPS MEET INTERPERSONAL NEEDS

A number of researchers have addressed the notion of interpersonal needs, among them William Schutz, the formulator of a three-dimensional theory of interpersonal behavior known as **fundamental interpersonal relations orientation** (FIRO), and Abraham Maslow, the creator of a well-known hierarchy of human needs.

We all need person-to-person contact. Without it, we feel lonely and isolated.

Fundamental interpersonal relations orientation: A three-dimensional theory of interpersonal behavior highlighting the needs for inclusion, control, and affection.

How much interest do you take in others? How would you describe your needs for inclusion?

According to Schutz, we meet three of our basic interpersonal needs through our relationships: inclusion, control, and affection. To various degrees, we have a need to include others and be included, to control others and be controlled, and to love others and be loved.[12] Thus, inclusion is about our perception of whether we are "in" or "out," control is concerned with whether we are "on the top" or "on the bottom," and affection measures how "close" we are to or how "far" we remain from another.[13] Let us see how these needs play out in our lives.

Inclusion relates to the extent to which we feel the need to establish and maintain a feeling of mutual interest with others—how much we take an interest in others, and vice versa. Most of us want to be included. We want others to acknowledge us and want to learn more about us. Some of us know what it feels like to be excluded— to be the last asked to join a team or work on a project, to be the last asked out, or to have to eat alone in the cafeteria because no one asks us to sit with him or her. When our **inclusion needs** goes unmet, we feel isolated and lonely; our health may even deteriorate. In contrast, when our inclusion needs are satisfied, we develop a sense of enhanced self-worth and feel fulfilled.

Control relates to our need to establish and maintain relationships that facilitate our experiencing satisfactory levels of influence and power. To varying degrees, we need to feel capable of having someone else in charge. We differ in how necessary it is for us to be a controlling or supporting player. When our **control needs** go unmet, we may conclude that others fail to value or respect our abilities and that, consequently, we are unable to make sound decisions, direct our future, or influence another's.

Affection relates to our need to give and receive love and to experience emotionally close (intimate) relationships. Should our **affection needs** go unfulfilled, we may feel unlovable and long for meaningful relationships that will keep us from being emotionally detached. In contrast, when our affection needs are met, we are comfortable sharing intimate and friendly relationships. Not every relationship develops into one based on love.

Typically, the need for inclusion impels us to build relationships. Once we do, these relationships also meet our control and affection needs. The extent to which we feel and are able to realize these needs varies. In fact, we can classify people according to their specific "need levels." If, for example, individuals rarely attempt to satisfy a specific need, we say their need level is deficient. On the other hand, if they are consumed with satisfying a specific need, we say their need level is excessive. People with a deficient need for inclusion are referred to as **undersocial**, those with a deficient need for affection are **underpersonal**, and persons with little need to control others are known as **abdicrats**. Those in whom these needs are excessive are referred to, respectively, as **oversocial**, **overpersonal**, and **autocrats**.

Individuals who are undersocial, for example, try to avoid interacting with others, preferring their privacy and alone time. Oversocial people, in contrast, continually seek to be with others. However, people in both sets, the undersocial and the oversocial, experience a similar fear of isolation. Equally afraid of being ignored or left out, they compensate for their fear using opposite strategies. The same holds true for individuals with deficient and excessive control needs. Abdicrats fear not being able to exert control, so they readily cede it; autocrats fear not having control, so they grab the reins of power. Finally, individuals

Inclusion need: The social need to feel a sense of belonging or mutual interest in relationship to others.

Control need: The need to establish and maintain relationships that allow one to experience satisfactory levels of influence and power.

Affection need: The need to give and receive love and to experience emotionally close relationships.

Undersocial: Having little need for inclusion.

Underpersonal: Having little need for affection.

Abdicrat: One who has little need to control another.

Overpersonal: Having an overriding need for affection.

Oversocial: Having an overriding need for inclusion.

Autocrat: One with a great need to control and dominate others.

who are underpersonal do their best to keep relationships superficial, while those who are overpersonal exhibit the opposite behavior—consistently trying to increase their closeness to others. Both sets of people, however, are motivated by the need for affection and a fear of being rejected.

Unlike people in the groups just described, many of us are quite satisfied with our relationships; we find our need levels fulfilled and express our needs comfortably and naturally. People in this group are described as *social* (comfortable with people or alone), *democratic* (willing to give or take orders depending on the situation), and *personal* (at ease sharing both close and distant relationships).

In contrast to Schutz, Abraham Maslow conceived of human needs as forming a pyramidal hierarchy, now known as **Maslow's needs hierarchy**, with our most basic needs located at or near the base and our higher-order needs closer to or at the apex (see Figure 12.1).[14] Viewed from a relational perspective, communication with others helps us meet our needs at each need level. Once our physiological and safety needs are met— the basic necessities of life (shelter, food, water, and safety), provided for us by family members or caregivers—we can move on to meeting our needs for belonging. These needs are usually satisfied through the attainment of a certain level of success in work, friendship, and love relationships and self-esteem. Ultimately, if we are fortunate, we find another who cares enough for us to help us in pursuit of realizing our full potential.

Figure 12.1 Maslow's Hierarchy of Needs

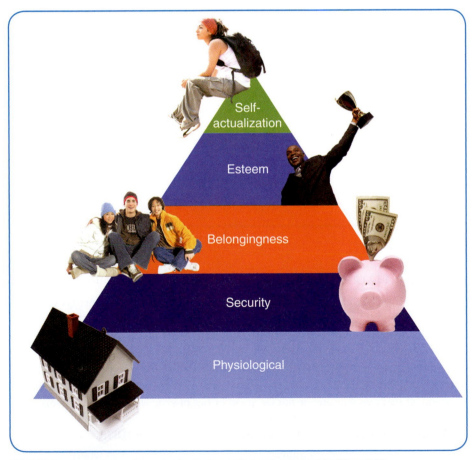

SOURCE: Abraham Maslow, *Toward a Psychology of Being*, New York: John Wiley, 1962.

Maslow's needs hierarchy: A five-level pyramidal hierarchy of human needs developed by Abraham Maslow.

What follows describes the "silencing" or isolation experienced by a cadet at the U.S. Military Academy at West Point. Consider how you would have responded if you were placed in a similar situation.

Upon hearing his name called, James J. Pelosi prepared himself for one last humiliating moment. As he approached the podium to accept his diploma, he expected to hear a chorus of boos. There were no boos, only silence. Upon returning to his seat, however, he was surprised by the handshakes he received from those around him. And this is how one of the strangest episodes in the history of the corps ended.

Why had James Pelosi expected to be booed by his peers? While a West Point cadet, Pelosi had been accused of cheating. Despite maintaining his innocence, he was convicted by the Honor Committee. Though his conviction was thrown out on appeal, Pelosi's punishment was not expunged. Even in the face of insufficient evidence to convict a person who stands accused of violating the Honor Code, the academy reserves the right to subject those it nonetheless believes guilty of a code violation to "the silencing." Thus, for his last two years at West Point, Pelosi was ostracized—virtually no one spoke a word to him. Most cadets are unable to withstand the pressure of such treatment and resign, but not James Pelosi. Steadfast in asserting his innocence and unwilling to bend under the punishment of having to live alone and eat every meal alone, of being repeatedly insulted and treated as if he didn't matter, and even though he lost twenty-six pounds, Pelosi persisted in continuing as a cadet.

Pelosi was among a handful of cadets who graduated after undergoing the silencing. When interviewed about the experience, he observed: "I've taken a psychology course and I know what isolation does to animals. No one at the Academy asks how it affects a person. Doesn't that seem strange?"

Answer these questions:

1. Would you have survived the treatment James Pelosi received? Why or why not?

2. How does Pelosi's experience compare with that of an individual bullied and/or taunted on the Internet by persons who urge others to ignore and ostracize her or him?

3. What role does resilience play in each of the preceding instances?

4. What steps would you advise others to take to cope with feelings of isolation?

SOURCES: For more detail, see "The Silencing," *Newsweek*, June 18, 1973, p. 42.

RELATIONSHIPS SERVE AS BEHAVIORAL ANCHORS

In addition to meeting our inclusion, control, and affection needs, relationships serve as points of reference for appropriate behavioral and emotional responses. They help us express grief, happiness, and a host of other feelings in culturally acceptable ways. By comparing how we react with how friends and family members react, and noting the common threads in our reactions, we become more comfortable and gain a greater sense of emotional stability. Thus, our contacts enable us to see how we stand in relationship to others and let us know whether or not we are in or out of sync with accepted norms.

RELATIONSHIPS FUNCTION AS COMMUNICATION CONDUITS

Relationships are a kind of communication pipeline; they are the places where communication about anything can occur. They give us the opportunity to talk about the

TRY THIS: *How Do You Feel about Being In/Out, Up/Down, or Close/Far?*

We frequently assume that others share with us the same needs for inclusion, control, and affection, but that may not necessarily be the case. First, answer the following questions. Then ask three men and three women from three different cultures to respond to the same questions.

1. How important is it to you to feel included as a part of a group?

_____ Extremely important

_____ Very important

_____ Neither important nor unimportant

_____ Very unimportnt

_____ Extremely unimportant

2. To what extent is your need to be included currently fulfilled?

_____ Totally fulfilled

_____ Very fulfilled

_____ Somewhat fulfilled

_____ Very unfulfilled

_____ Extremely unfulfilled

3. How important is it to you to be able to exert power and control in a relationship?

_____ Extremely important

_____ Very important

_____ Neither important nor unimportant

_____ Very unimportant

_____ Extremely unimportant

4. To what extent is your need to exert influence and power currently fulfilled?

_____ Totally fulfilled

_____ Very fulfilled

_____ Somewhat fulfilled

_____ Very unfulfilled

_____ Extremely unfulfilled

5. How important is it to you to be involved in a close or an intimate relationship—one based on love?

_____ Extremely important

_____ Very important

_____ Neither important nor unimportant

_____ Very unimportant

_____ Extremely unimportant

6. To what extent is your need for love fulfilled currently?

_____ Totally fulfilled

_____ Very fulfilled

_____ Somewhat fulfilled

_____ Very unfulfilled

_____ Extremely unfulfilled

To what degree do men and women from different cultures feel each need is important or unimportant, fulfilled or unfulfilled? Compare and contrast the need assessments of those whom you interviewed with your assessment of your own needs. What conclusions, if any, are you able to draw?

---

important and the trivial, the meaningful and the seemingly insignificant. They provide an audience for our self-disclosures. They provide the "someone" for us to talk to as we attempt to make sense of our life and experiences.

WHEN GOOD, RELATIONSHIPS HELP MAINTAIN OUR SENSE OF WORTH

To be sure, there are qualitative differences among our relationships. When healthy and functional, relationships enhance our sense of self. By supporting us, attending to us, and providing us with a sense of community, those with whom we share relationships help us preserve our self-esteem and opinions of our self-worth.

RELATIONSHIP CHARACTERISTICS

Various characteristics differentiate one relationship from another. We choose to spend more time with some people, perhaps because we have ties to them or they support our goals and are there for us when we need them. We distance ourselves from others, believing they may be threats to our well-being.

DURATION

How long did your longest relationship to date last? What about your shortest relationship to date? Why did one thrive while the other withered? Relational duration differs by relationship type. For example, you have known your mother from birth or since you were adopted. You may have known your best friend since you were five. Meaningful relationships require significant attention if they are to endure. In general, the stronger a relationship, the more time it has to develop and the longer it lasts.

Heavy-metal rocker Ozzy Osbourne has been married to music manager and television personality Sharon Osbourne for more than thirty years. How does that compare with your longest relationship to date?

CONTACT FREQUENCY

Duration and contact often go hand in hand. We are likely to engage in more frequent interaction with people to whom we are personally tied. The more frequent our contact, the greater our opportunity to understand one another and develop the ability to predict one another's behavior. Compare, for example, your ability to predict the behavior of a close friend with your ability to predict the behavior of an acquaintance. Probably because you and the close friend interact more frequently, you know that person better and thus are more accurate in predicting his or her behavior.

SHARING

The longer a relationship lasts, and the more frequent our contacts, the more information we are likely to share about ourselves. Usually this sharing of our innermost thoughts and feelings does not occur early in a relationship, but gradually, over a significant time.

SUPPORT

When we think about another person's needs and act to help meet those needs, we provide support. For instance, we may try to decrease the stress felt by another by helping him or her cope with problems or handle anxieties. We may also provide support for someone by alleviating his or her sense of isolation or loneliness and by being available to that person physically or emotionally whenever we are needed.

INTERACTION VARIABILITY

When the kinds of contacts we have with a single person vary, our relationship with him or her can be described as having greater breadth. For example, your authors work together writing books, socialize together, and live together. Thus, our interactions are characterized by greater variability than they would be if we were merely coauthors.

GOALS

We bring expectations and goals to our relationships. Often, for example, we expect those with whom we share relationships to be interested in us and in our welfare. We expect them to support us rather than to frustrate us, to help alleviate our fears rather than add to them. We expect significant others to be attentive and honest and to help us develop and understand ourselves. We also expect them to feel affection for us, to want to be with us, to enjoy our company, and, as we get closer, to want to share themselves with us.

WATCH THIS 12.1
For a video on supportive communication visit the student study site.

FORMING FRIENDSHIPS

We come into contact with many different people daily. Some of them we will never see again. Relationships with these people will never progress beyond the superficial; for all practical purposes, they will remain strangers to us.

Others we decide to get to know better. Some of these will become acquaintances; we will connect briefly when opportunities arise, but our interactions with them usually will be limited in quality and quantity. Typically, we simply drift away from each other. With others, however, we will develop long-lasting, meaningful friendships and/or romantic relationships. What are the forces that draw us toward some people and keep us together? What prevents us from developing relationships with others or ultimately pushes us apart?

It is impossible to have close relationships with everyone. We can characterize each of our relationships according to the amount and kind of closeness that we share. By exploring our different types of relationships, we can enrich our understanding of the nature of intimacy and the balance we strike between intimacy and distance with different people.[15]

THE NATURE OF INTIMACY

Intimacy is a measure of closeness.[16] Intimate closeness may involve physical contact, shared ideas and value principles, disclosure of emotional feelings, and participation in shared activities. While some **intimate relationships** exhibit all four qualities, others exhibit only one or two. The account of intimacy shared with acquaintances differs from the amount of intimacy shared with friends, which, in turn, differs from the amount of intimacy shared in romantic relationships.

Communication expectations for each type of relationship also differ. For example, we expect close friends and romantic partners to make more of an emotional investment toward understanding who we are than we would expect colleagues at work to exhibit. We count on the former group of people more and are more influenced by them, and we believe that others cannot easily replace their roles in our lives. (We discuss intimacy in greater detail in Chapter 13.)

THE NATURE OF ACQUAINTANCESHIP

Acquaintances are people we know, usually by name, with whom we converse when given the opportunity but with whom our interaction is typically limited in scope and quality. Unless we harbor a desire for more than acquaintanceship, rarely do we go out of our way to see an acquaintance, preferring to leave our meetings to chance.

Intimacy: A measure of closeness; sustained feelings of closeness and connection.

Intimate relationship: A relationship that involves a high degree of personal closeness or sharing.

Acquaintances: People one may know and converse with, but with whom one's interaction is typically limited in scope and quality.

TRY THIS: *Measuring Intimacy*

Think of five friends. Then locate each friend on the following relationship continuum according to the level of intimacy you share.

Names: _____

_____

_____

_____

_____

| (High) | 10 | 9 | 8 | 7 | 6 | 5 | 4 | 3 | 2 | 1 | (Low) |

Fill in each blank with as many of the five names as are applicable:

1. _____ and I reveal our deepest feelings and thoughts to each other.

2. _____ and I understand each other.

3. _____ and I rely on each other for help and support.

4. _____ and I trust each other.

5. _____ and I accept each other as we are.

6. _____ and I expect our relationship to last a long time.

7. _____ and I have a lot in common.

8. _____ and I enjoy doing things together.

9. _____ and I meet each other's needs.

10. _____ and I enjoy each other's company.

Based on your responses, with which person do you believe you share the most and the least intimacy? In most cases, the greater your interdependence with another, the more important and significant this person is in your life.

THE NATURE OF FRIENDSHIP

Over time, some acquaintanceships develop into **friendships**. Unlike acquaintances, friends voluntarily seek each other out, enjoy each other's company, and display a strong mutual regard. Friends accept each other, confide in each other, trust one another to keep confidences undisclosed, understand and provide emotional support to each other, share significant interests, and expect the relationship to endure.[17]

We are closer to some friends than we are to others. Our closest friends are those to whom we confide our innermost feelings and thoughts. We share a greater degree of intimacy with them, as evidenced by our willingness to become emotionally close to them. We also have the desire to continue learning more about them and sharing personal aspects of ourselves with them.

Friendship: A relationship between two people that involves the voluntary seeking out of one another and the displaying of a strong emotional regard for one another.

Friendships develop over time. Individuals who were once strangers can become intimate friends. As we progress from the initial stages of contact into a more planned but still casual friendship, we begin to increase our knowledge of and trust in each other, and both the depth and the breadth of the relationship increase. As our friendship intensifies, we are likely to become more "other-oriented," a quality we demonstrate by going out of our way for the other person, becoming more open and expressive toward and more accepting of one another.

Friendships are not only one-to-one experiences, however. Couples, not just individuals, also have friendships. In their book *Two Plus Two: Couples and Their Couple Friendships,* Geoffrey L. Greif and Kathleen Holtz Deal assert that couple relations are more complicated than one-to-one friendships. With a couple friendship, not only is there the couple-to-couple relationship involving all four people, but there are also the friendships that develop between the persons of the same and different genders. When you are part of a couple, being close with another couple and watching how they navigate their ups and downs can function as a model for how you might manage your relationship with your partner. When you see a partner interacting in ways another couple appreciates, you may also come to appreciate him or her more.[18]

Communication researcher and friendship expert W. K. Rawlins developed a six-stage model of friendship that provides a useful explanation of how this kind of relationship develops (see Table 12.2).[19] We discuss each of the six stages next.

Role-Limited Interaction. Friendships usually start with two people making limited initial contact in some context. For example, we might meet another at a sporting event, at work, in a restaurant, on a train, or in class. This initial meeting, or **role-limited interaction**, represents the first stage of friendship. During this stage, because we are unsure of how or if a relationship will develop, we relate somewhat tentatively. We possess little personal knowledge about each other, and we are reluctant to reveal personal information. We rely on polite exchanges, stereotypes of social roles, and standard scripts in our initial conversations.

The Big Bang Theory centers on the friendships and romances of physicists Sheldon Cooper (Jim Parsons, lower center) and Leonard Hofstadter (Johnny Galecki, top center). In one episode, Sheldon tries to overcome his poor social skills by employing a scientific approach to making friends: the "Friendship Algorithm."

TABLE 12.2 Models of Friendship and Relationships

Rawlins's Six-Stage Model of Friendship	Knapp and Vangelisti's Ten-Stage Model of Relationships
Role-limited interaction	Initiating
Friendly relations Moving toward friendship	Experimenting
Nascent friendship	Intensifying
Stabilized friendship	Integrating Bonding
Waning friendship	Differentiating Circumscribing Stagnating Avoiding Terminating

Role-limited interaction: An early stage of friendship characterized by a reliance on polite exchanges and standard scripts.

In a stable friendship, we trust each other and act in ways that confirm our trustworthiness.

Friendly Relations. During the next stage, we progress to **friendly relations**, in which we continue the effort to determine whether we have enough in common to continue building a relationship. We increase the amount of small talk as we test the waters to see whether interest in interacting is reciprocated. We become somewhat less guarded, a bit more openly expressive, and more interested in having the other respond to our overtures.

Moving toward Friendship. As our desire to be **moving toward friendship** increases, we cautiously step beyond conventional social rules and role playing, making small disclosures to demonstrate that we would like to expand our friendship. We invite the other to spend time voluntarily with us in a context outside the naturally occurring one we have shared to this point. We might, for example, ask a classmate if she would like to study with us, or ask someone we work with if he would like to stop at a coffee shop with us on the way home; we might even ask the person to join us at a party or to see a movie. Once we have the opportunity to interact more personally, naturally, and in a more relaxed setting, we may also reveal our attitudes, beliefs, and values to each other.

Nascent Friendship. As our moves toward friendship are reciprocated, we begin to consider ourselves friends. At this point, **nascent friendship**, significant changes in how we communicate with one another occur. We augment the social stereotypes and standards that once regulated our interactions and begin working out our own rules. We may, for instance, opt to get together to play tennis every Thursday afternoon, go to a movie Friday night, or have dinner together some Sundays. We select the activities we will do together, and our interactions become more regularized or patterned.

Stabilized Friendship. Once it is apparent that friendship will continue and we can count on each other to be there, we enter into a stage of **stabilized friendship**. We trust each other and respond to each other in ways that confirm our trustworthiness. We interact more frequently and across a greater number of settings; we give each other emotional support, share more intimate information, and reveal fears or vulnerabilities we keep secret from most others. We expect our friendship to continue.

Waning Friendship. Friendships do not maintain themselves. We need to work at them. Once we take a friendship for granted, or make less of a personal effort or investment to keep it going, we may find ourselves in the **waning friendship** stage. Why do once good friends drift apart? Sometimes, life circumstances, including interests, careers, or personal or family obligations, change. Such changes can alter friendship needs as individuals begin to participate in new activities and find new interests. In other cases, trust is violated or unspoken rules are broken, causing individuals to become less willing to disclose or to be more protective of personal information. Such feelings may also arise because one person habitually misbehaves by criticizing the other person, engages in binge drinking, is not forthcoming with support, or actively dislikes the other person's other friends or romantic partners. Sometimes friendships wane because people simply tire of or become bored with

Friendly relations: A phase of friendship during which an effort to preserve and strengthen the friendship is made if the parties have enough in common to build a relationship.

Moving toward friendship: The point in friendship formation when the parties make small disclosures in an effort to expand their relationship.

Nascent friendship: The stage in the development of friendship during which rules for regulating interaction are worked out.

Stabilized friendship: A stage in friendship development during which the parties behave as if they expect their friendship to continue for a long time.

Waning friendship: The stage in friendship development during with the parties drift apart.

each other; when this happens the friendship is likely to dissolve. Having run its course, it simply ends.[20]

But how do you end a friendship? How do you ultimately tell a once good friend that it's over? Some people just stop calling or are always too busy to get together, hoping their friend will eventually get the hint. Others fail to return texts. Facebook has normalized the practice of defriending, which allows you to remove a friend as you would a wrong word—with the click of a mouse. Not only is the person then out of your life, but so are all of his or her photos and status updates. Ending a friendship shares some similarities with divorce—some endings leave lasting resentments, but other friendships terminate without ill will, leaving open the possibility that at some point in the future you just might "friend" one another again—if only on Facebook.[21]

A little later in this chapter we will use Mark Knapp and Anita Vangelisti's ten-stage model of relationship formation (see Figure 12.3) to help us understand romantic relationships. Like friendships, romantic relationships develop in stages based on each party's perception of the amount of self-disclosing occurring and the kind of intimacy shared. For now, notice in Table 12.2 how the six friendship stages in Rawlins's friendship model correspond to the steps in Knapp and Vangelisti's ten-stage model.

ROMANCE: COMING TOGETHER AND BREAKING APART

The love we feel for the person we have a **romantic relationship** with is different from our love for friends or family. Even though approximately 50 percent of all marriages in the United States end in divorce, when we enter into marriage, typically we expect it to be permanent, and that expectation of permanence, at least in part, distinguishes a romantic relationship from others.

LOVE'S DIMENSIONS

Love has different dimensions. We can, for example, view it as passionate or as companionate. What's the difference? **Passionate love** is what we feel when we first fall in love; it signals our attraction for and focus on a single person. While some manage to sustain passionate love over a lifetime, it often decreases in intensity over time.[22] In contrast, **companionate love** increases over time. As a couple's feelings of trust and caring for one another grow, they engage themselves in one another's lives and mutually respond to one another's needs.

An alternative means of looking at types of love is attributed to sociologist John Alan Lee, who differentiated romantic relationships from nonromantic ones by describing them according to whether they are based primarily on *eros, ludis, storge, mania, pragma,* or *agape.*[23] The type of love experienced reveals the nature of the relationship shared. *Eros* (erotic love) is sexual love that brings couples together. *Ludis* is more like the game of love; partners seek affection and immediate gratification, but they don't see their relationship as lasting. They simply enjoy the idea of being in love. *Storge,* in contrast, is the kind of love we have for good friends and family members. It does not involve sex at all, though at one time or another we may find ourselves feeling sexual attraction. *Mania* is more like obsessive love, with a partner experiencing frequent relationship highs and lows because of his or her unyielding need for attention and/or low self-esteem. *Pragma* derives from the word *pragmatic*; arranged marriages, for example, are often planned for pragmatic

Figure 12.2 The Triangle of Love

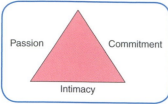

Commitment: The intention to remain in a relationship even if trouble occurs.

Passion: Intensely positive feelings of attraction that motivate one person to want to be with another.

Triangular theory of love: A theory developed by Robert Sternberg that states that varying combinations of intimacy, passion, and commitment create different types of love.

Manifest intimacy: Feelings of closeness and connection that are apparent to others.

Latent intimacy: Feelings of intimacy or connection not directly apparent to others.

Knapp and Vangelisti's ten-stage model of relationships: A model of relational development and deterioration created by Mark L. Knapp and Anita L. Vangelisti.

Relational culture: The ways in which the parties to a relationship work out the rules or routines of the relationship.

Relationship stages: Points used to characterize the nature of a relationship at any particular moment in its evolution.

reasons. *Agape* love has a spiritual quality, often being described as a love that is pure. One person devotes him- or herself to another but expects nothing in return. A minister and a congregation or a parent and a child are said to experience such love. Differentiating one type of love from another in this way makes love's many aspects clear.

THE TRIANGLE OF LOVE

What other characteristics differentiate romantic relationships? Researchers have concluded that the ingredients necessary for building a romantic love-based relationship are **commitment**, or an intention to remain in the relationship even if trouble occurs; **passion**, or intensely positive feelings of attraction that motivate each partner to want to be with the other person; and intimacy, or sustained feelings of closeness and connection.[24] According to Robert Sternberg's **triangular theory of love**, varying combinations of intimacy, passion, and commitment create different types of love (see Figure 12.2).[25] Every love relationship, says Sternberg, has these three elements in various amounts. For some couples intimacy dominates, with commitment and passion playing supporting roles. For others, little commitment to the relationship exists, but there is an abundance of passion and intimacy.

Sternberg asserts that intimacy, often the most central component within a love relationship, is the variable providing the foundation for love's development. It remains relatively stable over a relationship's course—or at least until the relationship partners no longer find the relationship satisfying and no longer feel emotionally close. Think of the warm and affectionate feelings you get when hugging someone you love. You feel close and connected. This is **manifest intimacy**. But we can also experience feelings of intimacy or connection that are not directly apparent to others; this is **latent intimacy**.

Passion, according to Sternberg, is love's "hot" component. Included in passion are sexual attraction and arousal, as well as motivation. Passion is the variable most important at the beginning of a love relationship, since it functions as an initial attractor. This does not mean that long-term relationships lack passion; rather, in developed relationships passion tends to occur in "sparks and spurts" rather than at a sustained high level.

The third component in Sternberg's love triangle is the "cooler" variable of commitment. A decision to love someone requires a commitment to maintain and sustain that love. Because commitment is based on decision making, it is the most stable component in the triangle and is the strongest predictor of relational satisfaction. Although any one element can exist without the others, all three are necessary for a romantic relationship and consummate love to exist.

LOVE'S STAGES

Knapp and Vangelisti's ten-stage model of relationships suggests that we perceive our relationships, including our romantic relationships, as escalating/intensifying, stabilizing, or deteriorating/atrophying over time as we grow closer and more intimate, become exceedingly comfortable with our **relational culture**—the rules or routines we have worked out for our relationship—or grow more distant or apart from each other. According to Knapp and Vangelisti, our relationships are in a constant state of flux: they grow either stronger or weaker with time. As they strengthen or weaken, they pass through some or all of the ten **relationship stages** they identify in their model and that we can use to characterize the nature of a relationship at any particular moment in its evolution (see Figure 12.3).[26] As you read about these stages, consider how, without

Figure 12.3 Relationship Stages

5 Bonding
4 Integrating
3 Intensifying
2 Experimenting
1 Initiating
6 Differentiating
7 Circumscribing
8 Stagnating
9 Avoiding
10 Terminating

True or False

3. *"What's up?" is a question that opens a communication channel between two people.*
True. Asking a question such as "What's up?" functions as a conversation opener.

labeling it either good or bad, you would describe a romantic relationship you are in currently.

Stage 1: Initiating. During the **initiating stage** of a relationship, we ask ourselves whether someone is appealing enough for us to initiate interaction with him or her. If the answer is yes, we display our interest in making contact and attempt to show why this person would, in turn, enjoy interacting with us. In other words, we do what we can to make the person perceive us as likable and friendly.

While in the past most love connections began with potential partners face-to-face, in increasing numbers, romantic relationships are initiating online—with many individuals relying on couple-matching websites to select their dating partners.

Communication during this phase is typically brief and formularized or ritualistic. We greet one another with a handshake, engage in phatic communication—superficial, casual interaction designed simply to open the channel between us, using such greetings as "How are you doing?" or "What's up?"—and search for an appropriate conversation opener, often opting to talk about an insignificant topic such as the weather, just so that contact will continue. Our goal is to make establishing a relationship possible. At the same time, we begin forming judgments about one another.

Stage 2: Experimenting. Once contact is initiated, we enter the **experimenting stage**. In this stage the objective is to determine if the relationship is worth pursuing. We want to reduce our uncertainty about each other. Researchers even call the theory that describes our thirst for acquiring information about another person *uncertainty reduction*.[27] As this theory explains, our goal during this phase is to learn enough about one another so that communication between us becomes predictable and understandable. As uncertainty dissipates we are better able to consider continuing a relationship.

At this stage, we keep our interaction casual—engaging in casual dating—as we probe the unknown in the effort to find out more. During our search for common ground, we use cultural, sociological, and psychological information to decide whether or not to continue interacting. We also are likely to engage in small talk about a wide variety of subjects, such as movies and television shows, books we are reading, courses we are taking, where we live, and our hobbies. In effect, we "audition for friendship."[28] During this process we may also discover possible areas for more meaningful conversation.

Initiating stage: The first phase in relational development, during which two individuals express interest in each other.

Experimenting stage: An early relational development phase during which the parties search for common ground.

Intensifying stage: A phase of relational development during which the amount of contact and self-disclosure the parties have increases.

Stage 3: Intensifying. As we become closer, our relationship enters the **intensifying stage**, with the amount of information we disclose to each other increasing. We talk about more serious ideas, share secrets, become better at predicting each other's behavior, use nicknames or affectionate expressions when conversing, and adopt similar postures or clothing styles. As our relationship increases in intimacy, we disclose much more personal information, increasing our personal vulnerability. Also during this stage, we begin to transform from individual "I"s into a "we."

Stage 4: Integrating. During the **integrating stage**, we become a couple; others perceive us as a "pair," a "package," or a "social unit," as the fusion of one "I" and another "I" is more fully realized. Our **interpersonal synchrony** also increases as we exhibit similar preferences for modes of dress; we act, speak, and think more alike; and we accelerate our level of sharing—of relaxation time, a car, even a bank account. As a result of the relationship's strengthening, we develop an even greater understanding and knowledge of each other, expect more from one another, and interact together in a wider array of settings.[29]

Stage 5: Bonding. In the **bonding stage**, we announce our commitment to each other in a public ritual that also lets the world in on the exclusiveness of our relationship. Our relationship is now formally recognized by such means as a wedding license or a prenuptial agreement. It begins to take on a new character, now guided by specific rules and regulations established by custom or law. Sometimes such a change causes us initial discomfort or feelings of rebellion as we adjust to it. The public ritual represented by marriage has taken on added significance in recent years across the United States as individual states have taken stances for or against same-sex marriage; individuals who support marriage equality for LGBT Americans argue that the civil unions available to them do not represent a formal bond equal in status to that of a marriage license.

Stage 6: Differentiating. The **differentiating stage** finds one of more partners attempting to reestablish or regain a sense of unique identity. Instead of continuing as a "we," we ask, "How do I differ from you?" In this way, we try to reassert an "I" orientation; individual differences, not similarities, become our focus.

As we differentiate ourselves, we may find ourselves experiencing more relational fights or conflicts.[30] We reindividualize joint possessions; "*our* friends" reverts to "*my* friends," "*our* bedroom" becomes "*my* bedroom," and "*our* children" become "*your* children" or "*my* children," depending on whether they have been bad or good.

Recognizing that differences exist between people who have bonded is not unusual as partners strive to regain some privacy or determine how to preserve commitment while allowing for independence. If we can't resolve our differences, however, and stresses persist, it may signal that the process of uncoupling is under way.

Stage 7: Circumscribing. The **circumscribing stage** finds the relationship continuing its deterioration; as a result, the parties constrict their communication, both in amount (they talk less about fewer topics) and in quality (they reveal less about feelings). They consciously try to limit subjects of discussion to those considered "safe." Questionable or sensitive areas are considered taboo and avoided. Phrases such as "Let's not talk about that," "That's not your concern," and "Let's just focus on . . ." are typical during this stage. As a result, interaction becomes more superficial; conversations have little if any depth, since

Marriage is a public ritual that confirms a relationship's exclusiveness.

Integrating stage: A phase of relational development in which the identities of the parties begin to merge.

Interpersonal synchrony: The exhibition of similarities; the interpersonal fusion of two individuals.

Bonding stage: A stage of relational development during which the parties symbolically demonstrate for others that their relationship exists.

Differentiating stage: A phase of relational development in which the parties reestablish their individual personal identities.

Circumscribing stage: A phase of relational development during which the partners start to lessen their degree of contact with each other and commitment to each other.

exchanging meaningful information and revealing intimate disclosures is absent. In effect, the parties are withdrawing both physically and mentally from the relationship.[31] They talk to each other only when they have to, no longer because they want to. The relationship suffers from fatigue; it exhausts them.

Stage 8: Stagnating. Relationships in the **stagnating stage** do not continue developing. Instead, they are virtually motionless—they stagnate. Communication between the parties is at a virtual standstill. Although the two may still share a common space, they no longer share each other. They feel that since there is no reason to talk with each other, they might as well say nothing. They close themselves off. In sum, their enthusiasm for maintaining the relationship is lost. The relationship is a shell of its former self. Exchanges feel strange and awkward. Conversation becomes stilted. The parties stiffen in each other's presence. The former partners perceive one another as strangers.

Stage 9: Avoiding. The **avoiding stage** has the partners closing communication channels. Because of the desire to stay away from each other, the parties take whatever steps are

Stagnating stage: A stage of relational development characterized by one person's decreasing interest in the other.

Avoiding stage: The stage of a relationship during which channels are closed as the parties attempt to refrain from contact with one another.

necessary to ensure they will not have to relate in any way. They do what they can to avoid coming together, since they know that getting together will be unpleasant and antagonistic. The running theme of this stage is "I don't want to see you anymore; I don't want to speak to you anymore; I don't want to continue the relationship." The relationship's end is in sight.

Stage 10: Terminating. The **terminating stage** finds the ties that once held the relationship together in shreds. The relationship is over. Depending on how both parties feel about the ending, this stage can be short-lived or prolonged, cordial or bitter. It may occur soon after the relationship's start or years later. Of course, both parties in a relationship may not necessarily move through all ten relationship stages at the same pace, and hence a partner who wants out often finds that the other person doesn't—at least not yet.

While there is an emotional component to ending a relationship, people say good-bye in different ways depending on how strong the emotional connection still is. If the emotional connection has been severed, for example, some do it with a note or a Facebook post, others with a text or over the phone, and still others in person or with a legal notice. While some couples who end a relationship remain friends, others expect—and want—never to speak to or see each other gain. While some are grateful for the good times they had together, others resent being replaced by another person. All relationships are terminated eventually by death; that does not mean, however, that saying good-bye comes easily or is pleasant. (We discuss death and grieving in Chapter 13.)

Not every relationship goes through each of these ten stages. Many never move beyond the experimenting stage, while others stabilize or are maintained at the intensifying stage, the bonding stage, or another stage. Stabilization occurs at the level both parties agree is satisfying and meets their needs. It is also possible not to proceed through the stages sequentially, but to skip one or more, jumping ahead toward greater intimacy or backward toward less. It is when partners are at odds regarding the optimum point for relationship stabilization that difficulties may develop.

Relationships often progress and retreat through the ten stages. We may advance in a relationship only to discover that we were more comfortable interacting at a more superficial level. Our relationships also grow and ebb at different rates. While some take a long time to deepen, others, especially those in which we perceive that we have little time to get to know one another, develop at a faster pace. The rate at which we grow toward or away from another depends on our individual needs and desires.

As we see, love relationships evolve. Typical romances today may involve such phases as "going out" when a teenager, "hooking up" or having a "friend with benefits" when a college student, seriously dating but delaying commitment when in your twenties, and marrying somewhere around thirty. Many people spend significant periods of their adult lives in committed relationships, but not necessarily married. Thus, we now also have different love relationship categories, such as the following: stay-over relationships, which are committed, monogamous partnerships, common among college students, that the parties find comfortable and convenient but do not call upon them to give up their independence; LAT (living apart together) relationships, which are committed relationships in which the parties maintain separate residences, common among those who are divorced and don't want to uproot their children or themselves; and LTA (living together apart) relationships, in which the parties have children together and continue

WHAT DO YOU KNOW?

True or False

4. *By talking about my friends instead of our friends, partners are able to bond more easily.*

False. By talking about my friends instead of our friends, partners enter the differentiating stage of their relationship.

Terminating stage: The stage of relational development during which the parties decide the relationship is over.

to cohabit even though their love connection is over, so that they can share parenting responsibilities and resources.[32]

Whatever the nature or status of a love relationship, romantic attraction probably played a role initially. We had to decide whether to pursue a relationship and came to a preliminary conclusion that our choice was acceptable—there was something about the other person that attracted us.

RELATIONSHIP ATTRACTORS

How do we decide whom we would like to meet or get to know better? Until we actually establish contact with someone, we cannot have a relationship. To be sure, typically we will not start a relationship with someone who turns us off. So, what is it that makes us want to keep our distance from some of the people we meet? What causes us to decide *not* to try to get closer? According to a survey of singles in America conducted for the dating website Match.com, the top five relationship turnoffs are having a disheveled or unclean appearance, appearing lazy, being too needy, lacking a sense of humor, and distance—that is, living more than three hours apart.[33]

That said, how do we identify those forces that do make us want to get to know some of the "strangers" we meet a lot better? When it comes to choosing the people with whom we *will* develop relationships, interpersonal attraction plays a key role. In fact, interpersonal attraction is the main reason we initiate contacts that we hope will develop into more meaningful relationships.

As you read about attraction, however, keep these points is mind: (1) Attraction is not necessarily mutual; we may find ourselves drawn to someone who does not reciprocate our feelings. (2) Attraction is not necessarily long-lived; we may discover that we were wrong about the qualities we thought another person possessed, or we may discover that the qualities that drew us toward him or her were unable to sustain our relationship. As interpersonal theorist Steve Duck notes, "When the attraction stage goes badly, then the rest of the potential relationship never materializes."[34]

WHAT DO YOU KNOW?

True or False
5. *Less talk about fewer topics increases a relationship's strength.*
False. Less talk about fewer topics is a sign of a deteriorating relationship.

The amount of attraction we feel for another depends on the nature of our relationship. We feel differently about our casual friends and our best friends, as we do about someone we hardly know and someone with whom we would like to be or have been intimate. Intimacy and attraction correlate positively. We are likely to be highly attracted to someone with whom we have become extremely close. As our relationship changes, so do our feelings of attraction.

Researchers identify a number of variables that influence how attracted or drawn we feel to another. Included among these are physical attractiveness, social attractiveness, task attractiveness, proximity, reinforcement, similarity, and complementarity (see Table 12.3).

TABLE 12.3 Relationship Attractors

Physical attractiveness	Physical appeal can lead to the initiation of a relationship.
Social attractiveness	Personality and demeanor can be engaging.
Task attractiveness	When we enjoy working together, we seek more interpersonal contact.
Proximity	We are apt to enjoy interacting with people who work or live near us.
Reinforcement	We tend to persist in interacting with people whose company we find personally rewarding.
Similarity	We are apt to like people whose way of thinking resembles our own.
Complementarity	We find ourselves attracted to people who are different from us but whose personalities complement ours in some way.

PHYSICAL ATTRACTIVENESS

Physical attractiveness serves as one of the main components we use to determine whom we want to interact with. How someone looks—whether it's the person's eyes, clothing, body shape, or some other aspect of appearance—determines whether or not we will find ourselves drawn to that person. For the most part, we prefer to initiate relationships with those we find physically appealing. Of course, there is no one universal standard of what an "attractive person" looks like. Cultural norms determine physical attractiveness factors. In many cultures, men judge physical attractiveness as more important in a partner than do women. In Japan, for example, diminutive females are judged to be the most attractive, whereas American males tend to prefer tall, slender women.[35] Of course, the mainstream media, via images in advertising, television programs, and films, convey standards and expectations of physical attractiveness as well.

SOCIAL ATTRACTIVENESS

We also consider a person's **social attractiveness**. Why do we desire to have a relationship with someone we judge to be socially attractive? From our vantage point, such a person possesses the kind of personality or interpersonal demeanor we admire. We simply feel comfortable interacting with him or her. Again, what is considered socially attractive varies among cultures. Asian men, for example, are said to find themselves attracted to women who appear introverted, gentle, or acquiescent.[36] Perceptions of physical attractiveness correlate with favorable personality attributions such as kindness, warmth, and intelligence.[37]

Physical attractiveness: Appeal based on physical qualities, which may lead to the initiation of a relationship.

Social attractiveness: Appeal based on an engaging personality and demeanor.

Even the most charming person may not inspire romantic desire in us. So, what is that causes us to come to think romantically about someone? While it is likely that the characteristics important to each of us in a romantic partner differ, research suggests that there is match between our ideal partner preferences and the process of initiating and maintaining a romantic relationship. In general, whether we have not yet met the person face-to-face or actually are in a relationship with a partner, if there is a match between our ideals and the traits we perceive that potential partner to have, a positive outcome for the relationship is likely.

What characteristics are most important to you in a romantic partner? With these traits in mind, how does either your current or a prospective partner measure up? For instance, how important to you are a partner's physical attractiveness, earning prospects, and warm characteristics?

Researchers have also used the nine-point agreement scales below to help in gauging romantic interest. You can use them now to express your romantic interest in either a current or a desired partner. Score your response to each statement with the number that represents your agreement level.

Agree   ___   ___   ___   ___   ___   ___   ___   Disagree

1   2   3   4   5   6   7   8   9

Passion

1. I feel a great deal of sexual desire for _____.
2. _____ is the only person I want to be romantically involved with.
3. _____ always seems to be on my mind.

Bondedness

1. It is important to me to see or talk to _____ regularly.
2. _____ is the first person I'd turn to if I had a problem.
3. If I achieved something good, _____ is the person I would tell first.
4. When I am away from _____, I feel down.

Desirability Alternatives

1. The people other than _____ with whom I might become involved are very appealing.
2. If I weren't dating _____ I would do fine; I would find another appealing person to date.

Relationship Satisfaction

1. I feel satisfied with my relationship with _____.
2. My relationship with _____ is close to ideal.
3. I want my relationship with _____ to last a very long time.
4. _____ is exactly the kind of person I would like to marry.
5. I intend to marry _____.
6. If _____ were to ask me to marry him/her tomorrow, I would say yes.

The lower your score, the greater your romantic interest.

SOURCE: Paul W. Eastwick, Eli J. Finkel, and Alice H. Eagly, "When and Why Do Ideal Partner Preferences Affect the Process of Initiating and Maintaining Romantic Relationships?," *Journal of Personality and Social Psychology,* 101, 2011, p. 1012–1032; and Ellen Berscheid and Pamela Regan, *The Psychology of Interpersonal Relationships,* Upper Saddle River, NJ: Prentice Hall, 2005.

Interpersonal attraction plays a key role in relationship development.

TASK ATTRACTIVENESS

Task attractiveness is another factor in whether or not we seek another's company. If we enjoy working with someone, we are apt to want to have more contact with him or her. We value the person's presence not just because he or she is adept at doing a job or enhances our productivity, but also because we find him or her engaging and want to sustain the interaction. As a result, what starts off solely as a business relationship may in time develop into a friendship.

PROXIMITY

If you think about those people with whom you enjoy interacting, you may find that for the most part they are individuals who work or live near you. **Proximity**, or physical nearness, influences attraction. Simply living or working in the same area increases opportunities to interact, share experiences, and form attachments. Common sense tells us that we are more apt to interact with people we see frequently. The more we interact, the more familiar we become, and the greater our chances of discovering other areas of common interest that could further increase a person's attractiveness in our eyes. Thus, the closer two people are geographically, the more likely it is they will be attracted to each other and develop an intimate relationship.

This is not to say that familiarity cannot also breed contempt. In fact, sometimes it does. According to researchers Ellen Berscheid and Elaine Hatfield Walster, the more closely people live, the greater the likelihood that they can come to dislike each other. Berscheid and Walster note, "While propinquity (or nearness) may be a necessary condition for attraction, it probably is also a necessary condition for hatred."[38] To what extent, if any, have your experiences revealed the truth of this claim?

REINFORCEMENT

Another factor influencing interpersonal attraction is **reinforcement**. We enjoy sustaining contacts that are rewarding, and we refrain from maintaining those we judge punishing. Consequently, all things being equal, we enjoy being in personally rewarding relationships. We like people who praise us more than those who criticize us. We are more attracted to individuals who like us than we are to those who dislike us. We seek to be in the company of people who cooperate with us more than we want to be among those who compete with or oppose us. But as is so often the case, too much of a good thing can backfire. Too much reinforcement can make us question another's sincerity or motivation. If someone becomes overzealous in praising us or disingenuously fawns over us, we begin to wonder what he or she really wants. As psychologist Elliot Aronson cautions, "We like people whose behavior provides us with maximum reward at minimum cost."[39] In other words, we are attracted to those with whom we can share a relationship that has few negative aspects or costs yet yields numerous incentives. When the opposite is true—that is, when the costs of a relationship outweigh its positive aspects or rewards—we tend to find the relationship unattractive.[40]

Task attractiveness: Appeal based in pleasure in working with another, which may lead one party to seek increased interpersonal contact with the other.

Proximity: Physical nearness.

Reinforcement: Behavior that is personally rewarding.

SIMILARITY

In general, we find ourselves attracted to people whose appearance, behavior, values, attitudes, experiences, beliefs, ideas, and interests are similar to ours, and who like and dislike the same things we do. Typically, we like people whose way of thinking resembles our own, more than we like those who disagree with us, especially when the issue under consideration is important to us. In fact, the more salient the issue, the more important being similar becomes. **Similarity** presents us with "social validation": it provides us with the input we need to confirm the "correctness" of a stance we have taken.

We also expect people with attitudes similar to ours to like us more than would those whose attitudes differ substantially from ours. By associating with and establishing relationships with people we perceive to be most like us, we play it safe. In fact, according to the **matching hypothesis** developed by Elaine Hatfield Walster and her colleagues, although you may be attracted to the most physically attractive people, you will most likely date and enter into a long-term relationship with someone similar to yourself in physical attractiveness.[41] The same holds true for those who hold ideas similar to ours; our attraction for each other tends to grow. We become "peas in a pod."

Similarity influences attraction. Do you date someone similar to you in attractiveness?

COMPLEMENTARITY

Not all research suggests that we develop relationships only with those who are like us. The variable of **complementarity** suggests that opposites attract. At times, instead of falling for someone who is our replica, we find ourselves attracted to someone very different. It may be because he or she exhibits one or more characteristics we admire but do not possess. Thus, an introverted person might be attracted to someone who is extroverted, or a submissive person might be interested in finding a dominant partner. You may enjoy conversing with someone whose position on an issue is diametrically opposed to yours. Interacting with our "opposites" can help us learn different ways of thinking. Opposites can be attracted to each other—just not as commonly or as easily as people who are more alike.

While each of the characteristics described above plays its part in our choice of a romantic partner, what we find attractive in a potential partner leads us to desire that person in particular. Which characteristic(s) drew you to your partner?

Recently, some airlines began allowing passengers to select their seatmates based on the perusal of information uploaded from fellow travelers' Facebook or LinkedIn profiles.[42] That way they can try to sit next to someone who seems interesting to them. The airlines call this "social seating." What would you look for in a potential seatmate? Do you think having such profiles available would improve your chances of meeting someone with whom you would not only like to begin a relationship but also continue to interact after landing? Why or why not?

Similarity: A like way of thinking between two people that results in attraction or social validation.

Matching hypothesis: The theory that we enter into a long-term relationship with someone similar to ourselves in physical attractiveness.

Complementarity: Attraction to a person who is different from oneself.

TRY THIS: *Attractors*

Whom are you attracted to? Use the rating scale below to identify why you find yourself attracted to a friend, a coworker, and a past or present romantic partner by placing one name in each blank and answering the questions with each of these persons in mind. Try to identify what dimensions your attraction for each of your chosen subjects is based on. For example, are you attracted because of physical, social, task, and/or other dimensions?

For each question, use this scale to make your ratings:

Agree				Disagree
1	2	3	4	5

1. I think _____ is particularly pretty or handsome.

2. I find _____'s looks appealing in whatever s/he wears.

3. I find spending time with _____ fun.

4. _____ fits in well with my friends.

5. I have confidence in _____'s ability to get a job done.

6. I believe _____ is an asset in most work situations.

7. I find living near _____ makes it easy for us to get together.

8. Living near _____ has made me like him/her more.

9. _____ makes me feel good about myself.

10. I really think that _____ likes me.

11. I have a lot in common with _____.

12. _____ and I have similar attitudes on important issues.

13. _____ and I are like night and day.

14. _____ helps me learn new ways of thinking.

To what extent, if any, is your attraction for each person based exclusively on one category? To what extent, if any, is it based on an amalgam of factors? How does the nature of your attraction for each of these persons influence the kind of relationship you share? Explain.

SOURCE: See C. H. Tardy, ed., *A Handbook for the Study of Human Communication: Methods for Observing, Measuring, and Assessing Communication Processes*, Norwood, NJ: Ablex, 1988.

CULTURE AND CONNECTION

Culture influences how and with whom we form relationships. Although we all have a need to make contact and connect with others, culture leads us to do these things in different ways. Culture even guides us in deciding whether to speak to strangers. Similarly, it teaches us how to spend our time and what to value. For instance, whereas some cultures value work as an end (Japan, for example), other cultures perceive work as a means to an end (Mexico, for example).[43]

Culture also guides us in understanding relationship customs and practices globally. For example, how we define who is a "stranger" reveals some of the challenges we face in interacting with persons from diverse cultures. In cultures that promote individualistic values, the concept of the stranger is easier to penetrate than it is in cultures that promote collectivistic values. Collectivistic culture members create strong in-group bonds to separate insiders from outsiders. For example, in Greek the word for "non-Greek" translates as "stranger"; in Korea, strangers are seen as "nonpersons."[44]

In most cultures, only loose connections exist between acquaintances. Because acquaintances do not usually confide in one another, they limit their conversations to ritualistic small talk. Even the topics of small talk may be culturally regulated. For example, although it may be perfectly acceptable in the United States to inquire about another's spouse, in some Arab countries it may be seen as a breach of etiquette to ask a male acquaintance about his wife.[45]

Culture guides us in understanding relationship customs and practices.

Intercultural conceptions of friendship may also vary. In some countries, such as Thailand, a person is accepted completely as a friend or not at all. For example, if you disapprove of any aspect of another's behavior, that person cannot be your friend.[46] In contrast, Americans typically simply choose not to discuss those aspects of their friends to which they take exception or with which they disagree, such as their political or religious beliefs.

Cultural expectations for friendships differ in other ways too. Whereas cultures with individualistic orientations refer to friends as "friends," cultures with collectivistic orientations refer to friends with labels typically reserved for family members in individualistic cultures: brother, sister, or cousin. The latter labels suggest that the bonds of friendship are not transient, but lasting.

Cultural customs concerning romance and marriage also vary widely. For example, in countries such as India and Afghanistan, parents arrange the marriages of their children. As a result, dating prior to marriage in these countries is rare. The same is true in many Middle Eastern countries; in some, such as Iran, dating is even against the law. In Central and South America, most young people do not date until they are well into their teens, and in Japan and Korea, significant dating first begins during college. In many European countries, dating is a group activity rather than a couples' activity.[47]

Because culture affects communication, it also affects our responses to those whose cultures differ from ours. By answering the following questions, you can remove barriers and improve your ability to communicate with others from different cultures.

DOES THE CULTURE PLACE MORE STRESS ON INDIVIDUALS OR ON SOCIAL RELATIONSHIPS?

While some cultures emphasize social relationships, others stress individualism. To determine what your culture has taught you, ask yourself if you give preference to your own private interests or the interests of the collectivity when interacting. In other words, are you likely to feel emotionally independent or dependent in the company of others? According to researchers, individualism lies at the very heart of American culture, while for members of other cultural groups, such as those from East Asian countries, the social relationship is paramount.[48]

DOES THE CULTURE PROMOTE THE DEVELOPMENT OF SHORT- OR LONG-TERM RELATIONSHIPS?

While Americans may find it easy to drop in and out of relationships and organizations, members of Far Eastern cultures believe that relationships ought to last and that individuals should show loyalty to others simply because they are obligated to each other. Because East Asian cultures share such a perspective, in these cultures business and personal relationships are mixed together, last longer, and are based on mutual expectations of reciprocity and congeniality. Thus, whereas Americans typically want to get right down to business, individuals from East Asian countries feel more comfortable if their business interactions occur on a more personal level, believing that for an effective business relationship to develop, a warm personal relationship must first exist.

DOES THE CULTURE VALUE RESULTS OR THE INTERACTIONAL PROCESS?

Americans are highly results-oriented, often wanting instant answers—even from a relationship. Compared with individuals from other cultures, they are more spontaneous in their interactions and more apt to reveal themselves to others. In contrast, in most Asian countries, people tend to be less revealing and more willing to devote significantly longer periods to getting to know each other.

By answering questions such as these, you can help to place a person's communicative behavior in an appropriate cultural context.

GENDER AND RELATIONSHIP FORMATION

Gender affects how we are taught to communicate, influencing our roles, the parts we play when interacting, and the rules or behavioral norms guiding our interactions and relationships with one another.

We learn the roles we perform. We are not born knowing how to enact them. Our learning, however, starts early—virtually as soon as we are born. For example, studies reveal that nurses in U.S. hospital nurseries handle boy and girl babies differently, raising the pitch of their voices as much as a third higher when talking to girls and using larger gestures when interacting with boys.[49]

In part because of the ways many in U.S. society interact, we are apt to develop different expectations for males and females. As a result, we may expect the members of the two sexes to behave differently, dress differently, play differently, and perform different jobs. On the other hand, people who grow up in families that treat males and females as equals are likely to develop or acquire views of their prospective roles that differ from the long-held traditional expectations.

Instrumental roles: Roles that are focused on getting things done; task-oriented roles.

Expressive roles: Roles focused on helping, supporting, nurturing, and being responsive to the needs of others; relationship-oriented roles.

Androgynous: Having both masculine and feminine traits.

In general, U.S. culture has taught that males are to perform **instrumental roles** and females are to perform **expressive roles**. The expectation is for males to focus on getting things done and for females to focus on helping, supporting, nurturing, and being responsive to others' needs. Consequently, male communication is primarily task-oriented and female communication is primarily relationship-oriented.

Over time, it has become possible and increasingly acceptable for males and females to be more **androgynous** in their roles—that is, to share both instrumental and expressive roles.

As perceptions of men and women have changed, so have expectations for them. When we view male and female roles as androgynous, we make it feasible for men and women to be behaviorally flexible and to display an array of what were once more limited, sex-typed characteristics. Thus, men can be both nurturing and competitive, and females can be both assertive and submissive.

As Rachel Bertsche, author of *MWF Seeking BFF: My Yearlong Search for a New Best Friend,* observes, friendship is terribly important in our lives.[50] Yet, too often it becomes a luxury, something we try to fit in after career and family. When compared with the friendships of men, women's friendships are often de-emphasized by the media, which often trivialize them while treating men's friendships with dignity and respect. Friends, however, are of vital importance to the members of both sexes, though not for the same reasons. When it comes to friendship, women choose women friends they can confide in.[51] Female friendships tend to be expressive, centering on sharing disclosures and developing loyalty and trust. Women focus on relational matters and are sensitive to what happens to their friends. Males, in contrast, have "chumships."[52] Instead of basing their friendships around talk, men tend to befriend other males with whom they share hobbies, play sports, and so forth. Whereas women's friendships emphasize face-to-face interaction, men's emphasize side-to-side interaction. On the other hand, male-female friendships tend to be more active and less intense than female friendships and more emotionally fulfilling and expressive than male friendships.

When women and men date, the women typically want to talk more than the men. Men tend to approach conversation functionally, with the goal of sharing information or solving problems, whereas women are more likely to view conversation as an ingredient essential to the relationship's development. Thus, it is often the woman who keeps the conversation going. Linguistic theorist Deborah Tannen explains that women use "rapport talk" while men use "report talk": women talk to establish and negotiate relationships; men talk to preserve independence and negotiate status.[53]

When selecting a romantic relationship partner, American men tend to look for stereotypically feminine women (women who are attractive, slim, and sexy), and women are likely to look for men with stereotypically masculine qualities (men who are ambitious, energetic, and strong).[54] Many American women also report that they expect their spouses to be their superiors in intelligence, ability, education, and job success.[55]

MEDIA, TECHNOLOGY, AND SOCIAL WORLDS

While the media and technology reflect existing societal expectations, we also use the portrayals and communication examples they feature as models of what to do or not do when building, maintaining, and ending relationships of our own.

MEDIA PORTRAYALS OF FRIENDSHIP AND ROMANCE

Media portrayals mimic cultural expectations for gender. As such, they further influence how we perceive men and women and shape our views of effective communication and relationships.

Until recently, media offerings for the most part featured dependent women and independent men, suggesting that incompetent women need to rely on men to succeed, that men are the breadwinners and women the caregivers, and that men are the aggressors and women the victims.[56] These depictions made their way into consciousness, causing us to limit our perceptions of ourselves and perpetuating unrealistic images of what we should be like and how we should interact when in one another's company. More recently, men have increasingly been portrayed in the media in ways echoing the false portrayals of women.[57] So-called reality programs, however, persist in portraying men stereotypically. For example, on *Jersey Shore* a prominent stereotype is the macho man, a man who demonstrates his manliness by degrading women.

Unfortunately, stereotypical depictions of women and men abound in advertisements as well. Advertisers persist in portraying men as central to women's lives and women as overly concerned with relationships, obsessed with appearance and youth, and emotionally dependent.[58] They depict women as sex objects—desirable not because of personal qualities but because of their bodies. Men are also held up as authorities, while women are depicted as the consumers who need to be told by male authorities which products they should be using.

Bridesmaids was a critical and commercial success, and the raunchy female-driven comedy challenged traditional Hollywood wisdom about how women should be portrayed in movies.

Similarly, in film and television offerings, men are often portrayed as aggressive, dominant, and engaged in exciting and instrumental activities, while women are portrayed as caregivers and nurturers who are dependent on men and preoccupied with romance.[59] Producers of media also stereotype. For example, films targeted at female audiences emphasize feelings, bonding, romance, and conversation, whereas male-targeted films emphasize carnage, zingy one-liners, and sex.

Technopoly: A culture whose thought world is monopolized by technology.

TECHNOLOGY: MEETING IN CYBERSPACE

Technology affects both communication and relationships. The late media scholar Neil Postman believed us to be living in a **technopoly**, a society in which all forms of cultural life are subordinate to technology.[60] Do you agree?

The Internet has brought social networks into our lives. We now develop some of our friendships and romantic relationships online. For centuries, the elite used paintings of themselves to represent their status and present themselves as they wished to be seen. Now this process has been expanded—we all have the ability to present digital portraits of ourselves to the world. We use these digital representations to connect with others—to "friend" them—on Facebook and other sites. In effect, we sell ourselves and promote our lifestyles. In the minds of some, the number of social network friends attracted (even if a majority of them are weak ties) is a status enhancer.[61] Being well liked becomes itself a preoccupation. Indeed, a large number of us keep careful count of online friends and Twitter followers, correlating our worth with their number.[62]

Interestingly, women update their status on Facebook more frequently than men do, making an average of twenty-one updates per week, while men average six. Women also comment more frequently on others' updates. Even in the online world, women take charge of social relationships.[63]

More and more friendships and romantic relationships are developing online.

It's not just about friends, however. While people still use singles bars, parties, cruises, and ads to meet potential romantic partners, the twenty-first century finds us also relying on the proliferation of sites such as Match.com, OkCupid, Chemistry.com, and eHarmony for romantic relationship building. We now shop for a love connection as we shop for everything else. While women are more likely than men to form personal relationships online, both use cyberspace to form friendships and romantic relationships, with increasing numbers of these transferring into real space. In fact, millions of Americans seek love on the Internet. Between 2007 and 2009, some 21 percent of heterosexual couples and 61 percent of same-sex couples in the United States met online, with their online descriptions revealing what they were looking for in a partner and what a partner should expect to find in them.[64]

When creating online descriptions, those seeking romantic partners tend to idealize themselves, bending the truth in the effort to put their best foot forward. Interestingly, they often seek others who are ethnically similar to themselves. More than three-quarters of white member contacts on online dating sites are with other white members. Black members, in contrast, are ten times more apt to contact white potential partners than black ones.[65] The woman with the best chance of having a male express interest is her is slightly underweight, whereas women prefer men slightly overweight—but financially well-off. According to researchers, however, these websites do not actually improve dating outcomes. The partner choices made by members are based on more than personality similarities and are not necessarily rational decisions.[66]

Why did online socializing take off? Why do large numbers of people find it a surrogate form of interpersonal communication? Unlike our more traditionally established relationships, relationships that are built online promote intimacy through mutual disclosure rather than physical attractiveness. According to communication researcher Joseph Walther, the online environment encourages interaction to become *hyperpersonal,* meaning we share in cyberspace information we would not share characteristically when face-to-face.

Perhaps this is because we feel less inhibited online and view our partners more positively, a perception that accelerates our feelings of closeness.[67]

In addition, online interactions help us maintain connections. "Away messaging," posts on Facebook, and numerous texts let our friends and significant others know what we are up to and vice versa. Researchers believe that those who use these means of communication do so because they do not want to be out of the loop. They also employ them to control others' impressions of them. For example, you can post a "social butterfly"-type message even if you are home watching a DVD. Or you can make a boy- or girlfriend think you're out with someone else when you're not. The best result is to return to a screen full of messages sent in response to your posts or texts. The worst is to return to an empty screen. Thus, responses to posts can serve as a litmus test of social capital.[68]

Now, even a cell phone can function as a matchmaker for love and friendship connections. Looking for love nearby is a common practice, and growing numbers of people now use cell phone applications to make instant dates based on the proximity of a prospect to the user's neighborhood.[69] Users post their profiles (sometimes only a picture) and scan lists of others who have done so. They exchange messages, and if a mutual interest surfaces, they can take it to the next step and decide where to meet. Applications include broadly targeted ones such as Blendr, OkCupid Locals, HowAboutWe, Jazzed, and Grindr, an app targeted to gay men. These apps offer opportunities for quick interaction (an advantage for the time-challenged), and users may decide soon after getting together whether they will do it again.

Despite the popularity of digital dating sites, some seeking to make a love connection are hiring "wingmen and -women"—people who specialize in picking up flirting signals—to pose as friends and accompany them to social gathering places. The wingman or -woman alerts the person who hires him or her to potential matches and helps to make seamless introductions to potential partners. Like the lead character in the popular film *Hitch,* these professional cupids excel at face-to-face conversation, a social skill sadly lacking in some who spend more and more time online.[70]

Thus, online social networks both facilitate and complicate relationship building. While they encourage mutual disclosures that help build intimacy, they also give users more control over how others perceive them than they otherwise would be able to exert. And by limiting face-to-face interaction, they may be impeding our ability to "think on our feet." We may be skilled at "conversing" with our fingertips, but this may not be a skill that carries over into our face-to-face encounters.

GAINING COMMUNICATION COMPETENCE: MASTERING RELATIONSHIP COMPLEXITIES

Relationships are complex. The more we can learn about how we form them and why they do or do not work, the better able we will be to deal with them. What can we do to improve our relationships? How can we develop better-balanced relationships? What do the media and technology forecast about relationships in the future, and what can or should we do about it?

UNDERSTAND THAT RELATIONSHIPS DON'T JUST HAPPEN

Working to improve relationships is a lifelong endeavor. We can work to develop meaningful relationships, or we can let them falter or wither away. By focusing on the nature of relationships and why we have them in the first place, we are able to discover what we will miss when one goes awry.

RECOGNIZE WHY WE NEED OTHERS

What happens to those who feel cut off from others? Feelings of isolation increase the risk of death. Lonely people die younger.[71] By being in relationships, we combat loneliness and experience belonging. Relationships provide us with a sense of inclusion. When they are lacking, we are often left with a sense of doom.

UNDERSTAND THE NATURE OF FRIENDSHIP AND ROMANTIC RELATIONSHIPS

People in healthy relationships enjoy the following:

- They look forward to being together because they enjoy each other's company.

- They accept each other as they are, are free to be themselves, and make few, if any, demands on the other person to change.

- They trust each other and are willing to put themselves in the hands of the other, because each assumes that the other will act in his or her best interest.

- They share a high level of commitment and are willing to help and support each other.

- They respect each other.

- They are willing to share personal information and engage in high levels of self-disclosure; as a result, they are better able to predict each other's behaviors and responses.

MEET THE CHALLENGES POSED BY MEDIA AND TECHNOLOGY

Our relational repertoire grows larger as the media and technological innovations make new ways of interacting possible. How we develop and grow future relationships may be different from how we grew and nurtured them in the past. We may become attracted to people in different ways and for different reasons. Originating, pacing, or repairing a relationship begun on the Internet may require us to have different skills than beginning, maintaining, or reinvigorating one established face-to-face. We need to remain open to using both traditional and new approaches to building meaningful relationships.

Susan and Bob are married and have two children. To ensure the lifestyle they want for their family, both Susan and Bob work more than forty hours per week. Though Bob tries to do his share of household chores, Susan somehow ends up more exhausted at week's end.

Susan figures out how to get the kids to and from soccer and softball practice, where they go after school, and how they spend their time on weekends. That seems fair to Bob, since he makes more money than Susan, or, as he puts it, "brings home the lion's share of the bacon," so they can afford to take great family vacations, buy designer clothes, and eat in fine restaurants.

Given Bob's position, Susan wonders how he will handle the latest news about her career.

Susan had nearly floated out of the CEO's office. Not only had she been promoted, she had also been given a substantial salary increase—she would now be making more money than her husband. Yet the excitement and pride she felt was tinged with concern and uncertainty because she wasn't sure how Bob would react to the news. She sat down at her desk, took a deep breath, took out her cell, and called Bob at his office. She told herself he should be pleased, since now they would have even more money to spend on those extras that help make their lives easier. Bob answered her call: "Hi, Susan. What's up?"

Consider these questions:

1. If you were Susan, would you reveal the truth to Bob?

2. How do you imagine Bob would respond if told the truth? What about if told a lie? Be specific.

3. If you were Bob, how would you react to the truth?

4. In what ways, or to what extent, do you think Susan's promotion and new salary will change Susan and Bob's relationship?

REVIEW THIS

CHAPTER SUMMARY

1 Discuss the functions relationships serve, identifying the characteristics that distinguish one relationship from another. Relationships help preserve our happiness and health; prevent our isolation; meet our needs for inclusion, control, and affection; offer a point of reference for checking if our behavior and emotional responses are culturally acceptable; serve as a communication pipeline; and maintain our sense of worth. We can compare and contrast relationships based on their duration, the frequency of interpersonal contacts, how much people reveal to each other, the kind of support they offer one another, the variability of their interactions, and their goals.

2 Use Rawlins's friendship model and Sternberg's triangle of love to explain the relationship spectrum, distinguishing among acquaintanceships, friendships, and romantic relationships. The stages of Rawlins's six-stage model of friendship are role-limited interaction, friendly relations, moving toward friendship, nascent friendship, stabilized friendship, and waning friendship. Sternberg's triangle of love identifies commitment, passion, and intimacy as necessary components in a romantic relationship.

3 Use Knapp and Vangelisti's relationship model to describe the stages a romantic relationship may pass through. Knapp and Vangelisti identify the following relationship stages: initiating (you decide if you are attracted to another), experimenting (you share information, looking for commonalities), intensifying (intimacy increases), integrating (your identities begin to merge), bonding (a public ritual makes clear your commitment to each other), differentiating (your differences begin to dominate), circumscribing (you restrict your sharing of information), stagnating (you decide further communication is pointless), avoiding (you keep your distance physically from one another), and terminating (you end your relationship). Not every relationship goes through all ten stages. Relationships may progress, retreat, advance again, and/or deteriorate. Relationship stabilization occurs at the level both parties agree is satisfying and meets their needs.

4 Describe the factors that influence interpersonal attraction. The primary motive for initiating a relationship is attraction. Among the variables influencing the amount of attraction are physical attractiveness, social attractiveness, task attractiveness, proximity, reinforcement, similarity, and complementarity.

5 Identify how culture, gender, the media, and technology influence relationship development. Culture influences the forming of relationships, determining attitudes toward strangers, including wheth love we feel for the person we have er or not we engage in ritualistic small talk. It also modifies attitudes toward friendship, romance, and marriage. Gender influences relationship roles and rules as well as the expectations developed for males and females. As perceptions of men and women change, androgyny has become more accepted. The media and technology tend to reinforce cultural and gender expectations, with stereotypical portrayals abounding. While shaping our image of an effective relationship, they can also help broaden our concept of acceptable means of interacting.

6 Identify specific techniques that can facilitate our mastery of relationship dynamics. Once we acknowledge that relationships don't just happen, recognize our need for others, understand the nature of friendship, and display the ability to meet the challenges the media and emerging technologies pose, we become better able to demonstrate mastery of relationship dynamics.

CHECK YOUR UNDERSTANDING

1. Can you list the functions that relationships fulfill in your life? (See pages 328–333.)

2. Can you use Rawlins's friendship model and Sternberg's triangle of love to summarize the similarities and differences between a relationship based on friendship and one based on love? If you were creating a list of rules to follow for friendship and romance, what rules would be on your list and why? (See pages 336–340.)

3. Can you create a ten-stage scenario to illustrate Knapp and Vangelisti's relationship model in action? (See pages 340–345.)

4. Can you explain which attraction factors are important to you and why? (See pages 345–349.)

5. Can you give examples of how your gender and/or culture or the media and technology you prefer have influenced the course of a relationship? (See pages 350–356.)

CHECK YOUR SKILLS

1. Can you recognize how isolation affects individuals? (See page 329; and *Analyze This,* page 332.)

2. Can you provide examples how inclusion, control, and affection needs differ among people with whom you share relationships? (See pages 329–331; and *Try This,* page 333.)

3. Can you identify the characteristics most important to you in choosing a friend and a romantic partner, using them to make relationship choices? (See pages 334–335.)

4. Can you compare and contrast the levels of intimacy you have in your relationships? (See page 335; and *Try This,* page 336.)

5. Can you chart the evolution of one of your relationships? (See pages 336–345; *Analyze This,* page 343; and *Try This,* page 345.)

6. Can you identify why you are attracted to some people but not to others? (See pages 345–350; and *Try This,* page 350.)

7. Can you recognize how culture and gender influence how you choose the people with whom you establish ties? (See pages 350–353; and *Try This,* page 354.)

8. Can you recognize when a media portrayal alters your thoughts about how to communicate in a relationship? (See pages 353–354.)

9. Can you decode online postings and use them to gauge your or another's social capital? (See pages 354–356.)

10. Can you diagnose the effectiveness of relational communication, and, if the communication is deemed ineffective, identify how to improve it? (See *The Case of the Job Promotion,* page 358.)

KEY TERMS

Relationships *328*

Fundamental interpersonal relations orientation *329*

Inclusion need *330*

Control need *330*

Affection need *330*

Undersocial *330*

Abdicrat *330*

Underpersonal *330*

Oversocial *330*

Autocrat *330*

Overpersonal *330*

Maslow's needs hierarchy *331*

Intimacy *335*

Intimate relationship *335*

Acquaintances *335*

Friendship *336*

Role-limited interaction *337*

Friendly relations *338*

Moving toward friendship *338*

Nascent friendship *338*

Stabilized friendship *338*

Waning friendship *338*

Romantic relationship *339*

Passionate love *339*

Companionate love *339*

Commitment *340*

Passion *340*

Triangular theory of love *340*

Manifest intimacy *340*

Latent intimacy *340*

Knapp and Vangelisti's ten-stage model of relationships *340*

Relational culture *340*

Relationship stages *340*

Initiating stage *341*

Experimenting stage *341*

Intensifying stage *341*

Integrating stage *342*

Interpersonal synchrony *342*

Bonding stage *342*

Differentiating stage *342*

Circumscribing stage *342*

Stagnating stage *343*

Avoiding stage *343*

Terminating stage *344*

Physical attractiveness *346*

Social attractiveness *346*

Task attractiveness *348*

Proximity *348*

Reinforcement *348*

Similarity *349*

Matching hypothesis *349*

Complementarity *349*

Instrumental roles *352*

Expressive roles *352*

Androgynous *352*

Technopoly *354*

STUDENT STUDY SITE

Visit the student study site at **www.sagepub.com/gambleic** to access the following materials:

- SAGE Journal Articles
- Videos
- Web Resources

- eFlashcards
- Web Quizzes
- Study Questions

I believe we're all secretly happy we can't figure our relationships out. It keeps our minds working.

—Jerry Seinfeld

INTIMACY AND DISTANCE IN RELATIONSHIPS

LEARNING OBJECTIVES

After completing this chapter, you should be able to demonstrate mastery of the following learning outcomes:

1. Define self-disclosure and intimacy.

2. Explain social penetration theory.

3. Describe the Johari window.

4. Define and explain the effects of relational dialectics.

5. Discuss when and how to maintain a relationship versus when to terminate one.

6. Define and explain toxic communication and identify the four stages in an abusive relationship.

7. Explain the grief cycle, describing what occurs when a relationship ends with a loved one's death.

8. Identify how culture, gender, the media, and technology influence notions of intimacy and disclosure.

9. Discuss strategies for handling closeness and distance in relationships more effectively.

How good do you imagine you would be at maintaining a romantic relationship if you and your significant other lived far apart from one another? This is a relationship challenge many college students face as they leave their hometowns to attend college and their romantic partners remain behind or select other colleges hundreds of miles away. Dual-career couples who work in widely separated locations, whether by choice or because of limited job availability, face similar problems.

While increasingly common, long-distance relationships can be fraught with complications—exposing the limits of technology, especially if one partner's faults surface and trust becomes an issue.[1] When one partner in a long-distance relationship idealizes the other, the relationship tends to stay more stable than even a geographically close one—that is, until the partners stage a reunion.[2]

> While increasingly common, long-distance relationships can be fraught with complications.

The 2010 romantic comedy *Going the Distance*, starring Drew Barrymore and Justin Long, explores the kinds of problems that can beset long-distance relationships. Erin and Garrett, the two distance-separated lovers, spend much time texting, Skyping, and calling one another in the effort to continue the relationship they began when both resided in the same town. Just working out a time when one of them can fly to see the other poses difficulties for them. In time, Erin and Garrett also find themselves arguing about such things as whether or not to have "phone sex."

A long-distance relationship may have a greater chance of success if both partners are willing to solve problems jointly and to be open to one another by engaging in self-disclosure.[3] If you were in a long distance relationship, do you think yours would make it?

WHAT DO YOU KNOW?

Before continuing your reading of this chapter, which of the following five statements do you believe to be true and which do you believe to be false?

1. Self-disclosure involves willingly revealing private information about ourselves to another person. T F

2. Self-disclosure carries no risks. T F

3. Intimacy and self-disclosure are positively related. T F

4. When disclosures occur too early in a relationship, the person being confided in is likely to feel uncomfortable. T F

5. While technologically equipped to handle a long-distance relationship, we may not be able to meet the emotional challenges such a relationship presents. T F

Read the chapter to discover if you're right or if you've made any erroneous assumptions.

ANSWERS: 1. T, 2. F, 3. T, 4. T, 5. T

Some of us are satisfied with our relationships and some of us are not. Some of us are in healthy and fulfilling relationships, while others of us are in poor relationships beset with problems and dangers. What happens when we want to deepen a friendship, develop a romance, extricate ourselves from a relationship we no longer find satisfying, or terminate a relationship we believe to be dysfunctional? In Chapter 12, we looked at different kinds of interpersonal relationships. In this chapter, we delve into those qualities that distinguish close interpersonal relationships from those that are more superficial or distant and satisfying relationships from those that are dysfunctional. When they are very good, close relationships help make us healthier and extend our lives, but when they are very bad and poorly handled, they may threaten both our health and our happiness.

We will explore how we know when a relationship is worth maintaining or deepening, how we can tell when a relationship is in need of repair or termination, and what we need to do to accomplish relational objectives. We will also look at how the death of a person with whom we have shared an intimate relationship affects us and what steps we need to take to rescue ourselves from grief so that we can cope and continue. Let us begin by looking at those qualities that differentiate our intimate and satisfying relationships from more superficial or distant ones.

Self-disclosure: The willing sharing of information about the self with others.

Norm of reciprocity: The expectation of self-disclosure equity in a relationship.

SELF-DISCLOSURE AND INTIMACY

In the age of social networking, managing how much other people know about you isn't easy. When and with whom are you most comfortable talking about yourself? Under what conditions and to whom do you reveal information about you that you normally keep to yourself?

When we self-disclose, we willingly reveal otherwise private information about ourselves to another person. By definition, messages of **self-disclosure** generally include personal facts about us that someone would be unlikely to discover on his or her own. Among Westerners, self-disclosure is a measure of closeness.[4] For this reason—and also because we do not usually intentionally reveal significant personal details about ourselves to many people—self-disclosure aids in the achievement of closeness or intimacy (as discussed in Chapter 12). Thus, as we disclose more about ourselves, our communication becomes more intimate; similarly, when we refrain from self-disclosing or backtrack in revealing personal information, our communication becomes less intimate and more impersonal.

Sometimes we use self-disclosure as a tool to get to know others.[5] Persons skilled in establishing connections offer self-disclosures that make it easier for a partner to reciprocate. They know that there are different depths of information and that the depth of disclosures should correlate positively with the appropriate relationship stage.[6]

Self-disclosure can be risky. By revealing our likes, dislikes, feelings, fears, strengths, and weaknesses, we increase our vulnerability, potentially subjecting ourselves to rejection and criticism. For that reason, we typically first reveal small amounts of low-risk information. For example, "My favorite color is blue because it reminds me of my grandmother." We save more risky disclosures, such as "I am an atheist" or "I don't think I ever want to get married," until we confirm that the other person is willing to match both the level and the nature of our disclosing behavior—that is, act in accordance with the **norm of reciprocity**.[7] According to the reciprocity norm, we expect to experience self-disclosure equity in our relationships—we expect that other persons will return our self-disclosures in kind. When another person reveals the same kind of information as we have revealed, we feel safer, display a greater willingness

True or False

1. *Self-disclosure involves willingly revealing private information about ourselves to another person.*

True. When we self-disclose, we share personal information about ourselves that the other person wouldn't otherwise know.

to move self-disclosing to a deeper level, and, over time, become even more willing to relate increasingly intimate information. In contrast, lack of such reciprocation indicates that the other person is not yet ready to openly disclose, that things need to go more slowly, or that our relationship may be one-sided and not likely to develop fully. The revealing of our most intimate information is reserved typically for only our very closest ongoing relationships.

If we are careless and inadequately or inappropriately engage in self-disclosure, others may view us negatively. The satisfactory development of our relationships hinges on our appropriate use of self-disclosures, which typically occur incrementally during the course of a positive relationship. In fact, we may judge a relationship's strength and health by assessing the breadth and depth of the information shared. **Relationship breadth** is related to the number of different topics we discuss with another. **Relationship depth**, in contrast, is reflected in how central the topics we discuss are to our self-concept, how much we reveal about ourselves, and how we feel about doing so. The depth of a relationship is seen in the degree of intimacy we are willing to divulge about specific areas of ourselves. The more we reveal, the deeper others are able to penetrate into our core.

Thus, self-disclosure and intimacy correlate positively in our relationships. Discovering another person's inner nature involves peeling back or penetrating the series of layers that protect the individual's inner self. The more layers we peel back or penetrate, the more is revealed about the person, and the closer we become.

SOCIAL PENETRATION THEORY

Social psychologists and communication practitioners use the model depicted in Figure 13.1 to describe how breadth and depth of communication relate. In the model, the outer circle represents the complete individual, composed of many different aspects (e.g., religion, work, school, social life). The aspects are, of course, different for each of us. Each wedge-shaped section of the circle represents one aspect of a person's life. The concentric rings indicate the information a person reveals during conversation, with the outer circles representing casual conversations and the inner circles representing very intimate conversations. By noting which segments of the circle are active in a relationship, we can use this model to illustrate the relationship's intimacy level.

To understand how the model works, it is necessary to understand **social penetration theory**, first proposed in 1973 by psychologists Irwin Altman and Dalmas Taylor.[8] According to this theory, relationships typically begin with relatively narrow breadth, in which we discuss few topics with each other, and shallow depth, in which our conversations about these topics remain relatively superficial. We may, for example, talk about where we grew up, what we are majoring in, and the kind of job we would like to hold. We depict this type of relationship as shown on the left-hand side of Figure 13.2; it is a casual relationship.

However, over time, the amount of intimacy we share increases and the level of intensity we feel deepens. As a result, highly intimate relationships have significant amounts of breadth and depth; the range of topics increases along with the amount of information revealed about the self and feelings. We may share our political and religious beliefs, eventually progressing to talking about our fears, talents, and secret ambitions. Such changes are shown on the right-hand side of Figure 13.2.

The social penetration model is useful for a number of reasons. First, it provides us with a two-dimensional depiction of our relationships, showing both the range

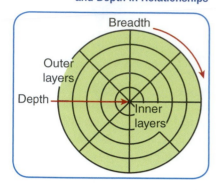

Figure 13.1 Altman and Taylor's Social Penetration Model: Breadth and Depth in Relationships

of topics we talk about and the extent to which we reveal ourselves through our conversations. Second, it enables us to understand why some of our relationships seem stronger than others. As a relationship increases in strength, we become more willing to discuss particular subjects and more comfortable revealing more about ourselves. Rather than limiting another's access to us (and our relationship circle), we give that person greater access, allowing her or him to move away from our circle's periphery and venture inward, toward its center—or our core. This increases our relational bonds. Thus, when your communication with someone lacks breadth or depth, although your relationship may be satisfying, it will likely remain quite casual. In order to change things, you would need to take steps to enhance the scope and nature of your interactions, perhaps by disclosing your personal values and sharing private feelings about yourself.

Figure 13.2 Social Penetration in a Casual and an Intimate Relationship

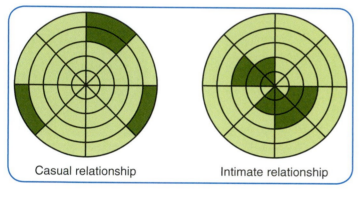

Casual relationship   Intimate relationship

At times, our desire to get to know someone better causes us to discuss topics at a depth we would normally reserve for those with whom we share a core intimate relationship. When such disclosures or revelations occur prematurely—before both partners are fully ready for a more intense relationship—they may contribute to feelings of discomfort in one or both of us. On the other hand, when we are ready to deepen the relationship, increases in breadth and depth occur naturally and cause little, if any, relational discomfort. We are likely to judge those who reveal too much to us too soon as indiscreet, untrustworthy, or just plain odd. We may even perceive those who try to get us to do more disclosing than we are ready for as pushy and overbearing.[9]

WHAT DO YOU KNOW?

True or False

4. *When disclosures occur too early in a relationship, the person being confided in is likely to feel uncomfortable.*

True. Premature disclosures may lead to relational discomfort.

Responses to the self-disclosure of positive and negative information are also time related. We tend to dislike those who disclose positive information about themselves in the very early stages of our relationship, especially if they brag about how talented they are. In contrast, the disclosure of negative information early in a relationship may be a positive, because, for some reason, we tend to be attracted to persons who are willing to be honest and take responsibility for their actions.[10] Thus, if a person tells you that he failed a course but then recommitted to studying and passed the course with an *A* the second time he took it, your respect for this person might actually grow.

Of course, it is neither possible nor desirable to have close relationships with everyone; every relationship has an optimal level. Current relationships that are more distant in scope and tone, if given the right opportunities, may become deeper and more significant. We need time to absorb information about each other. The satisfactory development of a relationship—whether a friendship or one more intimate and romantic—depends on our being able to pace or time our self-disclosures properly.

Social penetration theory reveals how opening the relational self to others is a process, not usually a single action, with some of our disclosures revealing more than others. There is a difference between saying "I love my job" and "I'm in love with my boss." The latter is a more significant revelation than the former, especially if it was never shared with anyone before.

TRY THIS: *Social Penetration—in Casual and Intimate Relationships*

Think about the nature of your conversations in four different relationships:

a. A new friendship

b. A long-lasting, meaningful friendship

c. A current relationship with a parent or caregiver

d. A romantic relationship

For each relationship, label the pie-shaped wedges of the corresponding diagram below with the various aspects of your life. Then color in the segments that correspond to the level of self-disclosures you share with the person. The resulting diagrams will illustrate graphically the amount of social penetration you have with each individual. How do the similarities and differences in your diagrams explain the different types of relationships? Explain.

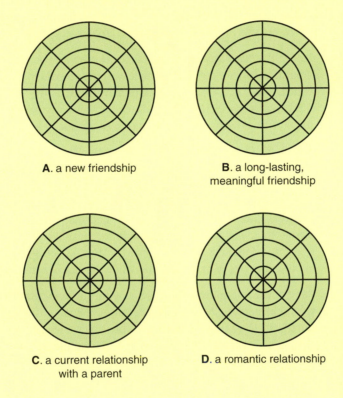

A. a new friendship

B. a long-lasting, meaningful friendship

C. a current relationship with a parent

D. a romantic relationship

THE JOHARI WINDOW AND SELF-DISCLOSURE

The **Johari window** is another model we can use to explore the roles that self-awareness and self-disclosure play in relationship building. "Johari" is a combination of the first names of the model's two creators: Joseph Luft and Harrington Ingham. The model uses a depiction

Johari window: A model containing four panes—the open area, the blind area, the hidden area, and the unknown area—that is used to explain the roles that self-awareness and self-disclosure play in relationship building.

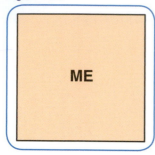

Figure 13.3

ME

of a window with four panes to help us explore how self-awareness and self-disclosure are relationship dependent—that how we view ourselves and how much we are willing to reveal varies among relationships.[11]

The entire window represents your self (see Figure 13.3). It is divided by two axes, creating four panes. The first axis includes what you do and do not know about yourself, and the second axis includes information that a specific person does or does not know about you. Let's look at the window's panes.

By dividing the window in half with an axis, we are able to depict what we do and do not know about ourselves (see Figure 13.4). Then by dividing the window still again with a horizontal axis, we are able to represent what another person does and does not know about us (see Figure 13.5). Finally, by putting the two axes together, we create four panes descriptive of a relationship (see Figure 13.6).

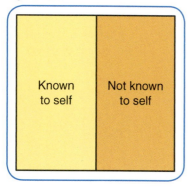

Figure 13.4

Known to self	Not known to self

Pane 1, the *open* area, represents information about you that is known both to you and to another person. For example, you may have divulged your religious background, tastes in food, or career aspirations. As you and the other person grow closer, the size of the open area grows larger.

Pane 2, the *blind* area, signifies information about you that the other person is aware of but that you are not. For example, you may consider yourself to be very confident, while another perceives you as extremely insecure. We learn of information in our blind area primarily through feedback. At times, we may feel we know so little about ourselves that we find it necessary to seek outside help to reduce our blind area's size.

Pane 3, the *hidden* area, signifies information that you know about yourself but are unwilling to reveal. For example, you may hesitate to reveal your fear of being left alone out of concern that another person will reject you and what you fear will actually happen. Items in the hidden area usually become known only as a result of self-disclosure, during which we reveal information about ourselves to another that he or she would not otherwise come to know. During this process information is moved from pane 3 into pane 1, the open area. Thus, as you share more about yourself with another, the size of pane 3 shrinks while the size of pane 1 grows.

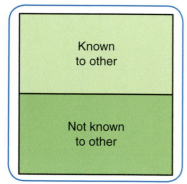

Figure 13.5

Known to other
Not known to other

Pane 4, the *unknown* area, signifies information unknown to both you and the other person. Pane 4 exists because we constantly learn new things about ourselves. Over time, education or life experience succeeds in bringing some of this pane's mysteries into the open. For example, we may discover that we have a previously unrecognized fear, prejudice, or talent. The more introspective we are, the smaller the size of our unknown area.

Because our development of self-awareness depends on our being able to gain information about the self, we need to be open to learning more about our blind and unknown areas. By understanding how others see us, we can also develop greater self-insight. Perspective taking is key to establishing meaningful relationships.

Similar to the way we use the social penetration model to represent our relationships, we can use the Johari window to represent how we feel about another person and how comfortable we are revealing personal information to him or her. Usually, as a new relationship begins, the information we discuss about ourselves is relatively superficial. If the person responds positively and reciprocates with disclosures of her or his own, we usually continue disclosing information. As a result, our relationship increases in trust,

When you have a responsive partner, do you tend to reveal more? When online, do you tend to disclose more than you would otherwise? Researchers have conducted studies to answer these two questions.

The thinking is that perceiving a relational partner as responsive should lead to more expressiveness. Research reveals this to be true, particularly if the discloser is low in self-esteem. In other words, partner responsiveness is less likely to enhance expressiveness when the discloser has high self-esteem. Thus, self-esteem appears to mediate disclosures. Do your experiences support this?

According to social penetration theory, the level of our sexual disclosure is reflective of how intimate we perceive our relationship to be. Research suggests that while there is a parallel relationship between the willingness of communicators to engage in sexual disclosure and relationship intimacy in real life, supporting the social penetration model, in cyberspace, males exhibit more willingness to engage in sexual disclosures than do females—a departure from the social penetration model. It seems that while females also have close online friends, they perceive real-life friendships to promote more self-disclosure. Can you provide examples from your own life that support these findings?

SOURCES: Amanda L. Forest, "When Partner Caring Leads to Sharing: Partner Responsiveness Increases Expressivity, but Only for Individuals with Low-Self-Esteem," *Journal of Experimental Social Psychology, 47,* 2011, p. 843–848.

Mu-Li Yang, Chao-Chin Yang, and Wen-Bin Chiou, "Differences in Engaging in Sexual Disclosure between Real Life and Cyberspace among Adolescents: Social Penetration Model Revisited," *Current Psychology, 29,* 2010, p. 144–154.

Cynthia M. H. Bane, Marilyn Cornish, Nicole Erspamer, and Lia Kampman, "Self-Disclosure through Weblogs and Perceptions of Online and 'Real-Life' Friendships among Female Bloggers," *Cyberpsychology, Behavior, and Social Networking, 13,* 2010, p. 131–139.

depth of self-other knowledge, and feelings of closeness. However, when two people in a relationship share little of the open area, for all practical purposes, interpersonal communication of any depth becomes unlikely. The less open person in the relationship typically is the one blocking relationship-building attempts, thereby limiting the amount of interpersonal communication possible.

Window A in Figure 13.7 shows a fairly impersonal relationship. The relatively large size of the unknown area and the relatively small size of the open area tell us that the persons involved in this relationship are not particularly introspective, are apt to withdraw from contact with one another, refrain from self-disclosing, and probably project images that announce their desire to be noncommunicative and not reveal a great deal of information. Thus, in such a relationship, all you may know about the other person is his taste in music because he plays the songs he has downloaded loudly enough for you to hear.

Window B shows a relationship with a dominant hidden area. This tells us that an individual sharing such a relationship fears exposure of some weakness and lacks trust in the other, believing that he or she

Figure 13.6 The Johari Window

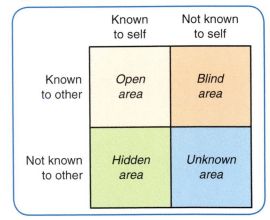

SOURCE: Joseph Luft, *Group Processes: An Introduction to Group Dynamics,* 3rd ed., Palo Alto, CA: Mayfield, 1984, p. 60.

Figure 13.7 Relationship Windows

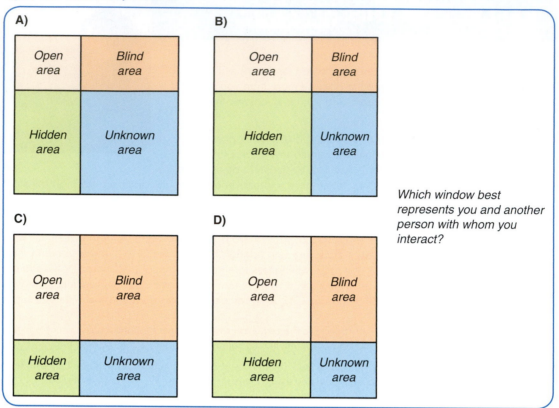

might exploit any information revealed. The person is likely to feel it necessary to create and maintain a facade in an effort to pretend to be something he or she is not. Perhaps the person is contemplating suicide but communicates no telling clue.

Window C shows a relationship with a dominant blind area. When involved in such a relationship, we usually are unaware of how we are affecting or being perceived by the other because we are overly concerned with our own self-presentation during our interactions. Maybe we don't think of ourselves as popular because we do not recognize how many friends we have or how many people care about us.

Window D depicts a relationship with a particularly large open area. Such a relationship usually involves significant self-disclosing and is characterized by candor, openness, and sensitivity to the needs and insights of the other. The individuals help each other to see into their blind areas, and they come to trust each other enough to share their most fundamental beliefs.

Thus, when we choose not to disclose information about ourselves to others, our windows have smaller open areas and larger hidden, blind, or unknown areas. In contrast, when we feel comfortable with another person and want to maintain or increase our feelings of closeness, our windows have larger open areas and smaller hidden, blind, and unknown areas.

As noted earlier in this chapter, self-disclosure and relationship success share a positive correlation. The higher the quality of our self-disclosures, the more satisfying we find the relationship. Feeling comfortable being honest and self-revealing are keynotes of relationship health, whether we are talking about the health of a marriage or grandchild-grandparent interaction.[12] This does not mean, however, that we should self-disclose without considering the risks—remember our discussion of trust in Chapter 9.

To evaluate the level of self-disclosure appropriate for you in a given relationship, ask yourself this series of questions:

1. Do I want to take the relationship to a deeper level?
2. Do I feel comfortable and safe doing so?
3. Is the disclosing I intend to do appropriate and relevant?
4. Will my partner reciprocate?
5. Will the disclosure have a positive impact on our relationship?

If you cannot answer all five of these questions with a yes, then it may not be the right time for you to self-disclose, or your relationship partner might not be the right person with whom you should share more information about yourself.

Disclosing personal information always carries some risk—both for you and for the other person. He or she may reject you or form a negative impression of you because of what you reveal. In addition, your disclosure may communicate a previously unknown weakness, and revealing the weakness may leave you with less control over the relationship. While what you disclose may help you feel more honest and forthcoming, the truth you reveal may hurt your partner. Or you may end up telling your partner more than he or she wishes to know.

On the other hand, self-disclosing can bring benefits and strengthen a relationship. Of course, developing a mutually satisfying relationship depends on more than reciprocal self-disclosing. Relationships worth having are going to evolve, and, as they do, we need to respond to the changes.

GO ▶

WATCH THIS 13.1
For a video on self-disclosure visit the student study site.

USING RELATIONAL DIALECTICS THEORY TO UNDERSTAND RELATIONSHIPS

As some relational forces pull us toward intimacy, opposing forces may pull us in the opposite direction. The road to a happy relationship is not always smooth. Partners do not necessarily want the same things from their relationship at the same time. Developed by communication theorist Leslie Baxter, **relational dialectics theory** explains the ups and downs and pushes and pulls that dynamic, healthy relationships experience.

While some models portray relationships developing in stages—recall both Knapp and Vangelisti's ten-stage model of relationships and Rawlins's six-stage model of friendship discussed in Chapter 12—others take into account that there is more to developing a relationship than whether it is new, has existed for a few years, or lasted decades. In fact, some theorists suggest that rather than proceeding though stages, a relationship never really stabilizes but instead evolves and changes over time as the parties sharing it repeatedly reevaluate and redefine their goals and needs while trying to manage the relationship's course. Since a relationship's context is ever changing, relational partners need to resolve a series of dialectical tensions—the opposing tensions or conflicts created when the goals and expectations of one partner clash with the goals and expectations of the other.

Relational dialectics theory: A theory that explores the pushes and pulls partners feel toward integration versus separation, stability versus change, and expression versus privacy.

Among the dialectical forces making relationship maintenance challenging are the push and pull partners feel toward integration versus separation, stability versus change, and expression versus privacy.[13] Dialectical tensions may occur in any interpersonal relationship in any context. According to Baxter, relationships experience both internal and external tensions. Internal tensions include how the partners communicate with each other, while external tensions occur between the partners and the rest of society.

INTEGRATION-SEPARATION

The dialectic of integration-separation focuses on the tension between the desire to be socially integrated and the desire to be self-sufficient. From an internal perspective, a person's desire for connection clashes with the need for autonomy. For example, we want to be connected to our partner but independent of him or her too. If you have ever felt smothered by a partner in a relationship, you were likely experiencing a need for more autonomy. On the other hand, if you have ever felt as if your partner was ignoring you or not giving you enough attention, you were probably expressing your desire for greater connection.

Externally, we express this pull-push dialectic by wanting to introduce our partner to others and at the same time wanting to keep him or her away from others—an inclusion-seclusion tension. Wanting to have our relationship included in a larger social network clashes with our desire to keep it private and personal.

STABILITY-CHANGE

Do you like to get comfortable in a relationship, or do you enjoy change? The internal manifestation of the stability-change dialectic suggests that there is a tension between desiring consistency or comfort in a relationship and desiring novelty or newness. For any relationship to last, each partner needs to be able to count on the other to perform certain relational roles. In other words, our lives need to have some nonvarying routines, or we would experience chaos daily. When our lives become nothing but routine and we feel we know everything about the other person, however, predictability rules, life becomes stale, and, as a result, we find ourselves longing for excitement and something different. But when relationships are characterized by too much novelty or surprise, we may feel overwhelmed by our lack of control.

Externally, this second pull-push dialectic manifests itself as tension between desiring to have a conventional relationship that conforms to social expectations and norms and desiring to demonstrate the uniqueness in our relationship.[14] For example, in the United

States, some act in conventional ways, working to fulfill the American Dream by holding a well-paying job with a dependable organization, owning a home, and supporting a family. Other Americans challenge this norm by opting to not settle down, marry, or have children.

EXPRESSION-PRIVACY

Do you disclose or keep things to yourself? The expression-privacy dialectic occurs when we desire openness in our relationships while still wanting to maintain a certain level of privacy. The internal tension between openness and privacy determines how much partners reveal to one another.[15] The push-pull here is between wanting to get closer by revealing thoughts and feelings and wanting to protect ourselves from criticism by withholding personal information that could increase vulnerability.

Externally, this dialectic manifests itself in how much we choose to reveal versus how much we conceal. For example, if your boss asks you what you think of a coworker's performance, do you tell the truth or keep your real thoughts to yourself? What do you tell your best friend about a dysfunctional romantic relationship? Do you reveal details about an abusive relationship or keep that information private? While we may want to reveal a relationship, we may think it best to conceal it from public scrutiny, fearing what could happen if others intervene. Unfortunately, such fears can allow an abusive relationship to continue.[16]

How much newness and novelty do you desire in your relationship?

WORKING THROUGH DIALECTICAL TENSIONS

Which of the preceding relational dialectics cause you the most problems? If you are like many partners, the dialectic producing the most tension in your close relationships is that of autonomy-connection, followed in descending order by predictability-novelty, inclusion-seclusion, openness-closeness, conventionality-uniqueness, and revelation-concealment.[17] Some researchers support the preeminence of autonomy-connection but believe that the tension surrounding the openness-closeness dialectic also significantly influences relational progress or deterioration.[18]

The real challenge lies in managing the problems created by the contradictory pushes and pulls. Researchers have identified a number of ways of handling these dialectical tensions practically.[19] Among them are denial, disorientation, spiraling alternation, segmentation, balance, integration, recalibration, and reaffirmation.

When you practice *denial,* you respond to one pole of a dialectical challenge while ignoring the other. For example, when caught between conflicting desires for autonomy and connection, you might opt for connection only, choosing to spend all your time with your partner. You satisfy one need while denying the other.

When you practice *disorientation,* you feel overwhelmed and opt to give in to feelings of utter helplessness. This response is nonfunctional, because all dialogue between you and your partner stops as you retreat into yourself.

The response of *spiraling alternation* finds you caught in a repetitive cycle of alternating tensions, causing you to move repeatedly from one side of the dialectic to the other. You might choose to draw close emotionally, but then argue that you need more space, only to draw close once more.

When you engage in *segmentation,* you and your partner isolate different relationship aspects and deal with them in separate situations of relational life. For example, you may choose to share some activities but have independent interests in other life spheres. You might emphasize different sides of the dialectic depending on the topic being discussed or the context in which find yourselves. For example, you might be open to discussing everything except politics or religion.

Balance is another compromise approach in which both partners see dialectical tension poles as legitimate and attempt to deal with their opposing needs by submerging the full strength of those needs. By engaging both sides of the dialectic—choosing to be moderately open or moderately connected, you strive to reach a midpoint that tips in neither direction.

Integration finds you responding to opposing forces without denying or diluting them. You might, for example, relish certainty but embrace its opposite by doing something that you have never done before on weekends.

When you *recalibrate* a relational tension, you reframe it. Though this tactic does not ensure a solution to the tensions, it does allow partners to redefine the nature of the challenge they face so that it is not perceived as a permanent oppositional pull or contradiction.

Finally, *reaffirmation* involves the realization by both partners that dialectical tensions will persist in relationships if only because relationships are rich and complex. Working through tensions becomes a promise of what the relationship can accomplish rather than a threat to its survival. We discuss relationship maintenance in greater depth in the next section.

Being adept at managing these pulls and pushes enhances relational comfort and prevents such tensions from contributing to a relationship's demise.

RELATIONSHIP MAINTENANCE

Though we may find the relationships we share satisfying and mutually rewarding, we still have to commit to working to maintain each one—that is, we need to engage in **relationship maintenance**. Should we grow lazy or careless, expecting a relationship to take care of itself, the relationship could end up suffering from a lack of nourishment and, if not tended to, waste away.[20]

Relationship maintenance: The work that is needed to keep a relationship healthy.

How can we keep a relationship healthy? First, we cannot let it go untended. We need to be mindful of it, make time for it, and demonstrate our commitment to it. According to researchers Kathryn Dindia and Leslie Baxter, we need to use the following strategies to maintain a relationship's health:

1. We need to take time to talk to one another and share our feelings and concerns in an open and honest manner.

2. We need to talk about *how* we talk to each other—that is, engage in *metacommunication* (as discussed in Chapter 6).

3. We need to rely on prosocial approaches, including showing that we affirm, support, and value our partner, being cheerful in each other's presence, and refraining from criticizing each other.

4. We need to celebrate the relationship itself by engaging in activities that mark the relationship's very existence and confirm its importance.

5. We need to have fun simply spending time together.[21]

To want to invest in and work at maintaining their relationship, partners need to feel treated fairly. According to equity theory, each partner needs to feel that both are equally committed to preserving the relationship, that neither is taking advantage of the other, and that the resources are being shared equitably. If one party in a relationship functions as a relationship weather vane, effectively in charge of relationship maintenance, that does not bode well for the relationship's future. When one party demonstrates concern and seeks to adapt but the other fails to do so, the relationship could be in danger.

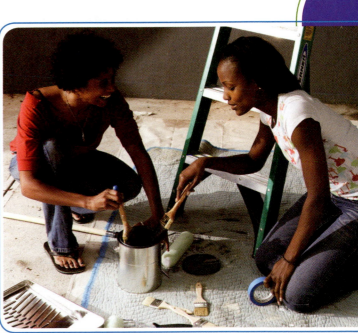

Relationships take work to maintain.

As a relationship's strength grows, the partners become more secure and feel less pressure to reciprocate every relationship contribution equally or quickly. Instead of focusing on the short-term relationship balance sheet, they focus on the long-term future, and thus they feel confident enough to postpone the personal rewards they expect their connection to each other to deliver. This, however, does not mean that the fairness quotient of the relationship can stay unbalanced too long without causing the partners to explore the nature of their interactions and to suggest changing the state of equity. By periodically assessing our relationship's equity and quality, we demonstrate our interest in its general state or climate, not merely in what we are currently gaining or losing by maintaining it.[22]

For those relationships that have the healthiest climates and make us feel the happiest, most rewarded, and most secure, we tend to perceive ourselves as investing equally in the relationship's well-being and its future. In contrast, when we believe we are the one investing more in the relationship, we tend to become resentful and might even conclude we are being "used." At the same time, when our partner makes more of a psychological or physical investment than we do, we could experience guilt. Either perceived imbalance reduces relationship satisfaction, possibly eroding the relationship's effectiveness and limiting or curtailing its future.[23] Once we believe a relationship has no future, we no longer perceive the need to weather bad times, and suddenly problems and conflicts we once would have handled easily or attempted to work out responsibly now appear insurmountable and

To evaluate a relationship, we may try to assess whether it is based on fairness or is one-sided.

Consider a relationship you are currently in and one that has terminated. Compare and contrast them based on the extent to which you and your current and former partner do or did each of the following:

1. Experience(d) feelings of being let down

2. Feel/felt rewarded

3. Share(d) resources

4. Feel/felt pressured to reciprocate the other's good deeds

5. Believe(d) the relationship survived only because of your or the other's efforts

6. Handle(d) and resolve(d) relational problems and conflicts fairly

Based on your responses, how important would you say fairness is to you in maintaining a satisfying relationship?

---

not worth the time or effort. When a relationship reaches this point, we also are less likely to trust one another. Thus, we tell each other less, and, as a result, we continue growing apart, as Knapp and Vangelisti's relationship model suggests.

RELATIONSHIP REPAIR: FIX IT OR END IT

When a relationship fails to satisfy or is no longer as satisfying as it once was, we need to decide whether we want to work to salvage or repair it and, if so, how to go about it. Of course, before we can take steps toward relationship repair or dissolution, we should identify what caused our relationship's communication climate to become negative in the first place.

IDENTIFY THE PROBLEM

The first task is to identify, as clearly as possible, why the relationship is not working. What is the problem? What exactly is it that you find dissatisfying?

As you learned in Chapter 2, the primary factor that leads to relationship problems and the creation of a negative relationship climate is a partner's sending disconfirming rather than confirming messages. Whereas **confirming messages** demonstrate that we value the relationship and our partner, disconfirming messages show our disregard. When we send **disconfirming messages**, we exhibit a lack of recognition of the other and his or her needs. We fail to acknowledge the other person's ideas or feelings. We refrain from supporting him or her, and we limit the amount of information we share. In effect, disconfirming messages announce to the other person that we are now of a mind to diminish or dismiss him or her. By our behavior, we let the other know we are ignoring him or her, that the person is unworthy of our serious attention, that because we now believe him or her to be insignificant, we are able to display a basic lack of concern for his or her needs. We may verbally abuse our partner, continually complain about his or her shortcomings, pretend he or she is not present, and make a concerted effort to prove our own importance by demonstrating that whatever we do matters, while the other's words and actions do

Confirming messages: Messages that convey value for another person.

Disconfirming messages: Messages that convey disregard for another person.

not count. Over time, the absence of confirmation curtails effective communication and reshapes the relationship into one that is very uncomfortable.

IDENTIFY STRATEGIES TO REPAIR THE PROBLEM

Next, partners need to agree on what to do to restore the relationship to a state each will find rewarding and reinforcing, one that affirms each party. This is the point at which we ask what kinds of changes, if any, we each would be willing to make in our behavior that could improve our satisfaction with the relationship, including its emotional tone or communication climate. For example, we take a giant step toward confirming the importance of our relationship with another if we (1) demonstrate our willingness to acknowledge the person's significance; (2) work to sustain both a verbal and a nonverbal dialogue that demonstrates our respect for him or her; (3) reflect back to that person that we care about, understand, and respect his or her feelings; and (4) encourage him or her to share thoughts and feelings with us.

DECIDE TO DISSOLVE OR SAVE THE RELATIONSHIP

Relationship repair depends on the partners being able to talk about what they feel and want from each other. When a relationship is stressed, the parties tend to exchange and perceive a lot more negativity than previously. Comments to each other become tinged with sarcasm. They argue more, and problems tend to escalate rather being resolved to their mutual satisfaction.[24] When partners fail to receive the rewards they expect, see no purpose in maintaining the relationship, or are unable to handle the strain that trying to maintain the relationship presents, they are liable to break up.

What kinds of changes are you willing to make should a relationship you share experience problems?

Unless mutually agreed to, breaking up is rarely easy. However, you can employ two key strategies to avoid an ugly scene. First, do not overpersonalize the relationship's end by feeling a need to blame yourself or your partner for the breakup. Asking questions such as "What's wrong with him?" or "How could I have been so stupid?" usually solves nothing. The fact is that sometimes circumstances rather than people cause a relationship to end.[25] Second, keep a sense of perspective and recognize that a relationship that does not survive probably was not meant to survive. When you are no longer able to meet each other's needs, or when you feel that the relationship is stifling your personal growth, it may be better to end it.

On the other hand, when one or both partners are motivated to repair the relationship, by questioning themselves and each other about the relationship and by making a commitment to change how each relates to the other, a couple can renegotiate the relationship, transform it, and facilitate its continued growth.

THE DARK SIDE OF RELATIONSHIPS: DYSFUNCTIONS AND TOXIC COMMUNICATION

In the United States, a woman is battered by an intimate partner approximately every fifteen seconds. Every day, four women die from violence committed by persons close to them. Some 50 percent of women have been physically or emotionally abused. It is estimated that

Relationship repair:
The work that is needed when a relationship fails to satisfy.

Women are often portrayed in the media as helpless against dangerous romantic men, as in this scene from *The Twilight Saga: New Moon,* in which Bella Swan (Kristen Stewart) is approached by the werewolf Jacob Black (Taylor Lautner).

85 percent of relationship abuse is perpetrated by males against females. Females, however, can also be highly verbally abusive toward their male partners. What is more, homosexual couples also experience partner abuse.[26] When a sexual relationship goes awry, why does it too often culminate in emotional or physical violence?[27]

While we may think of all romantic relationships as based in love, some have a dark side that makes them dysfunctional.[28] They are unhealthy, destructive, and characterized by episodes of **toxic communication**. Both physical and psychological forms of relational abuse are toxic and leave psychological scars from which victims find it difficult to recover. The fact that men commit most of the violence that is perpetrated against women underscores the unequal balance of power in many relationships. In general, men have been socialized to assert themselves, compete, and focus on outcomes, whereas society has conditioned women to defer, compromise, and focus more on nurturing others.

Why do some men abuse their partners? Why do too many women remain in these relationships? Perhaps it is because of learned myths such as "love can jump hurdles." As the media fill our minds with romantic notions of dangerous yet attractive male figures and charming but helpless females such as those featured in the *Twilight* books and films and the *Fifty Shades of Grey* novels, some women are apt to become overly dependent, leading to the toleration of abuse and contributing to increased physical and emotional risk.[29]

Romanticized notions encourage the abused to downplay relational violence by blaming it on uncontrollable passion or too much alcohol rather than on the abuser. As a result, both victim and aggressor ignore or reframe abusive incidents. Abusive persons have strong masculine gender orientations, relish controlling others, and aggressively seek to dominate. Victims who remain in such unhealthy relationships likely have been socialized into combining the emotionally supportive feminine role with one of learned helplessness and fear. Additionally, they probably have been socialized to be deferential and to value interpersonal harmony. When in a courtship relationship, the predominant theme the man enacts is control, while the predominant theme the woman enacts is dependence.[30] The perpetrators of violence against relational partners also take pains to isolate their partners from financial resources, leaving them without access to cash, checking accounts, or credit cards.[31]

Like friendships and romantic relationships, dysfunctional relationships pass through a predictable cycle of stages as illustrated in the model of the cycle of abuse (see Figure 13.8). During the first stage, relational tensions build in the abuser, who blames the partner for problems or for not being supportive and looks for an excuse to vent anger. In the second stage, the tensions erupt into violence and one or more battering incidents occur. In the third stage, the abuser experiences remorse and resolves to make it up to the victim, typically promising that it will never happen again. In the fourth stage, there is a lull in violence, and the victim again feels loved until relational tensions build and the cycle of abuse repeats.[32] For abuse to persist, the victim must be isolated from family and friends who could otherwise offer solace, support, and a means of escape.[33]

Toxic communication: Communication that is verbally or physically abusive.

Every 15 seconds in the United States a man beats a woman. Researchers contend that the abuse is promoted by cultural norms that espouse that males should be aggressive, in control, and dominant, and women should be submissive, loyal, and deferential.

1. Have you or anyone you know ever been involved in an abusive relationship?

2. If so, to what extent, if at all, do you believe the abuse was related to gender?

Figure 13.8 The Cycle of Abuse

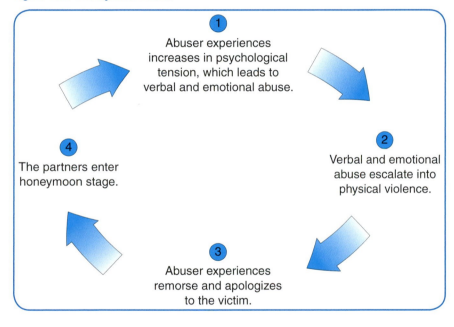

1. Abuser experiences increases in psychological tension, which leads to verbal and emotional abuse.

2. Verbal and emotional abuse escalate into physical violence.

3. Abuser experiences remorse and apologizes to the victim.

4. The partners enter honeymoon stage.

Why do some stay in unhappy relationships? Usually people stay because they want to. Why do some stay in abusive relationships? Most stay because they think they have to.[34] Relationships involving psychological or physical violence are ineffective, unhealthy, and often personally devastating. Violence has no place in any relationship. If you find yourself in an abusive relationship, do not think you can make it better by loving your partner more. That is not a viable solution. The best solution is to call the National Domestic Violence Hotline (at 1-800-799-SAFE, or 1-800-799-7233) for advice and then seek protection in a safe place such as a battered women's shelter. While all relationships encounter challenges, violence devalues the very meaning of love and is never an acceptable option.

RELATIONSHIPS AND DEATH: PROCESSING GRIEF

Not all relationship terminations are the result of a decision made by one or both parties to the relationship. Unfortunately, some of our strongest relationships terminate due to a loved one's death. Many report death to be the most painful of all relationship endings, and it is one that all of us will experience at some point in our lives. When a loved one dies, the surviving partner can be left with the feelings of loneliness and despair that may damage psychological and physical health. In fact, bereaved individuals are at greater risk than others for psychological problems as well as immune system and other health problems.[35] At the same time, however, some people may not be devastated by the death of a relational partner. Whether devastated or not, a person grieving should be allowed to recover in her or his own way.[36]

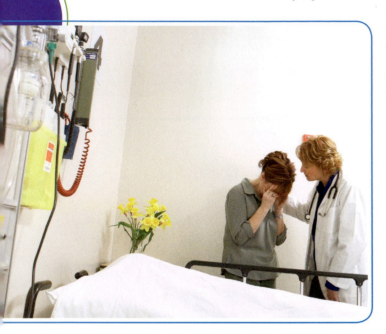

Some of our strongest relationships end with a loved one's death.

What steps can we take to rescue ourselves from grief? First, it is useful to understand the **grief process**, which has been characterized as consisting of five stages (see Figure 13.9). The first stage, denial, finds the griever trying to deny what has happened. Reality, however, prompts him or her to acknowledge the magnitude of the loss and the feelings of loneliness and social isolation accompanying it. The second stage, anger, leaves the person in grief feeling both helpless and powerless as he or she rages against the loss. During the third stage, guilt, the griever turns anger inward, regretting anything he or she might ever have done or said to hurt the person who has died. The grieving person feels as if a chapter in his or her life is left unwritten. This leads into the fourth stage, depression, during which the grieving person feels as if his or her former life is over and nothing will ever be right again. In fact, he or she finds it virtually impossible to envision a future. Finally, in the acceptance stage, the person realizes that while things will never again be the same, he or she will make it through and continue living.[37]

Figure 13.9 Working through Grief

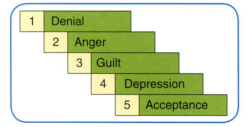

1. Denial
2. Anger
3. Guilt
4. Depression
5. Acceptance

During the mourning period, those closest to the person who has suffered the loss typically try to offer protection by shielding him or her from feeling sad. Denying sadness, however, rarely makes it go away. Rather than attempting to suppress or ignore feelings of sadness, mourners need to be permitted to experience and express it. Submerged grief usually does more harm than its expression. By allowing grieving persons to process their feelings, we help free them to continue with their lives.[38] Here, a social support network can play a critical role.

Grief process: A five-stage process during which the feelings a grieving individual experiences begin with denial and then pass through anger, guilt, and depression before resolving with acceptance.

Writing an obituary for the deceased loved one may also help a bereaved person to work through his or her grief. While the obituary produced may or may not provide accurate information on the person who died, writing it gives the person grieving the opportunity to recollect, honor, and commemorate what he or she appreciated most about the person who passed away while simultaneously facilitating the forming of memories. After the terrorist attacks of September 11, 2001, reporters for the *New York Times* interviewed the families of victims to help them create obituaries as tributes to those who had been killed.[39] Like a life story, an obituary performs the valuable act of remembering.[40]

Interestingly, an erroneous stereotype regarding romantic relationships in which one partner has died is that women grieve while men replace. Actually, significant numbers of both men and women form new intimate relationships over time after recovering from the deaths of romantic partners.

A separate issue related to death is that of "virtual immortality." What happens to a person's online existence after death? Does the cyberself pass away? Who has the power (and the passwords) to sort through a former digital life?[41]

CULTURE AND RELATIONAL INTIMACY

Culture mediates notions of intimacy, including ideas about self-disclosure and the expression of grief. Around the world, and even within U.S. culture, not all people necessarily approach intimacy in the same way. In fact, notions of intimacy vary from culture to culture. For example, the Japanese use friendship as a pathway to greater intimacy, while Americans rely more on romantic relationships to attain intimacy. Thus, the Japanese perceive best-friend relationships as more intimate than boy- or girlfriend relationships. On the other hand, both Japanese and Americans perceive strangers to be the least intimate relationship, see acquaintance relationships as less intimate than relationships with friends, and view best-friend relationships as more intimate than "just friends" relationships. These similarities in perception suggest that the stages of relationships discussed previously may cut across cultures.[42]

Within the United States, African Americans and Caucasians hold the most permissive sexual attitudes, while individuals of Asian, Latino, and Middle Eastern heritage typically display more conservative attitudes.[43] Similarly, both Caucasians and African Americans believe that talking about sexual intimacy is a sign of a strong relationship, whereas Asian and Hispanic Americans are much less likely to discuss their more intimate relationships.[44]

Notions of how much disclosure is appropriate also vary among cultures. Those born in the United States tend to be high disclosers, even demonstrating a willingness to disclose information about themselves to strangers.[45] This may explain why Americans seem particularly easy to meet, are proficient at cocktail-party conversation, and are perceived as exhibitionists by those from more nondisclosing cultures. Conversely, Japanese tend to do little disclosing about themselves to others except to the few people with whom they are very close. In general, Asians do not reach out to strangers. They do, however, demonstrate great care for each other, since they view harmony as essential to relationship nurturance. They work hard to prevent those they perceive as outsiders from obtaining information they believe to be unfavorable.[46]

Members of cultures with a strong group orientation do not value privacy as much as do members of cultures with an individualistic orientation. Thus, members of Arabic, Greek, and Spanish cultures have a lesser need for privacy in relationships than do members of Western or North American cultures.[47] Similarly, members of Western cultures depend on actions rather than words to cement trust. Westerners tend to perceive commitment as a bond connecting two people. Asians, Hispanics, and African Americans perceive commitment as a bond linking the members of groups.[48]

Members of diverse cultures also express and cope with grief differently. Relationship scholar Steve Duck notes that in some cultures it is acceptable to fall to the ground, cover oneself with dust, and wail loudly in a public display of grief; other cultures emphasize public composure and view the showing of such emotion as unacceptable.[49]

GENDER, INTIMACY, AND DISTANCE

Understanding alternative ways of developing and maintaining intimacy is an important part of our ability to sustain relationships. While both women and men value friendships and romantic relationships, they are apt to express closeness dissimilarly. For example, most men define intimacy in terms of what two people *do* together, whereas most women define it in terms of what they *talk about* together. Thus, men engage in shared activities as a means to achieve closeness, while women participate in shared emotional talk.[50] Men assume the value of a relationship; they don't feel a deep need to talk about it. Women, in contrast, feel that discussion of a relationship's dynamics is important. This can create relationship problems, because as men attempt to develop intimacy with women, they will plan activities, whereas women might prefer to be in a situation in which they would have an increased opportunity for talking and self-disclosing, not just doing.[51]

Men and women define intimacy differently.

Men and women also assign different weights to autonomy and connection. Because men are more likely to be socialized toward independence, they tend to prefer autonomy to interrelatedness; in contrast, women tend to need autonomy less and connection more. This preference disparity may lead a woman to think that her partner does not value their relationship and lead a man to think that his partner wants to consume his time with intrusive talk. What creates comfort for many women is the opposite of what creates discomfort for many men. Women likewise tend to disclose more intimate information to partners than do men. Perhaps this is because women have been encouraged to be more personal and open about their thoughts, feelings, and fears than men. Thus, men tend to ask women more questions about themselves than women ask of men. At the same time, women hope that their male partners will reciprocate with self-disclosures of their own voluntarily.[52] When it comes to disclosing intimate information, however, women are in the lead.

In general, women watch the progress of relationships more carefully. As a result, women tend to detect relationship troubles sooner and are apt to surpass men in both expressing feelings of vulnerability and providing emotional support. Whereas women are more comfortable revealing their feelings and providing overt expressions of **caring**, men tend to be at ease using covert caring signals such as teasing, joking, and providing companionship.

Caring: The level of emotional involvement we convey to one another.

Contrary to the image presented in romance novels and films, men are more likely to initiate a declaration of love than are women.[53] They are also more likely to fall in love first.[54] More often than not, a woman will wait until she hears her male partner say the "I love you" phrase before she reciprocates. Men have been socialized to take the lead in love.

ANALYZE THIS: *Feelings*

In the poem "To Women, as Far as I'm Concerned," D. H. Lawrence expresses his opinion of feelings.

The feelings I don't have, I don't have.

The feelings I don't have, I won't say I have.

The feelings you say you have, you don't have.

The feelings you would like us both to have, we neither of us have.

The feelings people ought to have, they never have.

If people say they've got feelings, you may be pretty sure they haven't got them.

So if you want either of us to feel anything at all

you'd better abandon all idea of feelings altogether.

Consider these questions:

1. With which, if any, of the poet's observations do you agree?

2. In what ways, if any, do you think the poet's perceptions express a male point of view? Explain.

SOURCE: "To Women, As Far As I'm Concerned", from THE COMPLETE POEMS OF D. H. LAWRENCE by D. H. Lawrence, edited by V. de Sola Pinto & F. W. Roberts, copyright © 1964, 1971 by Angelo Ravagli and C. M. Weekley, Executors of the Estate of Frieda Lawrence Ravagli. Used by permission of Viking Penguin, a division of Penguin Group (USA) Inc. Reproduced by permission of Pollinger Limited and The Estate of Frieda Lawrence Ravagli.

MEDIA AND TECHNOLOGY: THE DECLINE OF PRIVACY AND DISTANCE

Social networks enable us to keep in touch with those who live near and at a distance, some of whom we see regularly and others whom we may never see face-to-face, potentially making the Internet the ultimate noncontact, person-to-person network.[55] This is particularly important because of changing attitudes toward privacy and the reality that **long-distance relationships** are increasingly common.

The current economic and employment environment has made us more transient; in growing numbers, we are compelled to move to wherever jobs exist, to travel extensively for work, and to venture to distant training centers that require more time spent away from home. Yet we and our friends, family members, and significant others can commit to staying close and "staying together" psychologically although geographically apart. Certainly long-distance relationships are not new. When separated by distance, your grandparents and parents may have exchanged love letters. The Internet, however, has changed things in that some relationships that now exist may not have begun were it not for the **virtual communities** that brought the partners together.[56]

What impact does online interaction have on a relationship? In Chapter 12, we noted that interacting online facilitates hyperpersonal communication, likely precipitating greater intimacy and social attraction than would a comparable amount of face-to-face interaction.

Long-distance relationship: A relationship between individuals who are geographically separated.

Virtual community: A community that exists only in cyberspace.

Communicating online leads partners to construct idealized impressions of one another, heightening their expectations for the relationship and contributing to their continuing contact.[57]

What is more, Facebook users are more connected than ever. While the adage suggests there are "six degrees of separation" between any two people on the planet, the average Facebook user is but a mere 4.74 degrees away from any other user. Thus, the distances between us are narrowing. While some of our ties may be weak, they shrink the world, bringing us closer together nonetheless.[58]

When Facebook started, the amount of private information that members shared was minimal. Now members are able to share virtually everything. In addition, Facebook's Timeline keeps a record of each user's past posts, back to the account's creation, allowing others to gain a more comprehensive understanding of a person's online identity by providing a kind of life story.[59] Unless a user is vigilant about who can see old posts, however, his or her life can become almost literally an open book. The tug between privacy and transparency continues. Interestingly, active Facebook users are less concerned with privacy than are infrequent users.[60] How much of your Facebook past are you willing to reveal? What would you like concealed?

More than ever before in history, we are technologically equipped to handle the challenges of long-distance relationships. Previously, when individuals carried on such relationships, they were aware how the geographic distance created a special fragility in the relationships, which they were apt to characterize as tenuous and uncertain. Long-distance partners then lacked something we tend to take for granted: routine interactions about nothing—that is, talk about routine, seemingly unimportant daily events or activities.[61] Now we have the technological means to maintain frequent low-cost contact with those who are geographically distant from us, facilitating the small talk that increases relationship health, durability, and longevity. We have become more accessible—even immediately accessible—although miles apart. This sense of immediacy helps to nurture long-distance relationships by allowing the partners to sustain a sense of personal commitment and continuity. Because long-distance relationships no longer engender the decreased contact they were once known for, rather than concluding that a relationship should end because of geographic distance, we may now feel more equipped to cope. Technology serves up instant connectivity, allowing us to continue weaving our daily lives together. Even though far apart, we have the ability to feel the closeness required for relational depth.

Technology facilitates the development and maintenance of relationships in other ways as well. When communicating online, some of us actually become more talkative. There are fewer awkward silences and embarrassing moments. Some even feel less vulnerable talking about feelings online than they do face-to-face.[62]

Additionally, online journals—weblogs or blogs—facilitate emotional purging and self-other insight. Bloggers write about issues of importance to them, even reporting on painful traumas; the soliciting of reader feedback and the reading of each other's entries brings users closer together.[63]

GAINING COMMUNICATION COMPETENCE: HANDLING BOTH RELATIONAL CLOSENESS AND DISTANCE

By now it should be apparent that negotiating closeness and distance in relationships is complex. By considering the following questions you will be better able to select the level of closeness appropriate for you.

Work demands compel more and more of us to experience long-distance relationships. Interview three people of your generation (identifying their approximate ages and types of work) and three people from an older or younger generation (similarly identifying their approximate ages and types of work) regarding whether they expect to experience or have experienced a long-distance relationship (whether regional or international) because of job demands. Also ask them to describe what they consider to be the biggest hurdles of such relationships and how they have or would overcome them.

HOW IMPORTANT TO YOU IS THIS PERSON?

We typically want to get closer to and share more about ourselves with those whose friendship or romantic involvement is important to us. One measure of how important a person is in your life is the extent to which you are willing to invest time, effort, and energy to build and maintain a relationship with him or her.

ARE YOU WILLING TO INITIATE INTERACTION?

No matter how interested you and another person might be in one another, you stand little chance of developing a meaningful relationship unless you begin to communicate. If either of you hesitates or for some reason is unable to initiate contact, you are less likely to build the foundation needed for an effective relationship. Thus, it is necessary to use appropriate conversation openers that make the following situation unlikely:

> I decided to marry her. Courtship would be a mere formality. But what to say to begin the courtship? "Would you like some of my gum?" seemed too low-class. "Hello," was too trite a greeting for my future bride. "I love you! I am hot with passion!" was too forward "I want to make you the mother of my children," seemed a bit premature.
>
> Nothing. That's right, I said nothing. And after a while, the bus reached her stop, she got off, and I never saw her again.
>
> End of story.[64]

Being willing to initiate interaction is necessary to begin a relationship.

HOW MUCH AND WHAT KIND OF INTIMACY DO YOU DESIRE?

Many of us hope to realize emotional closeness with friends and lovers. We expect to reveal our inner selves and hope they will reciprocate. The ways we express intimacy, however, depend on our background. Some of us will build intimacy through expressive disclosure talk, while others will build it instrumentally by participating in activities together and by being there and doing things for one another.

HOW ACCEPTING ARE YOU OF THE OTHER PERSON?

To what degree are you able to accept the other person for who that person is and what he or she represents? Do you feel that in order for you to accept him or her fully, the other person must change? With our friends and lovers, we should feel that we can be ourselves, that we do not need to dissemble or put on a false front, and that we can reveal our feelings without having them or ourselves rejected.

HOW ARE YOU WILLING TO SUPPORT THE OTHER PERSON?

Support is a basic expectation of most relationships based on friendship or love.[65] We show support in different ways: by listening, talking through problems, empathizing, or being there in times of need or even when we disagree.

DO YOU RECOGNIZE THAT YOUR RELATIONSHIP WILL CHANGE?

Changes in relationships are a natural and a continuous part of the life cycle. Relationships evolve. They are dynamic. Relationship changes may challenge or upset us, excite or thrill us. We may welcome some changes, curse others, be delighted or disoriented by them. But they will continue. The people whose lives we touch, and vice versa, will influence us and change us in ways we are unable to predict. Our relationship choices, and whether we manage or mismanage them (expecting instant gratification or having the patience necessary for a meaningful relationship to grow) will affect and transform us.

CAN YOUR RELATIONSHIP SURVIVE THE DISTANCE TEST?

While we are likely to remain geographically close to those we see regularly, what do you imagine would happen to your friendships and romantic relationships if you had to relocate to a different part of the country or the world? Which of your relationships do you think would survive the test of distance? What specific steps would you take to secure intimacy and ensure the relationship's maintenance? How would you keep your lives interwoven? Would you rely on technology? Would you travel regularly to see one another?

DO YOU KNOW WHEN TO CONTINUE AND WHEN TO END A RELATIONSHIP?

Not every relationship should be sustained or maintained. When a relationship turns dark, is destructive, deteriorates into verbal or physical violence, or drains our energy and self-confidence, we need to end it before it does irreparable harm. However, there are some relationships we do not want to end, such as family relationships. In these cases, we may need to seek professional help.

Samantha sat down in her first-class seat. Her company had paid for her to travel coach, but she had used some of her frequent-flier miles to treat herself to a first-class return flight. After all, she told herself, she had sold more than anyone in her division, and she really deserved the upgrade.

The first-class seats were so-o-o comfortable. After texting her friend that she was on the plane and had just ordered a latte, Samantha settled in to read a magazine. She briefly gazed out the window, watching the last-minute preparations of the ground crew. Then Tom arrived and sat in the seat next to hers. From his opening greeting, Samantha knew that the flight might not be the dream flight she had envisioned; it would likely be awkward and uncomfortable instead.

"What are your plans for tonight?" Tom nonchalantly asked her. At first, Samantha thought he must be joking, and she smiled faintly. But he wasn't joking. He continued saying, "I have tickets to the hockey game. Want to go?"

Samantha answered that she had other plans, but added, "Thank you, anyway." Tom, however, pressed on: "I've just broken up with my girlfriend. Are you seeing anyone? Even if you are, what about tomorrow night, sweetheart?"

It wasn't just his sexist language that bothered her—it was the tone and content of the conversation. Tom acted as if they were vacationing together, as if he knew her well and could confide in her, when they didn't know each other at all. Not only had he skipped any rapport-building stages; he was also attempting to move too quickly for friendship between them to even have a chance of developing.

Samantha was uncertain how to handle the situation. She could ask to change her seat. She could tell Tom that he was bothering her and that she found his manner offensive. She could take out her phone and text a friend. She turned away from him and looked out the window.

Suddenly, the decision was no longer hers. Tom stood up and asked to change his seat. As the plane slowly pulled away from the gate, Samantha heard him asking someone else, "Would you like to go to a hockey game?"

Consider these questions:

1. If you had been in Samantha's position, how would you have responded to Tom?

2. What relationship-building mistakes, if any, do you think are exhibited in this case study?

3. What might Tom do differently if given the opportunity to replay his part?

CHAPTER SUMMARY

1 Define self-disclosure and intimacy. Self-disclosure occurs when we willingly tell others things about ourselves that they otherwise would not know. How much you reveal about yourself to another is a measure of closeness, or intimacy, in a relationship.

2 Explain social penetration theory. Each one of our relationships involves a different amount of intimacy and distance. In fact, we can describe every relationship we share in terms of its breadth, or the number of topics we talk about, and its depth, or how central the discussed topics are to our self-concept and how much we reveal about ourselves during our conversations. According to social penetration theory, most of our relationships begin with relatively narrow breadth and shallow depth. As the relationships grow and increase in strength, however, both breadth and depth increase also.

3 Describe the Johari window. The Johari window is a four-paned model used to explore the nature of relationships. The sizes of the panes signify what you do and do not know about yourself and what another person does and does not know about you. The four panes are termed the open area, the blind area, the hidden area, and the unknown area. As information is moved from the hidden, blind, and unknown areas into the open area, we engage in self/other disclosure and gain self-awareness and self-insight.

4 Define and explain the effects of relational dialectics. While some relational forces pull us toward intimacy, others pull us in the opposite direction. Relational dialectics reflect the dynamic nature of relational ties and tugs such as integration-separation, stability-change, and expression-privacy, tensions that we need to resolve.

5 Discuss when and how to maintain a relationship versus when to terminate one. We use relationship maintenance techniques to nourish relationships we find satisfying and mutually rewarding. This involves being mindful, taking time, and demonstrating commitment. Sometimes, if we cannot renegotiate or repair a relationship satisfactorily, we make the decision to dissolve it.

6 Define and explain toxic-communication and identify the four stages in an abusive relationship. Unfortunately, not all of our relationships are characterized by the presence of healthy patterns of communication. Some are dysfunctional, and in these the use of toxic communication is common. Dysfunctional relationships are also noted for the presence of verbal or physical abuse. Abusive relationships are characterized by four repeating stages: (1) the experiencing of psychological tension, to which the abuser responds by engaging in verbal and/or emotional abuse; (2) escalation into physical violence; (3) abuser remorse and apologies; and (4) a honeymoon stage until tensions increase again.

7 Explain the grief cycle, describing what occurs when a relationship ends with a loved one's death. The grief process consists of five stages: denial, anger, guilt, depression, and acceptance. Mourners need to be permitted to experience and express their feelings.

8 Identify how culture, gender, the media, and technology influence notions of intimacy and disclosure. Attitudes toward intimacy and disclosure differ from one culture to another. Members of different cultures may view strangers differently, hold more or less restrictive sexual attitudes, and engage in more or less self-disclosure. Like culture, gender influences preferences for developing and maintaining intimacy. Most men define intimacy in terms of what two people do together, whereas most women define it in terms of what they talk about together. Men and women also assign different weights to autonomy and connection. The media and technology also play roles in maintaining relationships, especially long-distance ones. We are a more transient society. Technology facilitates our committing ourselves psychologically to each other, though separated by great distance.

9 Discuss strategies for handling closeness and distance in relationships more effectively. Deciding how important another is to you, creating a climate fostering information seeking and giving, distinguishing the amount of intimacy desired, being accepting and supportive, acknowledging that changes occur in relationships, figuring out if a relationship can survive the distance test, and knowing when to end a relationship are necessary for gaining competence in handling closeness and distance in relationships.

CHECK YOUR UNDERSTANDING

1 Can you explain the relationship between self-disclosure and intimacy, using yourself or a close friend or relative to make your points? (See pages 364–365.)

2 Can you compare a relationship that has little breath and depth with one that has great breadth and little depth, and then with one that has both great breadth and great depth? (See pages 365–366.)

3 Can you use a Johari window to analyze one of your important relationships? (See pages 367–371.)

4 Can you summarize the dialectical tensions that can arise in a relationship? Which have arisen in your relationship with a family member? With a friend? With a romantic partner? In what ways are the tensions experienced similar and different? (See pages 371–374.)

5 Can you provide examples of how gender, culture, the media, and technology influence attitudes toward intimacy and distance in relationships? (See pages 381–384.)

CHECK YOUR SKILLS

1 Can you make sound decisions regarding to whom it is safe to reveal personal information about yourself? (See pages 364–365.)

2 Can you distinguish your relationships based on their breadth and depth? (See pages 365–366; and *Try This,* page 367.)

3 Can you determine when a relationship achieves its optimal level? (See pages 365–366; and *Reflect on This,* page 369.)

4 Can you use the Johari window to differentiate your relationships? (See pages 367–371; and *Try This,* page 372.)

5 Can you analyze the ways relational dialectics affect your relationships? (See pages 371–374; and *Try This,* page 374.)

6 Can you describe specifically what makes a relationship "fair" in your eyes? (See pages 374–376; and *Try This,* page 376.)

7 Can you make good decisions regarding when to try to repair a relationship and when to end it? (See pages 376–377.)

8 Can you identify when a relationship turns toxic and take the steps necessary to remove yourself from it? (See pages 377–379; and *Reflect on This,* page 379.)

9 Can you use cultural and gender differences to explain attitudes toward intimacy and distance? (See page 382; and *Analyze This,* page 383.)

10 Can you diagnose mistakes made during attempts to build a relationship? (See *The Case of the Plane Trip,* page 387.)

KEY TERMS

Self-disclosure *364*

Norm of reciprocity *364*

Relationship breadth *365*

Relationship depth *365*

Social penetration theory *365*

Johari window *367*

Relational dialectics theory *371*

Relationship maintenance *374*

Confirming messages *376*

Disconfirming messages *376*

Relationship repair *377*

Toxic communication *378*

Grief process *380*

Caring *382*

Long-distance relationship *383*

Virtual community *383*

STUDENT STUDY SITE

Visit the student study site at **www.sagepub.com/gambleic** to access the following materials:

- SAGE Journal Articles
- Videos
- Web Resources

- eFlashcards
- Web Quizzes
- Study Questions

chapter 14

*They always say that time
changes things, but you
actually have to change them
yourself.*

—Andy Warhol

RELATIONSHIPS IN OUR LIVES:
Family, Work, and
Health-Related Contexts

LEARNING OBJECTIVES

After completing this chapter, you should be able to demonstrate mastery of the following learning outcomes:

1. Discuss the nature of interpersonal communication in families, including the influences of culture, gender, the media, and technology on the interaction of family members.

2. Discuss the nature of interpersonal communication in the workplace, including how culture, gender, the media, and technology influence work relationships.

3. Explain the relationship between interpersonal communication and health, focusing on factors influencing the practitioner-client dyad and how culture, gender, the media, and technology influence health care–based relationships.

4. Identify how you can gain communication competence across contexts.

Our personal and professional relationships reflect how successful or unsuccessful we are in establishing a healthy work-life balance. If our professional life overshadows our personal life, relationships critical in the personal arena suffer. Similarly, if we neglect our professional life in favor of our personal life, we may end up looking for a new job. Jack Welch, the former head of General Electric, has argued that there is no such thing as work-life balance; instead, there are only work-life choices, which once made have consequences.[1]

More and more workers, however, are seeking work-life balance, and increasing numbers of employers are trying to help them. For example, to encourage its employees to achieve work-life balance and improve their ability to communicate their emotions and solve problems, Google offers hundreds of free classes, including a "Search Inside Yourself" seminar series, a course of study aimed at developing mindfulness. In the sessions, workers explore attention training, self-knowledge, and self-mastery.[2] Google employees work in a high-pressure environment in which criticism can be hard on egos, but perks such as volleyball courts, an indoor tree house, and apiaries alleviate some of the stress connected to the company's hard-driving culture.[3]

The attempt to achieve work-life balance does not diminish workplace importance, but it does symbolize that work is not everything. Workers with outside lives make better employees. Aware of this, many companies offer flextime schedules and let employees telecommute one or more days each week.

> **How good are you at balancing your personal and professional life?**

Work-life balance, as opposed to what used to be called work-family balance, is especially important to members of Gen X and Gen Y, also known as the Millennial Generation. Millennials expect flexibility; untethered from traditional workplaces, they get work done anywhere.[4]

Achieving work-life balance is especially essential for people who have jobs that are so stressful they can jeopardize health. For example, alcoholism, heart palpitations, eating disorders, and explosive temper are among the stress-related physical and emotional ailments associated with working in investment banking. As a result of their high-pressure jobs, investment bankers, traders, salespeople, and others like them can suffer personal emotional problems that exact a cost on their work and personal lives.[5]

Employers are not the only ones attending to this issue. An abundance of television offerings—including *Dr. Oz*, *The Doctors*, *The View*, *Teen Mom*, *Modern Family*, *Parenthood*, *Private Practice*, and *Grey's Anatomy*—address the topic of balancing work and personal and family responsibilities. Many, whether reality based, inspirational, or fictional, specifically explore the interface between personal and professional lives and health, providing models of the productive or unproductive handling of work-life stressors, together with effective or ineffective road maps for attaining work-life balance.

How good are you at balancing your personal life and your professional life?

WHAT DO YOU KNOW?

Before continuing your reading of this chapter, which of the following five statements do you believe to be true and which do you believe to be false?

1. Fewer than half of all American families include a married couple.　　T　F

2. If a family has more than two people, then its members live in triangles.　　T　F

3. Mindguards facilitate groupthink.　　T　F

4. An iron maiden is a woman who wears men's clothing.　　T　F

5. Cyberslacking occurs when you grow tired of playing online games.　T　F

Read the chapter to discover if you're right or if you've made any erroneous assumptions.

ANSWERS: 1. T; 2. T; 3. T; 4. F; 5. F

Family, work, and health communication are three contexts in which many of our most important interactions occur. How we interact and the kinds of relationships we share in each of these communication arenas influence our personal, economic, mental, and physical well-being. What happens in our family, on the job, and with our health has impacts on our sense of self and whether we feel physically and emotionally able to meet the daily challenges life presents.

Let us begin by exploring the nature of family communication. After all, much of what we know about communication stems from our upbringing. We apply the lessons we learned as children—including our internalization of family member functions, effective and ineffective communication patterns, and rules and responsibilities—to how we relate to others both at work and at play. It is in our family that we first learn how to create, maintain, and end relationships; how to express ourselves; how to argue; how to display affection; how to choose acceptable topics for conversation in mixed company; how work affects home life; how to cope with stress and illness; and more. What it means to be a family member and how the lessons we learned in childhood affect our health and relationship expectations are key issues to consider.

THE NATURE OF FAMILIAL COMMUNICATION

What is a family? Family communication researchers offer a number of definitions, including describing a family as a network of persons who live together and support each other,[6] as a group of intimates with strong ties of loyalty and emotion,[7] and as a group of two or more individuals who are interdependent because of their blood connection, legal bonds, and/or explicit verbal promise.[8] Some define family narrowly, others more broadly. We think family should be defined in terms of what it means to you. In other words, when you list the members of your family, in many ways you are revealing what family means to you.[9] Definitions of family need to be flexible and reflective of the diverse forms of contemporary families.

For some of us the concept of family brings to mind a picture of the traditional **nuclear family**, one that includes a mother, a father, and one or more children. Others picture a **blended family**, one that includes two adults—heterosexual, gay, lesbian, or transsexual— and children (biological or adopted) from one or both of the adults' previous relationships, as well as perhaps more from the current relationship. Others picture a **single-parent family** (also known as a primary-parent family), one in which the mother or father is solely responsible for the biological or adopted child(ren), effectively responsible for carrying out all parental obligations. Families also include committed partners who opt not to have children. As long as we are legally or emotionally connected to one or more people, we may consider ourselves part of a family.

Currently, more than half of all births in the United States are to single women, most of whom are not college educated.[10] In 1950, only 4 million Americans lived alone, approximately 9 percent of households. Today, according to 2011 census data, nearly 33 million Americans live alone, making up 28 percent of all households, which is nearly tied with the number of childless couples as the most prominent residential type.[11] Also of note, the Census Bureau reports that less than 50 percent of families in the United States include a married couple. That means that single adults or cohabiting opposite-sex or same-sex couples now head more than half of all U.S. households.[12]

Economic conditions and cultural preferences have increased the numbers of extended or intergenerational families living together—that is, in households shared by parents and their children along with the children's grandparents, and perhaps also aunts, uncles, and cousins. In recent years, economic conditions have led to a trend in which people of all age

Nuclear family: A household family unit that includes a mother, a father, and one or more children.

Blended family: A family with two adults and children from one or both of the adults' previous relationships as well as possibly children from the current relationship.

Single-parent family: A family in which one parent is solely responsible for the care of a biological or adopted child or children.

Figure 14.1 Percentage of One-Person Households in the United States, by Decade

SOURCE: Based on information from the U.S. Census Bureau.

groups have moved back to the family home, creating what has been labeled a **boomerang family** or an accordion family.[13] While some cultures have always lived in multigenerational households, this form of family living has not previously been the norm in the United States; demographers expect, however, that the numbers of U.S. households of this type will continue to increase for a while (see Figure 14.2).[14] Also increasing in number are **commuter families**, in which—again often for economic reasons—one or more members commute from a primary residence to a work location in a distant city, where they remain for periods.

In any discussion of family interaction, it is important to distinguish between family of origin and current family status. Your family of origin is the family in which you grew up. According to family therapist Virginia Satir, the family of origin provides the pattern for "peoplemaking."[15]

THE FAMILY AS COMMUNICATION SYSTEM

It is virtually impossible to assign a beginning or an end to communicative exchanges between family members. Familial exchanges are considered to be constantly in process, continually changing or evolving, providing us with a unique context for studying communication in which each member interprets experience based on his or her personal perspective.

There is a unique and dynamic interplay among family members. According to **systems theory**, the behavior of an individual family member can be understood only in relation to all family members and to the functioning of the family as a whole.[16] Family members are interdependent. The behavior of one family member affects the behavior of every other family member, both in and outside the family setting. Consequently, the verbal and nonverbal actions of one family member cannot be understood fully in isolation from those of other family members (remember our discussion of Watzlawick, Beavin, and Jackson's axioms of communication in Chapter 1).

Family Members Are Interdependent. To fully grasp the concept of family member interdependence, picture family members connected by pieces of rope. As one member moves, his or her movement tugs on or affects others. Sometimes as family members move

Boomerang families: Family households containing adult children who the family thought had left permanently but have unexpectedly returned.

Commuter family: A family that includes one or more members who commute from the household's primary residence to distant work location(s) and remain there for long periods of time.

Systems theory: An approach to communication that stresses the interaction of all elements in a communication network.

Figure 14.2 Multigenerational Households in the United States, 2000 and 2010

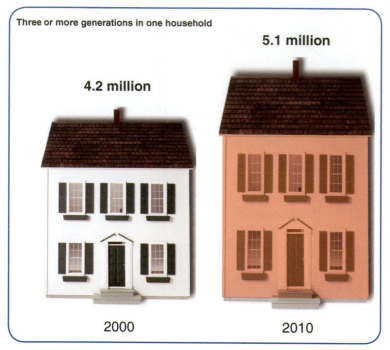

Three or more generations in one household

4.2 million
2000

5.1 million
2010

SOURCE: U.S. Census Bureau.

they tie each other up in knots, at other times they try to pull away from one another, and at still other times they give each other enough rope to experience the freedom necessary for personal growth.

The behavior of family members does not occur in a vacuum. When one person acts out, all have to adjust; any change in one part of the family system compels the entire system to adapt. Each member can cause the system to continue operating as it is or cause it to revise how it deals with situations, including the new and different. Any change in the family precipitates change in all members. Similarly, change in any one member precipitates change in the family.

The Family Is Greater than the Sum of Its Parts. Recall from Chapter 1 that the principle of nonsummativity tells us that the whole is greater than the sum of its parts. Summing up the characteristics of individual family members does not allow us to understand the family. Instead, we need to attend to how together the members of a family function as a whole, the ways in which they are connected, and the interaction patterns they use. By becoming more aware of the family system and discovering their part in it, including who they are and the connections between them and others, family members open the way to talking about their respective perceptions and any desire they may have to reshape either the roles members assume or the interaction patterns in use.

Families are complex and in flux. They need to be adaptive. Because they are made up of people, and people change as they age, families are continually dealing with change, processing new information, negotiating meaning, meeting member needs, and adapting to transitions. At the same time, members try to maintain a sense of stability and a balanced state in order to facilitate the family's maintenance.

None of this is easy. Change often leads to unresolved feelings, stress, and conflict. Families' attempts to meet such challenges and realize their goals reveal much about how they communicate. The systems process of *equifinality*, which asserts that initial system inputs do not determine outputs, reminds us that just as we can use different routes to reach a destination, different families may choose different pathways to reach similar goals.[17]

Family Members Engage in Mutual Influence. Family members are engaged in the complex process of mutual influence. As members decode, create, and share meaning, they interact and work out their relationships. Every family member, whether living or deceased, is connected to and has the ability to influence others in the family.

Every family has a unique communication dynamic.

FAMILY COMMUNICATION: ROLES AND RULES

Family members are expected to play certain roles in relation to each other and to the family as a whole. A role is a set of prescribed behaviors. Wage earner, homemaker, financial manager, child-care provider, and social planner are among the roles family members perform. In some families roles are shared; in others, each role is the primary responsibility of one family member. Whereas some families exhibit significant role versatility and turn taking in role performance, others adhere strictly to stereotypical role definitions. The family system sustains the roles that family members play. Today, family members play an expanding number of roles, a demand that may increase stress.

In families that practice healthy communication, roles relationships are constantly evolving. As the developmental stages of a family change, different family members may perform different roles. For example, some members may assume more responsibilities while others assume fewer. Family members who were advice givers may become advice takers, and vice versa. The late essayist and humorist Erma Bombeck refers to this switch in roles and power in a piece she wrote titled "When Did I Become the Mother, and the Mother Become the Child?"

Family members develop expectations for each other that, if realized, increase their satisfaction. For example, members of a family are expected to pull together to preserve the family unit and ensure its viability by helping each other survive everyday life and meeting each other's financial and emotional needs. Family members expect to receive emotional

ANALYZE THIS: *Transitions*

Begin by considering these questions: In what ways, if any, have the roles you play in your family evolved over time? To what extent are you satisfied/dissatisfied with your current roles?

In the following poem by Linda Pastan, the speaker reverses roles, offering us a mother's perception of her developing daughter:

To a Daughter Leaving Home

When I taught you

at eight to ride

a bicycle, loping along

beside you

as you wobbled away

on two round wheels,

my own mouth rounding

in surprise when you pulled

ahead down the curved path of the park,

I kept waiting

for the thud

of your crash as I

sprinted to catch up,

while you grew

smaller, more breakable

with distance,

pumping, pumping

for your life, screaming

with laughter,

the hair flapping

behind you like a

handkerchief waving

goodbye.

Now consider these questions:

1. What does the poem tell us about the parent-child relationship?

2. What does it tell us about the author's view of family?

SOURCE: "To a Daughter Leaving Home", from THE IMPERFECT PARADISE by Linda Pastan. Copyright © 1988 by Linda Pastan. Used by permission of W. W. Norton & Company, Inc. Used by permission of Linda Pastan, in care of the Jean V. Naggar Literary Agency, Inc. (permissions @jvnla.com).

support from one another. We expect the members of our family to support us no matter what. To this end, we make time for each other and recognize our obligation to help others in our family by providing social support and doing whatever we can to help them cope with everyday realities. What relational contributions do you make to your family? What relational benefits do you derive from it?

Families evolve. Members share a history and the prospect of a future. Past interactions, rituals, and celebrations pave the way for present exchanges and indicate the potential for mutually influential relationships to continue. What changes have you perceived in your family? What, in your opinion, causes family relationships to thrive or break off? For example, one of the challenges facing modern families concerns the emotional support that many aging parents need from their adult children. As Americans live longer, the parent-child relationship lasts longer. Thus, members of the so-called sandwich generation face dual responsibilities as they raise children of their own and take care of aging parents.

Family members share expectations for one another. Are yours realized?

Rules, or implied or spoken understandings, guide communication within families. Through repeated exposure, we come to recognize and internalize these rules.[18] Some rules are passed down through generations; others are new and are negotiated directly. Family rules regulate family interaction and, among other things, let members know how to divide tasks, who is in charge of what, and who talks and listens to whom, when, where, why, and under what conditions. For example, which, if any, of the following rules do members of your family accept?

- Children should be seen and not heard.
- Children should speak only when spoken to.
- Don't talk about family matters outside the family.
- No arguing at the dinner table.
- Never go into Mom and Dad's room.
- Don't lie.
- Don't answer back when scolded.
- Never raise your voice.
- Don't show when you have been hurt.
- Don't express fear.
- Don't ask for the car when Mom or Dad is in a bad mood.
- Don't interrupt an adult when he or she is speaking.

Individuals who perceive themselves as a family often occupy the same living space, requiring them to adapt to each other's personalities, expectations, and interaction styles. How have you and other family members adapted to accommodate one another?

Rules: Behavioral norms; implied or spoken understandings.

For example, in a boomerang family, when adult children the family thought had left permanently return home unexpectedly, a series of accommodations may be required on the part of all family members.

Through sustained interaction, we clarify our expectations regarding how family members should behave in relation to each other and toward us. Understanding these rules and their effects leads us to understand whether we communicate as effectively as we could and what rules, if any, we would like to renegotiate to improve family interaction. To survive in most families, we need either to follow or to renegotiate the rules prescribing and limiting family members' behavior.

COMMUNICATION PATTERNS IN FAMILIES

Families evolve habitual patterns of communication. Some patterns facilitate effective interaction, while others impede it.

Problematic Communication Patterns. In some families, the rules are too restrictive to be healthy. The term often used to describe a family with problematic communication is *dysfunctional*. When a family's rules prohibit a member from adequately expressing his or her feelings or needs, they also deter the sharing of important personal information and aspects of the self. Inhibiting a family member can be emotionally devastating and can harm the person in ways that may not become apparent for years. For example, if every time you bring a problem to your father he explodes with rage, you soon learn not to approach him with your problems. From such a parent you may also learn to express anger inappropriately.

Some families suffer from frequent episodes of *communication confusion,* or chaos. Instead of supporting one another, family members crash into each other. Instead of exhibiting family cohesion and pulling together emotionally, they come unglued. The communication characteristics of dysfunctional families enable at least one family member to inflict pain on or denigrate one or more other members systematically.

Among the harmful messages that may be communicated in dysfunctional families are physical, sexual, or emotional abuse; messages of worthlessness, intimidation, and manipulation; and the idea that one person has a right to use any and all compliance-gaining or power strategies to control fully the behavior of another. The targets of problematic or dysfunctional communication often blame themselves for causing such behavior in the first place. As a result of labeling themselves inadequate and the belief that they are powerless to control their lives, they lack the inner strength or self-confidence to counter the abuse they receive.

Family member behavior offers clues regarding family system issues and underlying problems. To operate successfully, we need to ensure that the costs of family life do not exceed the rewards. Parents and children who are insensitive to each other's needs often take increasingly dangerous steps to maintain their delicate sense of balance and assert control. This can lead to destructive, self-defeating behavior on both sides, behavior that demonstrates little if any concern for how others are affected. When we lack interpersonal sensitivity and fail to consider the feelings and need of those we live with, relationships deteriorate.

Abuse is never justified.

Productive Communication Patterns. More healthy or **productive family communication patterns** occur in families whose members have the freedom to express their feelings. The members of such families have the following qualities:

1. They are able to offer emotional and physical support to each other.

2. They are comfortable revealing their feelings and thoughts to one another.

3. They are confident about the family's ability to meet each member's needs.

4. They are flexible and open enough to adapt and respond to situations that produce conflict or unexpected change.

Communication is the greatest single factor that determines the health of family members and how they will interact.[19] Families whose members communicate effectively are healthy and more adaptable to changes in the family's power structure, role relationships, and rules.[20] They also are more willing to negotiate seemingly incompatible goals.

Your Family Network. We can learn a lot about how our family communicates by drawing a **family network** map.[21] A family can create such a map by taking the following steps:

1. Have one family member tack a large sheet of paper to the wall where all members can see it clearly.

2. Use a felt-tipped pen to draw a circle for each person who is a part of the family. If grandparents are part of the household, include circles for them on the row with the other adults. If someone was a part of the family but now is gone, represent that person with a filled-in circle.

3. To show how family members are connected, draw lines between the different pairs or roles. For example, a family may have marital pairs, parent-child pairs, and sibling pairs (see Figure 14.3).

Productive family communication patterns: Family communication styles that facilitate the expression of members' feelings and wants.

Family network: The relationships and connections within a family.

Figure 14.3 The Family Network: How Families Are Connected

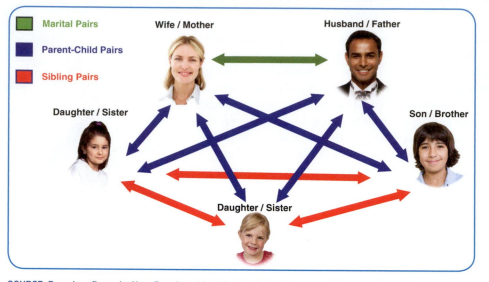

SOURCE: Based on figure in *New Peoplemaking*, Virginia Satir. Science and Behavior Books, Inc.

4. Identify what each role means to each family member.

5. Compare and contrast family role definitions. After sharing ideas, family members may develop new understandings about the members of their family and their relationships to one another.

6. Add network lines to the map by linking every family member with every other family member. As the lines for each person are drawn, that person should think about the particular relationship he or she has with every family member and describe how he or she feels about each connection.

The lines of the family network reveal that in families of more than two people, we do not live in pairs; we live in triangles. As Virginia Satir explains, a triangle is a pair plus one. However, because only two people can relate at one time, one person in the triangle is always the odd one out. This person faces a dilemma: break up the relationship between the other two, support it, or withdraw. The odd person's decision is critical in affecting how the family network operates.[22] Consider how a triangle looks from each family member's point of view. Family living is a complicated affair, and every family develops its unique patterns.

In more nurturing families, these relationships and the perceptions of family members are available and open to discussion by everyone. In less nurturing families, family members are unaware of these networks and their effects and are either unwilling or unable to discuss them. By discussing connections, however, family members can develop the insights they need for the family to function more effectively as a unit.

CULTURE AND THE FAMILY

Although the concept of family is universal, the nature of the family is not. Because culture shapes families, the word itself means different things to members of different cultures.

Families do not develop rules, beliefs, and rituals in isolation. How members think, act, and speak is drawn from the wider cultural context—both the culture the family members live in and the culture to which they trace their ancestry.[23]

Varying Family Composition. One culture's definition of family is no more correct or acceptable than another's—except, of course, to members of that specific culture. In many cultures the extended family household is the norm. For example, in Mexico it is standard for grandparents to live with their adult children and their grandchildren, not in retirement developments. In the United States, the nuclear family was considered the ideal household group for quite some time. Now, as a result of the economy and immigration, that norm is giving way as more people are living in multigenerational households rather than living alone or in nuclear families.[24]

Varying Communication Styles. Members of different cultures often differ in the extent to which they adhere to traditional sex roles, tolerate uncertainty and change, share or disclose their feelings and affections, retain individual identities, and assert individual rights.

Mexicans, for example, provide a very supportive environment to family members; as a result, Mexican children are raised to rely upon and provide support to the family unit. Mexicans judge their level of success based on the family's achievements. In contrast, children in the United States are taught from an early age to place a high value on individual ability and initiative.[25]

Varying Family Roles. Some families are more position-oriented than person-oriented, and vice versa. In **position-oriented families**, roles are more rigidly related to sex and age, whereas in **person-oriented families**, individual comfort levels and needs demarcate roles. Person-oriented families tend to practice democratic decision making, with roles negotiated, individualism fostered, and interaction between family members emphasized. Contrastingly, in position-oriented families, status and roles are ascribed, and members follow rules without questioning the authority figure or asking for reasons.[26] Thus, in some cultures, but not others, the sex of the parent determines who is in charge and who possesses the authority and power to influence other family members.

The family influences perception and communication as well. Chinese children, for example, are taught to respect and feel a lifelong obligation to their parents. The Chinese proverb "To forget one's ancestors is to be a brook without a source, a tree without a root" reflects this belief. In other cultures, such as India, it is common for males to be perceived as superior and for men and women to eat separately, or for the women to eat only once the men have finished. In Indian culture, boys usually have more freedom of expression than do girls.[27] In Japanese, Chinese, and Korean cultures, the father is the authority; other family members are subservient to him, while nurturing and caregiving fall to the mother.

However, it is important to remember that variation within cultures always exists. The family experience of one person will differ from that of another. As a result, when two people from different families decide to create a new family of their own, they may enter their partnership with different value systems as well as different role and rule definitions. Unless we talk about our differences and reveal our expectations, we may fail to clarify and check assumptions, clash regarding our roles and responsibilities, and be unable to negotiate our differences. This makes it more likely that we will fail to meet many of the challenges of family communication.

Position-oriented family: A family in which roles are rigidly related to sex and age.

Person-oriented family: A family in which flexible roles are nurtured.

TRY THIS: *Role Call*

How does your family distribute responsibilities among members? Use the chart below to indicate who has primary responsibility for each of the listed activities (a male, a female, or both) and how you feel about the role assignment.

Male/Female/ Both Responsible?	Role	How I Feel about This Role Assignment
	Cooking	
	Cleaning	
	Bill paying	
	Making investments	
	Decorating	
	Arranging/providing child care	
	Buying/maintaining a car	
	Home maintenance and repair	
	Scheduling the social calendar	
	Making travel plans	

Finally, how many members of your family are wage earners? In what ways, if any, does the amount of money a member earns affect his or her other responsibilities?

GENDER AND THE FAMILY

The family is an important source of our attitudes regarding gender and what it means to be male, female, gay, or transgender. Different families deal with such issues as gender identity and male and female authority and power in different ways. Through both overt and unconscious communication, families contribute to male and female **role assignments**. Consider your own family. To what extent do the notions it espouses regarding household roles, occupational choices, areas of responsibility, sources of emotional support, and how males and females should interact with sons and daughters and with each other reveal its feelings about gender issues?

The performance of specific family roles fulfills the following five functions:

1. The provision of basic resources such as food, clothing, and money

2. The provision of nurturance and support

3. The meeting of sexual needs

4. Personal and social development

5. The maintenance and management of the family unit, including decision making

Role assignments:
The parts individuals play in a relationship network.

In the United States, men were long given primary responsibility for meeting their families' financial needs. Now, however, women share this role. Similarly, while women were more likely than men to provide comfort, care, and warmth for family members, now these responsibilities also tend to be shared. Still, women devote more time to housework and child care than do men.[28] As you grew up, the role expectations held by your parents and other family members—the kinds of activities in which they encouraged you to engage, the kinds of emotional behaviors they expected you to exhibit—likely influenced your personal perceptions of what is and is not appropriate.

In addition to role assignments, parental communication affects gender expectations, traditionally by reinforcing cooperation, helpfulness, and nurturance in girls and competition, independence, industriousness, and assertiveness in boys.[29] Even today, some parents persist in treating boys more roughly to urge them to be aggressive while they treat girls more gently, encouraging them to be more physically reserved. Families that encourage children to grow up outside conventional gender roles are likely to exhibit broader sex-role views and broader communication repertoires than families in which traditional gender roles are strictly followed.

Parents communicate gender expectations to children in the ways they relate to their children, the clothes and toys they buy for them, the chores they assign to them, and how they speak to them. Girls, for example are often asked to help take care of and be responsible for other children, while boys are assigned to take care of things.[30] In addition, parents are likely to address boys in a more active, content-focused manner, whereas they address girls in softer tones, with content often focused on thoughts and feelings. Although children of both sexes are socialized regarding the importance of being masculine or feminine, positive changes are occurring in societal views of what constitute masculinity and femininity. The increased sharing of tasks by men and women correlates positively with increased disclosure and relationship maintenance.

MEDIA, TECHNOLOGY, AND THE FAMILY

What do we learn from the media, particularly "reality" shows and sitcoms, concerning family member communication? Television's images and models continue to offer distorted, stereotypical views of contemporary family members. Men are still presented as aggressive, confident, and powerful while women are depicted as obsessed with shopping, overly emotional, and highly sexualized.[31] Yet, there is hope. Some current media offerings present more complex depictions, showing men and women with combinations of qualities and responsibilities. The sitcom *Modern Family,* for example, depicts both traditional and nontraditional masculinity and femininity, with kind and gentle men, gay couples, and independent women. On the other hand, the comedy-drama *Desperate Housewives* capitalized on presenting strong, smart, but cunning and hypersexualized women who pursued their goals with a "no matter what" approach.

We see a variety of family types on television. We have singles living alone or together, divorced households, same-gender marriages, and

Modern Family finds humor in three interrelated families. The popular show has been praised for its fresh portrayal of contemporary family life but also criticized for relying on sitcom stereotypes.

dual-earner couples, just to name a few. This was not always the case. In years past, the predominant television family consisted of a legally married male and female and their children. We had, for example, the Nelsons of *The Adventures of Ozzie and Harriet,* the Cleavers of *Leave It to Beaver,* and the Stones of *The Donna Reed Show.* Members of these TV families lived in spotless homes; the moms packed lunches, the dads worked in white-collar jobs, and the general image was of a stable, warm, and loving family.[32]

As the years passed, alternative and nonnuclear families came to be featured. For example, *One Day at a Time* centered on a single-parent household, the household in *Kate & Allie* consisted of two divorced women and their kids, *My Two Dads* had male caregivers, *Eight Is Enough* showed a blended family, and *Diff'rent Strokes* featured an **integrated family**. In these shows, however, no matter the conflict depicted, it was quickly resolved—often without a disruption in family harmony. Rarely were we exposed to families with serious money issues, job-juggling problems, or child-care difficulties.

It was not until the late 1980s and the 1990s that working-class family life was deglamorized on American television with shows such as *Roseanne, Married . . . with Children,* and *The Simpsons.* With the advent of these shows we met overworked family members who disagreed, complained, spoke disrespectfully to one another, lacked social graces, and had to cope with economic hard times and threatening unemployment.[33]

Following on the heels of these shows were programs such as *Will and Grace,* which centered on the family-like relationship between a gay man and a heterosexual woman; *Six Feet Under,* featuring a family full of work-, health-, and relationship-challenged members; and the prototype "reality" series *The Real World,* which created temporary, artificial families of young adults.

Now, we have *Parenthood, Up All Night, Jersey Shore, The Good Wife, Modern Family,* and *Mad Men.* To what degree, if any, do the mediated images of families presented in shows like these influence the image of the kind of family you would like to have?

When it comes to technology, social media tools keep family members who may be widely dispersed across a state, a country, or the world closer by facilitating their continued interaction. For example, during the wars in Iraq and Afghanistan, deployed individuals were able to video-chat on Skype virtually daily. One soldier noted, "You could break away from the monotony of everyday stress and feel like you're back home for a bit."[34]

INTERPERSONAL COMMUNICATION AT WORK

Akin to its role in families, interpersonal communication sustains our work relationships. Whether we are in an entry-level position or function as CEO, our work-related activities depend on how well we negotiate the roles and rules of the environment. How well we communicate with others at work can make the difference between career success and failure. In fact, it is hard to imagine any work-related activity or function that does not depend on some form of interpersonal communication. Thus, in this section, we explore the role it plays at work.

Integrated family:
A family in which members are of different races and/or religions.

Whether we are concerned with management-employee relations, conflict resolution, decision making, problem solving, or leadership, good interpersonal skills are necessary. Determining why some organizations function well and "feel alive" while others "feel dead" may be as simple as identifying the kinds of interpersonal relationships and dynamic connectedness that the people who work in them have.[35]

1. While viewing a contemporary sitcom or drama that depicts a family, identify the following:
   a. The members of the family, their roles, and their relationships to one another
   b. The factors that seem to hold family members together
   c. The subjects about which family members communicate
   d. The nature of a conflict they experience
   e. How they resolve the conflict

2. Compare and contrast the television family with your own family. Based on your analysis, fantasize a sitcom or dramatic episode involving your family. What conclusions can you draw about the nature of communication in your own family?

RELATIONSHIPS ARE THE ORGANIZATION

Like family members, organizational personnel share interdependent relationships. In fact, were it not for their interaction, there would be no organization. Being savvy and knowledgeable about how to build person-to-person relationships is key to nurturing both individual and organizational growth. In Chapter 13, we discussed the effects of loneliness. Loneliness is not merely a personal issue. It can also be an organizational issue, limiting productivity and increasing employee anxiety. Like anger and happiness, loneliness may also be contagious. Having close relationships with colleagues—even just one—makes a difference.[36] Rugged individualism no longer dominates the thinking of successful organizations; team players are seen as more important. Thus, we need to take time to explore how a workplace organizes and energizes those who work in it. The more participants engage in the organization's life, the smarter and more effective the organization becomes and the greater the participants' emotional investment in it and support for it.[37]

Interpersonal communication sustains work relationships.

THE DYAD AND THE ORGANIZATION

As we noted in Chapter 1, the dyad, or two-person relationship, is the most basic level of interpersonal interaction. Numerous instances of dyadic interaction occur daily in organizational settings as coworkers interact with each other and organization leaders. The relationship level is where most of the organization's work gets done. It is also where most of the difficulties are encountered.

Communication in the workplace can flow either horizontally or vertically. Among the dyads formed in organizations are coworker relationships, in which communication flows horizontally; superior-subordinate or leader-follower relationships, in which communication flows upward and downward; worker-customer/client relationships, in which communication flows horizontally; and mentoring relationships, in which communication flows upward and downward. An increasing number of younger workers are mentoring top managers on how to use social media and other technology trends, a practice known as *reverse mentoring*.[38] Whatever the dyads' composition, the effectiveness of the workplace depends on the effectiveness of dyads.

A Question of Dependence and Independence. Some people in organizations are leaders, while others work with and under them. Although the organizations leaders and team members depend on each other, those people in leadership positions usually are able to exert varying degrees of control or power over others.

Leaders and their support people spend much of their time interacting. When their interactions are perceived as supportive, open, and honest, employees tend to find their jobs more satisfying. Another contributor to employee satisfaction is the degree of *argumentativeness* present. In this context, argumentativeness is not a negative; rather, it is the tendency to recognize controversial issues in communication situations, to present and defend positions taken on the issues, and to question the positions others have taken.[39] When workers perceive their bosses to be high in argumentativeness and low in verbal aggressiveness—that is, their managerial style neither blames nor denies workers the right to disagree—workers are likely to have higher levels of job satisfaction. Similarly, leaders value the same qualities in others. The nurturance of independent-mindedness, or allowing workers to express their opinions and interests without denying those of others, plays an important role in the relational satisfaction of all in the organization.[40]

This is not to suggest that we do not want to work with those who see things as we do. It is comfortable to work with people who share our goals and values. As you learned in Chapter 12, the more alike two people are, the more likely they are to interact. Yet, to sustain relational satisfaction (having relationships meet our needs), we also need to be comfortable expressing differences. That said, we like to work with and for others whose tolerance for disagreement is high.[41]

A Question of Trust. When workers perceive an organization's climate to be trusting and supportive, their relational satisfaction is generally high. A culture of openness makes genuine expressions of ideas and feelings possible. In contrast, if employees fear being punished for revealing true feelings, they will suppress them. Trust in one's leaders and coworkers is necessary for open communication. We are more likely to trust those whose behavior is consistent and who increase our own feelings of security.

Trust is built through risk and confirmation and destroyed through risk and disconfirmation (see Chapter 9). When you disclose your thoughts and feelings to a coworker and that person responds with acceptance, support, and cooperation, then reciprocates by disclosing feelings of his or her own, you are more apt to trust that person. We display trustworthiness by not exploiting another's vulnerabilities.

A Question of Perception. Workers who understand each other's job responsibilities and requirements, as well as the problems inherent in each, tend to exhibit higher morale and openness than those whose perceptions differ.[42] If, when communicating, employees are overly ambitious, exhibiting a burning desire to achieve and be promoted, then they are more likely to distort information as it is passed up to the organization's leadership in the effort to please. Thus, such employees may base their answers to questions on what they think the boss wants to hear, not on what they actually think. Leaders, in contrast, have been known to discount positive information about employees and pay more attention to

GO ▶

WATCH THIS 14.1
For a video on workplace perception visit the student study site.

critical information.[43] Recall from Chapter 3 that we see and hear what we expect to see and hear. Perceptions influence interpretations.

NETWORKS, INTERACTION, AND RELATIONSHIP SATISFACTION

Workplace networks are communication paths that affect the amount and type of communication employees send and receive. They also determine how freely ideas and feelings flow through the organization. **Organizational networks** may be formal, describing structured, established, official lines of communication, revealing who should be talking to whom and about what, or they may be informal, describing the unofficial channels of communication—who actually talks to whom and about what.[44] Workers network both off- and online, connecting with others to share resources, deepen knowledge, complete assignments, and fulfill goals.[45]

Just as in a family, an organization's network reveals the extent to which every member functions not as an isolated element but as an active member in relationships with others. Persons who occupy central positions in a network are more satisfied, have higher morale, and have greater ability to exert influence than those who occupy peripheral positions. Organizations that foster freedom, allowing workers to circulate and make new connections, tend to prosper.[46]

Communication networks can be formal or informal.

WORKING IN TEAMS

Although interaction at the dyadic level serves as the most basic unit for exploring organizational interaction, communication within and between teams is also central to organizations.

Create Healthy Work Climates. In his classic book *Communication within the Organization* Charles Redding notes the following components of an effective work climate: supportiveness, participative decision making, trust among group members, openness and candor, and high performance goals.[47] The healthier a work group's climate, the more effectively the team's members are able to work. Likewise, Douglas McGregor, an expert in organizational communication, attributes the effectiveness of work groups to the following characteristics:

1. The working atmosphere tends to be informal, comfortable, and relaxed.

2. There is ample discussion pertinent to the task at hand, in which virtually all participate.

3. Members understand, accept, and commit themselves to the group's task or objective.

4. Members listen to each other. Every idea put forth is given a fair hearing.

5. Disagreements are not suppressed. Rather, the reasons for disagreement are examined carefully as the group seeks to resolve them rationally rather than to dominate or silence dissenters.

Organizational networks: Patterns of communication in organizations.

6. Most important decisions are reached by consensus in which it is clear that everyone generally agrees and is willing to support the decision.

7. Criticism is frequent, frank, and relatively comfortable. There is little evidence of personal attack, either overt or hidden.

8. Members freely express their feelings.

9. When action needs to be taken, clear assignments are made and accepted.

10. The chairperson does not dominate, nor do members defer to the chair. In fact, the group's leadership shifts, depending on circumstances. The issue is not who controls the group but how the job is done.

11. The group is cognizant of its own operation.[48]

Practice Effective Decision Making. How well groups work depends at least in part on the nature of their decision making. To work effectively, groups are likely to rely on a number of methods designed to increase problem-solving effectiveness, among which are reflective thinking, brainstorming, and the conscious avoidance of groupthink.

Use Reflective Thinking. The **reflective thinking framework**, first proposed by John Dewey in 1910, remains a favored problem-solving approach. It consists of six steps:

1. What is the problem?

2. What are the facts of the situation? (Analyze the problem.)

3. What criteria must an acceptable solution meet?

4. What are the possible solutions?

5. Which is the best solution?

6. How can the solution be implemented?

For the reflective thinking framework to work effectively, the team's members need to suspend judgment and open themselves to all available ideas, facts, and opinions. To ensure this occurs, as they make their way through the sequence's steps, team members ask themselves questions such as the following:

1. Are we using all of the group's resources?

2. Are we using our time well?

3. Are we open to fact-finding and inquiry?

4. Are we listening to and demonstrating respect for each other?

5. Are we resisting pressuring those who disagree?

6. Is the atmosphere in which we are working supportive, trusting, and collaborative?

Reflective thinking framework: A problem-solving system designed to encourage critical inquiry.

Brainstorming: A technique designed to encourage idea generation.

Use Brainstorming. Still respected today as a technique for promoting the free flow of ideas during problem solving, **brainstorming** was devised in 1957 by communication practitioner Alex Osborn.[49] To ensure that brainstorming sessions are successful, team members need to follow these guidelines:

1. Temporarily suspend judgment. When an idea is put forth initially, do not evaluate or criticize it. Adverse criticism is forbidden.

2. Encourage freewheeling. It is easier to tame a wild idea than to give life to one that is inert.

3. Stress quantity of ideas. The greater the number of ideas, the better the chance of finding a good one.

4. Build on the ideas of other members. Modify, combine, and mix together ideas to generate different combinations or patterns.

5. Record all ideas. No idea censorship occurs.

6. Only after brainstorming is completed do members evaluate ideas for their usefulness and applicability.

Poorly managed groups kill ideas during the decision-making process. By following the preceding guidelines, groups can avoid shooting down ideas before they have had the chance to consider them fully. Defeatist phrases such as "That won't work" and "You've got to be kidding" should never be used.

Brainstorming encourages a free exchange of ideas.

While criticism is discouraged during the brainstorming process, after the brainstorming session ends it is important for team members to debate and reassess the contributions and viewpoints it has produced. Doing this enhances productivity. Dissent wakes up participants, encouraging them to dig beneath the surface of their ideas.[50]

Avoid Groupthink. The third strategy, the avoidance of **groupthink**, finds the group making a conscious effort not to pressure individual members to conform to the majority opinion in order to reach consensus.[51] Instead, the group works to realistically appraise alternative courses of actions thoroughly while ensuring that minority or unpopular views are expressed fully and listened to—rather than silenced by inappropriate pressures. When working in a group, members should be alert to the following symptoms of groupthink:

1. There is an *illusion of invulnerability*. Members feel so secure about a group decision that they ignore warning signs that the decision may be flawed. Instead, they let excessive optimism and risk taking lead the way.

2. Members use *rationalizations* to discount warnings.

3. There is an unquestioned belief in the *inherent morality* of the group and its actions.

4. Those who disagree with the group are *stereotyped* as evil, weak, or stupid. An "us" versus "them" attitude is fostered.

5. The group applies direct *pressure* to any members who question the stereotypes. The guiding ethic is that if you are a loyal member, you will not question the group's direction.

6. *Self-censorship* occurs as members strive not to have others perceive them as deviating from the group's consensus.

7. The *illusion of unanimity* causes group members to interpret silence as agreement.

8. Members serve as self-appointed *mindguards* in an effort to protect the group and its leader from adverse information.

WHAT DO YOU KNOW?

True or False
3. *Mindguards facilitate groupthink.*
True. Mindguards protect the leader from receiving dissenting information.

Groupthink: A communication dysfunction in which some group members attempt to protect the group's harmony by exerting irrational pressures on one or more members so that genuine opinions are suppressed.

Groups engaging in groupthink let a desire for consensus interfere with the need to think critically. The mental efficiency of the group deteriorates when members exhibit defensive avoidance and when healthy disagreements and conflicts are suppressed. There is little doubt that work groups that consciously seek to avoid becoming trapped by the dynamics of groupthink produce better decisions.

CULTURE AND THE WORKPLACE

Our shrinking world requires enhanced understanding of diverse cultures. Although the English language serves as the international language of business, there remain significant differences in how people around the world relate to each other at work.

For example, the **participative leadership** style evidenced in many American companies may be less effective and underused in countries where **authoritarian leadership** is practiced.[52] Authoritarian leaders use a dominating and directive communication style as they determine policies and make decisions that team members are expected to support. Participative leaders, in contrast, act as guides to team members who are free to identify goals, establish procedures, and reach their own conclusions. In organizations with participative leaders, virtually any member may fulfill any leadership function.

Similarly, the common American practice of organizations rewarding their best workers with bonuses would not be well received by Japanese workers, who are unaccustomed to being singled out and do not like receiving individual attention. The Japanese also are unaccustomed to the bluntness and independence often displayed by U.S. business representatives.

All of us can benefit from increasing our understanding of how cultural differences affect on-the-job relationships. As we explore some of these differences, however, keep in mind that characterizing a national work culture does not mean that every person in that country ascribes to that culture; individual variations and differences will always exist.

Are Workers Dominant or Submissive? Some cultures instill in their members a desire to dominate their environment, while others instill in them a desire to live in harmony with

Participative leadership: Leadership in which leaders act as guides to others who remain free to identify their own goals, establish their own procedures, and reach their own conclusions.

Authoritarian leadership: A style of leadership characterized by the use of dominating and directive communication.

it. Workers in the United States, for example, interact directly with each other, typically seeking to dominate their environment. Workers in Asian cultures, in contrast, work instead to preserve a sense of harmony, interacting with one another much more indirectly and often less offensively. American businesspeople generally prefer that others "get to the point" and "put all their cards on the table."[53] In contrast, Asian businesspeople try not to reveal their emotions, may practice avoidance, use third-party intermediaries, and go out of their way to help others save face.

Are Workers Individualistic or Collectivistic? Whereas workplaces in the United States, Great Britain, and Canada promote individualism, in other countries, such as Japan, China, and Israel, the emphasis is placed on group harmony and loyalty instead. As discussed in Chapter 7, in individualistic cultures individuals tend to think more of themselves, their individual goals, their personal potential for success, and the needs of their immediate families; in collectivistic cultures people are likely to show considerable allegiance to their organizations. Whereas individuality, independence, and self-reliance are important in individualistic cultures, making the "I" paramount, collectivistic cultures stress the "we." Members of individualistic cultures base decisions on what is good for the individual. Those in collectivistic cultures, in contrast, weigh the benefits to the individual and the benefits to the group and opt for what is best for the group. In such cultures, emphasis is given to belonging rather than to individual initiative. Members of individualistic cultures are known to use confrontational strategies when handling interpersonal issues. Members of collectivistic cultures characteristically do not, believing that "the nail that sticks up gets pounded down."

Do you prefer to work in a cubicle or in an open space?

How Do Workers Perceive the Need for Space? Members of different cultures perceive space differently. In the United States, for example, employees prefer private space and have a greater need for personal space than do members of other cultures. The harder it is to gain access to someone who works in an organization, the more important that person is perceived to be. In Japan, in contrast, leaders and followers often share the same space. Middle Eastern cultures also have a public orientation, often opting to mix workers and managers together in one space.[54]

In organizations, furniture may be used to communicate space needs. For example, when workers from the United States meet to talk they generally prefer a face-to-face arrangement or one in which their chairs are placed at right angles. Workers belonging to Asian cultures, however, generally prefer a side-by-side arrangement; the desire to avoid direct eye contact may account for this preference (see Figure 14.4).[55] What advantages and disadvantages do you see for each type of arrangement?

How Do Workers Perceive Time? Culture influences our perception of time. While persons in some societies are oriented toward the past, others, including those in the United States and Canada, place more emphasis on the present or the future. The business strategies used by organizations in these countries are not as concerned with where the organizations have been as they are with where they are now and where they will be five to ten years from

Figure 14.4 Preferred Furniture Arrangements: U.S. and Asian Cultures

Preferred by people in the United States		Preferred by Asian cultures
Face-to-face	Right angles	Side-by-side

now. Persons from Asian countries tend to be even more future-oriented, as we see in this description of a conversation that occurred some years back:

> A Chinese official matter-of-factly informed an ARCO manager that China would one day be the number one nation in this world. The American said he did not doubt that, considering the size of the country and its population, and the tremendous technological progress that will be made, but he asked, "When do you think that China will be number one?" The Chinese responded, "Oh, in four or five hundred years."[56]

Cultural preferences regarding time similarly affect whether someone thinks it rude for another to do two things at once, such as texting or reading e-mail during a meeting. In cultures with a monochromic time orientation, such as the United States, Germany, and Switzerland, time is perceived to be linear and segmented; in these cultures the belief is that only one thing should be done at a time. In cultures with a polychromic time orientation, such as Latin American and Middle Eastern cultures, time is perceived as more leisurely, and people rather than tasks are central. In these cultures, it is more acceptable to devote attention to several activities simultaneously. Thus, people in monochromic cultures schedule appointments, don't run late, and believe in following a plan. In polychromic cultures maintaining harmonious relations is seen as more important than the agenda; for people from these cultures, the concept of time is more flexible and more susceptible to interruption.[57]

What it means to be "on time" also differs among cultures. Being punctual for business meetings is very important in the United States, Germany, and Switzerland. In Latin American and Middle Eastern countries, however, businesspeople typically display a much more casual approach to punctuality. Arabs, for example, believe that God alone decides when things get accomplished.[58] Such an orientation may become frustrating for those who would like to take control to ensure that things get done.

How Diverse Are the Interpersonal Needs and Skills of Workers? Members of Asian cultures are likely to stress the meeting of collective needs, while among Americans meeting individual needs usually is the priority. Thus, while helping workers attain self-actualization may be a goal of U.S. organizations, in Asian cultures the goal is belonging. The personal achievement needs of workers differ from culture to culture.

The practice of interpersonal skills also differs. In some countries, such as Spain and Portugal, managers are likely to be more aware of employees' feelings and more concerned with their welfare, whereas German and French managers are less so. Whereas the Dutch appear quite willing to cooperate, the French are often the least willing. The Japanese tend to rely on objectivity in decision making, but in Latin American, intuition often rules. While managers in the United States and Latin American are often praised for having interpersonal competence, this does not mean they are perfect.[59] Consider this:

> A U.S. supervisor on an oil-rig in Indonesia, in a moment of anger, shouted at his timekeeper to take the next boat to shore. Immediately, he was surrounded by a mob of outraged, ax-carrying, Indonesian coworkers of the timekeeper. The supervisor had to barricade himself in his quarters in order to escape the mob. He learned an important cultural lesson, however: Never berate an Indonesian in public.[60]

Are Members of Different Generations Prepared to Work Together? While generational differences affect all relationships, their impact is especially visible in the workplace. In recent years, for the first time, some American workplaces have included employees from four generations. In ascending chronological order, they are the *Mature* or *Greatest Generation* (since 1930s), the *Baby Boomers* (since 1940s), *Generation X* (or Gen X; since 1960s), and *Generation Y,* also known as the Millennial Generation (since the 1980s). While members of older generations are catching up with Millennials in technological capabilities, they display different interests and values. And since the generation we were born into influences our communication, members of different generations need to understand one another in order to determine how best to work together.

How prepared are you to work with people from different cultures and generations?

For example, the members of the Matures are likely retired or soon to retire. They are known for hard work and respecting authority. Boomers, in contrast, seek personal fulfillment, expect to be employed long term, and thus display a sense of loyalty toward employers. They tend to be optimistic, involved, and not afraid to question authority. Members of Gen X are both individualistic and team players and seek more work-life balance than do the Boomers, who are typically overworked (and often described as workaholics). Generation Xers tend to be skeptical, challenging others. Members of Gen Y are reputed to feel special and entitled, but they are also team-oriented, technologically savvy, capable of multitasking, and achievement motivated.[61] Of course, not every person in a generation displays all of the characteristics generally associated with that generation.

What implications, if any, do you think the differences among generations have for you, your work life, and your relationships? For example, earlier in this chapter we noted the increasing use of reverse mentoring. Many older workers, however, don't enjoy being mentored by someone younger. Changing one's mind-set is key.

GENDER AND THE WORKPLACE

Cultural views of gender influence communication in organizational settings. Only a short time ago, the sexual division of labor was a fundamental feature of the workplace. Although

TRY THIS: *Culture Can Shock*

What happens when the communication customs of businesspeople from different cultures clash? What can be done to resolve the resulting problems? Consider the following observation of a business meeting made by practitioner Richard G. Linowes two decades ago. In your opinion, would it be equally true today?

Around a conference table in a large U.S. office tower, three American executives sat with their new boss, Mr. Akiro Kusumoto, the newly appointed head of a Japanese firm's subsidiary, and two of his Japanese lieutenants. The meeting was called to discuss ideas for reducing operating costs. Mr. Kusumoto began by outlining his company's aspirations for its long-term U.S. presence. He then turned to the current budgetary matter. One Japanese manager politely offered one suggestion, and an American then proposed another. After gingerly discussing the alternatives for quite some time, the then exasperated American blurted out: "Look, that idea is just not going to have much impact. Look at the numbers! We should cut this program, and I think we should do it as soon as possible!" In the face of such bluntness, uncommon and unacceptable in Japan, Mr. Kusumoto fell silent. He leaned back, drew air between his teeth, and felt a deep longing to "return East." He realized his life in this country would be filled with many such jarring encounters, and lamented his posting to a land of such rudeness.

SOURCE: Richard G. Linowes, "The Japanese Manager's Traumatic Entry into the United States: Understanding the American-Japanese Cultural Divide," *Academy of Management Executive*, November 1993.

the divisions are no longer so extreme, gender inequality and sexual discrimination still exist. Let us explore some of the prescriptive roles once accorded men and women, the ways in which these stereotypes devalued women's work, and efforts made to diminish such stereotypical assumptions.

Stereotypes of Women in Organizations. Almost a half century ago, organizational theorist and Harvard educator Rosabeth Moss Kanter observed that some organizations exhibited a tendency to classify women into one of four roles: sex object, mother, child, or iron maiden.[62] While some believe the accuracy and applicability of these stereotypes outdated, they continue to be debated. Let us explore each in turn.

The stereotype of women as sex objects is revealed in interactions between male and female coworkers and between male and female supervisors and those who work under them. Conversations in such dyads are likely to focus on a woman's appearance rather than on her performance. In 2011, an ABC News poll found that one in four women reported having experienced workplace sexual harassment.[63] According to the U.S. Supreme Court, sexual harassment is "unwelcome sexual advances, requests for favors, and other verbal or physical conduct of a sexual nature" when submission to or rejection of the conduct enters into employment decisions and/or the conduct interferes with work performance or creates a hostile work environment. The accusations against Republican presidential candidate Herman Cain in 2012 by women who used to work him when he headed the National Restaurant Association are illustrative of the problem's continued pervasiveness.

The stereotype of women as mothers also influences their treatment in organizations. When male coworkers or supervisors are in need of support or sympathy, they characteristically seek to interact with a woman rather than with another man. Also, working women who have children are believed to be less committed to their work than are men with children, causing women to be passed over more frequently for training and advancement opportunities.

The stereotype of women as children reinforces men's need to protect them. By asserting that women are not mature enough to make difficult decisions, men also restrict women's opportunities to lead.

The stereotype of women as iron maidens reflects the belief that women who succeed in achieving positions of power get there because of their unwomanliness—that is, because they possess characteristics such as independence, ambition, toughness, and forcefulness, all of which are usually associated with men.[64]

Any of these stereotypes may keep women from advancing in their careers. Because of perceived incompetence or perceived lack of femininity, women may be held back from realizing their full potential. Persisting to this day is a feeling among some that because women tend to be more affiliative and nurturing than men, they are less able to make tough decisions, not assertive enough, and too worried about disappointing others to be effective leaders.

Stereotypes of Men in Organizations. Men are also stereotyped in organizations, but, as communication expert Julia Wood observes, the stereotypes attributed to men tend to be more positive. In contrast to women, men are seen as sturdy oaks, fighters, and breadwinners.[65]

The stereotype of men as sturdy oaks suggests that men who are tough, self-sufficient, and in control of their feelings are "real men" and are thus of more value to the organization than are men who lean on others, complain, or give in to their fears. As a result, men sometimes choose to hide mistakes and suffer stress-related ailments in silence.

The stereotype of men as fighters reflects their training to be aggressive and committed to defeating any competitor. To illustrate their toughness, men wage war, figuratively and literally. For men, the battleground is work, and it, not family, sometimes comes first.

The stereotype of men as breadwinners reflects society's expectation that men be their families' primary wage earners. Frequently, a man's ability to earn a good income is a measure of his success. In fact, psychiatrist Willard Gaylin notes that "men commit suicide at a rate of seven to eight times as frequently as women in our culture, and they do so invariably because of perceived social humiliation that is almost exclusively tied to business failures."[66]

While these stereotypes of men have little if any validity, they also limit women's chances for comparable workplace growth.

Gender and Work-Life Balance. Women have struggled for quite some time to balance work and personal life, but in recent years it has become increasingly common for men to seek such balance as well. More and more men desire to spend time with their families and have their work reflect their interests. Some also work from home one or more days each week. Companies that have made allowances for the personal lives of women are similarly making allowances for the personal lives of men. Technology enables men and women to keep in touch with the office without always having to be there. What is more, greater emphasis is being placed on such "soft skills" as interpersonal communication and relationship building. In fact, social networking sites such as LinkedIn and Twitter have normalized the idea that an individual is the sum of his or her workplace relationships.[67]

WHAT DO YOU KNOW?

True or False
4. *An iron maiden is a woman who wears men's clothing.*
False. The phrase *iron maiden* represents a stereotype reflecting the belief that to succeed at work a woman must be unwomanly.

Work life and home life are colliding. What will you do to maintain work-life balance?

Leadership and Management Style. According to the International Women's Forum, the management styles of men and women tend to differ. Male managers describe their style in terms of a series of exchanges involving rewards or punishments for the actions of others. In contrast, female managers are more concerned with exhibiting **interactive leadership**—in encouraging and sharing both power and decision making with others.[68] Women leaders generally use more collaborative, participative communication to accomplish goals, whereas men rely on more directive communication strategies. Of note, qualities such as assertiveness, competitiveness, and instrumentality—usually associated with men—are valued in leaders. On the other hand, so are characteristics such as supportiveness, receptiveness, participation, and collaboration—communication skills more typically attributed to women.

When men and women are able to work together well, they complement and enhance each other's performance.[69]

Workplace Pathologies: Bullying and Sexual Harassment. Bullying and sexual harassment are examples of dysfunctional workplace behavior. All too prevalent, the unleashing of verbal or nonverbal hostility toward workers and the making of unwelcome sexual overtures or demands render the workplace an offensive and intimidating environment.

Bullying. Workplace bullying is all too common.[70] Anyone in an organization can be a bully's target. Workplace bullying generally involves verbal abuse and may include such behaviors as gossiping about a target, both on- and offline; insulting and threatening the target; acting unkindly toward, humiliating, and being harshly critical of the target; assaulting the target's dignity; denigrating the target publicly; and excluding the target from social functions. (Unlike school bullying, workplace bullying does not typically involve physical abuse.)

While most workplace bullies are male, bullies may operate in groups. They attack male and female targets in approximately equal numbers.[71] While peer-to-peer bullying occurs, most bullies are in higher-ranking positions than their targets. To combat bullying, workplaces need to communicate their opposition to it by establishing a policy of zero tolerance and taking action when it is observed or reported.

Sexual Harassment. The U.S. Equal Employment Opportunity Commission (EEOC) defines sexual harassment as unsolicited and unwelcome behavior of a sexual nature that makes the target uncomfortable. Members of either sex can be sexually harassed—usually for not living up to another's expectations for their gender. There are two categories of sexual harassment: quid pro quo ("something for something") harassment and harassment in which a hostile work environment is created by a pervasive pattern of unwelcome behavior related to a person's sex.

- *Quid pro quo harassment* makes employment opportunities dependent on the granting of sexual favors. Negative consequences are the cost of a refusal, and promotions and expensive gifts are common rewards.

Interactive leadership: Leadership that encourages the sharing of both power and decision making with followers and coworkers.

- *Hostile work environment harassment* includes sexual conduct such as the posting of sexually explicit photos, telling sexually charged jokes, making lewd remarks, using sexual gestures, and engaging in sexual banter that makes a worker uncomfortable and intimidates him or her.

In the United States, companies are not permitted to suspend or reassign employees who complain about being sexually harassed.[72] So, if you think you are being sexually harassed, report it. To educate their employees and to protect themselves, many workplaces now require that all employees attend programs aimed at the prevention of sexual harassment.

Because neither bullying nor sexual harassment has been eradicated from the workplace, both problems need to receive our continuing attention. We can help to reduce their incidence by challenging these behaviors when they occur.

Nick Hendricks (Jason Batemen, right) is the victim of workplace bullying by his boss, Dave Harken (Kevin Spacey, left), in the dark comedy film *Horrible Bosses.*

MEDIA, TECHNOLOGY, AND THE WORKPLACE

How have the pervasiveness of the media and technology influenced both perceptions and realities of the workplace? In what ways have they contributed to global thinking and personalization?

Media Portrayals. When depicted in the media as members of a workplace, women are sometimes shown having trouble juggling work and personal relationships. More frequently than men, women are shown discussing love interests, problems with their children, their clothing, or other nonwork issues, making them appear less professional.

Although television programs and films show the working lives of women characters, their personal lives and friends also loom as important. Men, in contrast, are usually presented as job focused and helpers of less competent women. Women also are shown to be overly concerned with appearance and spend significant amounts of time watching the men work.[73] Although some shows, such as *Bones, The Closer*, and *Scandal,* feature strong, intelligent, and capable women at work, many others, such as *Jersey Shore* and *Gossip Girl,* present female characters who are more focused on their appearance than on their work lives.

Technological Realities. Workplace communication is no longer limited to face-to-face interactions, phone conversations, or paper or e-mail memos. Newer technologies are redefining our work lives and making it more difficult for us to separate our work and personal lives. While technology affords us the freedom to work in multiple environments, including at home, it also means we are reachable 24/7.[74]

Many of us now spend significant segments of the day with our smart phones, laptops, and tablets, texting and/or tweeting. As a result of our dependence on technology, workplaces now typically offer employees coffee-bar-like conference rooms in which employees can meet face-to-face for casual interchanges and to bounce ideas off each other.

Virtual teams—teams made up of members who do not have to assemble physically to work together—abound in modern workplaces. Such teams, composed of persons who may live

True or False

5. *Cyberslacking occurs when you grow tired of playing online games.*
False. Cyberslacking occurs when you are at work but engage in nonwork activities online.

in different countries, locations, and time zones, can tackle and accomplish assignments quickly and efficiently—that is, if the technology is used appropriately and not for what is known as *cyberslacking*. Cyberslackers engage in non-work-related online activities—such as playing games, shopping, updating Facebook pages, and accessing problematic websites—during work hours.[75]

How technology is used in an organization often indicates whether its leaders care for and respect those who work in them. For example, do the organization's leaders rely on technology to deliver bad news, or do they do it personally? Firing an employee through a tweet or a text message is simply inappropriate.

By using social networking, you can facilitate communication and collaboration with your coworkers as well as among peers in your field. Cross-functional teams (teams that run across different areas of a company) create new social connections that facilitate the exchange and building of knowledge while fostering team members' embeddedness in one another's lives.[76] Multiteaming—that is, being a member of several teams—and publicly relating to coworkers through internal and personal social networking, including tweeting and retweeting, can also help enhance your professional visibility. As you share information and experiences online, you also extend your reach, widen your perspective, and advance your professional reputation by growing your social capital and driving others to your online presence.[77]

Increasing numbers of employers now turn to the Facebook profiles of both job applicants and employees to derive information about the individuals' character, personality, and potential for job success. Our online and professional lives are merging. For example, while it is illegal for a potential employer to ask some questions during an employment interview, the information that asking those questions might yield is often readily available on the Facebook page of the job candidate.[78]

INTERPERSONAL COMMUNICATION IN HEALTH CARE SETTINGS

The field of **health communication** is concerned with the study of human interaction in the health care process.[79] Just as we rely on interpersonal communication to enhance family and work-related relationships, we rely on it to enhance our ability to discuss our health. In fact, whether we succeed at maintaining our health or are able to help others maintain theirs may well depend on the following three factors:

1. How effective we are at interacting interpersonally in diverse health care settings

2. How capable we are at developing and maintaining effective health care relationships

3. How adept we are at using interpersonal communication to resolve health-related conflicts and solve health communication problems

Health communication: A field of study concerned with human interaction in the health care process.

While we acknowledge the importance of formal health care providers, the bulk of our communicative interactions about health occur not in formal health care settings but in more informal settings such as in our homes, over the Internet, or at our workplaces, when, for example, we converse with a coworker about a health matter and offer him or her our social support. It is probable that you offer others more social support than you realize. When you listen to a grieving parent or help someone search WebMD for information, you are offering social support. Social support enhances healing, reduces stress, and builds feelings of self-worth. Thus, receiving and offering social support can be health enhancing.[80]

THE CONSUMER–HEALTH CARE PROVIDER DYAD

There are four key functions of communication involved in the relationship between a health care consumer and a health care provider, each dependent on interpersonal communication:

1. *Diagnosis:* requires data gathering, data interpretation, and problem-solving skills

2. *Cooperation or compliance gaining:* requires skill in developing quality interactions that foster effective provider-patient interactions; involves eliciting consumer consent, including the following of prescribed measures

3. *Counseling:* relates to the provider's role as therapist and his or her effectiveness as a deliverer of therapeutic communication

4. *Educating:* involves the provider in disseminating information to others in the effort to reduce health risks and increase health care effectiveness

How can we improve our abilities to interact with each other to fulfill these functions? What can we do to ensure the sharing of sufficient information to facilitate correct diagnosis, needed cooperation, and proper treatment? The answers to these questions lie less in what we need to do alone and more in what we need to do together.

While medical advances have been significant, consumers continue to level charges of insensitivity, inability to empathize, lack of trust, and deficient listening skills against some health care providers. In fact, realizing that effective interpersonal communication and trust are essential for the creation of satisfactory provider-consumer relationships, medical schools are increasingly integrating communication training into their curricula. When it comes to communicating about health—the informing, influencing, and interpretation of health-based messages—how the messages are encoded, decoded, and interpreted is critical.

Sensitivity Matters. Provider insensitivity and consumer dissatisfaction are correlated. In contrast, interpersonal sensitivity and an awareness of the variables likely to facilitate full and honest disclosure in clients is of vital importance in maintaining the provider-consumer relationship. Consider your own situation with your medical provider. You likely become upset and apprehensive when your provider does not pay significant attention to your medical concerns. On the other hand, your compliance with your provider's recommendations, such as reducing your intake of salt or giving up foods high in sugar, probably increases when you feel you have been listened to.

Among the variables essential to the development of a good provider-consumer relationship are empathy, trust, honesty, confirmation, caring, and humor (see Chapters 8 and 9). Consumers prefer health care providers who are caring, friendly, and expressive.

Clear Communication Matters. To develop open and trusting provider-consumer relationships, we need to be skilled at exchanging health-based messages.[81] Finding the right words to use when communicating about health—particularly sexual health—can be difficult, but it is extremely important. Not talking about safe sex, for example, increases the chances that individuals will engage in risky behavior rather than healthful sexual practices.[82]

We need to be aware of the messages sent and received. Some messages frighten or confuse us. If we have difficulty describing or explaining our symptoms, others may be likely to misinterpret our words. Contributing to the clarity problem is the tendency for health care providers to use jargon, a practice that makes it more likely for us to misunderstand a diagnosis or treatment regimen and, thus, fail to comply with the provider's instructions. There are two key

How would you describe your physician's communication effectiveness?

message-sending strategies for providers that influence the consumer's willingness to comply: *emphasizing of expertise* ("If you comply with my recommendations to take time off from work and take the prescribed medication, your symptoms should decrease") and, if the consumer resists, *threats* ("If you fail to follow my recommendations, you're a prime candidate for a stroke").

Along with verbal messages, health care providers use a wide range of nonverbal communication cues—some that enhance and some that unintentionally undermine consumer compliance. By moving physically closer to clients, smiling, or exhibiting pleasant facial expressions, head nods, or vocal reinforcers such as "uh-huh," providers communicate high sensory involvement and caring, both enhancers of compliance. In contrast, by maintaining excessive distance from clients, frowning, or speaking in a cold voice, providers may cause clients to become less willing to follow instructions.

Perceptions Matter. In addition to misunderstanding each other, providers and consumers may misperceive or stereotype one another, further complicating their relationship. We sometimes have unreasonable performance expectations for health care providers—counting on them to pull a miracle cure out of a hat much as a magician pulls out a rabbit. Such perceptions make it highly unlikely that providers will be able to measure up in our eyes. At the same time, providers often stereotype health care consumers. For example, they may underestimate clients' intelligence or, based on assumptions related to age, sex, or level of attractiveness, fail to work with clients to foster honest exchanges of information and feelings.

Decision Making Matters. How decisions are made and who makes them also influence patient satisfaction, compliance with prescribed treatment, and recuperation. The **continuum of health care decision making** shown in Figure 14.5 identifies the factors at work.[83]

At the *physician control* end of the continuum, the provider is responsible for all decision making. In the past, this was the most common model. The mind-set was that because the physician has superior knowledge and abilities, the patient ought to trust him or her. In such a relationship, the physician does most of the talking, asks the majority of questions, frequently interrupts the patient, abruptly changes topics, or even ignores the patient. The interaction is dominated and controlled by the physician.

Continuum of health care decision making: A measure of health care provider-patient relationships, with physician control and patient control at opposing ends and collaboration at the midpoint.

Figure 14.5 Health Care Decision Making Continuum

Patient control				Physician control
	Patient autonomy	Collaboration	Patient abdication	

SOURCE: Deborah Ballard-Reisch, "Health Care Providers and Consumers: Making Decisions Together," in Barbara C. Thornton and Gary L. Kreps, eds., *Perspectives on Health Communication*, Long Grove, IL: Waveland Press, 1993, p. 70.

At the opposite end of the continuum is *patient autonomy*. In such a relationship, the patient exercises his or her right to self-determination and assumes complete responsibility for decision making. This is the opposite of what occurs in a patient-abdication relationship. The proliferation of health care information resources on the Internet has facilitated this option.

At the scale's midpoint is *collaboration*. In this kind of relationship, provider and patient share information, negotiate perspectives, and reach a mutually satisfactory decision. Typically more time-consuming than the alternatives, this approach preserves the patient's right to participate fully in decisions affecting his or her health and allows for more balanced interaction and consensus building.

CULTURE AND HEALTH COMMUNICATION

The cultural backgrounds of health care providers and the clients they treat often differ. While this does not necessarily cause problems, problems can surface if either fails to recognize how culture and prevailing stereotypes influence communication about health.

When it comes to health and perceptions of illness, it is important to consider an individual's beliefs, values, and attitudes. Beliefs, for example, influence those symptoms we are prone to consult a provider about, what we expect the provider to do, and how we are likely to react when confronting a health issue.

Due to both ethnocentrism and the bureaucratic nature of the Western health care system, American health care providers sometimes use an excess of technical phrases that their clients do not understand. Misunderstandings occur when persons from different cultures have conflicting ideas about the nature of disease and the meaning of illness. For instance, providers who fail to understand that persons from Asian cultures may perceive mental illness as dishonoring their family and community may be confused when an Asian consumer strongly denies being depressed even when all the symptoms suggest depression as a diagnosis.[84]

Providers may benefit from understanding how members of different cultures cope with and attempt to reduce the uncertainty that illness presents. Here communication specialist William B. Gudykunst's uncertainty reduction theory, which addresses the desire to gather enough information to make a social encounter predictable, plays a role. In high-context cultures such as Japan, uncertainty reduction predicts if individuals will follow group norms, while in low-context cultures such as the United States, the focus is on predicting the actions of individuals, not group behavior. A provider's having contact with the relatives and friends of clients from high-context cultures could help to reduce the provider's uncertainty.[85]

Cultural awareness can facilitate treatment. For example, knowing that the matriarch of a Hispanic family is the primary decision maker for all health-related matters facilitates the health care provider's communication with the rest of the family members.[86] Similarly, a provider's losing patience with culture-based taboos or beliefs— such as the dietary restrictions of a Hindu or an Orthodox Jew, or an African patient's belief in the healing powers of a certain amulet—will not help to resolve that person's medical condition.

When interacting with members of different cultures, health care providers can benefit from asking the following questions: What are the person's space needs? Does he or she respond to touch? What kind of eye contact will foster trust? Are there any special rules of protocol to follow? Are there any role models that might increase treatment compliance?

Women health care providers tend to spend more time with patients.

GENDER AND HEALTH CARE

Although current prime-time health-related television programs do include more interesting professional women than were featured years ago, the portrayals of female health care providers are often stereotyped. For examples, the female medical professionals depicted tend to be younger than the men, and they are rarely identified as the persons in charge. In addition, media depictions of men as sexual aggressors and women as sex objects contribute to the pathologizing of women's bodies and the legitimating of unhealthy and destructive behaviors such as anorexia and battering. Similarly, the emphasis on eroticism and sex in music videos and prime-time television helps to create a societal atmosphere that is conducive to risky sexual practices.

Research indicates that female health care providers tend to relate to their patients differently than do male practitioners. Consider the impact of this interchange between a male obstetrician and a patient:

Several years ago, Dr. Faith Frieden watched in dismay as a fellow obstetrician checked a patient who had begun bleeding during her pregnancy.

"Well," the doctor announced matter-of-factly, "you've miscarried."

His words of comfort? "These things happen. Some women miscarry before they even know they're pregnant."

True, Frieden thought, but if patients wanted merely a clinical explanation, they could consult a medical encyclopedia. What about a little kindness?[87]

On average, compared with their male counterparts, female health care providers spend more time with patients, interrupt less frequently, are more empathetic, elicit more medical information, and are more responsive to issues related to reproduction and sexuality. They also work harder to create a positive interpersonal climate. The health care provider's sex is also associated with the length of a patient's visit, with patient visits to female providers typically lasting longer than those to male providers.[88]

MEDIA, TECHNOLOGY, AND HEALTH CARE

The media and technology influence our interactions with health care providers as well as what we eat, what we drink, and how long we live.

Media Messages. As we have noted, prime-time television offerings contain high levels of sexual and occupational stereotyping. Media portrayals of medical practitioners also help to develop a distorted picture of illness and available medical treatments. Rarely do television dramas deal with the long-term consequences of illness; instead, week after week, they present examples of acute illness, crisis situations, and injuries. What is more, the health care providers portrayed in these shows make few diagnostic errors and frequently cure dire ailments. In addition, all too often the patient is not depicted as taking an active role in his or her care.

Television also provides many models of eating and drinking practices that are not conducive to maintaining good health. References to and the presence of unhealthy food abound. Yet, despite the fattening foods they consume and their unbalanced diets, with few exceptions, the characters are rarely overweight or out of shape. Such depictions may contribute to weight gain and dental problems in individuals who watch a lot of television.

Finally, the influence on health care consumers of talk shows such as *Dr. Oz* and *The Doctors* should not be discounted. Although they enable consumers to learn about health away from the tensions of a doctor's examining room, such programs cannot substitute for the one-to-one nature of the consumer–health care provider relationship.

Technology Messages. The Internet and computers have become thriving parts of the health care arena, enabling us, if we want to, to take more control over our medical futures than was previously possible. An abundance of websites are devoted to disseminating health-related information, and we can even chat with health care providers via Skype. Burgeoning electronic communities also facilitate health care consumer research and consumer-to-consumer interactions. Consumers are able to explore the medical literature and compare notes with others who experience the same symptoms and afflictions. Internet support groups may also facilitate recovery from illness and health maintenance.

Technology has improved not only our ability to process health-related information but also our ability to develop effective interpersonal relationships with health care practitioners, so that we are able to talk openly and candidly about our health and health-related issues. This improvement in communication can itself be health enhancing.

The health care arena has moved online. Which online sources do you trust?

GAINING COMMUNICATION COMPETENCE ACROSS CONTEXTS

In our highly mobile, stress-filled technological society, life is not static. Change, in fact, is the one constant in family, work, and health relationships. Family relationships transition or dissolve; new ones are created. Some family members experience health problems. Some leave the family as a result of divorce or relocation; others marry into the family. Some pass away; new members are born. Deaths, departures, and arrivals may elicit a range of emotions, from deep-seated grief, resentment, fear, and jealousy to happiness. Similar comings, goings, and health-related challenges occur in organizational life. We sometimes find ourselves needing to adapt by working through or renegotiating the nature of our relationships. To do this we rely on our powers of constructive observation, verbalization and discussion, problem solving, and joint decision making—keystones of effective interpersonal communication.

PREPARE TO HANDLE CONFLICT ACROSS CONTEXTS

You have a disagreement with a friend and choose to simply walk away. You disagree with a mechanic about the cost of repairing your car, but you pay up, telling yourself that you will never take your car to be fixed at that shop again. It is not so easy, however, to walk away from or escape family or work conflicts or disagreements with health care providers. To avoid creating "pressure-cooker" environments that can result in out-of-control situations, you need to rely on effective problem-solving and conflict resolution techniques (see also Chapter 11). As you do this, use the following rules to foster the sharing of perceptions:

1. Respond to what is going on rather than what you *think* is going on; clarify any ambiguous messages by describing discrepancies between the words spoken and the nonverbal message and asking for clarification.

2. Ask for help and emotional support when you need it.

3. Express your dreams and vision for the future.

4. Refrain from blaming and judging others.

5. Express your feelings directly without concealing them or becoming physically or verbally aggressive.

6. Observe your own behavior, noticing what you say, how you sound, and what you feel during an interaction.

RECOGNIZE THAT YOU CANNOT STAY AS YOU ARE OR ALWAYS BE HAPPY AND IN GOOD HEALTH

Whether it is in a family, work, or health-related context, it is important to be able to communicate honestly, admit when you have a problem, and seek help when you are unable to resolve it on your own. Follow these guidelines to address issues as they emerge:

1. Share responsibilities.

2. Maintain a high level of self-disclosure and trust.

3. Deal directly with unmet or unrealized expectations.

4. Deal directly with changing rules and role conflicts.

5. Ask questions.

6. Listen more, paying attention to verbal and nonverbal cues.

7. Remain open to change and be willing to relate to the person or condition that is, rather than the one that was.

LEARN ABOUT EACH OTHER

When you share effective interpersonal family, work, and health care relationships, you focus on and talk about issues that may help you adapt to change and face new situations and circumstances. Exhibiting an other-orientation—that is, focusing not just on yourself but on the other person's perceptions—facilitates this. Offer support when it is needed, take a sincere interest in another's welfare, use productive methods for coping with stress and illness, and use online resources to help maintain social and work networks and acquire knowledge relevant to your and others' well-being. Additionally, become aware of how cultural customs and gender practices affect relationships in different contexts.

"It seemed like such a good idea!," Jade moaned to Dominic, her husband. "I thought that for too long we've only been communicating on Facebook and that hosting a family reunion would be such fun and succeed in finally getting all of us together. Now I just want to call the whole thing off! Facebook is easier."

Both Jade and Dominic work full-time jobs. Taking their two kids, ages six and ten, to school and then to an array of after-school and weekend activities, making child-care arrangements, and serving as caregivers for an ailing grandparent (taking him to and from doctor visits), plus a host of other responsibilities, make their lives a constant juggling act. They see their siblings, parents, aunts and uncles, and cousins far less frequently than they did when they married fifteen years earlier. A family reunion seemed like the perfect way to see everybody again. So Jade had e-mailed a bunch of invitations.

It seemed that as soon as Jade pressed *send* she was flooded with a bunch of replies asking for more information. There were questions about the date and the food she would serve, requests for transportation, queries regarding who else was invited, and complaints about who should not have been invited—it seemed that everyone had advice to offer and a hidden agenda.

No one had told Dominic's parents in advance about the reunion, and they had already planned a vacation cruise. Uncle Fred was not speaking with cousin Jennifer. Cousins Olivia and Jason were going to be away on a business trip. Nieces Jane and Keri and nephews Elijah and Conner were committed to playing in assorted Little League and soccer games. Jade's mom did not want to stay overnight at Jade's home. Aunt Tessie would love to come, but she was under a doctor's care and needed someone to fly down to where she lived and escort her to the reunion.

Jade and Dominic were ready to cancel the reunion when their children started whining that they wanted to have a party.

Consider these questions:

1. What advice would you give Jade and Dominic about family, work, and health issues?

2. Have you or someone you know faced a similar situation? How was it resolved?

3. What kinds of attitudes or behavioral orientations would help turn this experience into a more positive one for Jade and Dominic?

REVIEW THIS

CHAPTER SUMMARY

1 Discuss the nature of interpersonal communication in families, including the influences of culture, gender, the media, and technology on the interaction of family members. The family is the core of early communicative and socialization experiences. It is, as Virginia Satir notes, "the factory where the person is made." According to systems theory, at any point in time, the behavior of one family member may be understood only in relation to the behavior of every other family member. Families are defined in many different ways, and many different family forms are common. In any family, however, members perform roles and have responsibilities. In addition to often sharing living space, they share a past, present, and future. They create rules that guide family communication and regulate family member interaction. A family's cultural background influences its preferred communication style and whether it is position- or person-oriented. The family is also the source of member attitudes regarding what it means to be male or female, directly influencing the roles and responsibilities of family members. Mediated images of family affect family member satisfaction; technological innovations enable family members to maintain contact with one another.

2 Discuss the nature of interpersonal communication in the workplace, including how culture, gender, the media, and technology influence work relationships. Those who work in organizations share interdependent relationships. As in any relationship, the dyad is the most basic level of interaction and at the heart of peer and leader-follower relationships.

The kinds of communication and the networks at play affect the organization's ability to fulfill its functions and facilitate employee morale and job satisfaction. Culture influences whether participative or authoritarian leadership is practiced. Whether employees are dominant or submissive, individualistic or collectivistic, and how they perceive space, time, and their needs are also affected by culture. In addition, cultural views of gender influence workplace roles, interactions, and expectations, and workplace relationships are influenced by both media portrayals and technological innovations.

3 Explain the relationship between interpersonal communication and health, focusing on factors influencing the practitioner-client dyad and how culture, gender, the media, and technology influence health care–based relationships. Persons in health-related settings rely on interpersonal communication as they present, process, and react to health-related messages. No matter the setting, it is important that both parties to an interaction be sensitive to each other's needs, have an awareness of mutual expectations, understand how their manner of encoding and decoding messages and interacting with others influences relations, and recognize how to overcome perceptual barriers. When not acknowledged, cultural influences and stereotypes can interfere with communication about health, leading to misunderstandings and affecting the delivery of health care. Media representations too frequently reinforce gender stereotypes and promote unhealthy practices. Technology is facilitating a more active role for health care consumers, fostering both consumer-provider interaction and ease of finding information and support online.

4 Identify how you can gain communication competence across contexts. In any context, constructive observation, verbalization and discussion, problem solving, and joint decision making enhance communication.

CHECK YOUR UNDERSTANDING

1 Can you evaluate the relational consequences of not attaining work-life balance? (See pages 391–392.)

2 Can you provide scenarios to explain how the family context influences the nature of interpersonal communication? How important to you is the performance of particular familial roles? (See pages 392–401.)

3 Can you offer examples of how gender, culture, the media, and technology influence both family and workplace relationships? (See pages 410–418.)

4 Can you explain the interface between healthy relationships and personal health? (See pages 418–423.)

5 Can you summarize steps you can take to enhance your interpersonal competence across contexts? (See pages 423–424.)

CHECK YOUR SKILLS

1 Can you explain your personal meaning for the word *family*? (See pages 392–393.)

2 Can you identify the factors that make family members interdependent? (See pages 393–394; and **Try This**, page 395.)

3 Can you analyze the roles and responsibilities of family members as well as the rules at work in a family? (See pages 395–398; **Analyze This**, page 396; and **Try This**, page 398.)

4 Can you recognize when a communication pattern creates a problem? (See pages 398–400.)

5 Can you observe how culture and gender influence behavioral preferences in families? (See pages 400–403; and **Try This**, page 402.)

6 Can you use techniques that increase communication effectiveness in the workplace? (See pages 408–410; and **Reflect on This**, page 410.)

7 Can you identify how the media and technology affect your behavior toward the members of your family? (See pages 417–418.)

8 Can you demonstrate awareness of how gender and cultural preferences, media images, and technological resources affect work relationships? (See pages 410–418; and **Try This**, page 414.)

9 Can you use clear communication when in health care settings? (See pages 419–421.)

10 Can you diagnose and overcome challenges created by family, work, and health issues? (See **The Case of the Problematic Reunion**, page 425.)

KEY TERMS

Nuclear family *392*

Blended family *392*

Single-parent family *392*

Boomerang family *393*

Commuter family *393*

Systems theory *393*

Rules *397*

Productive family communication patterns *399*

Family network *399*

Position-oriented family *401*

Person-oriented family *401*

Role assignments *402*

Integrated family *404*

Organizational networks *407*

Reflective thinking framework *408*

Brainstorming *408*

Groupthink *409*

Participative leadership *410*

Authoritarian leadership *410*

Interactive leadership *416*

Health communication *418*

Continuum of health care decision making *420*

STUDENT STUDY SITE

Visit the student study site at **www.sagepub.com/gambleic** to access the following materials:

- SAGE Journal Articles
- Videos
- Web Resources
- eFlashcards
- Web Quizzes
- Study Questions

Glossary

Abdicrat: One who has little need to control another.

Accenting: The use of nonverbal cues that underscore or emphasize parts of a verbal message.

Accommodative style: A style of resolving conflict that is unassertive and cooperative.

Acquaintances: People one may know and converse with, but with whom one's interaction is typically limited in scope and quality.

Active listening: A form of listening that involves the paraphrasing of a speaker's thoughts and feelings.

Adaptors: Unintentional movements of the body that reveal information about psychological state or inner needs, such as nervousness.

Affect displays: Unintentional movements of the body that reflect the intensity of an emotional state of being.

Affection need: The need to give and receive love and to experience emotionally close relationships.

Affectors: Factors that color responses to stimuli, including, but not limited to, culture, roles, biases, emotional state, past experiences, physical limitations, and capabilities.

Ageism: Discrimination against persons because of their age.

Aggressive expression style: A style of communication involving the open expression of one's needs, wants, and ideas even at the expense of another person.

Allness: A perceptual fallacy that allows a person to believe that he or she knows everything about something.

Allocentric orientation: A perspective displayed by people who are primarily collectivistic in their thinking and behaving.

Androgynous: Having both masculine and feminine traits.

Appreciative listening: Listening engaged in for pleasure.

Argot: The language used by members of a coculture.

Articulation: How individual words are pronounced.

Assertive expression style: A style of communication that is honest, clear, and direct.

Attending: Paying attention; the willingness to organize and focus on particular stimuli.

Attitude: A mental set or readiness that causes one to respond in a particular way to a given stimulus.

Attribution theory: A theory that posits that we assign meaning to behavior by ascribing motives and causes.

Authoritarian leadership: A style of leadership characterized by the use of dominating and directive communication.

Autocrat: One with a great need to control and dominate others.

Avoiding stage: The stage of a relationship during which channels are closed as the parties attempt to refrain from contact with one another.

Avoiding style: A style of resolving conflict that is unassertive and uncooperative.

Axioms of communication: A paradigm of universally accepted principles used for understanding communication.

Backchannel signals: Verbalizations one uses to tell another person that one is listening.

Balance theory: A mode of attitude change that demonstrates the desire to live in a state of equilibrium.

Behavioral pattern: A series of behavioral events occurring within a given context.

Beliefs: The building blocks of attitudes; one's assessment of what is true or false, probable or improbable.

Blended family: A family with two adults and children from one or both of the adults' previous relationships as well as possibly children from the current relationship.

Blindering: The unconscious adding of restrictions that do not actually exist.

Bonding stage: A stage of relational development during which the parties symbolically demonstrate for others that their relationship exists.

Boomerang families: Family households containing adult children who the family thought had left permanently but have unexpectedly returned.

Brainstorming: A technique designed to encourage idea generation.

Bullying: Repeated verbal or physical attacks or emotional harassment committed by one or more persons to intimidate or cause harm to one or more victims.

Bypassing: A communication problem that occurs when individuals think they understand each other but actually miss each other's meaning.

Caring: The level of emotional involvement we convey to one another.

Category-based processing: The processing of information about a person that is influenced by attitudes toward the group into which the person is placed.

Channel: A medium or passageway through which a message travels.

Chronemics: The study of how humans use time to communicate.

Circumscribing stage: A phase of relational development during which the partners start to lessen their degree of contact with each other and commitment to each other.

Client-centered interview: An interview during which the interviewer/practitioner helps the interviewee/client achieve his or her own insight and find solutions to problems he or she faces.

Client compliance: A client's following of measures prescribed for his or her care by a health care provider.

Closed-ended question: A question that forces the respondent to choose a specific response.

Closure: The process by which one fills in a missing perceptual piece.

Coculture: A group of people who share a culture within a society but outside its dominant culture.

Coercive power: The ability to deliver negative consequences in response to the action of another; power derived from force or the threat of force.

Cognitive dissonance: An aversive drive propelling one toward consistency.

Collaborative style: A style of resolving conflict that is high in both assertiveness and cooperativeness.

Collectivistic cultures: Cultures in which group goals are given a higher priority than individual goals.

Commitment: The intention to remain in a relationship even if trouble occurs.

Communication: A process involving both deliberate and accidental transfer of meaning.

Communication accommodation theory: A theory that asserts that we adjust our language patterns to reflect how we feel about another person.

Communication convergence: The matching of vocabulary, speaking rate, and use of pauses with another as part of building a relationship.

Communication divergence: The purposeful adoption of a style of speaking that contrasts with the style of speaking of a person from whom one desires to distance oneself.

Commuter family: A family that includes one or more members who commute from the household's primary residence to distant work location(s) and remain there for long periods.

Companionate love: Love that increases over time; love that engages a couple in one another's lives.

Comparison level for alternatives: A comparison of profits and costs derived from one relationship with those that might be derived from another relationship.

Competitive relationship: A relationship characterized by the presence of defensive and threatening behavior; a relationship in which one party aims to win, or to beat or outsmart the other party.

Competitive style: A style of resolving conflict that is high in assertiveness and low in cooperation.

Complementarity: Attraction to a person who is different from oneself.

Complementary relationship: A relationship based on difference in which the parties engage in opposite behaviors.

Comprehensive listening: Listening engaged in to gain knowledge.

Compromising style: A style of resolving conflict that is in the middle range in both assertiveness and cooperativeness.

Computer-mediated communication: Communication that uses computers as a means of linking individuals.

Confirmation: A communication that tells another person that his or her self-image is affirmed.

Confirming messages: Messages that convey value for another person.

Conflict resolution grid: A model that measures an individual's preferred style of handling conflict.

Conflict styles: Individuals' characteristic approaches to conflict with respect to measures of assertiveness and cooperativeness.

Connotative meaning: Subjective meaning; personal meaning.

Contact cultures: Cultures that encourage nonverbal displays of warmth, closeness, and availability.

Content conflict: A conflict that revolves around a matter of fact.

Context: The setting in which communication takes place.

Continuum of health care decision making: A measure of health care provider–patient relationships, with physician control and patient control at opposing ends and collaboration at the midpoint.

Control need: The need to establish and maintain relationships that allow one to experience satisfactory levels of influence and power.

Conversation: A relatively informal social interaction in which the roles of speaker and listener are exchanged in a nonautomatic fashion under the collaborative management of all parties.

Conversation deprivation: A lack of aural communication.

Conversational blunder: A faux pas; the uttering of something someone else is apt to find objectionable.

Conversational maintenance: Preservation of the smooth and natural flow of conversation.

Conversational rules: Behaviors that are established, preferred, or prohibited during social exchanges.

Conversational structure: The typical format for conversation, comprising the greeting, topic priming, the heart of the conversation, preliminary processing, and the closing.

Conversational turn taking: The simultaneous exchanging of the speaker and listener roles during a conversation.

Cooperative relationship: A relationship based on supportiveness, sharing, interdependent efforts, and trust.

Coping: The managing of emotions.

Cost-benefit theory: A theory that states that we work to sustain relationships that give us the greatest total benefit and that a relationship will be sustained only as long as perceived benefits outweigh emotional expenditures; also known as social exchange theory.

Counterfeit relationship: A relationship based on a lie.

Crazymaking behavior: Behavior believed to be at the root of dysfunctional conflict.

Critical or deliberative listening: Listening that involves working to understand, analyze, and assess content.

Cultural awareness: The ability to understand the role cultural prescriptions play in shaping communication.

Cultural lens: The influence of culture on perception.

Cyberbullicide: Suicide committed in response to online aggression.

Cyberspace: The virtual space that exists in an online or computer environment.

Debilitative emotion: An emotion that impedes a person's ability to function effectively.

Deception detection: The identification of a person's behavior that contradicts his or her words.

Defensive climate: The climate that results when a party to a relationship perceives or anticipates a threat.

Denotative meaning: Dictionary meaning; emotion-free meaning.

DESC script: A strategy for expressing one's own feelings and understanding the feelings of others; DESC is an acronym for describe, express, specify, and consequences.

Describing feelings: Revealing how another's behavior affects one without expressing any judgment of that behavior.

Descriptive statements: Statements that recount observable behavior without judgment.

Dialogue: An interactive process involving speaking and listening.

Dialogic listening: Listening that involves give-and-take between persons interacting as they cocreate a relationship.

Differentiating stage: A phase of relational development in which the parties reestablish their individual personal identities.

Directive interview: An interview that is tightly controlled and orchestrated by the interviewer or practitioner.

Disconfirmation: Communication that denies another person's significance.

Disconfirming messages: Messages that convey disregard for another person.

Displacement: A defense mechanism through which one releases anger or frustration by communicating feelings to people or objects perceived to be more accessible and less dangerous than the person who precipitated the feelings.

Displaying feelings: Overtly enacting one's feelings.

Dominant culture: The culture that has the most power.

Double message: The message that is communicated when words say one thing and nonverbal cues another.

Dramaturgical approach to human interaction: A theory, originated by Erving Goffman, that explains the role that the skillful enacting of impression management plays in person-to-person interaction.

Dyad: Two individuals interacting; a two-person relationship.

Dynamic process: A process that is ongoing, continuous, and in a state of constant flux.

Dysfunctional conflict: Conflict that creates one or more serious relationship problems.

Effect: The result of a communication episode.

Ego conflict: A conflict that revolves around an individual's self-worth.

Emblems: Deliberate movements of the body that are consciously sent and easily translated into speech.

Emoji icons: Whimsical pictures used to supplement emoticons.

Emoticons: Text-based representations of facial expressions and moods.

Emotion state: An emotion of limited endurance.

Emotion trait: An emotion that persists during person-to-person interactions regardless of whom one is interacting with.

Emotion contagion: The passing of a mood from person to person, influenced by individuals' ability to respond to emotion in kind or to exhibit a parallel response.

Emotional ineptitude: The inability to handle and control one's emotional responses.

Emotional intelligence: The ability to motivate oneself or to persist in the face of frustration; to control impulse and delay gratification; to regulate one's mood and keep distress from swamping the abilities to think, empathize, and hope.

Emotionally tone-deaf: Unable to listen empathetically.

Emotions: The feelings one experiences in reaction to one's surroundings.

Emotive language: Language that announces the user's attitude toward a subject.

Empathetic listening: Listening that involves understanding and internalizing the emotional content of a message.

Empathetic responsiveness: A listener's experiencing of an emotional response that corresponds with the emotions a speaker is experiencing.

Empathy: The ability to understand another's thoughts and feelings and to communicate that understanding to the person; the ability to comprehend another's point of view.

Equivocal language: Words that may be interpreted in more than one way.

Ethnocentrism: The tendency to perceive what is right or wrong, good or bad, according to the categories and values of one's own culture.

Euphemism: Less direct or inoffensive language substituted for blunt language.

Evaluative feedback: Feedback that reveals one's feelings or reactions to what one heard, providing a positive or a negative assessment.

Evaluative statements: Judgmental pronouncements.

Expectancy violation theory: A theory that addresses our reactions to nonverbal behavior and notes that violations of nonverbal communication norms can be positive or negative.

Expected self: The self that others assume one will exhibit.

Experimenting stage: An early relational development phase during which the parties search for common ground.

Expert power: Power derived from having special knowledge or skills that another thinks he or she needs.

Expressive roles: Roles focused on helping, supporting, nurturing, and being responsive to the needs of others; relationship-oriented roles.

Extensional orientation: The type of orientation one displays when not blinded by labels.

External feedback: Responses received from others.

Face-saving: The preservation of a person's dignity; may involve giving indirect answers to avoid hurting or embarrassing another person.

Facial Action Coding System: A virtual taxonomy of more than three thousand facial expressions used to interpret emotions and detect deception.

Facilitative emotion: An emotion that promotes effective functioning.

Fact-inference confusion: The tendency to treat observations and assumptions similarly.

Family network: The relationships and connections within a family.

Feedback: Information received in exchange for a message sent.

Feedforward: A variant of feedback sent prior to a message's delivery as a means of revealing something about to follow.

Field of experience: The sum of all the experiences that a person carries with him or her, which influences the individual's communication.

Figure-ground principle: A strategy that facilitates the organization of stimuli by enabling one to focus on different stimuli alternately.

Fixed-feature space: Space as defined by the permanent characteristics of an environment.

Flaming: The losing of emotional self-control while sending a message online.

Flame war: An exchange of out-of-control online messages.

Friendly relations: A phase of friendship during which an effort to preserve and strengthen the friendship is made if the parties have enough in common to build a relationship.

Friendship: A relationship between two people that involves the voluntary seeking out of one another and the displaying of a strong emotional regard for one another.

Frozen evaluation: A perceptual fallacy that discourages flexibility and encourages rigidity; an evaluation of a person that ignores changes.

Functional conflict: A conflict that develops a clearer understanding of needs, attitudes, or beliefs.

Fundamental attribution error: The overemphasis of internal or personal factors.

Fundamental interpersonal relations orientation: A three-dimensional theory of interpersonal behavior highlighting the needs for inclusion, control, and affection.

Gender: The socially constructed roles and behaviors that the members of a given society believe to be appropriate for men and women.

Gender differences: Differences between men and women according to social definitions and views of masculinity and femininity.

Gender identity: An inner sense of being male or female.

Gender prescriptions: The roles and behaviors that a culture assigns to males and females.

Genderlect: Deborah Tannen's term for language differences attributed to gender.

Grief process: A five-stage process during which the feelings a grieving individual experiences begin with denial and then pass through anger, guilt, and depression before resolving with acceptance.

Groupthink: A communication dysfunction in which some group members attempt to protect the group's harmony by exerting irrational pressures on one or more members so that genuine opinions are suppressed.

Halo effect: The perception of positive qualities in a person one likes.

Haptics: The study of how touch communicates.

Health communication: A field of study concerned with human interaction in the health care process.

Hearing: An involuntary physiological response in which sound waves are transformed into electrical impulses and processed by the brain.

High-context cultures: Cultures in which people tend to be very polite and indirect when interacting with others.

High-intensity conflict: Extreme conflict in which one party aims to destroy or debilitate the other.

High-monitored feedback: Feedback offered to serve a specific purpose; feedback that is sent intentionally.

Horn effect: The perception of negative qualities in a person one dislikes.

HURIER model: A model of listening that focuses on the following stages: hearing understanding, remembering, interpreting, evaluating, and responding.

"I" messages: Nonevaluative forms of feedback that reveal a speaker's feelings about the situation faced by another person.

Ideal self: The self one would like to be.

Idiocentric orientation: An orientation displayed by people who are primarily individualistic in their ways of thinking and behaving.

Illustrators: Bodily cues designed to enhance receiver comprehension of speech by supporting or reinforcing it.

Impression management: The exercising of control over one's behaviors in an effort to make the desired impression.

Inclusion need: The social need to feel a sense of belonging or mutual interest in relationship to others.

Indiscrimination: A perceptual barrier that causes one to emphasize similarities and neglect differences.

Individualistic culture: A culture in which individual identity is paramount.

Informal space or non-fixed-feature space: The invisible space each person carries around.

Initiating stage: The first phase in relational development, during which two individuals express interest in each other.

Instrumental roles: Roles that are focused on getting things done; task-oriented roles.

Integrated family: A family in which members are of different races and/or religions.

Integrating stage: A phase of relational development in which the identities of the parties begin to merge.

Intensifying stage: A phase of relational development during which the amount of contact and self-disclosure the parties have increases.

Intensional orientation: The type of orientation displayed when one responds to a label rather than to what the label actually represents.

Interaction model: A representation of communication as a back-and-forth process.

Interactive leadership: Leadership that encourages the sharing of both power and decision making with followers and coworkers.

Internal feedback: A person's response to his or her own performance.

Interpersonal communication: The ongoing, ever-changing process that occurs when one person interacts with another person, forming a dyad; communication occurring within a relationship.

Interpersonal competence: The ability to use appropriate communication to build and maintain an effective relationship.

Interpersonal conflict: A struggle between interdependent parties that occurs whenever one individual's thoughts or actions are perceived to limit or interfere with those of another; conflict that originates between two or more interdependent people.

Interpersonal deception theory: A theory that explains deception as a process based on falsification, concealment, or equivocation.

Interpersonal relationship: An association between two people through which the parties may or may not meet each other's social needs; a dyad.

Interpersonal synchrony: The exhibition of similarities; the interpersonal fusion of two individuals.

Intimacy: A measure of closeness; sustained feelings of closeness and connection.

Intimate distance: From skin contact to 18 inches from another person; the distance usually used by people who trust each other or who share an emotional bond or closeness.

Intimate relationship: A relationship that involves a high degree of personal closeness or sharing.

Intrapersonal communication: Communication requiring only a single communicator; communication with oneself.

Intrapersonal conflict: Conflict that originates within a single person.

Johari window: A model containing four panes—the open area, the blind area, the hidden area, and the unknown area—that is used to explain the roles that self-awareness and self-disclosure play in relationship building.

Kinesics: The study of human body motion.

Knapp and Vangelisti's ten-stage model of relationships: A model of relational development and deterioration created by Mark L. Knapp and Anita L. Vangelisti.

Language: A code or system of arbitrary symbols shared by a group and used by its members to communicate with each other.

Latent intimacy: Feelings of intimacy or connection not directly apparent to others.

Legitimate power: The type of power in which one party in a relationship controls the other.

Lie: The deliberate distortion or concealment of information; the intentional deception of another person to convince him or her of something one knows to be untrue.

Linear or unidirectional model: A representation of communication that depicts it as going in only one direction.

Linguistic determinism: The view that language shapes thinking.

Linguistic relativity: The view that languages contain unique embedded elements.

Listening: A voluntary psychological process consisting of the following stages: sensing, attending, understanding/interpreting, evaluating, responding, and remembering.

Long-distance relationship: A relationship between individuals who are geographically separated.

Low-context culture: A culture in which people typically exhibit a direct communication style.

Low-intensity conflict: Conflict in which the parties involved devise strategies to create a solution beneficial to both.

Low-monitored feedback: Feedback that is sincere and spontaneous; feedback delivered without careful planning.

Machiavellianism: The drive to control others.

Make-believe media: Media offerings that make us believe things that are not necessarily true.

Manifest intimacy: Feelings of closeness and connection that are apparent to others.

Manner maxim: The premise that when conversing one should use diction that is appropriate to the receiver and the interaction's context.

Maslow's needs hierarchy: A five-level pyramidal hierarchy of human needs developed by Abraham Maslow.

Matching hypothesis: The theory that we enter into a long-term relationship with someone similar to ourselves in physical attractiveness.

Media models: The images depicted in the mass media.

Mediated reality: The world as it is seen through the filter of the mass media.

Medium-intensity conflict: Conflict in which each of the persons involved wants to win.

Message: The content of communication.

Metacommunicative functions: Communication about communication.

Metaconversation: Conversation about conversation.

Microfacial/micromomentary expression: An expression lasting no more than one-eighth to one-fifth of a second that usually occurs when an individual consciously or unconsciously attempts to disguise or conceal an emotion and that reveals an actual emotional state.

Minimal justification for action: The principle that small rather than large incentives are more effective at creating dissonance and inducing attitude change.

Monologue: A communication process lacking in interactivity, during which one person speaks while another person listens.

Moving toward friendship: The point in friendship formation when the parties make small disclosures in an effort to expand their relationship.

Muted group theory: A theory that proposes that in a social hierarchy, the dominant group uses language to shape perceptions, effectively silencing or muting those with less power.

Nascent friendship: The stage in the development of friendship during which rules for regulating interaction are worked out.

Need for reassurance: The need to seek out information to confirm a decision.

Negative feedback: Responses that stop behavior in progress.

Negative Pygmalion: An individual who negatively influences one's perceptions of one's own abilities.

Noise: Anything that interferes with or impedes the ability to send or receive a message.

Nonassertive expression style: A style of communication characterized by hesitation in expressing one's feelings and thoughts.

Noncontact cultures: Cultures that discourage the use of nonverbal displays of warmth, closeness, and availability.

Nonevaluative feedback: Feedback that is nonjudgmental.

Non-fixed-feature space: *See* Informal space.

Nonfluencies: Hesitation phenomena; nonlinguistic verbalizations.

Nonlistening: A kind of deficient listening behavior in which the receiver tunes out.

Nonshareable goal: A goal that can be fully claimed and possessed by a single individual only.

Nonverbal communication: Communication that does not include words; messages expressed by nonlinguistic means; people's actions or attributes, including their use of objects, sounds, time, and space, that have socially shared significance and stimulate meaning in others.

Norm of reciprocity: The expectation of self-disclosure equity in a relationship.

Nuclear family: A household family unit that includes a mother, a father, and one or more children.

Olfactics: The study of the sense of smell.

Online disinhibition effect: The willingness to say what one really thinks or to misbehave when online.

Open-ended question: A question that allows the respondent free rein in answering.

Organizational networks: Patterns of communication in organizations.

Overattribution: The attributing of everything an individual does to a single or a few specific characteristics.

Overpersonal: Having an overriding need for affection.

Oversocial: Having an overriding need for inclusion.

Paralanguage: Messages sent using only vocal cues.

Participative leadership: Leadership in which leaders act as guides to others who remain free to identify their own goals, establish their own procedures, and reach their own conclusions.

Participative organization: An organization in which individuals perceive themselves to have significant ownership of and emotional investment in their work.

Passion: Intensely positive feelings of attraction that motivate one person to want to be with another.

Passionate love: The type of love that one feels when first falling in love.

Perceived self: A reflection of one's self-concept; the person one believes oneself to be when one is being honest with oneself.

Perception: The process used to make sense of experience.

Perceptual constancy: The tendency to maintain the way one sees the world.

Perceptual sets and selectivities: Organizational constructions that condition a readiness to perceive, or a tendency to interpret stimuli in ways to which one has been conditioned.

Perceptual shortcuts: The kinds of perceptions exhibited by lazy perceivers who rely on stereotypes to help them make sense of experience.

Personal distance: From 18 inches to 4 feet from a person; the distance at which we are most apt to converse informally.

Person-based processing: The processing of information about a person based on perceptions of the individual, not on his or her membership in a particular group.

Person-oriented family: A family in which flexible roles are nurtured.

Perspective taking: Adopting the viewpoint of another person.

Persuasive power: The ability of one party in a relationship to persuade the other party to act in a desired way.

Phatic communication: Superficial interaction designed to open the channel between individuals.

Physical attractiveness: Appeal based on physical qualities, which may lead to the initiation of a relationship.

Pitch: The highness or lowness of a voice.

Polarizing language: Language that describes experience in either-or terms.

Position-oriented family: A family in which roles are rigidly related to sex and age.

Positive feedback: Responses that enhance behavior in progress.

Positive Pygmalion: An individual who positively influences one's perceptions of one's own abilities.

Possible self: The self that one might become someday.

Power: The potential to influence others.

Power distance: The extent to which individuals are willing to accept power differentials.

Power-distance index: A measurement of where a culture rests on the power-distance scale.

Pragmatic code: The agreement to consider the context of an interaction, the interdependent nature of the relationship, and the goal of the exchange in deciphering meaning.

Prejudiced talk: Talk that includes racist, sexist, or ageist comments or comments denigrating any other kind of group.

Presentational facial expressions: Facial expressions that are consciously controlled.

Probing: A nonevaluative technique in which one solicits additional information from another.

Productive family communication patterns: Family communication styles that facilitate the expression of members' feelings and wants.

Pronunciation: The conventional treatment of the sounds of a word.

Proxemics: The study of how space and distance are used to communicate.

Proximity: Physical nearness.

Pseudoconflict: A situation that, while not an actual conflict, gives the appearance of one.

Public distance: A distance of 12 feet and beyond; the distance we use to remove ourselves physically from interaction, to communicate with strangers, or to address large groups.

Purr words: Words that register social approval.

Quality maxim: The premise that persons engaged in conversation do not offer comments known to be false.

Quantity maxim: The premise that persons conversing provide as much information as is needed to communicate a message's meaning and continue the conversation.

Racial profiling: A form of stereotyping attributed to racism.

Rate of speech: The speed at which a person speaks.

Rationalization: The provision of a logical or reasonable explanation for an unrealistic thought or feeling.

Reasoned sense making: The ability to predict and account for the behavior of a particular person.

Red-flag word: A word that triggers emotional deafness in the receiver, dropping listening efficiency to zero.

Referent power: Power that is based in other persons' respect for or identification with the power holder.

Reflected appraisal theory: A theory that states that the self a person presents is in large part based on the way others categorize the individual, the roles they expect him or her to play, and the behaviors or traits they expect him or her to exhibit.

Reflective thinking framework: A problem-solving system designed to encourage critical inquiry.

Regulators: Communication cues intentionally used to influence turn taking and to control the flow of conversation.

Reinforcement: Behavior that is personally rewarding.

Rejection: The negation of or disagreement with a self-appraisal.

Relational culture: The ways in which the parties to a relationship work out the rules or routines of the relationship.

Relational dialectics theory: A theory that explores the pushes and pulls partners feel toward integration versus separation, stability versus change, and expression versus privacy.

Relationship breadth: An aspect of a relationship measured by how many topics the parties discuss.

Relationship depth: An aspect of a relationship measured by how central the topics discussed are to the self-concepts of the individuals involved and how much the parties are willing to reveal about themselves and their feelings.

Relationship maintenance: The work that is needed to keep a relationship healthy.

Relationship repair: The work that is needed when a relationship fails to satisfy.

Relationship stages: Points used to characterize the nature of a relationship at any particular moment in its evolution.

Relationships: Social connections, of many different kinds, that, to varying degrees, meet our interpersonal needs.

Relevancy maxim: The premise that persons engaged in conversation do not purposefully go off on tangents or digress.

Representational facial expressions: Exhibited facial expressions that communicate genuine inner feelings.

Repression: The forgetting or denial of disturbing stimuli.

Resilience: The ability to cope with and recover quickly from disappointments.

Retrospective sense making: The ability to make sense of one's own behavior once it has occurred.

Reward power: Power based in the fact that one party in a relationship controls something valued by the other party.

Role assignments: The parts individuals play in a relationship network.

Role duality: The simultaneous performance of the roles of sender and receiver by the members of a dyad.

Role-limited interaction: An early stage of friendship characterized by a reliance on polite exchanges and standard scripts.

Role reversal: Imagining or acting by one party in a relationship or an exchange that he or she is the other party.

Roles: The parts that people play when interacting.

Romantic relationship: A love-based relationship built on commitment, passion, and intimacy.

Rules: Behavioral norms; implied or spoken understandings.

Sapir-Whorf hypothesis: A theory that proposes that language influences perception by revealing and reflecting one's worldview; language is determined by the perceived reality of a culture.

Schemata: The mental templates or knowledge structures that individuals carry with them.

Scripts: The general ideas that individuals have about persons and situations and how things should play out.

Selective attention: The means by which one focuses on certain cues while ignoring others.

Selective exposure: The practice of exposing oneself to people and messages that confirm one's existing beliefs, values, or attitudes.

Selective perception: The aspect of perception comprising selective exposure, selective attention, and selective retention, which enables individuals to see, hear, and believe only what they want to.

Selective retention: The recalling of things that reinforce one's thinking and the forgetting of things one finds objectionable.

Self-awareness: Personal reflection on and monitoring of one's own behavior.

Self-concept: The relatively stable set of perceptions one attributes to oneself.

Self-disclosure: The willing sharing of information about the self with others.

Self-efficacy: A positive belief in one's own abilities, competence, and potential.

Self-esteem: One's appraisal of one's own self-worth.

Self-fulfilling prophecy: A prediction or expectation that comes true simply because one acts as if it were true.

Self-image: The mental picture one has of oneself.

Self-serving bias: The overemphasizing of external factors as influences on one's behavior.

Semi-fixed-feature space: Space in which movable objects are used to identify boundaries and promote or inhibit interaction.

Semantic code: The agreement to use the same symbols to communicate.

Sex: The biological characteristics that define men and women.

Sexual harassment: Unwelcome sexual behavior that takes place in person or electronically.

Shareable goal: A goal that both parties to a conflict can possess.

Shared centrality: A communication network in which the ability to influence others is shared.

Silence: The absence of vocal communication.

Similarity: A like way of thinking between two people that results in attraction or social validation.

Single-parent family: A family in which one parent is solely responsible for the care of a biological or adopted child or children.

Small talk: Spontaneous conversation that lays the foundation for an interpersonal relationship.

Snap judgment: An evaluation made without reflection; an undelayed reaction.

Snarl words: Words that register social disapproval.

Social attractiveness: Appeal based on an engaging personality and demeanor.

Social comparison theory: A theory affirming that individuals compare themselves to others to develop a feel for how their talents, abilities, and qualities measure up.

Social distance: From 4 feet to 12 feet from another person; the interpersonal distance we usually use to conduct business or discuss nonpersonal issues.

Social identity model of de-individuation effects: A theory that states that each individual has different identities that make themselves visible in different situations.

Social intelligence: The ability to understand and relate to people.

Social learning theory: A theory that asserts that individuals learn at least some of what they know by observing others and then modeling the behaviors that they have observed.

Social penetration theory: A theory that states that relationships typically begin with relatively narrow breadth and shallow depth and develop both over time.

Speech-thought differential: The difference between the rate of speech and the rate at which speech can be comprehended.

Spotlighting: The highlighting of a person's sex for emphasis.

Stabilized friendship: A stage in friendship development during which the parties behave as if they expect their friendship to continue for a long time.

Stagnating stage: A stage of relational development characterized by one person's decreasing interest in the other.

Standpoint theory: A theory that one's place in the power hierarchy influences the accuracy of one's perception of social life.

Stereotypes: Rigid perceptions that are applied to all members of a group or to an individual over time, regardless of individual variations.

Substituting: The use of nonverbal cues that take the place of verbal cues.

Supportive climate: A climate in which the level of threat that individuals experience is reduced.

Supportive environment: An environment that builds trust and maintains each person's sense of worth.

Supportive feedback: Nonevaluative feedback that indicates that another's problem is viewed as important.

Symbol: Something that stands for something else.

Symmetrical relationship: A relationship in which the parties mirror each other's behavior.

Sympathetic responsiveness: Feeling for, rather than with, another.

Syntactic code: Conventions that guide word use; the agreement to use the same rules regarding word use.

Systems theory: An approach to communication that stresses the interaction of all elements in a communication network.

Task attractiveness: Appeal based in pleasure in working with another, which may lead one party to seek increased interpersonal contact with the other.

Technopoly: A culture whose thought world is monopolized by technology.

Telepresence: The sense of physically being in a different place or time through virtual reality.

Terminating stage: The stage of relational development during which the parties decide the relationship is over.

Territoriality: The claiming or identifying of space as one's own.

Therapeutic relationship: A relationship that increases one's level of interpersonal health.

Toxic communication: Communication that is verbally or physically abusive.

Transactional model: A representation of communication that depicts transmission and reception occurring simultaneously, demonstrating that source and receiver continually influence one another.

Triangle of meaning: A model that demonstrates the relationships that exist among words, things, and thoughts.

Triangular theory of love: A theory developed by Robert Sternberg that states that varying combinations of intimacy, passion, and commitment create different types of love.

Trigger cues: Cues that stimulate "click, whirr" programmed responses to persuasive appeals.

Trust: The belief that one can rely on another; made up of two components: trusting behavior and trustworthy behavior.

Trusting behavior: Behavior that accords with the belief that another will not take advantage of one's vulnerabilities.

Trustworthy behavior: Behavior that does not take advantage of another's vulnerabilities.

Turn-denying signals: Paralinguistic and kinesic cues that signal a reluctance to switch speaking and/or listening roles.

Turn-maintaining signals: Paralinguistic and kinesic cues that suggest that a speaker is not yet ready to give up the speaking role.

Turn-requesting signals: Paralinguistic and kinesic cues that let a speaker know that a listener would like to switch roles.

Turn-yielding signals: Paralinguistic and kinesic cues that indicate the readiness of a speaker to exchange the role of speaker for the role of listener.

Uncertainty reduction theory: A theory that states that individuals learn more about each other by monitoring their social environment.

Underpersonal: Having little need for affection.

Undersocial: Having little need for inclusion.

Value conflict: Conflict that revolves around the importance of an issue.

Values: One's ideas about what is important in life.

Virtual community: A community that exists only in cyberspace.

Visual dominance ratio: A figure derived by comparing the percentage of looking while speaking with the percentage of looking while listening.

Volume: The power or loudness of a voice.

Waning friendship: The stage in friendship development during with the parties drift apart.

Word mask: Ambiguous language meant to confuse.

Word wall: Language that impedes understanding.

Notes

CHAPTER 1

1. Aaron Smith, "Americans and Text Messaging," Pew Internet & American Life Project, September 19, 2011, http//pewinternet.org/Reports/2011/Cell-Phone-Texting-2011.aspx.
2. "Teens, Smart Phones & Texting," Pew Charitable Trusts, March 19, 2012, http://www.pewtrusts.org/our_work_report_detail.aspx?id=85899377053&category=56.
3. See, for example, E. Diener and M. E. P. Seligman, "Very Happy People," *Psychological Science,* 13, 2002, p. 81–84.
4. See Julia T. Wood, *Communication Theories in Action: An Introduction,* 9th ed., Boston: Wadsworth, 2011; and W. W. Wilmot, *Relational Communication,* New York: McGraw-Hill, 1999.
5. See Julia T. Wood, *Relational Communication,* 2nd ed., Belmont, CA: Wadsworth, 1997.
6. For a review of the research on interpersonal communication competence, see J. M. Wiemann and M. O. Wiemann, *Interpersonal Competence,* Newbury Park, CA: Sage, 1991.
7. I. Lau, C. Chiu, and Y. Hong, "I Know What You Know: Assumptions about Others' Knowledge and Their Effects on Message Construction," *Social Cognition,* 19, 2001, p. 587–600.
8. See Steve Duck," Relationships as Unfinished Business: Out of the Frying Pan and into the 1990s," *Journal of Social and Personal Relationships,* 7, 1990, p. 5.
9. See, for example, Kevin B. Wright, Lisa Sparks, and Dan O'Hair, *Health Communication in the 21st Century,* Malden, MA: Blackwell, 2007.
10. Erica Goode, "Rethinking Solitary Confinement," *New York Times,* March 11, 2012, p. 1, 19.
11. See Thomas Hora in Paul H. Watzlawick, Janet H. Beavin, and Don D. Jackson, *Pragmatics of Human Communication: A Study of Interactional Patterns, Pathologies, and Paradoxes,* New York: Norton, 1967.
12. William Schutz, *The Interpersonal Underworld,* Palo Alto, CA: Science and Behavior Books, 1966.
13. C. R. Berger, *Planning Strategic Interaction: Attaining Goals through Communication Action,* Mahwah, NJ: Lawrence Erlbaum, 1997.
14. William D. Cohan, "From Tweets to Blogs, We're Being Watched," *The Record* (Bergen County, NJ), July 31, 2011, p. O1, O4.
15. See also Richard West and Lynn H. Turner, *Understanding Interpersonal Communication,* 2nd ed., Boston: Wadsworth, 2011.
16. See Mark L. Knapp and John A. Daly, eds., *The SAGE Handbook of Interpersonal Communication,* 4th ed., Thousand Oaks, CA: Sage, 2011.
17. Watzlawick et al., *Pragmatics of Human Communication.*
18. Edward T. Hall, *The Silent Language,* New York: Fawcett, 1959.
19. William B. Gudykunst, *Bridging Differences: Effective Intergroup Communication,* 4th ed., Thousand Oaks, CA: Sage, 2004.
20. See Geert Hofstede, *Culture's Consequences: Comparing Values, Behaviors, Institutions, and Organizations across Nations,* 2nd ed., Thousand Oaks, CA: Sage, 2001.
21. See Edward T. Hall, *Beyond Culture,* New York: Doubleday, 1959.
22. See Julia T. Wood, *Gendered Lives: Communication, Gender, and Culture,* 9th ed., Boston: Wadsworth, 2011.
23. Elizabeth Fox-Genovese, *Feminism without Illusions,* Chapel Hill: University of North Carolina Press, 1991, p. 20.
24. Marshall McLuhan, *Understanding Media: The Extension of Man,* New York: McGraw-Hill, 1964.
25. Quoted in D. Kirkpatrick, "Here Comes the Payoff from PCs," *Fortune,* March 23, 1992, p. 93–102.
26. "Exactly How Much Are the Times A-Changin'?" *Newsweek,* July 26, 2010, p. 56.
27. A. Ramirez and S. Zhang, "When Online Meets Offline: The Effect of Modality-Switching on Relational Communication," *Communication Monographs,* 74, 2007, p. 287–310.
28. See "The Information: How the Internet Gets Inside Us," *The New Yorker,* February 14 and 21, 2011, p. 124–130.
29. For a discussion of contemporary breakups, see Benoi Denizet-Lewis, "It's Not U, It's Me:(," *New York Times Magazine,* August 7, 2011, p. 14.

CHAPTER 2

1. Lionel Tiger, "Zuckerberg: The World's Richest Primatologist," *Wall Street Journal,* February 6, 2012, p. A11.
2. See, for example, Amy Gonzales and Jeffrey T. Hancock, "Mirror, Mirror on My Facebook Wall: Effects of Exposure to Facebook on Self-Esteem," *Cyberpsychology, Behavior, and Social Networking,* 14, 2011, p. 41–49; and N. B. Ellison, C. Steinfield, and C. Lampe, "The Benefits of Facebook 'Friends': Social Capital and College Students' Use of Online Social Network Sites," *Journal of Computer-Mediated Communication,* 12:4, 2007, http://jcmc.indiana.edu/vol12/issue4/ellison.html.
3. As quoted in *Life* magazine, April 21, 1961.
4. S. I. Hayakawa and Alan R. Hayakawa, *Language in Thought and Action,* 5th ed., New York: Harcourt Brace Jovanovich, 1990. For a recent discussion of the self in relationship to others, see David Brooks, *The Social Animal: The Hidden Sources of Love, Character, and Achievement,* New York: Random House, 2011.
5. See Christopher J. Mruk, *Self-Esteem Research, Theory, and Practice: Toward a Positive Psychology of Self-Esteem,* 3rd ed., New York: Springer, 2006; and Don Hamacheck, *Encounters with the Self,* 3rd ed., Fort Worth, TX: Holt, Rinehart & Winston, 1992, p. 3–5.
6. See Lauren Slater, "The Trouble with Self-Esteem," *New York Times Magazine,* February 3, 2002, p. 44–47.
7. R. F. Baumeister, L. Smart, and J. M. Boden, "Relation of Threatened Egotism to Violence and Aggression: The Dark Side of High Self-Esteem," *Psychological Review,* 103, 1996, pp. 5–33.
8. R. Brooks and S. Goldstein, *Raising Resilient Children,* New York: Contemporary Books, 2001.
9. William James, *The Principles of Psychology,* New York: Dover, 1890.
10. Charles Horton Cooley, *Human Nature and the Social Order,* New York: Scribner's, 1912.
11. See, for example, C. Jaret, D. Teitzes, and N. Shapkina, "Reflected Appraisals and Self-Esteem," *Sociological Perspectives,* 48, 2005, p. 403–419.
12. Leon Festinger, "A Theory of Social Comparison Processes," *Human Relations,* 2, 1954, p. 117–140.
13. L. B. Whitbeck and D. R. Hoyt, "Social Prestige and Assortive Mating: A Comparison of Students from 1950 and 1988," *Journal of Social and Personal Relationships,* 11, 1994, p. 137–145.

14. D. M. Tice and J. Faber, "Cognitive and Motivational Process in Self-Presentation," in J. P. Forgas, K. D. Williams, and L. Wheeler, eds., *The Social Mind: Cognitive and Motivational Aspects of Interpersonal Behavior,* New York: Cambridge University Press, 2001, p. 139–156.

15. See Erving Goffman, *The Presentation of Self in Everyday Life.* Garden City, NY: Doubleday, 1959.

16. Kelly McGonical, *The Willpower Instinct,* New York: Avery, 2011.

17. Alina Tugend, "Bad Habits? My Future Self Will Deal with That," *New York Times,* February 25, 2012, p. B5.

18. Paul H. Watzlawick, Janet H. Beavin, and Don D. Jackson, *Pragmatics of Human Interaction: A Study of Interactional Patterns, Pathologies, and Paradoxes,* New York: Norton, 1967.

19. See Kim Giffin and Bobby R. Patton, "The Search for Self Identity," in *Fundamentals of Interpersonal Communication,* New York: Harper & Row, 1971; and George H. Mead, *Mind, Self and Society,* Chicago: University of Chicago Press, 1934, p. 144–164.

20. See Albert Bandura, *Self-Efficacy: The Exercise of Control,* New York: Freeman, 1997.

21. See, for example, Robert Rosenthal and Lenore Jacobson, *Pygmalion in the Classroom,* New York: Holt, Rinehart & Winston, 1968; and Len Sandler, "Self-Fulfilling Prophecy: Better Management by Magic," *Training Magazine,* February 1986.

22. Rosenthal and Jacobson, *Pygmalion in the Classroom.*

23. Lisa K. Libby, Greta Valenti, Allison Pfent, and Richard P. Eibach, "Seeing Failure in Your Life: Imagery Perspective Determines Whether Self-Esteem Shapes Reactions to Recalled and Imagined Failure," *Journal of Personality and Social Psychology,* 101, 2011, p. 1157–1173.

24. See, for example, Michael L. Hecht, Ronald L. Jackson II, and Sidney A. Ribeau, *African American Communication: Exploring Identity and Culture,* Mahwah, NJ: Lawrence Erlbaum, 2003.

25. Larry A. Samovar and Richard E. Porter, *Communication between Cultures,* Belmont, CA: Wadsworth, 1991; Richard Brislin, *Understanding Culture's Influence on Behavior,* Orlando, FL: Harcourt Brace Jovanovich, 1993, p. 47.

26. Samovar and Porter, *Communication between Cultures,* p. 91. See also Larry A. Samovar, Richard E. Porter, and Edwin R. McDaniel, *Communication between Cultures,* 7th ed., Boston: Wadsworth, 2010.

27. See Judith Martin and Thomas Nakayama, *Experiencing Intercultural Communication: An Introduction,* 3rd ed., New York: McGraw-Hill, 2008; and William B. Gudykunst and Stella

Ting-Toomy, *Culture and Interpersonal Communication,* Newbury Park, CA: Sage, 1988.

28. S. Kitayama and H. R. Markus, "Culture and Self: Implications for Internationalizing Psychology," in N. R. Goldberger and J. B. Veroff, eds., *The Culture and Psychology Reader,* New York: New York University Press, 1995, p. 44.

29. Harry C. Triandis, Kwok Leung, Marcelo J. Villareal, and Felicia I. Clack, "Allocentric versus Idiocentric Tendencies: Convergent and Discriminant Validation," *Journal of Research in Personality,* 19, 1985, p. 395–415.

30. J. A. Vandello and D. Cohen, "Patterns of Individualism and Collectivism across the United States," *Journal of Personality and Social Psychology,* 77, 1999, p. 279–292.

31. See, for example, W. B. Gudykunst, Y. Matsumoto, S. Ting-Toomey, T. Nishida, K. Kim, and S. Heyman, "The Influence of Cultural Individualism-Collectivism, Self-Construals, and Individual Values on Communication Styles across Cultures," *Human Communication Research,* 22, 1996, p. 510–543.

32. For a discussion of cultural variations in power distance, see Judith N. Martin and Thomas K. Nakayama, *Intercultural Communication in Contexts,* 5th ed., New York: McGraw-Hill, 2010.

33. Robert Atkinson, "The Universal Teenager," *Psychology Today,* October 1988. See also Amy Novotney, "R U Friends 4 Real?," *Monitor on Psychology,* 43, February 2012, p. 62.

34. Ibid.

35. Darlene Powell Hopson and Derek Hopson, *Different and Wonderful: Raising Black Children in a Race-Conscious Society,* Upper Saddle River, NJ: Prentice Hall, 1991.

36. See Philip Jordan and Maria Hernandez Reif, "Reexamination of Young Children's Racial Attitudes and Skin Tone Preferences," *Journal of Black Psychology,* 35, 2009, p. 388–403.

37. Quoted in Joel Wells, *Who Do You Think You Are?,* Chicago: Thomas More Press, 1989, p. 92–93.

38. Ibid, p. 93.

39. M. Kremar, S. Giles, and D. Helme, "Understanding the Process: How Mediated and Peer Norms Affect Young Women's Body Esteem," *Communication Quarterly,* 56, 2008, p. 111–130.

40. See, for example, C. M. Strong, "The Role of Exposure to Media Idealized Male Physiques on Men's Body Image," *Dissertation Abstracts International,* 65, 2005, p. 4306.

41. Julia T. Wood, *Gendered Lives: Communication, Gender, and Culture,* 9th ed., Boston: Wadsworth, 2011, p. 176.

42. Ibid.

43. Michael Parenti, "The Make Believe Media," *The Humanist,* November–December, 1990.

44. Lee Margulies, "Females Under-represented in Top U.S. Films, Study Says," *The Record* (Bergen County, NJ), May 17, 2012, p. BL4.

45. Stuart Ewen, *All Consuming Images: The Politics of Style in Contemporary Culture,* New York: Basic Books, 1988, p. 89.

46. Amanda Lenhart, Lee Rainie, and Oliver Lewis, *Teenage Life Online: The Rise of the Instant-Message Generation and the Internet's Impact on Friendships and Family Relationships,* Washington, DC: Pew Internet & American Life Project, 2001, http://www.pewinternet.org/~/media//Files/Reports/2001/PIP_Teens_Report.pdf.pdf.

47. For example, see B. Marcus, F. Machilek, and A. Schutz, "Personality in Cyberspace: Personal Web Sites as Media for Personality Expressions and Impressions," *Journal of Personality and Social Psychology,* 90, 2007, p. 1014–1031; and M. K. Matsuba, "Searching for Self and Relationships Online," *Cyberpsychology and Behavior,* 9, 2006, p. 275–284.

48. Sherry Turkle, *Alone Together: Why We Expect More from Technology and Less from Each Other,* New York: Basic Books, 2011, p. 12, 14, 178.

49. See Gonzales and Hancock "Mirror, Mirror on My Facebook Wall."

50. Christopher Carpenter, "Narcissism on Facebook: Self-Promotion and Anti-social Behavior," *Personality and Individual Differences,* 52, 2012, p. 482–486.

51. Tara Parker-Pope, "All about You," *New York Times Magazine,* May 20, 2012, p. 16.

52. Roni Caryn Rabin, "Internet Use Tied to Depression in Youths," *New York Times,* August 10, 2010, p. D6.

53. Lynda Edwards, "What Might Have Been," *New York Times,* January 2, 1994, sec. 9, p. 1.

54. Claudette Mackay-Lassonde, "Butterflies, Not Pigeonholes," *Vital Speeches of the Day,* January 1, 1994, p. 183.

CHAPTER 3

1. See, for example, Marian L. Houser, Sean M. Horan, and Lisa A. Furler, "Predicting Relational Outcomes: An Investigation of Thin Slice Judgments in Speed Dating," *Human Communication,* 10:2, 2007, p. 69–81.

2. Malcolm Gladwell, *Blink: The Power of Thinking without Thinking,* New York: Little, Brown, 2005.

3. See also Marian L. Houser, Sean M. Horan, and Lisa A. Furler, "Dating in the Fast Lane: How Communication Predicts Speed Dating Success," *Journal of Social and Personal Relationships,* 24, 2008, p. 749–768.

4. Houser et al., "Predicting Relational Outcomes."
5. See, for example, Paul W. Eastwick, Eli J. Finkel, and Alice H. Eagly, "When and Why Do Ideal Partner Preferences Affect the Process of Initiating and Maintaining Romantic Relationships?," *Journal of Personality and Social Psychology,* 101, 2011, p. 1012–1032.
6. Houser et al., "Dating in the Fast Lane."
7. Robert Lee Hotz, "Project to Explore Human Perception," *Wall Street Journal,* March 22, 2012, p. A2.
8. Jessica K. Witt and Dennis R. Profitt, "See the Ball, Hit the Ball," *Psychological Science,* 16, 2005, p. 937–938.
9. Joe Palca, "Can You Think Your Way to That Hole-in-One?," NPR Science, April 18, 2012, http://m.npr.org/news/science/150813843.
10. Patrick McGeehan, "Imagine His Shock. His Leg Had Vanished," *New York Times,* January 30, 2012, p. A15.
11. Ibid.
12. Adam Liptak, "Often Wrong but Rarely in Doubt: Eyewitness IDs Will Get a Fresh Look," *New York Times,* August 23, 2011; and Erica Goode and John Schwartz, "Police Lineups Start to Face Fact: Eyes Can Lie," *New York Times,* August 29, 2011, p. A1, A3.
13. Eric Schwitzgebel, *Perplexities of Consciousness,* Cambridge: MIT Press, 2011.
14. Stephen R. Covey, *The Seven Habits of Highly Effective People,* New York: Simon & Schuster, 1990, p. 28.
15. See, for example, Donna J. Haraway, "Situated Knowledges: The Science Question in Feminism and the Privilege of Partial Perspectives," in *Simians, Cyborgs, and Women: The Reinvention of Nature,* New York: Routledge, 1991; and Sandra Harding, ed., *The Feminist Standpoint Theory Reader: Intellectual and Political Controversies,* New York: Routledge, 2003.
16. See, for example, P. H. Collins, "Learning from the Outsider Within," *Social Programs,* 33, 1986, p. 514–532.
17. Sandra Harding, *Whose Science? Whose Knowledge? Thinking from Women's Lives,* Ithaca, NY: Cornell University Press, 1991.
18. See, for example, Charles R. Berger, "Uncertain Outcome Values in Predicted Relationships: Uncertainty Reduction Theory Then and Now," *Human Communication Research,* 13, 1986, p. 34–38.
19. See "Information Theory," *Encyclopedia Britannica Online,* http://www.britannica.com/EBchecked/topic/287907/Information-theory.
20. See, for example, Mark Changizi, "Masters of Distraction," *Wall Street Journal,* August 20–21, 2011, p. C9.
21. Quoted in Jonah Lehrer, "Learning How to Focus on Focus," *Wall Street Journal,* September 3–4, 2011, p. C12.
22. See Benedict Carey, "The Then and Now of Memory," *New York Times,* July 5, 2011, p. D4.
23. See, for example, Christopher Chabris and Daniel Simons, *The Invisible Gorilla and Other Ways Our Intuitions Deceive Us,* New York: Crown, 2010.
24. V. Nanusov, "It Depends on Your Perspective: Effects of Stance and Beliefs about Intent on Person Perception," *Western Journal of Communication,* 57, 1993, p. 27–41.
25. Sharon Begley, "The Memory of Sept. 11 Is Seared in Your Mind, But Is it Really True?" *Wall Street Journal,* September 13, 2002, p. B1.
26. Jill Harness, "Tricks Our Minds Play on Us," Neatorama, September 29, 2010, http://www.neatorama.com/2010/09/29/tricks-our-minds-play-on-us.
27. Saul Kassin, *Psychology.* 2nd ed., Upper Saddle River, NJ: Prentice Hall, 1998.
28. See, for example, Larry A. Samovar, Richard E. Porter, and Edwin R. McDaniel, *Communication between Cultures,* 7th ed., Boston: Wadsworth, 2010.
29. Ibid.
30. Donald R. Arkinson, George Morten, and Derald Wing Sue, "Minority Group Counseling: An Overview," in Larry A. Samovar and Richard E. Porter, eds., *Intercultural Communication: A Reader,* 4th ed., Belmont, CA: Wadsworth, 1982, p. 172.
31. Quoted in Erica Orden, "A Changed City: Reflections on 9/11," *Wall Street Journal,* September 6, 2011, p. A23.
32. Irene V. Blair, Charles M. Judd, Melody S. Sadler, and Christopher Jenkins, "The Role of Afrocentric Features in Person Perception: Judging by Features and Categories," *Journal of Personality and Social Psychology,* 83, 2002, p. 5–25.
33. See, for example, M. E. Hill, "Color Difference in the Socioeconomic Status of African American Men: Results of a Longitudinal Study," *Social Forces,* 78, p. 1437–1460.
34. See Alison L. Chasteen, "The Role of Age and Age-Related Attitudes in Perceptions of Elderly Individuals," *Basic and Applied Social Psychology,* 22, 2000, 147–156.
35. S. T. Fiske and S. L Neuberg, "A Continuum of Impression Formation, from Category-Based to Individuating Processes: Influences of Information and Motivation on Attention and Interpretation," in M. P. Zanna, ed., *Advances in Experimental Social Psychology,* vol. 23, New York: Academic Press, 1990, p. 1–74.
36. M. Snyder and P. K. Miene, "Stereotyping of the Elderly: A Functional Approach," *British Journal of Social Psychology,* 33, 1994, p. 63–82.
37. Ibid.
38. Irving J. Lee, *How to Talk with People,* San Francisco: International Society for General Semantics, 1982.
39. Mary Morain, ed., *Classroom Exercises in General Semantics,* San Francisco: International Society for General Semantics, 1980, p. 17–18.
40. J. W. Bagby, "A Cross-Cultural Study of Perceptual Predominance in Binocular Rivalry," *Journal of Abnormal and Social Psychology,* 54, 1957, p. 331–334.
41. Susan Page and Carly Mallenbaum, "Views Differ on Degree of Change since MLK," *USA Today,* August 18, 2011, p. 4A.
42. See Julia T. Wood, *Gendered Lives: Communication, Gender, and Culture,* 9th ed., Boston: Wadsworth, 2011.
43. See George Gerbner, Larry P. Gross, Michael Morgan, and Nancy Signorielli, "Growing Up with Television: The Cultivation Perspective," in Jennings Bryant and Dolf Zillmann, eds., *Media Effects: Advances in Theory and Research,* Hillsdale, NJ: Lawrence Erlbaum, 1994, p. 17–41.
44. See George Gerbner, Larry P. Gross, Michael Morgan, and Nancy Signorielli, "The 'Mainstreaming' of America: Violence Profile No. 11," *Journal of Communication,* 30, 1980, p. 10–29; and George Gerbner, "The Politics of Media Violence: Some Reflections," in Cees J. Hamelink and Olga Linné, eds., *Mass Communication Research: On Problems and Policies,* Norwood, NJ; Ablex, 1994.
45. See, for example, Robin L. Nabi, "Cosmetic Surgery Makeover Programs and Intentions to Undergo Cosmetic Enhancements: A Consideration of Three Models of Media Effects," *Human Communication Research,* 35, 2009, p. 1–27; and L. J. Shrum and Valerie Darmanin Bischak, "Mainstreaming, Resonance, and Impersonal Impact: Testing Moderators of the Cultivation Effect for Estimates of Crime Risk," *Human Communication Research,* 27, 2001, 187–215.
46. See Tom Postmes, Russell Spears, and Martin Lea, "Breaching or Building Social Boundaries? SIDE-Effects of Computer Mediated Communication," *Communication Research,* 25, 1998, p. 689–715.
47. See, for example, Russell Spears, Tom Postmes, Martin Lea, and Susan E. Watt, "A SIDE View of Social Influence," in Joseph P. Forgas and Kipling D. Williams, eds., *Social Influence: Direct and Indirect Processes,* Philadelphia: Psychology Press, 2001, p. 331–350.
48. Iowa State University, "Violent Video Games and Hostile Personalities Go Together," *Science Daily,* April 4, 2007, http://www.sciencedaily.com/releases/2007/04/070404162247.htm.
49. Sharon Begley, "The Kid Flunked, But He Sure Pays Attention," *Wall Street Journal,* May 29, 2003, p. B1, B8.
50. Sandra Blakeslee, "Video-Game Killing Builds Visual Skills, Researchers Report," *New York Times,* May 29, 2003, p. A1, A25.

51. Randall Stross, "The Second Screen, Trying to Complement the First," *New York Times,* March 4, 2012, p. BU5.

52. Marco R. Della Cava, "Attention Spans Get Rewired," *USA Today,* August 4, 2010, p. 1D, 2D.

53. Cathy N. Davidson, *Now You See It: How the Brain Science of Attention Will Transform the Way We Live, Work, and Learn,* New York: Viking, 2011.

54. Tim Mullaney, "Distractions for Workers Add Up," *USA Today,* May 18, 2011, p. 1B.

55. Patricia Cohen, "Internet Use Affects How We Remember," *New York Times,* July 15, 2011, p. A14; and Katherine Hobson, "Relying on Internet Affects the Way We Remember," *Wall Street Journal,* July 19, 2011, p. D2.

56. Peggy Orenstein, "I Tweet, Therefore I Am," *New York Times Magazine,* August 1, 2010, p. 11–12.

CHAPTER 4

1. See, for example, David Glenn, "Divided Attention: In an Age of Classroom Multitasking, Scholars Probe the Nature of Learning and Memory," *Chronicle of Higher Education,* February 28, 2010, http://chronicle.com/article/Scholars-Turn-Their-Attention/63746.

2. Ibid.

3. Faith Brynie, "The Madness of Multitasking," *Psychology Today,* Brain Sense blog, August 24, 2009, http://www.psychologytoday.com/blog/brain-sense/200908/the-madness-multitasking

4. These observations are attributed to Edward Guiliano, Ph.D., president of New York Institute of Technology, in "A New Game Plan for Learning," *NYIT Magazine,* Winter 2012, p. 4.

5. See, for example, R. Emanuel, J. Adams, K. Baker, E. K. Daufin, C. Ellington, E. Fitts, J. Himsel, L. Holladay, and D. Okeowo, "How College Students Spend Their Time Communicating," *International Journal of Listening,* 22, 2008, p. 13–28; L. Barker, R. Edwards, C. Gaines, K. Gladney, and F. Holley, "An Investigation of Proportional Time Spent in Various Communication Activities by College Students," *Journal of Applied Communication Research,* 8, 1981, p. 101–109; and Andrew Wolvin and Carolyn Coakley, "A Survey of the Status of Listening Training in Some *Fortune* 500 Corporations," *Communication Education,* 40, 1991, p. 152–164.

6. See Victoria J. Rideout, Ulla G. Foehr, and Donald F. Roberts, *Generation M²: Media in the Lives of 8- to-18-Year-Olds,* Menlo Park, CA: Henry J. Kaiser Family Foundation, January 2010, http://www.kff.org/entmedia/upload/8010.pdf.

7. See Denisa R. Superville, "Digitally Distracted: Hours Spent Wired Changing How Kids Think and Interact," *The Record* (Bergen County, NJ), May 15, 2010, p. A1, A8; and Rideout et al., *Generation M².*

8. M. L. Beall, J. Gill-Rosier, J. Tate, and A. Matten, "State of the Context: Listening in Education," *International Journal of Listening,* 22, 2008, p. 123–132.

9. See R. N. Bostrom, "The Process of Listening," in O. Hargie, ed., *Handbook of Communication Skills,* 3rd ed., New York: Routledge, p. 267–291; and Andrew Wolvin and Carolyn Gwynn Coakley, *Listening,* 5th ed., Dubuque, IA: Brown & Benchmark, 1996.

10. See Judi Brownell, *Listening: Attitudes, Principles, and Skills,* 3rd ed., Boston: Allyn & Bacon, 2006.

11. Cited in Arthur K. Robertson, *The Language of Effective Listening,* Carmel, IN: Scott Foresman Professional Books, 1991, p. 44–45.

12. Cathy N. Davidson, *Now You See It: How the Brain Science of Attention Will Transform the Way We Live, Work, and Learn,* New York: Viking, 2011.

13. See M. Imhof, "Who Are We as We Listen? Individual Listening Profiles in Varying Contexts," *International Journal of Listening,* 18, 2004, p. 36–45; and K. W. Watson, L. L. Barker, and J. B. Weaver, "The Listening Styles Profiles: Development and Validation of an Instrument to Assess Four Listening Styles," *International Journal of Listening,* 9, 1995, p. 1–13.

14. See, for example, M. Snyder, "A Gender-Informed Model of Couple and Family Therapy: Relationship Enhancement Therapy," *Contemporary Family Therapy,* 14, 1992, p. 15–31; and B. I. Omdahl, *Cognitive Appraisal, Emotion, and Empathy,* Mahwah, NJ: Lawrence Erlbaum, 1995.

15. L. A. Sapadin, "Friendship and Gender: Perspectives of Professional Men and Women," *Journal of Social and Personal Relationships,* 5, 1988, p. 387–403.

16. J. B. Weaver III and M. B. Kirley, "Listening Styles and Empathy," *Southern Communication Journal,* 60, 1995, p. 131–140.

17. Frank I. Luntz, *Win: The Key Principles to Take Your Business from Ordinary to Extraordinary,* New York: Hyperion, 2011.

18. See, for example, D. Grewal and P. Salovey, "Feeling Smart: The Science of Emotional Intelligence," *American Scientist,* 93, 2005, p. 330–339; and D. Goleman, *Emotional Intelligence,* New York: Bantam, 1995.

19. See, for example, Wolvin and Coakley, *Listening.*

20. R. Preiss and L. Wheeless, "Affective Responses in Listening," *Journal of the International Listening Association,* 3, 1989, p. 72–102.

21. See, for example, J. B. Bavelas and T. Johnson, "Listeners as Co-narrators," *Journal of Personality and Social Psychology,* 79, 2002, p. 941–952.

22. Quoted in Adam Bryant, "Want to Inspire? Don't Sugarcoat Your Feedback," *New York Times,* September 11, 2011, p. BU2.

23. Rachel Emma Silverman, "Yearly Reviews? Try Weekly," *Wall Street Journal,* September 6, 2011, p. B6.

24. John Stewart and M. Thomas, "Dialogic Listening: Sculpting Mutual Meanings," in John Stewart, ed., *Bridges Not Walls: A Book about Interpersonal Communication,* 6th ed., New York: McGraw-Hill, 1995, p. 184–201.

25. See, for example, H. S. Park and X. Guan, "Cultural Differences in Self versus Others' Self-Construals: Data from China and the United States," *Communication Research Reports,* 24, 2007, p. 21–28.

26. C. Y. Cheng, "Chinese Philosophy and Contemporary Communication Theory," in D. I. Kincaid, ed., *Communication Theory: Eastern and Western Perspectives,* New York: Academic Press, 1987.

27. See Stella Ting-Toomey, "Toward a Theory of Conflict and Culture," in William B. Gudykunst, Lea P. Stewart, and Stella Ting-Toomey, eds., *Communication, Culture, and Organizational Processes,* Beverly Hills, CA: Sage, 1985, p. 71–86.

28. Larry A. Samovar and Richard E. Porter, *Communication between Cultures,* 5th ed., Belmont, CA: Wadsworth, 2004, p. 211–212.

29. See T. S. Lebra, "The Cultural Significance of Silence in Japanese Communication," *Multilingua,* 6, 1987, p. 343–357.

30. William B. Gudykunst, *Bridging Differences: Effective Intergroup Communication,* 4th ed., Thousand Oaks, CA: Sage, 2004, p. 196–197.

31. Deborah Tannen, *You Just Don't Understand: Women and Men in Conversation.* New York: Morrow, 1990.

32. M. Booth-Butterfield, "She Hears . . . He Hears: What They Hear and Why," *Personnel Journal,* 44, p. 36–42.

33. M. Messner, "Boyhood, Organized Sports, and the Construction of Masculinities," in E. Disch, ed., *Reconstructing Gender,* Mountain View, CA: Mayfield, 1997, p. 57–73.

34. See Julia T. Wood, *Gendered Lives: Communication, Gender, and Culture,* 10th ed., Boston: Wadsworth, 2013, p. 127.

35. Diana K. Ivy and Phil Backlund, *Exploring GenderSpeak: Personal Effectiveness in Gender Communication,* New York: McGraw-Hill, 1994, p. 225.

36. B. R. Burleson, "Emotional Support Skills," in J. O. Green and B. R. Burleson, eds., *Handbook of Communication and Social Interaction Skills,* Mahwah, NJ: Lawrence Erlbaum, 2003.

37. N. Newcombe and D. B. Arnkoff, "Effects of Speech Style and Sex of Speaker

on Person Perception," *Journal of Personality and Social Psychology,* 37, 1999, p. 1293–1303.

38. A. Mulac, C. R. Incontro, and M. R. James, "Comparison of the Gender-Linked Language Effect and Sex Role Stereotypes," *Journal of Personality and Social Psychology,* 49, 1985, p. 1098–1109.

39. Davidson, *Now You See It,* p. 23–31.

40. Ibid.

CHAPTER 5

1. See, for example, V. Paul Poteat and Craig D. DiGiovanni, "When Biased Language Use Is Associated with Bullying and Dominance Behavior: The Moderating Effect of Prejudice," *Journal of Youth and Adolescence,* 39, 2010, p. 1123–1133.

2. Karen Sudol and Rebecca D. O'Brien, "Ravi Found Guilty, But Still Could Avoid Prison," *The Record* (Bergen County, NJ), March 17, 2012, p. A1, A6.

3. For an in-depth analysis of the Clementi/Ravi story, see Ian Parker, "The Story of a Suicide," *The New Yorker,* February 6, 2012, p. 37–51.

4. See, for example, Alonzo Westbrook, *Hip Hoptionary: The Dictionary of Hip Hop Terminology,* New York: Broadway, 2002.

5. C. K. Ogden and I. A. Richards, *The Meaning of Meaning,* New York: Harcourt Brace Jovanovich, 1930.

6. William Safire, "Traffic Talk," *New York Times,* February 28, 1982.

7. See, for example, Ralph Keyes, *Euphemania: Our Love Affair with Euphemisms,* New York: Little, Brown, 2011.

8. For a discussion of politeness in non-Western cultures, see M. S. Kim, *Non-Western Perspectives in Human Communication,* Thousand Oaks, CA: Sage, 2002.

9. William Lutz, *Doublespeak Defined,* New York: Harper Resource, 1999; and National Council of Teachers of English, "The 1999 Doublespeak Awards," *ETC.: A Review of General Semantics,* 56, 1999–2000, p. 484.

10. William Haney, *Communication and Organizational Behavior,* 3rd ed., Homewood, IL: Richard D. Irwin, 1973, p. 247–248.

11. See "Mokusatsu: One Word, Two Lessons,"www.nsa.gov/public_info/_files/tech_journals/mokusatsu.pdf.

12. Benjamin Lee Whorf, "Science and Linguistics," in John B. Carroll, ed., *Language, Thought, and Reality: Selected Writings of Benjamin Lee Whorf,* Cambridge: MIT Press, 1996.

13. William B. Gudykunst, "Uncertainty and Anxiety," in Young Yun Kim and William B. Gudykunst, eds., *Theories in Intercultural Communication,* Newbury Park, CA: Sage, 1988, p. 129.

14. Dean C. Barnlund, *Public and Private Self in Japan and the United States: Communicative Styles in Two Cultures,* Yarmouth, ME: Intercultural Press, 1989, p. 57; and Tomohiro Hasegawa and William B. Gudykunst, "Silence in Japan and the United States," *Journal of Cross-Cultural Psychology,* 29, 1998, p. 668–684.

15. See Richard E. Nisbett, "Living Together versus Going It Alone," in Larry A. Samovar, Richard E. Porter, and Edwin R. McDaniel, *Intercultural Communication: A Reader,* 12th ed., Boston: Wadsworth, 2009, p. 134–144.

16. Steve Duck, "Talking Relationships into Being," *Journal of Social and Personal Relationships,* 12, 1995, p. 535–540.

17. Howard Giles, Nikolas Coupland, and Justine Coupland, "Accommodation Theory: Communication, Context, and Consequence," in Howard Giles, Nikolas Coupland, and Justine Coupland, eds., *Contexts of Accommodation: Developments in Applied Sociolinguistics,* New York: Cambridge University Press, 1991, p. 1–68.

18. Y. Baruch and S. Jenkins, "Swearing at Work and Permissive Leadership Culture: When Anti-social Becomes Social and Incivility Is Acceptable," *Leadership and Organization Development Journal,* 28, 2006, p. 492–507.

19. Edward Sapir, *Selected Writings of Edward Sapir,* David W. Mandelbaum, ed. Berkeley: University of California Press, 1949, p. 162.

20. E. M. Rogers and T. M. Steinfatt, *Intercultural Communication,* Prospect Heights, IL: Waveland Press, 1998, p. 135.

21. B. L. Whorf, *Language, Thought, and Reality: Selected Writings of Benjamin Lee Whorf,* J. B. Carroll, ed., Cambridge: MIT Press, 1940/1956, p. 239.

22. Sapir, *Selected Writings,* p. 162.

23. Wendell Johnson, *People in Quandaries,* New York: Harper & Row, 1946.

24. See Fiona Cowie, *What's Within? Nativism Reconsidered,* New York: Oxford University Press, 1999.

25. Larry A. Samovar and Richard E. Porter, *Communication between Cultures,* Belmont, CA: Wadsworth, 1991, p. 152.

26. See, for example, Margaret K. Nydel, *Understanding Arabs: A Guide for Modern Times,* 4th ed., New York: Nicholas Brealey, 2005.

27. See, for example, Edwin R. McDaniel, Larry A. Samovar, and Richard E. Porter, "Understanding Intercultural Communication: The Working Principles," in Larry A. Samovar, Richard E. Porter, and Edwin R. McDaniel, eds., *Intercultural Communication: A Reader,* 12th ed., Boston: Wadsworth, 2009, p. 6–17.

28. Sharon Begley, "West Brain, East Brain: What a Difference Culture Makes," *Newsweek,* March 1, 2010, p. A6.

29. Lera Boroditsky, "Lost in Translation," *Wall Street Journal,* July 24–25, 2010, p. W3.

30. Nancy M. Henley, "Molehill or Mountain? What We Know and Don't Know about Sex Bias in Language," in Mary Crawford & Margaret Gentry, eds., *Gender and Thought: Psychological Perspectives,* New York: Springer-Verlag, 1989, pp. 59–78.

31. See, for example, J. Gastil, "Generic Pronouns and Sexist Language: The Oxymoronic Character of Masculine Generics," *Sex Roles,* 23, 1990, p. 629–643; and J. Y. Switzer, "The Impact of Generic Word Choices: An Empirical Investigation of Age- and Sex-Related Differences," *Sex Roles,* 22, 1990, p. 69–82.

32. Christina Passariello and Ray A. Smith, "Grab Your 'Murse,' Pack a 'Mankini' and Don't Forget the 'Mewelry,'" *Wall Street Journal,* September 8, 2011, p. A1, A12.

33. Deborah Tannen, "Gender Differences in Conversational Coherence: Physical Alignment and Topical Cohesion," in Bruce Dorval, ed., *Conversational Organization and Its Development,* Norwood, NJ: Ablex, 1990, p. 167–206.

34. Julia T. Wood, *Gendered Lives: Communication, Gender, and Culture,* 9th ed., Boston: Wadsworth, 2011.

35. Jennifer Coates, *Women, Men, and Language: A Sociolinguistic Account of Gender Differences in Language,* 2nd ed., New York: Longman, 1993.

36. See, for example, Karina Schumann and Michael Ross, "Why Women Apologize More than Men: Gender Differences in Thresholds for Perceiving Offensive Behavior," *Psychological Science,* 21, 2010, p. 1649–1655.

37. Campell Leaper and Rachel D. Robnett, "Women Are More Likely than Men to Use Tentative Language, Aren't They? A Meta-analysis Testing for Gender Differences and Moderators," *Psychology of Women Quarterly,* 35, 2011, p. 129–142.

38. Robin Lakoff, *Language and Woman's Place,* New York: Harper & Row, 1975.

39. See, for example, S. Mills, "Discourse Competence: Or How to Theorize Strong Women," in C. Hendricks and K. Oliver, eds., *Language and Liberation,* Albany: State University of New York Press, 1999, p. 81–97.

40. Deborah Tannen, *You Just Don't Understand: Women and Men in Conversation,* New York: Morrow, 1990.

41. Ibid., p. 42.

42. L. Tamir, *Men in Their Forties: The Transition to Middle Age,* New York: Springer, 1982.

43. J. Harwood, H. Giles, S. Fox, E. B. Ryan, and A. Williams, "Patronizing Young and Elderly Adults: Response Strategies in a Community Setting," *Journal of Applied Communication Research,* 21, 1993, p. 211–226.

44. Naomi Wolf, *The Beauty Myth,* New York: Morrow, 1991.

45. Susan F. Rasky, "Study Reports Sex Bias in News Organizations," *New York Times,* April 11, 1989, p. C22.

46. Howard Rheingold, "A Slice of Life in My Virtual Community," in Linda M. Harasim, ed., *Global Networks: Computers and International Communication,* Cambridge, MA: MIT Press, 1993, p. 61.

47. See Boyce Watkins, "Teacher Calls First-Graders 'Future Criminals,'" The Root, August 31, 2011, http://www.theroot .com/buzz/teacher-calls-first-graders-future-criminals.

48. Pamela Paul, "Cracking Teenagers' Online Codes," *New York Times,* January 22, 2012, p. ST1, ST9.

49. Stephanie Raposo, "Quick! Tell Us What KUTGW Means," *Wall Street Journal,* August 5, 2009, p. D1, D3.

50. See Carolyn Tagg, "A Corpus Linguistics Study of SMS Text Messaging," doctoral dissertation, University of Birmingham, March 2009.

51. Mike Hager, "OMG! Is Texting Ruining Our Language?," *PostMedia News,* April 9, 2012, http://www.canada.com/ technology/researcher+studies+impact+t ext+messaging+language/6428085/story .html.

52. Katie Riophe, "The Language of Fakebook," *New York Times,* August 15, 2010, p. 2; and Aimee Lee Ball, "Talking (Exclamation) Points," *New York Times,* July 3, 2011, p. 2.

53. Holly Corbett Bristol, "Women Set Casual Tone on Social Media (v. eexxcciittting!)," *USA Today,* December 8, 2011, p. 3D.

54. See Marketing Translation Mistakes, http:// www.i18nguy.com/translations.html.

CHAPTER 6

1. In "The Art of Original Filmmaking: Interview with Bérénice Bejo," The Writing Studio, http://www.writingstudio. co.za/page3974.html, as cited in "Business Communication Lessons from 'The Artist,'" Presence and Impact: The Art and Practice of Communication Mastery, March 8, 2012, http:// presenceandimpact.com/2012/03/08/ business-communication-lessons-from-the-artist-3; emphasis added.

2. See, for example, Mark L. Knapp, *Lying and Deception in Human Interaction,* Boston: Pearson, 2008; and Mark L. Knapp and Judith A. Hall, *Nonverbal Communication in Human Interaction,* 7th ed., Boston: Wadsworth/Cengage Learning, 2010.

3. See Paul Ekman, *Telling Lies: Clues to Deceit in the Marketplace, Politics, and Marriage.* New York: Norton, 1992.

4. Ibid, p. 43.

5. See David B. Buller and Judee K. Burgoon, "Interpersonal Deception Theory," *Communication Theory,* 6, 1996, p. 203–242.

6. Ibid.

7. See Paul Ekman, "Mistakes When Deceiving," in Thomas A. Sebeok and Robert Rosenthal, eds., *The Clever Hans Phenomenon: Communication with Horses, Whales, Apes, and People,* New York: New York Academy of Sciences, 1981, p. 269–278; Paul Ekman, *Emotions Revealed: Recognizing Faces and Feelings to Improve Communication and Emotional Life,* New York: Henry Holt, 2003; and Malcolm Gladwell, "The Naked Face," *The New Yorker,* August 3, 2002, p. 38–49.

8. Ekman, *Emotions Revealed.*

9. Quoted in Daniel Goleman, "Sensing Silent Cues Emerges as Key Skill," *New York Times,* October 10, 1989. See also Joe Navarro with Marvin Karlins, *What Every BODY Is Saying: An Ex-FBI Agent's Guide to Speed-Reading People,* New York: HarperCollins, 2008.

10. See H. D. Ellis and A. W. Young, "Are Faces Special?," in A. W. Young and H. D. Ellis, eds., *Handbook of Research in Face Processing,* Amsterdam: North Holland, 1989, p. 1–26.

11. See M. D. Alicke, R. H. Smith, and M. L. Klotz, "Judgments of Physical Attractiveness: The Role of Faces and Bodies," *Personality and Social Psychology Bulletin,* 12, 1986, p. 381–389.

12. D. S. Berry, "What Can a Moving Face Tell Us?," *Journal of Personality and Social Psychology,* 58, 1990, p. 1004–1014.

13. E. H. Hess and J. M. Polt, "Pupil Size as Related to Interest Value of Visual Stimuli," *Science,* 132, August 5, 1960, p. 349–350.

14. See C. L. Kleinke, "Gaze and Eye Contact: A Research Review," *Psychological Bulletin,* 100, 1986, p. 78–100.

15. M. Argyle and J. Dean, "Eye Contact, Distance, and Affiliation," *Sociometry,* 28, 1965, p. 289–394.

16. See Richard Bandler and John Grinder, *Frogs into Princes: Neuro Linguistic Programming,* New York: Real People Press, 1979; R. Dilts, *Roots of Neuro-Linguistic Programming,* Cupertino, CA: Meta, 1983; and M. Buckner, N. M. Meara, E. J. Reese, and M. Reese, "Eye Movement as an Indicator of Sensory Components in Thought," *Journal of Counseling Psychology,* 34:3, 1987, p. 283–287.

17. See M. LaFrance and C. Mayo, *Moving Bodies: Nonverbal Communication in Human Interaction,* 2nd ed., New York: Holt, 1978.

18. Paul Ekman and Wallace V. Friesen, *Unmasking the Face: A Guide to Recognizing Emotions from Facial Expressions,* Englewood Cliffs, NJ: Prentice Hall, 1984.

19. "Girl's Surgery Is Performed for a Smile, Doctors Hope," *New York Times,* December 15, 1995, p. 8.

20. Paul Ekman and Wallace V. Friesen, "The Repertoire of Nonverbal Behavior: Categories, Origins, Usage and Coding," *Semiotica,* 69, 1969, p. 49–97.

21. M. Argyle, *Bodily Communication,* 2nd ed., London: Methuen, 1988.

22. See P. D. Krivonos and M. L. Knapp, "Initiating Communication: What Do You Say When You Say Hello?," *Central States Journal,* 26, 1975, p. 115–125; and M. L. Knapp, R. P. Hart, and G. W. Friedrich, "Nonverbal Correlates of Human Leave Taking," *Communication Monographs,* 40, 1973, p. 182–198.

23. M. L. Knapp, "Nonverbal Communication: Basic Perspectives," in John Stewart, ed., *Bridges Not Walls: A Book about Interpersonal Communication,* 5th ed., New York: McGraw-Hill, 1990.

24. See M. Hodgins and K. Miyake, "The Vocal Attractiveness Stereotype: Replication and Elaboration," *Journal of Nonverbal Behavior,* 14, 1990, p. 97–112.

25. R. N. Bond, S. Feldsteen, and S. Simpson, "Relative and Absolute Judgments of Speech Rate from Masked and Content-Standard Stimuli: The Influence of Vocal Frequency and Intensity," *Human Communication Research,* 14, 1988, p. 548–568.

26. Edward T. Hall, *The Hidden Dimension,* New York: Doubleday, 1969.

27. A. G. Halberstadt, "Race, Socioeconomic Status, and Nonverbal Behavior," in A. W. Wiegman and S. Feldstein, eds., *Multichannel Integrations of Nonverbal Behavior,* Mahwah, NJ: Lawrence Erlbaum, 1985, p. 195–225.

28. See J. K. Burgoon, "Privacy and Communication," in M. Burgoon, ed., *Communication Yearbook 6,* Beverly Hills, CA: Sage, 1982, p. 206–249; J. K. Burgoon and L. Aho, "Three Field Experiments on the Effects of Violations of Conversational Distance," *Communication Monographs,* 49, 1982, p. 71–88; and J. K. Burgoon and J. B. Walther, "Nonverbal Expectations and the Evaluative Consequence of Violations," *Human Communication Research,* 17, 1990, p. 232–265.

29. Hall, *Hidden Dimension*; and A. Rapoport, *The Meaning of the Built Environment,* Beverly Hills, CA: Sage, 1982.

30. See U. J. Derliga, R. J. Lewis, S. Harrison, B. A. Winstead, and R. Costanza, "Gender Differences in the Initiation and Attribution of Tactile Intimacy," *Journal of Nonverbal Behavior,* 13, 1989, p. 83–96.

31. See D. K. Fromme, W. E. Jaynes, D. K. Taylor, E. G. Harold, J. Daniell,

J. R. Rountree, and M. L. Fromme, "Nonverbal Behavior and Attitudes toward Touch," *Journal of Nonverbal Behavior,* 13, 1989, p. 3–14.

32. S. E. Jones and A. E. Yarbrough, "A Naturalistic Study of the Message of Touch," *Communication Monographs,* 52, 1985, p. 19–56; and Argyle, *Bodily Communication.*

33. Nancy Henley, *Body Politics: Power, Sex, and Nonverbal Communication,* New York: Simon & Schuster, 1986.

34. S. Kaiser, *The Social Psychology of Clothing: Symbolic Appearances in Context,* 2nd ed., New York: Macmillan, 1990.

35. See, for example, M. S. Singer and A. E. Singer, "The Effect of Police Uniforms on Interpersonal Perception," *Journal of Psychology,* 119, 1985, p. 157–161.

36. Robin Givhan, "The Casual-Friday Campaign," *Newsweek,* August 15, 2011, p. 61.

37. Dahlia Lithwick, "Our Beauty Bias Is Unfair," *Newsweek,* June 14, 2010, p. 20; Jessica Bennett, "The Beauty Advantage," *Newsweek,* July 26, 2010, p. 46–48; Maureen Dowd, "Dressed to Distract," *New York Times,* June 6, 2010, p. WK11; and Harriet Brown, "For Obese People, Prejudice in Plain Sight," *New York Times,* March 16, 2010, p. D6.

38. See, for example, Hajo Adam and Adam D. Galinsky, "Enclothed Cognition," *Journal of Experimental Social Psychology,* 2012, doi:10,1016/j.jesp.2012.02.008.

39. Erinn Connor, "Now You Can Look Like the Drapers," *The Record* (Bergen County, NJ), February 8, 2012, p. F3.

40. Erinn Connor, "Watch Fashion Evolve on 'Mad Men,'" *The Record* (Bergen County, NJ), March 31, 2012, p. F1, F4.

41. N. Wade, "Scent of a Man Is Linked to a Woman's Selection," *New York Times,* January 22, 2002, p. F2.

42. N. Wade, "For Gay Men, Different Scent of Attraction," *New York Times,* May 10, 2005, p. A1, A14.

43. Lauran Neergaard, "Researchers Find Bad Times Really Do Stink," *The Record* (Bergen County, NJ), March 28, 2008, p. A6.

44. Max Luscher, *The Luscher Color Test,* New York: Simon & Schuster, 1980; and Max Luscher, *The Four Color Person,* New York: Simon & Schuster, 1980.

45. Ibid.

46. Katharine Q. Seelye, "We Call It Brown, They Call It 'Weekend in the Country,'" *New York Times,* June 30, 2011, p. A14, A18.

47. Robert Levine, "Waiting Is a Power Game," *Psychology Today,* April 1987, p. 30.

48. Peter Anderson, "Exploring Intercultural Differences in Nonverbal Communication," in L. A. Samovar and R. E. Porter, eds., *Interpersonal Communication: A Reader,* 5th ed., Belmont, CA: Wadsworth, 1998, p. 272–282.

49. See, for example, P. A. Andersen and H. Wang, "Unraveling Culture Cues: Dimensions of Nonverbal Communication across Cultures," in L. A. Samovar, R. E. Porter, and E. R. McDaniel, eds., *Intercultural Communication: A Reader,* 11th ed., Belmont, CA: Wadsworth, 2006, p. 250–266.

50. Larry A. Samovar, Richard E. Porter, and Edwin R. McDaniel, *Communication between Cultures,* 7th ed., Boston: Wadsworth, 2010, p. 260–265.

51. Larry A. Samovar, Richard E. Porter, and Lisa A. Stefani, *Communication between Cultures,* 3rd ed., Belmont, CA: Wadsworth, 1998, p. 159.

52. Michael L. Hecht, Ronald L. Jackson II, and Sidney A. Ribeau, *African American Communication,* 2nd ed., Mahwah, NJ: Lawrence Erlbaum, 2003. See also K. R. Johnson, "Black Kinesics: Some Nonverbal Communication Patterns in the Black Culture," in R. L. Jackson, ed., *African American Communication and Identities,* Thousand Oaks, CA: Sage, 2004, p. 39–46.

53. M. P. Orbe and T. M. Harris, *Interracial Communication Theory into Practice,* New York: Thompson Learning, 2001.

54. "If You're Minding Manners, One Gesture Isn't OK in Brazil," *The Record* (Bergen County, NJ), July 6, 2008, p. T1.

55. Austin Considine, "A Little Imperfection for That Smile," *New York Times,* October 23, 2011, p. ST6.

56. Judith A. Hall, *Nonverbal Sex Differences: Communication Accuracy and Expressive Style,* Baltimore: Johns Hopkins University Press, 1984, p. 3.

57. B. Ueland, "Tell Me More: On the Fine Art of Listening," *Utne Reader,* November/December 1992, p. 104–109; A. Mulac, "Men's and Women's Talk in Some Gender and Mixed Gender Dyads: Power or Polemic?" *Journal of Language and Social Psychology,* 8, 1989, p. 249–270.

58. J. F. Dovidio, S. L. Ellyson, C. F. Keating, K. Heltman, and C. E. Brown, "The Relationship of Social Power to Visual Displays of Dominance between Men and Women," *Journal of Personality and Social Psychology,* 54, 1988, p. 233–242.

59. K. Floyd, "Affectionate Same-Sex Touch: The Influence of Homophobia on Observers' Perceptions," *Journal of Social Psychology,* 140, 2000, p. 774–788.

60. See, for example, Nancy Briton and Judith Hall, "Gender-Based Expectancies and Observer Judgments of Smiling," *Journal of Nonverbal Behavior,* 19, 1995, p. 49; and Diane Hales, *Just Like a Woman,* New York: Bantam Books, 1999, p. 270.

61. Julia T. Wood, *Gendered Lives: Communication, Gender, and Culture,* 9th ed. Boston: Wadsworth, 2011, p. 130.

62. Antonia Abbey, Catherine Cozzarelli, and Kimberly McLaughlin, "The Effects of Clothing and Dyad Sex Composition on Perceptions of Sexual Intent: Do Women and Men Evaluate These Clues Differently?," *Journal of Applied Social Psychology,* 17, 1987, p. 108–126.

63. Tricia Romano, "A Tall Tale, but True: Men in Heels," *New York Times,* October 16, 2011, p. ST12; Alexis Tarrazi, "What's in Store: Brogues/Oxfords," *The Record* (Bergen County, NJ), October 16, 2011, F3.

64. Stephanie Clifford, "Men Step Out of the Recession, Bag on Hip, Bracelet on Wrist," *New York Times,* February 20, 2012, p. A1, B3.

65. See, for example, Bill Puka, "The Liberation of Caring: A Different Voice for Gilligan's Different Voice," *Hypatia,* 5, 1990, p. 59–82; and J. A. Hall, "Gender, Gender-Roles, and Nonverbal Communication Skills," in R. Rosenthal, ed., *Skill in Nonverbal Communication: Individual Differences,* Cambridge, MA: Oelgeschlager, Gunn & Hain, 1979.

66. Carol Gilligan, *In a Different Voice: Psychological Theory and Women's Development,* Cambridge, MA: Harvard University Press, 1982; and Carol Gilligan, Nona P. Lyons, and Trudy J. Hanmer, eds., *Making Connections: The Relational Worlds of Adolescent Girls at Emma Willard School,* Cambridge, MA: Harvard University Press, 1990.

67. See, for example, "Why We Flirt," *Time,* February 4, 2008; and Deborah A. Lott and Frank Veronsky, "The New Flirting Game," *Psychology Today,* January 1, 1999, http://www.psychologytoday.com/articles/199901/the-new-flirting-game.

68. Alan K. Goodboy and Maria Brann, "Flirtation Rejection Strategies: Toward an Understanding of Communicative Disinterest in Flirting," *Qualitative Report,* 15:2, 2010, p. 268–278.

69. See, for example, Jean Kilbourne, "The More You Subtract, the More You Add: Cutting Girls Down to Size," in Joan Z. Spade and Catherine G. Valentine, eds., *The Kaleidoscope of Gender: Prisms, Patterns, and Possibilities,* Belmont, CA: Wadsworth, 2004, p. 234–244.

70. Wood, *Gendered Lives,* p. 257–283.

71. Brandon Griggs, "Why Computer Voices Are Mostly Female," CNN, October 21, 2011, http://www.cnn.com/2011/10/21/tech/innovation/female-computer-voices/index.html?hpt.

72. Christopher De Vinck, "A Digital Hug," *The Record* (Bergen County, NJ), November 26, 2009, p. A23.

73. Judith Newman, "If You're Happy and You Know It, Must I Know, Too?" *New York Times,* October 23, 2011, p. ST2.

74. Nick Bilton, "Behind the Google Goggles, Virtual Reality," *New York Times,* February 23, 2012, p. B1, B2.

75. Aaron Wolfgang, *Everybody's Guide to People Watching,* Yarmouth, ME: Intercultural Press, 1995, p. 19.

76. H. S. Hodgkins and C. Belch, "Interparental Violence and Nonverbal Abilities," *Journal of Nonverbal Behavior,* 24, 2000, p. 3–24.

77. See, for example, N. Miczo, C. Segrin, and L. E. Allspach, "Relationship between Nonverbal Sensitivity, Encoding, and Relational Satisfaction," *Communication Reports,* 14, 2001, p. 39–48.

CHAPTER 7

1. Rachel Dodes, "The New Water Cooler Is a TV Show," *Wall Street Journal,* February 10, 2012, p. D4.

2. Jefferson Graham, "TV Networks Count on 'Social' TV Viewers," *USA Today,* May 3, 2012, p. 3B.

3. O. Weisman, I. M. Aderka, H. Hermesh, and E. Gilboa-Schectman, "Social Rank and Affiliation in Social Anxiety Disorder," *Behavior Research and Therapy,* 49, 2011, p. 399–405.

4. Elizabeth Bernstein, "Speaking Up Is Hard to Do: Researchers Explain Why," *Wall Street Journal,* February 7, 2012, p. D1, D4.

5. Steve Duck, *Understanding Relationships,* New York: Guilford, Press, 1991, p. 16. See also Steve Duck, *Human Relationships,* 4th ed., Thousand Oaks, CA: Sage, 2007.

6. Gerald Coffee, *Beyond Survival,* New York: Putnam, 1990.

7. See, for example, Susan Cain, *Quiet: The Power of Introverts in a World That Can't Stop Talking,* New York: Crown, 2012.

8. See, for example, Ed Keller and Brad Faye, *The Face-to-Face Book: Why Relationships Rule in a Digital Marketplace,* New York: Free Press, 2012.

9. Margaret L. McLaughlin, *Conversation: How Talk Is Organized,* Beverly Hills, CA: Sage, 1984.

10. Susan Shimanoff, *Conversational Rules,* Beverly Hills, CA: Sage, 1980, p. 57.

11. Steve Duck, *Human Relationships,* 3rd ed., Thousand Oaks, CA: Sage, 1998, p. 7. See also Duck, *Human Relationships,* 4th ed.

12. See, for example, Scott Jacobs and Sally Jackson, "Speech Act Structure in Conversation: Rational Aspects of Pragmatic Coherence," in Robert T. Craig and Karen Tracy, eds., *Conversational Coherence: Form, Structure, and Strategy,* Beverly Hills, CA: Sage, 1983, p. 47–66.

13. See Robert E. Nofsinger, *Everyday Conversation,* Newbury Park, CA: Sage, 1991, p. 6. For a discussion of criteria used to assess conversational effectiveness, see Daniel J. Canary, Michael J. Cody, and Valerie L. Manusov, *Interpersonal Communication: A Goals-Based Approach,* 3rd ed.,

Boston: Bedford/St. Martin's Press, 2003, p. 520–523.

14. Thomas E. Murray, "The Language of Singles Bars," *American Speech,* 60, 1985, p. 17–30.

15. Chris Kleinke, *Meeting and Understanding People,* New York: W. H. Freeman, 1986.

16. Gregory Stock, *The Book of Questions,* New York: Workman, 1987.

17. Mark L. Knapp, Roderick P. Hart, Gustav W. Friedrich, and Gary M. Shulman, "The Rhetoric of Goodbye: Verbal and Nonverbal Correlates of Human Leave-Taking," *Speech Monographs,* 40, August 1973, p. 182–198.

18. H. P. Grice, "Logic and Conversation," in P. Cole and J. L. Morgan, eds., *Syntax and Semantics,* vol. 3, *Speech Acts,* New York: Seminar Press, 1975, p. 41–58; and K. Lindblom, "Cooperating with Grice: A Cross-Disciplinary Metaperspective on Uses of Grice's Cooperative Principle," *Journal of Pragmatics,* 33, 2001, p. 1601–1623.

19. McLaughlin, *Conversation,* p. 88–89.

20. See, for example, K. Midooka, "Characteristics of Japanese Style Communication," *Media, Culture, and Society,* 12, 1990, p. 477–489; and Y. Gu, "Polite Phenomena in Modern Chinese," *Journal of Pragmatics,* 14, 1990, p. 237–257.

21. P. Brown and S. Levinson, *Politeness: Some Universals in Language Usage,* New York: Cambridge University Press, 1987.

22. Robert Lee Hotz, "Science Reveals Why We Brag So Much," *Wall Street Journal,* May 8, 2012, p. D1.

23. Diana I. Tamir and Jason P. Mitchell, "Disclosing Information about the Self Is Intrinsically Rewarding," *Proceedings of the National Academy of Sciences,* May 7, 2012, published online before print, doi:10.1073/pnas.1202129109, http://wjh.harvard.edu/~dtamir/Tamir-PNAS-2012.pdf.

24. Ibid.

25. William B. Gudykunst, *Bridging Differences: Effective Intergroup Communication,* 2nd ed., Thousand Oaks, CA: Sage, 1994, p. 83. See also William B. Gudykunst, *Bridging Differences: Effective Intergroup Communication,* 3rd ed., Thousand Oaks, CA: Sage, 1998.

26. Gudykunst, *Bridging Differences,* 2nd ed., p. 139.

27. See, for example, Stella Ting-Toomey and Leeva C. Chung, *Understanding Intercultural Communication,* 2nd ed., New York: Oxford University Press, 2012, p. 118–120; and Edward C. Stewart and Milton J. Bennett, *American Cultural Patterns: A Cross-Cultural Perspective,* 2nd ed., London: Nicholas Brealey, 2005.

28. Ibid.

29. T. S. Lebra, "The Cultural Significance of Silence in Japanese Communication," *Multilingua,* 6, 1987, p. 343–357.

30. Halim Barakat, *The Arab World: Society, Culture, and State.* Berkeley: University of California Press, 1993.

31. Ibid.

32. M. S. Morris, *Saying and Meaning in Puerto Rico,* Elmsford, NY: Pergamon, 1981, p. 135–136.

33. H. Yamada, "Topic Management and Turn Distributions in Business Meetings: American versus Japanese Strategies," *Text,* 10, 1990, 272–295.

34. See, for example, L. K. Acitelli, "Gender Differences in Relationship Awareness and Marital Satisfaction among Young Married Couples," *Personality and Social Psychology Bulletin,* 18, 1992, p. 102–110; and Julia T. Wood and Christopher C. Inman, "In a Different Mode: Masculine Styles of Communicating Closeness," *Journal of Applied Communication Research,* 21, 1993, p. 279–295.

35. Deborah Tannen, *You Just Don't Understand: Women and Men in Conversation,* New York: Morrow, 1990, p. 24–25.

36. Alice Greenwood, "Discourse Variation and Social Comfort: A Study of Topic Initiation and Interruption Patterns in the Dinner Conversations of Preadolescent Children," doctoral dissertation, City University of New York, 1989.

37. Deborah Tannen, *Gender and Discourse,* New York: Oxford University Press, 1994, p. 61–67.

38. See Sherry Turkle, *Alone Together: Why We Expect More from Technology and Less from Each Other,* New York: Basic Books, 2011; and Sherry Turkle, "The Flight from Conversation," *New York Times Sunday Review,* April 22, 2012, p. SR1, SR6–7.

39. Turkle, "Flight from Conversation," p. SR6.

40. Ibid.

41. Alison Gendar, "Let'salltalkovereachother," *Daily News,* October 18, 2011, p. 11.

42. See Amanda Lenhart, "Teens, Smartphones and Texting," Pew Internet & American Life Project, March 19, 2012, http://pewinternet.org/Reports/2012/Teens-and-smartphones.aspx; and Amanda Lenhart, "Teens, Cell Phones and Texting: Text Messaging Becomes Centerpiece Communication," Pew Internet & American Life Project, April 20, 2010, http://pewresearch.org/pubs/1572/teens-cell-phones-text-messages.

43. Robert Lee Hotz, "Decoding Our Chatter," *Wall Street Journal,* October 1–2, 2011, p. C1–C2.

44. See Roy Pea, Clifford Nass, Lyn Meheula, Marcus Rance, Aman Kumar, Holden Bamford, et al, "Media Use, Face-to-Face Communication, Media Multitasking, and Social Well-Being Among 8- to 12-Year-Old Girls," *Developmental Psychology,* 48, 2012, p. 327–336; Rachel Emma Silverman, "Study: Face Time

Benefits Preteens," *Wall Street Journal,* January 31, 2012, p. D2.

45. Ibid.

46. Pamela Paul, "A Blog as Therapy for Teenagers," *New York Times,* January 20, 2012, p. ST6.

47. Geert Lovink, *Zero Comments: Blogging and Critical Internet Culture,* New York: Routledge, 2008, p. 10.

48. McLaughlin, *Conversation.*

CHAPTER 8

1. Danielle Ofri, "Doctors Have Feelings, Too," *New York Times,* March 27, 2012, p. A27.

2. Ellen Peters, Daniel Västfjäll, Tommy Gärling, and Paul Slovic, "Affect and Decision Making: A 'Hot' Topic," *Journal of Behavioral Decision Making,* 19, 2006, p. 79–85.

3. See, for example, Robin L. Nabi, "Exploring the Framing Effects of Emotion: Do Discrete Emotions Differentially Influence Information Accessibility, Information Seeking, and Policy Preference?," *Communication Research,* 30, 2003, p. 224–247.

4. Daniel Goleman, *Emotional Intelligence,* New York: Bantam Books, 1995, p. x.

5. Ibid., p. 34. See also Daniel Goleman, *Social Intelligence,* New York: Bantam, 2006.

6. See Nico H. Frijda, *The Laws of Emotion,* New York: Lawrence Erlbaum, 2007; and Richard S. Lazarus, *Emotion and Adaptation,* New York: Oxford University Press, 1991.

7. James Gorman, "Laughter Feels So Good, Scientists Say, Because Guffaws Release Endorphins," *New York Times,* September 14, 2011, p. A14.

8. See Richard J. Davidson and Sharon Begley, *The Emotional Life of Your Brain,* New York: Hudson Street Press, 2012.

9. Carroll E. Izard, *Human Emotions,* New York: Plenum, 1977, p. 10.

10. Howard Gardner, *Multiple Intelligences: The Theory in Practice,* New York: Basic Books, 1993, p. 9.

11. See Davidson and Begley, *Emotional Life of Your Brain.*

12. I. Ruisel, "Social Intelligence: Conception and Methodological Problems," *Studia Psychologica,* 34, 1992, p. 281–296.

13. J. D. Mayer and P. Salovey, "The Intelligence of Emotional Intelligence," *Intelligence,* 17, 1993, p. 433–442.

14. See Goleman, *Emotional Intelligence,* p. 43.

15. Paul Ekman, *Darwin and Facial Expression,* New York: Academic Press, 1973.

16. Goleman, *Emotional Intelligence,* p. 6.

17. E. Nagourney, "Blow a Gasket for Your Heart," *New York Times,* February 11, 2003, F6.

18. American Psychological Association, "Strategies for Controlling Your Anger," October 2011, http://www.apa.org/helpcenter/controlling-anger.aspx.

19. "Psychologist Produces the First-Ever 'World Map of Happiness,'" *Science Daily,* November 13, 2006, http://www.sciencedaily.com/releases/2006/11/061113093726.htm.

20. Gorman, "Laughter Feels So Good," p. A14.

21. See, for example, Stephanie Armour, "After 9/11, Some Workers Turn Their Lives Upside Down," *USA Today,* May 8, 2002, p. A1, A2.

22. See, for example, Nick Powdthavee, *The Happiness Equation: The Surprising Economics of Our Most Valuable Asset,* New York: Icon Books, 2011.

23. Daniel Gilbert, "The Science Behind the Smile," interview by Gardiner Morse, *Harvard Business Review,* January–February, 2012, p. 85–90. See also Daniel Gilbert, *Stumbling on Happiness,* New York: Knopf, 2006.

24. Virginia Konchan, "Synthetic Happiness," *Michigan Quarterly Review* blog, February 17, 2012, http://www.michiganquarterly review.com/2012/02/synthetic-happiness.

25. James Gorman, "Survival's Ick Factor," *New York Times,* January 24, 2012, p. D1, D4.

26. Daniel Goleman, "A Feel-Good Theory: A Smile Affects Mood," *New York Times,* July 19, 1989, p. C1.

27. Robert Plutchik, "Emotions: A General Psychoevolutionary Theory," in Klaus R. Scherer and Paul Ekman, eds., *Approaches to Emotion,* Hillsdale, NJ: Lawrence Erlbaum, 1984, p. 197–219.

28. See, for example, Daniel Goleman, "Happy or Sad, a Mood Can Prove Contagious," *New York Times,* October 15, 1991, p. C1; and Ellen O'Brien, "Moods Are as Contagious as the Office Cold," *The Record* (Bergen County, NJ), November 15, 1993, p. B3.

29. B. Aubrey Fisher and Katherine L. Adams, *Interpersonal Communication: Pragmatics of Human Relationships,* New York: McGraw-Hill, 1994, p. 290.

30. Ibid.

31. Izard, *Human Emotions,* p. 5.

32. Goleman, "Happy or Sad."

33. Ibid.

34. Lazarus, *Emotion and Adaptation.*

35. Albert Ellis and R. Harper, *A New Guide to Rational Living,* North Hollywood, CA: Wilshire Books, 1977.

36. Joseph P. Forgas, "Affect and Person Perception," in Joseph P. Forgas, ed., *Emotion and Social Judgments,* New York: Pergamon, 1991, p. 288.

37. Sandra Metts and John Waite Bowers, "Emotion in Interpersonal Communication," in Mark L. Knapp and Gerald R. Miller, eds., *Handbook of Interpersonal Communication,* 2nd ed., Thousand Oaks, CA: Sage, 1994.

38. Cited in Elizabeth Bernstein, "Show Me the Love . . . or Not," *Wall Street Journal,* February 21, 2012, p. D1, D2.

39. See also Amir Levine and Rachel Heller, *Attached: The New Science of Adult Attachment and How It Can Help You Find—and Keep—Love,* New York: Tarcher, 2011.

40. J. W. Pennebaker, B. Rime, and V. E. Blankenship, "Stereotypes of Emotional Expressiveness of Northerners and Southerners: A Cross-Cultural Test of Montesquieu's Hypotheses," *Journal of Personality and Social Psychology,* 70, 1996, p. 372–380.

41. See, for example, K. Nishiyama, *Doing Business with Japan,* Honolulu: University of Hawaii Press, 2000.

42. Larry A. Samovar, Richard E. Porter, and Edwin R. McDaniel, *Communication between Cultures,* 7th ed., Boston: Wadsworth, 2010, p. 316.

43. J. A. Soto, R. W. Levenson, and R. Ebling, "Cultures of Moderation and Expression: Emotional Experience, Behavior, and Physiology in Chinese Americans and Mexican Americans," *Emotion,* 5, 2005, p. 154–165.

44. Stella Ting-Toomey, "The Matrix of Face: An Updated Face-Negotiation Theory," in William B. Gudykunst, ed., *Theorizing about Intercultural Communication,* Thousand Oaks, CA: Sage, 2005, p. 73.

45. Julia T. Wood and Christopher C. Inman, "In a Different Mode: Masculine Styles of Communicating Closeness," *Journal of Applied Communication Research,* 21, 1993, p. 279–295.

46. Scott Swain, "Covert Intimacy: Closeness in Men's Friendships," in Barbara J. Risman and Pepper Schwartz, eds., *Gender in Intimate Relationships: A Microstructural Approach,* Belmont, CA: Wadsworth, 1989, p. 71–86; and Drury Sherrod, "The Influence of Gender on Same-Sex Friendships," in Clyde Hendrick, ed., *Close Relationships,* Newbury Park, CA: Sage, 1989, p. 164–186.

47. Christopher Shea, "What's a 'Good Cry'?," *Wall Street Journal,* July 16–17, 2011, p. C4; A. M. Kring and A. H. Gordon, "Sex Differences in Emotion: Expression, Experience, and Physiology, *"Journal of Personality and Social Psychology,* 74, 1998, p. 686–703.

48. See, for example, E. J. Coats and R. S. Feldman, "Gender Differences in Nonverbal Correlates of Social Status," *Personality and Social Psychology Bulletin,* 22, 1996, p. 1014–1022.

49. D. J. Goldsmith and P. A. Fulfs, "'You Just Don't Have the Evidence': An Analysis of Claims and Evidence in Deborah Tannen's *You Just Don't Understand,*" in M. E. Roloff, ed., *Communication Yearbook 22,* Thousand Oaks, CA: Sage, 1999,

p. 1–49; and J. Swenson and F. L. Casmir, "The Impact of Culture-Sameness, Gender, Foreign Travel, and Academic Background on the Ability to Interpret Facial Expression of Emotion in Others," *Communication Quarterly,* 46, 1998, p. 214–230.

50. Judith A. Hall, *Nonverbal Sex Differences: Accuracy of Communication and Expressive Style,* Baltimore: Johns Hopkins University Press, 1984, p. 182–184.

51. Sharon Jayson, "Botox May Deaden Perception, Study Says," *USA Today,* April 22, 2011, p. 3A.

52. See, for example, Carolyn Zahn-Waxler, "The Development of Empathy, Guilt, and Internalization of Distress: Implications for Gender Differences in Internalizing and Externalizing Problems," in Richard J. Davidson, ed., *Anxiety, Depression, and Emotion,* New York: Oxford University Press, 2000, p. 222–265.

53. R. A. Buhrke and D. R. Fuqua, "Sex Differences in Same and Cross-Sex Supportive Relationships," *Sex Roles,* 17, 1987, p. 339–352.

54. Diane F. Witmer and Sandra Lee Katzman, "On-Line Smiles: Does Gender Make a Difference in the Use of Graphic Accents?," *Journal of Computer-Mediated Communication,* 2:4, 1997, http://jcmc.indiana.edu/vol2/issue4/witmer1.html.

55. Anthony Pratkanis and Elliot Aronson, *Age of Propaganda: The Everyday Use and Abuse of Persuasion,* New York: W. H. Freeman, 1992, p. 52.

56. Ibid., p. 54.

57. Funda Kivran-Swaine and Mor Naaman, "Network Properties and Social Sharing of Emotions in Social Awareness Streams," paper presented at the Association for Computing Machinery Conference on Computer Supported Cooperative Work, March 19–23, 2011, http://comminfo.rutgers.edu/~mor/publications/kivranswainescw2011.pdf; and Nasir Naveed, Thomas Gottron, Jérôme Kunegis, and Arifah Che Alhadi, "Bad News Travel Fast: A Content-Based Analysis of Interestingness on Twitter," paper presented at the Web Science Conference, June 14–17, 2011, http://journal.webscience .org/435/1/50_paper.pdf.

58. Scott A. Golden and Michael W. Macy, "Diurnal and Seasonal Moods Vary with Work, Sleep, and Daylength Across Diverse Cultures," *Science,* 333, September 30, 2011, p. 1878–1881.

59. Benedict Carey, "Study of Twitter Messages Tracks When We Are :)," *New York Times,* September 30, 2011, p. A16.

60. Jenna Wortham, "Whimsical Text Icons Get a Shot at Success," *New York Times,* December 7, 2011, p. B1, B10.

61. Martin Lindstrom, "You Love Your iPhone. Literally," *New York Times,* October 1, 2011, p. A21.

62. Albert Ellis, "Why Rational-Emotive Therapy to Rational Emotive Behavior Therapy?" *Psychotherapy,* 36, 1999, p. 154–159.

63. See, for example, A. M. Bippus and S. L. Young, "Owning Your Emotions: Reactions to Expressions of Self-versus Other-Attributed Positive and Negative Emotions," *Journal of Applied Communication Research,* 33, 2005, p. 26–45.

64. Albert Ellis, *A New Guide to Rational Living,* North Hollywood, CA: Wilshire Books, 1977.

65. C. Peterson, M. E. P. Seligman, and G. E. Vaillant, "Pessimistic Explanatory Style Is a Risk Factor for Physical Illness: A 35-Year Longitudinal Study," *Journal of Personality and Social Psychology,* 55, 1988, p. 23–27.

CHAPTER 9

1. Tim Cole, "Lying to the One You Love: The Use of Deception in Romantic Relationships," *Journal of Social and Personal Relationships,* 18, 2001, p. 107–129.

2. Christopher F. Chabris, "The Stranger Within," *Wall Street Journal,* June 15, 2011, p. A13.

3. Cole, "Lying to the One You Love."

4. Alice Park, "White Coats, White Lies: How Honest Is Your Doctor?," *Time,* February 9, 2012, p. 15.

5. Antoine de Saint-Exupéry, *The Little Prince,* K. Woods, trans., New York: Reynal & Hitchcock, 1943, p. 45.

6. See, for example, James Jaska and Michael W. Pritchard, *Communication Ethics: Methods of Analysis,* Belmont, CA: Wadsworth, 1988.

7. Abraham Maslow, *Motivation and Personality,* New York: Harper & Row, 1970.

8. Fred Luskin, *Forgive for Good,* San Francisco: HarperCollins, 2002.

9. Fred Luskin, "Four Steps toward Forgiveness," *Healing Currents Magazine,* September/October, 1996, http://www.coopcomm.org/essay_luskin.htm.

10. Linda Berlin, "Forgive: Stanford Program Teaches How to Let Go of Grudges," SFGate, September 24, 1999, http://www.sfgate.com/default/article/FORGIVE-Stanford-program-teaches-how-to-let-go-2906556.php.

11. F. M. Luskin, K. Ginzburg, and C. E. Thoresen, "The Effect of Forgiveness Training on Psychosocial Factors in College-Age Adults," *Humboldt Journal of Social Relations,* 29, 2005, p. 163–184. See a summary of this study on the Forgive for Good website, http://learningtoforgive.com/research/effect-of-forgiveness-training.

12. Luskin, "Four Steps toward Forgiveness.

13. A. H. Harris, F. M. Luskin, S. V. Benisovich, S. Standard, J. Bruning, S. Evans, and C. Thoresen, "Effects of a Group Forgiveness Intervention on Forgiveness, Perceived Stress, and Trait Anger: A Randomized Trial," *Journal of Clinical Psychology,* 62, 2006, p. 715–733. See a summary of this study on the Forgive for Good website, http://learningtoforgive.com/research/effects-of-group-forgiveness-intervention-on-perceived-stress-state-and-trait-anger-symptoms-of-stress-self-reported-health-and-forgiveness-stanford- forgiveness-project.

14. Cited in Jennifer Kavanaugh, "Getting Down to the Heart of Forgiveness," *Palo Alto Weekly,* February 10, 1999.

15. See John W. Thibaut and Harold H. Kelley, *The Social Psychology of Groups,* New York: John Wiley, 1959; Kenneth J. Gergen, Martin S. Greenberg, and Richard H. Willis, eds., *Social Exchange: Advances in Theory and Research,* New York: Plenum, 1980; and Dalmas Taylor and Irwin Altman, "Self-Disclosure as a Function of Reward-Cost Outcomes," *Sociometry,* 38, 1975, p. 18–31.

16. Ellen Berscheid, "Interpersonal Attraction," in Gardner Lindzey and Elliot Aronson, eds., *Handbook of Social Psychology,* 3rd ed., New York: Random House, 1985, p. 413–484.

17. Stephen R. Covey, *The Seven Habits of Highly Effective People,* New York: Simon & Schuster, 1989, p. 188.

18. Jack R. Gibb, "Defensive Communication," *Journal of Communication,* 2, 1961, p. 141–148.

19. Patrik Jonsson, "We're Becoming Truth-Challenged, and That's No Lie," *The Record* (Bergen County, NJ), July 24, 2011, p. O1, O4.

20. See, for example, James B. Stewart, *Tangled Webs: How False Statements Are Undermining America—From Martha Stewart to Bernie Madoff,* New York: Penguin Press, 2011.

21. See Sissela Bok, *Lying,* New York: Random House, 1989; and Steven A. McCornack and Timothy R. Levine, "When Lies Are Uncovered: Emotional and Relational Outcomes of Discovered Deception," *Communication Monographs,* 57, 1990, p. 119–138.

22. See, for example, Frank Bruni, "True Believers, All of Us," *New York Times,* August 7, 2011, p. SR3.

23. Walter Isaacson, *Steve Jobs,* New York: Simon & Schuster, 2011.

24. Carolyn Saarni and Michael Lewis, "Deceit and Illusion in Human Affairs," in Michael Lewis and Carolyn Saarni, eds., *Lying and Deception in Everyday Life,* New York: Guilford Press, 1993, p. 7.

25. Ibid., p. 8.

26. C. Camden, M. T. Motley, and A. Wilson, "White Lies in Interpersonal Communication: A Taxonomy and Preliminary Investigation of Social Motivations," *Western Journal of Speech Communication,* 48, 1984, p. 309–325.

27. See, for example, Matthew Feinberg, Robb Willer, Jennifer Stellar, and Dacher Keltner, "The Virtues of Gossip: Reputational Information Sharing as Prosocial Behavior," *Journal of Personality and Social Psychology,* 102, 2012, p. 1015–1030; Jennifer Coates, "Gossip Revisited: Language in All-Female Groups," and Jane Pilkington, "Don't Try to Make Out That I'm Nice! The Different Strategies Women and Men Use When Gossiping," in Jennifer Coates, ed., *Language and Gender: A Reader,* Malden, MA: Blackwell, 1998, p. 226–253 and p. 254–269; and Lubna Abdel Aziz, "Why We Gossip," *Al-Ahram Weekly* online, November 28–December 4, 2002, http://weekly.ahram.org.eg/2002/614/pe2.htm.

28. Suzanne Eggins and Diana Slade, *Analysing Casual Conversation,* London: Cassell, 1997.

29. Jack Levin and Arnold Arluke, *Gossip: The Inside Scoop,* New York: Plenum, 1987.

30. Robin Dunbar, *Grooming, Gossip, and the Evolution of Language,* Cambridge, MA: Harvard University Press, 1998.

31. Sameer Hinduja and Justin W. Patchin, *Bullying beyond the Schoolyard: Preventing and Responding to Cyberbullying.* Thousand Oaks, CA: Corwin Press, 2009. See also Sameer Hinduja and Justin W. Patchin, *Cyberbullying and Suicide* (Cyberbullying Research Summary), http://www.cyberbullying.us/cyberbullying_and_suicide_research_fact_sheet.pdf.

32. William B. Gudykunst, *Bridging Differences: Effective Intergroup Communication,* 2nd ed., Thousand Oaks, CA: Sage, 1994, p. 74–75.

33. See, for example, M. Hecht, S. Ribeau, and M. Sedane, "A Mexican-American Perspective on Interethnic Communication," *International Journal of Intercultural Relations,* 14, 1990, p. 31–55.

34. John G. Holmes and John K. Rempel, "Trust in Close Relationships," in Clyde Hendrick, ed., *Close Relationships,* Newbury Park, CA: Sage, 1989, p. 204.

35. See, for example, Ellen Goodman and Patricia O'Brien, *I Know Just What You Mean: The Power of Friendship in Women's Lives,* New York: Simon & Schuster, 2000; and Peter M. Nardi, ed., *Men's Friendships,* Newbury Park, CA: Sage, 1992.

36. Drury Sherrod, "The Influence of Gender on Same-Sex Friendships," in Clyde Hendrick, ed., *Close Relationships,* Newbury Park, CA: Sage, 1989, p. 164–186.

37. See, for example, Harry T. Reis, "Gender Differences in Intimacy and Related Behaviors: Context and Process," in Daniel J. Canary and Kathryn Dindia, eds., *Sex Differences and Similarities in Communication: Critical Essays and Empirical Investigations of Sex and Gender in Interaction,* Mahwah, NJ: Lawrence Erlbaum, 1998, p. 203–231.

38. Bella M. DePaulo, Jennifer A. Epstein, and Melissa M. Wyer, "Sex Differences in Lying: How Women and Men Deal with the Dilemma of Deceit," in Michael Lewis and Carolyn Saarni, eds., *Lying and Deception in Everyday Life,* New York: Guilford Press, 1993, p. 126–147.

39. Ibid.

40. Louis A. Day, *Ethics in Media Communications: Cases and Controversies,* Belmont, CA: Wadsworth, 1991, p. 279.

41. Susan Faludi, *Backlash: The Undeclared War against American Women,* New York: Crown, 1991; and Julia T. Wood, *Gendered Lives: Communication, Gender, and Culture,* 10th ed., Boston: Wadsworth, 2013.

42. Amitai Etzioni, "E-Communities Build New Ties, but Ties That Bind," *New York Times,* February 10, 2000, G7.

43. See, for example, Bruce E. Johansen, "Race, Ethnicity, and the Media," in Alan Wells, ed., *Mass Media and Society,* Lexington, MA: D. C. Heath, 1987, p. 441.

44. James E. Murphy and Sharon M. Murphy, "American Indians and the Media: Neglect and Stereotype," in Ray Heibert and Carol Reuss, eds., *Impact of Mass Media,* 2nd ed., New York: Longman, 1988, p. 312–322; and Beverly R. Singer, *Wiping the War Paint off the Lens: Native American Film and Video,* Minneapolis: University of Minnesota Press, 2001.

45. Jonathan Coleman, "Is Technology Making Us Intimate Strangers?." *Newsweek,* March 27, 2000, p. 12.

46. Cited in Cristen Conger, "Do People Lie More On the Internet?," ABC News online, March 5, 2011, http://abcnews.go.com/Technology/people-lie-internet/story?id=13060797.

47. See, for example, Catalina L. Toma, Jeffrey T. Hancock, and Nicole B. Ellison, "Separating Fact from Fiction: An Examination of Deceptive Self-Presentation in Online Dating Profiles," *Personality and Social Psychology Bulletin,* 34, 2008, p. 1023–1036.

48. Catalina L. Toma and Jeffrey T. Hancock, "What Lies Beneath: The Linguistic Traces of Deception in Online Dating Profiles," *Journal of Communication,* 62, 2012, p. 78–97.

49. Matt Richtel, "Young, in Love and Sharing Everything, Including a Password," *New York Times,* January 18, 2012, p. A1, A11.

CHAPTER 10

1. Stanley Milgram, *Obedience to Authority.* New York: Harper Perennial, 1974.

2. Dominic J. Packer, "Identifying Systematic Disobedience in Milgram's Obedience Experiments: A Meta-Analytic Review," *Perspectives on Psychological Science,* 3, 2008, p. 301–304.

3. See J. P. Dillard and L. J. Marshall, "Persuasion as a Social Skill," in J. O. Greene and B. R. Burleson, eds., *Handbook of Communication and Social Interaction Skills,* Mahwah, NJ: Lawrence Erlbaum, 2003, p. 479–513.

4. See "Social Anxiety Fact Sheet," Social Phobia/Social Anxiety Association, http://www.socialphobia.org/fact.html.

5. See Dan O'Hair, and Michael J. Cody, "Machiavellian Beliefs and Social Influence," *Western Journal of Speech Communication,* 51, 1987, p. 286–287.

6. See William W. Wilmot and Joyce L. Hocker, *Interpersonal Conflict,* 6th ed., New York: McGraw-Hill, 2001.

7. John R. French and Bertram Raven, "The Bases of Social Power," in Dorwin Cartwright, ed., *Studies in Social Power,* Ann Arbor: University of Michigan Press, 1959, p. 150–167; and Bertram H. Raven, Richard Centers, and Aroldo Rodrigues, "The Bases of Conjugal Power," in Ronald E. Cromwell and David H. Olson, eds., *Power in Families,* Beverly Hills, CA: Sage, 1975, p. 217–232.

8. Malcolm R. Parks, *Personal Relationships and Personal Networks,* Mahwah, NJ: Lawrence Erlbaum, 2007.

9. Scott Cutlip and Alan Center, *Effective Public Relations,* Englewood Cliffs, NJ: Prentice Hall, 1985, p. 122.

10. William B. Gudykunst, *Bridging Differences: Effective Intergroup Communication,* 2nd ed., Thousand Oaks, CA: Sage, 1994, p. 37.

11. See Milton Rokeach, *The Open and Closed Mind,* New York: Basic Books, 1960; and Milton Rokeach, *Beliefs, Attitudes, and Values,* San Francisco, CA: Jossey-Bass, 1970.

12. Eduard Spranger, *Types of Men: The Psychology and Ethics of Personality,* New York: M. Niemeyer, 1928.

13. E. J. Langer, "Rethinking the Role of Thought in Social Interaction," in J. H. Harvey, W. J. Ickes, and R. F. Kidd, eds., *New Directions in Attribution Research,* vol. 2, Hillsdale, NJ: Lawrence Erlbaum, 1978, p. 35–58.

14. Robert B. Cialdini, *Influence: Science and Practice,* 5th ed., Boston: Allyn & Bacon, 2009.

15. See, for example, G. R. Miller, F. Boster, M. E. Roloff, and D. Seibold, "MBRS Rekindled: Some Thoughts on Compliance Gaining in Interpersonal Settings," in M. E. Roloff

and G. R. Miller, eds., *Interpersonal Processes: New Directions in Communication Research,* Newbury Park, CA: Sage, 1987, pp. 89–116.

16. Fritz Heider, *The Psychology of Interpersonal Relations,* New York: John Wiley, 1958.

17. Leon Festinger, "Social Communication and Cognitions: A Very Preliminary and Highly Tentative Draft," in Eddie Haron-Jones and Judson Mills, eds., *Cognitive Dissonance: Progress on a Pivotal Theory in Social Psychology,* Washington, DC: American Psychological Association, 1999, p. 361.

18. Cialdini, *Influence.*

19. Richard E. Petty and John T. Cacioppo, *Communication and Persuasion: Central and Peripheral Routes to Attitude Change,* New York: Springer-Verlag, 1986, p. 7.

20. Geert Hofstede, *Culture's Consequences: Comparing Values, Behaviors, Institutions, and Organizations across Nations,* 2nd ed., Thousand Oaks, CA: Sage, 2001.

21. Michael L. Hecht, Mary Jane Collier, and Sidney A. Ribeau, *African American Communication: Ethnic Identity and Cultural Interpretation,* Newbury Park, CA: Sage, 1993, p. 97.

22. Hofstede, *Culture's Consequences.*

23. See Geert Hofstede, *Cultures and Organizations: Software of the Mind,* London: McGraw-Hill, 1991.

24. Jan Servaes, "Cultural Identity in East and West," *Howard Journal of Communication,* 1:2, 1988, p. 64.

25. See Mary Jane Collier, "Conflict Competence within African, Mexican, and Anglo American Friendships," in Stella Ting-Toomey and Felipe Korzenny, eds., *Cross-Cultural Interpersonal Communication,* Newbury Park, CA: Sage, 1991.

26. See, for example, J. M. Steil and K. Weltman, "Marital Inequality: The Importance of Resources, Personal Attributes, and Social Norms on Career Valuing and the Allocation of Domestic Responsibilities," *Sex Roles,* 24, 1991, 161–179; and W. Farrell, "Men as Success Objects," *Utne Reader,* May/June 1991, p. 81–84.

27. See, for example, Kenneth C. Dempsy, "Men and Women's Power Relationships and the Persisting Inequitable Division of Housework," *Journal of Family Studies,* 6, 2000, p. 7–24.

28. Graham Allen, *Family Life,* New York: Blackwell, 1993.

29. See, for example, Patricia S. E. Darlington and Becky Michele Mulvaney, *Women, Power, and Ethnicity: Working toward Reciprocal Empowerment,* New York: Haworth Press, 2003.

30. Jenny Anderson, "National Study Finds Widespread Sexual Harassment of Students in Grades 7 to 12," *New York Times,* November 7, 2011, p. A14.

31. See Associated Press, "National Study Finds Sexual Harassment Pervasive," November 14, 2011, available at http://www.in.gov/icrc/2557.htm.

32. Hilary Stout, "Less 'He Said, She Said' in Sex Harassment Cases," *New York Times,* November 5, 2011, p. BU10.

33. Julia T. Wood, *Gendered Lives: Communication, Gender, and Culture,* 9th ed., Boston: Wadsworth, 2011.

34. See Susan A. Basow, *Gender: Stereotypes and Roles,* 3rd ed., Pacific Grove, CA: Brooks/Cole, 1992.

35. Dwight E. Brooks and Lisa P. Hébert, "Gender, Race, and Media Representation," in Bonnie J. Dow and Julia T. Wood, eds., *The SAGE Handbook of Gender and Communication,* Thousand Oaks, CA: Sage, 2006, p. 297–317.

36. See, for example, Angela Watercutter, "*The Hunger Games*' Katniss Everdeen: The Heroine the World Needs Right Now," Wired.com, March 22, 2012, http://www.wired.com/underwire/2012/03/katniss-everdeen-hollywood-heroines/all/1.

37. James D. Ivory, "The Games, They Are a-Changin': Technological Advancements in Video Games and Implications for Effects on Youth," in Patrick E. Jamieson and Daniel Romer, eds., *The Changing Portrayal of Adolescents in the Media since 1950,* New York: Oxford University Press, 2008, p. 347–376.

38. Charles M. Blow, "The Bleakness of the Bullied," *New York Times,* October 15, 2011, p. A19.

39. See, for example, Susan Donaldson James, "Immigrant Teen Taunted by Cyberbullies Hangs Herself," ABC News, January 26, 2010, http://abcnews.go.com/Health/cyber-bullying-factor-suicide-massachusetts-teen-irish-immigrant/story?id=9660938; and Alfred P. Doblin "Through Tyler Clementi's Looking Glass," *The Record* (Bergen County, NJ), September 12, 2011, p. A13.

CHAPTER 11

1. W. Wagner, D. T. Ostick, and S. R. Komives, *Leadership for a Better World: Understanding the Social Change Model of Leadership Development—Instructor's Manual,* San Francisco: Jossey-Bass, 2007.

2. See, for example, D. H. Cloven and M. E. Roloff, "Sense-Making Activities and Interpersonal Conflict: Communicative Cures for the Mulling Blues," *Western Journal of Speech Communication,* 55, 1991, p. 134–158; and A. S. Rancer and T. A. Avtgis, *Argumentative and Aggressive Communication: Theory, Research, and Application,* Thousand Oaks, CA: Sage, 2006.

3. See, for example, Joyce L. Hocker and William W. Wilmot, *Interpersonal Conflict,* 3rd ed., Dubuque, IA: William C. Brown, 1991, p. 12; William W. Wilmot and Joyce L. Hocker, *Interpersonal Conflict,* 8th ed., New York: McGraw-Hill, 2011; Dudley D. Cahn, "Intimates in Conflict: A Research Review," in Dudley D. Cahn, ed., *Intimates in Conflict: A Communication Perspective,* Hillsdale, NJ: Lawrence Erlbaum, 1990; and Joseph P. Folger, Marshall Scott Poole, and Randall K. Stutman, *Working through Conflict,* 2nd ed., New York: HarperCollins, 1993.

4. See G. L. Welton, "Parties in Conflict: Their Characteristics and Perceptions," in K. G. Duffy, J. W. Grosch, and P. V. Olczak, eds., *Community Mediation: A Handbook for Practitioners and Researchers,* New York: Guilford Press, 1991, p. 105–118; and Laura K. Guerrero, Peter A. Andersen, and Walid A. Afifi, *Close Encounters: Communication in Relationships,* 2nd ed., Thousand Oaks, CA: Sage, 2007.

5. See, for example, Lavinia Hall, ed., *Negotiation: Strategies for Mutual Gain,* Newbury Park, CA: Sage, 1993; and F. F. Jordan-Jackson, Y. Lin, A. S. Rancer, and D. A. Infante, "Perceptions of Males and Females' Use of Aggressive Affirming and Nonaffirming Messages in an Interpersonal Dispute: You've Come a Long Way Baby?" *Western Journal of Communication,* 72, 2008, p. 239–258.

6. See R. Fisher and S. Brown, *Getting Together: Building Relationships as We Negotiate,* Boston: Houghton Mifflin, 1988.

7. Alan C. Filley, *Interpersonal Conflict Resolution,* Glenview, IL: Scott Foresman, 1975; Mark L. Knapp and Anita L. Vangelisti, *Interpersonal Communication and Human Relationships,* 2nd ed., Boston: Allyn & Bacon, 1994; and J. Gottman, "Why Marriages Fail," in K. M. Galvin and P. J. Cooper, eds., *Making Connections: Readings in Relational Communication,* 4th ed., 2006, p. 228–236.

8. Folger et al., *Working through Conflict,* p. 8–10.

9. G. R. Bach and P. Wyden, *The Intimate Enemy: How to Fight Fair in Love and Marriage,* New York: William Morrow, 1969, p. 3; A. M. Hicks and L. M. Diamond, "How Was Your Day? Couples' Affect When Telling and Hearing Daily Events," *Personal Relationships,* 15, 2008, p. 205–228; and L. N. Olson and D. O. Braithwaite, "'If You Hit Me Again, I'll Hit You Back': Conflict Management Strategies of Individuals Experiencing Aggression during Conflicts," *Communication Studies,* 55, 2004, p. 271–285.

10. G. R. Back and R. Deutsch, *Pairing,* New York: Peter Wyden, 1970; G. Back,

Stop! You're Driving Me Crazy, New York: Putnam, 1985.

11. John Stewart, ed., *Bridges Not Walls: A Book about Interpersonal Communication,* New York: McGraw-Hill, 1995, p. 401.

12. Robert R. Blake and Jane Srygley Mouton, *The Managerial Grid,* Houston: Gulf, 1964.

13. M. J. Papa and D. J. Canary, "Communication in Organizations: A Competence-Based Approach," in A. M. Nicotera, ed., *Conflict and Organizations: Communicative Processes,* Albany: State University of New York Press, 1995, p. 153–179; and Joyce L. Hocker and William W. Wilmot, *Interpersonal Conflict,* 5th ed., Dubuque, IA: Brown & Benchmark, 1998.

14. M. A. Gross and L. K. Guerrero, "Managing Conflict Appropriately and Effectively: An Application of the Competence Model to Rahim's Organizational Conflict Styles," *International Journal of Conflict Management,* 11, 2000, p. 200–226.

15. Sharon Anthony Bower and Gordon H. Bower, *Asserting Yourself: A Practical Guide for Positive Change,* updated ed., Reading, MA: Perseus Books, 1991, p. 111–113.

16. Adapted from ibid.

17. See, for example, Stella Ting-Toomey, and John G. Oetzel, *Managing Intercultural Conflict Effectively,* Thousand Oaks, CA: Sage, 2001.

18. Stella Ting-Toomey, "Intercultural Conflict Styles: A Face-Negotiation Theory," in Young Yun Kim and William B. Gudykunst, eds., *Theories in Intercultural Communication,* Newbury Park, CA: Sage, 1988.

19. See, for example, Stella Ting-Toomey, "Managing Conflict in Intimate Intercultural Relationships," in Dudley D. Cahn, ed., *Conflict in Personal Relationships,* Hillsdale, NJ: Lawrence Erlbaum, 1994.

20. Deborah Tannen, *The Argument Culture: Moving from Debate to Dialogue,* New York: Random House, 1998, p. 206.

21. See Stella Ting-Toomey and Jiro Takai, "Explaining Intercultural Conflict: Promising Approaches and Future Directions," in John G. Oetzel and Stella Ting-Toomey, eds., *The Sage Handbook of Conflict Communication,* Thousand Oaks, CA: Sage, 2006, p. 691–723.

22. William B. Gudykunst, *Bridging Differences: Effective Intergroup Communication,* 2nd ed., Thousand Oaks, CA: Sage, 1994.

23. Malcolm Boyd, "Empathy Can Span the Abyss," *Modern Maturity,* 1992. See also Leora Lawton, Merril Silverstein, and Vern Bengtson, "Affection, Social Contact, and Geographic Distance between Adult Children and Their Parents," *Journal of Marriage and the Family,* 56, 1994, p. 57–68.

24. Julia T. Wood, *Gendered Lives: Communication, Gender, and Culture,* 5th ed., Belmont, CA: Wadsworth, 2003, p. 202.

25. M. Fox, M. Gibbs, and D. Auerback, "Age and Gender Dimensions of Friendship," *Psychology of Women Quarterly,* 9, 1985, p. 489–502.

26. J. M. Gottman, "The Roles of Conflict Engagement, Escalation, or Avoidance in Marital Interaction: A Longitudinal View of Five Types of Couples," *Journal of Consulting and Clinical Psychology,* 61, 1993, p. 6–15.

27. J. M. Gottman, *What Predicts Divorce: The Relationship between Marital Processes and Marital Outcomes,* Hillsdale, NJ: Lawrence Erlbaum, 2004, p. 21.

28. Lev Grossman and Evan Narcisse, "Conflict of Interest: Video Games Based on America's Real Wars Are Big Business," *Time,* October 21, 2011, p. 70–75.

29. See Craig A. Anderson, "Violent Video Games: Myths, Facts, and Unanswered Questions," in Alison Alexander and Janice Hanson, eds., *Taking Sides: Clashing Views in Mass Media and Society,* 11th ed., New York: McGraw-Hill, 2011, p. 94–98.

30. See, for example, Robert Putnam, *Bowling Alone: The Collapse and Revival of American Community,* New York: Simon & Schuster, 2000.

31. Matt Ridley, "Internet On, Inhibitions Off: Why We Tell All," *Wall Street Journal,* February 18–19, 2012, p. C4.

CHAPTER 12

1. Andy Cohen, "*Housewives* and the Hill," Huffington Post, June 14, 2010, http://www.huffingtonpost.com/andy-cohen/housewives-and-the-hill_b_612040.html.

2. See Emily Impett, Amy Strackman, Eli J. Finkel, and Shelly L. Gable, "The Best of Times, the Worst of Times: The Place of Close Relationships in Psychology and Our Daily Lives," *Journal of Personality and Social Psychology,* 94, 2008, p. 808–823.

3. Sharon Jayson, "People Who Say They Feel Happy May Live 35% Longer," *USA Today,* November 1, 2011, p. 2A.

4. Steve Duck, *Understanding Relationships,* New York: Guilford Press, 1991, p. 1–2.

5. See H. K. Kim and P. McKenry, "The Relationship between Marriage and Psychological Well-Being," *Journal of Family Issues,* 23, 2002, p. 885–911.

6. See R. M. Kaplan and R. G. Kronick, "Marital Status and Longevity in the United States Population," *Journal of Epidemiology and Community Health,* 60, 2006, p. 760–765.

7. James J. Lynch, *The Broken Heart: The Medical Consequences of Loneliness,* New York: Basic Books, 1977.

8. Jean Seligmann with Nina Archer Biddle, "The Death of a Spouse," *Newsweek,* May 9, 1994, p. 57.

9. "Lonely People 'More Likely to Die Young,'" Daily Mail online, September 14, 2007, http://www.dailymail.co.uk/health/article-481791/Lonely-people-likely-die-young.html.

10. Duck, *Understanding Relationships,* p. 9.

11. Phyllis Korkki, "Building a Bridge to a Lonely Colleague," *New York Times,* January 29, 2012, p. BU8.

12. William C. Schutz, *The Interpersonal Underworld,* Palo Alto, CA: Science and Behavior Books, 1966, p. 18–20.

13. Ibid., p. 24.

14. Abraham Maslow, *Motivation and Personality,* 3rd ed., New York: HarperCollins, 1954; and Abraham Maslow, *Toward a Psychology of Being,* New York: John Wiley, 1962.

15. See, for example, Daniel Perlman and Anita L. Vangelisti, "Personal Relationships: An Introduction," in Anita L. Vangelisti and Daniel Perlman, eds., *The Cambridge Handbook of Personal Relationships,* New York: Cambridge University Press, 2006, p. 1–7.

16. Robert J. Sternberg, *The Triangle of Love: Intimacy, Passion, Commitment,* New York: Basic Books, 1988.

17. See David M. Buss and David P. Schmitt, "Sexual Strategies Theory: An Evolutionary Perspective on Human Mating," *Psychological Review,* 100, 1993, p. 204–232.

18. Geoffrey L. Greif and Kathleen Holtz Deal, *Two Plus Two: Couples and Their Couple Friendships,* New York: Routledge, 2012.

19. William K. Rawlins, "Friendship as a Communicative Achievement: A Theory and an Interpretive Analysis of Verbal Reports," doctoral dissertation, Temple University, Philadelphia, 1981.

20. See William K. Rawlins, *Friendship Matters: Communication, Dialectics, and the Life Course,* New York: Aldine de Gruyter, 1992; and William K. Rawlins, *The Compass of Friendship: Narratives, Identities, and Dialogues,* Thousand Oaks, CA: Sage, 2009.

21. Alex Williams, "It's Not Me, It's You," *New York Times,* January 28, 2012, p. ST1, ST8.

22. H. T. Reis and A. Aron, "Love: What Is It, Why Does It Matter, and How Does It Operate?," *Perspectives on Psychological Science,* 3, 2009, p. 80–86.

23. John Alan Lee, "A Typology of Styles of Loving," *Personality and Social Psychology Bulletin,* 3, 1977, p. 173–182.

24. Robert J. Sternberg, "A Triangular Theory of Love," *Psychological Review,* 93, 1986, p. 119–135; and Sternberg, *The Triangle of Love.*

25. Ibid.; and Robert J. Sternberg, "Triangulating Love," in Robert J. Sternberg and Michael L. Barnes, eds., *The Psychology of Love,* New Haven, CT: Yale University Press, 1988, p. 119–138.

26. See Mark L. Knapp and Anita L. Vangelisti, *Interpersonal Communication and Human Relationships,* 3rd ed., Boston: Allyn & Bacon, 1996.

27. See Charles R. Berger and James J. Bradac, *Language and Social Knowledge: Uncertainty in Interpersonal Relations,* London: Arnold, 1982.

28. Ibid.

29. See Laura K. Guerrero and Paul A. Mongeau, "On Becoming 'More than Friends': The Transition from Friendship to Romantic Relationship," in Susan Sprecher, Amy Wenzel, and John Harvey, eds., *Handbook of Relationship Initiation,* New York: Psychology Press, 2008, p. 175–194; S. Planalp and A. Benson, "Friends' and Acquaintances' Conversations I," *Journal of Social and Personal Relationships,* 9, 1992, p. 483–506; and S. Planalp, "Friends' and Acquaintances' Conversations II," *Journal of Social and Personal Relationships,* 10, 1993, p. 339–354.

30. Mark L. Knapp and Anita L. Vangelisti, *Interpersonal Communication and Human Relationships,* 2nd ed., Boston: Allyn & Bacon, 1992, p. 41.

31. See Lawrence B. Rosenfield and Daniella Bordaray-Sciolino, "Self Disclosure as a Communication Strategy during Relationship Termination," paper presented at the national meeting of the Speech Communication Association, Denver, November 1985.

32. Rose Pastore, "The New Lexicon of Love," *Psychology Today,* December 2011.

33. Sharon Jayson, "Many Singles Looking for Love, but Not Marriage, *USA Today,* February 2, 2012, p. 4D.

34. Duck, *Understanding Relationships,* p. 31.

35. Larry A. Samovar and Richard E. Porter, *Communication between Cultures,* 2nd ed., Belmont, CA: Wadsworth, 1995, p. 188.

36. Ibid., p. 190–193.

37. Ray Bull and Nichola Rumsey, *The Social Psychology of Facial Appearance,* New York: Springer-Verlag, 1988.

38. Ellen Berscheid and Elaine Hatfield Walster, *Interpersonal Attraction,* 2nd ed., Reading, MA: Addison-Wesley, 1978.

39. Elliot Aronson, *The Social Animal,* 11th ed., New York: Worth, 2012, p. 357.

40. For another discussion of how reinforcement or its lack influences relationships, see Michael E. Roloff, *Interpersonal Communication: The Social Exchange Approach,* Beverly Hills, CA: Sage, 1981.

41. See Elaine Walster, G. William Walster, and Ellen Berscheid, *Equity: Theory and Research,* Boston: Allyn & Bacon, 1978; and Elaine Hatfield and Susan Sprecher, "Matching Hypothesis," in Harry T. Reis and Susan Sprecher, eds., *Encyclopedia of Human Relationships,* vol. 2, New York: Sage, 2009, p. 1065–1067.

42. Nicola Clark, "Making the Skies Friendlier," *New York Times,* February 24, 2012, p. B1, B2.

43. William B. Gudykunst and Stella Ting-Toomey, *Culture and Interpersonal Communication,* Newbury Park, CA: Sage, 1988, p. 197–198.

44. Myron W. Lustig and Jolene Koester, *Intercultural Competence: Interpersonal Communication across Cultures,* 2nd ed., New York: HarperCollins, 1996, p. 243.

45. See Geert Hofstede, "Cross-Cultural Management II: Empirical Studies," *International Studies of Management and Organization,* 13, 1983, p. 46–74.

46. John Paul Feig, *A Common Core: Thais and Americans,* Yarmouth, ME: Intercultural Press, 1989, p. 50.

47. See, "Dating Customs around the World," FactMonster.com, 2000, http://www.factmonster.com/ipka/A0767654.html.

48. Hervé Varenne, *Americans Together: Structured Diversity in a Midwestern Town,* New York: Teacher's College Press, 1977.

49. Paul Bohannan, *We, the Alien: An Introduction to Cultural Anthropology,* Prospect Heights, IL: Waveland Press, 1992, p. 57.

50. Rachel Bertsche, *MWF Seeking BFF: My Yearlong Search for a New Best Friend,* New York: Ballantine, 2011.

51. Pharme M. Camarena, Pamela A. Sarigiani, and Anne C. Peterson, "Gender-Specific Pathways to Intimacy in Early Adolescence," *Journal of Youth and Adolescence,* 19:1, 1990, p. 19–32.

52. William Pollack, *Real Boys: Rescuing Our Sons from the Myths of Boyhood,* New York: Random House, 1998, p. 181.

53. Deborah Tannen, *You Just Don't Understand: Women and Men in Conversation,* New York: Morrow, 1990, p. 77.

54. S. Davis, "Men as Success Objectives and Women as Sex Objects: A Study of Personal Advertisements," *Sex Roles,* 23, 1990, p. 43–50; and J. E. Smith, V. A. Waldorf, and D. L. Trembath, "Single White Male Looking for Thin, Very Attractive . . . ," *Sex Roles,* 23, 1990, p. 675–685.

55. L. H. Ganong and M. Coleman, "Gender Differences in Expectations of Self and Future Partner," *Journal of Family Issues,* 13, 1992, p. 55–64.

56. Tannen, *You Just Don't Understand,* p. 238–244.

57. M. D. Vargas, "Domesticating Patriarchy: Hegemonic Masculinity and Television's Mr. Mom," *Critical Studies in Media Communication,* 19, 2002, p. 352–375.

58. Cynthia M. Lont, ed., *Women and Media: Content, Careers, Criticism,* Belmont, CA: Wadsworth, 1995.

59. See Jennifer L. Walsh and L. Monique Ward, "Adolescent Gender Role Portrayals in the Media: 1950 to the Present," in Patrick E. Jamieson and Daniel Romer, eds., *The Changing Portrayal of Adolescents in the Media since 1950,* New York: Oxford University Press, 2008, p. 132–164; and D. Smith, "Media More Likely to Show Women Talking about Romance than at a Job, Study Says," *New York Times,* May 1, 1997, p. B15.

60. Steve Lohr, "Reluctant Conscripts in the March of Technology," *New York Times,* September 17, 1995, p. 16.

61. Christine Rosen, "Virtual Friendship and the New Narcissism," in Mark Bauerlein, ed., *The Digital Divide,* New York: Penguin, 2011, p. 172–188.

62. See, for example, Charles Isherwood, "'Salesman' Comes Calling, Right on Time," *New York Times,* February 26, 2012, p. AR6, AR27.

63. Keith N. Hampton, Lauren Sessions Goulet, Cameron Marlow, and Lee Rainie, *Why Most Facebook Users Get More than They Give,* Pew Internet & American Life Project, February 3, 2012, http://pewinternet.org/Reports/2012/Facebook-users.aspx.

64. Stephanie Rosenbloom, "Love, Lies, and What They Learned," *New York Times,* November 13, 2011, p. ST1, ST8–ST9.

65. Ibid.

66. Eli J. Finkel, Paul W. Eastwick, Benjamin R. Karney, Harry T. Reis, and Susan Sprecher, "Online Dating: A Critical Analysis from the Perspective of Psychological Science," *Psychological Science in the Public Interest,* 13:1, 2012, p. 3–66.

67. See, for example, Joseph B. Walther, "Computer-Mediated Communication: Impersonal, Interpersonal, and Hyperpersonal Interaction," *Communication Research,* 23, 1996, p. 3–43; and J. R. Suler, "The Online Disinhibition Effect," *Cyberpsychology and Behavior,* 7, 2004, p. 321–326.

68. See, for example, Joyce Conen, "Making a Statement in Absentia," *New York Times,* March 20, 2003, p. G1, G4.

69. Jenna Wortham, "With an App, Your Next Date Could Be Just around the Corner," *New York Times,* November 3, 2011, p. A1, B4.

70. Jennifer Levitz, "On a Wingman and a Prayer: Singles Bow to Cupids-for-Hire," *Wall Street Journal,* January 6, 2012, p. A1, A10.

71. Lynch, *The Broken Heart.*

CHAPTER 13

1. Nina Lin, "Social Media Helps Couples Plug into Their Relationships," *The*

Statesman (Stony Brook University), February 13, 2012; http://www. sbstatesman.com/social-media-helps-couples-plug-into-their-relationships786.

2. Laura Stafford and Andy J. Merolla, "Idealization, Reunions, and Stability in Long-Distance Dating Relationships," *Journal of Social and Personal Relationships,* 24, 2007, p. 37–54.

3. Katheryn C. Maguire and Terry A. Kinney, "When Distance Is Problematic: Communication, Coping, and Relational Satisfaction in Female College Students' Long-Distance Dating Relationships," *Journal of Applied Communication Research,* 38, 2010, p. 27–46.

4. Valerian J. Derlega and John H. Berg, eds., *Self-Disclosure: Theory, Research, and Therapy,* New York: Plenum, 1987.

5. D. E. Miell, "Cognitive and Communicative Strategies in Developing Relationships," doctoral thesis, University of Lancaster, 1984.

6. See, for example, Patricia Parr, Rebecca A. Boyle, and Laura Tejada, "I Said, You Said: A Communication Exercise for Couples," *Contemporary Family Therapy,* 30, 2008, p. 167–173.

7. See, for example, B. Aubrey Fisher and Katherine L. Adams, *Interpersonal Communication: Pragmatics of Human Relationships,* New York: McGraw-Hill, 1994, p. 309.

8. Irwin Altman and Dalmas Taylor, *Social Penetration: The Development of Interpersonal Relationships,* New York: Holt, Rinehart & Winston, 1973.

9. Steve Duck, *Understanding Relationships,* New York: Guilford Press, 1991, p. 80.

10. Ibid.

11. Joseph Luft, *Group Processes: An Introduction to Group Dynamics,* 2nd ed., Palo Alto, CA: Mayfield, 1970.

12. See, for example, F. D. Fincham and T. N. Bradbury, "The Impact of Attributions in Marriage: An Individual Difference Analysis," *Journal of Social and Personal Relationships,* 6, 1989, p. 69–85; and V. G. Downs, "Grandparents and Grandchildren: The Relationship between Self-Disclosure and Solidarity in an Intergenerational Relationship," *Communication Research Reports,* 5, 1988, p. 173–179.

13. Leslie A. Baxter, "The Social Side of Personal Relationships: A Dialectical Perspective," in Steve Duck, ed., *Social Context and Relationships,* Newbury Park, CA: Sage, 1993, p. 139–165.

14. Ibid.

15. Sandra Petronio, "The Boundaries of Privacy: Praxis of Everyday Life," in Sandra Petronio, ed., *Balancing the Secrets of Private Disclosure,* Mahwah, NJ: Lawrence Erlbaum, 2000, p. 37–49.

16. Renate Klein and Robert M. Milardo, "Third-Party Influences on the Management of Personal Relationships,"

in Steve Duck, ed., *Social Context and Relationships,* Newbury Park, CA: Sage, 1993, p. 55–77.

17. D. R. Pawlowski, "Dialectical Tensions in Marital Couples' Accounts of Their Relationships," *Communication Quarterly,* 46, 1998, p. 396–416.

18. L. A. Baxter and L. A. Erbert, "Perceptions of Dialectical Contradictions in Turning Points of Development in Heterosexual Romantic Relationships," *Journal of Social and Personal Relationships,* 16, 1999, p. 547–569.

19. See, for example, L. A. Baxter, "Dialectical Contradictions in Relationship Development," *Journal of Social and Personal Relationships,* 7, 1990, p. 69–88; and E. M. Griffin, *A First Look at Communication Theory,* 5th ed., New York: McGraw-Hill, 2003, p. 157–170.

20. Duck, *Understanding Relationships,* p. 122.

21. Kathryn Dindia and Leslie A. Baxter, "Strategies for Maintaining and Repairing Marital Relationships," *Journal of Social and Personal Relationships,* 4, 1987, p. 143–158; and Kathryn Dindia, "A Multiphasic View of Relationship Maintenance Strategies," in D. J. Canary and L. Stafford, eds., *Communication and Relational Maintenance,* San Diego, CA: Academic Press, 1994, p. 91–112.

22. Duck, *Understanding Relationships,* p. 125–126.

23. Sharon S. Brehm, *Intimate Relationships,* 2nd ed., New York: McGraw-Hill, 1992.

24. Katherine A. McGonagle, Ronald C. Kessler, and Ian H. Gotlib, "The Effects of Marital Disagreement Style, Frequency, and Outcome on Marital Disruption," *Journal of Social and Personal Relationships,* 10, 1993, p. 385–404.

25. Duck, *Understanding Relationships,* p. 168–169.

26. Julie Mehta, "Tainted Love," *Current Health,* 32, January 2006, p. 18–21.

27. See Michael P. Johnson, "Violence and Abuse in Personal Relationships: Conflict, Terror, and Resistance in Intimate Partnerships," in Anita L. Vangelisti and Daniel Perlman, eds., *The Cambridge Handbook of Personal Relationships,* New York: Cambridge University Press, 2006, p. 557–576; and Susan Murphy-Milano, *Defending Our Lives: Getting Away from Domestic Violence and Staying Safe,* New York: Anchor/Doubleday, 1996.

28. See, for example, Brian H. Spitzberg and William R. Cupach, eds., *The Dark Side of Interpersonal Communication,* Mahwah, NJ: Lawrence Erlbaum, 2007.

29. Sally A. Lloyd and Beth C. Emery, *The Dark Side of Courtship: Physical and Sexual Aggression,* Thousand Oaks, CA: Sage, 2000, p. 27.

30. Sally A. Lloyd, "The Dark Side of Courtship," *Family Relations,* 40, 1991, p. 14–20.

31. M. F. Davis and S. J. Kraham, "Protecting Women's Welfare in the Face of Violence," *Fordham Urban Law Journal,* 22, 1995, p. 1141–1157.

32. Julia T. Wood, *Gendered Lives: Communication, Gender, and Culture,* Belmont, CA: Wadsworth, 1994, p. 202.

33. J. E. McConnell, "Beyond Metaphor: Battered Women, Involuntary Servitude, and the Thirteenth Amendment," *Yale Journal of Law and Feminism,* 4, 1992, p. 207–253.

34. M. P. Johnson, "Social and Cognitive Features of the Dissolution of Commitment to Relationships," in Steve Duck, ed., *Dissolving Personal Relationships,* New York: Academic Press, 1982, p. 51–73.

35. See George A. Bonanno, *The Other Side of Sadness: What the New Science of Bereavement Tells Us about Life and Loss,* New York: Basic Books, 2009; and James J. Lynch, *The Broken Heart: The Medical Consequences of Loneliness,* New York: Basic Books, 1977.

36. Hal Arkowitz and Scott O. Lilienfeld, "Grief without Tears," *Scientific American Mind,* November/December 2011, p. 68–69.

37. This process is described in Harold S. Kushner, *When Bad Things Happen to Good People,* New York: Schocken Books, 1981.

38. See, for example, Erica Goode, "Experts Offer Fresh Insights into the Mind of the Grieving Child," *New York Times,* March 28, 2000, p. F7, F12.

39. Janice Hume, "'Portraits of Grief,' Reflectors of Values: *The New York Times* Remembers Victims of September 11," *Journalism and Mass Communication Quarterly,* 80, 2003, p. 166–182.

40. S. K. Bonsu, "The Presentation of Dead Selves in Everyday Life: Obituaries and Impression Management," *Symbolic Interaction,* 30, 2007, p. 199–219.

41. See "Virtual Immortality," *The Record* (Bergen County, NJ), February 25, 2012, p. A 13.

42. William B. Gudykunst, "The Influence of Cultural Variability on Perceptions of Communication Behavior Associated with Relationship Terms," *Human Communication Research,* 13, 1986, p. 147–166; and Kyoko Seki, David Matsumoto, and T. Todd Imahori, "The Conceptualization and Expression of Intimacy in Japan and the United States," *Journal of Cross-Cultural Psychology,* 33, 2002, p. 303–319.

43. Susan Sprecher and Kathleen McKinney, *Sexuality,* Newbury Park, CA: Sage, 1993.

44. Robert Crooks and Karla Baur, *Our Sexuality,* 7th ed. Pacific Grove, CA: Brooks/Cole, 1999.

45. Gudykunst, "Influence of Cultural Variability."

46. See, for example, M. Kito, "Self-Disclosure in Romantic Relationships and Friendships among American and Japanese College Students," *Journal of Social Psychology,* 145, 2005, p. 127–140.

47. Carol Zinner Dolphin, "Beyond Hall: Variables in the Use of Personal Space in Intercultural Transactions," *Howard Journal of Communications,* 1, 1988, p. 28–29.

48. Stanley O. Gaines, Jr., "Relationships among Members of Cultural Minorities," in Julia T. Wood and Steve Duck, eds., *Under-studied Relationships: Off the Beaten Track,* Thousand Oaks, CA: Sage, 1995, p. 51–88.

49. Duck, *Understanding Relationships,* p. 12.

50. Scott Swain, "Covert Intimacy: Closeness in Men's Friendships," in Barbara J. Risman and Pepper Schwartz, eds., *Gender in Intimate Relationships: A Microstructural Approach,* Belmont, CA: Wadsworth, 1989, p. 71–86; and E. Paul and K. White, "The Development of Intimate Relationships in Late Adolescence," *Adolescence,* 25, 1990, p. 375–400.

51. Julia T. Wood and Christopher C. Inman, "In a Different Mode: Masculine Styles of Communicating Closeness," *Journal of Applied Communication Research,* 21, 1993, p. 279–295.

52. See, for example, Judy Cornelia Pearson, Lynn H. Turner, and William Todd-Mancillas, *Gender and Communication,* 2nd ed., Dubuque, IA: William C. Brown, 1991, p. 170–171.

53. W. F. Owen, "The Verbal Expression of Love by Women and Men as a Critical Communication Event in Personal Relationships," *Women's Studies in Communication,* 10, 1987, p. 15–24.

54. Brehm, *Intimate Relationships.*

55. Michelle M. Kazmer and Caroline Haythornthwaite, "Juggling Multiple Social Worlds: Distance Students Online and Offline," *American Behavioral Scientist,* 45, 2001, p. 510–529.

56. See Henry Jenkins, "Love Online," in Mark Bauerlein, ed., *The Digital Divide,* New York: Penguin, 2011, p. 160–165.

57. Artemio Ramirez, Jr., and Shuangyur Zhang, "When Online Meets Offline: The Effect of Modality Switching on Relational Communication," *Communication Monographs,* 74, 2007, p. 287–310.

58. John D. Sutter, "On Facebook, It's Now 4.74 Degrees of Separation," CNN.com, http://www.cnn.com/2011/11/22/tech/social-media/facebook-six-degrees/index.html?hpt.

59. Michaelle Bond, "Your Facebook Past on Display?," *USA Today,* November 3, 2011, p. 3B.

60. Ibid.

61. Duck, *Understanding Relationships,* p. 163.

62. Ruth Padawer, "Teens Get Closer from Afar with Instant Messages," *The Record*

(Bergen County, NJ), June 17, 2003, p. A1, A8.

63. Marilyn Elias, "You've Got Trauma, but Writing Can Help," *USA Today,* July 1, 2002, p. G6.

64. Alan Garner, *Conversationally Speaking,* New York: McGraw-Hill, 1989, p. 61.

65. See B. R. Burleson and W. Samter, "A Social Skills Approach to Relationship Maintenance: How Individual Differences in Communication Skills Affect the Achievement of Relationship Functions," in D. J. Canary and L. Stafford, eds., *Communication and Relational Maintenance.* Orlando, FL: Academic Press, 1994.

CHAPTER 14

1. Jennifer Rubin, "Jack Welch, Julia and the Fallacy of Working Women 'Having It All,'" *Washington Post* blog, May 4, 2012, http://www.washingtonpost.com/blogs/right-turn/post/jack-welch-julia-and-the-fallacy-of-working-women-having-it-all/2012/05/04/gIQAFjYU1T_blog.html

2. Caitlin Kelly, "Okay, Google, Take a Deep Breath," *New York Times,* April 29, 2012, p. BU1.

3. Ibid.

4. Jennifer Ludden, "When Employees Make Room for Work-Life Balance," *NPR Morning Edition,* March 15, 2010, http://www.npr.org/templates/story/story.php?storyId=124611210.

5. Leslie Kwor, "Hazard of the Trade: Bankers' Health," *Wall Street Journal,* February 15, 2012, p. C1, C2.

6. Kathleen M. Galvin, Carma L. Bylund, and Bernard J. Brommel, *Family Communication: Cohesion and Change,* 8th ed., Boston: Allyn & Bacon, 2012, p. 4.

7. Patricia Noller and Mary Anne Fitzpatrick, *Communication in Family Relationships,* Englewood Cliffs, NJ: Prentice Hall, 1993; and Lynn Turner and Richard West, *Perspectives on Family Communication,* New York: McGraw-Hill, 2005.

8. Laurie P. Arliss, *Contemporary Family Communication: Messages and Meanings,* New York: St. Martin's Press, 1993, p. 7.

9. See Jane Jorgenson, "Where Is the 'Family' in Family Communication? Exploring Families' Self-Definitions," *Journal of Applied Communication Research,* 17, 1989, p. 27–41.

10. Jason DeParle and Sabrina Tavernise, "Unwed Mothers Now a Majority Before Age of 30," *New York Times,* February 19, 2012, p. A1, A16.

11. Eric Klinenberg, "Living Alone Is the New Norm," *Time,* March 11, 2012, p. 60–62.

12. U.S. Census Bureau, 2009, American Community Survey, http://www.census.gov/acs/www.

13. See Katherine S. Newman, *The Accordion Family: Boomerang Kids, Anxious Parents, and the Private Toll of Global Competition,* New York: Beacon Press, 2012; and Rachel Louise Ensign, "When the Budget Calls for a Move Back Home," *Wall Street Journal,* November 27, 2011, p. B3.

14. Sharon Jayson, "All Together Now: Extended Families," *USA Today,* November 23–24, 2011, p. 1A, 2A.

15. Virginia Satir, *The New Peoplemaking.* Mountain View, CA: Science and Behavior Books, 1988.

16. Arliss, *Contemporary Family Communication,* p. 57.

17. L. Von Bertalanffy, *General System Theory: Essays on Its Foundation and Development,* New York: Braziller, 1968.

18. Galvin et al., *Family Communication.*

19. Satir, *New Peoplemaking,* p. 79.

20. David H. Olson and Associates, *Families: What Makes Them Work,* Beverly Hills, CA: Sage, 1983.

21. Satir, *New Peoplemaking,* p. 182–193.

22. Ibid.

23. See Monica McGoldrick, "Ethnicity, Cultural Diversity, and Normality," in Froma Walsh, ed., *Normal Family Processes,* 2nd ed., New York: Guilford Press, 1993.

24. Jayson, "All Together Now."

25. John W. Santrock, *Life Span Development,* 4th ed., Dubuque, IA: William C. Brown, 1992, p. 261.

26. Stella Ting-Toomey and Leeva C. Chung, *Understanding Intercultural Communication,* 2nd ed. New York: Oxford University Press, 2012, p. 68.

27. Julia T. Wood, *Gendered Lives: Communication, Gender, and Culture,* 9th ed., Boston: Wadsworth, 2011, p. 190.

28. Judy C. Pearson, *Communication in the Family: Seeking Satisfaction in Changing Times,* 2nd ed., New York: HarperCollins, 1993, p. 80.

29. Wood, *Gendered Lives,* p. 169–181.

30. Ibid.

31. See, for example, Dwight E. Brooks and Lisa P. Hébert, "Gender, Race and Media Representation," in Bonnie J. Dow and Julia T. Wood, eds., *The SAGE Handbook of Gender and Communication,* Thousand Oaks, CA: Sage, 2006, p. 297–317; and Jennifer L. Walsh and L. Monique Ward, "Adolescent Gender Role Portrayals in the Media: 1950 to the Present," in Patrick E. Jamieson and Daniel Romer, eds., *The Changing Portrayal of Adolescents in the Media since 1950,* New York: Oxford University Press, 2008, p. 132–164.

32. F. Earl Barcus, *Images of Life on Children's Television: Sex Roles, Minorities, and Families,* New York: Praeger, 1983.

33. Arliss, *Contemporary Family Communication,* p. 258–262.

34. Mike Chalmers, "Deployed? Facebook Puts Family in Your Face," *USA Today,* November 25, 2011, p. 3A.

35. See P. M. Sias, K. J. Krone, and F. M. Jablin, "An Ecological Systems Perspective on Workplace Relationships," in M. L. Knapp and J. A. Daly ed., *Handbook of Interpersonal Communication,* 3rd ed., Thousand Oaks, CA: Sage, 2002, p. 615–642; and Margaret J. Wheatley, *Leadership and the New Science,* San Francisco: Berrett-Koehler, 1994, p. 23.

36. Phyllis Korkki, "Building a Bridge to a Lonely Colleague," *New York Times,* January 29, 2012, p. BU8.

37. Marvin R. Weisbord, *Discovering Common Ground: How Future Search Conferences Bring People Together to Achieve Breakthrough Innovation, Empowerment, Shared Vision, and Collaborative Action,* San Francisco: Berrett-Koehler, 1992.

38. Leslie Kwoh, "Reverse Mentoring Cracks Workplace," *Wall Street Journal,* November 28, 2011, p. B7.

39. D. A. Infante and A. S. Rancer, "A Conceptualization and Measure of Argumentativeness," *Journal of Personality Assessment,* 45, 1982, p. 72–80.

40. D. A. Infante and W. I. Gorden, "Superiors' Argumentativeness and Verbal Aggressiveness as Predictors of Subordinates' Satisfaction," *Human Communication Research,* 12, 1985, p. 117–125; and D. A. Infante and W. I. Gorden, "Superior and Subordinate Communicator Profiles: Implications for Independent-Mindedness and Upward Effectiveness," *Central States Speech Journal,* 38, 1987, p. 73–80.

41. Virginia P. Richmond and James C. McCroskey, *Organizational Communication for Survival,* 4th ed., Boston: Pearson, 2009, p. 174–178.

42. Gerald M. Goldhaber, *Organizational Communication,* 5th ed., Dubuque, IA: William C. Brown, 1990, p. 214.

43. Fred Dansereau and Steven E. Markham, "Superior-Subordinate Communication: Multiple Levels of Analysis," in Fredric M. Jablin et al., eds., *Handbook of Organizational Communication: An Interdisciplinary Perspective,* Newbury Park, CA: Sage, 1987, p. 343–353.

44. Richmond and McCroskey, *Organizational Communication for Survival,* p. 27–28.

45. Dawn R. Gilpin, "Working the Twittersphere," in Zizi Papacharissi, ed., *A Networked Self: Identity, Community, and Culture on Social Network Sites,* New York: Routledge, 2011, p. 232–250.

46. Wheatley, *Leadership and the New Science,* p. 107.

47. Charles Redding, *Communication within the Organization,* New York: Industrial Communication Council, 1972.

48. Douglas McGregor, *The Human Side of Enterprise,* New York: McGraw-Hill, 1960.

49. Alex F. Osborn, *Applied Imagination,* New York: Scribner's, 1957.

50. Jonah Lehrer, "Groupthink," *The New Yorker,* January 30, 2012, p. 22–27.

51. Irving Janis, *Groupthink,* Boston: Houghton Mifflin, 1982.

52. See, for instance, Lisa A Mainiero, "Participation? Nyet. Rewards and Praise? Da!" *Academy of Management Executive,* August 1993, p. 87; and Diane H. B. Welsh, Fred Luthans, and Steven M. Sommer, "Managing Russian Factory Workers: The Impact of U.S. Based Behavioral and Participative Techniques," *Academy of Management Journal,* February 1993, p. 57–59.

53. Lillian H. Chaney and Jeanette S. Martin, *Intercultural Business Communication,* Englewood Cliffs, NJ: Prentice Hall, 1995, p. 41.

54. See, for example, *Diversity Leadership Guide,* Diversity Management Office, NASA, January/February 2007, http://www.grc.nasa.gov/WWW/NLS/LeadershipGuideJanFeb07.pdf.

55. Chaney and Martin, *Intercultural Business Communication.* See also C. Chiu, L. Mallorie, H. T. Keh, and W. Law, "Perceptions of Culture in Multicultural Space: Joint Presentation of Images from Two Cultures Increases In-Group Attribution of Culture-Typical Characteristics," *Journal of Cross-Cultural Psychology,* 40, 2009, p. 282–300.

56. Lennie Copeland and Lewis Griggs, *Going International: How to Make Friends and Deal Effectively in the Global Marketplace,* New York: Random House, 1985, p. 10.

57. Larry A. Samovar, Richard E. Porter, and Edwin R. McDaniel, *Communication between Cultures,* 7th ed., Boston: Wadsworth, 2010, p. 278.

58. Christopher Engholm, *When Business East Meets Business West,* New York: John Wiley, 1991.

59. See, for example, Geert Hofstede, *Culture's Consequences: Comparing Values, Behaviors, Institutions, and Organizations across Nations,* 2nd ed., Thousand Oaks, CA: Sage, 2001; and Anne-Marie Soderberg and Nigel Holden, "Rethinking Cross-Cultural Management in a Globalizing Business World," *International Journal of Cross-Cultural Management,* 2, 2002, p. 103–121.

60. See B. M. Bass and P. C. Burger, *Assessment of Managers: An International Comparison,* New York: Free Press, 1979.

61. Greg Hammill, "Mixing and Managing Four Generations of Employees," *FDR Magazine Online,* Winter/Spring 2005, http://www.fdu.edu/newspubs/magazine/05ws/generations.htm.

62. Rosabeth Moss Kanter, *Men and Women of the Corporation,* New York: Basic Books, 1977.

63. Gary Lange, "One in Four U.S. Women Reports Workplace Harassment," ABC News online, November 16, 2011, http://abcnews.go.com/blogs/politics/2011/11/one-in-four-u-s-women-reports-workplace-harassment. See also Julia T. Wood, "Telling Our Stories: Narratives as a Basis for Theorizing Sexual Harassment," *Journal of Applied Communication Research,* 4, 1992, p. 349–363.

64. Barbara Garlick, Suzanne Dixon, and Pauline Allen, eds., *Stereotypes of Women in Power: Historical Perspectives and Revisionist Views,* Westport, CT: Greenwood Press, 1992.

65. Wood, *Gendered Lives,* p. 234–235.

66. Willard Gaylin, *The Male Ego,* New York: Viking, 1992.

67. Rhymer Rigby, "Metro Males Find Their Place," *Financial Times,* January 31, 2012, p. 10.

68. Richmond and McCroskey, *Organizational Communication for Survival,* p. 114–117.

69. Wood, *Gendered Lives,* p. 250–251.

70. S. Magnuson and K. Norem, "Bullies Grow Up and Go to Work," *Journal of Professional Counseling, Practice, Theory, and Research,* 37:2, 2009, p. 34–51.

71. See Gary Namie and Pamela E. Lutgen-Sandvik, "Active and Passive Accomplices: The Communal Character of Workplace Bullying," *International Journal of Communication,* 4, 2010, p. 343–373.

72. J. F. Andronici and D. S. Katz, "The Right to Complain," *Ms.,* Spring 2007, p. 59.

73. See, for example, R. E. Thompson, "The Changing Face of Gender Issues in the 21st Century Workplace," *Physician Executive,* 31:1, 2005, p. 64–65; and J. N. Cleveland, M. Stockdale, and K. R. Murphy, *Women and Men in Organizations: Sex and Gender Issues at Work,* Mahwah, NJ: Lawrence Erlbaum, 2000.

74. S. Ladner, "Laptops in the Living Room: Mobile Technologies and the Divide between Work and Private Time among Interactive Agency Workers," *Canadian Journal of Communication,* 33, 2008, p. 465–489.

75. R. K. Garrett and J. N. Danziger, "Disaffection or Expected Outcomes: Understanding Personal Internet Use During Work," *Journal of Computer-Mediated Communication,* 13, 2008, p. 937–958; and R. K. Garrett, and J. N. Danziger, "On Cyberslacking: Workplace Status and Personal Internet Use at Work," *Cyberpsychology and Behavior,* 11, 2008, p. 287–292.

76. Mary Beth Watson-Manheim, "Exploring the Use of Social Network Sites in the Workplace," in Zizi Papacharissi, ed., *A Networked Self: Identity, Community, and Culture on Social Network Sites,* New York: Routledge, 2011, p. 169–182.

77. Gilpin, "Working the Twittersphere."

78. Rex W. Huppke, "Facebook Profile Can Predict Job Success," *Sun Sentinel,* March 12, 2012, p. 2D.

79. See Kevin B. Wright, Lisa Sparks, and H. Dan O'Hair, *Health Communication in the 21st Century,* Malden, MA: Blackwell, 2008, p. 5; and Gary L. Kreps and Barbara C. Thornton, *Health Communication: Theory and Practice,* 2nd ed., Prospect Heights, IL: Waveland Press, 1992, p. 2.

80. See J. B. Bowen, M. A. Stewart, and B. L. Ryan, "Outcomes of Patient-Provider Interaction," in T. L. Thompson, A. M. Dorsey, K. I. Miller, and R. Parrot, eds., *Handbook of Health Communication,* Mahwah, NJ: Lawrence Erlbaum, 2003, p. 141–161; S. Cohen and T. A. Wills, "Stress, Social Support, and Buffering Hypothesis," *Psychological Bulletin,* 98, 1985, p. 310–157; and T. Ferguson, "Health Care in Cyberspace: Patients Lead a Revolution," *The Futurist,* 31, November–December 1997, pp. 29–34.

81. For an early discussion of the value of interpersonal communication in health care settings, see T. L. Thompson, "Patient Health Care: Issues in Interpersonal Communication," in E. Berlin Ray and L. Donohew. eds., *Communication and Health,* Hillsdale, NJ: Lawrence Erlbaum, 1990, p. 27–50. See also V. Batenburg and J. A. Small, "Does a Communication Skills Course Influence Medical Students' Attitudes?," *Medical Teacher,* 19, 1997, p. 263–269.

82. Peggy Clarke, "Finding the Words to Communicate about Sexual Health," paper presented at the "Communication and Health" conference of the Speech Communication Association, Washington, DC, July 19–23, 1995, p. 2.

83. See also D. Ballard-Reisch, "A Model of Participative Decision Making for Physician-Patient Interaction," *Health Communication,* 2, 1990, p. 91–104.

84. Athena du Pre, *Communicating about Health: Current Issues and Perspectives,* Mountain View, CA: Mayfield, 2000, p. 157.

85. See Gary L. Kreps and Elizabeth N. Kunimoto, *Effective Communication in Multicultural Health Care Settings,* Thousand Oaks, CA: Sage, 1994; and D. E. Brashers, "Communication and Uncertainty Management," *Journal of Communication,* 51, 2001, p. 477–497.

86. See, for example, A. Ndiwane, K. H. Miller, A. Bonner, et al., "Enhancing Cultural Competence of Advanced Practice Nurses: Health Care Challenges in the Twenty-First Century," *Journal of Cultural Diversity,* 11, 2004, p. 118–121; and T. Randall, "Key to Organ Donation May Be Cultural Awareness," *Journal of the American Medical Association,* 285, 1991, p. 176–178.

87. Ruth Padawer, "Warming Trend: Increase in Female Doctors Brings a More Personal Touch to Medical Care," *The Record* (Bergen County, NJ), October 9, 1995, p. H1, H2.

88. Peter Franks and Klea D. Bertakis, "Physician Gender, Patient Gender, and Primary Care," *Journal of Women's Health,* 12, 2003, p. 73–80.

Photo Credits

xxiv. Digital Vision./Digital Vision/Thinkstock 2. Hemera Technologies/PhotoObjects.net/Thinkstock 2. PhotoObjects.net/PhotoObjects.net/Thinkstock 3. Photodisc/Photodisc/Thinkstock 3. Photodisc/Photodisc/Thinkstock 5. Noel Hendrickson/Photodisc/Thinkstock 6. Jupiterimages/Photos .com/Thinkstock 6. © Can Stock Photo Inc. / creatista 7. Thinkstock/Comstock/Thinkstock 7. Pixland/Pixland/Thinkstock 8. Creatas Images/Creatas/Thinkstock 9. Digital Vision./Digital Vision/Thinkstock 9. Burke/Triolo Productions/Brand X Pictures/Thinkstock 10. Jupiterimages/Brand X Pictures/Thinkstock 12. © iStockphoto.com/DrAfter123 12. © Can Stock Photo Inc. /gunnar3000 13. Thinkstock/Comstock/Thinkstock 13. Mike Powell/Photodisc/Thinkstock 16. © Can Stock Photo Inc. /fantasista 16. © iStockphoto.com/spfoto 17. Digital Vision./Digital Vision/Thinkstock 19. © iStockphoto.com/MotoEd 23. © iStockphoto.com/TadejZupancic 25. © iStockphoto.com/arekmalang 27. © John Reeves 27. CALVIN AND HOBBES ©1995 Watterson. Dist. By UNIVERSAL UCLICK. Reprinted with permission. All rights reserved. 28. © iStockphoto.com/pxl66 29. © iStockphoto.com/manley099 29. altrendo images/Stockbyte/Thinkstock 30. © iStockphoto.com/laflor 34. © Mike Kepka/San Francisco Chronicle/Corbis 36. IT Stock Free/Polka Dot/Thinkstock 37. Hemera Technologies/PhotoObjects .net/Thinkstock 38. © iStockphoto.com/garymilner 39. Digital Vision./Photodisc/Thinkstock 40. Photodisc/Photodisc/Thinkstock 41. BananaStock/BananaStock/Thinkstock 42. © Can Stock Photo Inc./afhunta 43. © iStockphoto.com/Alija 44. © iStockphoto.com/dial-a-view 46. Medioimages/Photodisc/Photodisc/Thinkstock 48. Digital Vision./Digital Vision/Thinkstock 49. Comstock/Comstock/Thinkstock 49. Brand X Pictures/Brand X Pictures/Thinkstock 51. © iStockphoto.com/HultonArchive 53. Goodshoot/Goodshoot/Thinkstock 55. Stockbyte/Stockbyte/Thinkstock 56. © iStockphoto.com/FarukUlay 57. Jupiterimages/Comstock/Thinkstock 60. Spencer Grant / Art Directors / Alamy 62. © iStockphoto.com/johnwoodcock 62. © Shelby Lessig 63. Include credit 64. © iStockphoto.com/kimberrywood 66. Digital Vision./Photodisc/Thinkstock 67. © iStockphoto.com/Tommydickson 68. © Can Stock Photo Inc. /wacker 70. United States Mission Geneva 72. Jupiterimages, Creatas Images/Creatas/Thinkstock 73. © Can Stock Photo Inc. / vicnt 74. Anup Shah/Photodisc/Thinkstock 76. Erik Snyder/Photodisc/Thinkstock 77.

Jupiterimages/liquidlibrary/Thinkstock 80. Archives du 7e Art/Columbia Pictures/Alamy 82. © Can Stock Photo Inc. / creatista 86. © iStockphoto.com/Alina555 90. © iStockphoto.com/aabejon 92. © iStockphoto.com/hocus-focus 92. Stockbyte/Stockbyte/Thinkstock 93. © iStockphoto.com/DoxaDigital 94. Photodisc/Photodisc/Thinkstock 95. Jupiterimages/Brand X Pictures/Thinkstock 97. © iStockphoto.com/diego_cervo 99. Thinkstock/Comstock/Thinkstock 100. © iStockphoto.com/Thomas_EyeDesign 102. Jupiterimages/Brand X Pictures/Thinkstock 103. © iStockphoto.com/RuslanDashinsky 104. Jupiterimages/Photos.com/Thinkstock 105. © iStockphoto.com/Ljupco 106. Marili Forastieri/Photodisc/Thinkstock 108. Digital Vision./Digital Vision/Thinkstock 111. David Sacks/Lifesize/Thinkstock 113. Michael Blann/Lifesize/Thinkstock 115. Thinkstock Images/Comstock/Thinkstock 118. Jupiterimages/Photos.com/Thinkstock 122. © Saed Hindash/Star Ledger/Corbis 124. Comstock Images/Comstock/Thinkstock 124. George Doyle/Stockbyte/Thinkstock 125. Digital Vision./Digital Vision/Thinkstock 126. © iStockphoto.com/Andrew_Howe 127. Jupiterimages/Photos.com/Thinkstock 127. Thomas Northcut/Lifesize/Thinkstock 129. Hemera Technologies/Ablestock/Thinkstock 131. Moviestore Collection/Alamy 132. © iStockphoto.com/EdStock 133. Digital Vision./Digital Vision/Thinkstock 133. © iStockphoto.com/CEFutcher 134. GRAND AVENUE ©2008 Steve Breen and Mike Thompson. Reprinted by permission of Universal Uclick for UFS. All rights reserved. 135. © iStockphoto.com/mrPliskin 135. Jupiterimages/Comstock/Thinkstock 140. Thomas Northcut/Photodisc/Thinkstock 141. Jupiterimages/Pixland/Thinkstock 142. Jupiterimages/Comstock/Thinkstock 143. Goodshoot/Goodshoot/Thinkstock 146. © iStockphoto.com/killis 150. Pictorial Press/Alamy 152. altrendo images/Stockbyte/Thinkstock 154. Jupiterimages/Comstock/Thinkstock 155. Christopher Robbins/Digital Vision/Thinkstock 156. Ryan McVay/Lifesize/Thinkstock 156. Jupiterimages/Photos.com/Thinkstock 157. Digital Vision./Digital Vision/Thinkstock 159. A. F. Archive/Alamy 160. © iStockphoto.com/Tempura 162. Jack Hollingsworth/Photodisc/Thinkstock 163. Thinkstock Images/Comstock/Thinkstock 165. Digital Vision./Digital Vision/Thinkstock 167. Digital Vision./Digital Vision/Thinkstock 168. © Can Stock Photo Inc. / creatista 170. Comstock Images/Comstock/Thinkstock 171. Ulrik Tofte/Lifesize/Thinkstock

172. Brand X Pictures/Brand X Pictures/Thinkstock 173. Jupiterimages/Photos.com/Thinkstock 173. Stockbyte/Stockbyte/Thinkstock 174. Moviestore Collection/Alamy 175. George Doyle/Stockbyte/Thinkstock 176. Michael Blann/Digital Vision/Thinkstock 177. © Can Stock Photo Inc. / foto_fritz 179. Hemera Technologies/AbleStock.com/Thinkstock 180. Jupiterimages/Polka Dot/Thinkstock 181. © Can Stock Photo Inc. / aaronamat 182. Jupiterimages/Brand X Pictures/Thinkstock 185. IS Stock/Valueline/Thinkstock 188. © iStockphoto .com/RapidEye 190. Thinkstock/Comstock/Thinkstock 191. © Can Stock Photo Inc. / diego_cervo 192. Brand X Pictures/Brand X Pictures/Thinkstock 194. Michael Blann/Digital Vision/Thinkstock 195. Jack Hollingsworth/Photodisc/Thinkstock 198. Yamini Chao/Digital Vision/Thinkstock 199. Everett Collection 200. Robert Koene/Photodisc/Thinkstock 201. © Can Stock Photo Inc. / micropix 202. Creatas Images/Creatas/Thinkstock 203. Hemera Technologies/AbleStock.com/Thinkstock 204. altrendo images/Stockbyte/Thinkstock 205. DILBERT ©2011 Scott Adams. Used By permission of UNIVERSAL UCLICK. All rights reserved. 205. Jupiterimages/Comstock/Thinkstock 207. David De Lossy/Photodisc/Thinkstock Chapter Opening Photo, 210. Digital Vision./Digital Vision/Thinkstock 212. Jupiterimages/Photos.com/Thinkstock 213. Brand X Pictures/Brand X Pictures/Thinkstock 214. Photodisc/Photodisc/Thinkstock 214. BananaStock/BananaStock/Thinkstock 215. Digital Vision./Digital Vision/Thinkstock 216. Jupiterimages/Brand X Pictures/Thinkstock 217. Maria Teijeiro/Digital Vision/Thinkstock 221. altrendo images/Stockbyte/Thinkstock 222. Donald Miralle/Lifesize/Thinkstock 223. BananaStock/BananaStock/Thinkstock 223. Ryan McVay/Photodisc/Thinkstock 224. Stockbyte/Stockbyte/Thinkstock 226. Showtime/Alamy 226. © iStockphoto.com/fotosipak 228. Jupiterimages/Photos.com/Thinkstock 230. D. Anschutz/Digital Vision/Thinkstock 234. Digital Vision/Digital Vision/Thinkstock 236. © iStockphoto.com/EdStock 237. Jupiterimages/Comstock/Thinkstock 238. © iStockphoto.com/nicolesy 240. Thinkstock Images/Comstock/Thinkstock 240. Ferdaus Shamim/ Contributor/WireImages/Getty Images 241. Thinkstock/Comstock/Thinkstock 242. Thinkstock/Stockbyte/Stockbyte/Thinkstock 245. Thinkstock Images/Comstock/Thinkstock 246. Jupiterimages/Polka Dot/Thinkstock 248. Carl Van Vechten 250. Jupiterimages/Comstock/Thinkstock 251. Jupiterimages/Brand X Pictures/Thinkstock

Index

workplace relationships and, 406
See also Truth
Hopson, D. P., 51
Horn effect, 65
Humor, 215
HURIER model of listening, 95–97, 96
Hurt, 239–240

Ibsen, H., 203
Ideal self, 42
Identity:
    culture/families and, 401
    differentiating stage of relationships and, 342
    fictional, 258
    gender/nonverbal communication and, 177
    individualistic/collectivistic cultures and, 47
    interpersonal relationships and, 4
    language and, 134, 138
    media and, 52
    online, 384
    self, 36–37
    technology and, 54
    technology/language and, 143
    See also Self
Idiocentric orientation., 48–49
Illustrators, 163
"I" messages, 111
    conflict resolution and, 313, 321
    differentiating stage of relationships and, 342
Impression management, 42
Inadequacy, 10
Inclusion:
    relationships and, 330
    social functions of interpersonal
        communication and, 16
Inclusion needs, 330
Independence:
    differentiating stage of relationships and, 342
    gender/families and, 402
    men and, 382
    monogamous partnerships and, 344
Indiscrimination, 75–76
Individualism:
    culture/relationships and, 351
    culture/workplace relationships and, 411
    families and, 401
    workplace relationships and, 405
Individualistic cultures, 23, 47–49, 50t
Influence, 265–266
    See also Power
Influence functions of interpersonal
        communication, 17
Informal space, 170
Information functions of interpersonal
        communication, 17
Ingham, H., 367
Ingratiation, 42
Initiating stage of relationships, 341
Instant messaging:
    channels and, 9
    deciding when to use, 1–2
    percentage of teens using, 2f
    technology/conflict resolution and, 319
    See also Technology
Instrumental roles, 352
Integrated families, 404
Integrating stage of relationships, 342
Integration, 373–374
Intellectual noise, 10t
Intensifying stage of relationships, 341, 342
    terminating stage of relationships and, 344
Intensional orientation., 134
Interaction constructs, 69
Interaction model of interpersonal
        communication, 13, 13f, 14t
Interactive leadership, 416
Internal feedback, 11
International Womens
        Forum, 415–416
Internet:
    friendship/romance and, 355
    health care and, 423
    power and, 287
    privacy/distance and, 383–384
    technology/perception and, 83

Interpersonal attraction, 345
Interpersonal communication, 3
    essential elements of, 7t
    linear model of, 12f
    models of, 5–14
    people and, 6–8
    relationships and, 3
Interpersonal competence, 4
Interpersonal conflict, 294
Interpersonal deception theory, 156, 157
Interpersonal influencers, 275f
Interpersonal relationships *See* Relationships
Interpersonal skills, 3
Interpersonal synchrony, 342
Intimate distance, 168
Intimate relationships, 335
    attraction and, 346
    circumscribing stage of relationships
        and, 342–343
    culture and, 176, 381
    culture/trust and, 255
    distance in relationships and, 363–364
    emotions and, 222
    expressing, 385
    eye movements and, 161
    friendships and, 336
    gender/distance and, 382
    measuring, 336
    nonverbal communication and, 183
    proximity and, 348
    romantic relationships and, 340, 342
    self-disclosure and, 364–365
    social penetration theory and, 365, 366
    technology/distance and, 383–384
    technology/friendship/romance and, 355, 356
    terminating stage of relationships and, 344
    touch and, 171
    trust and, 241, 256
    See also Relationships
Intrapersonal communication, 3
Intrapersonal conflict, 298
Intrapersonal intelligence, 213
Introverts:
    attraction and, 349
    conversations and, 191
Isolation:
    health/relationships and, 329
    psychological functions of interpersonal
        communication and, 14–15
    relationships and, 330, 357

Jackson, 21, 22
Jacobson, L., 46
James, W., 40
Jargon, 144
Jobs, S., 25
Johari window, 367–371, 368f, 369f
Johnson, W., 137
Jung, K., 210

Kanter, R. M., 414
Kinesics, 158t, 159–163
Kissing, 8–9
Kleinke, C., 194
Knapp, M., 196
Knowledge:
    about communication, 8
    cultural awareness and, 22–23
    effect and, 12
    effective interpersonal communicators and, 4
    impersonal relationships and, 7
    information functions interpersonal
        communication and, 17
    listening and, 95, 100
    noise and, 10
Kragen, K., xxiv

Labels, 133–134
Lakoff, R., 141
Landline phones:
    deciding when to use, 1–2
    percentage of teens using, 2f
Language:
    age and, 141–142
    assertive, 313–314

body, 115
defining, 124–126
emotive, 129–130
equivocal, 132–133
gender and, 139–141
labels and, 133–134
media and, 142–143
para, 165
polarizing, 130–131
politically correct, 131–132
thoughts affects, 138
Laptop computers, 417
Latent intimacy, 340
Lawrence, D. H., 382
Lazarus, R. S., 254
Leadership:
    authoritarian, 410
    interactive, 416
    participative, 410
Lee, J. A., 339
Lee, S., 81
Legitimate power, 269
    See also Power
Leifer, C., 52
Lesbians, 342, 392
    See also Homosexuals
Levin, J., 254
Levine, A., 221
Lies, 248
    effects of, 253
    reasons for, 252
    relationships and, 248–254
    statistical data on, 253t
    white, 251–252, 254
    See also Deception; Truth
Linear model of communication, 12, 14t
Linguistic determinism, 136–137
Linguistic relativity, 136–137
LinkedIn:
    messages impossible to erase, 19
    workplace relationships and, 415
    See also Social networking
Linowes, R. G., 414
Listening, 91, 93
    behaviors of poor, 105t
    conflict resolution and, 306
    effective/ineffective, 93–95
    ethics and, 103–107
    feedback and, 107–111
    gender's influence on, 113–114
    media and, 114–115
    people-oriented, 111–112
    stages of, 95–98, 97f
    styles of, 98–100, 99t
    technology and, 115
    time spent, 92
    types of, 98–103, 100t
Listening styles of conflict resolution, 113
    See also Conflict resolution
Living Together Apart (LTA) relationships, 344–345
Loneliness:
    grief and, 380–381
    relationships and, 334, 357
    workplace relationships and, 405
Long-distance relationships, 363–364
    surviving, 386
    technology/distance and, 383–384
Looking glass self, 40
Love relationships:
    abusive relationships and, 378
    conflict resolution and, 306–307
    different, 344
    evolution of, 344
    men/women and, 382
    relationships and, 241, 331
    romance and, 345
    stages of, 340–345
    technology/friendship/romance and, 355
    triangle of, 339f, 340
    types of, 339–340
    violence and, 379
    See also Romantic relationships
Low-context communication:
    culture and, 24, 49, 200
    culture/conflict resolution and, 315–316

relationships and, 241
workplace relationships and, 416
Richards, I. A., 124, 126
Rigid complementarity, 22
Rituals, 396, 400–401
Role assignments, 402
Role constructs, 69
Role duality, 8
Role-limited interaction, 337
Role reversal, 306
Roles:
    culture/families and, 401
    families and, 394, 395–404
    gender and, 51
    gender/relationships and, 352
    perception and, 66
    relational, 372
    self-concept and, 37, 40
    social functions of interpersonal
        communication and, 16–17
Romantic relationships, 339
    attraction and, 347
    characteristics of, 340
    culture/intimacy and, 381
    culture/relationships and, 351
    dark sides of, 377–379
    evolution of, 344
    gender/relationship formation and, 353
    stages of, 340–345, 341f
    trust/technology and, 258
    See also Love relationships; Relationships
Rosenthal, R., 46
Rules, 396–397
    context and, 11
    conversations and, 191, 192
    families and, 395–404
    grammatical, 125

Sadness, 213, 215–216, 222
    See also Emotions
Salander, L., 80
Sapir, E., 136–137
Sapir-Whorf hypothesis, 136–137, 137t, 138
Sarcasm, 377
Satir, V., 395, 400
Saxe, J. G., 76
Schemata, 66
    memory and, 67
    perception and, 69
Schutz, W., 16, 329–330
Scripts, 42, 66
Segmentation, 373–374
Seinfeld, J., 362
Selective attention, 65
Selective exposure, 65
Selective perception, 65
Selective retention, 65
Self See also Identity
    emotions and, 212
    future, 42–43
    in high/low-context cultures, 49
    in high/low-power-distance cultures, 49–50
    in individualistic/collectivistic cultures, 47–49
    relationships and, 333
    self-concept and, 37–39, 39f
Self-awareness, 36
Self-concept, 36–37, 36t
    gender and, 51–52
    how others shape, 40–44
    revising, 46–47
    self and, 37–39, 39f
    ways to strengthen, 55–56
Self-disclosure, 364
    conversations and, 198–199
    culture and, 381
    intimacy and, 364–365
    Johari window and, 367–371
Self-efficacy, 44
Self-esteem, 36–37, 36t
    culture/conflict resolution and, 315–316
    high/low, 39, 40
    lying and, 252
    relationships and, 241, 248, 331, 333
    self-disclosure and, 369

self-serving bias and, 69
self-worth and, 39–40
social networking sites and, 54
Self-fulfilling prophecy, 44–46
    story, 45f
Self-image, 36–37, 36t
    unrealistic, 47
Self-serving bias, 69
Self-worth:
    interpersonal communication and, 4
    self-concept and, 39
    self-esteem and, 39–40
Semantic code, 125, 125t
Semantic noise, 10t
Semi-fixed-feature space, 170
Separation, 372
    See also Divorce
Sex:
    culture/intimacy and, 381
    love and, 339
    romantic relationships and, 340
    self-disclosure and, 369
Sexism, 10
Sexual discrimination, 414
Sexual harassment, 285
    workplace relationships and, 416–417
Sexual health, 419
Sexual needs, 402
Sexual orientation:
    cyberbullying and, 287
    political correctness and, 131
Shareable goals, 299
    See also Goals
Shaw, G. B., 46
Shyness:
    conflict resolution and, 311
    noise and, 10
Sight:
    channels and, 9
    noise and, 10
Silence, 112
    communication styles and, 134
    culture/conversations and, 200–201
    nonverbal communication and, 167
Similarity, 346t, 349
Simon, H., 65
Sincerity, 348
Single-parent families, 392
Skills:
    assertive, 313
    conversational maintenance, 195
    coping, 241
    effective interpersonal communicators and, 4
    improving conversation, 206
    interpersonal, 3, 404
    practicing/applying, 28
    self-concept and, 46–47
    self-esteem and, 39–40
    social comparison theory and, 41
Skype:
    emotions and, 226
    health care and, 423
    listening and, 115
    long-distance relationships and, 363
    technology/conversations and, 205
Slang, 144
Small talk, 190, 195
Smart phones:
    conversations and, 202, 203, 205
    workplace relationships and, 417
Smell:
    channels and, 9
    messages and, 8
    noise and, 10
    nonverbal communication and, 173
Snap judgments, 77
Snarl words, 135
Social attractiveness, 346, 346t
Social comparison theory, 41–42, 41t
Social distance, 169
Social exchange theory, 241
Social functions of interpersonal communication, 16–17
Social identity See Identity
Social identity model of de-individuation effects, 82

Social intelligence, 213
Social learning theory, 317–318
Social media, 83
    See also Media
Social Network, 35
Social networking:
    deciding when to use, 1–2
    emotions and, 226
    friendship/romance and, 355
    LinkedIn, 19, 415
    percentage of teens using, 2f
    privacy/distance and, 383–384
    self-disclosure/intimacy and, 364
    strangers and, 4
    technology/conflict resolution and, 319
    trust and, 258
    workplace relationships and, 418
    See also Technology; Twitter
Social norms See Norms
Social penetration theory, 365–367, 366f
Social relationships, 351
Social setting, 11
Social support:
    grief and, 380
    health communication and, 418–419
Sound:
    channels and, 9
    noise and, 10
Speech-thought differential, 106
Speed dating, 61
Spiraling alternation, 373–374
Spirituality, 37
Spotlighting, 140
Spranger, E., 275
Stability, 372–373
Stabilized friendships, 338
    terminating stage of relationships and, 344
Stagnating stage of relationships, 343
Standpoint theory, 63
    gender/nonverbal communication and, 179
Stereotyping, 71
    age/language and, 141–142
    culture/conflict resolution and, 316
    culture/health communication and, 421
    friendships and, 338
    gender/conversations and, 202
    gender/emotions and, 223
    gender/health care and, 422
    gender/nonverbal communication and, 178
    gender/relationship formation and, 353
    grief and, 381
    health care providers/consumers and, 420
    indiscrimination and, 75–76
    language and, 139–140
    making words work and, 145
    media/friendship/romance and, 354
    media/health care and, 422
    media/language and, 142–143
    media/perception and, 81
    media/trust and, 257
    of men in organizations, 415
    perception and, 66, 69, 71–72, 74
    technology/perception and, 82
    vocal cues and, 166
    of women in organizations, 414–415
Sternberg, R., 340
Stimuli, 69–70
Stock, G., 195
Strategic ambiguity, 130
Streetcar Named Desire, 246–247
Stress:
    differentiating stage of relationships and, 342
    exercise and, 216
    families and, 394, 395
    gossip and, 255
    listening and, 95
    relationships and, 334
    social support and, 418–419
    work/life balance and, 391
Success:
    clothing/jewelry and, 172
    in college, 57
    individualistic/collectivistic cultures and, 47
    interpersonal competence and, 4